Managing
LIFE SKILLS

GLENCOE

Managing
LIFE SKILLS

Building Brighter Futures

Supports Financial Literacy

Patricia Clark, M.Ed., CFCS
Sue Couch, Ed.D.
Ginny Felstehausen, Ph.D.

Mc Graw Hill **Glencoe**

Glencoe

The *McGraw·Hill* Companies

Printed in the United States of America.

Send all inquiries to:
Glencoe/McGraw-Hill
4400 Easton Commons
Columbus, OH 43219

ISBN: 978-0-07-893386-8   (Student Edition)
MHID: 0-07-893386-2   (Student Edition)
ISBN: 978-0-07-894327-0   (Teacher Wraparound Edition)
MHID: 0-07-894327-2   (Teacher Wraparound Edition)

 4 5 6 7 8 9   QDB/LEH   15 14 13 12 11

Authors

Patricia Clark, M.Ed., CFSC
Family and Consumer Sciences
    Specialist
Mahomet, Illinois

Sue Couch, Ed.D.
Texas Tech University
Lubbock, Texas

Ginny Felstehausen, Ph.D.
Texas Tech University (Ret.)
Lubbock, Texas

Teacher Reviewers

Suzi Beck
Trenton R-9 School
Trenton, Missouri

Denise J. Watts Bowker
Capitol Hill High School
Oklahoma City, Oklahoma

Kathryn Cox, NBCT
Enloe Magnet High School
Raleigh, North Carolina

Tangela I. Frost, M.Ed., NBCT
Southern Alamance High School
Graham, North Carolina

Janet Hartline
Fort Payne High School
Fort Payne, Alabama

Vikki Jackson
Kathleen Middle School
Lakeland, Florida

Tammy Lamparter
Smyrna High School
Smyrna, Tennessee

Georgia Lash
Hillcrest High School
Simpsonville, South Carolina

Dawn Lewis
Coffee High School
Freshman Campus
Douglas, Georgia

Bettie O'Shields
Durham Public Schools
Durham, North Carolina

Amanda Riggen
Walker Career Center
Indianapolis, Indiana

Technical Reviewer

Angie Lustrick, CN, CPT
Nutritionist and
Certified Personal Trainer
Riverside, California

Scavenger Hunt

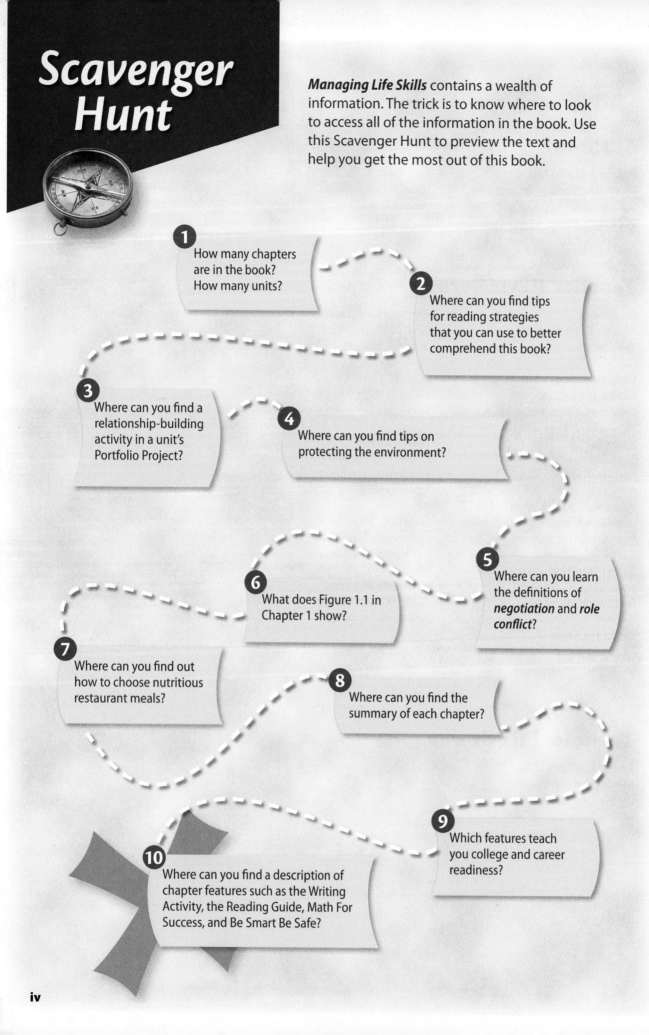

Managing Life Skills contains a wealth of information. The trick is to know where to look to access all of the information in the book. Use this Scavenger Hunt to preview the text and help you get the most out of this book.

1 How many chapters are in the book? How many units?

2 Where can you find tips for reading strategies that you can use to better comprehend this book?

3 Where can you find a relationship-building activity in a unit's Portfolio Project?

4 Where can you find tips on protecting the environment?

5 Where can you learn the definitions of *negotiation* and *role conflict*?

6 What does Figure 1.1 in Chapter 1 show?

7 Where can you find out how to choose nutritious restaurant meals?

8 Where can you find the summary of each chapter?

9 Which features teach you college and career readiness?

10 Where can you find a description of chapter features such as the Writing Activity, the Reading Guide, Math For Success, and Be Smart Be Safe?

Table of Contents

UNIT 1   Prepare for Independent Living   2

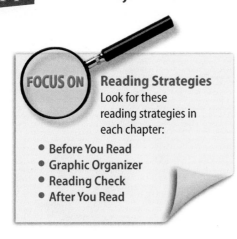

FOCUS ON **Reading Strategies**
Look for these
reading strategies in
each chapter:

- Before You Read
- Graphic Organizer
- Reading Check
- After You Read

Table of Contents

FOCUS ON

Academic Success
To help you succeed in your classes and on tests, look for these academic skills:

- Reading Guides
- Writing Tips
- Math For Success
- Science For Success
- Financial Literacy

Table of Contents

FOCUS ON Visuals
Images help you to comprehend key ideas. Answer the questions for all:
- Unit and Chapter Openers
- Photos and Captions
- Figures and Tables

Table of Contents

FOCUS ON Project-Based Learning

Projects throughout this book can help you use your skills in real-life situations:

- Real-world scenarios
- Step-by-step instructions
- Team- or individual- based learning

Table of Contents

FOCUS ON **Assessment**
Look for review questions
and activities to help you
remember important
topics.

- Reading Checks
- Section and Chapter Reviews
- Unit Thematic Projects

UNIT 8 Wellness, Nutrition, and Food Choices 516

Table of Contents

Table of Contents

FOCUS ON Online Resources
Look for the online icon and go to the book's Online Learning Center at **glencoe.com** for:

- Graphic Organizers
- Practice Tests
- Evaluation Rubrics
- Career Resources
- Additional Activities

Features Table of Contents

CCR College and Career Readiness

Are you prepared for life after you graduate from school? As you get ready to continue your education or enter the world of work, these features will teach you the skills you need to be prepared to succeed.

Pathway to College

Pathway to Your Career

Build Academic and Financial Literacy Skills

Do you know how to create a budget? Do you understand the technology behind alternative energy sources? Use these standards-based academic features to prepare you for independent living!

Financial *Literacy*

Math *For Success*

Science *For Success*

Build a Professional Portfolio

No matter what career path you choose, an organized job portfolio can help you get started. Following these Unit Portfolio Projects in order will result in having a well-rounded portfolio to use as you enter the world of work.

Unit Portfolio Projects

Strengthen Your Writing Skills

You will use a variety of writing skills in all your classes and in everyday life. Writing Activities uses different techniques to help you explore real-world topics.

Writing Activities

Learn 21st Century Skills

How can you be more organized? What is the best way to ask for feedback? Look for the Succeed in School and Life features in every section to help you improve in every class and prepare you for college or for your career.

Succeed in SCHOOL and LIFE

Think Critically and Weigh Opinions

Ethics, leadership, teamwork, and management skills are important for school and the workplace. Use these features to develop your own opinions and build character.

Two Views One World

Character In Action

Acquire New Life Skills

How can you manage your time more effectively? Do you know how to work better as part of a team? These activities and ideas show you how to apply leadership, teamwork, and independent living skills to everyday life.

Life On Your Own

HOW TO. . .

Become Involved in Your Community

Have you ever volunteered for a local organization? How can you save money and help the environment? These features can help you get involved in your community and make decisions and take actions that help the planet!

Get Involved!

Go Green!

Stay Healthy and Safe for Success

To succeed, you must take care of yourself physically and mentally. In these features, you will find tips to keep you healthy and strong and to help you stay safe in everyday situations.

Health & Wellness

TIPS

Be Smart Be Safe

To the Student

Begin the Unit

Get Ready for Independent Living!

Managing Life Skills takes you beyond school and helps prepare you for the real world, college, and careers. Use the My Journal writing activity to connect what you already know to the unit topics. Think about the people, places, and events in your own life. Are there any similarities with those in your textbook?

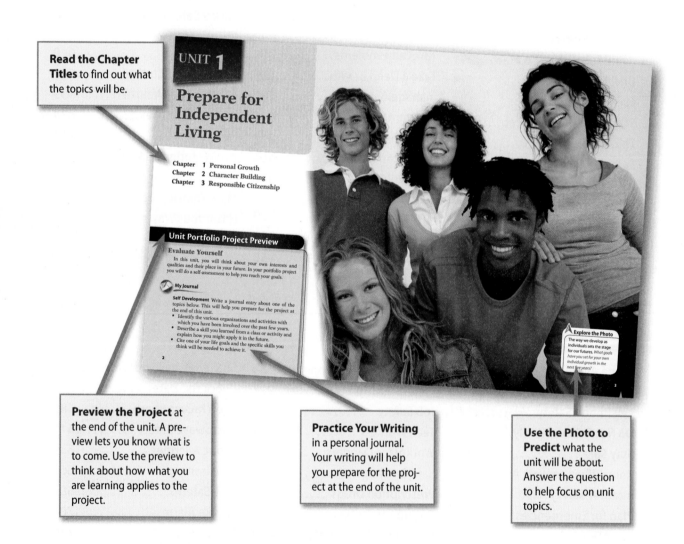

Read the Chapter Titles to find out what the topics will be.

UNIT 1

Prepare for Independent Living

Chapter 1 Personal Growth
Chapter 2 Character Building
Chapter 3 Responsible Citizenship

Unit Portfolio Project Preview

Evaluate Yourself

In this unit, you will think about your own interests and qualities and their place in your future. In your portfolio project you will do a self-assessment to help you reach your goals.

My Journal

Self Development Write a journal entry about one of the topics below. This will help you prepare for the project at the end of this unit.

- Identify the various organizations and activities with which you have been involved over the past few years.
- Describe a skill you learned from a class or activity and explain how you might apply it in the future.
- Cite one of your life goals and the specific skills you think will be needed to achieve it.

2

Explore the Photo
The way we develop as individuals sets the stage for our futures. What goals have you set for your own individual growth in the next five years?

3

Preview the Project at the end of the unit. A preview lets you know what is to come. Use the preview to think about how what you are learning applies to the project.

Practice Your Writing in a personal journal. Your writing will help you prepare for the project at the end of the unit.

Use the Photo to Predict what the unit will be about. Answer the question to help focus on unit topics.

Close the Unit

Build a Professional Portfolio to Showcase Your Skills

Every unit ends with a Unit Portfolio Project designed to explore an important issue from the unit while creating a project for a written and electronic skills portfolio. For each project, you will make decisions, do research, connect to your community, share what you have learned, and evaluate your work.

Read the Project Assignment and numbered steps. The assignment explains what you will need to do.

Follow the Project Checklist to make sure that you have done everything you need to complete your life skills project.

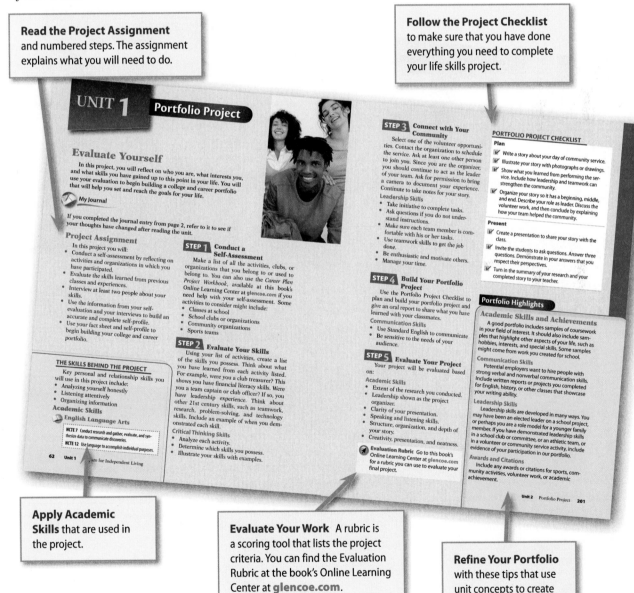

Apply Academic Skills that are used in the project.

Evaluate Your Work A rubric is a scoring tool that lists the project criteria. You can find the Evaluation Rubric at the book's Online Learning Center at **glencoe.com**.

Refine Your Portfolio with these tips that use unit concepts to create an interviewing resource.

Set a Purpose for Your Reading

Successful readers set a purpose for reading. Think about why you are reading this book, and how it will help you make plans for the future. Then use the chapter opener activities to target the skills you want to learn.

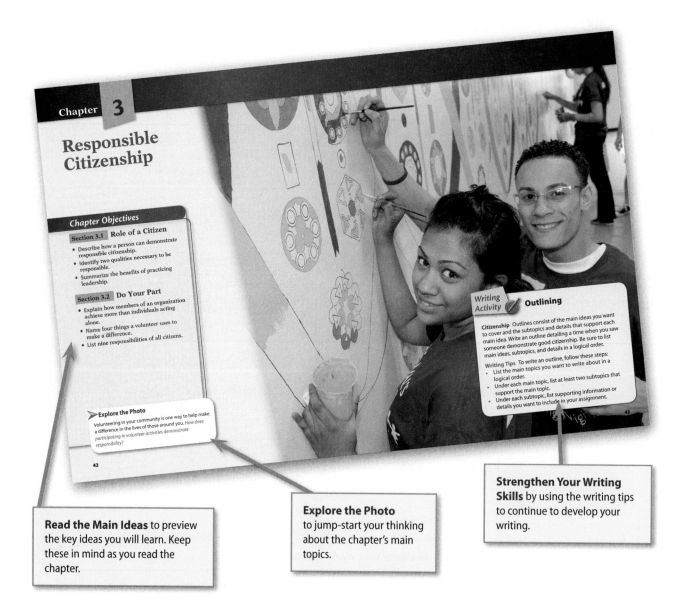

Chapter **3**

Responsible Citizenship

Chapter Objectives

Section 3.1 Role of a Citizen
• Describe how a person can demonstrate responsible citizenship.
• Identify two qualities necessary to be responsible.
• Summarize the benefits of practicing leadership.

Section 3.2 Do Your Part
• Explain how members of an organization achieve more than individuals acting alone.
• Name four things a volunteer uses to make a difference.
• List nine responsibilities of all citizens.

▶ **Explore the Photo**
Volunteering in your community is one way to help make a difference in the lives of those around you. *How does participating in volunteer activities demonstrate responsibility?*

42

Writing Activity 🖊 **Outlining**

Citizenship Outlines consist of the main ideas you want to cover and the subtopics and details that support each main idea. Write an outline detailing a time when you saw someone demonstrate good citizenship. Be sure to list main ideas, subtopics, and details in a logical order.

Writing Tips To write an outline, follow these steps:
• List the main topics you want to write about in a logical order.
• Under each main topic, list at least two subtopics that support the main topic.
• Under each subtopic, list supporting information or details you want to include in your assignment.

43

Read the Main Ideas to preview the key ideas you will learn. Keep these in mind as you read the chapter.

Explore the Photo to jump-start your thinking about the chapter's main topics.

Strengthen Your Writing Skills by using the writing tips to continue to develop your writing.

Review the Chapter

Check Your Understanding and Practice Critical Thinking

Use the chapter review to check your understanding of key concepts, and learn to use these concepts in real-world situations.

Read the Chapter Summary to review the most important ideas that you should have learned in this chapter.

Review Vocabulary and Key Concepts to check your recall of important ideas.

Critical Thinking takes your knowledge of the chapter further. If you have difficulty answering these questions, go back and reread the related parts of the chapter.

Projects and Activities give you the opportunity to practice what you have learned in the chapter.

Practice Academic Skills and connect what you have learned to your knowledge of language arts, math, science, and social studies.

Succeed on Tests with test-taking tips and practice questions.

FCCLA Connections help you connect with family and community.

Apply Real-World Skills to situations that you might find in your day-to-day life.

Chapter 3 — Review and Applications

CHAPTER SUMMARY

Section 3.1 Role of a Citizen
There are many opportunities for you to make a difference in the lives of others by being responsible, doing your share, and using your skills, time, and talent to help others. Show responsibility by being reliable and accountable at home, at school, and at work. Many responsible citizens take on leadership roles. These will help you develop your confidence and leadership skills.

Section 3.2 Do Your Part
Participating in organizations is a good way to make a difference. There are many different types of organizations. Volunteering is a great way to improve the lives of others while building your own skills. All citizens have certain rights and responsibilities. Taking an active role and being a responsible citizen can make your community a better place to live.

Vocabulary Review

1. Create multiple-choice test questions for each content and academic vocabulary term.

Content Vocabulary
◇ citizen (p. 45)
◇ citizenship (p. 45)
◇ accountable (p. 46)
◇ leadership (p. 49)
◇ collaboration (p. 50)
◇ outreach program (p. 52)
◇ volunteer (p. 53)
◇ service learning (p. 55)

Academic Vocabulary
■ clutter (p. 45)
■ chair (p. 46)
■ restrict (p. 56)
■ cultivate (p. 57)

Review Key Concepts

2. Describe how a person can demonstrate responsible citizenship.
3. Identify two qualities necessary to be responsible.
4. Summarize the benefits of practicing leadership.
5. Explain how members of an organization achieve more than individuals acting alone.
6. Name four things a volunteer uses to make a difference.
7. List nine responsibilities of all citizens.

Critical Thinking

8. Analyze You can support your school and community by treating everyone with respect. Why is it important to also follow this rule at home?
9. Extrapolate Expand what you learned about leadership roles. How is being a leader similar to being a mentor?
10. Recommend Your friend is planning to [...] Compile a list of volunteer opportunities [...] this career.
11. Analyze Teens sometimes feel that they [...] on their community. Based on the re[...] what are some things that teens c[...] do [...] the community?

Chapter 3 — Review and Applications

ACTIVE LEARNING

12. **Write a Children's Story** Children's books and TV programs often focus on teaching responsible behavior. Follow your teacher's instructions to form into pairs. Work with your partner to pick a specific aspect of responsibility that you feel would be helpful to teach a five-year-old. Each of you should create a character that a kindergarten-age child could relate to, such as a cute animal, a child, or a friendly fantasy creature. Give the names to the characters, and write a short story or television script to teach your lesson. Include descriptions or illustrations of your characters.

Family & Community Connections

13. **Research Organizations** Conduct research to identify a service organization in your community that interests you. Arrange to speak with a member of the organization. Ask the member about participation in the organization. For example, "How would someone volunteer? How many hours are required of participants? What types of projects does the organization do?" If possible, observe or participate in one of the organization's projects. Create a presentation to share the results of your interview. If you participated in a project, include a summary of your activities and feelings. Were you proud to help someone? Was it hard work? Was it fun?

21st Century Skills

Media Literacy Skills
14. **Analyze Citizens' Responsibility** Read a recent human interest story in a newspaper. Analyze the level of responsible citizenship shown by the people in the article. How did each person demonstrate responsibility? If a person showed a lack of responsibility, what could he or she have done better? Write a summary of your analysis.

Technology Skills
15. **Research Service Learning** Conduct research to find service learning ideas. Use a word processing or desktop publishing program to create an attractive flyer to encourage your classmates to participate in one or more of the opportunities. Give the Web addresses of the sites, where appropriate. Consider what skills and benefits could be gained from the service learning projects and include them in your pamphlet.

FCCLA Connections

Leadership Skills
16. **Increase Leadership Roles** As part of its mission, FCCLA encourages students to participate in leadership roles. Go to the FCCLA Web site to read about the Take the Lead unit of the Power of One program. Use this unit to develop a written plan to increase your participation in an organization such as FCCLA.

Academic Skills

English Language Arts
17. **Thank a Citizen** Think about a citizen in your community who has served as a role model to you or others. Write a letter to express your gratitude for the person's efforts and the results of his or her actions. Be sure to include a heading, greeting, body, closing, and signature.

NCTE 5 Use different writing process elements to communicate effectively.

Social Studies
18. **Inspire Others** Select a historical document or a famous speech given by a leader, such as the Gettysburg Address or a speech given by a civil rights leader. Review the document or speech and write an analysis of how you believe it inspires citizens to make a difference. What was the outcome of the document or speech? Is there specific language used that helped inspire others?

NCSS X A Civic Ideals and Practices Interpret the continuing influence of key ideals of the democratic republican form of government, such as individual human dignity, liberty, justice, equality, and the rule of law.

Mathematics
19. **Volunteer Hours** Volunteer work is important to Mae. Last year, she volunteered with a group that unites lonely senior citizen[...] the 2,400 hou[...] she spent 40[...] rest of that [...] work. What [...] teer work t[...]

Math Concept [...] sons of nu[...] ed in diffe[...] represent [...] 1:2 can al[...] 1 to 2, or [...]

Starting Hint Set [...] fraction, with 400 as the numerator and 2,000 as the denominator. Your answer should be a fraction in the lowest terms.

For more math practice, go [...] Math Appendix at the back of [...] book.

NCTM Number and Operation[...] Understand numbers, ways of representing num[...] relationships among numbers, and number system[...]

CCR College & Career Readiness

Being a responsible citizen means doing your part to make your school safe and supportive environment.
20. What can you do to help make your school safer and more supportive? Give specific examples.

Standardized Test Practice

TIMED WRITING
Take five minutes to consider the statement and write an answer to the question.

Test-Taking Tip Plan out your answer before you begin writing. Jot down the main points or details you want to focus on in the margins of your test. Refer to these points frequently as you write. This will help you remain focused.

Begin the Section

Reading Guides Prepare You for Academic Success

The Reading Guide at the beginning of each section contains study tools to help preview the concepts and vocabulary you will learn in the section. See if you can predict how section topics will relate to your own life.

Before You Read the main text predict what the section will be about.

Check Vocabulary lists for words you do not know. You can look them up in the glossary before you read the section.

Preview key concepts and the main idea before you read.

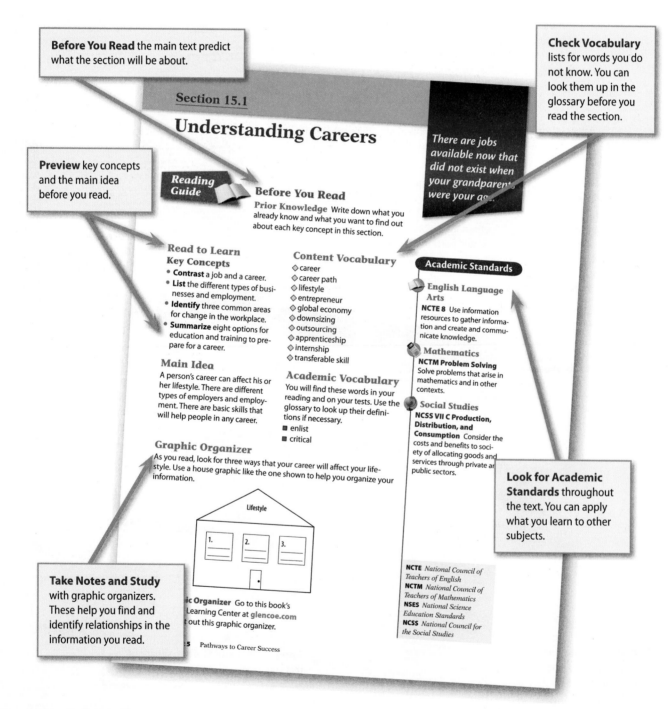

Take Notes and Study with graphic organizers. These help you find and identify relationships in the information you read.

Look for Academic Standards throughout the text. You can apply what you learn to other subjects.

Section 15.1

Understanding Careers

There are jobs available now that did not exist when your grandparents were your age.

Reading Guide

Before You Read

Prior Knowledge Write down what you already know and what you want to find out about each key concept in this section.

Read to Learn
Key Concepts
- **Contrast** a job and a career.
- **List** the different types of businesses and employment.
- **Identify** three common areas for change in the workplace.
- **Summarize** eight options for education and training to prepare for a career.

Main Idea
A person's career can affect his or her lifestyle. There are different types of employers and employment. There are basic skills that will help people in any career.

Graphic Organizer
As you read, look for three ways that your career will affect your lifestyle. Use a house graphic like the one shown to help you organize your information.

Lifestyle

1. ___ 2. ___ 3. ___

ic Organizer Go to this book's Learning Center at **glencoe.com** _ out this graphic organizer.

:5   Pathways to Career Success

Content Vocabulary
◇ career
◇ career path
◇ lifestyle
◇ entrepreneur
◇ global economy
◇ downsizing
◇ outsourcing
◇ apprenticeship
◇ internship
◇ transferable skill

Academic Vocabulary
You will find these words in your reading and on your tests. Use the glossary to look up their definitions if necessary.
■ enlist
■ critical

Academic Standards

English Language Arts
NCTE 8 Use information resources to gather information and create and communicate knowledge.

Mathematics
NCTM Problem Solving Solve problems that arise in mathematics and in other contexts.

Social Studies
NCSS VII C Production, Distribution, and Consumption Consider the costs and benefits to society of allocating goods and services through private and public sectors.

NCTE *National Council of Teachers of English*
NCTM *National Council of Teachers of Mathematics*
NSES *National Science Education Standards*
NCSS *National Council for the Social Studies*

Review the Section

Assess Your Progress with Self-Checks

The questions in the After You Read section closer can help you check your understanding. Be sure you can answer the questions in your own words before moving on to the next section.

Reading Checks let you pause to respond to what you have read.

Verify Your Understanding of key concepts in the section.

Develop Leadership Skills

A strong leader can make the difference between a successful team and an unsuccessful one. *What leadership roles are being fulfilled by the teen in this photo?*

Showing responsibility on the job benefits others as well as yourself. When all workers are reliable and have positive attitudes, morale is high. By helping one another, employees create a spirit of cooperation. Those who do business with such a company or organization are more likely to be satisfied customers.

✓ **Reading Check** **Recall** How can you show others that you are reliable?

Become a Leader

Check Your Answers online at this book's Online Learning Center at **glencoe.com**.

Section 5.1 After You Read

Life Skill Podcasts.

Review Key Concepts
1. Describe how personal development is a benefit of teamwork.
2. Explain three negative roles of team members.
3. Define compromise.

Practice Academic Skills

🖉 **English Language Arts**
4. Think about the different types of people you work with on a daily basis, such as classmates, coworkers, and friends. Consider the positive teamwork processes that you use with these people. List how these processes can benefit you in your career.

🌐 **Social Studies**
5. How you act as a team player is a way of expressing yourself and your values. It is a part of your identity. Write about ways you act as a team player. Do you use good communication skills? Do you respect differences? Do you do your fair share of the work? Explain how you developed your teamwork style. What influenced it?

🧭 **Check Your Answers** Check your answers at this book's Online Learning Center at glencoe.com.

NCTE 12 Use language to accomplish individual purposes.

NCSS IV D Apply concepts about the study of human growth and development, such as learning, behavior, and personality.

Chapter 5 Teamwork and Leadership Skills **151**

Practice Academic Skills with these cross-curricular activities.

Study with Features

College and Career Readiness

 Pathway to College

Learn skills to make a successful transition from high school to college.

Pathway to Your Career

Discover in-depth information on individual careers from each of the 16 career clusters.

 Succeed in **SCHOOL** and **LIFE**

Find information on how to improve the skills needed in classes and the real world.

Career Skills Handbook

This handbook can help you get ready to enter the world of work.

 Workplace Skills

Visit this book's Online Learning Center at **glencoe.com** for worksheets on choosing and preparing for a career and success at work.

 Career Resources Online

Visit this book's Online Learning Center at **glencoe.com** to find more information about career clusters and career skills.

Academic Solutions

Academic Standards

Standards are integrated into each chapter.

 Financial *Literacy*

Learn solid financial management skills and improve your math scores.

 Math For Success

Practice math skills with activities that relate to everyday life.

Math Skills Handbook

This handbook can help you better understand and apply mathematics concepts.

 Science For Success

Use scientific concepts and methods to explore the world around you.

 English Language Arts

Connect English language arts concepts to life skills.

 Writing Activity

Use your writing skills to describe events, create dialogues, and more.

 Standardized Test Practice

Improve your standardized test scores through practice quizzes and tips.

Reading Strategies

 Reading Skills Handbook

Get more from your reading with the information from this guide.

 Reading Guide

Discover the main idea, key concepts, content and academic vocabulary terms, and academic standards in one place at the beginning of each section.

 As You Read

Connect what you already know to new ideas you learn as you read.

 Vocabulary

Write down vocabulary words, and then find definitions in the text and in the glossary at the end of the book.

 Visuals

Examine photos and figures to reinforce content, and then answer the questions so you can better understand and discuss topics in the book.

Reading Check

Use these features to take a quick break and review the material you have just read.

21st Century Skills

▶ Life On Your Own
Discover how to better prepare yourself for life beyond school.

▶ Two Views One World
Use critical thinking to weigh two sides of an issue.

▶ Character *In Action*
Learn how to use character-building traits in school and life.

▶ 21st Century Skills & Applications
Apply skills you have learned to answer questions about everyday situations.

▶ Technology Skills
These chapter review activities can help you develop the skills you need to work well with today's technology.

▶ Interpersonal Skills
Visit this book's Online Learning Center at **glencoe.com** for worksheets on communication, leadership, conflict resolution, and positive relationships.

▶ Management Skills
Visit this book's Online Learning Center at **glencoe.com** for worksheets on managing time, money, information, technology, and problem solving.

Project-Based Learning

▶ Unit Portfolio Projects
Completing these projects will result in a job portfolio that you can use to apply for college and start your career.

▶ Rubrics
Visit this book's Online Learning Center at **glencoe.com** to access rubrics to help you evaluate your Unit Portfolio Projects.

Community Connections

▶ FCCLA Connections
Develop life skills through critical thinking, interpersonal relationships, and career preparation.

▶ Get Involved!
Discover opportunities to volunteer your skills at home, at school, and in your community.

▶ Family & Community Connections
Participate in activities with your family and the community at large.

▶ ACTIVE LEARNING
Get active by encouraging teamwork and working in collaboration with others.

Life Skills

▶HOW TO...
Use these step-by-step guides to practice important techniques.

▶ Health & Wellness TIPS
Use these tips to stay healthy and to improve your overall wellness.

▶ Be Smart Be Safe
Learn more about basic safety, and then expand your knowledge by writing about your experiences.

▶ Go Green
Use these tips to keep your school, home, community, and planet healthy.

▶ Food Labs & Recipes
Visit this book's Online Learning Center at **glencoe.com** for worksheets on kitchen skills, working in a foods lab, and preparing recipes.

▶ Sewing Labs
Visit this book's Online Learning Center at **glencoe.com** for worksheets with diagrams on a variety of sewing projects.

To the Student

 Online Learning Center Web Site

Extend and Enrich Learning

Managing LIfe Skills Online Learning Center provides resources to enrich and enhance learning.

Interactive Activities

- Interactive Games
- eFlashcards in English and Spanish
- Study-to-Go

Printable Activities & Projects

Additional classroom resources are available online:

- Food Labs and Recipes
- Sewing Labs
- Interpersonal Skills
- Workplace Skills
- Management Skills
- Graphic Organizers

StudentWorks Online

The StudentWorks Online is an interactive version of the textbook that can be accessed from the Online Learning Center. This version of the textbook is easy to read and search. It offers the same content as the printed text, as well as multimedia-enhanced content.

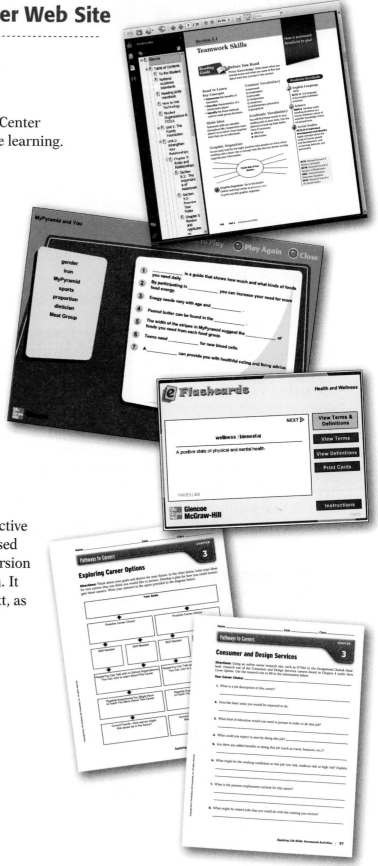

How to Access the Online Learning Center

The Online Learning Center provides access to a wide variety of student resources. Follow these steps to access the textbook resources at *Managing Life Skills* Online Learning Center

Step 1
Go to **glencoe.com**.

Step 2
Select **your state** from the pull-down menu.

Step 3
Select **Student/Parent**.

Step 4
Select **Family & Consumer Sciences**.

Step 5
Select **ENTER**.

Step 6
Click *Managing Life Skills* ©2011.

Step 7
Click **Student Center** to access a wide variety of textbook resources.

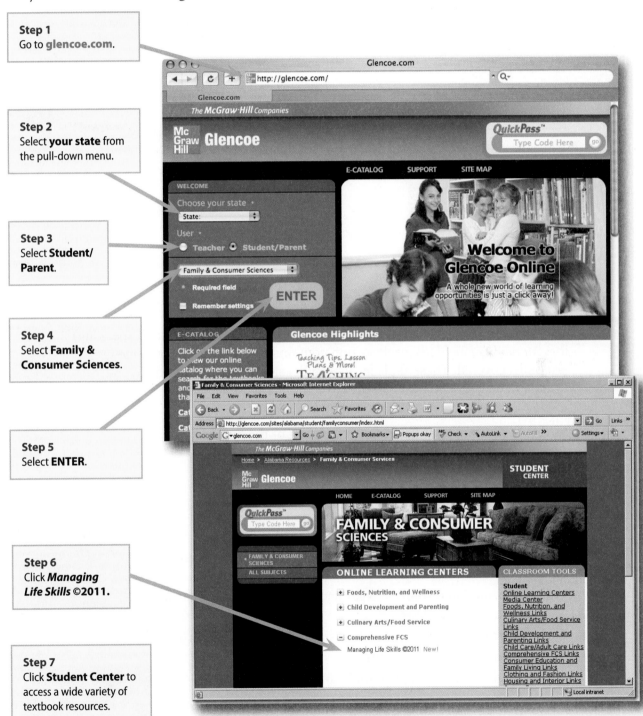

Prepare for Academic Success!

By improving your academic skills, you improve your ability to learn and achieve success now and in the future. It also improves your chances of landing a high-skill, high-wage job. The features and assessments in *Managing Life Skills* provide many opportunities for you to strengthen your academic skills.

Academic Standards Look for this box throughout the text to know what academic skills you are learning.

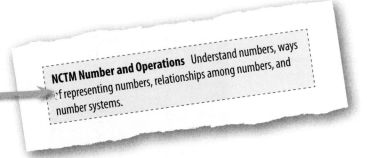

NCTM Number and Operations Understand numbers, ways of representing numbers, relationships among numbers, and number systems.

National English Language Arts Standards

To help incorporate literacy skills (reading, writing, listening, and speaking) into *Managing Life Skills*, each section contains a listing of the language arts skills covered. These skills have been developed into standards by the *National Council of Teachers of English* and *International Reading Association*.

- Read texts to acquire new information.
- Read literature to build an understanding of the human experience.
- Apply strategies to interpret texts.
- Use written language to communicate effectively.
- Use different writing process elements to communicate effectively.
- Conduct research and gather, evaluate, and synthesize data to communicate discoveries.
- Use information resources to gather information and create and communicate knowledge.
- Develop an understanding of diversity in language use across cultures.
- Participate as members of literacy communities.
- Use language to accomplish individual purposes.

National Mathematics Standards

You also have opportunities to practice math skills indicated by standards developed by the *National Council of Teachers of Mathematics.* *

- Algebra
- Data Analysis and Probability
- Geometry
- Measurement
- Number and Operations
- Problem Solving

Standards are listed with permission of the National Council of Teachers of Mathematics (NCTM). NCTM *does not endorse the content or validity of these alignments.*

National Science Standards

The *National Science Education Standards* outline these science skills that you can practice in this text.

- Science as Inquiry
- Physical Science
- Life Science
- Earth and Space Science
- Science and Technology
- Science in Personal and Social Perspectives
- History and Nature of Science

National Social Studies Standards

The *National Council for the Social Studies* is another organization that provides standards to help guide your studies. Activities in this text relate to these standards.

- Culture
- Time, Continuity, and Change
- People, Places, and Environments
- Individual Development and Identity
- Individuals, Groups, and Institutions
- Power, Authority, and Governance
- Production, Distribution, and Consumption
- Science, Technology, and Society
- Global Connections
- Civic Ideals and Practices

Reading Skills Handbook

▶ Reading: What's in It for You?

What role does reading play in your life? The possibilities are countless. Are you on a sports team? Perhaps you like to read about the latest news and statistics in sports or find out about new training techniques. Are you looking for a new dish to serve your family? You might be looking for advice about nutrition, cooking techniques, or information about ingredients. Are you enrolled in an English class, an algebra class, or a business class? Then your assignments require a lot of reading.

Improving or Fine-Tuning Your Reading Skills Will:

- ◆ Improve your grades.
- ◆ Allow you to read faster and more efficiently.
- ◆ Improve your study skills.
- ◆ Help you remember more information accurately.
- ◆ Improve your writing.

▶ The Reading Process

Good reading skills build on one another, overlap, and spiral around in much the same way that a winding staircase goes around and around while leading you to a higher place. This handbook is designed to help you find and use the tools you will need **before, during,** and **after** reading.

Strategies You Can Use

- ◆ Identify, understand, and learn new words.
- ◆ Understand why you read.
- ◆ Take a quick look at the whole text.
- ◆ Try to predict what you are about to read.
- ◆ Take breaks while you read and ask yourself questions about the text.
- ◆ Take notes.
- ◆ Keep thinking about what will come next.
- ◆ Summarize.

▶ Vocabulary Development

Word identification and vocabulary skills are the building blocks of the reading and writing processes. By learning to use a variety of strategies to build your word skills and vocabulary, you will become a stronger reader.

Use Context to Determine Meaning

The best way to expand and extend your vocabulary is to read widely, listen carefully, and participate in a rich variety of discussions. When reading on your own, though, you can often figure out the meanings of new words by looking at their **context,** or the other words and sentences that surround them.

Tips for Using Context

Look for clues like these:

◆ A synonym or an explanation of the unknown word in the sentence:
Elise's shop specialized in millinery, or hats for women.

◆ A reference to what the word is or is not like:
An archaeologist, like a historian, deals with the past.

◆ A general topic associated with the word:
The cooking teacher discussed the best way to braise meat.

◆ A description or action associated with the word:
He used the shovel to dig up the garden.

Predict a Possible Meaning

Another way to determine the meaning of a word is to take the word apart. If you understand the meaning of the **base,** or **root,** part of a word, and also know the meanings of key syllables added either to the beginning or end of the base word, you can usually figure out what the word means.

Word Origins Since Latin, Greek, and Anglo-Saxon roots are the basis for much of our English vocabulary, having some background in languages can be a useful vocabulary tool. For example, *astronomy* comes from the Greek root *astro,* which means relating to the stars. *Stellar* also has a meaning referring to stars, but its origin is Latin. Knowing root words in other languages can help you determine meanings, derivations, and spellings in English.

Prefixes and Suffixes A prefix is a word part that can be added to the beginning of a word. For example, the prefix *semi* means half or partial, so *semicircle* means half a circle. A suffix is a word part that can be added to the end of a word. Adding a suffix often changes a word from one part of speech to another.

Using Dictionaries A dictionary provides the meaning or meanings of a word. Look at the sample dictionary entry on the next page to see what other information it provides.

Thesauruses and Specialized Reference Books A thesaurus provides synonyms and often antonyms. It is a useful tool to expand your vocabulary. Remember to check the exact definition of the listed words in a dictionary before you use a thesaurus. Specialized dictionaries such as *Barron's Dictionary of Business Terms* or *Black's Law Dictionary* list terms and expressions that are not commonly included in a general dictionary. You can also use online dictionaries.

Glossaries Many textbooks and technical works contain condensed dictionaries that provide an alphabetical listing of words used in the text and their specific definitions.

Reading Skills Handbook

Dictionary Entry

Forms of the word

Part of speech

Numbered definitions

Example of use

Usage label

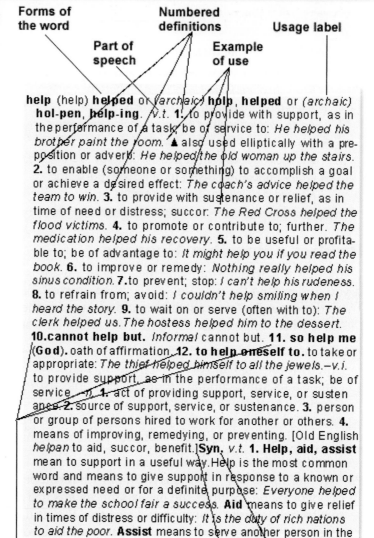

help (help) **helped** or *(archaic)* **holp, helped** or *(archaic)* **hol·pen, help·ing.** *v.t.* **1.** to provide with support, as in the performance of a task; be of service to: *He helped his brother paint the room.* ▲ also used elliptically with a preposition or adverb: *He helped the old woman up the stairs.* **2.** to enable (someone or something) to accomplish a goal or achieve a desired effect: *The coach's advice helped the team to win.* **3.** to provide with sustenance or relief, as in time of need or distress; succor: *The Red Cross helped the flood victims.* **4.** to promote or contribute to; further. *The medication helped his recovery.* **5.** to be useful or profitable to; be of advantage to: *It might help you if you read the book.* **6.** to improve or remedy: *Nothing really helped his sinus condition.* **7.** to prevent; stop: *I can't help his rudeness.* **8.** to refrain from; avoid: *I couldn't help smiling when I heard the story.* **9.** to wait on or serve (often with to): *The clerk helped us. The hostess helped him to the dessert.* **10.cannot help but.** *Informal* cannot but. **11. so help me (God).** oath of affirmation. **12. to help oneself to.** to take or appropriate: *The thief helped himself to all the jewels.—v.i.* to provide support, as in the performance of a task; be of service **—n. 1.** act of providing support, service, or sustenance. **2.** source of support, service, or sustenance. **3.** person or group of persons hired to work for another or others. **4.** means of improving, remedying, or preventing. [Old English *helpan* to aid, succor, benefit.] **Syn.** *v.t.* **1. Help, aid, assist** mean to support in a useful way. Help is the most common word and means to give support in response to a known or expressed need or for a definite purpose: *Everyone helped to make the school fair a success.* **Aid** means to give relief in times of distress or difficulty: *It is the duty of rich nations to aid the poor.* **Assist** means to serve another person in the performance of his task in a secondary capacity: *The secretary assists the officer by taking care of his corresponding.*

Idioms

Origin (etymology)

Synonyms

Recognize Word Meanings Across Subjects Have you learned a new word in one class and then noticed it in your reading for other subjects? The word might not mean exactly the same thing in each class, but you can use the meaning you already know to help you understand what it means in another subject area. For example:

Math Each digit represents a different place **value**.

Health Your **values** can guide you in making healthful decisions.

Economics The **value** of a product is measured in its cost.

▶ Understanding What You Read

Reading comprehension means understanding—deriving meaning from—what you have read. Using a variety of strategies can help you improve your comprehension and make reading more interesting and more fun.

Read for a Reason

To get the greatest benefit from your reading, **establish a purpose for reading.** In school, you have many reasons for reading, such as:

- to learn and understand new information.
- to find specific information.
- to review before a test.
- to complete an assignment.
- to prepare (research) before you write.

As your reading skills improve, you will notice that you apply different strategies to fit the different purposes for reading. For example, if you are reading for entertainment, you might read quickly, but if you are reading to gather information or follow directions, you might read more slowly, take notes, construct a graphic organizer, or reread sections of text.

Draw on Personal Background

Drawing on personal background may also be called activating prior knowledge. Before you start reading a text, ask yourself questions like these:

- What have I heard or read about this topic?
- Do I have any personal experience relating to this topic?

Using a KWL Chart A KWL chart is a good device for organizing information you gather before, during, and after reading. In the first column, list what you already **know,** then list what you **want** to know in the middle column. Use the third column when you review and assess what you **learned.** You can also add more columns to record places where you found information and places where you can look for more information.

K (What I already know)	W (What I want to know)	L (What I have learned)

Adjust Your Reading Speed Your reading speed is a key factor in how well you understand what you are reading. You will need to adjust your speed depending on your reading purpose.

Scanning means running your eyes quickly over the material to look for words or phrases. Scan when you need a specific piece of information.

Skimming means reading a passage quickly to find its main idea or to get an overview. Skim a text when you preview to determine what the material is about.

Reading for detail involves careful reading while paying attention to text structure and monitoring your understanding. Read for detail when you are learning concepts, following complicated directions, or preparing to analyze a text.

▶ Techniques to Understand and Remember What You Read

Preview

Before beginning a selection, it is helpful to **preview** what you are about to read.

Previewing Strategies

◆ Read the title, headings, and subheadings of the selection.
◆ Look at the illustrations and notice how the text is organized.
◆ Skim the selection: Take a glance at the whole thing.
◆ Decide what the main idea might be.
◆ Predict what a selection will be about.

Predict

Have you ever read a mystery, decided who committed the crime, and then changed your mind as more clues were revealed? You were adjusting your predictions. Did you smile when you found out that you guessed who committed the crime? You were verifying your predictions.

As you read, make educated guesses about story events and outcomes; that is, **make predictions** before and during reading. This will help you focus your attention on the text and will improve your understanding.

Determine the Main Idea

When you look for the **main idea**, you are looking for the most important statement in a text. Depending on what kind of text you are reading, the main idea can be located at the very beginning (news stories in a newspaper or a magazine) or at the end (scientific research document). Ask yourself the following questions:

• What is each sentence about?
• Is there one sentence that is more important than all the others?
• What idea do details support or point out?

Take Notes

Cornell Note-Taking System There are many methods for note taking. The **Cornell Note-Taking System** is a well-known method that can help you organize what you read. To the right is a note-taking activity based on the Cornell Note-Taking System.

Graphic Organizers Using a graphic organizer to retell content in a visual representation will help you remember and retain content. You might make a **chart** or **diagram,** organizing what you have read. Here are some examples of graphic organizers:

Venn Diagrams When mapping out a compare-and-contrast text structure, you can use a Venn diagram. The outer portions of the circles will show how two characters, ideas, or items contrast, or are different, and the overlapping part will compare two things, or show how they are similar.

Flow Charts To help you track the sequence of events, or cause and effect, use a flow chart. Arrange ideas or events in their logical, sequential order. Then, draw arrows between your ideas to indicate how one idea or event flows into another.

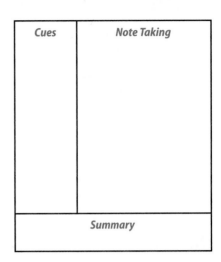

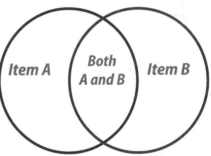

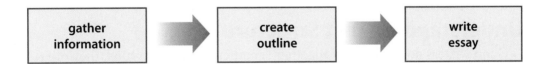

Visualize

Try to form a mental picture of scenes, characters, and events as you read. Use the details and descriptions the author gives you. If you can **visualize** what you read, it will be more interesting and you will remember it better.

Question

Ask yourself questions about the text while you read. Ask yourself about the importance of the sentences, how they relate to one another, if you understand what you just read, and what you think is going to come next.

Clarify

If you feel you do not understand meaning (through questioning), try these techniques:

> **What to Do When You Do Not Understand**
>
> ◆ Reread confusing parts of the text.
> ◆ Diagram (chart) relationships between chunks of text, ideas, and sentences.
> ◆ Look up unfamiliar words.
> ◆ Talk out the text to yourself.
> ◆ Read the passage once more.

Review

Take time to stop and review what you have read. Use your note-taking tools (graphic organizers or Cornell notes charts). Also, review and consider your KWL chart.

Monitor Your Comprehension

Continue to check your understanding by using the following two strategies:

Summarize Pause and tell yourself the main ideas of the text and the key supporting details. Try to answer the following questions: Who? What? When? Where? Why? How?

Paraphrase Pause, close the book, and try to retell what you have just read in your own words. It might help to pretend you are explaining the text to someone who has not read it and does not know the material.

▶ Understanding Text Structure

Good writers do not just put together sentences and paragraphs, they organize their writing with a specific purpose in mind. That organization is called text structure. When you understand and follow the structure of a text, it is easier to remember the information you are reading. There are many ways text may be structured. Watch for **signal words**. They will help you follow the text's organization. (Also, remember to use these techniques when you write.)

Compare and Contrast

This structure shows similarities and differences between people, things, and ideas. This is often used to demonstrate that things that seem alike are really different, or vice versa.

Signal words: similarly, more, less, on the one hand/on the other hand, in contrast, but, however

Reading Skills Handbook

Cause and Effect

Writers use the cause-and-effect structure to explore the reasons for something happening and to examine the results or consequences of events.

Signal words: so, because, as a result, therefore, for the following reasons

Problem and Solution

When they organize text around the question how?, writers state a problem and suggest solutions.

Signal words: how, help, problem, obstruction, overcome, difficulty, need, attempt, have to, must

Sequence

Sequencing tells you in which order to consider thoughts or facts. Examples of sequencing are:

Chronological order refers to the order in which events take place.

Signal words: first, next, then, finally

Spatial order describes the organization of things in space (to describe a room, for example).

Signal words: above, below, behind, next to

Order of importance lists things or thoughts from the most important to the least important (or the other way around).

Signal words: principal, central, main, important, fundamental

▶ Reading for Meaning

It is important to think about what you are reading to get the most information out of a text, to understand the consequences of what the text says, to remember the content, and to form your own opinion about what the content means.

Interpret

Interpreting is asking yourself, "What is the writer really saying?" and then using what you already know to answer that question.

Infer

Writers do not always state exactly everything they want you to understand. By providing clues and details, they sometimes imply certain information. To **infer** involves using your reasoning and experience to develop the idea on your own, based on what an author implies, or suggests. What is most important when drawing inferences is to be sure that you have accurately based your guesses on supporting details from the text. If you cannot point to a place in the selection to help back up your inference, you may need to rethink your guess.

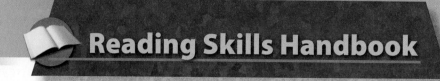

Draw Conclusions

A conclusion is a general statement you can make and explain with reasoning, or with supporting details from a text. If you read a story describing a sport where five players bounce a ball and throw it through a high hoop, you may conclude that the sport is basketball.

Analyze

To understand persuasive nonfiction (a text that discusses facts and opinions to arrive at a conclusion), you need to analyze statements and examples to see if they support the main idea. To understand an informational text (a text, such as a textbook, that gives you information, not opinions), you need to keep track of how the ideas are organized to find the main points.

Hint: Use your graphic organizers and notes charts.

Distinguish Facts from Opinions

This is one of the most important reading skills you can learn. A fact is a statement that can be proven. An opinion is what the writer believes. A writer may support opinions with facts, but an opinion cannot be proven. For example:

Fact: California produces fruit and other agricultural products.

Opinion: California produces the best fruit and other agricultural products.

Evaluate

Would you take seriously an article on nuclear fission if you knew it was written by a comedic actor? If you need to rely on accurate information, you need to find out who wrote what you are reading and why. Where did the writer get information? Is the information one-sided? Can you verify the information?

▶ Reading for Research

You will need to **read actively** to research a topic. You might also need to generate an interesting, relevant, and researchable **question** on your own and locate appropriate print and nonprint information from a wide variety of sources. Then, you will need to **categorize** that information, evaluate it, and **organize** it in a new way to produce a research project for a specific audience. Finally, **draw conclusions** about your original research question. These conclusions may lead you to other areas for further inquiry.

Locate Appropriate Print and Nonprint Information

In your research, try to use a variety of sources. Because different sources present information in different ways, your research project will be more interesting and balanced when you read a variety of sources.

Literature and Textbooks These texts include any book used as a basis for instruction or a source of information.

Book Indices A book index, or a bibliography, is an alphabetical listing of books. Some book indices list books on specific subjects; others are more general. Other indices list a variety of topics or resources.

Periodicals Magazines and journals are issued at regular intervals, such as weekly or monthly. One way to locate information in magazines is to use the *Readers' Guide to Periodical Literature*. This guide is available in print form in most libraries.

Technical Manuals A manual is a guide or handbook intended to give instruction on how to perform a task or operate something. A vehicle owner's manual might give information on how to operate and service a car.

Reference Books Reference books include encyclopedias and almanacs, and are used to locate specific pieces of information.

Electronic Encyclopedias, Databases, and the Internet There are many ways to locate extensive information using your computer. Infotrac, for instance, acts as an online readers' guide. CD encyclopedias can provide easy access to all subjects.

Organize and Convert Information

As you gather information from different sources, taking careful notes, you will need to think about how to **synthesize** the information—that is, convert it into a unified whole, as well as how to change it into a form your audience will easily understand and that will meet your assignment guidelines.

1. First, ask yourself what you want your audience to know.
2. Then, think about a pattern of organization, a structure that will best show your main ideas. You might ask yourself the following questions:

- When comparing items or ideas, what graphic aids can I use?
- When showing the reasons something happened and the effects of certain actions, what text structure would be best?
- How can I briefly and clearly show important information to my audience?
- Would an illustration or even a cartoon help to make a certain point?

What Is a Student Organization?

A student organization is a group or association of students that is formed around activities, such as:

- Family and consumer sciences
- Student government
- Community service
- Social clubs
- Honor societies
- Multicultural alliances
- Technology education
- Artists and performers
- Politics
- Sports teams
- Professional career development

A student organization is usually required to follow a set of rules and regulations that apply equally to all student organizations at a particular school.

Why Should You Get Involved?

Being an active part of a student organization opens a variety of experiences to you. Many student clubs are part of a national network of students and professionals, which provides the chance to connect to a wider variety of students and opportunities.

What's In It for You?

Participation in student organizations can contribute to a more enriching learning experience. Here are some ways you can benefit:

- Gain leadership qualities and skills that make you more marketable to employers and universities.
- Demonstrate the ability to appreciate someone else's point of view.
- Interact with professionals to learn about their different industries.
- Explore your creative interests, share ideas, and collaborate with others.
- Take risks, build confidence, and grow creatively.
- Learn valuable skills while speaking or performing in front of an audience.
- Make a difference in your life and the lives of those around you.
- Learn the importance of civic responsibility and involvement.
- Build relationships with instructors, advisors, students, and other members of the community who share similar backgrounds/world views.

Find and Join a Student Organization!

Take a close look at the organizations offered at your school or within your community. Are there any organizations that interest you? Talk to your teachers, guidance counselors, or a parent or guardian. Usually, posters or flyers for a variety of clubs and groups can be found on your school's Message Board or Web site. Try to locate more information about the organizations that meet your needs. Then, think about how these organizations can help you gain valuable skills you can use at school, at work, and in your community.

What Is FCCLA?

Family, Career and Community Leaders of America is a nonprofit national career and technical student organization for young men and women in Family and Consumer Sciences education in public and private school through grade 12. Everyone is part of a family, and FCCLA is the only national Career and Technical Student Organization with the family as its central focus. Since 1945, FCCLA members have been making a difference in their families, careers, and communities by addressing important personal, work, and societal issues through Family and Consumer Sciences education.

STAR Events Program

STAR Events (Students Taking Action with Recognition) are competitive events in which members are recognized for proficiency and achievement in chapter and individual projects, leadership skills, and occupational preparation. FCCLA provides opportunities for you to participate at local, state, and national levels.

What Are the Purposes of FCCLA?

1. Provide opportunities for personal development and preparation for adult life.
2. Strengthen the function of the family as a basic unit of society.
3. Encourage democracy through cooperative action in the home and community.
4. Encourage individual and group involvement in helping achieve global cooperation and harmony.
5. Promote greater understanding between youth and adults.
6. Provide opportunities for making decisions and for assuming responsibilities.
7. Prepare for the multiple roles of men and women in today's society.
8. Promote family and consumer sciences and related occupations.

UNIT 1

Prepare for Independent Living

Chapter **1** **Personal Growth**

Chapter **2** **Character Building**

Chapter **3** **Responsible Citizenship**

Unit Portfolio Project Preview

Evaluate Yourself

In this unit, you will think about your own interests and qualities and their place in your future. In your portfolio project you will do a self-assessment to help you reach your goals.

My Journal

Self Development Write a journal entry about one of the topics below. This will help you prepare for the project at the end of this unit.

- Identify the various organizations and activities with which you have been involved over the past few years.
- Describe a skill you learned from a class or activity and explain how you might apply it in the future.
- Cite one of your life goals and the specific skills you think will be needed to achieve it.

Explore the Photo

The way we develop as individuals sets the stage for our futures. *What goals have you set for your own individual growth in the next five years?*

3

1

Personal Growth

Chapter Objectives

Section 1.1 Be Your Best

- **Name** the four main categories of personality characteristics.
- **Describe** how a healthy self-concept can improve your confidence.
- **Demonstrate** the connection between personal growth and potential.

Section 1.2 Changes and Challenges

- **Explain** why the ability to adapt to change is an essential life skill.
- **Summarize** the personal qualities that can help you face life's challenges.

➤ Explore the Photo

When you feel good about yourself and your abilities, you feel more confident and in control. *When do you think that you are at your best?*

Writing Activity Freewriting

Who Am I? Suppose that you had to complete this sentence: "I am…" What would you say? What personal characteristics come to mind first? For five minutes, write whatever you can think of that describes who you are.

Writing Tips Use these tips to help you freewrite:
- Let your thoughts run free.
- Write down anything that comes to mind.
- Do not worry about grammar, spelling, or the order of your thoughts.
- Do not stop to reread, rephrase, or rethink.
- You can use fragments, words, and even doodles.

Be Your Best

When you feel great about yourself, life is much more enjoyable.

Reading Guide

Before You Read

Preview Take a few minutes to examine the images and features in this section. Discuss with a partner what you think this section will be about.

Read to Learn
Key Concepts

- **Name** the four main categories of personality characteristics.
- **Describe** how a healthy self-concept can improve your confidence.
- **Demonstrate** the connection between personal growth and potential.

Main Idea

Understanding yourself is the first step in becoming the person you want to be. A positive self-concept can help you realize your full potential.

Graphic Organizer

As you read, list traits that fall into the four main categories of personality characteristics. Use a chart like the one shown to help you organize your information.

Emotional Traits	Social Traits	Intellectual Traits	Moral Traits

Graphic Organizer Go to this book's Online Learning Center at **glencoe.com** to print out this graphic organizer.

Content Vocabulary

- ◇ personality
- ◇ introspective
- ◇ morality
- ◇ value
- ◇ self-concept
- ◇ self-esteem
- ◇ potential
- ◇ procrastination
- ◇ abstinence
- ◇ personal growth

Academic Vocabulary

You will find these words in your reading and on your tests. Use the glossary to look up their definitions if necessary.

- ■ apparent
- ■ evaluate

Academic Standards

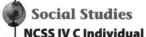

English Language Arts

NCTE 4 Use written language to communicate effectively.

Mathematics

NCTM Problem Solving Apply and adapt a variety of appropriate strategies to solve problems.

Social Studies

NCSS IV C Individual Development and Identity Describe the ways family, religion, gender, ethnicity, nationality, socioeconomic status, and other group and cultural influences contribute to the development of a sense of self.

NCTE *National Council of Teachers of English*
NCTM *National Council of Teachers of Mathematics*
NSES *National Science Education Standards*
NCSS *National Council for the Social Studies*

Get to Know Yourself

You have left childhood behind, and you are well on your way to independent living. Soon you will be responsible for making your own way in the world. Now is the time to think about what you hope your adult life will be like and what you want to achieve. What information and skills do you need to face life's challenges and achieve your personal and career goals? The choices you make will either positively or negatively affect your life, both now and in the future. Your journey through life begins with understanding who you are right now. You can build on this understanding and make a plan to become the kind of person you want to be in the future.

Your Personality

People come in all shapes and sizes and from different cultural backgrounds. They also come with distinctive personalities. Your **personality** is the combination of characteristics that makes you different from everyone else. Your unique personality includes your strengths and weaknesses, needs, and ways of expressing yourself.

At this stage in your life, you may have already experienced the physical and emotional changes that come with adolescence, or maybe you are in the midst of those changes right now. When you were younger, you probably spent a lot of time discovering and thinking about the world around you. As you get older, you may find yourself becoming more **introspective** (ˌin-trə-ˈspek-tiv), which means looking closely at your own feelings, thoughts, and motives. All of the changes and growth you have experienced up to this point have combined to form your unique personality. There are four main categories of personality characteristics: emotional, social, intellectual, and moral.

Emotional Emotion is a strong feeling about somebody or something. Every person feels the same basic emotions, such as happiness, love, fear, and anger, yet each responds to them individually.

Social In society, people meet, interact, and relate to one another in different ways. Some people prefer the company of others and dislike being alone. Others are just the opposite.

Intellectual As you gain experience and knowledge, you learn to solve more complex problems and make more mature decisions. Using your mind rather than your emotions to make decisions is a sign of intellectual maturity.

As You Read

Connect What do you typically reveal about yourself the first time you are introduced to someone?

◆ Vocabulary

You can find definitions in the glossary at the back of this book.

> ### What Makes Me Unique?
>
> You may share similar traits with others, but there is no one else just like you in the world. *Why is it important to know who you are and what makes you special?*

Moral **Morality** is a sense of right and wrong that guides decisions and actions. Morality is based on values. A **value** is an accepted principle or standard held by a person or a group. Values guide you through life and help you make decisions. Moral development is an important part of the maturing process. Teens who develop a reliable moral compass are more likely to make positive decisions. They are less likely to be lured into negative behaviors.

Your Choices

As a young adult, you will make more and more decisions that deal with issues of right and wrong behavior. Although you want to do what is right, sometimes it is not clear how you should act. Your parents and other adults in your life have set the standards for right and wrong behavior. It is up to you to apply these standards to your choices. For example, telling the truth and treating people fairly are commonly accepted standards of moral behavior. Lying and cheating are not. Parents, teachers, coaches, religious leaders, counselors, and other trusted adults can help you determine the right course of action in difficult situations.

The emotional, social, intellectual, and moral characteristics of personality become **apparent**, or clear, to others through behavior. Keep in mind, it takes time to get to know a person well and see the full depth of that person's personality.

✓ Reading Check **Explain** How can people be emotionally similar, yet different at the same time?

Self-Concept and Self-Esteem

The way you see yourself and the way you believe others see you is your **self-concept**. Think of it as a mental photograph of you. Sometimes people refer to self-concept as self-image or personal identity. It is based on your perception of your strengths and weaknesses, skills and talents, and many other qualities that make up your unique personality. When you have a positive self-concept, you like and accept yourself the way you are. This healthy attitude allows you to develop friendships with people who appreciate you for who you are. It helps you gain more independence from your parents as you mature and have more adult responsibilities. A positive self-concept can help you develop and reach goals and exhibit behaviors that challenge you physically and mentally.

Your self-concept is influenced by the experiences you have, by what people say to you, and by what you think about and say about yourself. Both negative and positive comments about you from family, friends, other people in your life, and yourself combine to help shape your self-concept. New experiences and interactions can change the way you view yourself.

It is important that you have a realistic self-concept. That means being honest about who you are and what matters to you. When you are realistic about yourself, you can take pleasure in your strengths and good qualities, acknowledge your weaknesses and limitations, and work on those areas that you can improve.

Your self-concept is directly related to your self-esteem. Your **self-esteem** is the value or importance you place on yourself. Self-esteem reflects how you feel about the picture you have of yourself in your mind. If you like yourself and have a positive self-concept, you will have high self-esteem. People who dislike the picture they have of themselves struggle with low self-esteem. Self-esteem can be higher at some times in your life than at others.

Self-esteem matters because it has a strong influence on your behavior and your well-being. When you feel good about yourself, you have more confidence. You are more likely to build healthy relationships. You avoid taking risks that will harm your health. High self-esteem generally leads to more responsible behavior. It also gives you a positive outlook and enables you to make the best of your life.

Positive and Negative Messages

Focus on the encouraging and positive messages you receive from people you trust to help you build a positive self-concept. Look at your personality, talents, and skills. What are some of the qualities that you like about yourself and that you value? When you remind yourself about your positive qualities, you are more likely to try new things. Having a positive self-concept does not mean you are perfect. No one is perfect. However, a positive self-concept can help you achieve your goals and improve your life.

Some people focus too heavily on their weaknesses and lose sight of their strengths. They might see themselves as too lazy, too shy, or as a failure. When people give too much attention to negative messages, they lose confidence in themselves. They may stop trying to improve. This is not to say that you should ignore all negative messages. You need to **evaluate**, or assess and examine, the messages you receive for any truth that they offer.

✓ **Reading Check** **Recognize** Why is it important to have a realistic self-concept?

Character?!
In Action

Accept Others
People want to be loved and accepted for who they are. Do not criticize others because they do not think the same way you do. Instead, try to understand their point of view. Focus on what makes them special. Rather than struggling to mold others into who you want them to be, encourage them to become who they want to be.

You Decide
Think of someone in your life who could use some support and encouragement. Describe what you can do to help.

▼ **Compliment Yourself**

Focus on the qualities you like about yourself to help you develop a positive self-concept. *What do you like about yourself?*

HOW TO... Boost Your Self-Esteem

Your self-concept and self-esteem affect every aspect of your life. Choosing to be a person with a positive outlook can help you when things are going well, but it becomes even more important when times are challenging. If your self-esteem is lower than it should be, work on developing a more positive view of yourself.

Learn to Accept Praise When someone compliments you, do not brush it off. People praise you because they feel that you really deserve it.

Focus on Your Strengths Everyone has talents. Remind yourself of the things you do well. Take time to participate in activities you enjoy.

Accept Yourself as You Are Do not compare yourself to others. Accept the fact that no one is perfect and that everyone has some faults. Simply work to improve yourself.

Learn from Your Mistakes Do not label yourself a failure. Instead, see mistakes as opportunities to figure out how you can do things differently in the future.

Use Your Strengths to Help Others Helping others shows you can accomplish something important. It also helps you feel good about yourself.

Take Responsibility for Your Own Life Learn how to deal with the different demands that are made of you. Managing your own life successfully will spur you to greater achievements.

Realize Your Potential

Like every other person, you have great **potential**, which is the capacity to develop, succeed, or become something more than you are right now. You were born with potential. You have strengths that can be developed. The challenge you face is to identify those strengths and make use of them. Like every other person, you can also be sidetracked from reaching your potential. This happens when certain attitudes, behaviors, or circumstances block progress.

Here are some suggestions for maximizing your potential:

- **Set Priorities** Once you decide what you want to accomplish, stay focused and avoid distractions.
- **Consider Interests and Activities** Make a list of your interests and activities and see how they fit in with your priorities.
- **Develop Supportive Friendships** Surround yourself with friends who encourage you to achieve your dreams.
- **Avoid Procrastination** The tendency to put off doing something until later is called **procrastination** (prō-ˌkras-tə-ˈnā-shən). Procrastination can often indicate an inability to set priorities and to be self-disciplined.
- **Be Health-Smart** Eat a variety of healthful food. Get enough sleep, and take time to exercise.
- **Practice Abstinence Abstinence** (ˈab-stə-nən(t)s) is the deliberate decision to avoid high-risk behaviors, including sexual activity and the use of tobacco, alcohol, and other drugs. Avoid behaviors that will keep you from reaching your full potential.

Be Smart Be Safe

Home Alone As a young adult, you may be spending more time home alone than ever before. What can you do to stay safe when you are by yourself, either in your parents' home, your dorm, or your apartment?

Write About It Write a list of safety tips for protecting yourself while you are home alone.

Life On Your Own

Build a Support Network

A strong sense of self-confidence will help you in every area of your life. It will help you master new skills and feel better about yourself when a situation does not go the way you expected. One way you can boost your confidence is to know who you can turn to for support when meeting life's challenges. Build a personal support network to help you reach your potential. Remind yourself that asking for help and accepting it are signs of strength, not weakness.

How It Works When you feel overloaded by school, family, work, and extracurricular activities, ask for support and encouragement. Supportive relationships take time to develop, so when you build your network, seek out people who really believe in you and want you to succeed. Include people who hold you accountable for your actions and who will challenge you to excel. Your network can be made up of trusted friends, parents, siblings, teachers, counselors, and others who want you to succeed.

Try It Out You are in your first year of college and have been living with a roommate in an apartment near campus. After a few months, you realize that the budget you came up with last summer is not quite working out. You do not have enough money to cover all of your expenses. You are worried about paying your bills, and it is affecting your sense of independence and your self-confidence. You know that you have made a mistake, but you are embarrassed to ask for help.

> *Your Turn* What is the first thing you should remind yourself? To whom might you turn for advice, help, or encouragement? How could you view this situation as a way to increase your confidence?

Personal Growth and Maturity

If Cassidy has the potential to be a veterinarian, does that mean she is certain to become one? The answer is no. Potential is simply the capacity you have. What matters is how you use that capacity. The key is to strive for personal growth by working toward your potential. **Personal growth** is learning and practicing new skills as you progress toward reaching your full potential. Growth has a mushrooming effect. That means the more you learn, the more you are able to learn, and the closer you move toward your potential. Personal growth is a lifelong process. You are never too mature to change and learn.

The desire to reach adulthood is normal and important. However, the real goal is not just turning a certain age, but to reach maturity. Maturity is not just about getting older. Maturity means reaching full development—physically, emotionally, socially, intellectually, and morally. People mature at different rates. Signs of maturity include independence, emotional control, dependability, and a willingness to work hard for what you want and need.

You are your most important asset. You can have a positive effect on the world when you develop positive qualities, skills, and attitudes. You will always be able to look back knowing that you made the best of your life.

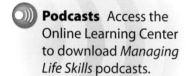

Section 1.1 — After You Read

Review Key Concepts

1. **Define** personality.
2. **Analyze** the role of self-esteem in responsible behavior.
3. **Explain** why procrastination limits your potential.

Practice Academic Skills

English Language Arts

4. Think about a time when someone used positive messages to encourage you to succeed. Write a paragraph that describes what the person said or did and how it made you feel. Then explain how you could use this experience to help someone else.

Social Studies

5. Take a look at your personality. What is it about your personality that attracts people to you? What traits do you and your friends or family have in common? What traits do you have that your friends or family do not? Write a paragraph about your favorite personality traits and how they were influenced.

Check Your Answers Check your answers at this book's Online Learning Center at **glencoe.com**.

NCTE 4 Use written language to communicate effectively.

NCSS IV C Describe the ways family, religion, gender, ethnicity, nationality, socioeconomic status, and other group and cultural influences contribute to the development of a sense of self.

Changes and Challenges

Reading Guide

Before You Read

Predict Look at the photos and figures in this section and read their captions. Write one or two sentences predicting what the section will be about.

Read to Learn
Key Concepts
- **Explain** why the ability to adapt to change is an essential life skill.
- **Summarize** the personal qualities that can help you face life's challenges.

Main Idea
You have the potential to become anything you want to be. Competence, confidence, and a positive attitude can help you reach your goals and achieve your full potential.

Content Vocabulary
◇ competence
◇ resiliency
◇ perseverance

Academic Vocabulary
You will find these words in your reading and on your tests. Use the glossary to look up their definitions if necessary.
■ accountable
■ initiate

Graphic Organizer
As you read, identify five actions you can take to help make positive changes. Use a web graphic organizer like the one shown to help you organize your information.

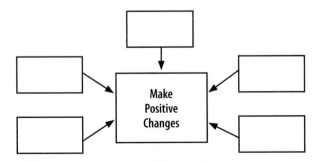

Make Positive Changes

Graphic Organizer Go to this book's Online Learning Center at **glencoe.com** to print out this graphic organizer.

Make Positive Changes

As You Read

Connect Think about a significant change you recently experienced. How did you react to it?

Some of life's changes are quick and easy to make. However, many changes are gradual, or taken one step at a time. Jaleesa wants to overcome her shyness. As a first step, she has decided to speak to someone new every day for one week. Philip is tired of being unable to find things in his cluttered room. He is committed to a major cleaning this weekend and to putting things away every night. Change can involve difficult or simple things. The ability to make changes and adapt, or adjust, to changes is an essential life skill.

Barriers to Change

Trying to make a positive change is not always easy. It takes effort and confidence. Barriers to change include thinking you have to do it all yourself, forgetting that change takes time, and procrastinating. In order to help overcome these barriers, make a plan for change, set goals, and be **accountable**, or responsible, for your own actions and attitudes.

Opportunities for Change

Some people look for opportunities to change in order to make life better or more interesting. Maybe you want to expand your talents and skills by learning to play a sport or a musical instrument. Maybe you want to tackle something more personal, like building relationships with distant relatives. If you are unhappy with some aspect of your life, look for ways to change it. Ask others who have made a similar change how they did it. Develop a plan of action. Confide in people you trust, and hold yourself accountable for the changes you want to make. To do this, you will need two special qualities: competence and confidence. They work hand in hand.

Developing Competence

Vocabulary

You can find definitions in the glossary at the back of this book.

An Olympic athlete, a top musician, and an inspirational teacher are each highly competent people. **Competence** (ˈkäm-pə-tən(t)s) is having the qualities and skills needed to perform a task or participate fully in an activity. You can, of course, be competent without being an Olympic champion. There are degrees of competence.

If you want to make a change, you need to develop or improve your competence in the related areas. Once you have committed to a change, brainstorm ways you can gain the competence needed. The people around you, and even the people that they know, may be willing to help you. School, of course, is an obvious resource. Books, newspapers, and Web sites may have useful information. There are many opportunities for learning, and you should learn how to recognize them. You are already competent in some areas. Continue to improve those skills as well as develop new ones. Doing so can enrich your life and help you improve the lives of others.

Build Competence

To become competent, you need opportunities to learn and practice the skills involved. *What can this teen do to become more competent when his car needs repairs?*

Gaining Confidence

Confidence means you believe in yourself and in your abilities. People who have this positive attitude display it in their actions. Luisa, for example, wondered if she could get a part in the school play. Though she worried about stage fright, her confidence won out, and she decided to audition. Her positive attitude showed and helped her get a part. Here are some common characteristics you often observe in confident people:

- **Self-Assurance** Because they believe in themselves, confident people stand up for themselves and for what they value. They are proud, but not arrogant.
- **Self-Control** Since they realize that their actions affect their own life and the world around them, people with confidence carefully consider what they do before they do it. They use reason, rather than emotion, to decide what to do and when to act.
- **Willingness to Take Reasonable Risks** Confident people are willing to take risks to achieve their goals, but they know where to draw the line. A skateboarder who wants to improve skills may try new tricks and jumps but knows better than to skate without safety gear.
- **Positive Self-Concept and High Self-Esteem** Confident people know that no one is perfect, but they work to improve their weaknesses. They feel good about what they have learned and achieved and keep trying to do better.

Confidence grows stronger each time you succeed. Your increased confidence makes you more willing to work toward building and strengthening your competencies. In other words, competence builds confidence, and vice versa. You see this principle in action all the time. A winning team is inspired to practice harder to win again. Receiving a high grade in class gives a student the encouragement to strive for other high grades. You can put this cycle to work in your own life to make the changes that you want to make.

Succeed in **SCHOOL** and **LIFE**

Learn from Disappointment

No one wants to do poorly on a test. However, disappointment and even failure are natural parts of success. Setbacks can be turned into positive experiences when you learn from them and use them to improve next time.

Confidence Is Learned

No one is born confident. *What can be gained from making an extra effort and taking risks?*

Setting Goals for Change

Feeling confident and competent provides a sense of power and purpose. You begin to realize that you can become the person you want to be and work to create the kind of life you want for yourself. Taking action that will lead you in these directions begins with setting goals and continues with making those goals a reality.

When you set goals and successfully achieve them, your confidence will grow. You will likely discover that you can make things happen in your life when you are willing to try. For now, remember that change is a gradual process. It can be worked on one step at a time. Be patient with yourself.

✓ **Reading Check** **Define** What is competence?

Meeting Life's Challenges

Change is a part of life. Some changes are expected. For example, you know that life will change when you move out on your own. When you move out, you face the challenge of settling in, making new friends, and building a different life. There may be other changes, however, that catch you off guard. For example, you or a family member could lose a job unexpectedly. If this happened, you would face multiple challenges, such as dealing with the sudden loss of income while looking for a new job. Even some of the positive changes that you **initiate** (i-'ni-shē-,āt), or cause to happen, can be challenging. Imagine that you take a part-time job working three evenings a week. You would have to learn the job, make an effort to get along with your coworkers, and find a way to get your homework and chores done with less time available. Change can bring gain or loss, joy or frustration. No matter what happens, you can count on change occurring throughout your life.

Like change, challenges are a part of life, and everyone has to deal with them. Some people, however, face more serious challenges than others. The challenges presented by disabilities, discrimination, and poverty sometimes seem impossible to overcome, yet there are many examples of people who conquer them. In general, a person's attitude toward challenges determines whether they give up or achieve success.

Challenges of the Teen Years

The changes that occur during adolescence can make any teen feel insecure. One teen struggles to fit in at school. Another is uncomfortable with a changing body. Still another feels especially sensitive about what people think about him. If any of this sounds familiar, do not worry. Every adult you know was a teen once. The children you know will become teens some day. Although it may seem like it at times, you are not alone. There are steps you can take to make things easier. **Figure 1.1** can give you some ideas for coping with the ups and downs of adolescence.

A Positive Attitude

Few people go through life without hitting a few bumps along the way. Some people hit more bumps than others. Those bumps can either get you down or get you going. What keeps some people working toward achieving their goals while causing others to give up? It is all a matter of attitude. Your attitude is your way of looking at the world and the people in it. People with a positive attitude usually get along well with others, and they tend to be enthusiastic and cheerful most of the time. They complete tasks, even the ones they do not enjoy, without complaining or trying to avoid them.

Go Green

When you choose to "go green," you help the environment and you help yourself. Set a positive example for others by doing something as simple as reusing plastic food storage bags instead of throwing them away after one use.

Figure 1.1 Coping with Changes

Change Happens During the adolescent years, your life can change when you least expect it to. *What other periods in a person's life might be especially challenging?*

WHAT YOU CAN DO	HOW IT CAN HELP
Look ahead.	People sometimes look longingly at the past, wishing that changes had not happened. Turning back the clock, however, is simply impossible. Those who look ahead realize that the changes of adolescence are moving them in an exciting direction.
Think positively.	Changes present opportunities. They can also signal personal growth. The strong emotions that sometimes hit you, for example, are a sign of deepening feelings that will help you form strong relationships.
Take advantage of new abilities.	As a young adult, you are continuing to develop a greater sense of concern for others. You can use this to make positive changes in your family, school, and community.
Get help when you need it.	Almost everyone needs help at one time or another. Adults, including your parents, have lived through adolescence themselves and can often suggest ways of handling its challenges.
Participate in physical activities.	Play a sport, take a swim, or go for a walk or run. As you exercise, your brain releases chemicals called endorphins, which reduce feelings of anxiety and improve your mood.
Eat the right foods.	Make sure to get plenty of protein, dairy, and whole-grains fortified with vitamin B_{12}. Studies show this vitamin reduces depression and increases energy. Avoid sugar and caffeine. These ingredients cause mood and energy swings.
Volunteer in your community.	Helping others is great on its own, but it can also be very rewarding and make you feel better about yourself.
Look for ways to make new friends.	Rather than spending long hours in your room, take advantage of opportunities to make new friends. Positive friendships can help improve your confidence and self-esteem, and they can help you develop important social skills.

Some people develop qualities that help prepare them to meet life's challenges head on. They are able to adapt by being willing to make necessary changes. **Resiliency** (ri-'zil-yən-sē) is the ability to recover from or adjust to change or misfortune. **Perseverance** (ˌpər-sə-'vir-ən(t)s) is sticking to an action or belief, even when it is difficult. Adaptability, resilience, and perseverance, along with a positive attitude, help people keep going even when they feel discouraged.

There will be times, of course, when you feel discouraged and overwhelmed. Those are the times when you need to work on keeping a positive attitude. Accept that some things cannot be changed. Work on changing those things that you can change. Do not focus on your negative feelings. Instead, focus on what you can achieve. A positive attitude is a powerful thing.

Sources of Support

As you look toward the future, realize that others are willing to help you meet your challenges in life. Family, friends, religious leaders, school counselors, and teachers are all possible sources of support. Do not be afraid to ask for help if you need it. Others know what it is like to make changes and face challenges. Remember, too, that others may need your help. Be ready to listen and encourage friends and family members. Giving to others benefits you, making you feel more confident and competent as you see what you can contribute to another person's life.

Two Views One World

How Do You Feel About Change?

Change is something that every person has to deal with, yet people greet it with different attitudes and responses.

Samantha: I guess you'd call me impatient, but I get bored when things stay the same for too long. I don't even like taking the same way to school each day. To me, change is opportunity. Think of the great inventions and discoveries we wouldn't have if people weren't willing to try something new. Think of the fun and excitement we'd miss. To me, change means progress.

Devin: Have you ever noticed that "change" is one letter away from "chance"? Making a change is risky. I don't have any trouble with giving up something to gain something better. But I like to be sure that what I gain is worth more than what I'm giving up—not only now, but in the long run, too. I'd also like to know that it is worth the trouble. I don't want to go through the hassle just to be disappointed.

Seeing Both Sides
What words tell you the feelings behind each attitude expressed above?
What advice would be helpful for both points of view?

 **You Are Not Alone**

As you face the challenges of the future, remember that you do not have to face them by yourself. *What should you do when you need help?*

 Podcasts Access the Online Learning Center to download *Managing Life Skills* podcasts.

Section 1.2 After You Read

Review Key Concepts

1. **Interpret** this statement: Competence builds confidence, and confidence builds competence.

2. **Identify** strategies you can use to keep a positive attitude when you face difficult challenges.

Practice Academic Skills

 English Language Arts

3. Write a letter to a friend who has great potential, but is not making an effort to develop it. Use words and phrases that have the power to encourage, motivate, and support your friend.

 Social Studies

4. Choose a technology product that you use often, such as a music player, cell phone, or a hairdryer. Outline the changes made to the product over time. Identify factors that led to the change. How were the changes accepted by those who use the product? Consider how changes in technology address common challenges people face.

Check Your Answers Check your answers at this book's Online Learning Center at **glencoe.com**.

> **NCTE 5** Use different writing process elements to communicate effectively.

> **NCSS VIII A** Identify and describe both current and historical examples of the interaction and interdependence of science, technology, and society in cultural settings.

Pathway to Your Career

Personal Trainer

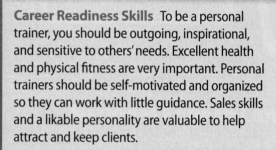

What Does a Personal Trainer Do?

Personal trainers work with clients to determine physical fitness levels and to set and reach fitness goals. They create customized exercise plans, demonstrate various exercises, and help clients improve their techniques. They often create records to keep track of clients' progress, and they may also give their clients advice on how to change their lifestyles to improve their fitness. They usually work one-on-one or in small groups in gyms and clients' homes.

Career Readiness Skills To be a personal trainer, you should be outgoing, inspirational, and sensitive to others' needs. Excellent health and physical fitness are very important. Personal trainers should be self-motivated and organized so they can work with little guidance. Sales skills and a likable personality are valuable to help attract and keep clients.

Education and Training Most personal trainers must be certified to begin working with clients. An increasing number of facilities prefer that personal trainers have a bachelor's degree in a field related to health or fitness. Personal trainers often do not receive on-the-job training and are expected to know how to do their jobs when they are hired.

Job Outlook Job opportunities for personal trainers are projected to increase faster than the average for all occupations due to the general trend of job growth in health clubs and fitness facilities and an increasing interest in fitness and health.

Critical Thinking Conduct research to learn about a typical workday in the life of a personal trainer, and summarize your findings. What interests, abilities, and personal priorities might draw someone to a career as a personal trainer?

Career Cluster  College & Career Readiness

Human Services Personal trainers work in the Personal Care Services pathway of this career cluster. Other jobs in this cluster include:

- Elementary School Counselor
- Market Researcher
- Barber
- Cosmetologist
- Events Specialist
- Buyer
- Credit Counselor
- Nail Technician
- Adult Day Care Worker
- Banker
- Food Service Worker
- Consumer Advocate
- Skin Care Specialist
- Party Planner

Explore Further The Human Services career cluster contains five pathways: Early Childhood Development and Services, Counseling and Mental Health Services, Family and Community Services, Personal Care Services, and Consumer Services. Choose one of these pathways to explore further.

 Career Clusters To learn more about career clusters, go to this book's Online Learning Center at **glencoe.com**.

CHAPTER SUMMARY

Section 1.1
Be Your Best

Personality is the combination of characteristics that make you unique. Your self-concept and self-esteem affect every aspect of your life. Boost your self-esteem by focusing on your strengths and using those strengths to help others. You have the potential to become whatever you want. The process of personal growth helps you reach your potential.

Section 1.2
Changes and Challenges

Change can involve difficult or simple things. It is important to be able to adjust to changes you cannot control and focus on changes that can improve your life. Overcome barriers and try viewing changes as opportunities. Competence, confidence, and a positive attitude give you the power to make successful changes and achieve your goals.

Vocabulary Review

1. Use each of these content and academic vocabulary terms in a sentence.

Content Vocabulary
◇ personality (p. 7)
◇ introspective (p. 7)
◇ morality (p. 8)
◇ value (p. 8)
◇ self-concept (p. 8)
◇ self-esteem (p. 9)
◇ potential (p. 11)

◇ procrastination (p. 11)
◇ abstinence (p. 11)
◇ personal growth (p. 12)
◇ competence (p. 14)
◇ resiliency (p. 18)
◇ perseverance (p. 18)

Academic Vocabulary
■ apparent (p. 8)
■ evaluate (p. 9)
■ accountable (p. 14)
■ initiate (p. 16)

Review Key Concepts

2. Name the four main categories of personality characteristics.
3. Describe how a healthy self-concept can improve your confidence.
4. Demonstrate the connection between personal growth and potential.
5. Explain why the ability to adapt to change is an essential life skill.
6. Summarize the personal qualities that can help you face life's challenges.

Critical Thinking

7. Analyze What might happen to people who mature in age, but who do not grow in other ways?
8. Examine Think of someone you know who is working to achieve his or her potential. How is he or she successful in reaching goals?
9. Make Judgments Choose a famous person in entertainment, sports, politics, or history. What characteristics make him or her appear confident? Does this person ever seem insecure? Explain your answer.
10. Predict Imagine what your future will be like based on your current self-concept. What changes could you make to improve your self-concept and strengthen your ability to reach your full potential?
11. Draw Conclusions How could having too much confidence or an inflated sense of self-esteem be a negative trait in a person?

ACTIVE LEARNING

12. Thank-You List Feeling grateful, or thankful, can contribute to a positive outlook. For example, imagine that you were having difficulty in your science class, and a classmate helped you prepare for the next test. Her help, as well as your doing well on the test, would likely make you feel grateful. For one week, make a list of at least five things that you were thankful for each day. At the end of the week, look over your lists. How often were your friends and family included in the lists? How often were material

things listed? What else made you feel grateful? Write a paragraph to explain how being thankful and expressing thankfulness can contribute to a positive outlook.

Family & Community Connections

13. Comment Log People are often their own harshest critics. How often have you heard yourself say, "There's no way I'm going to pass this test," or "My skin looks terrible!" Do you ever hear similar words from your peers? Perhaps you have a co-worker who jokingly says, "I don't know why they hired me—I don't know what I'm doing!" For three days, pay special attention to conversations around you. Listen to conversations at home, at school, at work, or anywhere you might hear people talking. Keep a log of the negative things you hear people say about themselves, even if they appear to be joking. Review your log at the end of the third day. What faults do people seem to criticize most in themselves? What can you do to encourage others to develop more positive attitudes about how they view themselves?

21ˢᵗ Century Skills

Technology Skills

14. Book Search Conduct research to find books about personal growth and self-esteem. Choose at least two books from each category that appeal to you. Using spreadsheet software, enter the title, author or authors, and a brief summary of the main focus of each book. Include the reasons for your choices.

Creativity Skills

15. Celebration Scrapbook Create a scrapbook that celebrates you. Include photos, mementos, and writings that represent the good things about you and your life. Every other day for a week, look at your scrapbook or collection. How has it improved your self-esteem?

FCCLA Connections

Self-Direction Skills

16. Power of One As part of its mission, FCCLA encourages students to create self-directed projects that focus on finding and using personal power. Read about the Power of One program on the FCCLA Web site. Choose a unit such as A Better You, and write an outline for an essay that you could submit to FCCLA.

Academic Skills

English Language Arts

17. Look for Clues Read a biographical article about a well-known person. Look for clues about the individual's personality. What is his or her attitude toward life? What is revealed about his or her self-image? What qualities seem to link success and happiness? Which qualities seem to have a negative effect? Compare your findings to those of your classmates.

> **NCTE 2** Read literature to build an understanding of the human experience.

Social Studies

18. Influences on Development How does society affect personality development and self-esteem? What role does family, religion, ethnic group, nationality, or gender play in development? What effect does the media have? What do you think has the most influence on you? Explain your conclusion.

> **NCSS IV C Individual Development and Identity** Describe the ways family, religion, gender, ethnicity, nationality, socioeconomic status, and other group and cultural influences contribute to the development of a sense of self.

Mathematics

19. Rent Comparison One of the most important choices you will make when you are ready to live on your own is where to live. Suppose you must decide between downtown and the suburbs. Compare rents to make your decision. A one-bedroom apartment downtown rents for $600. A one-bedroom apartment in the suburbs rents for 75% of the cost of the downtown apartment. What is the rent in the suburbs?

Math Concept **Multiplying by Percents** To determine the cost of the apartment in the suburbs, multiply the cost of the downtown apartment by 75%.

Starting Hint Change the percent to a decimal by moving the decimal point two places to the left. 75% becomes .75, which you will multiply by $600.

 For more math practice, go to the Math Appendix at the back of the book.

> **NCTM Number and Operations** Understand numbers, ways of representing numbers, relationships among numbers, and number systems.

 ## Standardized Test Practice   **CCR** College & Career Readiness

MULTIPLE CHOICE
Read the question. Then read each answer choice. Choose the best answer.

> **Test-Taking Tip** In a multiple-choice test, pay attention to key words in the question and each answer choice. In this question, the key words are "positive attitude." Which answer choice specifically refers to positive attitude?

20. Which situation best describes a person with a positive attitude?
a. Gene tries to convince his friend that he should not eat so much sugary foods.
b. Hilary lets Amanda copy her notes from biology class.
c. Ashley expresses sincere thankfulness to others.
d. Dwayne completed his degree, so he thinks he has enough education.

Character Building

➤ **Explore the Photo**

Participating in activities that benefit others is one of many ways to build character. *How can the activity shown in this photo be beneficial to your community and to your personal development?*

Writing Activity

Making Lists

Whom Do You Admire? Explore your ideas to clarify your thinking and find a focus for your writing. One useful technique for exploring ideas is making lists. Choose three people you admire. For each person, make a list of the traits you admire. Then review all the lists and underline related ideas. Which idea could be used as a writing topic?

Writing Tips Use these tips to help you make lists:
- Start with a key word or phrase.
- Add ideas, phrases, and thoughts as they occur to you.
- Do not worry about keeping your ideas in order.
- Review your lists to look for related ideas.

Character and Values

Reading Guide

Before You Read

Preview Choose a content or academic vocabulary word that is new to you. When you find it in the text, write down the definition.

Read to Learn
Key Concepts
- **Explain** why character is vital to personal growth and to society.
- **Outline** the ways in which values are acquired.

Main Idea
Values are the foundation upon which character is built. Values serve as a guide to setting your personal standards and making ethical decisions.

Content Vocabulary
◇ character
◇ consequence
◇ mentor
◇ conscience

Academic Vocabulary
You will find these words in your reading and on your tests. Use the glossary to look up their definitions if necessary.
■ model
■ reflect

Academic Standards

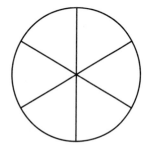
English Language Arts
NCTE 2 Read literature to build an understanding of the human experience.

Science
NSES A Develop understandings about scientific inquiry.

Social Studies
NCSS III J People, Places, and Environments Analyze and evaluate social and economic effects of environmental changes and crises resulting from phenomena such as floods, storms, and drought.

NCTE *National Council of Teachers of English*
NCTM *National Council of Teachers of Mathematics*
NSES *National Science Education Standards*
NCSS *National Council for the Social Studies*

Graphic Organizer
As you read, identify six guidelines that can help you act according to your values. Use a pie chart like the one shown to help you organize your information.

Graphic Organizer Go to this book's Online Learning Center at **glencoe.com** to print out this graphic organizer.

What Is Character?

Character is the development and application of commonly held principles which promote personal growth, establish good citizenship, and support society. People who have character possess moral strength and integrity. They understand the difference between right and wrong. They accept and live by principles such as honesty, dignity, respect, and caring.

Can you think of a time when you were faced with a choice between right and wrong, or selfish and unselfish? People face those types of choices every day. What they choose to do shows their character.

Character and Well-Being

Character affects your choice of friends, activities, interests, and behaviors. Character promotes your well-being. When you abide by the expectations, rules, and laws of your family, school, and community, you are more likely to behave responsibly and make thoughtful decisions.

Character also promotes the well-being of society. Most people would not want to live in a world in which lying, stealing, and cheating were considered normal behaviors. In order for society to function well, people must cooperate with one another. Character traits such as responsibility, respect, and mutual trust are essential to that process.

Developing character is a process that requires conscious effort. It does not just happen. Families, teachers, friends, and people in the community can all help you develop character. When they **model**, or demonstrate, character, you are likely to make the same traits a part of who you are. They can also provide support and set expectations that encourage you to build your character.

The choices you make and their consequences will give you lots of experience in developing character. A **consequence** (ˈkän(t)-sə-ˌkwen(t)s) is something that follows as a result of an action or choice. A consequence can be positive or negative. For example, Brandon lied to his parents about finishing his homework so he could practice his soccer drills. When his grades dropped, he was kicked off the soccer team. Brandon learned from his poor decisions. Today, he is responsible about doing his schoolwork and has won back his parents' trust and his place on the team. As you continue to mature, your struggles and successes will help you strengthen your character.

You may know a special person who helps you develop character by being a mentor. A **mentor** is a person who acts as a teacher and a guide. This person may be a relative, a friend, or someone in your community who invests time and energy to help you grow.

> ✓ **Reading Check**　**Connect**　How does personal character promote the well-being of society?

As You Read

Connect Which people in your life have had the most influence on your value system?

◆ **Vocabulary**

You can find definitions in the glossary at the back of this book.

Succeed in SCHOOL and LIFE

Stand Up for Yourself

With a trusted friend or adult, act out difficult situations and practice being assertive. Remember to stand your ground and be true to your personal values. You should never feel embarrassed about sticking up for what matters to you.

Role Models and Mentors

People reveal their character by their words, their actions, and by what they choose to do with their lives. *What common traits are found in good role models and mentors?*

Get Involved!

Be a Mentor

Why not volunteer to be a mentor? Most communities have organizations, such as *Big Brothers Big Sisters*, that pair up young adults with children who need guidance and mentoring. These one-to-one relationships can be positive for both participants. Volunteering your time to be a mentor can lead to brighter futures for all involved, and help build stronger communities.

Recognizing Values

Values are the foundation upon which character is built. Values are beliefs and ideas about what you think is important. Your actions, the decisions you make, and the kind of person you are all **reflect**, or reveal, your values.

Your values influence and guide all aspects of your life, including your relationships, decisions, and goals. For example, people with integrity have high principles and standards. They resist social pressure to do what they think is wrong, and they live by their values. In sports, a good sportsperson observes the rules of fair play, respects teammates and opponents, and wins and loses gracefully. People who possess the value of fairness show this kind of good sportsmanship in all of their actions. Compassionate people actively show concern for the well-being of people, animals, and the environment. It is important to be authentic, or real. Authentic people are honest—they tell the truth and admit to wrongdoing or mistakes. Look at the feature on page 29 for more values and how they are commonly expressed.

Universal Values

Many values, such as integrity, fairness, and compassion, are universal, or common, to all societies. Although universal values are held around the world, people place different levels of importance on them. Even among your own friends, you may share similar values but express them differently. You may show respect by choosing your words carefully to avoid hurt feelings. Your friend may think it is respectful to be very honest and blunt, even if her words stir up debate or disagreement.

HOW TO . . . . Express Values

You may express universal values every day without even knowing it. Your actions can show others that your character is built on a strong foundation of values. Values are expressed in what you say and in how you say it, and they show in what you are willing to stand up for. When universal values are upheld, life is better for individuals, families, and communities.

Responsibility Be accountable for your choices and actions. This involves making decisions and accepting the consequences of your choices and behaviors. It also means doing your fair share. Getting your homework done on time is just one example of responsible behavior you demonstrate every day.

Trustworthiness Trustworthy people can be taken at their word. Honor your commitments and do what you say you will do. Stand by your family, friends, and country.

Respect Show high regard for yourself and for others. Be tolerant of differences. Even better, view differences as reasons to celebrate. Deal peacefully with anger, insults, and disagreements. People who show respect are not hateful or cruel. Respecting elders is one of many ways to show respect.

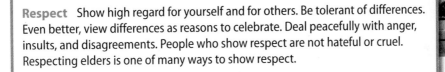

Self-Discipline You are in charge of your behavior. Demonstrate hard work and be self-directed. Do not wait to be told what to do. Take initiative in pursuing goals and activities. If you want a place on the track team, start a supervised and disciplined training routine.

Citizenship Respect authority and obey laws and rules. Show that your community is important to you by volunteering at school and in the community. When the time comes, exercise your right to vote. Your good citizenship shows when you use your time and skills to help others in your community.

Acquiring Values

You began to acquire, or obtain, values as soon as you were born. Values are learned both directly, through teaching, and indirectly, through observation. The family home is usually the first place where values are taught and observed. Families often teach one another to share, show respect, and care for one another. You also learn values in school and in your community.

Religion and culture also play a major role in the formation of values. For many people, religious beliefs and teachings provide guidelines to live by. Likewise, cultural traditions teach people what is important in a particular culture.

Society teaches values through laws, for example, which very clearly set forth what is important. You learn that safety is valued because of laws that set speed limits and require people to wear safety belts. You know that honesty is valued because people who steal or lie are punished.

Media messages, too, can influence how values are formed. For example, some advertisements imply that having fun and looking good are more important than values such as respect for yourself and others. Some movies and television shows reinforce the values that you have learned elsewhere, while others do not.

Live by Your Values

All your life you will examine your values and live by them. Strong values help you make wise choices when faced with negative influences. Here are some guidelines that can help you act according to your values:

• **Consider the consequences.** Ask yourself: Will taking this action result in harm to me or to anyone else? Will it cause me to do anything illegal? Will it get me in trouble at home?

 Messages in the Media

Many television and radio programs, magazines, Web sites, and advertisers have their own agenda, or underlying messages, to promote. *What have you seen in the media that may come into conflict with your personal values?*

Family Values

This family makes a special effort to spend quality time together. *What does that tell you about their values?*

- **Listen to your conscience.** The thinking that leads you to do what is right rather than wrong is called your **conscience** ('kän(t)-shən(t)s).
- **Turn to your family.** Your parents and older family members were teens once. Asking for help or advice from a parent may be difficult at times, but it can help strengthen relationships.
- **Gain knowledge.** When faced with a decision involving values, learn more before you act. Ask questions.
- **Evaluate the source.** Before accepting what others encourage you to do or believe, look at the source. Is it reliable? Use reason and logic to reach your decision.
- **Talk to others.** When you have doubts or concerns, talk to adults you trust and respect. Responsible people can help you sort things out.

 Podcasts Access the Online Learning Center to download *Managing Life Skills* podcasts.

Section 2.1 After You Read

Review Key Concepts

1. **Describe** how a mentor can help you develop character.
2. **Explain** why it is said that values are the foundation upon which character is built.

 Check Your Answers Check your answers at this book's Online Learning Center at **glencoe.com**.

Practice Academic Skills

 English Language Arts

3. An activist is a person who acts to bring about social or political change. Read about the life of a social activist. For example, choose a civil rights leader, a suffragist, a politician, or an educator. Write a brief essay about his or her achievements. Explain how the person's values and character played a part in what was accomplished.

> **NCTE 2** Read literature to build an understanding of the human experience.

 Social Studies

4. When a natural disaster occurs, most people react in a way that reflects their character. For example, a person who is generally kind and compassionate is likely to find a way to help victims. Research a natural disaster that affected a large community. What specific actions were taken by the community to provide relief and to rebuild?

> **NCSS III J** Analyze and evaluate social and economic effects of environmental changes and crises resulting from phenomena such as floods, storms, and drought.

Standards and Ethics

Standards, values, and ethics are the foundation of your character.

Reading Guide

Before You Read

Predict Read the key concepts and vocabulary terms on this page. Write one or two sentences predicting what you think the section will be about.

Read to Learn
Key Concepts
- **Describe** how personal standards can help you take control of life experiences.
- **Define** ethical behavior.

Main Idea

Personal standards are based on your values, and they guide your behavior. Ethical choices are based on what is fair and right.

Content Vocabulary
◇ personal standard
◇ proactive
◇ peer pressure
◇ discretion
◇ ethics

Academic Vocabulary

You will find these words in your reading and on your tests. Use the glossary to look up their definitions if necessary.
- conduct
- value

Academic Standards

 **English Language Arts**

NCTE 4 Use written language to communicate effectively.

 **Mathematics**

NCTM Problem Solving Solve problems that arise in mathematics and in other contexts.

Social Studies

NCSS I C Culture Apply an understanding of culture as an integrated whole that explains the functions and interactions of language, literature, the arts, traditions, beliefs and values, and behavior patterns.

Graphic Organizer

As you read, list four questions you can ask yourself when setting personal standards. Use a graphic organizer like the one shown to help you organize your information.

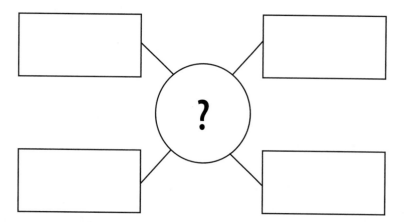

Graphic Organizer Go to this book's Online Learning Center at **glencoe.com** to print out this graphic organizer.

NCTE *National Council of Teachers of English*
NCTM *National Council of Teachers of Mathematics*
NSES *National Science Education Standards*
NCSS *National Council for the Social Studies*

Setting Your Standards

Your values are the basis for many decisions in your life. You already understand that actions resulting from your decisions bring positive or negative consequences. As you mature, you are more able to predict what those consequences might be. It is time to begin setting personal standards for how you will behave in certain types of situations.

A **personal standard** is a rule or principle you set for yourself. It guides your behavior by defining what you do and do not do. Your personal standards are like your own code of **conduct**, or behavior. It is a commitment to yourself about how you will act.

Eloisa set a personal standard that she will not get into a car with someone who has been drinking alcohol. After a party, Eloisa chose not to ride with a friend who had been drinking, and she called her parents instead. Eloisa had already decided how to handle such a situation and had simply followed through. Setting personal standards ahead of time is a way of being proactive. Being **proactive** means you take the initiative to think and plan ahead for situations you might encounter. Proactive people take control of life experiences rather than letting life experiences control them.

As Eloisa's situation shows, it helps to think about your personal standards before you are in a situation you might not be ready to handle. Personal standards help prevent you from making choices based on the mood of the moment or on **peer pressure**, the influence of others in your age group. You will learn more about peer pressure and peer influence in Chapter 6.

As You Read

Connect What helps you decide what is right and what is wrong?

Vocabulary

You can find definitions in the glossary at the back of this book.

Be Proactive

Take advantage of the life experiences of trusted adults by talking to them before facing difficult situations. *How can this help you make better choices?*

Figure 2.1
Plan Ahead

Know What To Do As you mature, you will be expected to make more and more decisions without input from others. *What are some examples of decisions that will no longer be made for you?*

POTENTIAL PROBLEM	QUESTIONS TO ASK YOURSELF
Conflict Values	What situations tend to put my values in conflict with others?
Expectations	When do I feel uncomfortable about what I think people expect of me?
Pressure	In what situations do I tend to feel pressured into being someone I do not want to be, or doing something I do not want to do?
Compromise	What types of situations make me feel like I am compromising, or giving in?

Values Guide Your Standards

At the heart of each of your personal standards are your values. If you **value**, or attach importance to, responsibility, your personal standards will reflect responsibility. Part of being proactive and planning ahead includes thinking about potential problems and preparing for them. **Figure 2.1** lists questions you can ask yourself that can help guide your decisions as you set personal standards.

Guidelines to Follow

As you build your value system and set your personal standards, you need to be prepared to keep, defend, adjust, and strengthen your values. Sound judgment and discretion will assist you. **Discretion** is the good judgment and sensitivity needed to avoid embarrassing or upsetting others, and to keep sensitive information private.

When thinking about new issues, be cautious and consider how your personal standards apply to the issues. When taking a position, be sure your reasoning is clear and logical. Below are guidelines that you can use as you develop a value system that will serve you well throughout life.

Follow the Rules of Society The rules of society are based on values that respect life, property, and truth. Rules and laws are created because order is needed for security and progress. Therefore, such acts as stealing and cheating are not allowed. Following laws and rules builds strength in society. It also makes you a stronger person. People who follow the laws gain respect and opportunity in society. Laws, of course, are changed when necessary.

Learn from Others Watch what goes on around you. Learn from the mistakes and the successes of others. Knowing about the experiences of other people can help you strengthen your own values. Look at each source of information carefully to see if its influence is positive. Talk to an adult you trust such as a family member, teacher, coach, or school counselor. The adult may be able to help you clarify your values.

Health & Wellness TIPS

Handling Peer Pressure

Peer pressure can cause enormous amounts of stress, which can lead to both physical and mental health problems. To deal with peer pressure:

► Spend time with friends who make you feel happy and accepted as you are.

► Walk away from any situation if you feel uncomfortable because of peer pressure.

Know What You Value Think about what is important to you. That will help you know what your values are. If you know this, your values will be there when you need them.

When Values Are Confusing

As you mature, you become more involved with people and events outside of your family and your circle of friends. You will be more aware of how people's values can sometimes conflict. Many issues are not clear cut. You may not be sure what is right. You may see reasons that support both sides of an issue. You may question why some people believe as they do when your beliefs are just the opposite.

It is important to stay true to the values and personal standards you have set for yourself. Some values can cause debate. It is not easy to take a stance on a controversial issue about which people have very different views. It may be impossible to come to an agreement. Society and individuals can be torn by conflicting values, especially in matters that involve tolerance and respect.

Read the questions again in Figure 2.1, and think of situations that fit each question. Imagine how you might respond in each situation, and consider possible consequences. Which responses have the most positive outcome for you and others? Which best reflect your values and the character you want to show? Use your values to set your own rules, principles, and guidelines by which to act. Then when you find yourself in these types of situations, remind yourself of your personal standards and act accordingly.

✓ **Reading Check** **Relate** What is the relationship between personal standards and values?

Succeed in SCHOOL and LIFE

Commitment
Consider joining or starting a pledge program in your school. Students sign a written pledge of standards they will follow in a particular area, such as behavior at school, sportsmanship, driving, dating, or alcohol and drug use. Signing a pledge helps to reinforce your commitment to something that matters to you.

Life On Your Own

Demonstrate Good Character Traits

Practicing good character traits, such as honesty, kindness, and respect, is something that will make your life easier and more enjoyable. If you treat others well, they will usually treat you well in return. This skill will help you with your friendships, family relationships, business interactions, and even casual acquaintances.

How It Works Have you ever heard the expression, "What goes around comes around"? Think about what it means. Imagine a new student walks into the cafeteria at lunch and has no place to sit. You wave her over to sit at your table. In the future, perhaps she or someone else will show you the same kindness.

Try It Out You need to choose groups to work on a project in one of your classes. Your teacher tells you that you can select your own groups of three or four students. You and your two closest friends have already formed your group when you notice one student who has not been selected. You do not know this student well, and you know your group of three will work well together and have fun.

Your Turn Come up with a solution to this situation. Would you try to include this student into your group? How could you do so without ruining your group dynamic? What could you gain by including this student? What would the student gain?

Making Ethical Choices

In addition to defining your values and setting your personal standards, you also develop your character by making ethical choices. Ethical choices are the choices you make based on your ethics. **Ethics** are the principles and values that guide the way you live. They are based on what is fair, right, just, caring, and best for all people involved. Making the right choice based on values and standards is a true indication of your character.

Code of Ethics

A common example of an ethical dilemma is a story a father, having no means of income or support, who has to steal food to feed himself and his starving family. It is wrong to steal, but it is also wrong for your family to starve. Fortunately, most ethical dilemmas are more clearcut, meaning that if you use your values to guide your decision making, the answer should be clear.

Ethical decisions may or may not involve legal considerations. For example, it is not illegal to gossip or spread rumors at school, but you know those are unethical, or wrong, behaviors. A code of ethics is not something you are born with. It does not develop overnight. You may be influenced by others in your life, but for the most part, your personal code of ethics takes shape as you confront the issues and problems of daily life. It develops over time as you make decisions about what is right and what is wrong.

Deenie faced an ethical choice one weekend. It was track season, and she had a big meet on Sunday. It was also her sister's sixteenth birthday, and a party was planned for Saturday night. On her list of things to do, she had to write a report on Friday's chemistry lab results, buy her sister's birthday gift, finish her creative writing project, and go to track practice. Clearly, she had overcommitted herself, and she called her friend Gayle to vent about her hectic schedule. Gayle, who is also her lab partner in chemistry class, offered to let Deenie copy her report on the lab results. What do you think Deenie should do?

You will experience similar types of problems throughout your life. As you mature, some problems will become easier to solve, while others may not. However, the better you know and trust your values, standards, and ethics, the more likely it is that you will make good choices.

Character in Action

Values and ethics mean nothing without action. First you learn them. Then you live by them. Your actions can show people your real values. You can also use your values to focus on others, not just yourself.

When you develop positive values, set personal standards, and make ethical choices, you show your character in action. Neenah, for example, does her part to make sure that students with physical disabilities feel included rather than left out. Her peers have come to admire Neenah for her caring and respect for others. Neenah puts her values, words, and actions together to make a difference for others.

You, too, can put your character into action. The "Character in Action" features throughout this book present different character traits and suggest actions to take for situations you might experience. They present opportunities for you to develop your character.

Developing character is a learning process. There are times when you will make a poor choice and fail to act on your values and standards. Learn from the experience and move on. Be careful, but give yourself room to grow. Character is rooted in positive values and expressed in a person's actions. A true test of character is when you live by your values and standards, even when no one is there to see you do it.

Character?! In Action

Discretion

Showing sensitivity in order to avoid embarrassing others is called discretion. It requires that you stop and think about how your words or actions may affect the other person.

You Decide

Scott works evenings at a nice restaurant downtown. It is Saturday night, and the couple at one of his tables is enjoying their first date. After their meal, Scott learns that the man's credit card has been declined. How can Scott return to the table and alert the man without embarrassing him in front of his date?

 Podcasts Access the Online Learning Center to download *Managing Life Skills* podcasts.

Section 2.2   After You Read

Review Key Concepts

1. **Recall** how your personal standards serve as guidelines for your behavior.
2. **Identify** the principles upon which ethics are based.

Practice Academic Skills

 English Language Arts

3. Imagine that your coach has asked you to create a list of rules for the judges who will determine next year's cheerleading team. Assume that many of the people trying out may be good friends with the judges. Also assume that there may be friction between some judges and potential team members. Write a list of rules to remind judges how to conduct themselves in an ethical manner when voting.

 Social Studies

4. Describe a typical problem teens face, such as peer pressure or arguments with parents. What kinds of decisions are often related to the problem? Consider possible reactions to this problem. What might cause other teens to make different decisions from the ones you would make?

 Check Your Answers Check your answers at this book's Online Learning Center at **glencoe.com**.

> **NCTE 4** Use written language to communicate effectively.

> **NCSS I C** Apply an understanding of culture as an integrated whole that explains the functions and interactions of language, literature, the arts, traditions, beliefs and values, and behavior patterns.

Pathway to College

Continuing Education

Is College My Best Option?

This is a very important question that every high school student will ask himself or herself at some point. There is no right answer, but it is a decision that can affect the rest of your life. It is important that you educate yourself before making the decision and give it the serious thought it deserves.

Does college guarantee success?

Having a college degree opens many doors. There are many people who find success and happiness without a degree. However, it is important to keep in mind that more and more employers want to hire applicants with degrees. You can find work without a degree, but more options are available when you have a degree.

What can I learn if I continue my education?

In college, students read books, have discussions with other students, learn new skills, and learn from experts in their fields. These experiences encourage students to think, ask questions, explore new ideas, and further develop academically. Students will expand their knowledge and skills, learn how to express themselves more clearly, and increase their understanding of local, national, and global issues.

What are some of the benefits of going to college?

Going to college creates opportunities. College graduates have an edge in the job market over those who have not experienced higher education. Additionally, a student who attends college usually earns more than a person who does not. According to a recent U.S. Census Bureau finding, a person with a bachelor's degree or higher earned approximately 50 percent more on average than a person with only a high school diploma.

Hands-On

College Readiness Create a list of pros and cons for continuing your education after high school. Think about the long term as well as the short term. Consider all the possibilities, such as community college, vocational school, or a four-year college or university. Go over the list with your parents or guardians, and ask a guidance counselor for his or her input.

Path to Success

CCR ☆ College & Career Readiness

Identify Your Goals When considering a college degree, think about what you want out of life and whether or not a degree will help you achieve it.

Talk to Others You are not the first person to make this decision. Talk to older siblings or friends to get their ideas and advice.

Explore Your Options Consider community college, trade and technical schools, four-year schools, and distance learning.

Seek Guidance Part of your school guidance counselor's job is to help you with decisions like this.

Think Long-Term Try to think about not only what you want your life to be like next year, but what you want it to be like in 20 years.

Be Confident Worrying that college or continuing your education in other ways might be too difficult should not be a factor in making your decision.

 Go to this book's Online Learning Center at **glencoe.com** to learn more about college and career readiness.

CHAPTER SUMMARY

Section 2.1
Character and Values

Building character is a lifelong process. Families, teachers, friends, and others in the community help develop your character. The choices you make and their consequences are a reflection of your character. Character is built on a foundation of values. Universal values include respect, fairness, responsibility, caring, and honesty. Having strong values helps you face difficult situations with confidence.

Section 2.2
Standards and Ethics

Personal standards guide your behavior by defining what you do and what you do not do. Planning ahead and knowing your standards can help you react appropriately in difficult situations. Ethics help you make decisions based on what is right, fair, just, caring, and best for all involved. Values, standards, and ethics develop as you mature, and they provide a framework that helps you make good choices.

Vocabulary Review

1. Write your own definition for each content and academic vocabulary term.

Content Vocabulary
- character (p. 27)
- consequence (p. 27)
- mentor (p. 27)
- conscience (p. 31)
- personal standard (p. 33)
- proactive (p. 33)
- peer pressure (p. 33)
- discretion (p. 34)
- ethics (p. 36)

Academic Vocabulary
- model (p. 27)
- reflect (p. 28)
- conduct (p. 33)
- value (p. 34)

Review Key Concepts

2. **Explain** why character is vital to personal growth and to society.
3. **Outline** the ways in which values are acquired.
4. **Describe** how personal standards can help you take control of life experiences.
5. **Define** ethical behavior.

Critical Thinking

6. **Connect** Identify two personal values, and explain how each can affect relationships.
7. **Interpret** Explain the meaning of this statement: Character is always there—even when no one is looking.
8. **Predict** How can personal values have an impact on future generations?
9. **Evaluate** Can the media, such as TV, radio, the Internet, newspapers, and magazines, affect one's personal values? Explain your answer.
10. **Apply** Consider the ethical principles in this situation: At the mall food court, a woman walks away from her table without realizing that a $20 bill has fallen out of her pocket. You are the only person who sees this happen. What do you do?
11. **Defend Your Position** Explain why you agree or disagree with this statement: Character can be developed to a degree, but for the most part, you are either born with good character or you are not.

Family & Community Connections

ACTIVE LEARNING

12. Weigh Options Follow your teacher's instructions to form groups. With your group, write a conclusion to this story: Mandy, a new student, felt great to be included in a group at school. Everything seemed fine at first, but then some people in the group started pressuring her to cut class with them. She really likes these people, but she does not want to cut class because she knows it is wrong, and she does not want to get in trouble at school or at home. To conclude this story, consider Mandy's options for dealing with the situation. What are the possible outcomes of each situation?

13. Observe Parental Influence Find three opportunities to watch parents interact with their children. For example, you may observe interactions at a playground, in a store, or at school. Pay attention to how parents teach habits, both directly and indirectly, that promote both positive and negative character development. How are the children influenced by what the parents do or say? Compare the interactions you observed. What similarities did you find in your observations? What differences did you notice? Write a summary that describes your observations and explains how decisions and behavior are influenced by parents.

21st Century Skills

Collaborative Skills

14. Code of Ethics Follow your teacher's instructions to form teams. With your team members, develop a code of ethics for students. Create a list of 10 guidelines based on the ethical principles, beliefs, values, and actions that your team considers most important. When your code is complete, ask for your teacher's permission to post it in the classroom.

Technology Skills

15. Evaluate a Web Site Values are reflected in Web sites. Locate three Web sites that promote a cause, such as a charity or fundraiser. Identify values that are reflected in the content and design of the Web site. Evaluate each site to determine which universal values are represented.

 **Connections**

Planning Skills

16. Manage Work and Life As part of its mission, FCCLA encourages students to create a plan for achieving the lifestyle they want. Many people picture their work life as a series of jobs that reflect what is most important, such as job satisfaction or certain benefits. What kind of work will align with your values? How do you imagine your work life will affect your family and your community? Write two or more paragraphs to describe a lifestyle that reflects your values.

Academic Skills

 English Language Arts

17. Create a Character Profile Think about your favorite fictional characters. What do you admire about them? What do they have in common? Using this information, create a profile of a character that represents the most admirable traits of your favorite characters. Describe the values, standards, and ethics that shape his or her character. How would your character handle difficult situations you have experienced?

> **NCTE 12** Use language to accomplish individual purposes.

 Science

18. Environmental Consciousness Concern for the environment is a value that has become very important to people.

Procedure Research recycling facilities near you. Find out what items can be recycled. Develop a plan to recycle those items. Discuss with family and friends how you can use your plan to work together to positively impact your environment.

Analysis Prepare a report that summarizes your plan and what it can do for the environment. Present it to the class.

> **NSES F** Develop understanding of environmental quality.

 Mathematics

19. Fundraiser A home near Central High School was recently damaged by a fire. Patrick and Mary Ellen, students at Central High School, wanted to do something to help, so they organized a bake sale at the school to raise money for the affected family. During the three hours of the bake sale, the students served 144 customers. If the customers were spaced evenly throughout the event, how many customers did they serve in the first 20 minutes?

Math Concept **Proportions** You can set up two equal ratios, also called a proportion, to relate a quantity you already know to another you are solving for. Use a variable such as x to represent the unknown amount in the second ratio. Solve the proportion by using cross products (multiply the numerator of one fraction by the denominator of the other and vice versa).

Starting Hint Convert 3 hours to minutes. Then solve for x: $144/180 = x/20$.

 For more math practice, go to the Math Appendix at the back of the book.

> **NCTM Algebra** Represent and analyze mathematical situations and structures using algebraic symbols.

Standardized Test Practice

 CCR College & Career Readiness

Test-Taking Tip In a true/false test, budget your time. Read all of the questions and statements, then answer the ones you know first. As time allows, reread the ones you skipped and try to answer them. Many times your first guess is the correct answer.

TRUE/FALSE
Read each of the statements and determine whether they are true or false.

20. People are born with a code of ethics.
21. A mentor acts as a teacher and guide.
22. Advertisers are always careful to promote universal values.

Chapter 3

Responsible Citizenship

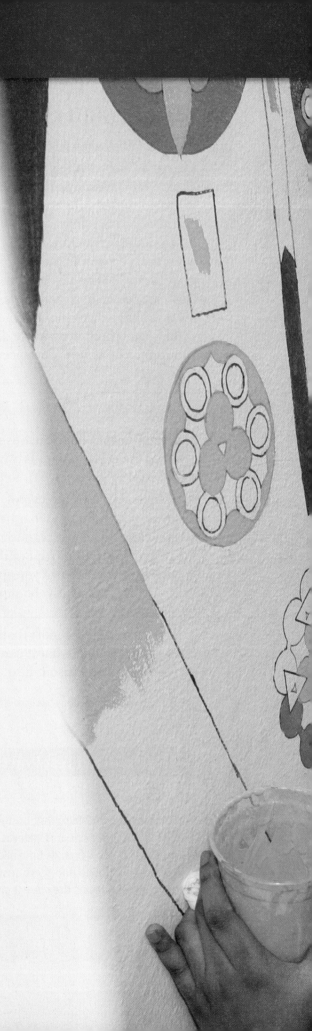

Chapter Objectives

Section 3.1 The Role of a Citizen

- **Describe** how a person can demonstrate responsible citizenship.
- **Identify** two qualities necessary to be responsible.
- **Summarize** the benefits of practicing leadership.

Section 3.2 Get Involved

- **Explain** how members of an organization achieve more than individuals acting alone.
- **Name** four things a volunteer uses to make a difference.
- **List** nine responsibilities of all citizens.

▶**Explore the Photo**

Volunteering in your community is one way to help make a difference in the lives of those around you. *How does participating in volunteer activities demonstrate responsibility?*

Writing Activity — Outlining

Citizenship Outlines consist of the main ideas you want to cover and the subtopics and details that support each main idea. Write an outline about a time when you saw someone demonstrate good citizenship.

Writing Tips To write an outline, follow these steps:
- List your main topics in a logical order.
- Under each main topic, list at least two subtopics that support the main topic.
- Under each subtopic, list supporting information or details you want to include in your assignment.

The Role of a Citizen

What roles do you play in your community?

Reading Guide

Before You Read

Understanding Write down questions as you read. Many of them will be answered as you continue. If they are not, you will have a list ready for your teacher when you finish.

Read to Learn
Key Concepts
- **Describe** how a person can demonstrate responsible citizenship.
- **Identify** two qualities necessary to be responsible.
- **Summarize** the benefits of practicing leadership.

Main Idea
There are many opportunities for you to make a difference. You can do this by showing responsibility and building leadership skills.

Content Vocabulary
◇ citizen
◇ citizenship
◇ accountability
◇ leadership
◇ collaboration

Academic Vocabulary
You will find these words in your reading and on your tests. Use the glossary to look up their definitions if necessary.
■ capacity
■ chair

Academic Standards

English Language Arts
NCTE 5 Use different writing process elements to communicate effectively.

Mathematics
NCTM Number and Operations Compute fluently and make reasonable estimates.

Social Studies
NCSS X E Civic Ideals and Practices Analyze and evaluate the influence of various forms of citizen action on public policy.

Graphic Organizer
As you read, identify five characteristics that employers look for in a responsible employee. Use a star organizer like the one shown to help you organize your information, placing each characteristic in a different point of the star.

Responsible Employees

Graphic Organizer Go to this book's Online Learning Center at **glencoe.com** to print out this graphic organizer.

NCTE *National Council of Teachers of English*
NCTM *National Council of Teachers of Mathematics*
NSES *National Science Education Standards*
NCSS *National Council for the Social Studies*

Make a Difference

Life is more than discovering who you are, taking care of yourself, and developing your character. Although these personal growth activities take up a major portion of your time and energy, they are not your only purpose. You can also make a difference in the lives of others. Emma, for example, helps at the food pantry once a week. Carlos tutors in an adult literacy program twice a month. Liang and other members of his 4-H club walk a mile-long section next to the highway embankment every month to pick up litter.

As you have grown older, you have gradually developed your **capacity,** or potential, to think of others. As a preschooler, you were probably taught to share. Throughout your childhood, you learned that your actions can have an impact on others. Now you are learning to reach out to help others improve their lives. Your world is expanding as you move toward adulthood.

Many opportunities exist for you to make a difference at home, at school, at work, and in the community. Start by looking around you and identifying an opportunity for improvement. Then do your part. You should take pride in your community, and by doing your part, you can help others feel pride as well.

A community becomes stronger because of the actions of good citizens. A **citizen** is a member of a community, such as a school, city, state, or country. Each citizen has rights and responsibilities, which you will learn more about in the next section. The way that you handle your responsibilities as a citizen is known as **citizenship**. By taking responsibility for yourself and your actions, you show responsible citizenship.

As you think about making a difference, remember that every effort counts. Whether you pick up the clutter around your home, organize a community fundraiser, or volunteer to read to young children, you are doing your part to make a difference. Sometimes you may work alone; other times you will team up with other people. You may have total responsibility for a task, or you may play a supporting role. Sometimes you may be the leader, and other times a team member. In whatever way you are involved, you can have a positive impact on the people you are working with and working for, and on society as a whole.

✓ Reading Check

Define What is a citizen?

As You Read

Connect Think of someone who has made a positive difference in your life. What did her or she do that affected you?

◆ Vocabulary

You can find definitions in the glossary at the back of this book.

∨ Do Something

You can volunteer your time to help individuals or to help a whole community. *What can you do to make a difference in your community?*

Show Responsibility

No matter how you choose to make a difference, you will be expected to be responsible, do your share, and support others. Being responsible means you are both reliable and accountable. When you accept **accountability**, you are willing to accept the consequences of your actions and your words.

How can you convince others that you have these qualities? You can show that you are reliable by keeping your word and doing what you say you will do. To show that you are accountable, if something goes wrong and it is your fault, do not blame others. Instead, acknowledge your mistakes and take steps to correct them and learn from them. For example, when only two students showed up at a committee meeting, Holly realized that she had forgotten to call people and let them know that the day of the meeting had changed. She apologized to the committee chair, or officer, and to the students who showed up. That evening she noted on her calendar when she should call members about the next meeting.

You have many opportunities to show responsibility. For example, you can show personal responsibility by wearing a seat belt. Following family rules is one way to show responsibility to your family. You can be responsible in school by completing your assignments on time. Arriving on time shows responsibility at work. Taking action in your community to make life better for all shows responsibility to society as a whole. You can let friends, family members, classmates, teammates, and coworkers know they can count on you by sticking to your commitments.

 Help at Home

Helping other family members shows that you care about them and that you take responsibility for your family's well-being. *What tasks do you do at home that demonstrate responsibility?*

At Home

Some teens try to get away with doing the fewest chores possible. A more mature approach would be to go beyond the minimum. Part of being mature means that you accept responsibilities and take the feelings of others into consideration. Erin, for example, had been washing dinner dishes since she was nine years old. As a teen, she started cooking with her father. She decided that it would be a good way to help out more, spend more time with her dad, and learn a new skill. Do your jobs willingly, and take on other chores without being asked. Offer to lend a hand when someone needs help. Be willing to listen if someone has a problem and needs to talk. You may already have discovered how much these things are appreciated. A teen who willingly contributes to the family earns the respect, gratitude, and cooperation of others in the family.

At times, however, showing responsibility requires something more than doing chores. For example, Neva listened as her stepsister Carley talked about borrowing their mother's car. Their mother was out of town, and Carley thought it would be exciting to take some of her friends out for a ride. Neva grew concerned. Carley had just earned her driver's license and had very little driving experience. Although she knew her message would not be welcomed by Carley, Neva trusted in the strength of their relationship. She decided it was time to have a conversation with Carley.

Character In Action

Show Compassion

Compassion means being aware of others' suffering and having the desire to help. It is more than just pity. It means that if you see someone in a bad situation, you think, "How can I help?" instead of, "I'm glad that's not me." Feeling compassion is a sign of maturity.

You Decide

If you see a homeless person on the street and feel sorry for that person, are you feeling compassion or pity? What is the difference? What is an example of each?

Two Views One World

Are Leaders Born or Made?

Some people think leadership is something you either have or do not have, while others think it is a skill you can develop.

Celina: Each person is born with certain talents, just like you're born with a certain eye color, and you'll be happier and more effective if you stick with what you're good at. If you're not comfortable as a leader and you try to force it, you won't enjoy it or be good at it. We're born into these roles, and we can't make ourselves be different from how we are.

Alex: You limit people by calling them either leaders or followers, because everyone has both inside of them. You can choose which part of yourself to develop. If you aren't comfortable as a leader, you can practice and eventually become an effective leader. Experience is more important than your natural tendency. Just like learning how to play the piano, you can learn how to be a leader.

Seeing Both Sides

Which of these viewpoints do you agree with? Why? Do you think they could both be right?

Succeed in SCHOOL and LIFE

Show School Spirit

Showing school spirit is a good way to make friends, have fun, and help your school. You can show school spirit by joining a sports team or another school group such as the school newspaper or debate team. You can also attend sports events, join the pep club or the community service committee, run for student body, or even wear school colors.

"What if you have an accident?" Neva asked. "What if somebody gets hurt?" As they talked, Neva brought up other possible consequences. At first, Carley was irritated. Eventually, however, she realized that Neva was right and that she asked the questions because she cared. Carley decided to give up her plan. In this situation, both girls showed responsibility.

In School

You show responsibility at school by going to class on time and doing your homework. But this is just the beginning. Being responsible also means doing your part to make your school a safe and supportive environment. When students and staff work together to make a difference in their school, it usually becomes a better place to learn and achieve. See **Figure 3.1** for ways you can make a contribution to your school.

On the Job

It is not surprising that employers value responsibility so highly. They need employees who arrive at work on time, follow directions, work efficiently, follow workplace rules, and are dependable. Responsible employees feel personally accountable for the tasks assigned to them and do what is necessary to accomplish those tasks.

Employees who demonstrate responsibility are more likely to receive positive reviews, raises, and promotions. Those who do not show responsibility may be disciplined or fired. Alex, for example, habitually shows up late at the fast-food restaurant where he works. His coworkers are upset at having to work longer and harder because they are short-staffed. After many warnings, the manager told Alex that if he is late one more time, he will be fired.

Figure 3.1   Responsibility at School

A Little Goes a Long Way   There are many ways that you can contribute to your school. *Can you think of anything to add to this list?*

ACTION	DESCRIPTION
Protect school property.	Students in many schools have stopped graffiti and vandalism. They know an attractive school is better for everyone. When money is not needed for repairs, other programs benefit, such as athletics, clubs, art, and music.
Help others having difficulty.	Everyone is stronger in some subjects than others. When classmates help one another, everyone benefits. Sometimes just listening can improve someone else's situation.
Treat everyone with respect.	Disrespect, bullying, and harassing others lower morale and have a negative impact on learning. Respect lifts morale and encourages learning.
Work to improve your school.	By participating in your student government or other groups and clubs, you can work toward goals that benefit the entire student body.
Support school events.	Your presence helps others do their best.
Show your school spirit in positive ways.	Putting down another school at a game or competition only gives your school a negative reputation. Instead, wear your school colors and cheer for your classmates.

◀ **Develop Leadership Skills**

A strong leader can make the difference between a successful team and an unsuccessful one. *What leadership roles are being fulfilled by the teen in this photo?*

Showing responsibility on the job benefits others as well as yourself. When all workers are reliable and have positive attitudes, morale is high. By helping one another, employees create a spirit of cooperation. Those who do business with such a company or organization are more likely to be satisfied customers.

✓ **Reading Check** **Recall** How can you show others that you are reliable?

Become a Leader

As a responsible citizen, you may be asked to take on a leadership role. **Leadership** is the ability to direct and motivate a team or group to achieve its goals. Leaders influence the actions of others. In essence, they inspire others and show them the way through example and direction.

There are many opportunities for leadership roles in organizations, teams, and groups. You might be a committee chair in a school club, captain of a sports team, or a manager of employees. Organizations look for people who have the right skills for specific leadership roles. For example, a caring individual would be a good choice to lead a team reaching out to help others. Strong organizational and math skills would be needed for the position of finance committee chair.

Having capable leaders helps organizations attract and keep members and make a difference. Typically, people in leadership roles coordinate their group's efforts. Leaders make sure all members are working toward their goals and focusing on their objectives.

For some people, taking on a leadership role is scary and uncomfortable. For others, it is a natural step in their personal growth.

There are many Web sites that will help you calculate your carbon footprint, or the amount of greenhouse gas emissions you generate. Once you know the size of your carbon footprint, you can come up with strategies to reduce it.

Whether you are new to leadership or have much experience, consider the benefits:

- You gain experience in communicating your ideas to a variety of people in different ways.
- You learn to resolve conflicts.
- You develop competence and confidence as you guide others.
- You learn and practice skills that will be useful at work and in your family throughout your life.

The combined, cooperative efforts of everyone in a group is called **collaboration** (kə-ˌla-bə-ˈrā-shən). In any group, success comes from collaboration. Leaders set the example of collaboration. They make sure each person's ideas are welcomed and respected. Every person is encouraged to participate and contribute. How well do the groups you belong to collaborate?

Many leadership positions last for a certain time period, such as one school year. At the end of that time period, another person may take over the role. Rotating leadership positions allows an organization, team, or group to fulfill its mission and meet its goals without placing too much pressure on individual members. New leaders also bring fresh ideas, and more people are given the chance to develop leadership skills. Everyone benefits. You will learn more about teamwork and leadership skills in Chapter 5.

 Podcasts Access the Online Learning Center to download *Managing Life Skills* podcasts.

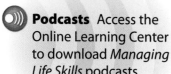

Section 3.1 — After You Read

Review Key Concepts

1. **List** four places where you have opportunities to make a difference.
2. **Describe** three ways to show responsibility and support at school.
3. **Explain** the role of collaboration in a group.

Practice Academic Skills

English Language Arts

4. Suppose that you are running for class president. Think of two or three areas that could use improvement in your school. Use those ideas to create a poster for your campaign. Be sure to use language and graphics that will attract the attention and respect of your classmates.

Social Studies

5. Many citizens write letters to government officials to express their approval or disapproval of laws and policies. Think of a law or policy that affects teens, such as driving limitations or minimum wage laws. Write a letter to express your thoughts about the law or policy. Be sure to include details that support your opinion. Do you think such letters can influence public policy? Why or why not?

 Check Your Answers Check your answers at this book's Online Learning Center at **glencoe.com**.

NCTE 5 Use different writing process elements to communicate effectively.

NCSS X E Analyze and evaluate the influence of various forms of citizen action on public policy.

Get Involved

Reading Guide

Before You Read

Vocabulary Divide a piece of paper into three columns. Label the first column: Vocabulary. Label the second column: What is it? Label the third: What else is it like? Write down each vocabulary word, and answer the questions as you read the section.

Read to Learn
Key Concepts

- **Explain** how members of an organization achieve more than individuals acting alone.
- **Name** four things a volunteer uses to make a difference.
- **List** nine responsibilities of all citizens.

Main Idea

Participating in organizations and volunteer activities are effective ways to make a difference in your community. Citizenship comes with both rights and responsibilities.

Graphic Organizer

As you read, look for six ways you can become actively involved in an organization. Use a graphic organizer like the one shown to help you organize your information.

Ways to be Involved in Organizations

 **Graphic Organizer** Go to this book's Online Learning Center at **glencoe.com** to print out this graphic organizer.

Content Vocabulary

◇ outreach program
◇ volunteer
◇ service learning

Academic Vocabulary

You will find these words in your reading and on your tests. Use the glossary to look up their definitions if necessary.

■ restrict
■ cultivate

Academic Standards

English Language Arts

NCTE 4 Use written language to communicate effectively.

Social Studies

NCSS X B Civic Ideals and Practices Identify, analyze, interpret, and evaluate examples of citizens' responsibilities.

NCTE *National Council of Teachers of English*
NCTM *National Council of Teachers of Mathematics*
NSES *National Science Education Standards*
NCSS *National Council for the Social Studies*

Participate in Organizations

As You Read

Connect What are some organizations for teens in your school?

◆ Vocabulary

You can find definitions in the glossary at the back of this book.

One effective way to make a difference is to become involved in an organization that interests you. Members of an organization can accomplish much more than they can as individuals. Members develop a sense of responsibility and obligation to the organization's mission or purpose. Organizations combine the talents, skills, energy, and resources of members to achieve their goals.

Many organizations make a difference in the lives of their members and in society. School organizations such as Family, Career and Community Leaders of America (FCCLA) and community outreach organizations are two examples. An **outreach program** is a program that offers assistance or services to the community, usually as an act of charity or goodwill. Consider joining your school's student government, or take part in a youth and government organization. You may be interested in participating in a religious organization that encourages teens to help others. Some organizations, such as the Family, Career and Community Leaders of America (FCCLA) and SkillsUSA, have service and outreach projects.

You will make a bigger difference if you become actively involved in the organization you choose. Encourage yourself and others to:
- Attend meetings regularly.
- Understand the mission, goals, and activities of the group.
- Participate on a committee.
- Follow through with assigned tasks and responsibilities.
- Develop leadership skills, and improve teamwork skills.
- Recruit new members, and promote the organization.

Organizations Build Leaders

Organizations like FCCLA help students develop leadership skills. FCCLA helps students who are interested in careers in the family and consumer sciences. Participating in the group allows teens to build job skills by taking leadership roles.

In organizations like FCCLA, opportunities for leadership are limited only by your abilities and energy. You might work as a committee chairperson or a chapter officer, coordinating projects and managing people. If selected by the nominating committee, you can run for office at the district, regional, state, or national level. If elected, you will participate in planning and work groups and gain experience in public speaking.

Becoming a leader in organizations such as FCCLA provides valuable experience. Interviewing with the nominating committee is good preparation for a college or job interview. Speaking in front of large audiences, managing projects, and dealing with people are skills you can use in your future career. Many students do not get this experience until they enter the working world. Joining an organization like FCCLA can give you a head start.

✓ **Reading Check** **Define** What is an outreach program?

▶ Get Involved!

Animal Shelters and Humane Societies

If you like animals, why not spend some time helping out at a local animal shelter or humane society? Most shelters depend on volunteers to exercise, feed, and interact with the animals. When you walk rescued dogs, it is not just the animals that get a workout. You can benefit, too, from both the exercise and the companionship.

Volunteering in Your Community

In communities everywhere, people make a difference in the lives of other people through volunteering. A **volunteer** is someone who puts caring into action by offering services free of charge. When you volunteer, you offer your enthusiasm, talents, skills, and time to improve the lives of others.

Some people volunteer from a sense of duty. Others do it because they care deeply about a cause. Lionel, for example, is a high school senior planning to major in architecture. He is determined to become a Peace Corps volunteer and work to help people construct affordable homes. Lionel is willing to dedicate his time, energy, and knowledge volunteering for his local branch of Habitat for Humanity to make a difference in the world.

Benefits of Volunteering

Every community has needs. Community programs meant to meet those needs often have low operating budgets and must rely on the work of volunteers to be effective. How much they can do is directly linked to how many willing hands are extended. One way to help is to donate money. What if you do not have money to spare? There is much more to helping your community than giving money. People who volunteer generally do not expect anything in return. However, volunteering can bring benefits you may not expect, and that can be worth much more than money.

Succeed in SCHOOL and LIFE

Join, Join, Join!

There are so many ways to reach out and get involved. You could volunteer at the local library, organize a walkathon, foster a homeless animal, or become a part of community politics. Joining the community helps both you and your neighbors. You donate your time to help others, and in return, you meet people, have new experiences, and exchange ideas.

Life On Your Own

Practice Citizenship

Some parts of being a good citizen are mandatory, or required, such as paying taxes and obeying laws, but other parts are optional. You can choose how you want to practice citizenship, but it should be a priority in your life. Every individual has the power to make a difference, both positively and negatively.

How It Works Being a good citizen can mean so many different things. It can be as simple as shoveling or sweeping the driveway of an elderly neighbor, or as involved as organizing a recycling program in your community. Think about the time, skills, knowledge, and interests you have. Everyone has something he or she can add to the community. By being a good citizen, you are helping others, but because you are improving your community, you are also helping yourself.

Try It Out You are thinking about volunteering at the Special Olympics, and you invite a close friend of yours to volunteer with you. You are surprised when she says, "I don't have any responsibility to that organization. My only responsibilities are to myself. I only have so much time, and I need to focus on myself. I don't have any extra time to do something that doesn't directly help me."

> **Your Turn** How would you respond to this? What would you say to your friend to try to change her mind? What is wrong with this type of thinking? What would happen if everyone felt this way?

Being Social
Social interaction can be fun, but did you know it is also good for you? Studies have shown that lonely people have higher blood pressure, get less exercise, and are more fatigued. Follow these tips:

▶ Say yes! When you are asked to join in an activity, go for it.

▶ Make time for social activities.

▶ Welcome opportunities to make new friends and meet new people.

Although you receive no money for volunteer work, it brings many rewards. You learn job skills and gain valuable work experience that you can include on your college applications and on job résumés. You can also develop a network of people who share your interests. This network may lead to friendships, further training and skill development, or information about job opportunities. You will likely work with people of different ages and from different areas of the community. This enables you to interact with a variety of people and learn more about the community you live in. Finally, one of the most rewarding benefits is that helping others brings you feelings of self-worth and fulfillment.

Ways to Help

Many teens want to volunteer but are not sure how to start. You might not know how or where to direct your efforts. A good way to begin is to take a look at yourself. Consider your interests, skills, and schedule. What are you interested in? Are there any causes that particularly concern you? What issues or problems have touched your life or the lives of people you know? Have you been moved by news stories about a particular need in your community or the larger world?

Also think about what activities you are good at and what you like to do. You will want to choose a volunteer activity that you not only believe is worthwhile but that you will also enjoy. If you enjoy what you are doing, you will be more likely to stick with it. For example, do you prefer working inside or outside? Do you enjoy talking with older people or playing with young children? Consider the skills you would like to share or learn and the amount of time you have to give.

Now you are ready to start looking for a volunteer opportunity that matches your interests, skills, and schedule. You can find ideas for volunteering by talking to a school counselor or your neighbors, reading the newspaper, or checking your community's Web site. Some communities have an agency that keeps track of opportunities for volunteers in the area. Here are just a few of the many ways you might volunteer:

- Help at a local food bank, homeless shelter, senior citizens' center, or animal shelter.
- Participate in a charity walkathon or race.
- Join Habitat for Humanity, which helps build or renovate houses for low-income families.
- Coach a Special Olympics team.
- Help beautify your community by planting flowers or building bike trails.
- Take part in a neighborhood cleanup campaign.
- Counsel others on a teen hotline.
- Help with a campaign to combat violence, drunk driving, or drug abuse.
- Work with a recycling or hazardous waste removal program.

 Help Others, Help Yourself

Volunteering helps build life skills while improving your community.
What life skills might these teens be developing?

Service Learning

An effective way to help others is through a service learning project. **Service learning** involves taking what you learn in the classroom and using it to meet a community need. Students often choose and plan a service learning experience in partnership with their school and a community agency or organization. Many times students receive classroom credit for their work. Service learning also provides opportunities for students to learn new skills and to explore and investigate various careers.

Check to see whether your school already has a service learning program in place. If you find that your school does not have a program, a school counselor or teacher may be willing to help you develop a service learning project that will meet a community need. For example, Heidi is interested in a career in law enforcement. Inspired by her personal interest, she contacted her local police department as well as school security officers. She enlisted the help of her civics teacher, and together they created a service learning project that helped to improve community-police relations and neighborhood safety. Her involvement helped make her community a better place to live. What ideas do you have for a possible service learning experience?

✓ Reading Check **Recall** What are three things to consider when looking for volunteer work?

 **Be Smart Be Safe**

Neighborhood Crime Watch Neighborhood crime watch groups are groups of citizens dedicated to reducing crime and increasing the overall sense of peace and safety in a neighborhood. These groups improve communication among neighbors and between citizens and law enforcement.

Write About It Neighborhood crime watch has proven to be effective. Write a paragraph hypothesizing about why you think this is true.

Citizens' Rights and Responsibilities

Remember that you are a citizen of your country, your school, and your community. Citizens of the United States have certain rights, including the right to receive an education and to be protected by the police. U.S. citizens also have the right to practice any religion they wish and to express their feelings about anything, as long as they do not harm others.

Citizenship also brings with it certain responsibilities. Volunteering is one way to show responsibility as a citizen. Here are some other basic responsibilities that citizens share:

- **Respect others' rights.** Treat other people as you expect to be treated. Show respect for individuality, needs, and property.
- **Obey laws.** Communities and countries make laws for the good of all. You have a responsibility to obey the laws.
- **Prevent and report crime.** Fighting crime means more than avoiding criminal activity. It begins with prevention. You have a responsibility to report crimes you are aware of and to cooperate with police investigations. In these ways, you help prevent further crimes, protecting yourself and others.
- **Comply with emergency and security procedures.** In a severe drought, for example, citizens may be asked to **restrict**, or limit, their water usage. Cooperating with security measures, such as allowing a bag search at a public event, helps keep everyone safe.
- **Pay taxes.** Many government services are financed by taxes. Citizens are required to pay their share of taxes or risk punishment. Once you begin earning an income, you will pay taxes on it.
- **Stay informed.** Keep up with local, national, and international news to stay aware of events and policies. This helps you make informed decisions and take responsible actions.
- **Participate in government.** When people attend meetings and voice their opinions, they can change government policies. What the public says influences those in leadership positions. You also influence government policies by taking part in elections. When you reach age 18, you are eligible, or legally qualified, to vote in national, state, and local elections. If you feel that a person in office is not doing a good job, you can vote for somebody else. At any age, you can help candidates by working on their campaigns. You may even run for office one day.

Be a Responsible Citizen

Responsible citizens are proud to support their community by voting. *What other actions can you take to show support for your community?*

- **Perform jury duty when called.** You may be called to serve on a jury after you reach age 18. The jury system is a crucial part of a justice system. Jurors listen to evidence presented in a trial and then, in agreement with other jurors, reach a verdict based on the evidence.

- **Serve in the military if called.** Young people in the United States can volunteer to serve in the military, but they are not required to do so in times of peace. However, there have been times of war and crisis when people have been called to serve in the military.

Citizens who truly care about their communities actively work to make them better for all. They are willing to volunteer to help others, and they accept responsibility for their civic duties.

Whatever you do, do not just sit back and do nothing. Do something! Do not think that the actions of one individual do not matter. They do! They matter to you as well as to others. As a family member, student, employee, leader, volunteer, and citizen, whatever productive steps you take are significant. When you develop the habit of helping, you **cultivate**, or encourage, an attitude of caring. Then you discover what a difference you really can make. When you take an active role in your community, you can make it a better place to live.

 Podcasts Access the Online Learning Center to download *Managing Life Skills* podcasts.

Section 3.2 After You Read

Review Key Concepts

1. **List** three leadership skills you can learn in an organization that you can use in your future career.

2. **Identify** three resources you can use to find out about volunteer opportunities.

3. **Recall** how you can respect the rights of other citizens.

 Check Your Answers Check your answers at this book's Online Learning Center at **glencoe.com**.

Practice Academic Skills

 English Language Arts

4. Suppose you and your best friend want you to do some volunteer work together. Write a letter to your friend describing what type of volunteer work you feel would be useful and enjoyable for the two of you. Consider your common talents, skills, and available time. Be sure to explain why you think the proposed options is most suitable.

> **NCTE 4** Use written language to communicate effectively.

Social Studies

5. Choose one of the responsibilities of citizens that is discussed in the text. Write a paragraph explaining what you think that responsibility means and how you can practice it in your own life. Offer an example of a time when you or someone you know demonstrated the chosen responsibility.

> **NCSS X B** Identify, analyze, interpret, and evaluate examples of citizens' responsibilities.

Pathway to Your Career

Postal Service Worker

What Does a Postal Service Worker Do?

Postal Service workers have many jobs within the Postal Service including processing, sorting, and delivering mail and packages. They also provide customer service and sell postage supplies in post offices. Jobs within the Postal Service include clerk, mail carrier, mail sorter, and mail processor. Both incoming and outgoing mail needs to be sorted and then delivered to urban and rural residences and businesses throughout the United States.

Career Readiness Skills Clerks and mail carriers must have good interpersonal skills because they often need to interact with the public, answering questions and responding to complaints. The ability to read quickly and accurately and a good memory are also helpful skills.

Education and Training Applicants must have a good command of English. There are no specific education requirements. Newly hired workers receive on-the-job training from experienced workers and additional instruction when new equipment or procedures are introduced. Postal Service workers must be at least 18 years old and either be U.S. citizens or have permanent resident-alien status.

Job Outlook Employment is expected to experience little change over the next ten years. The overall stable employment of mail carriers and clerks will be offset by a decline in the need for sorters and processors, as those jobs become more and more automated.

> **Critical Thinking** As e-mail, texting, and social networking Web sites become more and more widely used, how do you think these changes in technology will affect the Postal Service industry? Will the changes be positive, negative, or both?

Career Cluster

College & Career Readiness

Government and Public Administration Postal Service workers work in the Public Management and Administration pathway of this career cluster. Other jobs in this cluster include:

- Lobbyist
- Submarine Officer
- Ambassador
- Tax Auditor
- Global Imaging Systems Specialist
- Immigration Officer
- Mayor
- Aviation Safety Officer
- Cargo Inspector
- Combat Aircraft Pilot
- Census Clerk
- Border Inspector
- Election Supervisor

Explore Further The Government and Public Administration career cluster contains seven pathways: Governance, National Security; Foreign Service; Planning; Revenue & Taxation; Regulation; and Public Management & Administration. Choose one of these pathways to explore further.

 Career Clusters To learn more about career clusters, go to this book's Online Learning Center at **glencoe.com**.

CHAPTER SUMMARY

Section 3.1
The Role of a Citizen

There are many opportunities for you to make a difference in the lives of others by being responsible, doing your share, and using your skills, time, and talent to help others. Show responsibility by being reliable and accountable at home, at school, and at work. Many responsible citizens take on leadership roles. These will help you develop your confidence and leadership skills.

Section 3.2
Get Involved

Participating in organizations is a good way to help make a difference. There are many different types of organizations. Volunteering is a great way to improve the lives of others while building your own skills. All citizens have certain rights and responsibilities. Taking an active role and being a responsible citizen can make your community a better place to live.

Vocabulary Review

1. Create multiple-choice test questions for each content and academic vocabulary term.

Content Vocabulary
◇ citizen (p. 45)
◇ citizenship (p. 45)
◇ accountability (p. 46)
◇ leadership (p. 49)

◇ collaboration (p. 50)
◇ outreach program (p. 52)
◇ volunteer (p. 53)
◇ service learning (p. 55)

Academic Vocabulary
■ capacity (p. 45)
■ chair (p. 46)
■ restrict (p. 56)
■ cultivate (p. 57)

Review Key Concepts

2. Describe how a person can demonstrate responsible citizenship.
3. Identify two qualities necessary to be responsible.
4. Summarize the benefits of practicing leadership.
5. Explain how members of an organization achieve more than individuals acting alone.
6. Name four things a volunteer uses to make a difference.
7. List nine responsibilities of all citizens.

Critical Thinking

8. Analyze You can support your school and community by treating everyone with respect. Why is it important to also follow this rule at home?
9. Extrapolate Expand what you learned about leadership roles. How is being a leader similar to being a mentor?
10. Recommend Your friend is planning to pursue a career as a teacher. Compile a list of volunteer opportunities to help him or her prepare for this career.
11. Analyze Teens sometimes feel that they are too young to have an impact on their community. Based on the responsibilities discussed in the text, what are some things that teens can do to fulfill their citizenship roles in the community?

ACTIVE LEARNING

12. Write a Children's Story Children's books and TV programs often focus on teaching responsible behavior. Follow your teacher's instructions to form into pairs. Work with your partner to pick a specific aspect of responsibility that you feel would be helpful to teach a five-year-old. Each of you should create a character that a kindergarten-age child could relate to, such as a cute animal, a child, or a friendly fantasy creature. Give the  names to the characters, and write a short story or television script to teach your lesson. Include descriptions or illustrations of your characters.

Family & Community Connections

13. Research Organizations Conduct research to identify a service organization in your community that interests you. Arrange to speak with a member of the organization. Ask the member about participation in the organization. For example, "How would someone volunteer? How many hours are required of participants? What types of projects does the organization do?" If possible, observe or participate in one of the organization's projects. Create a presentation to share the results of your interview. If you participated in a project, include a summary of your activities and feelings. Were you proud to help someone? Was it hard work? Was it fun?

21st Century Skills

Media Literacy Skills

14. Analyze Citizens' Responsibility Read a recent human interest story in a newspaper. Analyze the level of responsible citizenship shown by the people in the article. How did each person demonstrate responsibility? If a person showed a lack of responsibility, what could he or she have done better? Write a summary of your analysis.

Technology Skills

15. Research Service Learning Conduct research to find service learning ideas. Use a word processing or desktop publishing program to create an attractive flyer to encourage your classmates to participate in one or more of the opportunities. Give the Web addresses of the sites, where appropriate. Consider what skills and benefits could be gained from the service learning projects and include them in your pamphlet.

 Connections

Leadership Skills

16. Increase Leadership Roles As part of its mission, FCCLA encourages students to participate in leadership roles. Go to the FCCLA Web site to read about the Take the Lead unit of the Power of One program. Use this unit to develop a written plan to increase your participation in an organization such as FCCLA.

Academic Skills

English Language Arts

17. Thank a Citizen Think about a citizen in your community who has served as a role model to you or others. Write a letter to express your gratitude for the person's efforts and the results of his or her actions. Be sure to include a heading, greeting, body, closing, and signature.

> **NCTE 5** Use different writing process elements to communicate effectively.

Social Studies

18. Inspire Others Select a historical document or a famous speech given by a leader, such as the Gettysburg Address or a speech given by a civil rights leader. Review the document or speech and write an analysis of how you believe it inspires citizens to make a difference. What was the outcome of the document or speech? Is there specific language used that helped inspire others?

> **NCSS X A Civic Ideals and Practices** Interpret the continuing influence of key ideals of the democratic republican form of government, such as individual human dignity, liberty, justice, equality, and the rule of law.

Mathematics

19. Volunteer Hours Last year, Mae volunteered with a group that supports senior citizens. Of the 2,400 hours she worked last year, she spent 400 hours volunteering. The rest of that time was spent doing paid work. What was the ratio of her volunteer work time to her paid work time?

Math Concept   Ratios Ratios are comparisons of numbers that can be represented in different forms. Usually, ratios are represented in simplest form. The ratio 1:2 can also be expressed as 1 out of 2, 1 to 2, or ½.

Starting Hint Calculate the number of paid hours worked. Then set up the ratio as a fraction, with volunteer hours as the numerator and paid hours as the denominator. Your answer should be a fraction in the lowest terms.

 For more math practice, go to the Math Appendix at the back of the book.

> **NCTM Number and Operations** Understand numbers, ways of representing numbers, relationships among numbers, and number systems.

Standardized Test Practice

 CCR College & Career Readiness

TIMED WRITING
Take five minutes to consider the statement and write an answer to the question.

> **Test-Taking Tip** Plan out your answer before you begin writing. Jot down the main points or details you want to focus on in the margins of your test. Refer to these points frequently as you write. This will help you remain focused.

Being a responsible citizen means doing your part to make your school a safe and supportive environment.

20. What can you do to help make your school safer and more supportive? Give specific examples.

Evaluate Yourself

In this project, you will reflect on who you are, what interests you, and what skills you have gained up to this point in your life. You will use your evaluation to begin building a college and career portfolio that will help you set and reach the goals for your life.

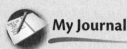 **My Journal**

If you completed the journal entry from page 2, refer to it to see if your thoughts have changed after reading the unit.

Project Assignment

In this project you will:

- Conduct a self-assessment by reflecting on activities and organizations in which you have participated.
- Evaluate the skills learned from previous classes and experiences.
- Interview at least two people about your skills.
- Use the information from your self-evaluation and your interviews to build an accurate and complete self-profile.
- Use your fact sheet and self-profile to begin building your college and career portfolio.

THE SKILLS BEHIND THE PROJECT

Key personal and relationship skills you will use in this project include:
- Analyzing yourself honestly
- Listening attentively
- Organizing information

Academic Skills

 English Language Arts

> **NCTE 7** Conduct research and gather, evaluate, and synthesize data to communicate discoveries.
>
> **NCTE 12** Use language to accomplish individual purposes.

STEP 1 Conduct a Self-Assessment

Make a list of all the activities, clubs, or organizations that you belong to or used to belong to. You can also use the *Career Plan Project Workbook*, available at this book's Online Learning Center at **glencoe.com** if you need help with your self-assessment. Some activities to consider might include:
- Classes at school
- School clubs or organizations
- Community organizations
- Sports teams

STEP 2 Evaluate Your Skills

Using your list of activities, create a list of the skills you possess. Think about what you have learned from each activity listed. For example, were you a club treasurer? This shows you have financial literacy skills. Were you a team captain or club officer? If so, you have leadership experience. Think about other 21st century skills, such as teamwork, research, problem-solving, and technology skills. Include an example of when you demonstrated each skill.

Critical Thinking Skills
- Analyze each activity.
- Determine which skills you possess.
- Illustrate your skills with examples.

STEP 3 Connect with Your Community

Select at least two people who know you well to interview about your personal skills. One person should be someone in your age group, and the other person should be a trusted adult, such as a parent, teacher, or work manager. Ask these people what they believe your strengths and skills are and why they believe you have those skills. Also ask them what skills you could work on to make yourself more well-rounded and valuable to a prospective college or employer.

Interview Skills
- Prepare your questions beforehand.
- Listen attentively to the other person.
- Take clear and accurate notes.
- Ask for clarification if you do not understand something.
- Thank the person for his or her time.

STEP 4 Compile What You Have Learned

Use the Portfolio Project Checklist to plan and give an oral report to share what you have learned with your classmates.

Speaking Skills
- Rehearse what you are going to say before your presentation.
- Speak clearly and concisely.
- Use visual aids to reinforce your speaking points.

STEP 5 Evaluate Your Project

Your portfolio project will be evaluated based on:

Academic Skills
- Accuracy and completeness of the information you compiled
- Organization and neatness of your information
- Speaking and listening skills

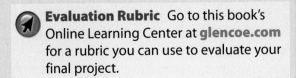 **Evaluation Rubric** Go to this book's Online Learning Center at **glencoe.com** for a rubric you can use to evaluate your final project.

PORTFOLIO PROJECT CHECKLIST

Plan
- ✔ Compare the list of skills from your self-evaluation to the list of skills from your interviews.
- ✔ If any of the skills differ, analyze why you think they do. Were you unrealistic in the skills you felt you possess? Did others recognize skills you missed?
- ✔ Create a document that lists all of the skills and strengths you possess, along with an example of a time when you demonstrated each one.

Present
- ✔ Make a presentation to your class to share your evaluation and discuss what you learned. Explain how you learned or demonstrated skills and strengths.
- ✔ Invite the students to ask questions. Answer any questions. Demonstrate in your answers that you respect their perspectives.
- ✔ Place your self-evaluation in your portfolio. Share your portfolio with your teacher.

Portfolio Highlights

College and Career Portfolio

A college and career portfolio is a collection of information about a person, including documents, projects, and work samples that showcase a person's academic and professional skills, talents, accomplishments, and qualifications.

Personal Information
Your portfolio will include the information needed for a job search or for applying for college. Many college or employment applications will ask for information such as interests, current and previous addresses, employers, and schools. It is important to have all of this information in one place.

Portfolio Format
Your portfolio can be a paper portfolio gathered in a folder or binder, a digital portfolio with electronic files, or a combination. Work with your teacher to determine which format will work best for you and your skills and experiences.

Save Your Work
Your portfolio can be used throughout your life to keep track of your academic and career goals and accomplishments. Keep it updated with new information, activities, and skills.

UNIT 2

Interpersonal Skills

Unit Portfolio Project Preview

Conduct Career Research

In this unit, you will look at the different types of skills you have developed or need to develop. In your portfolio project you will form connections between those skills and your future plans.

 My Journal

Making Matches Write a journal entry about one of the topics below. This will help you prepare for the project at the end of this unit.

- Identify three to five careers in which you are interested and explain why they would be good choices.
- Describe the types of information you might need about a career area before you pursue it further.
- Explain how you would go about getting information about specific career areas.

Explore the Photo

Interpersonal skills can help you get along better with others now and in your future. *Why do you think communication and teamwork are so important in healthy relationships?*

Chapter 4

Communication Skills

Chapter Objectives

Section 4.1 **Communicating with Others**

- **Explain** the differences between verbal and nonverbal communication.
- **Name** three ways to clearly communicate with others.
- **List** ways to listen actively and effectively.

Section 4.2 **Other Forms of Communication**

- **Describe** four ways to ensure effective communication by phone.
- **Outline** ways to create effective written communication.
- **Explain** how good communication skills impact everyday life.

➤ **Explore the Photo**

Most people have countless conversations in a day. *Why are good communication skills so important?*

Writing Activity   Dialogue

Sending the Right Messages You send messages to people through words, actions, and even your appearance. Write a short dialogue between two people that shows what you know about positive communication. Add notes about how each person reacts to the other person.

Writing Tips Use these tips to help you write a dialogue:
- Let the people in your dialogue express themselves and their purpose through the words you write.
- Use language that sounds real and appropriate to the people talking.
- Use quotation marks appropriately.

Communicating with Others

Reading Guide

Before You Read

What You Want to Know Based on the information on this page, write a list of what you want to know about this section. As you read through the section, write down the heads that provide that information.

Read to Learn

Key Concepts

- **Explain** the differences between verbal and nonverbal communication.
- **Name** three ways to clearly communicate with others.
- **List** ways to listen actively and effectively.

Main Idea

Communication combines verbal and nonverbal messages that convey your thoughts and feelings. Good communication is clear and free of mixed messages.

Content Vocabulary

- ◇ communication
- ◇ verbal communication
- ◇ nonverbal communication
- ◇ body language
- ◇ eye contact
- ◇ "I" message
- ◇ tone
- ◇ mixed message
- ◇ assertive
- ◇ aggressive
- ◇ passive
- ◇ active listening
- ◇ feedback
- ◇ interject

Academic Vocabulary

You will find these words in your reading and on your tests. Use the glossary to look up their definitions if necessary.

- ■ barrier
- ■ hinder

Graphic Organizer

As you read, list three communication barriers and possible solutions. Use a table like the one shown to help you organize your information.

Barrier	Solutions

 Graphic Organizer Go to this book's Online Learning Center at **glencoe.com** to print out this graphic organizer.

Academic Standards

 English Language Arts

NCTE 5 Use different writing process elements to communicate effectively.

 Mathematics

NCTM Problem Solving Apply and adapt a variety of appropriate strategies to solve problems.

 Social Studies

NCSS V B Individuals, Groups, and Institutions Analyze group and institutional influences on people, events, and elements of culture in both historical and contemporary settings.

NCTE *National Council of Teachers of English*
NCTM *National Council of Teachers of Mathematics*
NSES *National Science Education Standards*
NCSS *National Council for the Social Studies*

The Communication Process

Communication is the process of sending and receiving messages between people. Communication involves at least one person sending messages and another receiving them. Sometimes messages are not interpreted by the receiver as planned. This can end in confusion, and sometimes it can hurt relationships.

Good communication skills can help you avoid misunderstandings with people at home, in school, or in the workplace. Often people use **verbal communication**, which means sending messages with words and the sound of your voice. You use words to communicate face to face, on the phone, and in writing. **Nonverbal communication** is sending messages without words, often through facial expressions and gestures. People combine verbal and nonverbal messages to communicate their thoughts and feelings.

Barriers to Communication

It is important to be aware of barriers, or obstacles, that can prevent messages from being sent and received as intended. Here are some common traps people fall into when communicating:

- **Misunderstandings and Unclear Messages** If you have ever arrived at an event on the wrong day, you know how easy it is for messages to get confused. To avoid misunderstandings, pay attention and double check information.
- **Poor Listening Skills** Some people do not listen because they are too focused on their own thoughts. Others simply are not paying attention. Blocking out distractions and focusing on what someone is saying are important communication skills.
- **Language and Culture** People who have limited language skills may find it hard to say exactly what they mean. Listeners need to make an extra effort to understand. Culture, beliefs, values, and customs can also influence the way messages are interpreted. The best way to overcome cultural misunderstandings is to learn about and respect cultural differences.

As You Read

Connect What communication skills help you at school?

Vocabulary

You can find definitions in the glossary at the back of this book.

> **Avoid Misunderstanding**
>
> Good communication skills help ensure that messages get through clearly. *Have you ever misunderstood what someone said to you? What caused the problem?*

The way you carry your body, your facial expressions, and your gestures all send messages, just as your words do. *What do the gestures in this photo express?*

Adapt to Communication Challenges

There are other obstacles you may encounter when trying to communicate. Some people have visual or hearing impairments. Others may have challenges reading written texts, such as e-mail. Here are some ways communication challenges are being met:

- **Braille** People who have visual impairments can use the Braille alphabet to read with their fingertips.
- **Sign Language** This is a specific set of hand signals and gestures used by and for people with hearing impairments.
- **Technology** Speech synthesizers convert text into speech. Screen magnification software makes computer screens easier to read. Texts are typed messages sent through cell phones.

✓ **Reading Check** **Recall** What are some ways to meet communication challenges?

The Messages You Send

People who express themselves most clearly are aware of what they say and how they say it. Effective communication is a skill that can be learned, practiced, and improved.

Body Language

You can send messages without using words. **Body language** is a person's posture, facial expressions, gestures, and way of moving. **Eye contact** is direct visual contact with another person. Eye contact shows that you are interested, friendly, and sincere. Be aware, though, that in some cultures, eye contact can be considered inappropriate or even rude. Your appearance matters, too. What people say is more important than how they look, but clothes and grooming do send messages. Take care of your appearance to show that you respect others and yourself.

✓ **Be Smart Be Safe**

Cell Phone Safety Many states have passed laws making it illegal to talk on a cell phone while driving. This is because cell phones are distracting. You should never use a cell phone while you drive, walk alone at night, ride a bike, or do any other activity requiring concentration.

Write About It Research your state's laws about cell phone use while driving. Are there any laws about texting while driving? What about using a hands-free device? What happens if you are caught? Summarize your findings.

Send "I" Messages

An **"I" message** is a statement that allows you to say how you feel and what you think. "I" messages have three parts:

1. "I feel ..." (name an emotion, like disappointment or anger)
2. "when you ..." (say what behavior bothers you)
3. "because ..." (explain why it bothers you)

An example might be, "I feel angry when you interrupt me when I'm speaking because it makes it seem like you don't value my input." "I" messages are less likely to cause negative feelings, which interfere with communication. "You" messages often lead to attacks and accusations. "I" messages help both participants stay reasonable, focus on the underlying problem, and solve it together.

Use the Right Tone

Tone is the way a person says something to indicate what he or she is feeling or thinking. The tone of voice you use can add meaning to the words you say. A positive message can sound negative if it is said with sarcasm or boredom. If you say the same words enthusiastically, the message becomes positive. If you want to express sympathy, use a gentle tone. If you ask someone to help you, use a polite tone. Be aware of how the words you speak sound. This can help you send the messages you want to send.

Avoid Mixed Messages

Sometimes you might say one thing but your body language says another. When your words and body language do not communicate the same thing, you send a **mixed message**. Mixed messages cause confusion. People will not know whether to believe what you say or what they see. Practice thinking about what message you want to send and making sure your body language matches your words.

Life On Your Own

Be a Respectful Listener

Being a good listener will help you develop strong relationships by encouraging people to share things with you and open up to you. Also, if you show people respect by being a good, active listener, they will be more likely to show you that same respect in return.

How It Works Get rid of distractions, such as the television and telephones. Keep a positive attitude, and stay open-minded. Give nonverbal feedback, such as nodding and smiling. Let the speaker finish talking without interruption. Wait until the speaker is done before sharing your opinion.

Try It Out You are trying to have a serious conversation with a friend to get some advice from her, but you feel that she is not really listening. She keeps looking at her watch and checking her cell phone for text messages, and she does not look like she is paying attention. She has been nodding while you talk, but she does not seem focused on what you are saying.

> **Your Turn** How would this situation make you feel? How might this affect your relationship with your friend? What could she do differently to make you feel that she is listening to you?

Time and Place

Knowing when and where to communicate can improve communication as well. Sometimes it is best to speak your mind immediately. At other times it is wiser to wait. In choosing when and where to talk to someone, keep these tips in mind.

Be sure that the other person is willing and able to listen. Asking your mother something serious the minute she walks in the door from work is probably not a good idea. Wait until she is more receptive, or open and approachable.

Avoid times when your emotions might **hinder**, or get in the way of, your message. If you are angry, calm down before talking. If you are confused, take time to figure out what you want to say. Consider your listener's emotions, too. You are more likely to communicate effectively if both of you are calm and focused.

Make sure the other person is not distracted. Choose a time and place when the receiver can concentrate on the message and when you are unlikely to be interrupted.

Communication Styles

The way you speak can be just as important as what you say. You are more likely to get your message across if you are assertive. Being **assertive** means that you express your ideas and opinions firmly and with confidence. You show, through your communication style, that you mean what you say. People are more likely to listen to assertive speakers and to take them seriously.

Being assertive is not the same as being aggressive. People who are **aggressive** are overly forceful and pushy. They are often angry or frustrated. They think that by being aggressive they will persuade others. Often, the opposite happens. Many people react to aggressive behavior by rejecting the message and walking away.

People who have a **passive** communication style keep their opinions to themselves and give in to the influence of others. Some passive people are too timid to express an opinion. Others do not know what their opinions are. They find it easier to follow the crowd. This communication style can lead people to not have a say in what is going on or to make unwise choices.

✓ Reading Check **Identify** What are three terms that describe different communication styles?

The Messages You Receive

Sending clear messages is just as important as accurately interpreting the ones you receive. Other people want you to pay attention to and understand what they have to say. In that way, they are no different from you.

Dealing with Criticism

Criticism is spoken or written opinions that point out someone's shortcomings. Criticism can be beneficial when it is meant to help you improve a quality about yourself. This is called constructive criticism. For example, Geneva was upset when her drama teacher told her she needed to work much harder on memorizing her lines. However, it forced Geneva to take an honest look at herself and her habits. She realized that she should be working harder and that her teacher wanted her to do well in the play. Keep an open mind and consider comments that seem intended to help you.

Ignore criticism that is spiteful or inaccurate. People have a right to express their opinions. However, you do not have to respond to negative comments. Nor is there anything to be gained from dwelling on personal attacks. Learn to distinguish between helpful and unhelpful criticism. Focus on what is helpful.

Active Listening

Active listening is concentrating on what is said so that you understand and remember the message. It helps promote real understanding. People who make an effort to listen are less self-absorbed and more likely to learn from others. When you show an interest in what people have to say, you help them feel that they have something worthwhile to offer. **Figure 4.1** lists several strategies for receiving messages the way they were intended.

Succeed in SCHOOL and LIFE

Ask for Feedback

If you wonder how you are doing in a certain subject or what your teacher thinks of your idea for an upcoming paper, ask! Teachers have many ideas and a lot of experience. They are great and often underused resources. Do not be afraid to reach out to your teacher or to ask for feedback.

| Figure 4.1 | Active Listening Strategies |

Show an Interest It can be tempting to prepare a response while the other person is speaking. *Why should this be avoided?*

Keep an open mind. Set aside your opinions and be prepared to listen to the other person's point of view.	**Eliminate distractions.** If the music or TV is too loud, turn it off or move to a quieter place. Also, eliminate your own daydreams.	**Listen with a purpose.** Think about why you are listening. For example, you listen to your friends' problems to let them express their feelings.
Control negative emotions. If the speaker's message upsets you, focus on staying calm and listening. Then you can present your views.	**Focus your attention.** Think about what is being said, not how you will respond.	**Make eye contact.** Look the speaker in the eye, and keep your expression open and interested.
Do not cut the speaker off. Let the person who is speaking finish at his or her own pace.	**Concentrate.** Focus on what the speaker is actually saying, not what you expect him or her to say.	**Avoid judgments.** Resist judgment until the speaker is finished. You may miss a chance for understanding.

Feedback

An important part of any two-way communication is giving feedback. **Feedback** occurs when a listener lets a speaker know that he or she is trying to understand the message being delivered. When the other person is upset and needs to unload negative feelings, show empathy. Empathy is the ability to identify with and understand somebody else's feelings or problems. Use phrases that show you understand, like "That sounds unfair" or "You must have been so hurt." Do not feel you need to solve the problem. Having someone who will listen may be all that the speaker needs. There are different ways that you can provide useful feedback:

- **Interject** Do not interrupt, but when the speaker takes a moment to pause, interject. To **interject** is to insert something into a discussion. Make a comment or gesture that encourages him or her to continue.
- **Express** Show your interest by asking questions that lead to more conversation.
- **Restate** In your own words, restate what the speaker said to you. Then ask the person whether you understood the message correctly.

 Show an Interest

One way to show an interest in a conversation is to choose an appropriate place to talk. *What can you do to make sure you can talk in peace?*

 Podcasts Access the Online Learning Center to download *Managing Life Skills* podcasts.

Section 4.1 After You Read

Review Key Concepts

1. **Explain** how language and culture can affect communication.
2. **Describe** the dangers of mixed messages.
3. **Explain** how accepting criticism is an important listening skill.

Practice Academic Skills

 English Language Arts

4. Imagine you need to speak with a friend about something he or she did that hurt your feelings. Write a short paragraph explaining how and where you would discuss your issues. Use information from this section to make your decisions.

 Social Studies

5. Conduct research to find a culture different from your own, but geographically close. Compare and contrast the ways in which the cultures communicate with one another and with nearby people outside of the culture. Make a list of the differences and similarities that you find.

 Check Your Answers Check your answers at this book's Online Learning Center at **glencoe.com**.

> **NCTE 5** Use different writing process elements to communicate effectively.

> **NCSS V B** Analyze group and institutional influences on people, events, and elements of culture in both historical and contemporary settings.

Other Forms of Communication

Reading Guide

Before You Read

Create an Outline Use the section's heading titles to create an outline. Make the titles Level 1 main ideas. Add supporting information to create Level 2, 3, and 4 details. Use the outline to predict what you are about to learn.

Technology makes it easier to communicate— but is that always a good thing?

Read to Learn
Key Concepts

- **Describe** four ways to ensure effective communication by phone.
- **Outline** ways to create effective written communication.
- **Explain** how good communication skills impact everyday life.

Main Idea

Special skills are required to avoid confusion and unclear messages when you are not able to communicate face to face.

Content Vocabulary

◇ text message
◇ clarification

Academic Vocabulary

You will find these words in your reading and on your tests. Use the glossary to look up their definitions if necessary.

■ foster
■ convey

Academic Standards

English Language Arts

NCTE 4 Use written language to communicate effectively.

Social Studies

NCSS X C Civic Ideals and Practices Locate, access, analyze, organize, synthesize, evaluate, and apply information about selected public issues—identifying, describing, and evaluating multiple points of view.

Graphic Organizer

As you read, write four steps you should take before sending written communication. Use a flowchart like the one shown to help you organize your information.

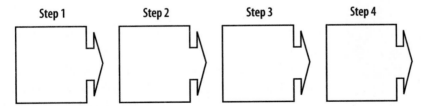

Step 1 Step 2 Step 3 Step 4

Graphic Organizer Go to this book's Online Learning Center at **glencoe.com** to print out this graphic organizer.

NCTE *National Council of Teachers of English*
NCTM *National Council of Teachers of Mathematics*
NSES *National Science Education Standards*
NCSS *National Council for the Social Studies*

Phone Calls and Text Messages

As You Read

Connect How many different ways do you connect to people throughout the day?

Vocabulary

You can find definitions in the glossary at the back of this book.

Cell Phones

Cell phones help us stay connected to the people in our lives. *How can you ensure you are not disturbing others with your cell phone conversations?*

A **text message** is a message sent in text form and designed to appear on the viewing screen of a cell phone or other electronic devices. When you talk on a phone or send a text message, you cannot see the person to whom you are speaking, and you cannot be seen. Neither of you can "read" facial expressions or other body language. You cannot nod or smile to encourage the person to keep talking. Misunderstandings are more frequent without the benefit of face-to-face interaction. Using active listening and providing feedback become even more important. Here are some other tips:

- **Find a convenient time.** When you call someone, ask, "Do you have time to talk?" If someone calls you when you are busy, ask if you can call back. If you are rushed or distracted, you will not be able to give your attention to the caller.
- **Find a convenient place.** Try to find a quiet place to make your call or send your text. Calling from a busy mall could make it hard for your listener to hear you.
- **Avoid disturbing other people.** A ringing cell phone or a beeping keypad can be intrusive and annoying, especially in a theater, library, classroom, or quiet restaurant. Turn off your cell phone or set it to vibrate instead of ring. If you need to make or answer a call, step outside.
- **Leave clear messages.** If you need to leave a voice mail message, think carefully about what you want to say. Let the listener know when you called and the reason for your call.

✔ **Reading Check** **Explain** Why can calling or sending a text message be more difficult than communicating face to face?

Communicating in Writing

Throughout history, people have communicated by writing letters. Today, e-mail and texting are significant means of written communication. Good writing and reading skills help you communicate with your friends and family. These skills are also essential in the workplace. Many jobs require you to write memos and reports or to read and understand written instructions.

Whatever form of writing you choose, the same guidelines apply. Consider the person receiving your message, the purpose of your message, and the subject about which you are writing. The words you choose can determine the tone of your message. Choose your words carefully. Even when written instead of spoken, a tone can "sound" light-hearted, apologetic, or angry.

Keep these suggestions in mind when writing:

- **Organize your thoughts before you start.** Make notes, list the points you want to cover, and decide on the sequence you want to follow.
- **Pay attention to the tone you use.** The letter you write when applying for a job requires a formal, respectful tone. You can be more casual when writing to a friend. Do not forget the tone you **convey**, or express, in your e-mail signature and name. Are they appropriate for a cover letter or a résumé?
- **Keep it simple.** Use straightforward language and make your points clearly. Do not make it hard for your reader to understand the reason for your message.
- **Check that you have made all your points.** Proofread your work before you send it. Check your spelling and grammar. Spell-check may not catch the misuse of some words. You might also accidently leave out a word that changes the meaning of your message.

Read messages you receive carefully. When you read messages, focus on the reason for the message. Try to understand what the person is saying. Follow up with any questions you have.

✓ Reading Check **Understand** When you communicate in writing, what is the best way to make sure you are clearly understood by your reader?

Succeed in SCHOOL and LIFE

Accept Criticism
Though it may be difficult to hear, constructive criticism can actually be helpful. Most jobs have some sort of review process through which your manager or supervisor provides feedback on your job performance. Though these situations can be intimidating, try thinking about them as opportunities to learn how you can improve and advance.

Two Views One World

Are Cell Phones Beneficial or Distracting?

Cell phones are convenient, and every year, more and more people become cell phone dependent. But cell phones can also be annoying and even isolating.

Ryan: I can't imagine life without my cell phone. I use it to make plans with friends, call people if I'm going to be late, and I even have music and games on my phone. My parents love it because they can always get in touch with me. Having a cell phone makes me feel like I'm always connected and like I can get whatever information I need. I think it's a great modern convenience that I'm convinced I couldn't live without.

Olivia: Everywhere I look, someone is on a cell phone. I don't want to hear people's private conversations when I'm on the bus or at the store. It's annoying when someone won't look at me because she's busy texting someone else. Everyone is constantly looking down at the little screen in their hands instead of at the world around them. Cell phones have their place, but I think we're too dependent on them.

Seeing Both Sides
Do you think these viewpoints are valid? Do you have a cell phone on which you depend? Come up with three rules you think cell phone users should follow to avoid irritating those around them.

HOW TO... Write Effective E-mail

E-mail has become a major form of communication in our society, with billions of e-mails being sent every day. While e-mail can serve many different purposes, there are certain standards expected for e-mail use. These tips are good guidelines to keep in mind regarding e-mail conduct.

Write a Meaningful Subject Line A good subject line indicates the content and purpose of the e-mail. Subject lines help recipients decide how important an e-mail is and are also sometimes used to sort and search e-mails.

Do Not Assume Privacy E-mail is not secure. E-mail is also easily and often forwarded, and many companies consider employee e-mail company property. To be safe, do not send e-mail messages that would embarrass you if they became public.

Proofread E-mail should be proofread just like letters sent in the mail. Spelling, grammar, and punctuation are important. Use spell-check on your e-mail before hitting send.

Keep Messages to the Point E-mail should be focused, readable, and as brief as possible. As you are writing, keep in mind the purpose of your e-mail, and avoid being wordy.

Be Careful with Group E-mail Send group e-mail only when it is helpful to every recipient. Use the "Reply All" function only when collective input is required.

Communication and Relationships

Good communication is essential to good relationships. This is true on a personal level, in the workplace, and in society in general. Good communicators know how to express themselves so that others will understand them. They also know how to receive messages in constructive ways. Diplomats, for example, must communicate with people from different countries to do their job well. They need excellent communication skills to make sure they do not offend anyone. They also understand how to resolve problems when communication breaks down.

When you realize that there may be a misunderstanding in communicating, try to clear the air between you and the other person as quickly as possible. Many arguments can be avoided if you ask for **clarification**, which means to make something clearer with further explanation. When you ask for clarification, you clear up mistakes and lessen confusion.

In the workplace, you need to get along with people of different ages, genders, cultures, backgrounds, and abilities. Communicating effectively increases understanding and cooperation at home, with friends, at work, and in the community. It can also help you understand interactions better in places where you may not meet someone face to face, such as on a social networking site. Understanding can **foster**, or encourage, good feelings, stronger relationships, and better communication.

Health & Wellness TIPS

Express Yourself

Bottling up your emotions can be harmful to your health. It can lead to irritability, depression, negative explosions of emotion, and even abuse of alcohol and drugs. Follow these tips to express yourself:

► Confide in someone.
► Think about your feelings.
► Speak your mind.

Podcasts Access the Online Learning Center to download *Managing Life Skills* podcasts.

Section 4.2 — After You Read

Review Key Concepts

1. **Describe** a good setting for a phone conversation.
2. **Explain** why paying attention to the tone of your message is especially important in written communication.
3. **Summarize** how clarification can help you avoid arguments.

Practice Academic Skills

English Language Arts

4. Think about the words, slang, and abbreviations you use every day with your friends in speech, text messages, and instant messages. Write a paragraph explaining why those terms and phrases may be acceptable in a casual setting but inappropriate in other situations.

Social Studies

5. Conduct research to find a famous historical speech that addressed a public issue. Write a short essay that explains the purpose of the speech. How did the words and phrases used help get the message across to the audience?

Check Your Answers Check your answers at this book's Online Learning Center at **glencoe.com**.

NCTE 4 Use written language to communicate effectively.

NCSS X C Locate, access, analyze, organize, synthesize, evaluate, and apply information about selected public issues—identifying, describing, and evaluating multiple points of view.

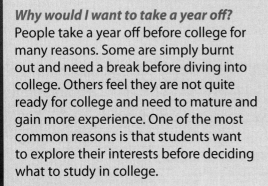

What Is a Gap Year?

After thirteen years of school, you may want a break. This is called a "gap year" because it is a year that fills the possible gap between high school and college. You could use the time to volunteer, intern in a field in which you are interested, or start learning another language. While taking a gap year is not the right choice for everyone, many students are taking advantage of this opportunity.

Why would I want to take a year off?
People take a year off before college for many reasons. Some are simply burnt out and need a break before diving into college. Others feel they are not quite ready for college and need to mature and gain more experience. One of the most common reasons is that students want to explore their interests before deciding what to study in college.

If I know I want to take a year off, when should I apply to college?
Even if you know you want to take a year off, it is still a good idea to apply for college during your senior year. Many colleges will defer your acceptance for a year. If you are still in high school, it will be easier to get letters of recommendation from your teachers, and you will have the support of your school guidance counselor, teachers, and other classmates.

If I decide to take a year off, what are some of my options?
Your options are practically limitless and range from studying art restoration in Italy to working on a ranch in Montana. If you can imagine it, you can most likely make it happen. However, some of the most common gap year activities include doing community service, participating in a foreign exchange program, working, and getting an internship. Taking a gap year requires careful planning.

Hands-On

College Readiness Imagine that you have decided to take a year off before college. Research your options, and decide which one you think would be best for you. Describe your ideal year off, and explain why you think this gap year activity would be a good fit and how it would help you in the future. Be sure to explain how the activity you chose would help you grow and develop as a person.

Path to Success

☆ **College & Career Readiness**

Get in First It is almost always a good idea to get into college and then postpone it for a year.

Imagine There are almost infinite options for what to do during a gap year. What do you want to learn?

Plan Getting the most out of your gap year requires a lot of thought, planning, and preparation.

Talk About It Taking a year off is a very important and serious decision, so be sure to discuss it with your parents and guidance counselor.

Think Carefully Taking a year off is not for everyone. Be sure it is something you really want.

Be Smart Your year off should teach you something and expand your horizons. It should not be used just to postpone college.

 Go to this book's Online Learning Center at **glencoe.com** to learn more about to learn more about college and career readiness.

CHAPTER SUMMARY

Section 4.1
Communicating with Others

Communication involves sending and receiving verbal and nonverbal messages. Verbal messages use words, while nonverbal messages are sent without the use of words. "I" messages help you communicate how you feel and what you think without hurting the feelings of other people. Body language, eye contact, and personal appearance all contribute to the messages you send.

Section 4.2
Other Forms of Communication

When you are not communicating face-to-face, you cannot depend on body language and facial expressions, so you must really focus on being clear. Telephone etiquette involves choosing an appropriate time and place to call or text and avoiding distractions. When communicating in writing, you need to consider to whom you are writing, the purpose of your message, and the subject of your message.

Vocabulary Review

1. Label each of these content and academic vocabulary terms as a noun, verb, or adjective.

Content Vocabulary
- communication (p. 69)
- verbal communication (p. 69)
- nonverbal communication (p. 69)
- body language (p. 70)
- eye contact (p. 70)
- "I" message (p. 71)
- tone (p. 71)
- mixed message (p. 71)
- assertive (p. 72)
- aggressive (p. 72)
- passive (p. 72)
- active listening (p. 73)
- feedback (p. 74)
- interject (p. 74)
- text message (p. 76)
- clarification (p. 79)

Academic Vocabulary
- barrier (p. 69)
- hinder (p. 72)
- convey (p. 77)
- foster (p. 79)

Review Key Concepts

2. Explain the differences between verbal and nonverbal communication.
3. Name three ways to clearly communicate with others.
4. List ways to listen actively and effectively.
5. Describe four ways to ensure effective communication by phone.
6. Outline ways to create effective written communication.
7. Explain how good communication skills impact everyday life.

Critical Thinking

8. Analyze How does nonverbal communication affect a verbal message?
9. Assess How can humor be misunderstood when you are not communicating face to face? Provide examples.
10. Recognize Assumptions Why do what you wear and your grooming have an important effect on the image you present to others?
11. Hypothesize How can listening skills positively or negatively affect a conversation?

ACTIVE LEARNING

12. Co-Write a Script With your teacher's permission, find a partner. With your partner, discuss common mistakes people tend to make when communicating with each other. After your discussion, write two scripts for a conversation about any topic you like. In the first script, write a scene in which two people illustrate poor communication skills. In the second script, rewrite the same scene to illustrate good communication techniques that resolve the issues that arose in the first dialogue.

Family & Community Connections

13. Role Models Talk to an adult in your family or in your community who you think has good communication skills. With his or her permission, observe a casual conversation between this person and someone else. Avoid taking notes during the conversation. Pay attention to the topic of the conversation, the body language of both participants, and the way they react to each other. Immediately after the conversation, write down your observations. What did they talk about? What skills from this chapter did they put into action? What did they do or say that was effective? Did they do or say anything that was ineffective? Explain your answers.

21st Century Skills

Information Literacy Skills

14. Research Online With permission from your teacher or parents, go online to research American Sign Language and Braille. Discuss interesting facts that you find about the history and use of these communication tools in our society. Use a word processing program to summarize your findings.

Collaboration Skills

15. Charades Follow your teacher's instructions to form small groups. Play charades, a game in which one person silently provides a visual or acted clue for a word or phrase, such as the title of a book, play, or movie, for the rest of the group to guess. Allow each person in the group to present his or her guess. In a short essay, describe the challenges presented when people must communicate without speaking.

 Connections

Communication Skills

16. Promoting Good Communication As part of its mission, FCCLA encourages students to promote positive communication in their home and community. Use FCCLA's Stop the Violence program to create a presentation that shows other teens how to use positive communication skills during conflicts. Deliver your presentation to the class or FCCLA chapter.

Academic Skills

 English Language Arts

17. Language Hurdles When someone is learning a new language, idioms can be difficult for him or her to understand. Idioms are phrases like "hold your horses," which means "be patient." Think of five common English language phrases that might be misunderstood by someone who is not a native English speaker. Explain what the phrases mean in a way someone who is learning English could understand them.

> **NCTE 4** Use written language to communicate effectively.

 Social Studies

18. Cultural Differences Sometimes people from different cultures can misunderstand each other's body language. Choose a region of the world that has a culture very different from yours. Conduct research to learn how body language is interpreted in similar and different ways around the world.

> **NCSS I B Culture** Predict how data and experiences may be interpreted by people from diverse cultural perspectives and frames of reference.

 Mathematics

19. Calculate Square Roots Your debate team has been invited to participate in a competition. You want to draw attention to your team with a colorful poster, and the organizers said the poster can be no more than 25 square feet in size. You want your poster to be a perfect square. What are the largest dimensions each side can have to fit the organizers' guidelines?

Math Concept **Squares and Square Roots** The square root of a number is one of two equal factors of the number. The notation $\sqrt{}$ indicates the square root.

Starting Hint Find the square root of 25 in order to determine the largest possible dimensions a square poster can have.

 For more math practice, go to the Math Appendix at the back of the book.

> **NCTM Measurement** Apply appropriate techniques, tools, and formulas to determine measurements.

 Standardized Test Practice   **CCR** College & Career Readiness

TRUE/FALSE
Read the passage, and then decide if the statements that follows are true or false.

> **Test-Taking Tip** Make sure you understand the full statement. All parts of a statement must be correct for the statement to be true. Statements that contain words such as *all, none, never,* or *always,* or that have unsupported opinions, are often false.

Interference, such as background noise, the television, and radio, can disrupt communication.

20. The conversations of other people can be considered background noise.

21. Background noise is always distracting.

22. Always make sure that you avoid distractions when having a serious conversation.

Chapter 5

Teamwork and Leadership Skills

Chapter Objectives

Section 5.1 Teamwork Skills

- **Summarize** the benefits of teamwork.
- **Describe** characteristics of a strong team player.
- **Identify** the three methods used to make group decisions.

Section 5.2 Leadership Skills

- **Analyze** characteristics of effective leadership.
- **Explain** the four most common leadership styles.
- **Determine** the importance of resolving group conflict.

➤ Explore the Photo

Working in teams at school and within your community prepares you for the future. *In what way can participating in a team environment at school prepare you for your future career?*

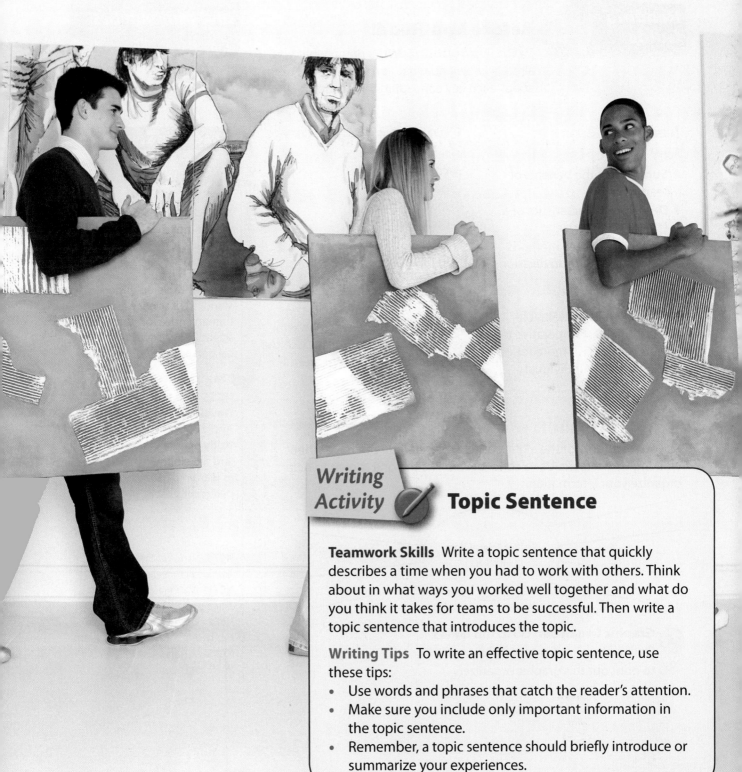

Writing Activity

Topic Sentence

Teamwork Skills Write a topic sentence that quickly describes a time when you had to work with others. Think about in what ways you worked well together and what do you think it takes for teams to be successful. Then write a topic sentence that introduces the topic.

Writing Tips To write an effective topic sentence, use these tips:

- Use words and phrases that catch the reader's attention.
- Make sure you include only important information in the topic sentence.
- Remember, a topic sentence should briefly introduce or summarize your experiences.

Teamwork Skills

Teamwork is a key to success in families, schools, workplaces, sports, and communities.

Reading Guide

Before You Read

Prior Knowledge Write down what you already know and what you want to find out about each key concept in this section.

Read to Learn

Key Concepts

- **Summarize** the benefits of teamwork.
- **Describe** characteristics of a strong team player.
- **Identify** the three methods used to make group decisions.

Main Idea

Teamwork skills are valuable throughout life. Cooperative team players accomplish more together than they can as individuals.

Content Vocabulary

◇ teamwork
◇ cooperation
◇ persuade
◇ majority rule
◇ compromise
◇ consensus
◇ parliamentary procedure
◇ groupthink

Academic Vocabulary

You will find these words in your reading and on your tests. Use the glossary to look up their definitions if necessary.

- effective
- alternative

Academic Standards

English Language Arts

NCTE 12 Use language to accomplish individual purposes.

Science

NSES G Develop understanding of science as a human endeavor, nature of scientific knowledge, historical perspectives.

Social Studies

NCSS IV D Individual Development and Identity Apply concepts about the study of human growth and development, such as learning, behavior, and personality.

NCTE *National Council of Teachers of English*
NCTM *National Council of Teachers of Mathematics*
NSES *National Science Education Standards*
NCSS *National Council for the Social Studies*

Graphic Organizer

As you read, look for the eight positive roles people can have when working with a team. Use a concept web like the one shown to help organize your information.

Positive Roles of Team Members

Graphic Organizer Go to this book's Online Learning Center at **glencoe.com** to print out this graphic organizer.

What Is Teamwork?

Teamwork involves working with others to achieve a common goal. It is based on the principle that people working together can accomplish more than individuals working alone. Many teams start out with some good ideas, but they also face challenges in learning to work together successfully. When people develop teamwork skills, they are more likely to succeed when working with others.

Teamwork is a key to the success of families, schools, workplaces, and communities. In your family, you may work together to clean up the kitchen after a meal. Maybe you have worked on a group project in school. Your local school board and city or town council are examples of teamwork in your community.

As You Read

Connect What are some reasons you would want to work with a team?

Benefits of Teamwork

Learning to be an **effective**, or successful, member of a team is a skill that will always be useful. In the workplace, employers recognize that many goals can be accomplished only through teamwork. Some businesses depend almost entirely on a teamwork approach. In these companies, managers do not tell employees what to do. Instead, teams of employees are responsible for choosing their own methods of reaching the goals that have been set. A sense of teamwork in the workplace increases productivity and builds a feeling of company loyalty.

Since teamwork is so important in the workplace, now is the time to learn and practice teamwork skills. School provides many opportunities. You can participate in class projects, sports, and organizations such as Family, Career and Community Leaders of America (FCCLA). These experiences can help make you both a productive student and a desirable job candidate.

Teamwork has many benefits, both for the group as a whole and for individual team members. These benefits include:

- **Efficiency** Projects can be completed in less time if people work together.
- **Combined Strengths** The variety of skills that various team members bring to a project is a plus. Combining individual strengths enhances the quality of the results.
- **Mutual Support** It is easy to procrastinate or become discouraged when working alone on a difficult project. On team projects, team members can offer support and encouragement.
- **Job Satisfaction** By giving and receiving positive feedback and making progress, team members feel that their contributions are worthwhile.

Vocabulary

You can find definitions in the glossary at the back of this book.

Accomplish Goals Together

When individuals come together and work in harmony, they can create a whole that is greater than the sum of its parts. *What do musicians need to do to work well as a team?*

Get Involved!

Teamwork in Your Community

Choose a successful volunteer group in your community, such as a food bank or Habitat for Humanity. Interview someone who volunteers for that group. How does the group focus on teamwork and leadership? Why do the group's members work well together? What could you gain by joining this group?

- **Personal Development** Teamwork helps you develop skills, gain self-confidence, and learn from others. For example, if you served as student council representative during your freshman year, you may gain the confidence to run for a higher position the following year.
- **Improved Relationships** Teamwork offers opportunities to build and strengthen relationships. Working together can lead to a lasting bond among team members.

✓ **Reading Check** **Explain** What are the benefits of teamwork in the workplace?

Characteristics of Team Players

Cooperation is associating with others for mutual benefit. Imagine trying to pull a huge, heavy box by tying ropes to it. If everyone grabs a rope and pulls in a different direction, nothing is accomplished. Only by pulling together in the same direction will the team achieve its goal.

Cooperative team members coordinate their efforts. They are willing to do what is necessary to complete a job, and they accept responsibility for team results. **Figure 5.1** describes ways people can be team players and show cooperation.

Taking on Roles

Members of a team play different roles to help achieve the team's goals. For example, an orchestra needs musicians and a conductor. A ball team needs players and a coach. You need team members who have different skills and who contribute those skills to the team's success.

Figure 5.1 **How to Be a Team Player**

Active Participation Putting these ideas into practice will help make you a valued member of any team. *How could competition among team members affect the people and the work?*

Be willing to contribute. Let the team know how you can be most useful. Team success depends on using members' knowledge, skills, and ideas effectively.	**Use good communication skills.** In team meetings, express your ideas clearly and listen attentively. Communicate effectively between meetings.	**Respect differences.** Show respect for every team member, regardless of age, ability, gender, and culture. Everyone has something to contribute.
Avoid competing with other team members. Being on a team means focusing on group success, not personal success.	**Do your fair share.** Take on as much as you can handle, and be sure to complete your tasks. Accept responsibility for the jobs assigned to you.	**Focus on team goals.** The team's goals are your top priority. Do not get sidetracked by unrelated goals or personal goals.
Work to resolve conflicts. If team members disagree, help find a workable solution while respecting others' opinions.	**Support team decisions.** Accept responsibility for carrying out team decisions, even if you do not agree with them.	**Pitch in to help others.** If someone on the team has a tough job or falls behind, be supportive. If you can, offer to lend a hand.

Figure 5.2 **Roles of Team Members**

Leaders Need Followers Not every team has members who play these roles, but you may recognize some of these roles in team members with whom you have worked. *Which roles have you played?*

POSITIVE ROLES	NEGATIVE ROLES
Initiator: a person who gets things moving **Coordinator:** a person who organizes team resources **Leader:** a person who takes responsibility for moving the team forward **Harmonizer:** a person who tries to build good relationships among team members **Encourager:** a person who praises other people's ideas **Seeker:** a person who asks questions **Innovator:** a person who has creative ideas **Peacemaker:** a person who helps the team deal with conflict	**Avoider:** a person who refuses to actively participate **Dominator:** a person who tries to control other team members **Blocker:** a person who rejects everyone else's ideas **Distracter:** a person who turns attention away from the team's primary goal

When any group of people comes together, there will be a variety of personalities. Sometimes the personalities work well together, and other times they may clash. When you participate in a team, ask yourself what role or roles you are playing. Do they assist the team's progress, or do they get in the way? See **Figure 5.2** for the types of roles often found in teams.

✓ **Reading Check** **Define** What role does an innovator play within a team?

How Teamwork Works

Teams work together for common purposes. Teams' time frames can vary. In a large corporation, team projects often require weeks, months, or years to complete. Whatever the team's purpose or time frame, successful teams use similar processes to achieve their goals.

Team members trust, support, and rely on one another. They appreciate each person's efforts and ideas. This mutual support helps them cooperate to achieve their goals and build team spirit.

Dividing Tasks

Teams function best when all team members understand what is expected of them. Everyone should be asked to contribute, and responsibilities should be distributed fairly. If people feel they are expected to do too much, frustrations can build. If they are asked to do too little, they may feel they are not a valued part of the team. The workload of team members should be fairly balanced.

Successful teams assign tasks in ways that make the best possible use of the knowledge and skills of all members. The prom committee asked Elena to present its plans to the entire class. They chose her because of her excellent speaking skills and her ability to persuade others. To **persuade** (pər-ˈswād) is to encourage someone to believe something, especially by giving good reasons for doing so.

Succeed in **SCHOOL** and **LIFE**

Understand Teamwork

Teamwork can be intimidating to people who are shy or insecure or who do not have well-developed skills. When working on teams in school and throughout your life, keep this in mind and look for ways to help people overcome their insecurities and embrace the opportunity to learn.

Reaching a group decision may not be easy, but it is an important process. *What are the advantages of involving the whole team in decision making?*

Making Group Decisions

When teams are faced with important decisions, they must find a way to reach an agreement. Team members must be willing to listen to and consider different points of view. The method used to reach a decision will depend on the group and the situation. For example:

- **Majority rule** is a democratic process in which decisions are made by voting. All team members vote on an issue, and the majority opinion must be accepted. One disadvantage is that it creates winners and losers.
- **Compromise** is a settlement of differences in which each side makes concessions or sacrifices. Team members each give up some of what they want. The result is a solution that is not totally satisfying to anyone, but that everyone agrees will help the team meet its goals.
- **Consensus** (kən-'sen(t)-səs) means agreement by the entire group, and everyone's ideas are taken into account. The final decision must be agreeable to everyone. If any member of the team has a strong objection, an **alternative**, or another option, must be found. Consensus building may take a long time, or it may not be possible at all. Even if the team does not reach a consensus, the process can help clarify the issues being discussed.

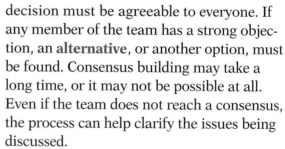

Science For Success

Collaboration in Scientific Research

There are many methods of collaboration, or teamwork, that are used to enhance the pursuit of scientific knowledge.

Procedure Follow your teacher's instructions to work with a partner and conduct research about how collaboration has affected scientific research. Identify at least three benefits of collaborative research.

Analysis Create a short report or class presentation about how specific collaboration methods have helped scientific research.

NSES G Develop understanding of science as a human endeavor, nature of scientific knowledge, historical perspectives.

Parliamentary Procedure

Parliamentary procedure is a set of rules for conducting meetings in an orderly way. This democratic method ensures that even though majority rules, the rights of the minority are protected. Many government bodies, professional associations, and student organizations use this procedure.

The basic rules of parliamentary procedure include:

- **Motion** This is a method of introducing a topic to the group for discussion.
- **Second** If other members agree, they second the motion.
- **Debate** Members present opinions about the motion.
- **Motion to Amend** During the debate, members can propose changes to the original motion.
- **Division of Question** This breaks up the motion so each part can be considered.
- **Vote** When the debate ends, the group votes.

Avoid Groupthink

Sometimes groups work well together, yet make poor decisions. Irving Janis, a researcher who studied how groups work together, coined the term "groupthink" to explain why this can happen. **Groupthink** refers to a faulty decision-making process caused by a strong desire for group agreement. Groups engaging in groupthink consider only a few alternatives before selecting a course of action. They ignore information that does not support the action they decide to take. Team members with opposing opinions are pressured to agree with the majority.

Groupthink is a barrier to successful teamwork. Teams can avoid groupthink by being open and accepting of diverse opinions and by encouraging critical evaluation of all ideas. Teams made up of people with diverse backgrounds and experiences are less likely to engage in groupthink.

Health & Wellness TIPS

Avoid Taking on Too Much

Being a good group member means doing your part. However, you cannot say yes to everything. If you overcommit yourself, you can negatively affect your health. Be realistic when agreeing to take on projects.

 Podcasts Access the Online Learning Center to download *Managing Life Skills* podcasts.

Section 5.1 — After You Read

Review Key Concepts

1. **Describe** how personal development is a benefit of teamwork.
2. **Explain** three positive roles of team members.
3. **Define** compromise.

Practice Academic Skills

 English Language Arts

4. Think about the different types of people you work with on a daily basis, such as classmates, coworkers, and friends. Consider the positive teamwork processes that you use with these people. List how these processes can benefit you in your career.

 Social Studies

5. How you act as a team player is a way of expressing yourself and your values. It is a part of your identity. Write about ways you act as a team player. Do you use good communication skills? Do you respect differences? Do you do your fair share of the work? Explain how you developed your teamwork style. What influenced it?

Check Your Answers Check your answers at this book's Online Learning Center at **glencoe.com**.

NCTE 12 Use language to accomplish individual purposes.

NCSS IV D Apply concepts about the study of human growth and development, such as learning, behavior, and personality.

Leadership Skills

Reading Guide

Before You Read

Look It Up If you read or hear an unfamiliar word while reading this section, look it up in the glossary at the back of this book or in a dictionary. Before long, this practice will become a habit.

Read to Learn
Key Concepts
- **Analyze** characteristics of effective leadership.
- **Explain** the four most common leadership styles.
- **Determine** the importance of resolving group conflict.

Main Idea
Effective teams need strong leaders to guide the team to accomplish the team's goals. Leaders guide and influence others.

Content Vocabulary
◇ role model
◇ commitment
◇ delegate
◇ ethical leadership
◇ leadership style

Academic Vocabulary
You will find these words in your reading and on your tests. Use the glossary to look up their definitions if necessary.
◼ vision
◼ quality

Academic Standards

 **English Language Arts**

NCTE 4 Use written language to communicate effectively.

 **Mathematics**

NCTM Problem Solving Build new mathematical knowledge through problem solving.

Social Studies

NCSS I A Culture Analyze and explain the ways groups, societies, and cultures address human needs and concerns.

Graphic Organizer

As you read, pick out the four styles of leadership. Identify one unique characteristic of each leadership style. Use a chart like the one shown to organize your information.

Leadership Style	Unique Characteristic

 Graphic Organizer Go to this book's Online Learning Center at **glencoe.com** to print out this graphic organizer.

NCTE *National Council of Teachers of English*
NCTM *National Council of Teachers of Mathematics*
NSES *National Science Education Standards*
NCSS *National Council for the Social Studies*

Effective Leadership

To be effective, teams need good leadership. Leadership provides the direction and motivation that helps a team or group achieve its goals. Whether the goal is to plan a class project, organize a family reunion, or run a small business, every team needs a leader.

Some leaders are chosen or elected. Others take a leadership role when they see a need to do so. For example, Ryan heard that a fire had damaged the home of a friend in his math class. He wanted to help, but he knew he could not provide the new household goods the family needed. So Ryan decided to brainstorm with some of his classmates about ways they could help. Together they organized a school-wide fundraiser to help the family. In this case, Ryan's leadership made things happen.

Leadership Skills

People like Ryan serve as role models. A **role model** is a person who sets an example for others. When you serve as a role model and others follow your example, your ability to make a difference extends beyond your own actions.

What leadership skills did Ryan demonstrate in helping his classmate's family? First, he had the **vision**, or ability to imagine, what he wanted to achieve. He could see that while he alone could do little to help the family, he could make a difference by inspiring and persuading others to help. In addition, Ryan demonstrated the commitment to take action. People show **commitment** when they pledge to do something in the future and follow through on their pledge. Ryan's skill of persuasion convinced others to share his vision. Without these leadership skills, he could not have achieved his goal.

As You Read

Connect Why do you think a leader needs a vision?

Vocabulary

You can find definitions in the glossary at the back of this book.

Succeed in SCHOOL and LIFE

Learning to Lead

Sometimes quieter team members have good ideas that are not heard because more outgoing team members take over the discussion. More outgoing members often energize a team, which is an asset, but team leaders need to be sure to take advantage of all team members' skills and personality traits.

Motivation

A good leader knows how to guide and motivate others. *What might happen if a group tried to accomplish a goal without a leader?*

Below are other important skills leaders need. Ask yourself which skills you already have and which you need to work on.

- **Communicating Clearly** Good leaders consciously choose what they say and how they say it. They understand the importance of body language, and they are careful to avoid sending mixed messages. Good leaders are active listeners and provide feedback to show that they are sincerely trying to understand other people's points of view.
- **Motivating Others** Effective leaders offer guidance, praise, and encouragement to motivate team members. Some members appreciate public recognition for their efforts, while others might be shy about being praised. Leaders must learn which approach each person responds to best.
- **Managing** Good leaders understand the big picture. They are skilled in planning, organizing, and implementing a project. They know how to make the best use of the skills and resources of the team members to get the job done.
- **Delegating** Effective leaders avoid the temptation to do all the work themselves. Instead, they **delegate**, which means they assign tasks to other team members. They try to match the abilities of team members to the tasks. This helps other team members gain experience and strengthen their skills.
- **Making Decisions** Leaders must understand and use the decision-making process. They involve others in identifying and evaluating alternatives and selecting the best course of action. They are willing to reconsider when decisions do not work out.
- **Solving Problems** Good problem-solving skills help effective leaders face challenges. They work with their team to analyze alternatives and find creative solutions.

Life On Your Own

Make Humor a Part of Teamwork

As team members work to achieve their goals, many challenges can arise. When a problem proves especially tough, frustration can build and tempers can flare. The resulting conflict distracts the team's focus away from solving the original problem. Using humor to lighten the team's mood can help calm nerves and open lines of communication.

How It Works Your goal is to unite the group, not divide it. Never make fun of other team members or laugh at their ideas. If things starts to get tense, try making a silly suggestion: "It looks like we can't decide. Maybe we should use 'rock, paper, scissors.'" Pointing out the humorous side of the situation can break the tension and allow the team to refocus.

Try It Out You are the leader of a group that is trying to plan and build a float for the homecoming parade. You do not have much money with which to work, and the parade is two weeks away. So far, every idea suggested for the float has been voted down as being too difficult, too expensive, or not good enough. Some committee members are becoming angry and losing their motivation to be involved in the meeting.

Your Turn Come up with a way to lighten the mood of this meeting. How could you help committee members see the humor in the situation? How could doing so help the team work together more effectively?

Leadership Qualities

Think about some of the leaders you know, such as friends, classmates, teachers, coaches, family members, and community leaders. What special **quality**, or characteristic, does each person have? What qualities do they have in common? In addition to leadership skills, successful leaders need personal qualities that encourage people to follow their lead. Chances are that the successful leaders you know are dependable, enthusiastic, and honest. These are qualities common to many successful leaders.

Leaders also need the courage to face difficulties and take risks. A positive attitude is very helpful, too. Leaders must believe that they can reach their goals and communicate that belief to their team. A sense of responsibility is essential. Leaders must accept responsibility for their actions to gain the respect of others. A sense of humor also helps. Team members may be more willing to make an effort for a leader who exhibits positive leadership qualities and makes the work enjoyable.

Math For Success

Calculate a Tip

Rima is a supervisor at a non-profit company that raises money to build affordable homes. She has taken her employees out for a team-building lunch. Rima decided to pay the bill herself so that the company can use more of their funds for the home-building efforts. The final bill is $92.50. If Rima leaves $110 including tip, what percentage did she leave as a tip?

Math Concept **Finding a Percent** To find what percent a number is of a second number, divide the first number by the second number. Multiply the result by 100 and add the percent symbol.

Starting Hint Determine the amount of the tip by subtracting $92.50 from $110. Divide this tip amount by the original bill amount ($92.50), and multiply by 100 to get the percent.

 For more math practice, go to the Math Appendix at the back of the book.

NCTM Problem Solving Build new mathematical knowledge through problem solving.

Ethical Leadership

Leaders must do what is needed to get a job done. However, there is more to leadership than just doing things right. Leadership is also about doing the right thing. An effective leader practices ethical leadership. **Ethical leadership** is leadership based on ethical principles.

How do leaders demonstrate ethical principles? They tell the truth and keep their promises. They have respect for themselves and for others, including people different from them. Ethical leaders accept responsibility for the consequences of their actions. They play by the rules and treat people fairly. Many work to make a difference in their communities.

As a leader, you must be concerned about your behavior not only for yourself but because of the example you set for others. Remember that leadership is not about seeking recognition for yourself. True leadership involves serving other people and working toward a common group goal.

 Set an Example

Taking the lead in cleaning up your community is one way to make a difference. *What are some other examples of ethical leadership?*

✓ **Reading Check** **Identify** What are some of the qualities of ethical leaders?

Sharing Leadership

Sometimes you might find yourself sharing a leadership position. To minimize conflict, start by getting to know the other person. Learn how you each communicate, delegate, and solve problems. Discuss the team's goals. Look for ways to distribute the work and leadership, capitalizing on each of your strengths.

You Decide

Think of a specific classmate. If you two were sharing leadership, what strengths might each of you bring to the partnership? How might this affect the way you divide responsibilities?

Leadership Styles

Think about some of the political leaders you have seen on television. Some have an energetic style of speaking, while others are more reserved. If you could observe these leaders as they work with others behind the scenes, you would find that, just as they do not have the same style of speaking, they do not all use the same style of leadership. **Leadership style** refers to a leader's pattern of behavior when directing a team. The style that is chosen may depend on the leader's personality as well as the situation.

The four most common leadership styles are authoritarian, democratic, integrated, and laissez-faire. Authoritarian leaders take charge of every aspect of the team, from the smallest details to the outcome. Democratic leaders make decisions with the group. Integrated leaders focus on helping the individual team members form good working relationships. Laissez-faire [ˌle-ˌsā-ˈfer] is a French term that means "leave alone" or "let people do as they choose." Laissez-faire leaders sit back and let the team function on its own.

Different styles of leadership are appropriate for specific situations (see **Figure 5.3**). For example, in a crisis, an authoritarian style would allow for quick decisions. In a situation in which team members have never worked together before, an integrated style might be more appropriate. If a team task is particularly complex, a democratic leadership style would encourage everyone to contribute. Laissez-faire leadership might work best with team members who are highly motivated and capable of moving forward independently. Successful leaders are able to vary their leadership style to suit the situation.

✓ **Reading Check** **Explain** Why do successful leaders vary their leadership style?

Figure 5.3	**Four Styles of Leadership**

Different Ways to Lead There is more than one approach to leadership.
What may leaders take into account when choosing which style to use?

STYLE	CHARACTERISTICS	ADVANTAGES	DISADVANTAGES
Authoritarian	Leader makes decisions using his or her own judgment, and then tells others what to do.	The team process is efficient and orderly. Decisions can be made quickly.	Team members' ideas are not used. Without input, members may lack commitment.
Democratic	Leader encourages team members to express their opinions. Decisions are made by the majority.	Everyone is welcome to contribute. Team members support decisions and work to carry them out.	Team process is more complex. There are more disagreements, and decisions tend to take longer.
Integrated	Leader emphasizes maintaining group harmony and helping team members build good relationships.	Team may reach better decisions. Decisions are more likely to be based on consensus.	Team-building process is time-consuming. There is a lot of work for the leader.
Laissez-faire	Leader takes a "hands-off" approach and lets the group function on its own.	Leaders may come from the group. The group is empowered. There is less work for the leader.	Team process lacks organization and is inefficient. There is less accountability.

Resolving Group Conflict

Conflict is a natural part of teamwork and leadership. Any time people work together, there will be opposing ideas and interests that lead to disagreements. If team members have very different personalities, maintaining harmony can be very challenging, especially for the leader.

Whatever the source of conflict, the important thing is how leaders respond to it. Facing conflict and working through the issues can have positive results. It can bring problems into the open, strengthen relationships, and lead to better team decisions. On the other hand, unresolved conflict is a major obstacle to team progress. The conflict resolution strategies explained in Chapter 7 can help you resolve conflicts in positive ways.

As a leader, there are ways you can help prevent some conflicts and keep others from escalating.

- Focus on trying to understand other people's ideas.
- Give people credit for having good ideas, even when you do not agree with them.
- Use differences of opinion as opportunities to examine creative new alternatives.
- Do not get irritated about things that do not matter.
- Maintain a positive attitude.
- Above all, stay focused on the team goals. They are the reason your team exists.

Go Green!

Instead of buying a new book or magazine to read, borrow one from the library or from a friend. Sharing books and magazines is a great way to reduce waste and reuse materials.

Podcasts Access the Online Learning Center to download *Managing Life Skills* podcasts.

Section 5.2 — After You Read

Review Key Concepts

1. **Describe** why a sense of humor is a good quality for a leader.
2. **Define** the laissez-faire leadership style.
3. **Explain** what can cause conflict in groups.

Check Your Answers Check your answers at this book's Online Learning Center at **glencoe.com**.

Practice Academic Skills

English Language Arts

4. Imagine you have been asked to interview a person who is running for student body president of your school. Write five questions you could ask that would help you find out about the person's leadership skills and style.

> NCTE 4 Use written language to communicate effectively.

Social Studies

5. Conduct research to find a well-known leader from world history. Analyze the skills and qualities that helped that person become an effective leader. Give examples that illustrate each skill or quality.

> NCSS I A Analyze and explain the ways groups, societies, and cultures address human needs and concerns.

Public Relations Specialist

What Does a Public Relations Specialist Do?

Public relations specialists speak for organizations that want to communicate consistently and professionally with the public. They are responsible for a company's image and must establish a good relationship with the media to create positive publicity. They draft press releases, contact media officials, set up public events, and plan and prepare speeches for company officials.

Career Readiness Skills Public relations specialists should be outgoing, self-confident, creative, team-oriented, and open to new ideas. They should have strong communication skills that they can adapt to a variety of audiences. Decision-making, problem-solving, and research skills also are important.

Education and Training Employers usually prefer to hire candidates with college degrees, especially in the fields of journalism, communications, or advertising. Work experience in the type of organization represented is useful, as is experience with a school publication or radio or television station.

Job Outlook Employment is projected to grow faster than average as an increasingly competitive business environment boosts demand for good public relations specialists. However, heavy competition for entry-level jobs is also expected as more and more people are attracted to this fast-growing profession.

Critical Thinking Find an example in the media of a problem that a company has experienced recently, such as financial troubles, a product recall, or other bad press. Imagine you are a public relations specialist for this company. Draft a press release explaining the problem. Interpret the situation to make it sound more positive. This is often called "spinning" the story in favor of one side or the other.

Career Cluster

CCR ☆ College & Career Readiness

Business, Management, and Administration
Public relations specialists work in the Management pathway of this career cluster. Here are some other jobs in this career cluster:

- Payroll Manager
- Bookkeeper
- Library Assistant
- Personnel Recruiter
- Entertainment Manager
- Office Manager

- Entrepreneur
- Receptionist
- Sports Manager
- Accountant
- Corporate Trainer
- Art Director
- Treasurer
- Price Analyst

Explore Further The Business, Management and Administration career cluster contains six pathways: Management; Business Financial Management & Accounting; Human Resources; Business Analysis, Marketing & Communications; and Administrative & Information Support. Choose one of these pathways to explore further.

 Career Clusters To learn more about career clusters, go to this book's Online Learning Center at **glencoe.com**.

CHAPTER SUMMARY

Section 5.1
Teamwork Skills

Teamwork skills are valuable throughout life and have a variety of benefits. By cooperating, team players can accomplish more than they can as individuals. The different roles that team members play can help or hinder the team's success. Sometimes groups work well together but make poor decisions. Teams must find ways to divide tasks fairly and make effective group decisions.

Section 5.2
Leadership Skills

Effective leaders usually have specific skills and qualities, and they practice ethical leadership. Different leadership styles can be useful depending on the situation. There are four common leadership styles many leaders use. Most groups face conflicts that they must work to resolve. Good leaders encourage team members to find solutions and maintain good relationships.

Vocabulary Review

1. Write each of the vocabulary terms below on an index card and the definitions on separate index cards. Work in pairs or small groups to match each term to its definition.

Content Vocabulary
◇ teamwork (p. 87)
◇ cooperation (p. 88)
◇ persuade (p. 89)
◇ majority rule (p. 90)
◇ compromise (p. 90)
◇ consensus (p. 90)
◇ parliamentary procedure (p. 90)
◇ groupthink (p. 91)
◇ role model (p. 93)
◇ commitment (p. 93)
◇ delegate (p. 94)
◇ ethical leadership (p. 95)
◇ leadership style (p. 96)

Academic Vocabulary
■ effective (p. 87)
■ alternative (p. 90)
■ vision (p. 93)
■ quality (p. 95)

Review Key Concepts

2. **Summarize** the benefits of teamwork.
3. **Describe** characteristics of a strong team player.
4. **Identify** the three methods used to make group decisions.
5. **Analyze** characteristics of effective leadership.
6. **Explain** the four most common leadership styles.
7. **Determine** the importance of resolving group conflict.

Critical Thinking

8. **Evaluate** Is there such a thing as a natural leader, or must people learn to be leaders? Give reasons for your answer.
9. **Analyze** Which leadership style do you prefer when you are the leader? Why? Which style do you prefer when someone else is leading? Why?
10. **Recognize Assumptions** What role does popularity play in leadership?
11. **Compare** How do the qualities of team players relate to group conflict prevention?

ACTIVE LEARNING

Family & Community Connections

12. Teamwork Skit Follow your teacher's instructions to form into groups with your classmates. Together, look over the part of this chapter that discusses characteristics of a strong team player. With your group, write and act out a short skit illustrating the characteristics of a good team player. After working with the group, evaluate the teamwork that your group used while creating the skit. Did

any group members compromise on any part of the work? Did certain people have specific roles within the team?

13. Demonstrate Leadership Imagine that you have been asked to lead a meeting for a club at your school. When you are ready to start the meeting, several people continue talking to one another instead of paying attention. Their talking is disrespectful to you as the leader, and it is starting to annoy the other people in attendance. Explain how you, as a leader, would deal with this situation. Would you practice a certain leadership style? Do you consider this a conflict, and if so, what would you do to prevent the conflict from getting worse? Write a short outline of the steps you would take to deal with this situation. Be prepared to share your explanation with your class.

⭐ 21st Century Skills

Management Skills

14. Assess Your Skills Make a plan for improving your teamwork skills. Start by listing the skills and qualities that team members need. Evaluate yourself honestly in each area, and then identify the one in which you need the most improvement. What resources can help you build this skill or quality? What specific steps can you take?

Problem-Solving Skills

15. Resolve Group Conflict Sara is the captain of her school volleyball team and is planning a car wash fundraiser. Some of the team members disagree with one another about who should do what at the car wash. The players will not listen to one another to hear different options because they all have ideas about how the car wash should be planned. Sara wants the car wash to be a fun day for the team and wants to resolve the conflict. Write a letter to Sara offering your advice.

 Connections

Technology Skills

16. Desktop Publishing As part of its mission, FCCLA encourages students to improve their computer skills. Imagine that you need to create a poster advertising an event held by a student organization at your school. Follow your teacher's instructions to form into groups. Work together and use your computer skills to produce an attractive poster publicizing the event. Focus on the leadership opportunities that are available. Your poster should showcase your technology skills and have an eye-catching design.

Academic Skills

 ### English Language Arts

17. Interpret Information Many people have made different statements about leadership. Indira Gandhi said, "I suppose leadership at one time meant muscles, but today it means getting along with people." Consider this quote as you skim back through this chapter. Prepare a brief oral presentation about how the information in this chapter relates to Gandhi's quote. Do you agree or disagree with her quote? Why? Share your report with the class.

> **NCTE 2** Read literature to build an understanding of the human experience.

 ### Social Studies

18. Research World Leaders Conduct research to develop a list of past and present world leaders. Choose leaders of both genders from a variety of cultures, political movements, and governments. Select one person from the list, and write a short summary about that person's leadership style. Support your choice of leadership style with specific examples from the person's life.

> **NCSS II D Time, Continuity, and Change** Systematically employ processes of critical historical inquiry to reconstruct and reinterpret the past.

 ### Mathematics

19. Compare Housing Costs Ricky is currently paying $675 a month to lease a one-bedroom apartment. The cost of utilities is included in the rent. Ricky and Patrick met two years ago on the varsity football team. Now, as college freshmen, they are thinking about renting a two-bedroom house together near campus. The monthly rent for the house is $900, not including utilities. Utilities will cost an extra $300 a month. Ricky and Patrick have agreed to split all costs evenly. Calculate how much the move would save or cost Ricky each month.

Math Concept **Multi-Step Problems** Solving word problems sometimes requires several mathematical steps. Read the situation carefully to identify the steps and the sequence of the steps.

Starting Hint First, find how much Ricky would pay each month in the two-bedroom house: ($900 + $300) ÷ 2. Then subtract this from Ricky's current rent to find the difference between the two.

 For more math practice, go to the Math Appendix at the back of the book.

> **NCTM Problem Solving** Solve problems that arise in mathematics and in other contexts.

 ## Standardized Test Practice

 CCR College & Career Readiness

MULTIPLE CHOICE
Choose the phrase that best completes the statement.

> **Test-Taking Tip** In a multiple-choice test, the answers should be specific and precise. Read the question first, and then read all the answer choices. Eliminate answers that you know are incorrect.

20. A(n) _____ is a team player who offers creative ideas.
   a. seeker
   b. innovator
   c. blocker
   d. encourager

Chapter 6

Peer Pressure and Refusal Skills

Chapter Objectives

Section 6.1   Peer Pressure

- **Summarize** internal and external influences on decisions.
- **Identify** two ways that peer pressure can be positive.
- **List** six areas of consequences that result from negative peer pressure.

Section 6.2   Refusal Skills

- **Describe** three ways to effectively manage peer pressure.
- **List** four refusal skills that you can use to deal with peer pressure.
- **Identify** the best way to protect yourself from risky behaviors.

> **Explore the Photo**
>
> Peers can be one of the strongest influences on a teen's decisions. *Why is it important to find friends who share your values?*

Writing Activity

Summarizing

Pressure from the Media Look at print, radio, television, or Internet ads, and find an ad for a product you have never tried. Analyze the ad to determine what message it is promoting. Is it positive? Is it biased? Is it useful or helpful? Write a paragraph summarizing what you learned.

Writing Tips Use these tips to help you summarize:
- Present what you learned in your own words.
- Keep your summary brief and to the point.
- Summaries should cover only the most important points and major supporting details.

Peer Pressure

Even simple decisions are influenced by multiple factors.

Reading Guide

Before You Read

Be Organized A messy environment can be distracting. To lessen distractions, organize an area where you can read this section comfortably.

Read to Learn

Key Concepts

- **Summarize** internal and external influences on decisions.
- **Identify** two ways that peer pressure can be positive.
- **List** six areas of consequences that result from negative peer pressure.

Main Idea

Actions and decisions are influenced by both internal and external pressures. Peer pressure can be either positive or negative.

Content Vocabulary

◇ internal pressures
◇ external pressures
◇ media

Academic Vocabulary

You will find these words in your reading and on your tests. Use the glossary to look up their definitions if necessary.

- compelling
- aggressive

Academic Standards

English Language Arts

NCTE 12 Use language to accomplish individual purposes.

Mathematics

NCTM Number and Operations Understand numbers, ways of representing numbers, relationships among numbers, and number systems.

Science

NSES A Develop understandings about scientific inquiry.

Social Studies

NCSS IV G Individual Development and Identity Compare and evaluate the impact of stereotyping, conformity, acts of altruism, and other behaviors on individuals and groups.

NCTE *National Council of Teachers of English*
NCTM *National Council of Teachers of Mathematics*
NSES *National Science Education Standards*
NCSS *National Council for the Social Studies*

Graphic Organizer

As you read, identify three sources of external pressure that can influence your decisions. Use a web organizer like the one shown to help you organize your information.

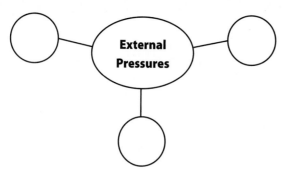

External Pressures

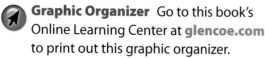

Graphic Organizer Go to this book's Online Learning Center at **glencoe.com** to print out this graphic organizer.

Influences on Decisions and Actions

Raul was getting his books out of his locker when his friends, Charlie and Antonio, stopped by. "Today's the day!" Charlie whispered. "We're cutting classes this afternoon to go to the lake. You're coming with us, aren't you?" Raul grinned. Cutting class sounded fun and daring. He was about to say yes, but then he hesitated. If he cut class, he would miss art, his favorite class. He would also miss history class, and he has been struggling in history lately. If he were caught skipping, he would get a Saturday detention, and he would be punished at home, too.

Raul thought about his choices. He wanted to go and have fun with his friends. Maybe cutting a few classes was not such a big deal. On the other hand, their friendship should not depend on doing everything the others wanted to do. Also, he was worried about missing classes and getting caught. After thinking it over for a minute or two, Raul made his decision. "Count me out, guys," he said as he headed toward the art room.

Like Raul, you have most likely been tempted to do things that were not in your best interest. Making decisions in such circumstances is not always easy. You might feel pressure because you want to please your friends, but you also want to do what is right for you.

Decisions are actually influenced by a number of pressures, both internal and external. Understanding these different pressures and their effects on you can help you make better choices.

As You Read

Connect Think about a recent decision you made. What influenced your decision?

Succeed in SCHOOL and LIFE

Integrity in the Workplace

It is important to develop and maintain integrity in the workplace. This includes never wasting your time at work. If you are getting paid but not working, you are not demonstrating integrity.

> ### The Media's Influence
>
> It is important to analyze advertisements to separate fact from fiction. *What might this teen be thinking as she looks at this magazine advertisement?*

Science For Success

Vocabulary

You can find definitions in the glossary at the back of this book.

Internal Pressures

Internal pressures are pressures that come from within you. They are the result of the expectations that you set for yourself. These expectations are generally developed from the values you learn from family and society as you grow older.

For example, Trevor works very hard to excel at school. Although his teachers and family expect a lot from him, Trevor always tries to exceed those expectations. He gets high grades and is involved in school activities. However, this year Trevor is struggling in his physics course. His perfect grade point average is sliding. He is afraid that if he asks for help from the teacher or other students, they might think less of him. Trevor is dealing with the internal pressure he feels to be perfect, smart, and successful without any help. These internal pressures are influencing his decisions.

External Pressures

External pressures are pressures that come from outside sources. Three of the most influential external pressures are the media, your family, and your peers. Can you think of other external pressures that might influence your decisions?

Media

Think about all the messages you receive from the media. **Media** are channels of mass communication, such as newspapers, magazines, radio, television, movies, and Web sites. You are surrounded by these messages every day. Advertisements can have an especially strong influence on your decisions about everything from the jeans you wear to the shampoo you choose. You can make better choices if you realize how **compelling**, or strong, an influence the media can be.

Family

Your family members can help you make important decisions. Even when they are not around, they can have a strong influence on you. When faced with an important decision, you might ask yourself what your family would think about the decision. This is because your family generally has your best interests in mind. The amount of influence your family has on your decisions will vary based on many factors including the size of your family and your relationships with different family members.

Peers

As a teen, you probably feel strong pressure from other teens. The influence of other people in your age group is called peer pressure. Teens tend to be more sensitive to peer pressure than adults are. One reason is that in your teen years, you are still discovering who you are and what is important to you. It is natural to seek approval and acceptance from other teens. Peer pressure can be open and direct, like the pressure Raul felt to skip classes. It also can be more subtle, like being influenced to listen to the same music as your peers.

✓ Reading Check **Define** What is media?

Go Green

Set a good example for others. Instead of buying bottled water which generates a lot of container waste, use reusable bottles and a water filter to purify tap water. This way, you can help the environment and save money at the same time.

Positive Peer Pressure

Peer pressure is often thought of as a bad thing. But there is such a thing as positive peer pressure. The most obvious way that peer pressure can be positive is when peers encourage one another to develop new skills and to get involved in worthwhile activities. Perhaps you can remember a time when friends gave you the confidence to try out for the school play or cheered you on in a sporting event. Positive peer pressure can help motivate people and give people a feeling of acceptance and belonging.

For example, Celeste heard about a project to build a playground for children in a neighborhood that did not have one. She volunteered to help and also called some of her friends and encouraged them to sign up as well. Some of her friends recruited other friends. Before long, 34 teens had volunteered to help with the project, all because of Celeste's initiative. Celeste's efforts are an example of positive peer pressure.

✓ Reading Check **Explain** How is cheering for someone at a sporting event a form of positive peer pressure?

◄ **Family Influence**

One of the biggest influences in a teen's life is family. *What parts of your life are affected by the influence of your parents and other family members?*

It is important to be able to separate positive peer pressure from negative peer pressure. *What are some signs that your peers may be exerting negative peer pressure?*

Negative Peer Pressure

Peer pressure is negative when it influences you to do something that conflicts with your values, makes you feel uncomfortable, or puts you in danger. Teens who start to use alcohol, tobacco, or other drugs often do so because of peer pressure. Negative peer pressure can make some teens feel pressured to join gangs, shoplift, break their curfews, allow peers who are driving to drive recklessly, or become involved in a sexual relationship. They know that these activities are risky, dangerous, and possibly even deadly. They also know that giving in to such pressures could negatively affect their health and their future. However, what they often do not know is how to resist the pressure.

Many teens lack confidence and often feel that giving in to certain pressures will help them gain friends and popularity. Resisting negative pressure from peers can be difficult, especially when you want to feel like a member of the group. Peers sometimes use insults, threats, or other forms of intimidation to convince people to do things. **Aggressive**, or overly pushy, behavior like this is a sign that peer pressure is negative rather than positive. After all, if someone wants you to do something that is in your best interest, threats are not needed. A real friend will not do or say anything to hurt you, physically or emotionally.

Financial *Literacy*

Long-Term Costs

You want to show a friend who is pressuring you to smoke cigarettes that, in addition to not being good for your health, it is also not financially worth it. If one pack of cigarettes costs $6.35, calculate the cost of smoking one pack a day for one year. Then calculate the cost of smoking a pack a day for 10 years.

Math Concept **Multiplication by Ten** When multiplying a number by ten, simply move the decimal to the right one place.

Starting Hint Calculate the cost of smoking a pack of cigarettes every day for a year by multiplying the cost of one pack by the number of days in a year. Multiply the one-year cost by 10 to find out how much smoking for 10 years would cost.

Math For more math practice, go to the Math Appendix at the back of the book.

> **NCTM Number and Operations** Understand numbers, ways of representing numbers, relationships among numbers, and number systems.

Facing the Consequences

It can be easier to resist negative peer pressure if you know the risks attached to it. Giving in to negative peer pressure can have serious consequences that can affect you, and others, for years to come. Consequences generally occur in one or more of six basic areas: physical, emotional, legal, social, educational, and consequences to others.

Physical Consequences

People who allow others to pressure them into using alcohol, tobacco, or other drugs pay for it with their health, and it is never worth the cost. Many drugs are linked to serious health problems such as heart disease, cancer, and harmful changes in the brain.

Teens who allow themselves to be pressured into sexual activity run the risk of contracting a sexually transmitted infection. Many of these infections are incurable or even fatal. There is also the possibility of pregnancy, which can pose health risks to the mother and child, and other risks for teen parents and their children. You will learn more about the risks of sexual activity in Chapter 21.

Peer pressure can also lead people to try activities that could cause physical injuries. Someone who has never ridden a skateboard before should not be pressured into learning to use a skateboard without wearing protective gear.

Emotional Consequences

When people do something that goes against their values, they usually feel guilty. Their self-esteem may suffer because they realize that they failed to stand up for their beliefs. Often they feel worried and stressed about the results or potential results of their actions.

Legal Consequences

When peer pressure leads to illegal acts, the consequences can be severe. If you break the law and are caught and arrested, you may be convicted and penalized with a fine, or even sentenced to jail. A criminal record can interfere with your future educational and work opportunities.

> ### Possible Repercussions
>
> It is important to think about all of the possible consequences of giving in to negative peer pressure. *How could the legal consequences of an action affect future educational or work opportunities?*

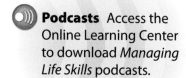
 Podcasts Access the Online Learning Center to download *Managing Life Skills* podcasts.

Social Consequences

Those who give in to negative peer pressure also run the risk of losing friendships that they value. Teens who join a gang, for example, will find that the gang takes over their life. They may be pressured to end friendships with peers who are not in the gang.

Sometimes it may seem as though giving in to pressure is a way to make friends. However, people who have the strength and confidence to stand up to peer pressure often avoid making friends with people who are easily swayed.

Educational Consequences

Negative peer pressure leads some teens to actions that affect their academic lives. Doing something you know is wrong can result in stress that can cause your grades to suffer. Getting caught cheating on a test or copying a research paper can impact your grade point average, your ability to graduate, and your future educational opportunities.

Consequences for Others

Most decisions you make affect not only you, but other people as well. Actions that are harmful to your health can have emotional, and sometimes financial, consequences for your family. Doing something that is dishonest or illegal can cause friends and family to feel betrayed. When you weigh your choices and make decisions, always consider how others might be affected.

Section 6.1 **After You Read**

Review Key Concepts

1. **Compare and contrast** internal and external peer pressure.

2. **Give** an example of how positive peer pressure can influence someone to get involved in volunteering for a local charity.

3. **Describe** ways in which peer pressure can be negative.

Practice Academic Skills

English Language Arts

4. Write a short story with two endings about a teen responding to peer pressure. In one ending, describe the consequences of the teen giving in to negative peer pressure. In the other ending, describe what happens when the teen successfully resists the peer pressure.

Social Studies

5. The desire for acceptance often leads teens to acts of conformity, such as dressing a certain way. Susan wants to fit in with the popular girls by wearing similar clothes, but her mother would prefer to save money rather than spend it on expensive clothing. Write a paragraph describing how this situation might impact Susan's behavior.

 Check Your Answers Check your answers at this book's Online Learning Center at **glencoe.com**.

NCTE 12 Use language to accomplish individual purposes.

NCSS IV G Compare and evaluate the impact of stereotyping, conformity, acts of altruism, and other behaviors on individuals and groups.

Refusal Skills

You have the power to say no and mean it!

Reading Guide

Before You Read

Helpful Memory Tools Successful readers use tricks to help them remember. For example, the acronym HOMES is a memory aid where each letter stands for one of the five Great Lakes (Huron, Ontario, Michigan, Erie, and Superior). As you read this section, look for opportunities to make up your own memory aids.

Read to Learn
Key Concepts
- **Describe** three ways to effectively manage peer pressure.
- **List** four refusal skills that you can use to deal with peer pressure.
- **Identify** the best way to protect yourself from risky behaviors.

Main Idea
Having strong values and good refusal skills can help you be prepared to manage peer pressure.

Graphic Organizer
As you read, look for the four qualities that show a firm sense of self. Use a pie chart like the one shown to help you organize your information.

 Graphic Organizer Go to this book's Online Learning Center at **glencoe.com** to print out this graphic organizer.

Content Vocabulary
◇ sense of self
◇ refusal skills

Academic Vocabulary
You will find these words in your reading and on your tests. Use the glossary to look up their definitions if necessary.
- waver
- conviction

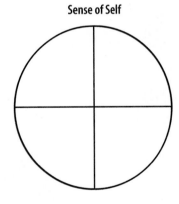
Sense of Self

Academic Standards

English Language Arts
NCTE 12 Use language to accomplish individual purposes.

Social Studies
NCSS IV C Individual Development and Identity
Describe the ways family and other group and cultural influences contribute to the development of a sense of self.

NCTE *National Council of Teachers of English*
NCTM *National Council of Teachers of Mathematics*
NSES *National Science Education Standards*
NCSS *National Council for the Social Studies*

Manage Peer Pressure

As You Read

Connect Think of a time when you resisted peer pressure. What strategies did you use?

Ronda, a senior, transferred to a new school after her father accepted a new job in a new city. As a senior, she felt very out of place with the other students who had been together since freshman year. She wanted to fit in, so when she was invited to a party within her first week of school, she jumped at the chance to make new friends. Unfortunately, the party was to take place at a house where no adults would be present and where alcohol would be served. Ronda wanted to make new friends, but in her heart she knew that this was not a good way to start her senior year.

When you learn to manage peer pressure, you can benefit from its positive effects and avoid its negative consequences. You will know when to go along with the crowd and when to hold back. Refusing to go along may not be easy, even when you know it is the right choice. In the end, though, you will feel better about yourself and avoid the consequences of unwise choices. Your stand might also set an example for others. Some teens go along with the crowd because they do not know how to say no. Your refusal might give others the courage to make better decisions.

Knowing what is right for you involves having a strong sense of self. A **sense of self** is your idea of who you are, based on your emotions, personality, and the ways you perceive the world. People who are able to manage peer pressure generally have a strong sense of self, know how to prepare for peer pressure, and practice assertiveness. You may need to improve your strength in these areas, but understanding their importance can help you do so.

◆ Vocabulary

You can find definitions in the glossary at the back of this book.

➤ Eliminate the Negative

Surrounding yourself with those who share your goals and values makes it easier to avoid negative peer pressure. *How are these teens demonstrating positive peer pressure?*

Know Yourself

To deal with negative peer pressure, you need a firm sense of self. This includes knowing your values, priorities, and goals. What matters to you? What do you want your life to be like? What kind of impression do you want to make on friends, family members, teachers, and employers? When you know these things, you will find it easier to make decisions and stick to them. This, in turn, will give you confidence to stand up to people who exert negative pressure on you. Several qualities work together to help you develop a firm sense of self.

Develop a Strong Value System

Having a strong set of values will help you recognize and deal with difficult situations. For example, if your health is important to you, it should be easier to resist any pressure to use tobacco. Use what you have been taught by your family and other responsible adults to develop a value system that you can use to guide your decisions and actions.

Have Confidence in Your Own Judgment

Trust your own judgment and instincts. When you are pressured to do something that you feel is wrong, remember that you are more qualified than your peers to determine what is right for you. Trust your conscience, your inner voice that tells you what is right and what is wrong.

Have High Self-Esteem

When you feel good about yourself, you are less concerned about gaining the approval of others. If you have high self-esteem, you will also have a strong sense of self-worth. People with healthy self-esteem are less likely to give into negative pressure. You can be more confident in saying no when people pressure you.

Focus on Your Priorities

When you focus on your priorities, you are less likely to be influenced by negative peer pressure. Become involved in positive activities that will help you achieve the personal goals you have set. This kind of behavior sets a positive example for others.

Prepare for Peer Pressure

A great tactic for resisting peer pressure is planning ahead. Anytime you are prepared for a situation, you will feel more confident. Follow these three steps to help you prepare:

1. Identify people and situations that are most likely to influence or pressure you into doing something you do not want to do.
2. If possible, avoid those people and situations. When it is not possible to avoid them, think about how and why they might be a problem. Write down the reasons you would use refusal skills to say no.

Character In Action

Stay True to Yourself

Staying true to who you are shows strong character. We are all swayed by our friends, family, the media, peer pressure, and other outside sources, but it is important to know who you are and keep your values and priorities in mind as you make decisions.

You Decide

There is a difference between staying true to oneself and being stubborn and closed-minded. Explain what you think the difference is.

Succeed in SCHOOL and LIFE

Set Your Priorities

A typical teen's life is very busy. Between sports, school, homework, time with family, time with friends, volunteer work, and other extracurricular activities, it is hard to know what to focus on and how to get it all done. If you can prioritize your activities, it will help you make decisions and make sure you fit in what is most important to you.

Develop Self-Esteem

Having good self-esteem can lead to a healthier lifestyle. Low self-esteem is linked to depression, and a lack of self-esteem often leads to people being pressured into harmful behaviors. To increase your self-esteem:

▶ Do not downplay the positive parts of your life.

▶ Focus on your successes.

▶ Set yourself up for success with achievable goals.

3. On your own or with a friend, practice different ways of responding to the situations. By thinking it through and practicing, you can decide which method will work best for you.

If you have already decided what to do when faced with a pressure situation, you are more likely to follow through with an assertive, well-planned response. This process allows you to be prepared to handle the pressure. It also gives you the confidence to stand by your values.

Practice Assertiveness

Knowing what is important to you gives you the confidence to be assertive. People who are assertive state their positions firmly but respectfully. They do not **waver**, or go back and forth between possible choices, when other people pressure them. Learning to be assertive will help you say no and stand by your decision.

Maggie's boyfriend, Lucas, tried to persuade Maggie to go to a party at his friend's house. She knew that there had been drugs and underage drinking at a party there last year. "No, I don't want to go," she told Lucas. "If there's trouble, we could be arrested and I won't take that risk. Besides, I'd have to lie to my parents, and I won't do that."

Maggie's assertiveness makes her position clear. Her self-esteem, strong values, and knowledge of the risks made it easier for her to be assertive. Lucas showed he was a true friend by accepting Maggie's answer rather than pressuring her to change her mind.

✓ **Reading Check** **Paraphrase** How can you effectively prepare for peer pressure?

Life On Your Own

Your Life, Your Decisions

It is easy to get caught up in the moment, especially as a teen, and go along with what your friends are doing without actually making the decision yourself. But it is important that you keep your values in mind. If you do not feel right about doing something, do not do it, even if others are.

How It Works When you are faced with a decision, be sure to think of the big picture. How will you feel about your decision in a week, a month, or a year? What are the possible consequences of the decision? How will it affect others?

Try It Out Roger and his two friends have been harassing Jordan. At first, it seemed like harmless fun. Lately, though, Roger has noticed some changes in Jordan. He has gotten quieter and started sitting alone at lunch. Yesterday, he turned down an invitation to go for a swim, which he usually loves to do. Roger is starting to feel like things have gone too far, but when he tried to talk to his friends about it, they shrugged it off, telling him not to be so uptight. Now Roger does not know what to do. He wonders if he should tell someone at school what is going on, but he does not want to get his friends in trouble.

> **Your Turn** Why might Roger decide to tell someone at school about the harassment? Why might he decide not to? If you were in Roger's situation, what would you do? Explain your answer.

Using Refusal Skills

You probably want to fit in and be part of a group. At the same time, you need to be true to yourself and maintain your individuality. That is why refusing to do something your peers are pressuring you to do is rarely easy. You need to know when to say no, and how to say it with **conviction**, or confidence and certainty.

Fortunately, you can benefit from the experience of others. Many people have developed effective ways to say no. **Refusal skills** are communication strategies that can help you say no when you are urged to take part in behaviors that are unsafe, bad for you, or that go against your values.

Learning Refusal Skills

Refusal skills are simple but powerful. Arming yourself with good refusal skills will prepare you to manage negative peer pressure effectively. Four simple refusal skills are:

- **Change the subject.** If someone is trying to talk you into doing something you do not want to do, you can often ease the pressure by talking about something else.
- **Do not apologize.** You do not need to explain or justify your decision if you do not want to.
- **Reject the action, not the person.** Be sure that you do not insult people when you refuse to go along with a suggested activity. Rather, keep the focus on the action.
- **Use humor.** Firm but humorous statements can let people know you are not interested without putting them on the defensive. Be sure you say these statements in a joking manner so people do not feel you are trying to belittle, or criticize, them.

For additional refusal skills, read the feature on the next page. Remember that some of these skills work better in certain situations. Also, you may be more comfortable with some of these skills than with others. Practice using a variety of these skills until you figure out what works best for you. Remember that having a strong sense of self will help give you the confidence to use these refusal skills.

Skills for Life

Peer pressure does not disappear when you become an adult. The refusal skills that you learn now will be useful throughout your life. There will always be people who pressure you to go against your better judgment. You may encounter them in the workplace, in your personal life, and in the community. Learning how to stand up to negative peer pressure will help protect you from the consequences of poor decisions. It will also help you get where you want to go in life.

✓ **Reading Check** **Define** What are refusal skills?

Be Smart Be Safe

Stay Safe Not being able to say no when you need to can be dangerous. Giving in to negative peer pressure can lead to harmful behavior, such as trying drugs or alcohol. Learning how to say no allows you to feel good about yourself, and it could even save your life!

Write About It Think of a situation that happened to you or a friend in which someone did not say no and ended up in a potentially dangerous situation. Write a description of the event. What could this person have done to avoid the harmful situation?

HOW TO . . . Say "No"

Saying yes and going along with your friends and peers might seem like the easiest option at the time, but knowing how to say no is an essential life skill. Feeling pressured to say yes can lead to people being involved in too many activities, which can lead to stress and fatigue. It can also lead to people finding themselves in dangerous situations. Sometimes saying no to someone else is a way of saying yes to yourself.

Say What You Mean State your position clearly and firmly. Avoid mixed messages by making sure your body language reinforces what you are saying.

Stay in Control Try not to get angry or upset. You can better control the situation if you stay calm, and you will be able to state your position more clearly if you remain composed.

Make Eye Contact You can say no more forcefully if you look straight at the other person while you are refusing. This shows strength and confidence, and it will help you convince people that you mean what you say.

Suggest an Alternative Try reversing the pressure. If you suggest an alternative that is a better idea or more fun, you take the pressure off yourself and put it on the other person.

Plan Ahead Decide in advance what you will do when faced with problem situations. You can even practice what you would say in problem situations you think might arise.

Walk Away As a last resort, if someone refuses to take no for an answer, walk away from a situation. Remember, no one should make you do anything you do not want to do.

Avoid Risky Behaviors

It is easy to assume that bad things will not happen to you, but certain behaviors greatly increase the odds that they will. Some of these risky behaviors include:

- using alcohol and tobacco.
- using illegal drugs.
- participating in sexual activity.
- driving recklessly.
- participating in extreme sports and foolish stunts.

These are only a few. You can probably think of other risky behaviors that you have done or been pressured to do. All of these behaviors are risky because they can put people's health and, in some cases lives, at risk. When people combine risky behaviors, such as driving too fast while not wearing their seat belt, they increase their chances of suffering serious consequences. Most people know these behaviors are dangerous, but they participate because of external pressure. Remember that these pressures can come from different sources, such as the media or your peers.

The most effective way to stay safe and protect yourself from harm is to practice abstinence. Abstinence, as you learned in Chapter 1, is a deliberate decision to avoid high-risk behaviors, including sexual activity and the use of tobacco, alcohol, and other drugs. Using your refusal skills and choosing to abstain from risky behaviors will help you achieve and maintain wellness.

 Podcasts Access the Online Learning Center to download *Managing Life Skills* podcasts.

Section 6.2 After You Read

Review Key Concepts

1. **Explain** how a strong sense of self can help you manage peer pressure.
2. **Describe** how humor can be useful when saying no.
3. **Clarify** what makes an action a risky behavior.

 English Language Arts

4. Songs and poems can sometimes be used to help you learn and remember important information. Write a song or a poem to help you remember at least two of the refusal skills that you feel would be most helpful to you. If you choose to write a song, it can be set to music from an existing song, or you can make up an original melody.

 Social Studies

5. Family plays a large role in influencing your sense of self. Families teach values and help family members develop confidence and self-esteem. Write a paragraph describing at least one value that you have learned from your family. How was the value taught or modeled? Why is this value important to you?

 Check Your Answers Check your answers at this book's Online Learning Center at **glencoe.com**.

> **NCTE 12** Use language to accomplish individual purposes.

> **NCSS IV C** Describe the ways family and other group and cultural influences contribute to the development of a sense of self.

What Is Community College?

Community college is a two-year government-supported college that offers both technical and general education associate degrees. They tend to be more affordable than four-year colleges and offer career-oriented degrees, such as fashion design or computer certification programs. Community college student bodies are often quite diverse with regard to age, experience, and employment status.

What are some of the benefits of attending community college?

There are many reasons for why community college might be a good choice. It usually costs significantly less than state or private colleges and universities. Also, if you are unsure about what you want to study, community college can allow you to explore different subject areas before deciding. Community colleges also have more flexible schedules, including part-time options and online courses.

What are the benefits of community college?

Many students use community college as a bridge between high school and a four-year college or university. It can be a good way to save money and to establish a strong grade point average before transferring. Community college can be a great way for you to take college-level courses while building your academic skills.

Can a degree from a community college help me get a job?

Community colleges are often career-oriented, so they provide opportunities for you to connect with employers. Community colleges communicate with potential employers to learn what fields are hiring and what skills the market currently demands. Community college counselors can help you make decisions about your career path, or help you meet transfer requirements.

Hands-On

College Readiness Go online and find the Web site of a community college near you. Find information on the classes and areas of study that community college offers. Think about which area of study interests you most. Write a paragraph identifying this area of study, and explain why it is the one that you are most interested in. What types of jobs could you get with a degree in this area of study?

Path to Success

 College & Career Readiness

Get a Taste Community college can be a way to "test drive" a specific career field.

Enjoy Flexibility Community college allows you to choose days and times that fit your personal schedule.

Consider the Cost Tuition and fees can be much less expensive than four-year colleges.

Think About Location Community colleges are often close to home.

Be Career-Focused Community colleges offer many programs leading directly to a career.

Take Advantage Preparing students to transfer to a four-year institution is one of the purposes of community college.

 Go to this book's Online Learning Center at **glencoe.com** to learn more about college and career readiness.

CHAPTER SUMMARY

Section 6.1
Peer Pressure

Decisions and actions are influenced by both internal and external pressures. Positive peer pressure helps you develop new skills and build confidence. Negative peer pressure can influence people to do things that go against their values. Giving in to negative peer pressure can have serious consequences, both for you and for others.

Section 6.2
Refusal Skills

To manage peer pressure, you should develop a strong sense of self, prepare for situations, and practice being assertive. Learning and developing refusal skills can help you resist negative peer pressure and stand up for your values. The most effective way to protect yourself from risky behaviors is by practicing abstinence.

Vocabulary Review

1. Use at least six of the following vocabulary terms to write a brief essay about a day in the life of a teenager.

   Content Vocabulary
   - ◇ internal pressures (p. 106)
   - ◇ external pressures (p. 106)
   - ◇ media (p. 106)
   - ◇ sense of self (p. 112)
   - ◇ refusal skills (p. 115)

   Academic Vocabulary
   - ■ compelling (p. 106)
   - ■ aggressive (p. 108)
   - ■ waver (p. 114)
   - ■ conviction (p. 115)

Review Key Concepts

2. **Summarize** internal and external influences on decisions.
3. **Identify** two ways that peer pressure can be positive.
4. **List** six areas of consequences that result from negative peer pressure.
5. **Describe** three ways to effectively manage peer pressure.
6. **List** four refusal skills that you can use to deal with peer pressure.
7. **Identify** the best way to protect yourself from risky behaviors.

Critical Thinking

8. **Plan** Think of an activity you want one of your friends to participate in with you. Write a brief plan that describes how you could use positive peer pressure to encourage your friend's interest.
9. **Predict** Think of two different situations in which you might need to use refusal skills as an adult.
10. **Apply** Imagine that a friend tries to convince you to get a tattoo but you do not want to. Identify two refusal skills that could be effective in this situation, and explain why you chose those two.
11. **Infer** Suppose a friend invites you to a college party. How might your family influence your decision?

12. Practice Refusal Skills Follow your teacher's instructions to form into partners or small groups. Work together to come up with two scenarios in which you might need to plan ahead to resist negative peer pressure. For inspiration, think of realistic situations that you have experienced in your own life. Decide with your group or partner which refusal skills would work best in your scenarios. Then take turns practicing those skills. Decide which method is most likely to work for each of you in the given scenario.

13. Find Relevance Interview three trusted adults. Ask each adult to recall a situation in which he or she had to respond to peer pressure. Create a three-column chart to record the results of your interviews. In the first column, give a brief description of each situation. In the second column, write down how the person responded. In the third column, write down which, if any, of the refusal skills discussed in the text was used in the situation described. If the person used a different refusal skill from what is in the text, record it in the third column. If the person gave in to the pressure, note in the third column which refusal skill might have been useful in his or her situation.

⭐ 21st Century Skills

Research Skills

14. Research Consequences Many teens find it difficult to resist the pressure to use alcohol. This can have physical consequences by damaging your health. Find out what other consequences exist for teens who drink alcohol. Categorize each of the consequences in one of the six areas discussed in the text. Write a brief summary of your findings.

Technology Skills

15. Analyze Online Ads Use the Internet to locate advertisements that target teens. Analyze the techniques used by the advertisers to persuade teens to buy or use the products or services. Use presentation software to create a presentation showing the ads you chose, as well as your analysis of them. Include in your analysis how you think online advertising techniques do or do not differ from television advertisements.

 **Connection**

Interpersonal Skills

16. Be a Positive Influence As part of its mission, FCCLA encourages students to develop interpersonal communication skills. Ask students, teachers, and other staff to find out what types of bullying occur at your school. Research community or online resources that offer positive ways of dealing with bullies. Plan a program that will help bully-proof your school. You can use this project to complete the STOP the Violence program in FCCLA.

Academic Skills

 English Language Arts

17. Learning from Literature Follow your teacher's instructions to form into groups. Choose a novel or short story with a teen as the main character. Read the story, looking for examples of peer pressure. How did the pressure affect the characters? Compare your ideas with the other members of your group. Share your results with the class.

> **NCTE 11** Participate as members of literacy communities.

 Science

18. Stress and Your Health Peer pressure and the desire to fit in often lead to undue stress in teens, which can lead to physical illness.

Procedure Conduct research to find out how stress can affect health, both mentally and physically.

Analysis Create a presentation explaining how stress can make people sick. In your presentation, mention specific health problems that can be caused by stress induced from peer pressure.

> **NSES F** Develop understanding of personal and community health.

 Mathematics

19. Comparing Measurements In math class, the teacher asks Purcell and Bethany to compare the lengths of two lines. One line is 8 inches long, and the other line is 19 centimeters long. Cassandra, another student in the class, tells them that the line measuring 19 centimeters is longer. Bethany agrees with Cassandra because she does not want to appear argumentative. Purcell gives the matter some thought and says he thinks the 8-inch line is longer. Who is correct?

Math Concept **Unit Conversions** Centimeters are a measurement of the metric system, while inches are a measurement in the customary system. To compare measurements, you should convert both numbers to the same system.

Starting Hint 1 inch = 2.54 centimeters. Multiply 8 inches by 2.54 to convert it to centimeters.

 For more math practice, go to the Math Appendix at the back of the book.

> **NCTM Measurement** Apply appropriate techniques, tools, and formulas to determine measurements.

 ## Standardized Test Practice

CCR College & Career Readiness

ANALOGIES
Select the pair of terms that best expresses a relationship similar to that expressed in the capitalized pair.

> **Test-Taking Tip** Analogies are relationships between two words or concepts. Common relationships in analogy questions include cause and effect, part-to-whole, general classification and specific example, and synonym or antonym.

20. JAIL : LEGAL CONSEQUENCE
   a. plan ahead : negative peer pressure
   b. guilt : emotional consequence
   c. media : internal pressure
   d. refusal skill : peer pressure

Chapter 7

Conflict Resolution Skills

Chapter Objectives

Section 7.1 **Consequences of Conflicts**

- **List** reasons why conflicts occur.
- **Summarize** the possible positive and negative effects of conflict.
- **Explain** how to prevent violence that results from conflict.

Section 7.2 **Settling Conflicts**

- **Compare** two methods of preventing conflict.
- **Describe** the steps you can take to resolve a conflict.

▶ Explore the Photo

You can maintain good relationships with others if you understand conflicts and how to resolve them. *What might be the cause of conflicts with other students at school?*

Writing Activity

Describe an Event

Compromise Conflicts can sometimes be resolved by compromising, or giving up something to find a solution that everyone agrees is fair. Write a description of a time when you compromised. Explain how the compromise helped to resolve a conflict.

Writing Tips To write a description of an event, follow these steps:

- Tell what happened.
- Explain how you felt before and after the event.
- Use details that make the event come to life for the reader.

Consequences of Conflicts

> Conflict can have both positive and negative consequences.

Reading Guide

Before You Read

Stay Engaged One way to stay engaged when reading is to turn each of the headings into a question, and then read the section to find the answers. For example, *Results of Conflict* might be *What are the results of conflict?*

Read to Learn

Key Concepts

- **List** reasons why conflicts occur.
- **Summarize** the possible positive and negative effects of conflict.
- **Explain** how to prevent violence that results from conflict.

Main Idea

There are many different causes of conflicts. Although some results of conflict can be positive, many results are negative. Violence is the most extreme negative result.

Graphic Organizer

As you read, list five examples of negative results of conflict. Use a web like the one shown to help you organize your information.

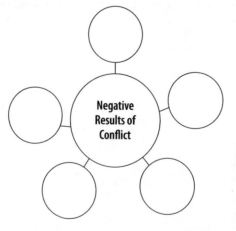

Negative Results of Conflict

 Graphic Organizer Go to this book's Online Learning Center at **glencoe.com** to print out this graphic organizer.

Content Vocabulary

- ◇ conflict
- ◇ power struggle
- ◇ prejudice
- ◇ violence
- ◇ bully

Academic Vocabulary

You will find these words in your reading and on your tests. Use the glossary to look up their definitions if necessary.

- ■ trivial
- ■ progress

Academic Standards

English Language Arts

NCTE 5 Use different writing process elements to communicate effectively.

Social Studies

NCSS VI F Power, Authority, and Governance Analyze and evaluate conditions, actions, and motivations that contribute to conflict and cooperation within and among nations.

NCTE *National Council of Teachers of English*
NCTM *National Council of Teachers of Mathematics*
NSES *National Science Education Standards*
NCSS *National Council for the Social Studies*

Why Conflicts Happen

Cassie was angry when she called her older brother Steve on his cell phone. "Where are you? I have to leave for work in 10 minutes, and you said you would drive me there."

"Sorry, Cassie," came Steve's reply. "I'm across town with some friends right now. You'll have to find another way to get to work." Cassie was angry. She knew she could take the bus, but this would make her late for work. Her supervisor would be annoyed, she would lose some of her pay because of her tardiness, and it was all Steve's fault. "Just wait until I see him tonight," Cassie muttered.

Cassie's situation is a conflict. A **conflict** is a clash among people who have opposing ideas or interests. Some conflicts are trivial ('tri-vē-əl), or minor, and can be quickly resolved. Others are serious and take time and effort to resolve. The worst kinds of conflict are those that lead to violence.

Knowing the origins of conflicts can help you avoid or prevent them. Here are some of the basic causes of conflicts:

- **Poor Communication** Cassie's conflict with Steve could be the result of poor communication. She may not have made it clear that she needed a ride to work. He may not have realized that she was relying on him. Misunderstandings like this are at the heart of many conflicts.
- **Power Struggles** A **power struggle** happens when individuals or groups feel a need to be in control. An example of a small power struggle is trying to control the TV remote control. A more serious power struggle could happen in the workplace when coworkers clash over roles and responsibilities.
- **Personality Differences** People who have different values, goals, and attitudes are more likely to argue than those who have the same values and attitudes. For example, imagine you are working on a project with a partner. If you are a careful person, you might clash with someone who rushes and does not pay attention to detail.
- **Jealousy** This strong emotion can cause feelings of resentment or hostility. We often think of romantic relationships when we think of jealousy. But jealousy can happen in other situations as well. You might feel jealous when another student receives an award that you felt you deserved.
- **Prejudice** People who are prejudiced cannot easily accept people who are different. **Prejudice** ('pre-jə-dəs) is an unfair judgment or opinion made without knowing all of the facts. Prejudice has been a major cause of conflict throughout history.

✓ Reading Check **Explain** How can personality differences create conflict?

As You Read

Connect What are some ways you might try to avoid a conflict?

◆ Vocabulary

You can find definitions in the glossary at the back of this book.

▼ Power Struggles

Power struggles can happen when two individuals or groups are trying to be in control. *How are power struggles in games different from other power struggles?*

Results of Conflict

Conflict is a fact of life and is not always a bad thing. Disagreements occur in almost all relationships. When you know how to deal with a conflict and **progress**, or move forward, toward a solution, you benefit in a number of ways. Poorly handled conflicts, on the other hand, can have long-term harmful effects.

Positive Results of Conflict

Think about the last time you settled a disagreement with a family member or friend. Did you learn something that was helpful? Working to resolve a conflict is a valuable experience. It helps you develop your problem-solving skills and communicate effectively. You also learn to get along with people who do not agree with you, a skill that will help you now and in the future.

Making an effort to resolve a conflict can strengthen a relationship. When you explain your views and learn how the other person feels, you get to know each other better. Agreeing to resolve the conflict together shows that each person values the relationship.

Working to resolve a conflict can also sometimes result in a more imaginative solution. Learning to cooperate with someone may create a better solution than insisting on having your own way.

Negative Results of Conflict

As Tyrone thought about a recent disagreement he had with a friend, the angry feelings returned. His muscles tightened, and his stomach felt queasy. The argument had never been settled, and he was not sure it ever would be. Can you relate to the way Tyrone felt? If so, you know that unresolved conflict can have some serious negative effects. Here are some examples:

- **Negative Emotions** Think about a time when you had a serious disagreement with someone. Did you feel anger, frustration, fear, pain, humiliation, or sadness? All of these negative emotions can be felt during a conflict.

Succeed in **SCHOOL** and **LIFE**

Deal with Personal Issues

It is important to know how to deal with personal issues so that they do not interfere with your studies. You need to be able to recognize when a situation is serious enough that it must be addressed. Once a serious situation arises, deal with it as soon as possible instead of letting it get worse. Do not fool yourself into believing you can handle everything alone. Sometimes you need to ask for help.

- **Stress** Conflict causes stress. Stress, in turn, can cause headaches, digestive problems, anxiety, and other physical and mental problems. People who experience stress caused by serious conflict may have trouble sleeping, feel very tired, and find it hard to concentrate.
- **Hurtful Words** In the heat of anger, it is easy to say the wrong thing and hurt another person's feelings. Remember, once something has been said, it cannot be "unsaid."
- **Damaged Relationships** Conflicts can break up families and friendships. Some family feuds are never resolved and last a lifetime. In the workplace, conflicts can cause difficulties for coworkers and, in extreme cases, may even cause people to lose their jobs.
- **Violence** When tempers flare, arguments can sometimes get out of hand and lead to violence. **Violence** is the use of physical force to injure someone. The result may be serious injury or even death. All negative effects of conflict are troubling, but violence is the most serious, both for the individuals involved and for society as a whole.

Health & Wellness TIPS

Exercise to Fight Stress

Exercising regularly has been proven to be a good way to reduce stress. Exercise improves your mood, decreases the production of stress hormones, and produces feel-good hormones called endorphins. Try these tips:

▶ Create an exercise schedule, and stick to it.
▶ Exercise with a buddy.
▶ Pick exercise you enjoy.

✓ **Reading Check**　**Describe** How can stress affect the body?

Two Views One World

What Do You Think About Violence in the Media?

Is violence in the media a cause or an effect of violence in real life? Is it possible to make such a clear distinction?

Sarah: News shows emphasize the most violent stories. Murder trials make headlines. TV shows and movies are full of explosions, car chases, and shootings. Because we are constantly exposed to these violent images, we have become desensitized to them. Kids are learning that using violence is an acceptable way to react to situations. The responsible thing to do is to decrease the amount of violence shown in the media.

Ryan: The world is a violent place with or without violence in the media. Look at all the wars throughout history. There's a lot of violence in the media, but that's just because it is reflecting reality. Violence in entertainment is nothing new. The human race has always been violent, and many people are entertained by violence. To reduce violence in the media, we need to first reduce violence in the real world.

Seeing Both Sides
Do you agree more with Sarah or Ryan? Why? Do you think they can both be right? Do you think the media has a responsibility to decrease the amount of violence it covers?

Violence

If everyone were skilled in conflict resolution, violence might not be a problem in modern society. Unfortunately, that is not the case. From fights between rival gangs to violent acts on school grounds to violent actions on a date, violence is a distressing reality.

Factors that Affect Violence

Why do some people resort to violence? Sometimes it is because they do not know how to solve conflicts in constructive ways. Violence may be the only way they know how to express anger. Such behavior may be acquired during childhood. Children learn violence from adult role models, sometimes from adults in their own families. They see violence on television and in sports, video games, movies, and other forms of media. Some people believe that violence in the media contributes to violence in society.

According to a study done by the U.S. Department of Justice, gang members are more likely than other teens to participate in illegal activities, engage in violent behavior, and become victims of violence themselves. Once a person is in a gang, it is hard to get out. Gang leaders demand loyalty and use threats and fear to keep members from leaving.

Easy access to weapons contributes to violence. Many schools have installed metal detectors and other security devices to prevent weapons from being brought onto school property.

Another factor that plays a part in violence is drug or alcohol abuse. Drug addicts often use violence when they need money to support their drug habit. In addition, people under the influence of alcohol or drugs are less able to control their emotions. This means they are more likely to become violent if they get involved in a conflict.

| Figure 7.1 | Deal with Bullying |

School Bullies   Most bullying occurs at school. *How can this affect students' ability to achieve educational goals?*

Show confidence.	Bullies choose easy targets. Carry yourself with pride, look people in the eye, and be friendly to others.
Ignore verbal abuse.	Show no reaction to insults or cruel jokes. Bullying is like a game that takes two or more to play. The game ends when you do not play.
Stand up for yourself.	Forcefully tell the bully to stop the behavior. Avoid responses that will provoke further attacks. Leave calmly.
Stand up for others.	Defend someone who is being abused, and encourage others to do the same. Bullies often back down when faced with a display of courage.
Talk to an adult.	Tell a parent, teacher, or other trusted adult if you are bothered by a bully. Take a friend if you need support.
Put safety before possessions.	If a bully demands that you hand over a possession, do it. Your physical well-being is more important than any material item. Report the incident to a trusted adult.

Bullying

A **bully** is an aggressive person who intimidates, abuses, or mistreats people. Bullies are motivated by many reasons. Some may be unhappy and insecure. Others are jealous of the person they target. Still others struggle with deeper personal issues. Bullies taunt, tease, torment, and humiliate those who are weaker or different in order to feel a sense of importance. Bullies may believe they are earning respect, but it is only fear and resentment that they instill in their victims. For some, the abuse confirms the low opinion they hold of themselves. They need help dealing with their insecurity and anger. Very often, the conflict is within themselves rather than with their victims. This makes it difficult, if not impossible, for mediation and conflict resolution techniques to be useful when dealing with a bully.

Most bullies will eventually leave you alone if you show confidence and ignore their verbal abuse. They are looking for any sort of reaction, and if you do not give them one, they will eventually find an easier target. If you are being bullied by e-mail, block the bully's messages. If a bully does not stop harassing you, you need to get help. Do not hesitate to talk to a parent, teacher, guidance counselor, coach, or other trusted adult. See **Figure 7.1** on the previous page for guidelines that can help you deal with a bully.

 Podcasts Access the Online Learning Center to download *Managing Life Skills* podcasts.

Section 7.1 — After You Read

Review Key Concepts

1. **Explain** how prejudice can lead to conflict.
2. **Identify** some positive effects of conflict.
3. **Outline** ways to take positive action against bullying.

 Check Your Answers Check your answers at this book's Online Learning Center at **glencoe.com**.

Practice Academic Skills

 English Language Arts

4. Many people think that there is too much violence in the media. Write a script for the opening of a newscast using stories that do not feature violence. You may use real stories, or you may create your own stories.

> **NCTE 5** Use different writing process elements to communicate effectively.

Social Studies

5. Major and minor conflicts happen constantly all over the world. Conduct research to find stories about conflicts between individuals, businesses, groups, or nations. Choose one, and write a one-page summary of each side of the conflict. Summaries should be neutral, which means that each side of the conflict should be reported fairly, without supporting either side's arguments or actions.

> **NCSS VI F** Analyze and evaluate conditions, actions, and motivations that contribute to conflict and cooperation within and among nations.

Settling Conflicts

Learn to resolve conflicts before they get out of hand.

Reading Guide

Before You Read

Buddy Up for Success One advantage of sharing your notes with a buddy is that it allows you to fill in any gaps in each other's information.

Read to Learn
Key Concepts

- **Compare** two methods of preventing conflict.
- **Describe** the steps you can take to resolve a conflict.

Main Idea

It is best to prevent conflicts before they develop by adapting your behavior and examining your attitude. If a conflict cannot be avoided, try resolving it through negotiation or mediation.

Graphic Organizer

As you read, look for the three steps used for workplace mediation. Use a chain-of-events organizer like the one shown to help you organize your information.

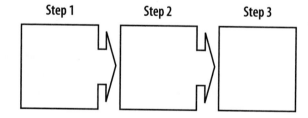

Step 1   Step 2   Step 3

Graphic Organizer Go to this book's Online Learning Center at **glencoe.com** to print out this graphic organizer.

Content Vocabulary

◇ peer education
◇ negotiation
◇ win-win solution
◇ mediation
◇ peer mediation

Academic Vocabulary

You will find these words in your reading and on your tests. Use the glossary to look up their definitions if necessary.

■ adapt
■ project

Conflict Prevention

The best way to deal with conflict is to keep it from happening in the first place. If you know someone who tends to start arguments, stay away from that person if you can. If you get involved in a minor disagreement, try to maintain perspective and look at the big picture. Do not start arguing about something small that you will probably forget about tomorrow. Maintain a sense of humor. Let the other person see that you are not planning to argue.

As You Read

Connect How have you solved conflicts in the past?

Adapt Your Behavior

Sometimes the easiest way to prevent a conflict is to **adapt** to, or change to match, the other person's behavior. This approach works best when a situation bothers one person more than the other.

Riley, for example, was annoyed that his friend James was late almost every time they went somewhere together. Instead of confronting James and causing a conflict, Riley decided to plan for James being late. If he was supposed to pick James up, Riley asked him to be ready 10 minutes sooner than they really needed to leave. That way, James could be late and they would still get where they were going on time.

Examine Your Attitude

Some people **project**, or display outwardly, an attitude that causes conflict. Liz, for example, felt that people were always criticizing her and doing things to annoy her. She complained to her friend Marisa about it. Marisa told her, "I think you need an attitude adjustment."

Marisa was probably correct. People like Liz are always on the defensive. They take even the mildest remark as a personal insult. Often they misinterpret other people's words and actions. This type of attitude often results in constant conflict and unhappiness.

Liz took a closer look at herself and her attitude. She realized that her defensiveness was connected to her own negative feelings about herself. She began to work to improve her self-esteem and develop a more positive attitude. She taught herself to react to people differently. This helped her to avoid focusing on things that cause conflict.

If you feel that other people are often in conflict with you, ask yourself: Am I overly defensive? Do I misinterpret other people's words and actions? Do I have an attitude that causes conflict? Thinking about questions like these can lead to greater self-awareness and help you adjust your attitude, if necessary.

Violence Prevention

The first step in preventing violence is to understand that it is never an acceptable way to settle differences. Choose nonviolent actions, and encourage your peers to do the same. If you find yourself in a conflict that involves threats, violence, or weapons, walk away. It takes a strong person to walk away from a situation like that, but your life and well-being are worth more than winning any argument.

Vocabulary

You can find definitions in the glossary at the back of this book.

Succeed in SCHOOL and LIFE

The Art of Negotiation

Negotiation skills will be useful to you in all parts of life. However, they will be especially useful in the workplace. To negotiate well, choose the right time and place, listen more than you talk, be open to other points of view, and look for creative solutions. To prevent unnecessary conflict, avoid blaming and name-calling, attack the problem instead of the person, and try to understand others' positions.

You can also work with others to reduce violence in your school and community. One of the most effective ways to reduce youth violence is through peer education. **Peer education** is a program that is based on the principle of teens teaching teens. It works because young people are more likely to listen to their peers than to adults. Other examples of positive ways to take action against violence include:

- **Educate Yourself** Knowing how youth violence affects your community can motivate you to take action. Find out how many teens have been arrested for violent crimes or weapons possession in your neighborhood. How many have been victims of violence? How many are gang members?
- **Find Violence Prevention Resources** You can get information from school officials, community leaders, law enforcement officials, parent-teacher groups, and social service organizations.
- **Recognize Warning Signs** People who are at risk of becoming violent usually show warning signs. These may include drug and alcohol use, prejudice, social withdrawal, and threats.
- **Report Potentially Violent Situations** Tell a responsible adult if you hear or see threats of violence. Not all threats turn into violent acts, but it is wise to play it safe. Share your concerns to help protect yourself and others.
- **Avoid Gang Influence** Do not be lured into a gang. Gang membership puts you at greater risk to inflict, or cause, violence. It also puts you at a greater risk of being a victim of violence. Also, encourage your peers to avoid gang influence.

✓ **Reading Check** **Describe** What are three characteristics of an attitude that causes conflict?

Conflict Resolution

If a conflict does happen, it is in the interests of everyone involved to work together to find a resolution. You can start by using the problem-solving skills from Chapter 9. When trying to reach a positive resolution, keep two goals in mind. The first goal is to find a fair solution. You want to agree on a solution that is acceptable to all parties. The second goal is to preserve the relationship. Ultimately, you want to preserve or strengthen the relationships involved.

Negotiation

Conflict resolution involves negotiation. **Negotiation** (ni-ˌgō-shē-ˈā-shən) is communication about a problem with the goal of finding a fair solution. Negotiation is used at all levels of society. Friends negotiate when they decide which movie to see. Labor unions negotiate with employers over contracts. Nations negotiate to make trade and peace agreements.

For negotiation to be successful, everyone who is involved in a conflict must be willing to play a part. They must be willing to respect other viewpoints and accept responsibility for finding a solution that works. Just as poor communication can cause conflict, good communication is key to resolving conflict.

The ideal outcome of negotiation is a win-win solution. A **win-win solution** is a solution that benefits everyone involved and has no real drawbacks for anyone. You must use creative thinking and be willing to explore options to find a win-win solution.

Suppose a family is planning where to go on a weekend trip. If one member of the family insists on a vacation spot that the others will not enjoy, that person wins and the others lose. A win-win solution would be finding a different location that the whole family will enjoy.

When a win-win solution is not possible, other outcomes need to be explored. Here are some other ways to resolve a conflict:

- **Compromise** In a compromise, each party agrees to give up something to reach a solution that satisfies everyone. Compromise is sometimes called the "fair-fair solution." Each side gets something they want, but not everything. For example, when two children agree to take turns playing with a toy instead of having it all to themselves, that is a compromise.

Life On Your Own

The Importance of Forgiveness

When someone has wronged you, it is normal to feel hurt and angry. However, knowing how to forgive is an essential life skill. Being unable to forgive can lead to ruined relationships, isolation, stress, unhappiness, and loneliness. Often, forgiving someone will make you feel better and give you a sense of peace.

How It Works Forgive the person, not the action. You can still be upset about what happened while forgiving the person. Remember that everyone makes mistakes. Express yourself; it might help to explain why you felt so hurt or angry. Look for the positive. Often, even the most negative experiences have at least some positive results. Practice empathy, and try putting yourself in the other person's place. It can help to talk to a parent or trusted adult to get an opinion from someone outside of the situation.

Try It Out Imagine one of your close friends had a party and did not invite you. The next week at school, everyone is talking about how much fun the party was, and you feel left out, hurt, and confused about why you were not invited. Remembering all the time you and your friend have spent together and the parties to which you invited her, you feel like you will not be able to forgive her.

Your Turn Could there be a reason your friend did not invite you to the party? What could be gained from forgiving your friend? If you forgave your friend, would that be a sign of weakness? What would you do in this situation?

Trust Others, Trust Yourself

Trust is the basis for effective communication, stable relationships, and fulfilling interactions. To trust others, you need to look for the good in people, talk openly, and be trustworthy yourself. Even if you have been hurt in the past, try to rid yourself of the fear of being hurt again.

You Decide
Being able to trust others is important, but you can also trust too much. If you are too trusting, people might take advantage of you. When does trust turn into a lack of judgment?

- **Agree to Disagree** Some conflicts cannot be resolved because it is clear that the parties will not change their points of view. For example, if you and your uncle hold strongly opposing political views, trying to convince each other to change is probably pointless. Agreeing to disagree and simply accepting that you have different opinions instead of arguing may be the best solution.

- **Withdraw** Sometimes finding a solution seems impossible. Tempers get frayed. Negotiations go nowhere. In such cases, it may be best to withdraw, or walk away, for a while. Walking away gives both parties time to calm down and collect their thoughts. They can resume negotiations later, when they have new ideas or are more willing to compromise.

Mediation

When other attempts to settle conflict are not successful, mediation can help. **Mediation** (ˌmē-dē-ˈā-shən) is settling a conflict with the help of a neutral third party. This process is widely used to resolve conflicts in families, the workplace, schools, and communities.

The word mediate literally means "to be in the middle." As a person in the middle, the mediator does not make judgments or decide how to resolve the conflict. Instead, the mediator helps people find a fair solution that satisfies both sides. The mediator is there to help, but the parties involved in conflicts are responsible for finding the solutions

Mediation can be formal, with a trained mediator. Formal mediation is used when a conflict lasts for a long time or gets in the way of normal living. Mediation can also be informal. For example, you might ask a family member to help if you have a disagreement with a friend. Sometimes just talking things over with a third party can help the people involved in a conflict reach a solution.

Mediation is a good way to resolve conflicts in the workplace. Many workplace complaints involve perceived discrimination. For example, a worker who feels that he or she has been treated unfairly because of age, gender, religion, or race may file a complaint. Other workplace conflicts involve disputes about responsibilities, space, and equipment.

Workers can request mediation whenever they believe it will help resolve a dispute. All parties involved must voluntarily agree to mediate the problem. The mediator then arranges a session in which the parties try to resolve their differences. Information shared during the mediation session is confidential, which means that the information is not shared with anyone.

▼ Meeting Halfway

The best outcome for a conflict is one in which both parties are happy with the resolution. *What would happen if only one party was happy with the resolution?*

Employers believe that mediation offers several benefits. It allows people to be heard and to develop ways of dealing with a dispute by creating their own solutions. Equally important, it clears the air and reduces workplace stress.

Peer Mediation

Peer mediation is a process in which specially trained students help other students resolve school-related conflicts peacefully. Peer mediators remain neutral. They often see solutions that those involved in the conflict are too upset to see. One of their goals is to keep everyone calm. Peer mediators are trained to see things through the eyes of those involved in the conflict. They learn to ask questions that help students clarify their feelings and thoughts.

To be successful, the students involved in the conflict must be willing to participate in peer mediation. Discussions are confidential, or private. Students will speak more freely if they know that no one else will know what is said.

Peer mediation works partly because the mediators are students themselves. They understand their peers' attitudes and viewpoints. They can relate to the issues involved. They use language that students can understand. The widespread success of peer mediation programs shows the value of this conflict resolution technique.

Get Involved!

Become a Peer Mediator

Many schools have peer mediation programs in which students help other students resolve disputes. Peer mediation has proven to be effective, and it helps improve the self-esteem, listening skills, and critical thinking skills of all students involved. It also improves the school climate, encourages learning, and reduces disciplinary actions and the frequency of fights.

 Podcasts Access the Online Learning Center to download *Managing Life Skills* podcasts.

Section 7.2 — After You Read

Review Key Concepts

1. **Summarize** how examining your attitude can lead to better self-awareness.
2. **Compare and contrast** three options to a win-win solution for resolving a conflict.

Practice Academic Skills

 English Language Arts

3. Re-read the example about Liz and Marisa from the Examine Your Attitude section on page 131. Follow your teacher's instructions to form small groups. Discuss possible consequences of Liz not listening to Marisa. Would Liz's friendship with Marisa have changed? Would Liz have changed her attitude on her own? After your discussion, write a short essay on the group's findings.

 Social Studies

4. Use print and Internet resources to research an ongoing conflict between two or more nations. What are the root causes of the conflict? How has the conflict changed over time? What solutions have the nations tried? Have mediators been used? Have any resolution efforts been successful? Create a time line using the information you have gathered.

Check Your Answers Check your answers at this book's Online Learning Center at **glencoe.com**.

NCTE 11 Participate as members of literacy communities.

NCSS II B Apply key concepts such as time, chronology, causality, change, conflict, and complexity to explain, analyze, and show connections among patterns of historical change and continuity.

Pathway to Your Career

Lawyer

What Does a Lawyer Do?

Lawyers, also called attorneys, represent people in criminal or civil trials. They present evidence and argue to support their client's cause. Lawyers also give advice to their clients about their legal rights and responsibilities, and suggest courses of action. In general, lawyers research and interpret laws and judicial decisions. Then they relate the laws and their interpretations of the laws to the circumstances faced by their clients.

Career Readiness Skills Potential lawyers must have strong verbal and written communication skills. Lawyers need to be able to reason well, form clear arguments, and show determination. Creativity is helpful when interpreting law. Lawyers must have an eye for detail and quick thinking abilities.

Education and Training Becoming a lawyer usually takes four years of undergraduate study followed by three years of law school. Some law schools have part-time courses of study that take longer to complete. You must then pass the bar exam in the state in which you wish to practice law.

Job Outlook Employment for lawyers is expected to grow at an average rate over the next 10 years. Population growth and more business activity should increase the demand for lawyers.

Critical Thinking There are many types of lawyers, including employment, divorce, environmental, and bankruptcy lawyers. Research different types of lawyers, and pick one type that you think will grow in demand due to current and projected societal patterns and changing demographics. Summarize your findings.

Career Cluster

CCR ☆ College & Career Readiness

Law, Public Safety, Corrections & Security
Lawyers work in the Legal Services pathway of this career cluster. Other jobs in this cluster include:

- Park Ranger
- Judge
- Private Detective
- Life Guard
- Paralegal
- Investigator
- Law Clerk
- Air Marshall
- Court Reporter
- Police Officer
- Warden
- Fire Fighter
- Ambulance Driver
- Port Security Specialist
- Parole Officer
- Ski Patrol
- EMT

Explore Further The Law, Public Safety, Corrections & Security career cluster contains five pathways: Correction Services; Emergency & Fire Management Services; Security & Protective Services; Law Enforcement Services; and Legal Services. Choose one of these pathways to explore further.

 Career Clusters To learn more about career clusters, go to this book's Online Learning Center at **glencoe.com**.

CHAPTER SUMMARY

Section 7.1
Consequences of Conflicts

Conflicts happen between people with opposite ideas or interests. Causes of conflicts include poor communication, power struggles, personality differences, jealousy, and prejudice. Sometimes conflict can lead to positive outcomes, but many times it results in negative consequences, including violence. Prevent violence by educating yourself, finding resources, seeing warning signs, reporting potential violence, and avoiding gang influence.

Section 7.2
Settling Conflicts

The best way to deal with conflicts is to prevent them. To do this, adapt your behavior and examine your attitude. Try to find fair solutions and preserve relationships. Negotiation and compromise can work when people communicate about a problem to find a fair solution. Mediation can help when people are unable to resolve a conflict on their own. Peer mediation is used by schools to settle differences between students.

Vocabulary Review

1. Arrange the vocabulary words below into groups of related words. Explain why you put the words together.

Content Vocabulary
- conflict (p. 125)
- power struggle (p. 125)
- prejudice (p. 125)
- violence (p. 127)
- bully (p. 129)
- peer education (p. 132)
- negotiation (p. 133)
- win-win solution (p. 133)
- mediation (p. 134)
- peer mediation (p. 135)

Academic Vocabulary
- trivial (p. 125)
- progress (p. 126)
- adapt (p. 131)
- project (p. 131)

Review Key Concepts

2. **List** reasons why conflicts occur.
3. **Summarize** the possible positive and negative effects of conflict.
4. **Explain** how to prevent violence that results from conflict.
5. **Compare** two methods of preventing conflict.
6. **Describe** the steps you can take to resolve a conflict.

Critical Thinking

7. **Appraise** What qualities do you believe a good mediator must have?
8. **Analyze** Why are conflict resolution techniques, such as mediation and negotiation, ineffective on bullies?
9. **Predict** Jonas and Mariana are in conflict over who owns a book. What do you think might happen if the conflict is not resolved properly?
10. **Argue** During a discussion, a student says he believes that violence is sometimes necessary to resolve a conflict. How would you react to this?
11. **Relate** Margot has been confronted by a friend who says that Margot promised to call with homework notes. Margot does not remember promising this, but does not want to damage the friendship. What would you advise Margot to do to end the conflict?

ACTIVE LEARNING

Family & Community Connections

12. Misunderstanding Messages Follow your teacher's instructions to gather in a large group as a class. Select one person to be the message giver and one person to be the message receiver. The message giver should whisper a message into the ear of another person. The message should be whispered from person to person until it reaches the receiver. How did the message change as it was passed along? How might a misunderstood message lead to conflict? Discuss as a class.

13. Interview a Professional Locate a professional in your community who works in one of the careers mentioned in the Law, Public Safety, Corrections, & Security career cluster on page 136. Interview the professional about the conflicts he or she encounters on the job and how he or she resolves them. Are the conflicts minor or major? Did he or she receive any special training to deal with conflict? If not, ask how he or she has learned from experience to deal with conflict. After the interview, create a visual presentation to illustrate the information you have learned. Be prepared to share your presentation with your class.

★ 21st Century Skills

Cooperative Learning Skills

14. Be a Mediator Follow your teacher's instructions to form groups of three. Decide on a conflict topic, then role-play the conflict between two people, with the third person acting as a peer mediator helping to find a solution. Switch places until everyone has had a turn as the peer mediator. What was the true role of the mediator? Was it difficult to stay neutral? As a group, give a five-minute oral report on your experience.

Technology Skills

15. Violence Prevention Follow your teacher's instructions to form small groups. Imagine your group has been asked to develop a public service announcement for teens on ways to prevent violence at school. To make your public service announcement, use technology options, such as presentation software, the Internet, videos, or music. Use information from this chapter as the basis for your presentation. Be prepared to show your presentation to the class.

 Connections

Interpersonal Skills

16. See the Other Side As part of its mission, FCCLA encourages students to address important personal issues. Resolving conflicts means understanding both sides of an issue. Think about a recent conflict you have experienced. Write a paragraph explaining your side of the conflict. Then write a second paragraph summarizing the other person's point of view.

Academic Skills

 English Language Arts

17. Keep a Conflict Log Keep a week-long log in which you list all the events and incidents that caused conflict in your life. Write down how each event made you feel and what you did to handle it. At the end of the week, analyze your entries to see what patterns show. Summarize what you learned about how you handle conflict in a brief report.

> **NCTE 7** Conduct research and gather, evaluate, and synthesize data to communicate discoveries.

 Social Studies

18. Research the United Nations Go online to learn more about the work of the United Nations in resolving international conflicts. Focus on how the United Nations tries to achieve the goal of keeping conflicts from developing into wars. Use your research to create a storyboard about the skills the United Nations uses in conflict resolution.

> **NCSS IX G Global Connections** Describe and evaluate the role of international and multinational organizations in the global arena.

 Mathematics

19. Compromise You have decided to make an effort to include more physical activity in your weekly routine. This week, you are going on a hike with your friend. You want to hike for 2½ hours, but your friend wants to hike for only 45 minutes. You suggest that you both compromise and split the difference. What amount of time should you suggest as a compromise?

Math Concept **Averages** To find the average of a group of numbers, add all the numbers together and divide the sum by the quantity of numbers you have added.

Starting Hint Convert the hours you want to spend hiking into minutes. There are 60 minutes in an hour, so 2 and a half hours would equal 150 minutes (60×2.5). Add 150 minutes to the 45 minutes your friend wants to spend hiking.

 For more math practice, go to the Math Appendix at the back of the book.

> **NCTM Algebra** Use mathematical models to represent and understand quantitative relationships.

 Standardized Test Practice   **College & Career Readiness**

FILL IN THE BLANK
Read the sentence, and choose the best word to fill in the blank.

> **Test-Taking Tip** When answering a fill-in-the-blank question, silently read the sentence with each of the possible answers in the blank space. This will help you eliminate wrong answers. The best word results in a sentence that is both factual and grammatically correct.

20. A _____ happens when people or groups feel a need to be in control.
a. personality difference
b. power struggle
c. damaged relationship
d. negotiation

UNIT 2 Portfolio Project

Conduct Career Research

In this project, you will analyze your career interest areas and begin researching different careers. You will organize your research into useful information you can quickly refer to in your college and career portfolio.

My Journal

If you completed the journal entry from page 64, refer to it to see if your thoughts have changed after reading the unit.

Project Assignment

In this project you will:
- Evaluate career interest groups to determine what your interests are.
- Research the 16 career clusters.
- Choose one career cluster that matches your career interest areas, and learn about the pathways and jobs within that cluster.
- Research information about the jobs you choose to select.
- Conduct an interview or arrange to job shadow a professional for at least one of the identified jobs.
- Organize your research and findings for your portfolio using a graphic organizer.

THE SKILLS BEHIND THE PROJECT

Key personal and relationship skills you will use in this project include:
- Using resources effectively
- Evaluating information
- Communicating respectfully

Academic Skills

English Language Arts

> **NCTE 1** Read texts to acquire new information.
>
> **NCTE 8** Use information resources to gather information and create and communicate knowledge.

STEP 1 Determine Your Career Interest Areas

Based on your self-evaluation from the Unit 1 Portfolio Project, determine your career interest areas. You can also use the *Career Plan Project Workbook* from this book's Online Learning Center at **glencoe.com**. Career interest groups are based on what you are good at doing and what you enjoy and value.

STEP 2 Research Career Clusters

Conduct research to learn about the 16 career clusters, and choose one that interests you. Each cluster includes several pathways. For your cluster, list its pathways and any jobs that interest you within those pathways. Choose two or more jobs that appeal to you. Use career research resources to find information about the jobs, including education required, tasks involved, and academic and technical skills required.

Research Skills
- Take clear notes on your research, and keep them organized for future reference.
- Use reliable sources of online information, such as the U.S. Department of Labor's *Occupational Outlook Handbook* or Glencoe's Career Clusters Web site at **careerclusters.glencoe.com**.
- Accurately document your sources.

STEP 3 Connect with Your Community

Choose one of the jobs researched in Step 2, and arrange to interview or job shadow a trusted adult in that profession. Develop a list of questions about topics you would like to know more about, such as job conditions, skills needed for the job, or advancement possibilities. Many of your questions may be answered during a job shadow. If any of your questions are not answered, ask for clarification.

Interpersonal Skills

- Be polite and professional when interviewing or job shadowing.
- Pay attention to the interviewer as you take your notes.
- Always thank the professional for his or her time. Consider sending a thank you note.

STEP 4 Organize Your Research

Use the Portfolio Project Checklist to create a graphic organizer to share what you have learned with your classmates.

Organization Skills

- Use a graphic organizer that is appropriate for the information you want to share.
- Draw or write neatly to ensure legibility.

STEP 5 Evaluate Your Project

Your portfolio project will be evaluated based on:

Academic Skills

- Thoroughness of your research
- Presentation of your graphic organizer
- Communication skills

Evaluation Rubric Go to this book's Online Learning Center at **glencoe.com** for a rubric you can use to evaluate your final project.

PORTFOLIO PROJECT CHECKLIST

Plan

☑ Determine what type of graphic organizer you could use to best organize and share the information you have learned about the jobs.

☑ Create the graphic organizer, including facts for all the jobs. If you learned additional information during your job shadowing or interview, conduct more research to find information for the other jobs.

☑ Consider using colors to easily identify similar information, or all the information for a single job.

Present

☑ Present and explain your graphic organizer to the class. Describe your reasons for choosing the jobs and style of your graphic organizer.

☑ Invite the students to ask questions. Answer any questions. Demonstrate in your answers that you respect their perspectives.

☑ Place your research notes and graphic organizer in your portfolio. Share your portfolio with your teacher.

Portfolio Highlights

Continue to Explore

Your college and career portfolio is intended to be a continually evolving tool. Researching many careers can help you know what training and preparation you need to begin now.

Career Interest Areas

Your interests have likely changed over the past few years. We continue to grow throughout our lives. Periodically re-evaluate your career interests.

Career Clusters

As you now know, there are thousands of careers within the 16 clusters. Continue researching jobs that interest you. This is especially important if you find that your career interests are changing.

Update Your Portfolio

As you continue your research, save your notes and sources in your portfolio so you will have an organized career research reference. Create a tab or folder within your portfolio just for career research.

UNIT 3

Management Skills

Unit Portfolio Project Preview

Develop a Career Plan

In this unit, you will examine ways to manage the general demands of an independent life. In your portfolio project you will use goal setting concepts to help build a successful plan.

My Journal

Setting Goals Write a journal entry about one of the topics below. This will help you prepare for the project at the end of this unit.

- Describe a time when you set a goal and successfully met that goal.
- Give examples of short-term, medium-term, and long-term goals.
- Explain how setting goals creates learning opportunities, whether or not the goal is actually met.

Explore the Photo

Although each of us is unique, we all face challenges in life. *What methods have you used to overcome your own life's challenges?*

Chapter 8

Learning to Manage

Chapter Objectives

Section 8.1 Goals and Resources

- **Discuss** reasons for and influences on priorities.
- **Explain** the different types of goals and their benefits.
- **Identify** resources that help people achieve their goals.

Section 8.2 Management in Action

- **Compare** strategies for making the most of resources.
- **Outline** the four steps of the management process.

▶ Explore the Photo

Goals can be big or small, group or individual. *What goals must you achieve to graduate from high school?*

Writing Activity   Blog

A Personal Goal A blog, short for Web log, is a Web site in the form of an online journal. Bloggers write their reflections and opinions, as they would in traditional journals. However, as with anything posted online, blogs can be viewed publicly. Identify a goal you achieved. Write a blog about the experience, including what you set out to do, what went right or wrong, and how you feel about it now.

Writing Tips To write a blog, follow these steps:
- Date your blog.
- Include your observations and reflections about the topic.
- Write your blog in the first person.
- Do not censor yourself. Let the words flow naturally.

145

Goals and Resources

Use resources wisely to help set big and small goals.

Before You Read

Pace Yourself Short blocks of concentrated reading are more effective than one long session. Focus on reading for 10 minutes. Take a short break. Then read for another 10 minutes. This will help you remember what you read.

Read to Learn
Key Concepts
- **Discuss** reasons for and influences on priorities.
- **Explain** the different types of goals and their benefits.
- **Identify** resources that help people achieve their goals.

Main Idea
Manage your life by deciding on priorities and setting goals. Once you have set your goals, you need to determine which resources you will need to achieve them.

Content Vocabulary
◇ prioritize
◇ goal
◇ short-term goal
◇ medium-term goal
◇ long-term goal
◇ fixed goal
◇ flexible goal
◇ resource

Academic Vocabulary
You will find these words in your reading and on your tests. Use the glossary to look up their definitions if necessary.
■ essential
■ unique

Academic Standards

English Language Arts
NCTE 6 Apply knowledge of language structure and conventions to discuss texts.

Social Studies
NCSS IV H Individual Development and Identity Work independently and cooperatively within groups and institutions to accomplish goals.

Graphic Organizer
As you read, look for definitions of the five types of goals. Write the definitions in the boxes under each type of goal. Use a tree organizer like the one shown to help you organize your information.

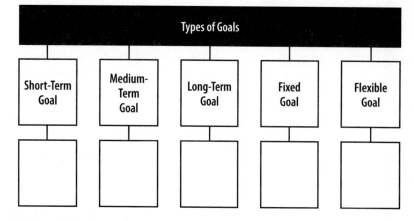

Types of Goals

Short-Term Goal	Medium-Term Goal	Long-Term Goal	Fixed Goal	Flexible Goal

Graphic Organizer Go to this book's Online Learning Center at **glencoe.com** to print out this graphic organizer.

NCTE *National Council of Teachers of English*
NCTM *National Council of Teachers of Mathematics*
NSES *National Science Education Standards*
NCSS *National Council for the Social Studies*

Establish Priorities

Managing your life starts with determining your priorities. What plans do you have for the years ahead? Perhaps you have so many ideas about what you want that sorting them out seems overwhelming. Accomplishing everything right away may not be reasonable or even possible. That is why you need to prioritize. When you **prioritize** (prī-'ȯr-ə-ˌtīz), you decide which goals and activities are most important to you. Priorities are based on values, interests, skills, and your stage in the life cycle. Identify your priorities to give you direction as you set goals and manage your resources.

Needs and Wants

Establishing your priorities starts with taking a close look at your needs and wants. Needs are things you must have for survival, such as food, clothing, and shelter. Wants, on the other hand, are things that you desire but that are not **essential** (i-'sen(t)-shəl), or necessary.

It is easy to think that certain wants are needs. If you already have several pairs of shoes, do you really need another pair? You might need transportation to get to work, but having an expensive car is a want. Being able to tell the difference between needs and wants is essential to setting priorities.

The Role of Values

When you set priorities, you should also examine your values. Values are the beliefs and ideas that guide your life. They help you determine what is more important, less important, or unimportant. If you value good health, for instance, good nutrition and exercise may be priorities. If you value education, then getting good grades, graduating, and being accepted into college may be priorities. Your values help steer you toward what is right for you and away from activities that are not in your best interest.

Differing Priorities

Priorities differ from person to person. For instance, Josh loves sports. He plays on the school's basketball team and watches sports on TV. His brother, Kevin, thinks sports are boring. He prefers to work on his digital photo album. In spite of the difference, spending time together is a high priority for both of them. They like to talk, watch science fiction movies, and go hiking together.

Right now, your list of priorities might include getting your driver's license or finding a part-time job. When you graduate, what do you think your priorities will include? How might they change if you get married and start a family? Changes in life often cause your priorities to shift.

✓ **Reading Check** **Explain** Why do priorities vary from person to person?

As You Read

Connect What are your priorities right now?

◆ Vocabulary

You can find definitions in the glossary at the back of this book.

Be Smart Be Safe

Internet Safety Online social networking Web sites allow you to share opinions and meet new people. However, you must be careful. To stay safe online, never reveal personal information, never agree to meet strangers, and let only people you know to access your information.

Write About It Make a list of information you probably want to keep private and so should not make available online. Keep this list handy, and refer to it when you are sharing online.

Share Your Goals

Sometimes it can help to share your goals. For example, if you have a specific goal at work and you share it with your manager, the two of you can work together to come up with a plan for you to achieve your goal. Your manager might have valuable and helpful suggestions. Also, by sharing your goals with someone else, that person can help you plan and succeed.

Find Time for Fun

Your priorities affect many of the choices you make, from how you spend your free time to the goals you set for the future. *How do you fit hobbies and fun activities into your daily routine?*

Set Goals

Once you know your priorities, you can set appropriate goals. A **goal** is something you consciously aim to achieve and for which you are willing to plan and work.

Like priorities, your goals are personal. You and your friends probably have a common goal of graduating, but may have very different career goals. That is because the goals you choose are influenced by your own needs, wants, values, and priorities.

It is not just individuals who set goals. Families, businesses, communities, and other groups set goals as well. A family's goal might be to save enough money for a down payment on a home. A business might set a goal of increasing productivity by 10 percent. A community might set a goal of building a new recreation center.

Even though people and groups have different goals, they set them for the same reasons. Goals provide direction and a sense of purpose. Without goals, it is easy to drift along without making progress. If you realized late in life that you had accomplished very few of the things you wanted to do in your life, how would you feel? Achieving goals gives you a sense of accomplishment and improves your self-esteem. By becoming comfortable with setting and working toward goals now, you can make your life more fulfilling.

Short-Term and Long-Term Goals

A **short-term goal** is something you want to complete soon, like today or this week. Examples are baking brownies for a bake sale, completing a science project, or finishing reading a book.

A **medium-term goal** is something that will take a bit longer, perhaps six months or a few years. Examples are preparing to compete in a gymnastics competition, saving enough money to buy a new laptop, or mastering a musical instrument.

A **long-term goal** is something you plan to complete much later, perhaps many years into the future. Examples are getting a college degree, taking a vacation, becoming a dentist, or having a family. A long-term goal can seem overwhelming if viewed as a single task. Breaking it down into several short- and medium-term goals can make it seem more manageable and reachable.

Fixed and Flexible Goals

A **fixed goal** is one that can be met only at a certain time. If you want a part in the school musical, for instance, you will need to be ready for auditions. Fixed goals are often tied to specific dates.

A **flexible goal**, on the other hand, has no definite time limit. Building your savings is an example of a flexible goal. It is ongoing, and the amount of money saved can vary. However, if you are saving to buy a laptop before the new school year, that is a fixed goal.

Fixed and flexible goals can be short-term, medium-term, or long-term. Preparing to take the SAT test in six months is a fixed, medium-term goal. Preparing for next week's history test is a fixed, short-term goal. Distinguishing between fixed and flexible goals can help you better manage your time. To set achievable goals, try these tips:

- **Analyze your goals.** Is the goal short-, medium-, or long-term? Is it fixed or flexible? Do you need to break it down? Should you tackle it now or later?
- **Be realistic.** Challenging goals can inspire you to learn and seek new experiences. However, it is important to be realistic. Choose goals that challenge you, but that can be reached.
- **Be specific.** State goals in specific terms so you can measure progress. "Work out at least 30 minutes five days a week" is a better goal than "Be more physically active."
- **Put goals in writing.** Often, the act of writing something down makes you more likely to follow through. Try posting your goals where you will see them often.

✓ **Reading Check** **Recall** How can you make a long-term goal more manageable?

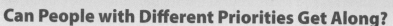

Two Views One World

Can People with Different Priorities Get Along?

What happens when people have different priorities? Is there a way to reach an understanding?

Antonio: My friends don't understand why I won't go out with them more often. I mean, I like having fun, but right now schoolwork and my part-time job come first. I just wish my friends would try to understand my priorities. I don't mean to hurt their feelings, but sometimes when they ask me to go to a movie or a party with them, I have to say no to get done what I need to get done.

Huan: It's true that things like school and jobs are important, but it's not healthy to spend all your time on serious stuff. Other things in life are just as important, like spending time with friends and family and just relaxing. What is the point of working all the time if you never take time to enjoy what you earn? And studying is a good thing, but if you study all the time, you'll burn out.

Seeing Both Sides
Have both teens based their priorities on values? What values? Why is awareness important for people with different priorities to get along?

Break it Down

Big goals seem less daunting when broken down into smaller goals. *Why is it so important to have a goal and take steps toward achieving it?*

Identify Your Resources

To reach your goals, you need to manage your resources. A **resource** is something or someone that can help you achieve a goal. Resources fall into four main categories: human, material, community, and natural. Everyone has resources, though in varying amounts, depending on individual situations. Learning to recognize your available resources is the first step in managing them.

Human Resources

Human resources are found within yourself and other people. Knowledge is a human resource that consists of everything you read, observe, and learn. Your skills are the things you can do, such as use a computer, swim, paint, play piano, or build furniture.

Creativity is another human resource. Creativity is what enables you to come up with original solutions to problems and **unique** (yu'-'nēk), or distinctive, ways of expressing yourself. Time and energy are human resources that you need to achieve goals. Family and friends are also human resources. You might be able to use their knowledge, skills, creativity, time, and energy in addition to your own.

Material Resources

Material resources are all the physical objects you can use to reach your goals. Material resources include tools, equipment, and other possessions. Money is probably the most recognized material resource. If your goal is to learn how to dance, money can help you reach that goal by allowing you to pay for lessons.

Technology has expanded both the type of material resources that are available and what they can do. Think of all the ways in which computers, portable entertainment devices, GPS devices, cell phones, satellites, and lifesaving medical equipment have changed people's lives.

Get Involved!

Volunteer at a Museum

There are many types of museums, including art, history, science, and maritime museums. Most museums welcome volunteers. Opportunities could range from giving tours to helping with a Web site to organizing exhibitions. Volunteering at a museum is a way to give back to your community, meet new people, and learn new skills and information.

Community Resources

Communities also offer resources that can help you enjoy life, improve your skills, and solve problems. These include schools, libraries, hospitals, museums, parks, and theaters. Places of worship, shopping malls, and public transportation are other examples of community resources.

The businesses in your community provide access to many resources. Through them, people are able to learn new skills, earn money, and purchase products they need or want. People in the community can also provide valuable help. Teachers can expand your learning. School counselors and other trusted adults can help you deal with problems. Doctors, dentists, and other medical professionals can help you stay healthy.

Natural Resources

The resources found in nature include air, water, soil, plants, and minerals. Some, such as clean air and drinking water, are necessary for survival. People have also come to depend on sources of fuel such as gas, oil, and coal. Without natural resources, your options would be severely limited. For these reasons and more, natural resources, like any other resources, need to be used wisely.

Take a Look Around
People make use of community resources every day, such as this museum. *What other examples of community resources are available in your area?*

 Podcasts Access the Online Learning Center to download *Managing Life Skills* podcasts.

Section 8.1   After You Read

Review Key Concepts

1. **Distinguish** between needs and wants.
2. **Explain** why having goals is important.
3. **List** four examples of human resources.

Practice Academic Skills

 English Language Arts

4. Imagine that you are asked to be on a committee to help teens set and achieve goals. Create a brochure that explains what a goal is, defines different types of goals, and demonstrates how to set a realistic goal. Use artwork to make your brochure more appealing.

 Social Studies

5. Use Internet and print resources to find the history of a local, state, or national law. What goals did the law's authors set to get the law passed? What resources did they use to achieve their goals? Write a summary that describes your findings.

Check Your Answers Check your answers at this book's Online Learning Center at **glencoe.com**.

NCTE 6 Apply knowledge of language structure and conventions to discuss texts.

NCSS IV H Work independently and cooperatively within groups and institutions to accomplish goals.

Management in Action

Manage your time wisely to accomplish your goals.

Reading Guide

Before You Read

Use Color Try using different colored pens to take notes. This can help you learn new material and study for tests. You might use red for vocabulary terms and definitions, blue for explanations, and green for examples.

Read to Learn
Key Concepts
- **Compare** strategies for making the most of resources.
- **Outline** the four steps of the management process.

Main Idea
You can use resources wisely by following different resource management strategies. The management process includes four steps: planning, organizing, implementing, and evaluating.

Content Vocabulary
◇ resourceful
◇ management process
◇ contingency plan
◇ implement

Academic Vocabulary
You will find these words in your reading and on your tests. Use the glossary to look up their definitions if necessary.
■ define
■ consider

Academic Standards

English Language Arts
NCTE 12 Use language to accomplish individual purposes.

Mathematics
NCTM Problem Solving Apply and adapt a variety of appropriate strategies to solve problems.

Social Studies
NCSS IV H Individual Development and Identity Work independently and cooperatively within groups and institutions to accomplish goals.

Graphic Organizer
As you read, look for the four different strategies for using resources. Use a spider graphic organizer like the one shown to list the four strategies, along with a short explanation of each.

Strategies for Using Resources

Graphic Organizer Go to this book's Online Learning Center at **glencoe.com** to print out this graphic organizer.

NCTE *National Council of Teachers of English*
NCTM *National Council of Teachers of Mathematics*
NSES *National Science Education Standards*
NCSS *National Council for the Social Studies*

Management Skills

You may see the word *management* and think of the business world. But management skills are used by everyone, every day. One of the many challenges of the teen years is to learn to manage your own life. Over the next few years you will need to decide how you will earn a living, spend your time, use your resources, and reach your goals. This may sound intimidating, but fortunately, managing, like many other life skills, is something you can learn, practice, and improve upon.

Learning the basics of managing now will help you both in the short term and in the long term. It will help you determine your priorities, set career and personal goals, use your resources effectively, and find ways of balancing your work and social life.

Put Your Resources to Work

Now that you can identify resources, it is time to learn how to manage them. You need to understand the limits of your resources and know how to make the most of them. In other words, you need to be resourceful. People who are **resourceful** are able to use creative problem solving to manage available resources wisely. The ability to come up with creative, efficient ways to manage resources helps people deal with both everyday situations and unusual challenges. Resourceful people use several strategies to make the most of their resources. These strategies include expanding, exchanging, conserving, and substituting resources.

Expand Resources

Some resources, such as your knowledge and skills, can be expanded, which means you can add to your supply. To improve your drawing skills, for example, you might take lessons and practice drawing every day. To learn more about car care and repair, you could read books, do online research, take a class, or work with someone experienced.

Personal energy is another resource that you may be able to increase. Energy comes from eating nutritious foods, being physically active, and getting enough rest. Your energy level also depends on your attitude. A positive attitude gives you more energy and enthusiasm. That makes it easier to overcome obstacles and get things done.

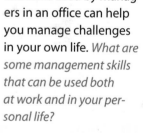

As You Read

Connect What does the word *manage* mean to you? Write a brief definition.

▶ **Vocabulary**

You can find definitions in the glossary at the back of this book.

▼ **More than Business**

The skills used by managers in an office can help you manage challenges in your own life. *What are some management skills that can be used both at work and in your personal life?*

Exercise Your Creativity

Being able to think creatively is a valuable resource, both at school and in the workplace. Just like a physical muscle, you need to exercise your imagination to make it strong. With mental workouts, you can make your imagination stronger and more flexible. Brainstorming, challenging yourself, and trying to think "outside the box" encourage creative thinking.

Conserve Resources

Some resources cannot be increased because the supply is fixed. In this case, you need to make the most of what you have by conserving resources, or using them in the most efficient way possible.

Time is a good example. While everyone has 24 hours in each day, some people get everything done on time while others struggle with deadlines. Everyone can learn to better use time through planning and wise choices. You will learn more about time management in Chapter 10.

Taking care of your possessions is another way to conserve resources. Giving possessions the right care will keep them usable as long as possible. It will also save you money.

Community resources also need to be cared for so they remain available for others. Whenever you use a community resource, it is your personal responsibility to care for it. Do your part, whether it is cleaning up after a picnic or returning library materials on time.

Exchange Resources

Have you ever exchanged resources with someone else? Perhaps you traded clothes with a family member or offered your time to help a friend.

Quong wants to learn how to play the guitar. His sister has loaned him her guitar and is teaching him the basics. In return, she knows she can count on Quong to help her with any computer problems.

Your family, friends, and people in the community may have resources that they are willing to share with you. Do not be afraid to ask for help when you need it. You, in turn, should be ready to return the favor.

Life On Your Own

The Importance of Setting Realistic Goals

If your goals are too easy to reach, they will not challenge you. However, if your goals are too difficult to reach, you might get discouraged and give up. When setting goals, it is important to find a "happy medium" that makes you push yourself but that, with hard work, you have a chance of meeting.

How It Works When setting goals, be precise. Include starting dates, times, and amounts so that you can properly measure your achievements. It can also be helpful to write down goals. If you have multiple goals, prioritize them so you can avoid feeling overwhelmed. Set goals over which you have as much control as possible. Try to avoid goals that depend on factors that are outside of your control.

Try It Out A few months ago, you realized your grades were not as high as you wanted them to be. You wanted to set an academic goal that would motivate you to get better grades, so you set a goal to spend more time studying, especially before tests. However, you have not been able to meet this goal, and you are starting to feel discouraged.

> *Your Turn* How could you change the original goal to make it more realistic? What should you have done differently from the start?

Substitute Resources

In some situations, resources that are plentiful can be substituted for others that are in short supply. Suppose that your grandmother's birthday is next week, and you do not have much money to spend on a gift for her. You do, however, have the time, skills, and creativity to make a gift yourself. You might decide to frame a photo that you took or make a book of coupons for tasks you are willing to do for her. By substituting the resources you have for the money you lack, you can accomplish your goal.

✓ Reading Check

Understand Why is it important to conserve some resources?

The Management Process

By now, you know the importance of establishing priorities, setting goals, and maximizing resources to meet those goals. But how do you put it all together? How can you bridge the gap between just thinking about your goals and making them happen?

What you need is a systematic way of working toward your goals. Fortunately, just such a system exists. The system to manage the steps needed to accomplish something is called the **management process**, and it is useful for all kinds of situations. The management process involves four steps: planning, organizing, implementing, and evaluating.

Keep in mind that this management process does not **define**, or outline and describe, everything included in management. Being a good manager involves a variety of skills, including decision making, problem solving, communication, leadership, organization, critical thinking, and creative thinking.

Think of the management process as a road map that helps you find the most effective ways to use resources and achieve your goals. You are more likely to reach any significant goal if you use this process. It works whether you are trying to accomplish goals on your own or as part of a group. The more complex the task or project, the more important the management process becomes.

Planning

There is an expression that says, "If you fail to plan, you plan to fail." What do you think this saying means? Do you often find yourself scrambling to finish a big project at the last minute? Lack of planning might be the reason. When you take time to plan, you can get more done.

Self Management

Most goals require resource management. *How do you think this teen accomplished her goal of doing well on her science project?*

Character?!
In Action

Fulfill Your Commitments

When you make a commitment to yourself or to others, you are making a promise. If you do not meet your commitments, people will start to view you as unreliable. Management skills, such as planning and organizing, can help you keep the commitments you have made.

You Decide

Think about a commitment you made that you were able to fulfill and one that you were not. How did each situation make you feel? What did you do differently in the situation in which you were able to meet your commitment?

There are several steps involved in successful planning:

- **Identify Your Goals** What do you want to accomplish? Put it into words, and write it down. Also identify the secondary goals that fill in the specific details. For example, if you are planning an anniversary party for your parents, some of your goals might be to invite guests, provide food, and present the couple with a gift from the family.

- **Establish Your Priorities** With goals, it is important to **consider**, or take into account, which ones matter most. If you are not able to complete everything, you will need to make choices. Use what you have learned about priorities to decide which of your goals are most important.

- **Assess Your Resources** Make a list of the resources available to help you meet your goals. If you include family and friends as resources, be sure they are able and willing to help.

- **Create a Task List** Based on the available resources, decide how you will accomplish each goal. Will you buy pre-prepared food, make it yourself, or ask everyone to bring something? Then make a list of the steps you will need to complete. Try to include even the smallest details.

As you plan, anticipate possible problems. Then develop a **contingency plan** (kən-'tin-jən(t)-sē 'plan), or a different course of action that could help you overcome potential obstacles and ensure success. If you plan to serve food outdoors, what will you do if it rains?

Organizing

After you make your plans, the next step is to get organized. Good organization is essential for tasks to go smoothly. There are two main steps to getting organized:

- **Create a Schedule** How much time will you need to perform each task on your list? Which tasks must be completed first? Develop a sequence of events that charts your course of action. If you are trying to meet several goals, look for efficient ways to juggle the different tasks required. For example, buying party supplies and shopping for a gift might be combined into one errand.

- **Gather Your Resources** What resources do you need? Are they ready to use? Check that any equipment you need is in good working order. If other people will be working with you, get together and decide how to coordinate your efforts.

Implementing

Now that you are done planning and organizing, it is time to implement your plan. To **implement** a plan means to put it in action. Use your resources and follow the task list according to your schedule. As you work through your plan, track your progress. If you have problems, consider turning to your backup plan.

Evaluating

You might think that after planning, organizing, and implementing, the management process is complete. However, one final step remains. After you have finished your work, you need to evaluate your plan and how well you carried it out. Doing so will help you manage more successfully in the future.

Start by evaluating your results. Did you accomplish your goals? If you met your goals, what helped you to succeed? What could you have done to make things go even more smoothly? If some goals did not get accomplished, try to analyze what happened. Did you set goals that were too ambitious? Did you forget to include something? Did a problem arise that you did not anticipate?

Evaluating helps you learn from your experiences. Each time you use the management process, you will get better at it. By the time you have more responsibilities and more complicated goals to meet, managing will be second nature.

Go Green

Start or join a community garden. Community gardens are shared neighborhood spaces where residents can grow flowers, fruits, and vegetables. They create green spaces and provide a place for people to meet and socialize.

 Podcasts Access the Online Learning Center to download *Managing Life Skills* podcasts.

Section 8.2   After You Read

Review Key Concepts

1. **Differentiate** between exchanging resources and substituting resources.
2. **Summarize** why evaluating is an important part of the management process.

Practice Academic Skills

 English Language Arts

3. Choose a task. Think about the resources that are needed to complete the task. Choose one resource that you think is the most important for getting the task done. Use persuasive language to write a paragraph describing the steps in the task and explaining why you think this resource is the most important.

 Social Studies

4. Follow your teacher's instructions to form small groups. Imagine your group has been asked to determine what foods are the most popular in your school's cafeteria. As a group, decide how you will get the information, what tasks need to be done, and what resources you will need. Discuss your group's findings with the class.

Check Your Answers Check your answers at this book's Online Learning Center at **glencoe.com**.

> **NCTE 12** Use language to accomplish individual purposes.

> **NCSS IV H** Work independently and cooperatively within groups and institutions to accomplish goals.

Pathway to College
Vocational Schools

What Are Vocational Schools?

Vocational schools, also called trade or technical schools, focus on giving graduates skills they can use in the job market. They offer classes in fields like construction, health care, and culinary arts. Their purpose is to prepare you for a job in a specific industrial trade. After graduating, you should be able to successfully enter the job market.

What is the difference between vocational school and community college?

While community colleges offer both technical and non-technical training, vocational schools focus only on trade and technical training. Community college credits are almost always transferable to four-year schools, while vocational school credits often are not. This means you usually do not use vocational school as a bridge into a four-year school. Also, community colleges are public, while vocational schools are usually private.

Why should I consider vocational school?

Vocational schools train you for a specific career, trade, or profession. It is a good option for people who are sure about what job they eventually want to have. Vocational schools have many of the same advantages that community colleges have, including affordable tuition, flexible schedules, and workforce preparation.

What specific trades can I learn at a vocational school?

Common options include automotive studies, plumbing, electronics, aviation, business, culinary arts, interior design, fashion, photography, architecture, music production, acting, Web design, welding, cosmetology, skin and nail care, hairstyling, teaching, health care, law, criminal justice, animation, audio production, filmmaking, broadcasting, graphic design, video game design, real estate, computer technology, travel, tourism, and hospitality.

Hands-On

College Readiness Pick a trade that is commonly studied at vocational schools and that you are interested in. Research this trade to find out more about it. Write a paragraph explaining why you picked this trade, what information you found out about it, what jobs you can get with a degree or certification in that trade, and what those job prospects look like.

Path to Success

☆ College & Career Readiness

Know What You Want Vocational school is a better option if you know what you want to study there.

Compare Programs Study the information from various schools so you can be sure you pick the right one.

Ask Questions What are the facilities like? What is the average class size? Who are the instructors? What is the program's success rate?

Do Research Check out the school's Web site. Also, go to the U.S. Department of Education's Web site for valuable information.

Ask Around Talk to previous and current students. This is a great way to get more information about a school.

Take Care of Business Make sure you understand exactly what it will cost and when and how you are expected to pay.

 Go to this book's Online Learning Center at **glencoe.com** to learn more about college and career readiness.

CHAPTER SUMMARY

Section 8.1
Goals and Resources

Managing life starts with determining your priorities. You must understand the difference between needs and wants, and know what role your values play in setting priorities. Once you know your priorities, you can set goals. Goals can be short-term, medium-term, long-term, fixed, or flexible. Identify the resources available to you to help you accomplish your goals.

Section 8.2
Management in Action

Management skills can be used every day to help you use your resources wisely. You can expand, conserve, exchange, and substitute your resources to help you manage. The management process gives you a systematic way to work toward achieving your goals. The management process includes four steps: planning, organizing, implementing, and evaluating.

Vocabulary Review

1. Write each of the vocabulary words below on an index card and their definitions on separate index cards. Work in pairs or small groups to match each word to its definition.

Content Vocabulary
- ◇ prioritize (p. 147)
- ◇ goal (p. 148)
- ◇ short-term goal (p. 148)
- ◇ medium-term goal (p. 148)
- ◇ long-term goal (p. 148)
- ◇ fixed goal (p. 148)
- ◇ flexible goal (p. 149)
- ◇ resource (p. 150)
- ◇ resourceful (p. 153)
- ◇ management process (p. 155)
- ◇ contingency plan (p. 156)
- ◇ implement (p. 157)

Academic Vocabulary
- ■ essential (p. 147)
- ■ unique (p. 150)
- ■ define (p. 155)
- ■ consider (p. 156)

Review Key Concepts

2. **Discuss** reasons for and influences on priorities.
3. **Explain** the different types of goals and their benefits.
4. **Identify** resources that help people achieve their goals.
5. **Compare** strategies for making the most of resources.
6. **Outline** the four steps of the management process.

Critical Thinking

7. **Evaluate** Are needs and wants the same for everyone? Could one person's need be another's want? Support your answer with examples.
8. **Propose** You are planning a friend's welcome-home party, but your funds are limited. What could you do that would cost little or no money?
9. **Predict** What could happen if you fail to use the management process?
10. **Analyze** You have a friend who claims fitness is his main priority, but he spends a lot of time watching TV. What does this say about his values?
11. **Describe** What factors could cause you to change strategies for how you would use a resource?

ACTIVE LEARNING

12. Step-By-Step Guide Follow your teacher's instructions to form small groups. Choose a simple task, such as replacing a light bulb, making a peanut butter and jelly sandwich, or adding a number to your cell phone address book. List all the necessary resources and the sequence of steps needed to complete the task. As a group, describe each step in detail, and have someone act out the task. Evaluate the results, and adjust the directions as needed. Use this information to create a detailed, easy-to-follow, step-by-step guide for carrying out the task.

Family & Community Connections

13. Media Analysis Find an article online, in a newspaper, or in a magazine about a person who demonstrates or represents a specific value. The article can be about any type of person and any type of value as long as the value he or she is representing or demonstrating is clear. Examine how that person may have used the value you identified to create a priority. Be ready to support your theory with details and examples. Prepare and give a brief report to the class, identifying the person you chose, and describing the value you found in the article. Explain how the value is shown in the article, and list any priorities that you think might have been affected by the value.

21st Century Skills

Technology Skills

14. Examine Management Software Learn about a software program that is designed to help businesses manage tasks and resources. You might gather information from the Web site of the software company or from product reviews in magazines. Prepare a report that explains how the software could be beneficial to the management process.

Planning Skills

15. Management Diagram Choose a long-term goal. Identify at least six different short- and medium-term goals that could contribute to the long-term goal you chose. Create a graphic organizer that shows how the short-and medium-term goals relate to the long-term goal. Add any details to the short- or medium-term goals that you feel are important.

FCCLA Connections

Interpersonal Skills

16. Interview a Leader As part of its mission, FCCLA encourages students to use interpersonal skills to accomplish tasks. Find someone who you consider to be a leader, and interview that person about his or her management process style. What factors does that person consider most important when setting and accomplishing goals? What steps does he or she take to organize and complete tasks? Transcribe your notes from your interview.

Academic Skills

 English Language Arts

17. Write a Book Report Choose a book that includes a character striving to complete a goal. What steps did the character take to try to achieve the goal? What resources were or were not available? Did the character reach the goal? What factors affected whether or not the goal was achieved? Write a two-page book report describing the goal, the resources, and the outcome.

> **NCTE 11** Participate as members of literacy communities.

 Social Studies

18. Government Connection Choose a local, national, or international government program that interests you. Find out what the program's priorities are, what goals have been set, and what is being done to manage available resources. Prepare a brief oral report detailing your findings.

> **NCSS VI I Power, Authority, and Governance** Evaluate the extent to which governments achieve their stated ideals and policies at home and abroad.

 Mathematics

19. Volume You made a 12-quart (693-cubic inch) pot of soup that you want to transfer into smaller containers for cooling. Each rectangular container is 12 inches long, 10 inches wide, and 2 inches deep. How many smaller containers are needed to hold all the soup?

Math Concept **Find the Volume of a Box**
Volume is the amount of space inside a solid object. The volume of a box is obtained by multiplying its length by its width by its height (or depth).

Starting Hint Calculate the volume in cubic inches of one container by multiplying its length (12 inches) by its width (10 inches) by its height (2 inches). Divide this number into the volume of soup (693 cubic inches) to determine the number of containers needed. Round up to the next whole number.

 For more math practice, go to the Math Appendix at the back of the book.

> **NCTM Geometry** Use visualization, spatial reasoning, and geometric modeling to solve problems.

 Standardized Test Practice

 College & Career Readiness

READING COMPREHENSION
Read the passage. Then answer the question.

> **Test-Taking Tip** Read the passage carefully, identifying key statements as you go. Answer the question based only on what you just read in the passage, not on your previous knowledge.

Every task can be broken down into multiple smaller, detailed steps. Organized people understand that breaking tasks down into multiple steps is an essential first step in the planning phase of the management process.

20. According to this passage, what type of people understand why it is important to break up tasks into detailed steps?

Chapter 9

Decisions and Problem Solving

Chapter Objectives

Section 9.1 Making Decisions

- **Describe** the different influences on choices.
- **Outline** the decision-making process.

Section 9.2 Solving Problems

- **List** the characteristics of a practical problem.
- **Summarize** the steps in the REASON process.

> ## Explore the Photo
>
> Teens make many decisions as they grow, mature, and move toward adulthood. *What types of decisions might a teen typically face?*

The board in the background shows:

$$+ b^2 = c^2$$

$$\sin = \frac{opposite}{hyp}$$

$$\cos = \frac{adjacent}{hyp}$$

$$\tan = \frac{opposite}{adjacent}$$

$$\tan 47$$

Writing Activity

Write an Introductory Paragraph

Making Decisions An introductory paragraph introduces readers to the topic of a paper and gives them an idea of what they will read. Imagine you are going to write a paper about the difficulties of making decisions. Create an introductory paragraph that includes a topic sentence and supporting details that help introduce the rest of the paper.

Writing Tips To write an introductory paragraph, follow these steps:
- Decide first what the point of your paper is, and then write the introductory paragraph.
- Use a story, question, or quote to get readers' attention.
- Use correct grammar and spelling.

Making Decisions

The decisions you make can affect you and everyone around you.

Reading Guide

Before You Read

Adjust Reading Speed Improve your comprehension by adjusting your reading speed to match the difficulty of the text. When the text is complex, slow down and, if necessary, reread it. Reading slowly may take longer, but it will help you understand and remember more.

Read to Learn

Key Concepts
- **Describe** the different influences on choices.
- **Outline** the decision-making process.

Main Idea

There are many different types of influences, including internal and external. These affect the choices you make, and your choices have an impact on you and on others.

Content Vocabulary
◇ dilemma
◇ decision-making process

Academic Vocabulary

You will find these words in your reading and on your tests. Use the glossary to look up their definitions if necessary.
■ foundation
■ impact

Academic Standards

English Language Arts

NCTE 5 Use different writing process elements to communicate effectively.

Social Studies

NCSS I B Culture Predict how data and experiences may be interpreted by people from diverse cultural perspectives and frames of reference.

Graphic Organizer

As you read, think about the various internal and external influences on choices. Use a Venn diagram like the one shown to help you categorize influences as internal, external, and both.

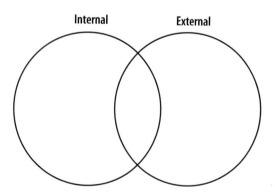

Internal   External

Graphic Organizer Go to this book's Online Learning Center at **glencoe.com** to print out this graphic organizer.

NCTE *National Council of Teachers of English*
NCTM *National Council of Teachers of Mathematics*
NSES *National Science Education Standards*
NCSS *National Council for the Social Studies*

Examine Decisions and Problems

Have you ever watched a carpenter or a mechanic select a tool or combination of tools for a particular job? Because of their skills and experience, these workers know which tools they need. Just as a carpenter or mechanic selects the right tools for the job, you need to select the best ways to help you make decisions and solve problems. This chapter will give you several options for your tool kit. With practice, using these tools will become second nature to you.

Every day you face problems and must make decisions. Some are so ordinary that you may not even be aware that you are making them. Others are difficult dilemmas. A **dilemma** is a situation in which you must choose between alternatives that could have serious consequences. These situations may seem so complicated that it is hard to know how to think through the issues and make the best decision.

You are more likely to make good choices if you are proactive. You learned in Chapter 2 that proactive people anticipate future decisions or problems and take action. They do not ignore a problem, hoping that it will go away. They act as soon as they realize that something needs to be done, and they do not let the fear of making a wrong decision stand in their way. They do not expect others to make their decisions for them. Proactive people recognize and accept responsibility for their own decisions and actions.

Influences on Choices

Whether you are faced with a decision or a problem, there are many factors that influence the choices you make. Some come from within yourself and others from outside. Some influences promote wise choices. Others get in the way and may lead you to make poor choices. Some common influences include:

- **Attitude** How do you react when you are confronted with decisions or problems? Do you view them as unwelcome hurdles or as opportunities for growth? Facing decisions and problems does not have to be a negative experience. With a positive attitude, you can often recognize more options. Staying optimistic can help you view decisions and problems as interesting challenges and learning experiences.

- **Emotions** Have you ever made a decision on impulse because of how you felt at the time? Your emotions can have a powerful effect on the choices you make. They can sometimes lead to poor decisions or stand in the way of solving a problem. The strategies explained in this chapter can help you avoid these pitfalls.

As You Read

Connect What is the difference between a decision and a problem?

◆ **Vocabulary**

You can find definitions in the glossary at the back of this book.

Take Action

If you are proactive, you plan for the future. *How is this person being proactive?*

Ethical Decisions

We make decisions every day, and many of them do not involve right or wrong. However, some choices are about doing the right thing. Decisions often happen quickly but the consequences can last a lifetime, so careful consideration is important. Your code of ethics can help you decide.

You Decide

Robyn knows a classmate cheated on a test. She does not want to get involved, but the class is graded on a curve, so the cheating student's grade will affect everyone else's grades. What should Robyn do?

- **Values, Goals, and Priorities** These are the foundation, or base, upon which wise choices are made. Make decisions and solve problems in a way that reflects the values you hold, the goals you want to achieve, and the priorities you have set.

- **Ethics** Your ethics are the principles and values that guide the way you live, based on what you believe is just and fair. For example, one of your ethical standards might be, "I will not hurt others by spreading gossip." Ethics help you make choices that are best for everyone involved, not just for you.

- **Family** Your family has guided your development, taught you values, and modeled ways to make decisions and solve problems. Their influence continues as you make more decisions for yourself. You can turn to them when you have trouble making choices.

- **Peers** Your peers also influence your choices, although their influence may not always be positive. As you make choices about what to do or how to behave, be your own person. You do not have to do something just because everyone else seems to be doing it. Distinguish between positive and negative peer influence. You are always personally responsible for the choices you make.

- **Media** A great deal of information comes to you through the media. Newspapers, magazines, radio, television, movies, and Web sites all present facts, fiction, and opinions. Much of the information is meant to influence your thinking and your choices. Awareness will help you deal with media influence.

- **Society and Culture** Your family, peers, and the media are just part of the larger society and culture in which you live. Cultural traditions, religious beliefs, societal expectations, and current trends can influence the choices you make.

- **Economic Factors** The options that families and individuals have when making decisions or solving problems may depend in part on their financial resources. Choices about how to spend and save money, in particular, are influenced by how much money there is. Good management can help you make the most of your financial resources.

✓ Reading Check **Contrast** What is the difference between values and ethics as an influence on choice?

The Decision-Making Process

Every choice has consequences. Sometimes the consequences are immediate and affect only you. Other times, they last a long time and also affect others. The consequences can be positive, negative, or a combination of the two. Before you make choices, think about their impact, or the effect that they have. The stronger the potential impact, the more thought you should put into the choice.

It is easy to overlook the impact of your choices on others. You want to act independently and make your own decisions. Though this is normal, remember that nearly every choice you make has an impact on others in some way.

Making decisions is a part of life. Some of the decisions you will make over the next few years are critical because they will give your life direction and purpose. As you enter adulthood, you will become responsible for all of your decisions. Your ability to make good decisions can have a significant impact on the quality of your life.

Fortunately, there is a process to help you make the best choices for each situation. The **decision-making process** is a six-step procedure for making thoughtful choices. Read the feature on page 168 to learn the six steps of the decision-making process.

Where Do Ethics Fit In?

You were introduced to the concept of ethics in Chapter 2. Now you are beginning to see how your code of ethics fits into your life and the lives of others. You must make choices about what is right and fair for all who are involved. How can you determine whether a decision is ethical? Try using the questions below. They can help you to apply an ethical standard to your choice or action.

- **What would happen if everyone made this choice?** This question helps you decide if you would be willing to accept the consequences if others made the choice or took the action.
- **What if I were the person being affected by this choice?** This question encourages you to switch roles with other people involved in your decision. If you were the person being affected by your choice, would you still see the choice as being fair?

Succeed in SCHOOL and LIFE

Take Time to Look Back

One of most overlooked parts of successful decision making is reviewing the results. This is especially important in the workplace, and it will help you become a more effective employee. Often, people make a decision and move on. But it is important to note the results of your actions and identify any issues encountered along the way. This allows you to learn from each experience and make any necessary adjustments for the next time.

Two Views One World

How Do You Make a Decision?

Some believe it is better to think every decision through thoroughly.
Others believe it is better to just follow your instincts and decide quickly.

Ethan: The best decisions I've made came after I learned the facts and thought things through. If I'm having trouble making a decision, it's usually a sign that I need more information. Sure, it takes time, but it saves time in the end because you don't waste time trying to undo bad decisions. When I consider the cost of making bad decisions, I know it's worth the effort and patience to think through each decision carefully.

Celina: Yes, it's important to think decisions through, but if you think about things for too long, you may miss opportunities. Also, if you try to think of every possibility, you may never make the decision. It's impossible to know for sure that every decision you make is right. But you don't want to spend your whole life over-thinking everything. Sometimes you just need to follow your instincts, make the decision, and hope for the best.

Seeing Both Sides
Do both teens take decision making seriously? What explains their differing methods? What compromise about making decisions might they agree to?

HOW TO .... Make Decisions

As you grow older and gain more responsibilities, your ability to make good decisions becomes more and more important. The six-step decision-making process can help you focus on the main issue, identify all possible courses of action, and choose wisely.

1. Identify the decision. You are more likely to make a good choice if you can clearly spell out what you are trying to decide. Why do you need to make a decision? What do you hope to accomplish? Who else will be affected by the decision?

2. List possible options. Gather the information that will help you make a good decision. You might want to do research or ask for advice. Then think of as many possible courses of action as you can.

3. Evaluate the pros and cons of each option. What would be the positive and negative results of each alternative? Remember to consider how others will be affected.

4. Make a choice. After carefully weighing the options, select the one that will have the most positive outcome overall.

5. Act on your decision. Identify what you need to do to put your decision into action. Then do it.

6. Evaluate your choice. Afterward, look back at the results of your decision. Did you make the best choice? How did your decision affect others? Accept responsibility for the results, and learn from them.

- **What would happen if my circumstances were slightly different and I made this choice?** This question checks to see whether your choice or action would be justified under other circumstances. If it is, the choice or action is probably ethical.
- **Which choice will have the most positive consequences for the most people?** This question focuses on what would happen to everyone involved as a result of your choice. The most ethical decision is the one with the most positive consequences.

Not understanding the impact of your choices can sometimes cause you to hurt others unintentionally. Christa, for example, decided to get a part-time job to earn some money. She got a job at the supermarket, working two afternoons a week. Her mom pointed out that taking the job meant that Christa could no longer watch her younger sister after school. As a result of Christa's decision, her mother had to arrange for her younger daughter to be taken care of by trusted neighbors two days a week.

Considering the impact of your decisions on others will help you make better choices. You are more likely to think through the consequences and possible outcomes and make the wisest choice. If Christa had thought through the impact of her choice, she might have arranged to work weekends instead of afternoons.

The decision-making process helps you focus on the main issue. It reminds you to find possible courses of action and to examine each one. Finally, you can improve your decision-making skills by evaluating the decision you made.

 Podcasts Access the Online Learning Center to download *Managing Life Skills* podcasts.

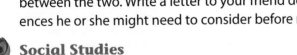

Section 9.1   After You Read

Review Key Concepts

1. **Review** the ways in which your family can influence your choices.

2. **Assess** how you can tell if a choice is ethical.

Practice Academic Skills

 English Language Arts

3. Imagine that a friend has been offered two different part-time jobs: one as a short-order cook at a restaurant and one as a commissioned salesperson at a clothing store. Your friend must make a choice between the two. Write a letter to your friend describing the influences he or she might need to consider before making the choice.

 Social Studies

4. Use online and print resources to examine the values of at least two cultures different from your own. What values do the other cultures have that are different from your own values? How could different values affect the choices that someone might make? Explain your answers in a two-page essay. Cite your sources.

Check Your Answers Check your answers at this book's Online Learning Center at **glencoe.com**.

NCTE 5   Use different writing process elements to communicate effectively.

NCSS I B   Predict how data and experiences may be interpreted by people from diverse cultural perspectives and frames of reference.

Solving Problems

Some problems are complicated and may require a process to solve.

Reading Guide

Before You Read

Create an Outline Use this section's heading titles to create an outline. Make the titles Level 1 main ideas. Add supporting information to create Level 2, 3, and 4 details. Use the outline to predict what you are about to learn.

Read to Learn
Key Concepts
- **List** the characteristics of a practical problem.
- **Summarize** the steps in the REASON process.

Main Idea

Practical problems have common characteristics and should be examined before taking action. The REASON process for problem solving can help you think through complicated problems.

Content Vocabulary

◇ practical problem
◇ context
◇ practical reasoning
◇ REASON process

Academic Vocabulary

You will find these words in your reading and on your tests. Use the glossary to look up their definitions if necessary.

■ aspect
■ reliable

Academic Standards

English Language Arts

NCTE 12 Use language to accomplish individual purposes.

Mathematics

NCTM Number and Operations Understand numbers, ways of representing numbers, relationships among numbers, and number systems.

Social Studies

NCSS IV G Individual Development and Identity Compare and evaluate the impact of stereotyping, conformity, acts of altruism, and other behaviors on individuals and groups.

NCTE *National Council of Teachers of English*
NCTM *National Council of Teachers of Mathematics*
NSES *National Science Education Standards*
NCSS *National Council for the Social Studies*

Graphic Organizer

As you read, you will discover four aspects of practical problems that you should examine. Use a herringbone organizer like the one shown to identify the four aspects.

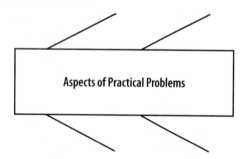

Aspects of Practical Problems

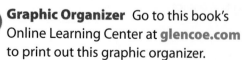

Graphic Organizer Go to this book's Online Learning Center at **glencoe.com** to print out this graphic organizer.

Practical Problems

The decision-making process is useful when you have a specific choice to make. Sometimes, however, you must deal with more than just a single decision. You may face a practical problem. A **practical problem** is a complex situation that has many elements and involves making several choices that are related to one another. Practical problems require thinking about values and ethics, not just facts. Learning how to solve practical problems is one of the most valuable life skills that you can have.

Jamal's dilemma is a good example of a practical problem. He feels that his father and his stepmother, Julie, expect him to do too many chores around the house. He works hard to keep up his grades, he is on the baseball team, and he has a part-time job. Jamal feels like whenever he tries to relax, his father or Julie find some other chore for him to do. Also, they often expect him to look after his stepbrother and his sister at a moment's notice. Jamal feels like they are asking too much of him.

Jamal usually does what his parents ask, but sometimes he feels like saying, "Why do all these chores have to be done right now? I just want to have a little time to myself." Jamal feels trapped and overwhelmed by his parents' expectations, and sometimes he feels like they are being unfair. However, he also realizes that his father and Julie work very hard and need to rely on him. He wants to please his parents. At the same time, he feels that he has a right to some free time. This is a good example of a practical problem because it has many aspects and no clear solution.

As You Read

Connect What complicated problems have you faced?

◆ Vocabulary

You can find definitions in the glossary at the back of this book.

▲ Practical Problems

Deciding what electives to take is a decision that affects other decisions. When you select one elective, you are giving up the chance to take others. *How did you decide to take the electives you are currently taking?*

Math For Success

Characteristics of Practical Problems

Have you ever, like Jamal, faced a complicated problem that left you feeling overwhelmed and confused? You will certainly face more as you confront any challenging **aspect**, or part, of your future. You will need to make decisions regarding college, your career, relationships, marriage, family, and more.

Although every practical problem is unique and different, they all share certain common characteristics:

- **Practical problems are complex.** They usually involve several different issues, and the way to deal with those issues is often unclear. To find a solution, you need to examine the issues. Jamal, for instance, is dealing with his role in his family, schoolwork, job expectations, involvement in sports, and time-management issues.

- **Practical problems have unique circumstances.** Two people with similar problems will approach the problems from different perspectives because of their unique circumstances. Jamal looks at his situation from the point of view of a young man whose life has been disrupted by divorce and the introduction of new family members—his stepmother Julie and a step brother. Julie's perspective, of course, is very different. She may feel like an outsider trying to fit in. Both people may also arrive at two different solutions, both of which may work or not work for each individual.

- **Practical problems affect others.** They may involve family, friends, classmates, coworkers, and even members of the community. Because of this, it is important to consider others' needs and feelings when resolving such problems. Jamal recognizes that his father and stepmother work long hours and depend on him. He has to consider the rest of the family as he works through his problem.

- **Practical problems involve ethical choices.** You must consider your ethics and values when determining what is the right thing to do. What ethical principles might affect Jamal's situation?

- **Practical problems require action.** They do not resolve themselves. You need to identify and weigh both the positive and negative consequences of each possible option. Only then can you make the best choice. After a choice is made, you must act to set the solution in motion.

Examine Practical Problems

When you are faced with a practical problem, start by examining the situation. You cannot get a complete picture of a situation unless you look at it from all angles. As you examine a practical problem, pay attention to the following four aspects of the problem.

Context

Just as no two people are exactly alike, no two practical problems are identical. Each problem has its own context to consider. **Context** refers to all of the conditions surrounding a problem or situation. To examine the context of the problem, ask yourself questions such as: What factors are influencing the situation? Of what aspects of this situation do I need to be aware? How do they affect the problem?

In Jamal's case, he is dealing with a situation in which both parents work and his siblings need care. He needs to consider those circumstances as he resolves the problem.

Desired Ends

Think about what ends, or outcomes, are desired. What conditions must be met for everyone involved to feel that the problem has been successfully resolved? Keep in mind that your values influence the outcome you want. The same is true of the others involved.

Means

Consider the means, or methods, that might be used to reach the desired ends. What are possible ways to achieve the desired outcome? For each possible strategy, think about who would take action, what resources could be used, and what steps would need to be taken.

Consequences

The actions taken will affect you and others. Ask yourself: What might be the positive and negative results of my actions? Who will be affected and how? What are the risks and benefits of each possible course of action?

This process of examining and asking questions about a practical problem is called **practical reasoning**. Unlike the decision-making process, practical reasoning is not a step-by-step method. Instead, you are likely to move back and forth among the aspects listed above as you work through the problem. Practical reasoning requires time and thought.

✓ **Reading Check** **Identify** When faced with a practical problem, what should you do first?

Be Smart Be Safe

Plan for Emergencies
Emergencies happen when you least expect them. Often you will have to decide how to respond in a split second. Thinking about how you should respond beforehand can help you be better prepared.

Write About It Write an emergency response plan in case there is a fire in your home. If you need help, look online for examples. Discuss your plan with your family.

Sources of Advice

One of the major influences in your life and on the choices you make is your family. *What do you think this means for practical problems in your life?*

Think Positively

Decision making can be viewed as positive or negative. Many scientists believe that keeping a positive outlook can help you reduce stress. Reducing stress can help to keep you healthy. You can think positively about a situation by focusing on positive aspects of the situation, by being around other people who think positively, and by finding humor in everyday life.

The REASON Process

Once you have examined a practical problem, you may find it helpful to use another problem-solving tool. The **REASON process** is similar to the decision-making process, but this tool is meant to help you think through and solve practical problems. You can remember the elements of this process by thinking of the word REASON. Each letter in the word represents one element in the process:

- **Recognize** the primary problem.
- **Evaluate** information.
- **Analyze** alternatives and consequences.
- **Select** the best choice.
- **Outline** and take action.
- **Note** the results of actions taken.

The best way to understand the REASON process is to see it being used. As you read about how Jamal solved his problem, notice how he used the different elements in the process and how they relate to one another.

Recognize the Primary Problem

A practical problem may involve several issues that are all tangled together, and it can be difficult to recognize which is the main problem. Try to identify the main issue or the root cause. Once you have identified it, make that your focus. Take the other factors into consideration, but do not get sidetracked by issues that are not really related to the main problem.

Life On Your Own

Tips for Solving Problems

No matter how careful you are in life, you are going to run into problems at some point. If you do not know how to solve your problems, you might become frustrated. This could lead to your reacting quickly instead of clearly thinking through the problem.

How It Works Clarify what the problem is, and confirm that your problem is not simply the result of a misunderstanding. It is important to get advice. Talk to people you trust to see what they think about the situation. If possible, calmly and rationally approach the individual with whom you have the problem. See if you can work together to resolve the problem. Be sure to listen to the other person. Be open to compromise.

Try It Out You were assigned a big project for class. You and a friend bounced ideas off each other, but you did your work separately. However, when you turn in your projects, the teacher feels there is too much similarity among the two projects. Your teacher wants you both to redo your projects.

> **Your Turn** If you were faced with this situation, how would you deal with it? Whom would you try to talk to first? What would you say? If that did not work, what would you do next?

When Jamal tried to analyze his situation, it took him a while to find the real issue. "This problem is really confusing," he thought. "It isn't just the chores they ask me to do. I feel like I'm continually racing around trying to keep up with homework, the team, my job, and my responsibilities at home. Maybe the problem is that I don't have time for everything."

As he thought about the time issue, he considered dropping baseball or his part-time job. Then he asked himself why he was always so frustrated and angry at home. Finally he realized that the main issue was really deeper. "I just want Dad and Julie to understand some of my needs," he thought. "It's really more about that than the other stuff."

Evaluate Information

Next, think about what information you need to solve the problem. Look for information from **reliable**, or trustworthy, sources. You do not need every available piece of information. You just need enough solid information to better understand your situation and make a choice.

Jamal thought about what information might help him see the problem more clearly. He grabbed a pen and paper and jotted down how much time he spends each week doing chores, and the amount of time he spends helping out with the kids. He also wrote down how much time he spends on himself, including study time, ball games and practice, and just relaxing. Jamal found that writing it all down gave him a more defined perspective.

Analyze Alternatives and Consequences

Think of what options you have. What are the short-term and long-term consequences of each option? How do your options fit in with your values, goals, priorities, and ethics? Consider both the positive and negative consequences for you and for others.

In addition to the notes he wrote to clarify the problem, Jamal listed some alternatives for finding a resolution to his problem:

- Do nothing for now, and just keep up the best I can.
- Ignore some of Dad's and Julie's requests and start living my own life.
- Tell Dad and Julie how I feel, and talk with them about negotiating new guidelines.

Over the next week, Jamal gathered information and continued to think through his alternatives. He made a chart showing the consequences of different options. **Figure 9.1** on the next page shows what his chart looked like.

Evaluate Your Options

The teen in this photo decided to learn how to knit her own sweaters to save money and have fun. *What information do you think she had to gather before pursuing this activity?*

Succeed in SCHOOL and LIFE

Write It Down

You are constantly exposed to all kinds of information. Even if are sure you will remember something, write it down. Writing things down gives you a written record you can refer to later. Also, the act of writing something down actually reinforces it in your memory. Write down notes, ideas, goals, problems, pro and con lists, assignments, due dates, and to-do lists.

Figure 9.1 **Jamal's Alternatives**

Examine Outcomes A chart like this can help you analyze the consequences of each alternative. *Why would you want to examine the consequences of each alternative?*

ALTERNATIVE	POSITIVE CONSEQUENCES	NEGATIVE CONSEQUENCES
Don't do anything now, but just keep up the best I can.	**+ Me:** Not much. I'll learn how to do various chores. **+ Family:** They'll reap the benefits of my work.	**– Me:** Anger and frustration; tension will increase; communication will decrease. **– Family:** They will not understand my anger and tension; problems could get worse.
Ignore their requests and start living my own life.	**+ Me:** I can do what I want when I want, and I have time to relax. **+ Family:** None.	**– Me:** I'll get into trouble for not doing chores when they want; constant conflict. **– Family:** They'll be frustrated and angry; there will be increased tension.
Tell Dad and Julie how I feel, and talk with them about negotiating new guidelines.	**+ Me:** I voice my concerns; I show I'm maturing and becoming more responsible; my family might understand. **+ Family:** They accept I'm growing up; we all work on relationships and expectations.	**– Me:** The time and energy needed to have conversation and work out solution. The solution might not be acceptable to me. **– Family:** They might resent my asking for time for myself.

Select the Best Choice

Which is the wisest choice for you? There may be more than one acceptable solution to the problem. Select an option that has a positive outcome for both you and others. Make sure it is workable for your situation and resources.

As he reflected on his options, Jamal said to himself, "The best and right choice is to talk with Dad and Julie. It won't be easy, though. I need to explain that with baseball and work, I have more demands on my time than I had last fall. The information I've gathered will help them see that. I hope they'll understand that I'm responsible and that I do help out, but that I need more control over how I plan and use my time. I know it's tough for Dad and Julie having to care for three of us and make enough money, but I'm sure we can work something out. I'm still willing to help, but things need to be handled differently."

Outline and Take Action

Once you have chosen an option, create a step-by-step plan to solve the problem. Identify and gather the resources you need to carry out your plan. Think about possible barriers to your plan and options for overcoming them.

Jamal decided to talk to his father and Julie on Sunday. That is usually the day they are most relaxed. He thought, "I'll have to think through how to tell them about my feelings so they will not get defensive. That will be my biggest challenge. I do not want to look like I'm complaining, but I do want to solve this problem."

Note the Results of Actions Taken

Finally, after you have made your decision and acted on it, look back on the outcome of your actions. Did they have positive results? If the results were not what you expected, think about how you could achieve a better outcome next time.

Several weeks after talking with his parents, Jamal looked back on how it went. "Dad and Julie really listened to what I had to say, and it has made a difference," he thought. "Now we have a plan for my weekly responsibilities. I make sure I get my chores done, and Dad and Julie make sure I have some time to relax. I don't feel nearly as stressed and frustrated anymore. All of us are doing better. I definitely made the right choice."

Jamal found that the REASON process was an effective tool for solving his practical problem. He also realized that resolving a problem can be a very satisfying experience. Not only did he solve some issues that were very important to him, but he also showed his parents that he is a caring, considerate, and responsible young adult on his way to independence.

When you work through a decision or problem, use the tools you have learned about to make the wisest choice for yourself and others. When you do this, you will build character, gain knowledge and wisdom, learn about yourself, and develop the ability to make wise choices.

It is important to consider the consequences of everything you do. Keep environmental consequences in mind as you go through your daily routine to discover small changes you can make. For example, taking shorter showers will reduce water use and lower your water bills.

 Podcasts Access the Online Learning Center to download *Managing Life Skills* podcasts.

Section 9.2 After You Read

Review Key Concepts

1. **Analyze** how examining the desired ends helps you deal with a practical problem.

2. **Describe** the conditions you must consider when you select the best choice for a problem.

Practice Academic Skills

 English Language Arts

3. Think of a practical problem you recently had and how you solved it. Create a list of the steps you used to solve the problem. Relate each of your steps to the steps of the REASON process. Then write a paragraph about the alternatives you examined and the results of the action you took. Include what you might do differently next time.

 Social Studies

4. Stereotypes toward individuals or groups can slow or stop the problem-solving process. Conduct research on stereotypes, and write a paragraph explaining what they are and how they might hinder the ability to find a solution to a problem.

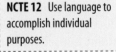 **Check Your Answers** Check your answers at this book's Online Learning Center at **glencoe.com**.

NCTE 12 Use language to accomplish individual purposes.

NCSS IV G Compare and evaluate the impact of stereotyping, conformity, acts of altruism, and other behaviors on individuals and groups.

Pathway to Your Career

Bank Teller

What Does a Bank Teller Do?

Bank tellers are employees who receive and pay out money. They cash checks, accept deposits and loan payments, and process withdrawals. Tellers give out cash during the day and are responsible for its safe and accurate handling. They sell savings bonds and travelers' checks and they sometimes accept payment for customers' utility bills and charge cards.

Career Readiness Skills Being a teller requires care, organization, and attention to detail to avoid and recognize errors. They must have strong mathematics skills and be comfortable handling large amounts of money. They should enjoy interacting with the public and have strong customer service skills.

Education and Training Bank tellers usually have a high school diploma, but a college degree is often not required. However, a degree in a related field, such as business or accounting, will make the employee more competitive. Office or customer service work experience can be helpful, as can knowledge of word processing and spreadsheet software. Bank tellers often get on-the-job training.

Job Outlook Employment of tellers is expected to grow about as fast as the average for all occupations. Job openings will increase as banks open new offices and stay open longer. However, automation and technology will reduce the need for tellers who perform only routine transactions.

Critical Thinking Find a bank online or in your community. Call its human resources department, and ask for a job description of a bank teller. Write a paragraph to summarize your findings. Then describe how you imagine a typical day at work for a bank teller.

Career Cluster

CCR ☆ College & Career Readiness

Finance Bank tellers work in the Banking & Related Services pathway of the Finance career cluster. Here are some other jobs in this career cluster:

- Loan Officer
- Auditor
- Credit Report Provider
- Controller
- Claims Investigator
- Underwriter
- Personal Financial Advisor
- Loan Processor
- Operations Manager
- Economist
- Investment Advisor
- Repossession Agent
- Debt Counselor
- Treasurer
- Credit Analyst
- Title Researcher

Explore Further The Finance career cluster contains four pathways: Financial & Investment Planning; Business Financial Management; Banking & Related Services; and Insurance Services. Choose one of these pathways to explore further.

 Career Clusters To learn more about career clusters, go to this book's Online Learning Center at **glencoe.com**.

CHAPTER SUMMARY

Section 9.1
Making Decisions

You face problems and make decisions every day. Being proactive will help you make good choices and act on them. Influences on choices include attitude, emotions, values, goals, priorities, ethics, family, peers, media, society, culture, and economic factors. The choices you make can have an impact on you and on others. Ask yourself questions to determine if a choice is ethical.

Section 9.2
Solving Problems

Practical problems are complex, have unique circumstances, affect others, involve ethical choices, and require action. Practical problems should be examined for context, desired ends, means, and consequences. The REASON process can help you think through and solve problems. Resolving problems and making wise choices can help you build character and gain knowledge.

Vocabulary Review

1. Create a fill-in-the-blank sentence for each of these vocabulary terms. The sentence should contain enough information to help determine the missing word.

   Content Vocabulary
   ◇ dilemma (p. 165)
   ◇ decision-making process (p. 167)
   ◇ practical problem (p. 171)
   ◇ context (p. 173)
   ◇ practical reasoning (p. 173)
   ◇ REASON process (p. 174)

   Academic Vocabulary
   ■ foundation (p. 166)
   ■ impact (p. 166)
   ■ aspect (p. 172)
   ■ reliable (p. 175)

Review Key Concepts

2. **Describe** the different influences on choices.
3. **Outline** the decision-making process.
4. **List** the characteristics of a practical problem.
5. **Summarize** the steps in the REASON process.

Critical Thinking

6. **Examine** Find a print or online advertisement. How does the ad try to influence your thinking and choices?
7. **Interview** Ask a friend or family member how he or she solves problems. Compare his or her method with the REASON process.
8. **Predict** What do you think might happen if you decided not to consider the impact on others of alternative solutions to problems?
9. **Conclude** Which influence on choices do you think is most important?
10. **Propose Solutions** Your friend is considering cheating on a test. Is this decision ethical? What other, better solutions could you propose?
11. **Analyze** You want to get a part-time job, but your parents worry it may harm your schoolwork. What is the context of this problem? What would you need to consider before deciding on a solution?

ACTIVE LEARNING

12. Influences on Choice Survey five people about which of the following they think is the most important influence on choices we often have to make: attitude, emotions, values, ethics, family, peers, media, society, or economics. Figure out what percent of the people surveyed named each style. Make a bar chart of the results. What conclusions can you draw from the survey results? Write a summary to explain.

Family & Community Connections

13. Ask a Counselor One of the hardest things about solving a problem can be to identify what the primary problem is. Find a school, peer, or professional counselor in your area. Ask him or her for advice about the best ways to recognize the primary problem in a complex situation. What questions does he or she suggest people ask themselves? What suggestions can he or she give you about how you can tell that you have identified the primary problem? Take notes during your discussion, and then write a brief report on your interview, summarizing what you learned.

21st Century Skills

Financial Literacy Skills

14. Charity Programs Imagine that you volunteered to donate money to have brochures made for a charity event. The event is in two weeks, and the cost to have the brochures made by a professional will be $100. You make $35 per week at your part-time job. Do you have enough money to make the programs? If not, what other suggestions can you offer?

Technology Skills

15. Internet Problem-Solving Resources Follow your teacher's instructions to do an Internet search on problem-solving resources. What types of resources did you find? What type of advice did they offer? Make a list of the resources, and write a paragraph explaining any differences between the advice given by the resources and the problem-solving tools discussed in this chapter.

FCCLA Connections

Self-Management Skills

16. Avoid Snap Decisions As part of its mission, FCCLA encourages students to make careful decisions and assume responsibilities. You have learned that practical problems require careful thinking to find a good solution. Sometimes, however, our emotions cause us to make snap decisions, or decisions made quickly without consideration. How can you keep emotions from taking over a problem-solving process to avoid snap decisions? Write a paragraph to explain.

Academic Skills

English Language Arts

17. Rate Yourself Choose five decisions you made recently. For each, list everyone who was affected. By each name, put a plus sign if the decision's impact was positive or a minus sign for a negative impact. Rate yourself on how well you considered the effects of your choices. Write a paper explaining the rating.

> **NCTE 7** Conduct research and gather, evaluate, and synthesize data to communicate discoveries.

Science

18. Examine a Problem Regular exercise should be an important part of everyone's life. However, many people do not get enough exercise. This can have adverse effects on their health.

Procedure Conduct research on the effects of not getting enough exercise.

Analysis Make a chart showing what can happen if you do not get enough exercise. Include tips on how to add exercise to everyday activities.

> **NSES A** Develop understandings about scientific inquiry.

Mathematics

19. Calculate a Budget Budgets are important. They can help you avoid money problems. Imagine you are making a budget. You determine that your basic needs require 75 percent of your monthly income. The items you list as "wants" cost another 15 percent. Your monthly income is $2,000. How much are you spending on wants?

 Percent A percent is a ratio that compares a number to 100.

Starting Hint You can rewrite the percent (15%) as a fraction. When doing this, 15 is the numerator and 100 is the denominator. Convert the fraction to a decimal. Multiply this decimal by the $2,000. Remember to put the decimal point in the correct place in your answer.

 For more math practice, go to the Math Appendix at the back of the book.

> **NCTM Number and Operations** Understand numbers, ways of representing numbers, relationships among numbers, and number systems.

 Standardized Test Practice

CCR College & Career Readiness

OPEN-ENDED RESPONSE
An open-ended response requires more than a yes or no answer. It can usually be answered with one or two sentences. Write one or two sentences to answer the questions.

Test-Taking Tip Open-ended test questions most often require a specific response rather than an opinion. They may include definitions, comparisons, or examples.

20. How do proactive people respond to problems?

21. What are ethics?

22. What is the definition of a practical problem?

Chapter 10

Manage Time and Money

Chapter Objectives

Section 10.1 Manage Time

- **Identify** the steps in making a to-do list.
- **Compare and contrast** procrastination and over scheduling.
- **Summarize** the importance of managing leisure time.

Section 10.2 Manage Money

- **Describe** the importance of managing money.
- **Define** financial discipline.
- **List** the categories in a budget.

> ➤ **Explore the Photo**
>
> Time and money are important resources. *Why is it important to carefully manage resources like time and money?*

Writing Activity

Write a First Draft

Procrastination When you procrastinate, you put something off until later that could be done now. Procrastination can cause problems, such as:

- It costs time and money.
- It keeps you from focusing on more important tasks.
- It makes you feel stressed.

Write a first draft of a one-page paper that describes a person who procrastinates too much. Offer suggestions to the person to help him or her complete tasks on time.

Writing Tips Use these tips to help you write a first draft:

- Arrange your ideas in an order that makes sense.
- Organize your draft into paragraphs.
- Make sure that each paragraph is organized around one main idea.

Manage Time

Manage time wisely to achieve your goals.

Before You Read

Prepare with a Partner Before you read, work with a partner. Read the titles of the heads, and ask each other questions about the topics that will be discussed. Write down the questions you both have about each section. As you read, answer the questions you have identified.

Read to Learn
Key Concepts

- **Identify** the steps in making a to-do list.
- **Compare and contrast** procrastination and over scheduling.
- **Summarize** the importance of managing leisure time.

Main Idea

Identify responsibilities and goals, make a do-to list, establish priorities, and make a schedule to plan your time. Avoid procrastination and over scheduling. Manage your leisure time wisely.

Graphic Organizer

As you read, look for five strategies used by efficient time managers. Use a description wheel like the one shown to help you list the strategies.

Time Management Strategies

Graphic Organizer Go to this book's Online Learning Center at **glencoe.com** to print out this graphic organizer.

Content Vocabulary

◇ task management
◇ responsibility
◇ deadline
◇ over scheduling
◇ dovetail

Academic Vocabulary

You will find these words in your reading and on your tests. Use the glossary to look up their definitions if necessary.

■ motivation
■ interfere

Academic Standards

English Language Arts

NCTE 2 Read literature to build an understanding of the human experience.

Mathematics

NCTM Number and Operations Understand the meanings of operations and how they relate to one another.

Social Studies

NCSS IV F Individual Development and Identity Analyze the role of perceptions, attitudes, values, and beliefs in the development of personal identity.

NCTE *National Council of Teachers of English*
NCTM *National Council of Teachers of Mathematics*
NSES *National Science Education Standards*
NCSS *National Council for the Social Studies*

Taming the To-Do List

Have you ever noticed that some people seem to have more time than others? That is because they understand time management and know how to make the best use of their time. Experts in time management have developed techniques that work and can be learned and used by anyone. Even if you manage time well already, you most likely still have room to improve.

An important part of time management is task management. **Task management** means keeping track of the tasks you need and want to accomplish and making sure you complete them. This includes creating a to-do list, or task list, and keeping it under control. By studying time management and learning from others, you can quickly learn how to manage your to-do list.

Identify Responsibilities and Goals

Before making a to-do list, look at the big picture, considering what you need and want to accomplish. Think about different areas of your life, such as family, school, job, friends, and personal life. For each area, identify your responsibilities and goals.

A **responsibility** is a task you are required to do. Responsibilities at home might include preparing dinner, caring for a sibling, or doing household chores. You also need to schedule time for school responsibilities, such as homework and studying. It also takes time to maintain friendships and family relationships. Personal care responsibilities, such as getting enough sleep, eating well, and exercising, also affect your schedule. All these responsibilities guide the way you use your time.

You also have goals you want to accomplish in the different areas of your life. These affect how you manage your time, too. For example, someone who wants to maintain a strong relationship with a faraway friend finds time to stay in touch through letters, phone calls, or e-mail. A person who wants to become a better swimmer schedules time for practice. A student whose goal is to achieve a high test score spends time preparing for the exam. In each situation, a goal is the underlying **motivation** for, or driving force behind, the activity.

As You Read

Connect How many responsibilities do you have at home and at school?

◆ **Vocabulary**

You can find definitions in the glossary at the back of this book.

> **Working Toward a Goal**
>
> Having a goal to work toward, such as getting a promotion at work, provides an incentive to use your time wisely. *How do your goals influence the way you spend your time?*

Creating a To-Do List

A to-do list can help you organize your time better. *What types of items should go on a to-do list?*

Make a To-Do List

A to-do list helps you keep track of your responsibilities and goals. How and when you make your list is up to you. Some people use electronic planners, while others keep to-do lists written down on paper.

Whatever method you choose, be sure to update your list regularly. Some people update their lists daily, others weekly. Write down everything that you need to accomplish. You may wish to organize your list into categories, such as school assignments, chores, and so on. If a project on your list seems too big or overwhelming, break it down into smaller tasks.

Establish Priorities

Few people have time to do everything they want to do. That is why they set priorities. They decide which tasks are most important and focus on them first. To do this, they look at deadlines. A **deadline** is a time or date by which a task must be completed. For example, a task with an immediate deadline usually has a higher priority than a task with a later deadline or no fixed schedule.

A simple way to prioritize is to decide whether tasks must be done, should be done, or are optional. Do tasks that must be done first, because they have a high priority. Then, as time permits, you can work on tasks that should be done. Finally, if you still have time, you can work on the optional tasks. Low-priority items may eventually be given a higher priority on future lists.

Plan Your Schedule

Once you have identified your responsibilities and goals, made your to-do list, and established your priorities, you can plan your schedule. Use a calendar to keep track of things that must happen at specific times, such as a dentist appointment or team practice. Plan each day by looking at both your calendar and your to-do list. First, see what is scheduled on your calendar. Then choose one or more tasks from your list to accomplish, based on priorities and time available. Plan a specific time to do them. Try to give yourself some flexibility in case a task takes longer than expected. After you have completed a task, check it off on your to-do list. You will feel good when you see how much you have accomplished.

✓ **Reading Check** **Explain** How do deadlines affect priorities on to-do lists?

Use Time Wisely

Keeping track of tasks is just one part of time management. You also need to make the best use of the time you have. Not every day needs to be loaded with accomplishments, but too much wasted time can keep you from reaching goals.

Try to identify your personal time traps. Do you spend too much time talking or texting on the phone, Web surfing, or watching television? It is okay to include relaxing activities in your routine, but when they **interfere** with, or negatively affect, the rest of your life, you need to make some changes. That means avoiding time traps and using strategies that work.

Time Traps to Avoid

Time traps prevent you from using your time effectively. Two of the most common time traps are procrastination and over scheduling.

Procrastination

People often put off doing tasks that they dislike. As you learned in Chapter 1, this tendency to put off doing something until later is called procrastination. Why is procrastination a problem? When you put things off, you are more likely to have to rush through them at the last minute. When you rush, you are more likely to make mistakes or do a poor job. Here are some tips that will help you avoid procrastination:

- **Do unpleasant tasks first.** You will feel better knowing they are out of the way.
- **Do your best to avoid distractions and interruptions.** These can often be hard to resist. Make an effort to stay focused.
- **Set up a schedule.** This can help you beat the urge to put them off. Give yourself a time limit.
- **Take a small step to get started.** If something seems overwhelming, divide it into smaller steps.

Succeed in SCHOOL and LIFE

Get Organized

Being disorganized wastes time and energy. If you are constantly forgetting homework assignments or trying to find a specific book, you are not getting things accomplished. Try some of these tips:

- Use color-coded folders and notebooks.
- Use clear book covers.
- Organize your locker.
- Develop a daily schedule.
- Keep your workspace neat and clean.

> ### A Sense of Accomplishment
>
> Finishing the tasks on your to-do list will give you a sense of accomplishment. *What should you do once you finish a to-do list task?*

Over Scheduling

As a musician, Geoff was always eager to get involved in anything musical that was going on. At the beginning of the school year, he joined the orchestra and also signed up for keyboard lessons. Later, when some classmates auditioned for a musical and asked him to accompany them, he agreed to do so. Soon Geoff realized that it was all too much.

Trying to accomplish too many things in a limited amount of time is called **over scheduling**. Over scheduling is a problem for many people. They end up with so much to do that they cannot do anything well. They feel overwhelmed and stressed out. It is better to be realistic about how much you can do with your time than to find yourself overloaded.

If over scheduling is a problem for you, learn how to say no. Practice responses that allow you to decline gracefully. You might say something like, "I'm sorry, but I just cannot take on another project right now." Then stick to your decision.

Time-Tested Strategies

Efficient time managers avoid the time traps you have just read about. Here are some other strategies they practice and recommend:

- **Be Prepared and Organized** Before you begin a task, think about what you need to accomplish it. It does not need to be complicated. For example, when you are cleaning your room, take the vacuum cleaner and dusting supplies with you on one trip. Making several trips for supplies slows you down.
- **Allow Enough Time** Mistakes are more likely to occur when you rush through tasks. Doing a task right the first time usually takes less time than doing it over again.
- **Dovetail Activities** When you **dovetail** (ˈdəv-ˌtāl) activities, you overlap them to save time. For example, if you have to go to the bank and buy groceries, do both errands in one trip.
- **Be Realistic** Understand what you can accomplish given your time and resources. Do not set impossible goals. Schedule tasks that can be accomplished in the time you have available.
- **Be Flexible** Not everything goes as planned. If you are flexible, you can adjust your schedule to include unexpected events.

✓ **Reading Check** **Define** What is a time trap?

Value Others' Time

One way to show respect to others is to value their time. Be on time when you meet a friend or arrive for an appointment. If you are delayed and have to keep someone waiting, call ahead and let the person know. This way, he or she can make other plans instead of spending time waiting for you.

You Decide

Being on time is just one way to show that you respect another's time. What are some other ways? Write a list.

Manage Leisure Time

You might think that leisure time does not require any time management. It is easy to relax and have fun, right? Yet many people are so busy that they do not relax. Leisure is an important part of a balanced lifestyle, and good time managers make sure that they include relaxation in their schedules. They also make sure that they get the most out of their leisure time. If you have ever spent an afternoon watching television but later wished that you had done something more fulfilling, you will understand the need to manage leisure time.

When you plan your leisure time, include time to spend alone as well as time with family members and friends. Then figure out how you want to spend the time. Choose activities that relax and refresh you. You may need to set aside a couple of hours for some activities, such as working on a puzzle, sketching, or going on a bike ride. Others activities, such as writing a letter or calling a friend, can be done in smaller amounts of time. The key to managing leisure time is balance. Give yourself enough time to relax, but not so much time that you fail to meet your responsibilities.

Podcasts Access the Online Learning Center to download *Managing Life Skills* podcasts.

Section 10.1 After You Read

Review Key Concepts

1. **Give examples** of how to prioritize items on a to-do list.
2. **Explain** how to keep from over scheduling your time.
3. **Describe** what might happen if you do not schedule your leisure time.

Practice Academic Skills

English Language Arts

4. Reading can be a good activity when you have extra leisure time. Find a short story that you enjoy reading. Reread the story, and think about why you enjoy the story and how you feel after reading it. Then write two paragraphs explaining why you enjoy the story and how this enjoyment can serve you in your leisure time.

Social Studies

5. Time management priorities can change over time. Create two priority lists: one that shows the priorities of a high school student and one that shows the priorities of an adult who is living alone with a full-time job. Compare the two lists. How are the priorities different? What do these differences say about how priorities change? Write a paragraph to explain your answer.

Check Your Answers Check your answers at this book's Online Learning Center at **glencoe.com**.

> **NCTE 2** Read literature to build an understanding of the human experience.

> **NCSS IV F** Analyze the role of perceptions, attitudes, values, and beliefs in the development of personal identity.

Manage Money

Using a budget can help you manage your money.

Reading Guide

Before You Read

What You Want to Know Write a list of what you want to know about this section. As you read, write down the heads in this section that provide that information.

Read to Learn

Key Concepts
- **Describe** the importance of managing money.
- **Define** financial discipline.
- **List** the categories in a budget.

Main Idea

Your personality affects the way you manage money. Know your priorities to create financial goals. A budget can help you keep track of how you earn and spend money.

Content Vocabulary
◇ budget
◇ income
◇ expenses

Academic Vocabulary

You will find these words in your reading and on your tests. Use the glossary to look up their definitions if necessary.

■ spontaneous
■ discipline

Academic Standards

English Language Arts

NCTE 7 Conduct research and gather, evaluate, and synthesize data to communicate discoveries.

Social Studies

NCSS V C Individuals, Groups, and Institutions
Describe the various forms institutions take, and explain how they develop and change over time.

Graphic Organizer

As you read, you will discover information on short-term and long-term financial goals. Use a main idea chart like the one shown. In the third box, describe each type of goal. In the fourth box, list an example.

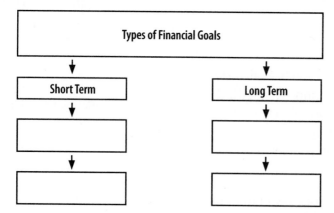

Types of Financial Goals → Short Term → Long Term

Graphic Organizer Go to this book's Online Learning Center at **glencoe.com** to print out this graphic organizer.

NCTE *National Council of Teachers of English*
NCTM *National Council of Teachers of Mathematics*
NSES *National Science Education Standards*
NCSS *National Council for the Social Studies*

Money Matters

Just like time, when you manage your money wisely, you seem to have more of it. Right now you might not have much money to manage, but it is not too early to start learning. Careful money management enables you to:

- live within your means.
- meet goals to purchase special items.
- prepare for financial emergencies.
- gain and maintain a sense of financial independence.

Attitudes Toward Money

Personality and attitude affect the way people manage money. People who are cautious by nature are careful about spending money and generally find it easy to save. Those who are more **spontaneous** (spän-'tā-nē-əs), or impulsive, may spend more freely and save less.

Attitudes affect the way people manage money. For some people, money provides a sense of security. Knowing that money is there to pay bills and cover financial emergencies is comforting.

Other people use money to satisfy their desire for power or status. They use money to acquire possessions and even more money. It is important to never allow money, or a lack of money, to determine one's value as a person.

✓ **Reading Check**   **Explain** What can good money management enable you to do?

Financial Priorities and Goals

Managing your money effectively starts with examining your goals and priorities. With priorities, needs must always come first. As a teen you probably do not have to pay for groceries, utilities, and housing, but once you live on your own, you will.

If you have money left after meeting your needs, you can decide on your next priorities. To do that, you must consider your values. Which is more important to you: saving for college or buying a used car? Would you rather buy new clothes or save for a vacation? Would you prefer to spend less on rent by sharing an apartment or spend more to have a place of your own?

As You Read

Connect On what types of things do you spend your money?

Vocabulary

You can find definitions in the glossary at the back of this book.

Money Management

Learning the basics of money management now will help you prepare for more responsibility in the future. *How will your financial responsibilities grow as you get older?*

You need to understand your own attitudes toward money. This will allow you to plan better and help prevent you from making poor financial decisions. When you need to make money decisions together with others, such as a roommate or spouse, it is important to recognize and respect other people's attitudes, especially when they differ from your own.

Look at your values and priorities to establish financial goals. You will have both short- and long-term goals. Short-term goals, such as a buying a new outfit, are less expensive and can be met in a short period of time. Long-term financial goals, such as paying for college, are more costly and may take months or years to meet.

Working Toward a Goal

Keeping a budget allows you to more easily work toward your goals. *What financial goals can you use a budget to reach?*

One Step at a Time

Every day you receive many messages about ways to spend your money. Advertisers work hard to persuade you to buy things you do not need. It may be tempting to wear the latest fashions or to see new movies as soon as they are released. Right now, with few financial responsibilities, you may be able to spend freely on such wants. Once you are living on your own, though, you might have to do without them sometimes. Developing financial **discipline**, or self-control, now will make it easier for you to manage your money later.

Having financial discipline means taking care of needs before wants. It means being patient and thinking carefully about your purchases. When you are disciplined, you acquire wants gradually and thoughtfully and save money for future needs.

✔ **Reading Check** **Interpret** How might advertisers affect your spending habits?

Using a Budget

Good money managers use a budget to help them plan and track their spending. A **budget** is a plan for spending and saving money. If you have a budget, you are more likely to spend and save wisely. A budget will also help you avoid running out of money between your allowance or paycheck. You can use a computer and financial software for budgeting, but a pencil, paper, and a calculator can work just as well. To create a budget, you need to evaluate and track your income and expenses. You must then keep up your budget to make sure that you are spending and saving as planned.

Be Smart Be Safe

Use ATMs Safely Automated teller machines (ATMs) make depositing and withdrawing money from your bank easy. However, ATMs can also be dangerous, as criminals sometimes use them as an opportunity to rob people.

Write About It Research tips for using ATMs safely. What should you do and not do while using ATMs to decrease the chance that someone will try to rob you?

Estimate Income

Your **income** is the money you make. It might come from an allowance, take-home pay from full- or part-time jobs, or odd jobs. List your sources of income and the amount for each for the same period of time, either weekly or monthly. If your income varies, estimate the average amount.

Estimate Expenses

Expenses are the items on which you spend money. The best way to be sure you do not overlook expenses is to track where your money goes for a period of time. Record every item on which you spend money and how much it cost. Two types of expenses are:

- **Fixed Expenses** These are expenses that do not vary in amount and that you must pay regularly. Examples include car payments, insurance premiums, and your phone bill.
- **Flexible Expenses** These expenses vary in amount and are less predictable. They include school supplies and clothes as well as optional items, such as movies.

After tracking your expenses for a period of time, group them into categories like clothing, entertainment, and gifts. Total each category. Use this information to decide how much to allow for each spending category in your budget. You may be surprised by how much you spend on certain items. Remember that the expenses you recorded during one week or month might not reflect all your expenses over time. Build extra room in your budget for savings and for unexpected expenses.

Health & Wellness TIPS

Spend to Save

Finding ways to save money is a good idea, but there are some areas where you should not pinch pennies. Avoiding the doctor to save money is a bad idea that could be dangerous. A serious illness usually costs more than preventive care. Going to the doctor for regular checkups actually saves money in the end.

Life On Your Own

Consider Costs and Benefits

Every decision has costs and benefits that need to be considered. Looking at your options can reveal which offers the most benefits at the lowest cost. For example, if you are trying to decide whether to take piano lessons, the costs would be paying for the lessons and the time spent practicing. The skill you acquire and the pleasure you get from playing would be the benefits.

How It Works When you weigh various options, look at all the costs and benefits, including money, time, effort, enjoyment, and what you might have to give up. Keep in mind that some of these costs and benefits will matter more than others, depending on the situation and your priorities. Ask yourself what each cost or benefit is worth to you, both now and over time. Be sure to consider how others will be affected as well.

Try It Out Mitch has a two-person lawn care business. It is almost spring, and Mitch is worried that his old lawnmower will not last the summer. The new, more powerful model he wants is more than he can afford right now. One option is to buy the mower with his credit card, but it would take him six months to pay off the balance, and he would have to pay interest. His other option, saving enough money to pay cash, would take four months. Competition for clients is fierce, and Mitch knows that if he loses customers, he might not get them back.

> **Your Turn** Thinking about Mitch's situation, list all of the potential costs and benefits you can think of for each of his options. Given his situation, what would you advise him to do? Explain why.

Plan for Savings

Savings should be listed as an item under expenses in your budget. Many people say they are going to save, but do not get around to it. Others say they will save whatever they have left over at the end of a week, but then find that nothing is left over. The best way to create savings is to treat them like any other expense. Act like savings are a mandatory part of your budget, another one of your fixed expenses. This way, you will build up savings that will be available in case you have unexpected expenses or an emergency or want to make a big purchase. If you have an expensive goal in mind, such as college or a vacation, you will need to save even more.

Balance the Budget

To balance your budget, compare your total income to your total expenses. If your income is greater than your expenses, you can spend or save the excess. If your income is less than your expenses, look for ways to increase your income or reduce your expenses. A sample monthly budget is shown in **Figure 10.1**.

As part of preparing a budget, ask yourself whether or not you are satisfied with the way you have been spending your money. You may decide that you should reduce the amount of one or more of your flexible expenses. For example, you might decide you are going to try to bring a packed lunch from home three days a week instead of eating at the cafeteria. Doing this will allow you to save the money you would have spent on lunches from the cafeteria. This will mean you can save more money that you can use to reach a long-term goal.

A realistic budget is one that you can actually follow. For example, if you think you spend too much on snacks, do not try to eliminate all snacks from your diet. Instead, reduce the amount you allow yourself to spend. Avoid buying snacks from vending machines and bring healthful snacks from home. By doing this, you can save money and improve your health.

Figure 10.1 Sample Monthly Budget

Balancing Budgets A simple budget helps you plan your income and expenses and keep them balanced. *What is meant by a balanced budget?*

INCOME		FIXED EXPENSES		FLEXIBLE EXPENSES	
Allowance	$70	Savings	$30	School lunches	$30
Paycheck	$250	Cell phone bill	$45	Food away from home	$20
		Payment to parents for guitar	$15	Entertainment	$20
		Guitar lessons	$50	Gifts	$10
		Car payment to parents	$100	Clothing	$30
TOTAL INCOME: $320		**TOTAL EXPENSES: $350**			

Choose How to Spend Money

Making a budget is all about making choices. *What choices were likely made by this teen to save for the down payment on a car?*

Follow Your Plan

A budget is useful only if you follow it. Once you have set up your budget, continue to record your income and expenses. Set aside time each week or month to compare your actual income and expenses with your budget. Constantly review your budget to see if you need to make adjustments. Reviewing your income and expenses regularly makes it easier to stay in control of your spending and see where your money goes. By following your budget, you can make sure that you do not live beyond your means and can save for future needs.

Maintaining a budget is easy once you get used to it. It is easier to learn money management skills now, when you have fewer funds to manage. This means you will be well prepared for the more complex money management you will need to do in the future. You will learn more about financial management in Chapter 14.

 Podcasts Access the Online Learning Center to download *Managing Life Skills* podcasts.

Section 10.2   After You Read

Review Key Concepts

1. **Discuss** how someone who is spontaneous or impulsive with money might behave.
2. **Determine** what priorities should come first when managing money.
3. **Explain** why you should review your income and expenses regularly.

Check Your Answers Check your answers at this book's Online Learning Center at **glencoe.com**.

Practice Academic Skills

 English Language Arts

4. Follow your teacher's instructions to go online and investigate budgeting software. Take notes about what the software can do. Then create an advertisement for budgeting software using information from the notes you took. Include benefits that potential buyers would get from creating a budget in your ad, using information from this section. Turn in the ad and your notes to your teacher.

NCTE 7 Conduct research and gather, evaluate, and synthesize data to communicate discoveries.

 Social Studies

5. Use Internet and print resources to research bankruptcy. Find a case of a company that went through a bankruptcy, and examine the reasons why the bankruptcy was necessary. Write a summary about what bankruptcy is, and describe the company's story.

NCSS V C Describe the various forms institutions take, and explain how they develop and change over time.

College Counseling

What Is College Counseling?

Part of your school guidance counselor's job is to walk you through the many steps of the college application process. Planning and preparing for college can be overwhelming. Your guidance counselor will use his or her valuable experience and knowledge to make sure nothing is missed and all options are explored.

When should I start talking to my guidance counselor about college?
It is never too early! Talking to your guidance counselor while in high school can be very helpful. He or she can help you plan a course of study with your educational goals in mind. However, it is also never too late. Your guidance counselor will be able to help you, no matter what stage of the process you are in.

What are some questions I should ask my guidance counselor?
There are many questions you might want to ask your guidance counselor, including: What courses are required and recommended for college preparation? What do I need to do to prepare for the SAT®/ACT®? What kinds of grades do different colleges require? What activities can I do on my own to get ready for college? Are there any college fairs nearby? Do you have any information to help me start exploring my interests?

In what ways can my guidance counselor help me prepare for college?
Guidance counselors can help in many ways. They can help you select your classes, keeping your goals in mind. If necessary, they can help you come up with a plan to improve your grades. They can give you information on how to prepare for the SAT/ACT. They can help you review your transcript to make sure you are on track, and they can help you with your college application essays and recommendations.

Hands-On

College Readiness Imagine you are going to speak with your school guidance counselor about college for the first time. Think about what you would want to talk about and what questions you would want to ask. Write a list of these topics and questions. Your list of questions should include at least some that are not listed on this page.

Path to Success

CCR ☆ **College & Career Readiness**

Start Early Factor in additional time for unanticipated errors and delays and to make sure your plan is strategized well in advance of your graduation.

Be Responsible While a guidance counselor can help, it is up to you to take control of your future.

Be Organized Make a chart to keep track of each college's requirements, and mark a calendar with your application deadlines.

Ask Questions Your guidance counselor is there to answer your questions, no matter what they might be.

Reach Out While your guidance counselor might contact you, do not wait for this to happen. Take the initiative and proactively seek help.

Relax! The college application process can be stressful. Try not to let it get you down.

 Go to this book's Online Learning Center at **glencoe.com** to learn more about college and career readiness.

CHAPTER SUMMARY

Section 10.1
Manage Time

Using time management and task management techniques can help keep you organized. First, identify your responsibilities and goals. Use these to create a daily or weekly to-do list. You may wish to organize your to-do list using priorities such as deadlines. Use the to-do list to plan a schedule for each day. Avoid time traps such as procrastinating and over scheduling. Manage your leisure time, too.

Section 10.2
Manage Money

Your personality and attitude affect how you manage money. Needs should always come first when deciding on priorities. Use values and goals to establish your financial priorities. You must have financial discipline to keep from spending too much. A budget can help you plan for spending and saving. Budgets list income and expenses and should be balanced. Follow through with your budget.

Vocabulary Review

1. Use these content and academic vocabulary terms to create a crossword puzzle on graph paper. Use the definitions as clues.

Content Vocabulary
◇ task management (p. 185)
◇ responsibility (p. 185)
◇ deadline (p. 186)
◇ over scheduling (p. 188)
◇ dovetail (p. 188)
◇ budget (p. 192)
◇ income (p. 193)
◇ expenses (p. 193)

Academic Vocabulary
■ motivation (p. 185)
■ interfere (p. 187)
■ spontaneous (p. 191)
■ discipline (p. 192)

Review Key Concepts

2. **Identify** the steps in making a to-do list.
3. **Compare and contrast** procrastination and over scheduling.
4. **Summarize** the importance of managing leisure time.
5. **Describe** the importance of managing money.
6. **Define** financial discipline.
7. **List** the categories in a budget.

Critical Thinking

8. **Predict** What might happen if someone with an overloaded schedule took on more responsibilities? What might happen if someone went through his or her day without a plan?
9. **Evaluate** Your friend has a report that is due in two days, but she is tired and has decided not to do it now. Do you agree with her decision?
10. **Classify** Make a list of the expense categories you would use to prepare a personal budget. Identify which are fixed and which are flexible.
11. **Distinguish** Over which expenses do you have more control: fixed or flexible? Why?

Family & Community Connections

ACTIVE LEARNING

12. Use a To-Do List Make a to-do list for tomorrow. Set your priorities for the day by assigning the letter A, B, or C to each task, with A being tasks that you must complete, B being tasks that you should complete, and C being tasks that you would like to complete but do not have to. As you complete each item on your to-do list, cross it off. At the end of the day, evaluate your list. Write a paragraph about how this time management tool worked or did not work for you. What did you learn from the experience? Share your findings with the class.

13. Conduct an Interview Talk to a trusted older adult who you think manages his or her money well. Interview this adult about his or her money management skills. Does this person follow a budget? What is this person's attitude toward savings? How has this person's attitude toward money changed over his or her lifetime? What events in his or her life affected how he or she manages money? Does this person behave any differently toward money now than he or she did in the past? Take notes during your interview. Use your notes to create a poster to display the events and changing attitudes that affected the adult's money management. Your posters should be informative and eye-catching. Share your poster with the class.

21ˢᵗ Century Skills

Technology Skills

14. Investigate Time Planners Research one or more technology products designed to manage time and schedules, such as personal organizers, or planning software. Evaluate them according to features, ease of use, and cost. Create a one-page summary of your findings, including whether you would use the product and why.

Stress Reduction Skills

15. Identify Time Traps Time traps can create stress in your life. Reflect on the past 24 hours. Identify strategies you could have used to manage your time more effectively and eliminate stress. Write a paragraph explaining how these strategies might have changed your day.

 Connections

Decision Making Skills

16. Identify Financial Goals As part of its mission, FCCLA encourages students to make decisions and assume responsibilities. Identify two short-term and two long-term financial goals. Decide how much money and time you would need to reach those goals. Is the time and money spent worth the benefits gained from the goal? Create a spreadsheet to show the goals and resources needed. Include a column for notes on whether the goal is worth the resources spent.

Academic Skills

English Language Arts

17. Write Questions Financial planners can help people create and follow budgets and plan how to save money. If you were to interview a financial planner, what questions would you ask about how to find ways to save money? What do you want to find out? Write 10 questions that you could ask a financial planner during the interview to find out useful information.

> **NCTE 12** Use language to accomplish individual purposes.

Social Studies

18. Time Management and Business
Investigate the ways that time management techniques are used in the business industry. Choose one technique that could be applied in your home or at school. Prepare a diagram or a description of the technique, and present it to the class.

> **NCSS V C Individuals, Groups, and Institutions** Describe the various forms institutions take, and explain how they develop and change over time.

Mathematics

19. Calculate Dimensions Chloe works at a department store and has been asked to calculate the dimensions of some boxes. The volume of the boxes can be no more than 1,800 cubic inches. To accommodate the products, the length must be 15 inches and the height 10 inches. What should the width of the boxes be?

Math Concept **Dimensions and Volume**
To calculate the volume of a three-dimensional figure use the formula: $V = l \times w \times h$. This formula means that Volume (V) equals length (l) times width (w) times height (h).

Starting Hint Use the information that you have to create an equation for the volume of the box. Use w to represent the width: $V = 15 \times w \times 10$. Solve for w.

 For more math practice, go to the Math Appendix at the back of the book.

> **NCTM Measurement** Apply appropriate techniques, tools, and formulas to determine measurements.

Standardized Test Practice

CCR College & Career Readiness

TRUE/FALSE
Read the Using a Budget section on page 192. Then determine whether this statement is true or false.

Test-Taking Tip Before deciding whether a statement is true or false, carefully read the text to which it relates. Then slowly review both the statement and the text again. Pay close attention to words. One word can make the difference between a true statement and a false one.

20. You cannot create a budget without the right computer software.
a. True
b. False

Chapter 11

Manage Technology and Information

Chapter Objectives

Section 11.1 Manage Technology

- **List** the benefits and drawbacks of technology.
- **Assess** how to use technology effectively.

Section 11.2 Manage Information

- **Explain** how to analyze information using critical thinking.
- **Describe** how copyrights can affect your use of information.

Explore the Photo

Technology and information systems affect many different parts of people's lives. *What parts of your life do these things affect?*

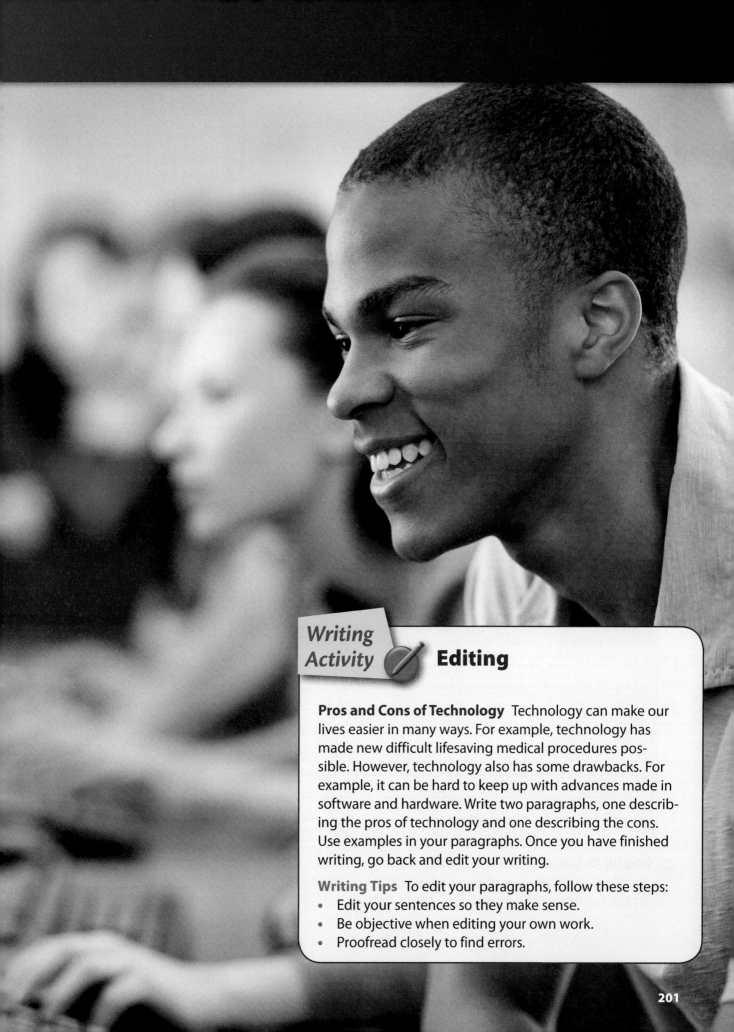

Editing

Pros and Cons of Technology Technology can make our lives easier in many ways. For example, technology has made new difficult lifesaving medical procedures possible. However, technology also has some drawbacks. For example, it can be hard to keep up with advances made in software and hardware. Write two paragraphs, one describing the pros of technology and one describing the cons. Use examples in your paragraphs. Once you have finished writing, go back and edit your writing.

Writing Tips To edit your paragraphs, follow these steps:
- Edit your sentences so they make sense.
- Be objective when editing your own work.
- Proofread closely to find errors.

Manage Technology

Constantly changing technology affects everyone's lives.

Reading Guide

Before You Read

Use Notes As you are reading, keep a note pad handy. Whenever you come across a concept or term you are unfamiliar with, write the word or question down. After you have finished this section, look up the terms or try to answer your questions based on what you have read.

Read to Learn

Key Concepts

- **List** the benefits and drawbacks of technology.
- **Assess** how to use technology effectively.

Main Idea

Technology affects everyday life in both positive and negative ways. You can use technology as a resource itself or with other resources.

Content Vocabulary

- ◇ technology
- ◇ obsolete

Academic Vocabulary

You will find these words in your reading and on your tests. Use the glossary to look up their definitions if necessary.

- ■ coordinate
- ■ enable

Graphic Organizer

As you read, look for nine benefits of technology and one example of each. Use a matrix like the one shown to organize your information.

Benefits of Technology	Example

 Graphic Organizer Go to this book's Online Learning Center at **glencoe.com** to print out this graphic organizer.

Academic Standards

English Language Arts

NCTE 12 Use language to accomplish individual purposes.

Science

NSES E Develop understandings about science and technology.

Social Studies

NCSS II B Time, Continuity, and Change Apply key concepts such as time, chronology, causality, change, conflict, and complexity to explain, analyze, and show connections among patterns of historical change and continuity.

NCTE *National Council of Teachers of English*
NCTM *National Council of Teachers of Mathematics*
NSES *National Science Education Standards*
NCSS *National Council for the Social Studies*

The Impact of Technology

Technology is the application of science to help people meet their needs and wants. It has an impact not only on individuals and families, but also on society as a whole. Technology makes it possible for people to live more comfortably. It reduces the need for physical labor, giving people more time for enjoyment. It contributes to better health and longer life spans. It enables people to feel more connected to the wider world. However, all of this does not necessarily mean that technology makes people happier. As you will learn, technology affects people in both positive and negative ways.

As You Read

Connect What technology devices have you used in the last 24 hours?

Benefits of Technology

Most people would agree that the benefits of technology vastly outweigh its drawbacks. The use of technology has had a positive impact on many parts of our everyday lives.

- **Communication** Modern communication technology started with the telephone. Today, you can fax documents and leave voice mail messages. You can also send and receive e-mails, documents, photographs, and videos via computers. With cell phones, you can send text messages, pictures, and videos. The Internet also offers social networking, blogging, and micro-blogging Web sites. There have never been so many options for communicating with other people.
- **Health Care** People can use the Internet to find information about a variety of medical conditions. Health care professionals use technologies like CAT scans, MRIs, PET scans, and ultrasound to visualize the internal structure of the body to find and diagnose diseases. Lasers, robotics, and other high-tech instruments have made surgery faster and less invasive. The invention of pacemakers, electronic devices that regulate the beating of the heart, allows people with heart conditions to live long and normal lives.

Vocabulary

You can find definitions in the glossary at the back of this book.

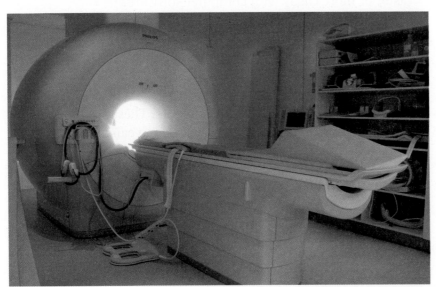

Technology Advantages

Technology has improved our lives in many ways. *How do you think modern technology has improved medicine and health care?*

Succeed in SCHOOL and LIFE

Share Your Schedule

Scheduling is an important life skill that allows you to plan, set goals, and accomplish things. One way to make scheduling more effective is to share your schedule with others, such as coworkers and friends. This allows people to know when you are busy and free, so they can plan around that knowledge. Technology can help. There are many electronic and online scheduling programs that make it easy to share your schedule.

- **Transportation** Air travel and mass transit systems are complex. They would be difficult to **coordinate**, or organize to work together, without the help of computers. Cars and other vehicles also contain computers that keep them functioning properly and warn drivers of problems. Some vehicles have global positioning systems that show maps and give drivers directions. Hybrid vehicles use two or more power sources to achieve better fuel economy. Space programs have sent telescopes, cameras, and people into space to explore.

- **Safety and Security** Developments in technology help protect people and property. Examples include vehicle air bags and anti-theft devices, motion lights, home security systems, motion detectors, smoke detectors, and airport screening systems. Monitoring systems allow many older people who have health problems to live independently.

- **Production** The use of robots has revolutionized manufacturing, increasing efficiency and quality. Computers are used to design and assemble products and to track shipments. Agricultural technology has helped increase the production and safety of food products.

- **Personal Productivity** Think of all the ways technology helps you get more done in less time. Think about how much quicker it is to type an e-mail and hit send than it is to handwrite a letter and mail it. How much time and effort have you and your family saved because of home appliances, such as dishwashers and clothes washers and dryers? What tasks can be completed faster or more easily with computer software?

- **Education** Distance learning and online classes allow students to earn degrees without attending regular classes. Students and teachers can interact at their convenience through online discussion boards.

- **Finance and Retail** Many supermarkets and other retail stores have electronic checkout scanners. These scanners also help them track inventory. Online shopping can **enable**, or help, you to make purchases without leaving home. You can make financial transactions at any hour of the day using computers, a phone, or automated teller machines (ATMs).

- **Entertainment** Technology brings many entertainment options into the home. This technology includes on-demand television, high-definition channels and movies, digital video, gaming stations, and digital music players.

Drawbacks of Technology

Despite its many benefits, technology also has some negative side effects. Chief among these are the stress and frustration associated with rapid and continual change. People sometimes find it hard to keep up with technology and learn new ways of doing things. Some people fear or resist the changes that technology brings. Some of the drawbacks of technology include:

- **Frustration** There is no doubt that technology can be frustrating. Just when you master one device or process, something new replaces it, or upgrades are requied to make it work. Moreover, new methods are not always user-friendly. Have you ever tried to call a company for information, only to find that you must work your way through several menus before you can talk to a real person? Malfunctions occur, computers crash, and computer viruses spread. Even something that seems minor, like a temporary power failure, can cause major frustrations for people who have become dependent on technology.

- **Health** Technology can also have negative effects on people's physical and social health. Hours spent working at a computer can result in back problems, eye strain, and wrist injuries. Poor health caused by a lack of physical activity is another risk. Spending hours watching television, playing computer games, or surfing the Internet can prevent people from interacting face to face.

- **Buying Decisions** The complexity of new technology can make it hard for consumers to make buying decisions. When you do not understand the features on competing products, choosing the right one becomes quite difficult. Also, the costs of some technology can be quite high, especially when it is first introduced, and many products require training to use.

- **Pollution** Technology has resulted in the invention and development of big industries, factories, and an increase in the use of cars and airplanes. While these are all forms of technological progress, they are also associated with serious environmental issues, such as air, water, light, and noise pollution as well as global warming.

- **Privacy Issues** Though information technology has made communication faster and more convenient, it has also created privacy issues. From cell phone signal interceptions to e-mail hacking to identity theft, people are now increasingly worried about their private information becoming public.

- **Job Security** While technology may have streamlined the business process, in many cases, it has also led to human workers being replaced by technology. This means some positions have been done away with, causing people to lose their jobs.

✓ **Reading Check** **Explain** Why might new technology make people worry about their privacy?

Be Smart Be Safe

Electrical Cords Electrical cords are a source of household fires every year. Never cover a cord with a rug or other object as this prevents heat from escaping. Always replace worn or cracked cords.

Write About It Find two additional tips or suggestions on how to safely use electrical or extension cords to decrease the chance of an electrical fire. Write them down, and share them with the class.

E-waste refers to broken, discarded, or obsolete electronic devices. Many of these devices contain materials that make them hazardous. We must be careful about how we dispose of them. Most communities have organizations that reuse or recycle electronics.

Use Technology

Managing technology can help you enjoy its benefits and minimize its drawbacks. A good way to start is to look at the relationship between technology and other resources.

Like any resource, technology can be used to improve your life and meet your goals. You can use the Internet, for example, to gather information about competing products before deciding what to buy. You can use instant messaging to communicate with a friend who has moved far away.

In addition to being its own resource, technology is also a tool that helps you manage other resources. Financial software helps people manage their money. Databases help people organize information. Scheduling software helps you manage your time.

However, technology can also be a drain on resources, like time and money. Many high-tech devices are expensive. It takes time to figure out what technology you need and to learn how to use and maintain it.

Fortunately, there are resources to help you manage the use of technology. Many manufacturers offer help installing new equipment or solving problems. Books and training programs give you information and help you develop skills by providing practice exercises.

Impact of Technology

Because of the fast pace of change, using new technology can sometimes be confusing. *What sources of help are available for new technology?*

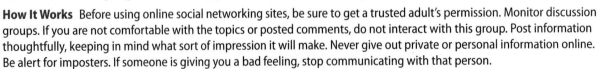

Life On Your Own

Stay Safe on Social Networking Sites

Just like the real world, the virtual world has kind, well-meaning people and dangerous, dishonest people. However, on the Internet, it is often harder to distinguish between these two types. That is why, when you use the Internet, you must take steps to protect yourself. Safety is particularly important on online social networking sites. Remember that the information you give in such settings is available to just about anyone.

How It Works Before using online social networking sites, be sure to get a trusted adult's permission. Monitor discussion groups. If you are not comfortable with the topics or posted comments, do not interact with this group. Post information thoughtfully, keeping in mind what sort of impression it will make. Never give out private or personal information online. Be alert for imposters. If someone is giving you a bad feeling, stop communicating with that person.

Try It Out Francesca has met someone on an online social networking site, and he seems really nice. He is her age, and she has recently discovered that they share very similar tastes in music and movies. He is a really great listener, and they have been chatting online and sending e-mails. He recently asked her for her real name and address because he wants to send her a DVD of his favorite movie that he thinks she will really like.

> *Your Turn* What do you think of this boy's behavior? Do you think he is actually who he says he is? Why or why not? If you were Francesca's friend, what advice would you give her in this situation?

Strategies for Using Technology

How can you avoid the pitfalls and drawbacks of using technology? How can you stay in control of the technology in your life and use it to your advantage? You can enjoy technology's benefits, knowing that it enhances the quality of your life instead of detracting from it. Try keeping these strategies in mind to make the most of technology:

- **Keep a Positive Attitude** A positive attitude helps you see that the benefits of technology are real and usually outweigh the drawbacks. For example, using a computer for word processing saves time, even if you may occasionally lose your work because of a software problem.

- **Be Patient** Set aside time for learning about new equipment or software. Do not expect to master it immediately. Be patient if you have to wait for files to download or for answers from technical support. Ask yourself what difference a few seconds or minutes will make.

- **Maintain Healthy Work Habits** When working at a computer, sit with your shoulders straight and your back supported. Take regular breaks, and do stretching exercises. If your eyes are bothering you, take a break, adjust the lighting in the room, or try an anti-glare screen. Compensate for the time you spend at a computer by being physically active at other times.

- **Maintain Interpersonal Relationships** Do not isolate yourself by spending too much time alone with television, computers, and video games. Nothing can replace positive interactions with friends and family members. Spending time using technology is fine, but be sure you make time in your schedule to spend time with people, too. It is important to include time in your life for the people you care about.

Figure 11.1 Internet Safety Guidelines

Protect Yourself Whenever you use the Internet, you need to take steps to protect your privacy and avoid harassment, such as unpleasant online exchanges. *What can you do if someone harasses you?*

GUIDELINES TO STAYING SAFE ONLINE
Use your primary e-mail address only with trusted friends and family. Use a different address for communicating with people you do not know.
Keep your passwords private. Do not share them with anyone or write them down where they might be found.
Do not give out personal information such as your name, address, or phone number. Remember that information you make available online can be viewed by almost anyone.
Be careful what you say online. Nothing on the Internet is completely private.
Remember that people are not always who they say they are online. You know only what they choose to tell you.
Use the preference options to block e-mails, chat messages, or instant messages from anyone who is bothering you.
If someone is harassing you, save the messages and any information that might help identify the person. Tell a trusted adult. Contact the police, if necessary.

- **Make Wise Consumer Choices** Buy new technology when you need it, not just because there is a new version of last year's product. Some manufacturers want you to think that as soon as a new product comes out, the old version becomes obsolete. **Obsolete** (ˌäb-sə-ˈlēt) means out of date and no longer useful. In reality, this is often not true. There may be only a few new features or design changes in the latest version. Consider your priorities, your budget, and the cost of the new item, and determine to what extent the product or service will actually improve your life.

- **Help Others Develop Technology Skills** When family members, friends, and coworkers help one another develop technology skills, everyone benefits. Jordan gave his grandmother his old computer and taught her how to use e-mail. Now she has an easier way to keep in touch with family and friends, and she loves looking at pictures of her family online.

- **Protect Your Privacy** Do not give people personal information over the phone, by e-mail, or on the Internet unless you know you can trust them. Make sure you are on a secure site when buying online before you give any credit card information. Remember that it is called the World Wide Web, meaning anyone in the world can access your information. Share your e-mail address only with family members and trusted friends. See **Figure 11.1** on the previous page for more information on Internet safety guidelines and ways to protect your privacy when you are online.

Section 11.1 — After You Read

Review Key Concepts

1. **Review** the health problems that can be caused by using technology.

2. **Explain** how technology can be used with other resources.

Practice Academic Skills

 English Language Arts

3. New technology can be intimidating for some people. Should people who fear or resist new technology be left alone, or should they be encouraged to understand and use new equipment and methods? Write your opinion in a paragraph, and give reasons for your answer.

 Social Studies

4. Create a time line of important technological advances that have happened over the past 30 years. Include information about each advance, as well as an image to represent it. Be prepared to share your time line with the class.

Check Your Answers Check your answers at this book's Online Learning Center at **glencoe.com**.

NCTE 12 Use language to accomplish individual purposes.

NCSS II B Apply key concepts such as time, chronology, causality, change, conflict, and complexity to explain, analyze, and show connections among patterns of historical change and continuity.

Manage Information

Reading Guide

Before You Read

Two-Column Notes Two-column notes are a useful way to study and organize what you have read. Divide a piece of paper into two columns. In the left column, write down main ideas. In the right column, list supporting details.

Read to Learn

Key Concepts

- **Explain** how to analyze information using critical thinking.
- **Describe** how copyrights can affect your use of information.

Main Idea

There is more information available now than ever before. You must use critical thinking skills to evaluate information. Find reliable sources, and use information wisely. Respect ownership rights.

Content Vocabulary

◇ critical thinking
◇ copyright
◇ plagiarism

Academic Vocabulary

You will find these words in your reading and on your tests. Use the glossary to look up their definitions if necessary.

■ flourish
■ determine

Academic Standards

English Language Arts

NCTE 8 Use information resources to gather information and create and communicate knowledge.

Mathematics

NCTM Problem Solving
Solve problems that arise in mathematics and in other contexts.

Social Studies

NCSS VIII B Science, Technology, and Society
Make judgments about how science and technology have transformed the physical world and human society and our understanding of time, space, place, and human-environment interactions.

NCTE *National Council of Teachers of English*
NCTM *National Council of Teachers of Mathematics*
NSES *National Science Education Standards*
NCSS *National Council for the Social Studies*

Graphic Organizer

As you read, you will learn three ways to respect the ownership rights of those who have copyrighted material. Use a web organizer like the one shown to help you organize your information.

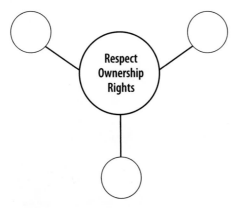

Respect Ownership Rights

 Graphic Organizer Go to this book's Online Learning Center at **glencoe.com** to print out this graphic organizer.

Evaluate Information

You are living in what is known as "the information age." More people have access to more information than ever before. Much of this information explosion is due to communication technology. Television brings news from around the world as it happens. The Internet continues to **flourish**, or be successful, putting information from countless Web sites at your fingertips. Traditional information sources, such as newspapers, magazines, and books, are also still sources of a lot of information.

Having access to so much information is beneficial in many ways. However, it also presents challenges. How do you know whether information is reliable? How can you judge its significance? How can you avoid being overwhelmed by too much information?

Critical Thinking

To evaluate information, you need to use critical thinking. **Critical thinking** means applying reasoning strategies to make sound judgments. For example, one such strategy is distinguishing fact from opinion. A fact can be verified by research, while an opinion is what someone thinks or believes. If you recognize that a statement is opinion, how does that affect the way you interpret it? In most cases, you will want to consider the opinion, but make up your own mind based on facts. Critical thinking is an essential skill for the information age. To be a critical thinker, you need to analyze information instead of just accepting it. To do this, ask yourself:

- How is the information presented? Is it factual and logical, or is it trying to stir up my emotions?
- Is enough valid evidence given to support each conclusion that is being drawn?
- Does the evidence really point to the conclusion? Might there be a different explanation?
- Is the information balanced, or does it present only one side of the story? Are certain key facts conveniently ignored? How could I find out more?

As You Read

Connect What sources do you use to find information?

Vocabulary

You can find definitions in the glossary at the back of this book.

**Information Sources**

Information can come from many different sources. *What are some differences among various information sources?*

Identify Reliable Sources

One key aspect of critical thinking is assessing whether information comes from a reliable source. Do not just assume that all the information you receive is true. You need to be able to determine if the content of the source is fact, opinion, or persuasion. Is what you are reading or hearing trying to inform you or convince you? Reading something in a book does not guarantee that it is correct. Anyone can create a Web site, so information found on the Internet may or may not be accurate. A friend or neighbor may tell you something that he or she believes is true but that turns out to be incorrect. Before you allow information to influence your judgment, you need to check it out and make sure that it is reliable, unbiased, and true.

✓ **Reading Check** **Recognize** What is the difference between fact and opinion?

HOW TO . . . . Evaluate Sources

Just because you read something in print or on your computer screen, do not assume it is accurate or reliable. It is crucial to evaluate whether or not the source of the information is balanced and trustworthy You need to ask yourself questions such as: What is the purpose? Who is the author? Why should I believe this information? How timely is the information? Try these tips when evaluating sources:

Look for Dates Most articles, books, and Web sites will mention the date the information was first published. If this date is very old, perhaps newer and more accurate information is available.

Be Skeptical Phrases such as "scientists have discovered" or "doctors believe" do not mean anything unless they are backed by hard facts. If an article mentions a scientific study, find out who conducted the study and who paid for it.

Evaluate the Source Look for details about authors or others cited as sources. Are they qualified? Make sure they are legitimate experts in their fields. Try to determine whether the information might be biased.

Confirm Information Check the information against other sources. See if the other sources give similar information.

Determine the Source If you read something in a magazine, check to see who wrote the article and what sources the author cites. If you are using a Web site, look at the URL. Does it come from .com, .org, .edu , or .gov?

Math For Success

How Many Semesters?

Yelena knows if she wants to get ahead in her job, she needs to keep up with technology trends. She is enrolling in a graphic design course in the evenings after work. She has to complete a total of 36 credits, and she can take only 3 credits per quarter. If there are 4 quarters per year, how long will it take for her to complete her course?

Math Concept **Word Problems** When a word problem involves multiple steps, it is helpful to outline the information before you solve it.

Starting Hint List the information you already have: total number of credits needed (36), number of credits per quarter (3), and the number of quarters per year (4). The information you are looking for is the number of years needed to complete the course.

Math For more math practice, go to the Math Appendix at the back of the book.

NCTM Problem Solving Solve problems that arise in mathematics and in other contexts.

Use Information Effectively

Once you have found reliable information, you must **determine**, or decide between possibilities, how you can use it most effectively. Often, you will need to organize and summarize the information so it is useful to you. Just gathering the information is not usually enough. For instance, when you research competing products, you might want to list the advantages and disadvantages of each by their features, use, care, and cost.

Sometimes you may not know how much information to gather. Getting too much information may lead to information overload and an inability to make a decision. But you must also be sure to gather enough information to make an informed decision. Be sure to get information from several reliable sources, and check them against one another. However, do not try to get all the available information on a particular topic or else you will be searching for information forever.

Two Views One World

Is the Internet a Good Source of Information?

The Internet is sometimes referred to as the information superhighway, but for some people, it is more like being lost without a map.

Devin: The Internet is incredible, and I don't think I could live without it. Whatever information I'm looking for, be it the best seafood restaurant in my area or the date World War II ended, I can find it online. Learning and researching are so much easier now that we have the Internet. It lets me gather facts and opinions, compare different sources, and connect with people to share ideas and get answers.

Erica: I really don't like looking things up online. I spend hours wading through useless information and visiting unhelpful Web sites. And since anyone can basically write whatever he or she wants, when I do find what I need, I worry about whether it's accurate. I can find just as much information at a good library, without all the frustration and wasted time, and in a library, I know I can trust the information I find.

Seeing Both Sides
With which of these Internet experiences do you agree? What strategies can help you find more useful Web sites with less searching?

Respect Ownership Rights

Even though the information you find in published works and on the Web is freely available, it is not necessarily free to take and use. Music files, pictures, articles, and other materials are all created by someone. In many cases, that person owns the copyright to the information. **Copyright** gives legal rights to the people and companies that produce original works. It gives them control over the way their works are used and the right to profit from their efforts.

Using copyrighted material without permission is a form of plagiarism. **Plagiarism** ('plā-jə-,ri-zəm) happens when someone takes part of another person's original work and uses it as if it were his or her own work. If you copy a passage from an online site and paste it into an essay without citing the source, you are plagiarizing. Plagiarism is illegal because it violates copyright law. It is also unethical. If you plagiarize, you are taking credit for something you did not create. Plagiarism is a growing problem because so much information is available through electronic sources. New technologies are being developed to catch people who steal copyrighted material.

If you use information from someone else's work, give that person credit. You can also summarize the information in your own words. Another way to respect copyrighted material is to quote short extracts exactly, clearly indicating the source. Respect the ownership rights of people who create original works. This will help ensure that creative people will continue to provide new works that enrich everyone's life.

Get Involved!

Bridge the Digital Divide

Volunteer to teach adults computer skills. Computer technology is growing very quickly. It is common nowadays for kids and teens to have better computer skills than older adults. For example, you might teach an older adult how to navigate the Internet and find important information on the Medicare Web site.

 Podcasts Access the Online Learning Center to download *Managing Life Skills* podcasts.

Section 11.2 After You Read

Review Key Concepts

1. **Discuss** how you might interpret information that is an opinion.

2. **Determine** why plagiarism has become a more serious problem in the information age.

Practice Academic Skills

 English Language Arts

3. Use print and Internet resources to research the legal and ethical issues related to plagiarism. Use the information you find to write an article for the school newspaper, explaining the meaning of copyright and discouraging students from plagiarizing. Make sure you cite all your sources in your article.

 Social Studies

4. Choose a new technology that interests you. Research how it works, what it replaces, what its advantages are, and the implications of its use. Prepare a visual presentation for the class that illustrates the new technology and the process it replaces.

 Check Your Answers Check your answers at this book's Online Learning Center at **glencoe.com**.

NCTE 8 Use information resources to gather information and create and communicate knowledge.

NCSS VIII B Make judgments about how science and technology have transformed the physical world and human society and our understanding of time, space, place, and human-environment interactions.

Pathway to Your Career

Software Engineer

What Does a Software Engineer Do?

Software engineers combine computer science and mathematics to design, develop, test, and evaluate the software and systems that make computers work. To do this, they create detailed sets of instructions that tell computers what to do. Software engineers work on many different types of software, including word processing, business applications, computer games, and operating systems.

Career Readiness Skills Software engineers should enjoy working with computers and numbers and have strong problem-solving skills. They need to be detail-oriented and able to concentrate for long stretches of time. They should also be curious and motivated, because to be successful, they will need to be continuously learning throughout their careers.

Education and Training Most software engineers have bachelor's degrees, usually in computer science or software engineering. Graduate degrees are preferred for many of the more complex jobs. To stay competitive, software engineers must keep up with the latest technology.

Job Outlook Software engineers are one of the occupations projected to grow the fastest over the next decade. This will occur as businesses continue to apply new technologies, try to make their computer systems as efficient as possible, and try to keep their computer systems current.

Critical Thinking To determine the impact of technology on career options and choices, write a paragraph identifying at least four industries that use computers. Why might these industries need software engineers?

Career Cluster

CCR ☆ College & Career Readiness

Science, Technology, Engineering & Mathematics Software engineers work in the Engineering & Technology pathway of this career cluster. Other jobs in this cluster include:

- Biologist
- Aerospace Engineer
- Toxicologist
- Mathematician
- Cartographer
- Oceanographer
- Economist
- Agricultural Engineer
- Paleontologist
- Electrical Engineer
- Mining Engineer
- Geologist
- Archeologist
- Physicist
- Chemist
- Zoologist
- Anthropologist

Explore Further The Science, Technology, Engineering, & Mathematics career cluster contains two pathways: Engineering & Technology and Science & Math. Choose one of these pathways to explore further.

 Career Clusters To learn more about career clusters, go to this book's Online Learning Center at **glencoe.com**.

CHAPTER SUMMARY

Section 11.1
Manage Technology

Technology can help people meet their needs and wants. There are many benefits of using technology, but there are also many drawbacks. Managing technology properly can help you enjoy its benefits and minimize its drawbacks. Technology is both a resource and a tool to manage other resources. You can use strategies to stay in control of technology.

Section 11.2
Manage Information

There is a wide variety of information available today. You must use critical thinking skills to analyze the information you receive and determine that it comes from reliable sources. Organize and summarize information so that it is more useful to you. Respect ownership rights, and do not plagiarize other people's work.

Vocabulary Review

1. Write a memo about using technology and information to the class. Use each of these vocabulary words in your memo.

Content Vocabulary
◇ technology (p. 203)
◇ obsolete (p. 208)
◇ critical thinking (p. 210)
◇ copyright (p. 213)
◇ plagiarism (p. 213)

Academic Vocabulary
■ coordinate (p. 204)
■ enable (p. 204)
■ flourish (p. 210)
■ determine (p. 212)

Review Key Concepts

2. List the benefits and drawbacks of technology.
3. Assess how to use technology effectively.
4. Explain how to analyze information using critical thinking.
5. Describe how copyrights can affect your use of information.

Critical Thinking

6. Analyze Why is it more important than ever to evaluate the reliability of information? What are the best ways to do this?
7. Differentiate What do you think the difference is between critical thinking and creative thinking? How can each play a role in managing technology and information?
8. Assess Overall, do you think technology has a positive or negative impact on your life? Explain your answer.
9. Predict What kinds of jobs in today's workplace are most likely to be eliminated by technology? What kinds are least likely to be eliminated? Why do you think so?
10. Communicate Your friend has decided to place a photo of himself on a social networking site. The photo was taken in front of his house, and his street sign is in the background. What would you say to your friend?
11. List How has technology changed learning? List several ways in which your learning process involves technology.

ACTIVE LEARNING

12. Observe and Report Spend at least one hour observing at least five people using a computers, either in your school's computer lab or at the library. Note their posture and how they are sitting, and look for signs of fatigue or eye strain. After observing people at computers, write down what you remember about the users' postures and behaviors. Then, using what you learned in this chapter, use this information to create a brochure to help people reduce fatigue and eye strain from using computers. Your brochure should be informative, easy to read, attractive, and eye catching.

Family & Community Connections

13. Public Technology Resources Find out where there are computers available for the public to use in your community. Find someone who is in charge in one of these places, and ask that person the following questions: Is there a charge to use the computers? Are there rules for using them? What are your hours? Is there often a line or a waiting list to use the computers? Is there a time limit for using the computers? Are there online or wireless network connections? Who pays for the networks? Are printers available? Is there a charge to use the printers? Is people's computer use monitored in any way? Take notes during your interview. Write a paragraph to share your findings, summarizing what you found out about this community resource.

⭐ 21st Century Skills

Technology Skills

14. Use Presentation Software Using appropriate software, prepare a presentation for your class in which you explain and illustrate how to manage technology effectively. Use the ideas in the chapter as a starting point, but add ideas and examples from your own experience.

Decision-Making Skills

15. Evaluate Information Find information on the same topic from two different sources: one that you consider reliable and one that you consider unreliable. Explain how you decided on the reliability of each source.

 Connections

Information Skills

16. Consider Technology Purchases As part of its mission, FCCLA encourages students to prepare for adult life. Imagine you have visited a computer store. The salesperson has told you that your current computer is now out of date. How can you evaluate this statement and know whether you need to make a new technology purchase? Follow your teacher's instructions to form small groups and discuss any strategies.

Academic Skills

English Language Arts

17. Persuasive Essays Write two essays, each trying to convince the reader of the same thing. In one, base your argument on reason. In the other, base your argument on emotion. Exchange essays with a classmate. What words and phrases signal the use of reason or emotion? Which is more persuasive?

> **NCTE 4** Use written language to communicate effectively.

Science

18. Accidental Discoveries Many times, new technology has resulted from an accidental discovery made while researching some other topic.

Procedure Find an example of a new technology that was discovered by accident or as a by-product of another discovery. Research the circumstances surrounding the discovery, and take notes.

Analysis Using your notes, write a report on what led to the discovery.

> **NSES E** Develop understandings about science and technology.

Mathematics

19. Presenting Data You are asked to create a chart for a presentation on your company's budget expenditures. The budget was spent in the following way: 65% employee salaries, 15% rent for office space, 10% utilities expenses, 8% maintenance expenses, and 2% miscellaneous expenses. Use a compass and ruler or computer software to create a pie chart that represents these data.

Math Concept **Pie Charts** A pie chart illustrates data as pieces of a whole. They are useful to show how data relate to one another. The size of the pie piece corresponds to the percentage of the whole represented by that piece of datum.

Starting Hint Draw a circle, and divide it into the number of percentages listed.

 For more math practice, go to the Math Appendix at the back of the book.

> **NCTM Number and Operations** Understand numbers, ways of representing numbers, relationships among numbers, and number systems.

Standardized Test Practice

 College & Career Readiness

TRUE/FALSE
Read each statement. On a separate piece of paper, write T if the statement is true and F if the statement is false.

Test-Taking Tip For true/false questions, look for clue words that usually make a statement false. Some of these words are always, all, only, none, and very. Words such as usually and generally are often used with true statements.

20. Technology is always beneficial.

21. If many other sources give similar information, the source you are using is most likely reliable.

Develop a Career Plan

In this project, you will build a career plan based on your career interest decisions and career research. Building a career plan will involve setting short-term, medium-term, and long-term goals that will help you achieve your career goal.

My Journal

If you completed the journal entry from page 142, refer to it to see if your thoughts have changed after reading the unit.

Project Assignment

In this project you will:

- Choose your long-term career goal to begin a career plan.
- Use your long-term goal to set medium-term and short-term goals.
- Review the requirements needed for your desired career.
- Research admission requirements for post-secondary education and training.
- Develop a skills improvement plan.
- Use your research and goals to develop a realistic plan for achieving your career goal.

THE SKILLS BEHIND THE PROJECT

Key personal and relationship skills you will use in this project include:
- Making good decisions
- Setting achievable goals
- Asking for advice

Academic Skills

English Language Arts

> **NCTE 4** Use written language to communicate effectively.
>
> **NCTE 7** Conduct research and gather, evaluate, and synthesize data to communicate discoveries.

STEP 1 Set Your Goals

Based on the work you did in the previous Unit Portfolio Projects, you are ready to develop a career plan. The first step is to state your long-term goal. This goal would be the career you would like to have. Based on that, determine your medium-term goals. These might include:
- Jobs that will give you needed skills and experience
- Education or training
- Career networking

STEP 2 Research Requirements and Refine Your Goals

Based on your medium-term goals, you will need to research which will help you to establish your short-term goals. For example, based on the education or training required for your goal, find out what the admission requirements are for the schools or programs you need.

Research Skills
- Use reputable Web sites and publications, such as the U.S. Department of Labor's online *Occupational Outlook Handbook*.
- Talk to counselors or trusted adults to get information.
- Keep the notes on your research neat and organized.

STEP 3 Develop a Skills Improvement Plan

Use your evaluation from the Unit 1 Portfolio Project to determine which employability skills you would like to work on improving. Ask for advice from a counselor or professional in your desired field to determine which skills are most crucial for attaining your desired job. Then develop strategies for how you will work toward obtaining and developing those skills. These strategies will function as the short-term goals to be included in your career plan.

Planning Skills

- Use a variety of resources and tools.
- Identify activities to be completed and the best sequence in which to complete them.
- Establish a schedule for activities, and follow that schedule.

STEP 4 Build Your Portfolio Project

Use the Portfolio Project Checklist to plan and create your goal checklist to share your goals with your classmates.

Presentation Skills

- Speak clearly and concisely.
- Make and maintain eye contact with your audience.
- Be sensitive to the needs of your audience.

STEP 5 Evaluate Your Project

Your portfolio project will be evaluated based on:

Academic Skills

- Organization of your presentation
- Communication skills
- How thoughtfully you express your ideas

Evaluation Rubric Go to this book's Online Learning Center at **glencoe.com** for a rubric you can use to evaluate your final project.

PORTFOLIO PROJECT CHECKLIST

Plan

☑ Use the short-term goals you developed in Steps 2 and 3 to create a checklist of the short-term goals you can accomplish to reach your long-term goal.

☑ Develop a visual, such as a career ladder, to illustrate your career plan. Conduct online research to see examples of career plans and career ladders.

☑ Share your career plan with a guidance counselor or a professional in your desired field. Adjust your plan as needed according to the feedback you receive.

Present

☑ Present your long-term goal to the class along with the medium- and short-term goals you will need to accomplish to reach your long-term goal.

☑ Invite the students to ask questions. Answer any questions. Demonstrate in your answers that you respect their perspectives.

☑ Place your notes, checklist, and final career plan in your portfolio. Share this with your teacher.

Portfolio Highlights

Map Out Your Future

Career goals are like a road map to your future. As with a road map, you need to be prepared for detours along the way to your career goal. Be flexible, but always keep your long-term goal in mind.

Visualize Your Goal

A career plan, or career ladder, is a visual image of the steps you need to take to achieve your long-term career goal. This can help you to see where you are in reaching your goals and what your next career step might be. Keeping your career plan in your portfolio will allow you to have it on hand for easy reference at any time.

Modifying Your Goals

Remember that your career plan is not set in stone. Your goals and the time you spend on them can, and probably will, change over time. If you are not reaching your goals, you need to figure out why you are stuck. Maybe your goal was unrealistic. Maybe your interests or priorities have changed. You might need to revise your goals to renew your motivation.

UNIT 4

Consumer Skills

Unit Portfolio Project Preview

Prepare Your Résumé

In this unit, you will explore the role of the consumer in society. In your portfolio project, you will look at ways to advertise your own abilities in pursuit of financial security.

My Journal

Understanding Your Value Write a journal entry about one of the topics below. This will help you prepare for the project at the end of this unit.

• Describe some of the general skills and qualities you think are important for a successful life.
• Summarize the reasons why you are a valuable member of society.
• Explain how a person's attitude may be more important than his or her amount of experience in life.

Explore the Photo

Consumers are constantly faced with choices and decisions. *How can you make sure that you make wise decisions as a consumer?*

Chapter 12

Be a Savvy Consumer

> **Explore the Photo**
>
> Consumers purchase products as well as services, such as haircuts and auto repair work. *What are some services that you often purchase?*

Writing Activity — Write a Letter

Making a Complaint Imagine that you bought a new computer and after two months of use, the computer stopped working. You took it back to the store and were told that they would not honor the warranty. They claimed that the problem was caused by software you downloaded. You do not feel this meets the terms of the warranty. Write a complaint letter to the manufacturer.

Writing Tips To write a complaint letter, follow these tips:
- Use a standard business letter format, and type your letter, if possible.
- Describe the problem, including all possible details.
- Clearly state what action you would like to be taken. Are you asking for a repair or a refund?
- Proofread to correct errors in grammar, usage, spelling, and punctuation.

Consumer Rights and Responsibilities

Consumers have the power to influence the marketplace.

Reading Guide

Before You Read

Cause and Effect A cause is an event or action that makes something happen. An effect is a result of a cause. Ask yourself, "Why does this happen?" to help you recognize cause-and-effect relationships in this section.

Read to Learn

Key Concepts

- **Describe** the importance of teens in the consumer population.
- **Identify** seven consumer rights and their corresponding responsibilities.
- **Explain** why the availability of information is important to consumers.
- **Summarize** two decisions that must be made before making a consumer complaint.

Main Idea

Consumers have rights and responsibilities. There are sources of information to help you as a consumer. Steps can be taken to resolve consumer problems.

Graphic Organizer

As you read, look for eight sources of consumer information. Use a diagram like the one shown to help you organize your information.

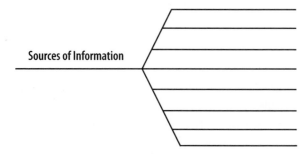

Sources of Information

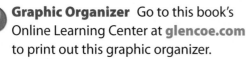

Graphic Organizer Go to this book's Online Learning Center at **glencoe.com** to print out this graphic organizer.

Content Vocabulary

◇ consumer
◇ redress
◇ consumer advocate
◇ small-claims court

Academic Vocabulary

You will find these words in your reading and on your tests. Use the glossary to look up their definitions if necessary.

- collectively
- vacuum

Academic Standards

English Language Arts

NCTE 4 Use written language to communicate effectively.

Science

NSES C Develop an understanding of organization in living systems and behavior of organisms.

Social Studies

NCSS V F Individuals, Groups, and Institutions Evaluate the role of institutions in furthering both continuity and change.

NCTE *National Council of Teachers of English*
NCTM *National Council of Teachers of Mathematics*
NSES *National Science Education Standards*
NCSS *National Council for the Social Studies*

Your Role as a Consumer

A **consumer** is someone who buys and uses products or services. Consumers have rights, such as the right to choose. They also have responsibilities. Just as important, consumers have power. They have the power to influence the marketplace.

The Power of Consumers

You may not think that you are exercising power every time you buy shampoo or choose where to get a haircut. However, consumers **collectively**, or as a group, have a great deal of power. Through their buying decisions, they determine which goods are produced and which services are offered. If too few consumers buy a certain product, it will be taken off the market. The manufacturer will have to offer better choices or risk going out of business.

Consumers play a significant role in the economic system as a whole. When consumers feel optimistic about the economy, they are more likely to spend money. When consumers spend more money, employers hire more workers. When more workers are employed, more people have money to spend. In these circumstances, the economy grows. The opposite is also true. When consumers lack confidence, they spend less and economic growth slows.

You may not realize it, but your opinion matters. Teens make up an important part of the consumer population. In addition to spending their own money, they influence their parents' purchases.

Influences on Consumer Spending

You do not make your consumer decisions in a **vacuum**, or free from outside influences. Your family, your peers, and the media, as well as your needs, wants, and values, guide you toward how you spend your money.

- **Family** Family members affect your decisions both directly and indirectly. For example, you may buy a certain brand of soap because it is what your parents use.
- **Peers** You might ask your friends for advice. You might decide to buy certain brands because that is what your peers are buying.
- **Media** Ads on the radio, the Internet, television, and in magazines are powerful influences.
- **Other Influences** Society, culture, your financial resources, your interests, and technology also play roles in your spending decisions.

✓ **Reading Check** **Define** What is a consumer?

As You Read

Connect Where would you go first to shop for new clothes? Why?

📖 **Vocabulary**

You can find definitions in the glossary at the back of this book.

▼ **Influencing the Market**

When you choose to buy one product over another, you are directly affecting the marketplace. *How can consumers more consciously use this power?*

Get Involved!

Organize a Collection Drive

Many people have things they do not want or no longer need. Help your community by collecting those things and donating them to a community organization that can use them or sell them. Tips to run a successful collection drive include specifying what type of things you are accepting, publicizing through advertising and word of mouth, and making the donation process as easy as possible.

Rights and Responsibilities

The role of consumer comes with rights and responsibilities. The government has created many laws to protect consumers. These laws regulate the sale of goods and services ranging from food and cars to health insurance and home loans. They ensure that businesses treat consumers fairly. They also give consumers the right to redress. **Redress** (ri-'dres) is the right to seek legal remedy when laws are violated. Consumer protection is provided at the federal, state, and local levels by agencies set up to enforce these laws.

Along with each legal right is a corresponding responsibility. To benefit from their rights, consumers must stand up for themselves and take appropriate action. **Figure 12.1** on the next page explains the basic consumer rights and the corresponding responsibilities.

✓ **Reading Check** **Recall** How does the government protect consumers?

Gathering Information

As Figure 12.1 shows, consumers have the right to be informed about products and services and the responsibility to use the information that is available to them. This makes the availability of information very important for consumers. This right and responsibility also raise two questions: "Where do I find the information I need?" and "How can I judge the information's usefulness and reliability?"

Science For Success

Consumers in Nature

Some biological organisms are categorized as consumers. A consumer that eats plants is an herbivore, while a consumer that eats animals is a carnivore. A consumer that eats both is an omnivore.

Procedure Select 10 different animals and conduct research to find out if they are herbivores, carnivores, or omnivores. Then interview 10 people to find out what types of foods they consume.

Analysis Create two graphs to illustrate your findings, one for the animals and one for the people. Write a paragraph stating why you think the animals are different types of consumers. Why are people different types of consumers?

NSES C Develop an understanding of organization in living systems and behavior of organisms.

Sources of Information

Learn about the goods and services and about the company that supplies them before you make a purchase. You can gather information from a wide variety of sources.

- **Government Agencies** The Federal Trade Commission, the Federal Citizen Information Center, and the Consumer Product Safety Commission are among the federal agencies that assist consumers. In many states, the attorney general's office handles consumer affairs.
- **Consumer Organizations** Nongovernment consumer groups include the National Consumers League, Consumers Union, and the Better Business Bureau. Like the government agencies, they offer consumer education, protection, and other services.

Figure 12.1 Consumer Protections and Obligations

Protection and Duties Consumer rights help protect buyers. *Whom do the responsibilities protect?*

CONSUMERS HAVE THE RIGHT TO:	CONSUMERS HAVE THE RESPONSIBILITY TO:
Safety. Consumers should be protected against being harmed by a product.	**Use products safely.** Consumers should use products as directed by the manufacturer.
Be informed. Consumers should be given the facts about goods and services and should be protected against false and misleading advertising.	**Use information.** Consumers should obtain information about the goods and services they intend to buy and use it to make evaluations.
Choose. Consumers should have access to a variety of goods and services at competitive prices.	**Choose carefully.** Consumers should use their intelligence when choosing products and services.
Be heard. Consumers have the right to speak out and to help shape consumer laws and regulations.	**Speak up.** Consumers should let their opinions on consumer issues be known.
Redress. Consumers are entitled to replacements or refunds of unsatisfactory products and to take legal action when laws are violated.	**Seek redress.** When a consumer is not satisfied with a product or service, he or she should take action and request a refund or replacement.
Consumer education. Consumers have the right to learn about consumer issues.	**Learn.** Consumers should use the information available to them to become more effective consumers.
Service. Consumers have the right to expect courtesy and responsiveness from businesses.	**Reward good service.** Consumers should show appreciation for businesses that provide good service and merchandise.

- **Media Sources** Television, radio, the Internet, magazines, and newspapers carry information about products and services. The quality of the information will vary. Consumer magazines such as *Consumer Reports*, published by the Consumers Union, generally provide the most objective information.
- **Advertising** You can learn about product availability, price, and selling features from advertisements. However, since they are trying to sell you something, advertisements are not a good source of objective information.
- **Packaging** Product packaging generally provides information on the contents of the package and instructions for use. Inserts may also provide information.
- **Salespeople** Customer service representatives and salespeople are often a good source of information about the products or services that they sell. Be aware, however, that they may be more interested in selling than in giving unbiased information.
- **Research Studies** Study findings are often reported in the news. Although this information can help you make decisions about products, you need to examine its accuracy. Studies or reports may be biased, simplify results, or give only partial information.
- **Other Consumers** Among the most useful sources of information are people you know who have used a service or product you are interested in. However, as you consider their recommendations, remember that your needs and standards may differ from theirs.

Succeed in **SCHOOL** and **LIFE**

Buying School Supplies

Having appropriate and adequate school supplies is an important part of succeeding in school. Be sure you have enough essential supplies, such as paper, pencils, and binders. However, there are ways to save when buying school supplies. Stock up during sales. Compare unit prices and buy in bulk. Reuse old school supplies. Just because you used something last year does not mean it cannot be used again this year.

Verify Health Claims

Many products advertise that they will make you healthier, including some foods, vitamins, supplements, exercise equipment, and cosmetics. Be sure to verify these claims. Read labels very carefully, especially the fine print, which might tell a different story. You can also do research to find out more about the product.

Evaluate Information

Not all consumer information is provided with the consumer's best interests in mind. You should, therefore, carefully evaluate any information that you obtain. Here are some ways to do this:

- **Consider the source.** What authority or expertise does the source have? Expert sources are more reliable than anonymous sources or people who are not qualified.
- **Look for signs of bias.** Does the source seem to be favoring a particular product or service? Is there a reason for this bias? A product review in a magazine, for example, might be biased because the manufacturer advertises in the magazine. Be sure to be on the lookout for any opinion that seems one-sided.
- **Distinguish between opinion and fact.** Opinions about a product might include that it is easy to use, will perform better than competitors' items, and will enhance your life. Facts provide detailed information that can be verified.
- **When in doubt, check it out.** If something sounds too good to be true, it probably is. If you have doubts about the claims made for a product or service, check other sources. You may find that someone is making exaggerated claims.

✓ **Reading Check**) **Paraphrase** Why might salespeople give biased information?

Resolving Consumer Problems

Sometimes, despite all your best efforts, you end up buying something that is unsatisfactory in some way. Perhaps the power button on the remote control for your new television does not work, or the cordless drill was missing a part when you took it out of the box. Maybe a sweater shrank when you washed it, even though you followed the care instructions. These kinds of consumer problems can be resolved. Businesses want satisfied customers and will usually work to settle a complaint.

Making a Complaint

Before you make a complaint, determine what you want to achieve. Do you want a defective item to be replaced or repaired? Or would you prefer a refund or a merchandise credit? If a service was performed poorly, do you want the provider to do it over or to refund your money? By knowing what you want and asking for it, you are more likely to be satisfied with the response to your complaint.

Next, decide how and to whom you will make your complaint. Depending on the situation, you might contact the company that makes a product or the retailer that sold it to you. You might make a complaint in person, by phone, or in writing.

- **In Person** If you purchased an item at a store, you can make your complaint in person. You might start with the sales clerk who helped you originally, or you might ask for a manager. Many stores have a customer service department to handle customer complaints. Make sure that you have your receipt. Explain exactly what is wrong with the product, and propose your solution for dealing with it. Be polite but firm. Remember that you have bargaining power and that stores usually want to settle consumers' complaints.

- **By Phone** Making a complaint by phone is similar to doing it in person. Be sure to have all the necessary information ready including what the problem is, when and where you purchased the item, and what solution you want. Describe the problem clearly. Write down the name of the person with whom you spoke, the date, and the action discussed. Keep this information in case you need to follow up on your call.

- **In Writing** If complaining in person or by phone does not work, you can write a letter. Clearly and politely state the problem, what you have done so far to resolve it, and what solution you are seeking. Again, keep your tone polite and reasonable. Enclose copies of the sales receipt and other relevant documents. Always keep the original documents for yourself. Also keep a copy of the letter.

Taking Further Action

If your first attempt to resolve a complaint is unsuccessful, try again. For example, if speaking to a store clerk does not bring the desired results, you might ask to see a manager. If a phone call is ineffective, write a letter. If after several attempts you are still unable to settle the problem, there are sources you can turn to for assistance.

- **Government Agencies** The same agencies that offer consumer information also help protect consumers and handle complaints. You can contact the nearest Federal Information Center to learn which federal agency can best help with your particular problem. State and local agencies are listed in the phone book. The Internet is also a good resource.

> **Consumer Advocacy**

Organizations such as the Better Business Bureau can help consumers get redress when they receive unsatisfactory service. *What steps should you take before you seek assistance from a consumer advocacy group?*

CUSTOMER COMPLAIN[T]

Better Business Bureau, Inc.

IMPORTANT: COMPLETE ALL 4 SECTIONS

1 | DATE PROBLEM OCCURRED | DATE(S) YOU COMPLAINED TO COMPANY | TO WHOM
BRAND NAME OR MANUFACTURER | MODEL NAME OR NUMBER | DATE PURCHASED
AMOUNT INVOLVED $ | HAS THIS GONE TO COURT? YES ☐ NO ☐ |

2 | COMPANY PHONE NUMBER | COMPANY FAX NUMBER | YOUR

COMPANY

NAME
STREET
CITY | STATE | ZIP

3 YOUR COMPLAINT IS? (ALSO BE SURE TO ENCLOSE **2 COPIES** EACH

BBB

- **Business Groups** A person or organization who works on behalf of consumers is called a **consumer advocate**. These advocates investigate business practices, expose unfair or dangerous situations, and encourage the passage of laws to protect consumers. Perhaps the best known of many business and industry groups that assist consumers is the Better Business Bureau (BBB). The BBB is an organization of businesses that promises to follow fair business practices. It provides reports on local businesses and helps resolve consumer complaints against its members and other businesses in the community. You might also ask your local chamber of commerce to help you with a consumer complaint. This organization represents and serves businesses in a specific town or city.

- **Legal Action** If a complaint is not settled, you may wish to take legal action. Minor complaints can be settled in small-claims court. A **small-claims court** is a court in which claims under a certain amount are settled by a judge. Although you have to pay a minimal fee to file a claim in small-claims court, you do not have to hire a lawyer or pay legal fees.

If you have a serious complaint that cannot be heard in a small-claims court, you may wish to hire a lawyer and file a lawsuit. This can be an expensive and time-consuming process. Local legal aid agencies may be able to assist you if you cannot afford a lawyer.

 Podcasts Access the Online Learning Center to download *Managing Life Skills* podcasts.

Section 12.1 After You Read

Review Key Concepts

1. **Identify** three influences on consumer spending.
2. **Explain** what redress means for consumers.
3. **List** four tips to remember when evaluating information.
4. **Summarize** how consumer advocates help consumers.

Practice Academic Skills

English Language Arts

5. Suppose that you bought two shirts online. When they arrived, one was the wrong size. Write an e-mail to the company you ordered from explaining the mistake and asking for it to be corrected.

Social Studies

6. Consumer advocates often encourage new laws to help protect the rights of consumers. Choose a particular consumer group, and conduct research to find a law that the group has helped to enact or is currently working to help enact in government. Write a paragraph to share what you learned.

 Check Your Answers Check your answers at this book's Online Learning Center at **glencoe.com**.

NCTE 4 Use written language to communicate effectively.

NCSS V F Evaluate the role of institutions in furthering both continuity and change.

Consumer Safety

Reading Guide

Before You Read

Create a KWL Chart Create a chart with three columns labeled "What I Know," "What I Want to Know," and "What I Learned." Read the Key Concepts, and fill in the first two columns. Fill in the last column after you read this section.

Read to Learn

Key Concepts

- **Describe** at least five ways identity theft can happen.
- **Identify** five common types of fraud.
- **Summarize** why it is important for consumers to act responsibly.

Main Idea

There are steps to take to protect yourself from identity theft and other forms of fraud. Every consumer must act responsibly.

Graphic Organizer

As you read, look for six things you can do to help prevent identity theft. Use a graphic organizer like the one shown to help you organize your information.

Identity Theft Prevention!

 Graphic Organizer Go to this book's Online Learning Center at **glencoe.com** to print out this graphic organizer.

Content Vocabulary

◇ identity theft
◇ fraud
◇ telemarketing
◇ pyramid scheme
◇ chain letter
◇ Ponzi scheme
◇ return policy
◇ shoplifting

Academic Vocabulary

You will find these words in your reading and on your tests. Use the glossary to look up their definitions if necessary.

■ recover
■ goods

Academic Standards

 English Language Arts

NCTE 7 Conduct research and gather, evaluate, and synthesize data to communicate discoveries.

 Mathematics

NCTM Number and Operations Understand numbers, ways of representing numbers, relationships among numbers, and number systems.

 Social Studies

NCSS VI C Power, Authority, and Governance Analyze and explain ideas and mechanisms to meet needs and wants of citizens.

NCTE *National Council of Teachers of English*
NCTM *National Council of Teachers of Mathematics*
NSES *National Science Education Standards*
NCSS *National Council for the Social Studies*

Protect Your Privacy

As You Read

Connect When have you given out personal information as a consumer?

Consumers give out personal and financial information when applying for credit cards, opening bank accounts, making certain purchases, completing product registration forms, answering telephone surveys, or filling out forms on Web sites. Many consumers are concerned about how their personal and financial information is used and who has access to it. They want to protect their privacy and keep personal information from falling into the wrong hands.

Many companies are aware of this concern and now ask for less personal information. When you fill out a form, look for required fields and optional fields. In addition, the government has enacted laws to restrict what companies can do with the information they collect from you. You should read any privacy policies you receive. Find out how your information is shared and what choices you have. If you do not receive a privacy policy from a company you deal with, ask for it.

Identity Theft

 **Vocabulary**

You can find definitions in the glossary at the back of this book.

Identity theft is the illegal use of an individual's personal information for fraudulent purposes. Identity theft can have serious and long-lasting consequences for victims. They may spend months or years trying to resolve the problems caused by it. The process can also be quite costly. During the process, the victims may find it difficult or even impossible to get credit cards, car loans, or home loans.

How Does It Happen?

Identity theft begins when someone gains access to personal information such as your name, address, date of birth, Social Security number, or bank or credit card account numbers. There are several ways that identity thieves obtain personal information:

- steal your wallet or purse with your identifying information
- steal your mail, including pre-approved credit offers, bank and credit card information, tax information, or new checks
- turn in a change-of-address form to redirect your mail
- retrieve discarded checks, credit card bills, bank statements, or receipts from trash cans or dumpsters
- watch over your shoulder as you use an ATM
- steal personal information using computers and the Internet
- steal records from a business or its computer system
- pose as bank representatives or government agencies to get you to reveal information over the phone or through e-mail

In addition to using your credit or debit account to run up charges, thieves may open a new credit account in your name. They may change the mailing address on credit card accounts so that the bills go elsewhere, delaying your discovery of the theft. They may forge checks and empty your bank account. They use the information to order new services, such as cell phone service, in your name. All of these actions can harm your financial reputation.

HOW TO.... Avoid Identity Theft

Identity theft is a crime. An identity thief will use personal information to commit additional crimes, such as spending your money or running up debts in your name. Identity theft begins when someone gains access to your personal information, such as your name, Social Security number, date of birth, credit card number, or passwords. To decrease the chances of having your identity stolen, follow these guidelines:

Secure Your Mail Drop your bills into public mailboxes instead of your home or apartment mailbox. If you go on vacation, ask a friend to pick up your mail or ask the post office to hold your mail.

Choose Creative Passwords Combinations of letters and numbers make the best passwords. Do not choose obvious passwords like birth dates or names. Do not share your passwords. Change them often.

Destroy Documents Shred or tear up documents such as bank and credit card statements. Cut up expired credit cards before throwing them away.

Use Secure Internet Sites Make sure both your wireless computer connection and the Web sites you visit are secure.

Be Safe at ATMs Make sure no one is watching when you use an automated teller machine. Block the view when you enter your personal identification number (PIN).

Keep Personal Information Private Do not give out personal information over the phone, by mail, or by e-mail, and only give it out when you are positive it is safe to do so.

What You Can Do

If you suspect that your identity has been stolen, take action immediately. First, contact the three major credit reporting agencies (Equifax, Experian, and TransUnion) so that a security alert can be placed on your file, including a statement that creditors should contact you for permission before opening any new accounts in your name. Next, call any banks or credit card companies about accounts that have been tampered with. Ask the representative what steps you should take. Follow up with letters, including details from the call such as the date, time, and the person with whom you spoke. Keep copies of all correspondence. Call any other creditors you have to alert them to the situation in case the thief tries to use your other credit cards or accounts. Finally, file a police report. Keep a copy of the police report in case creditors ask for proof of the crime. You can also file a report with the Federal Trade Commission (FTC) by phone or on its Web site. You might also want to contact the Privacy Rights Clearinghouse, a nonprofit consumer information and advocacy organization, for more information on dealing with identity theft.

Reading Check **Define** What is identity theft?

Guard Against Fraud

Identity theft is just one example of fraud. **Fraud** is deceitful conduct for personal gain. People who engage in fraud lie, make misleading statements, divert money from legitimate causes, sell products, or engage in other practices that persuades victims to spend or invest their money.

Types of Fraud

Every year, millions of people become victims of fraud. Many of them never **recover**, or get back, their money. Common types of fraud to be aware of include telemarking schemes, pyramid schemes, chain letters, Ponzi schemes, and Internet fraud.

- **Telemarketing Schemes** Selling products and services by telephone is called **telemarketing**. Not all telemarketing is fraudulent. However, some telemarketers persuade victims to buy expensive products or services. Victims send money and receive a cheap or worthless item. Others talk victims into investing money in schemes that "cannot fail." Some convince people to give money to a charity, but then keep the money.

Be Smart Be Safe

Watch Out for Phishing
Phishing is a criminal process in which identity thieves pretend to be someone else to trick people into providing personal information, such as user names, passwords, or credit card details.

Write About It Research phishing to find information on how people can avoid it and protect themselves from it. Summarize your findings in a short report.

- **Pyramid Schemes** A get-rich-quick plan based on recruiting more and more participants is called a **pyramid scheme**. People pay a fee to join, and then recruit others who also pay a fee and bring in more participants. In theory, people who stay in the pyramid long enough receive the money paid by new recruits. In fact, pyramid schemes are impossible to sustain. The people who start them often make money, but the later recruits lose everything that they paid in. Pyramid schemes are based on false promises and are illegal.
- **Chain Letters** A **chain letter** is a specific type of pyramid scheme in which a letter or an e-mail message encourages people to send copies of the letter to others, along with money. Participants are promised that they will receive money as the number of participants multiplies. Chain letters collapse after a short while, robbing most participants of their money.
- **Ponzi Schemes** Another type of pyramid scheme is known as a Ponzi scheme. A **Ponzi scheme** ('pän-zē 'skēm), named after Charles Ponzi who developed the scheme in the 1920s, is one in which investors are promised high profits from fake sources. Early investors are paid off with funds from later investors and then encouraged to take more and bigger risks.
- **Internet Fraud** Chain letters and pyramid schemes are now facilitated via the Internet. Criminals are always coming up with new ways to scam people. According to the Federal Bureau of Investigation's Internet Crime Complaint Center (IC3), Internet auction fraud and e-mail scams are the most reported offenses. Protect yourself and your computer by deleting any unsolicited e-mail.

Life On Your Own

Internet Fraud

Internet fraud refers to any type of fraud scheme that uses online services, such as chat rooms, e-mail, message boards, or Web sites, to conduct fraudulent transactions or solicit money from victims. Some online auction and retail sites send consumers items worth less than what was promised, or they may never send the items. Others claim to be verifying credit card information when, in fact, they are stealing that information.

How It Works Things that might indicate Internet fraud include: businesses that will not reveal their locations or give addresses; insisting that payment be made before information is sent; high-pressure offers good only for a short time; and any offer that seems too good to be true. If you think you have been a victim of fraud, report it to the Federal Trade Commission or the National Fraud Information Center.

Try It Out You receive an e-mail directing you to a Web site that is conducting a contest in which you could win a cruise ship vacation. You can easily enter your credit card number to pay the small $20.00 fee, and then you can enter the contest. The Web site seems professional and legitimate. It even explains that you will have to give the company money to pay taxes on your prize, should you win.

Your Turn What would you do if you received this e-mail and went to this Web site? Are there any warning signs that would make you suspicious? If so, what are they?

**Consumer
Courtesy**

The golden rule, "treat others as you want to be treated," is important for consumers to remember. *How do you feel when you receive great customer service?*

Protect Yourself

As a savvy consumer, you must always be on the lookout for fraud so you can recognize it before you become a victim. To help you avoid becoming a victim of fraud:

- **Do not believe all claims.** Remember, if it sounds too good to be true, it probably is.
- **Ask for details in writing.** Legitimate companies will have no problem sending written details of a product, plan, or promise.
- **Ask for the phone number of the company.** Make sure you call back before agreeing to any deal, and check the company out with the Better Business Bureau if possible to make sure it is legitimate.
- **Use the Internet.** Although the Internet can be used to commit fraud, you can use it to educate and protect yourself. Visit government Web sites to learn how to recognize Internet scams and fraud. Look for the ".gov" suffix at the end of the domain name to confirm that you are looking at a legitimate government Web site.

If you have been a victim of fraud, or if you believe someone is trying to deceive you, you need to report it. This can help keep others from being victimized as well. You can file a consumer complaint form and get more information by contacting the Federal Trade Commission or the National Fraud Information Center.

✓ **Reading Check** **Paraphrase** How is a pyramid scheme supposed to work?

Shop Responsibly

The role of consumer comes with both rights and responsibilities. Just as you expect a business to act honestly and fairly, a business expects you to do the same. Your actions toward other consumers and toward the businesses you deal with affect far more than just yourself. They also affect the welfare of other people, businesses, and even the economy. Make sure that you act in a responsible manner.

Follow the Rules

The rules for returning or exchanging merchandise is a store's **return policy**. Make sure you are aware of and follow a store's return policy. Some stores give store credit only, not refunds. Other stores give you the option of exchanging your returned item for something else. Most stores set time limits for the return of items. Stores expect returned items to be undamaged and unused.

Dishonesty, such as purchasing an item of clothing with a plan to return it after wearing it, costs business owners, and ultimately consumers, millions of dollars each year. **Shoplifting** is the theft of merchandise from a store by shoppers, and it is a particularly serious problem. Stores not only lose income because of stolen items, but they are also forced to spend money to prevent theft. The costs of security guards, cameras, and anti-theft tags are passed on to consumers as higher prices. Shoplifting has serious consequences, including fines, arrest, a criminal record, and imprisonment.

Be Considerate

Responsible consumers understand their rights and responsibilities. They expect to be treated fairly, and they are fair and honest themselves. When you shop or use a service, be considerate. Be courteous when you interact with employees, whether in person, by phone, or by e-mail.

You would not want to buy clothes that had been torn when someone tried them on. Your fellow consumers do not want damaged **goods**, or products, either. Treat merchandise with care. If you decide not to purchase an item, put it back where it belongs.

Enjoy your power as a consumer. Choose goods and services that meet your needs, show courtesy, and do your part to avoid and prevent crime against consumers.

 Podcasts Access the Online Learning Center to download *Managing Life Skills* podcasts.

Section 12.2   **After You Read**

Review Key Concepts

1. **Describe** three steps for victims of identity theft to take.
2. **Explain** what you should do if you have been a victim of fraud.
3. **Clarify** how shoplifting affects both stores and consumers.

Practice Academic Skills

 English Language Arts

4. People often panic when they discover they have been victims of credit card theft. Create a flyer telling people what to do if their credit card is stolen. Include a reminder to keep all personal and financial information secure.

 Social Studies

5. Since 1914, the Federal Trade Commission (FTC) has had the goal of protecting consumers' rights. Conduct research to find out more about the role of the FTC and how it affects you as a consumer. Write a brief report to share what you learn.

 Check Your Answers Check your answers at this book's Online Learning Center at **glencoe.com**.

NCTE 7 Conduct research and gather, evaluate, and synthesize data to communicate discoveries.

NCSS VI C Analyze and explain ideas and mechanisms to meet needs and wants of citizens.

Pathway to College — Choosing the Right College

How Do I Choose the Right College?

Deciding which college to attend is a very important decision. Should you stay close to home or move away? Should you go to a four-year college or a two-year college? Should you go to a college in a big city? Should you pick a college that specializes in a specific field? These are just some of the questions you will need to ask yourself.

What are some things I should consider when selecting a college?

There are many different things you should think about when trying to decide which college to attend. The size of the student body is important. Location is also something you need to think about. Find out about campus life, including housing, extracurricular activities, athletics, and social clubs. Cost is another key aspect, including possible scholarships or financial aid packages. You also want to make sure that the college offers classes in the area you want to study. You might also want to find out about the geographic, ethnic, racial, and religious diversity of the students.

Are there different types of colleges?

Yes, and different types of colleges suit different types of people. Liberal arts colleges offer a broad base of courses in humanities. Universities are generally bigger than colleges, with larger classes and more class options. Community colleges offer two-year degrees in technical programs that prepare you for the job market. If you have a clear idea about what you want to do, a specialized college might be a good choice. You will also need to decide between public colleges, which are usually less expensive, and private colleges, which are often smaller and more expensive. Finally, you might want to consider a special interest college, such as a single-gender or religious college.

Hands-On

College Readiness Think about what you learned in this feature about factors you should consider when choosing a college. Write a list of what matters to you in a college. Then go online to find colleges that match your list, eliminating those that do not meet your requirements. There are many Web sites that allow you to search for colleges by various features.

Path to Success

College & Career Readiness

Start Early College might seem far away, but it is closer than you think. Start your decision-making process early.

Talk It Over There are many people you can talk to about this decision, including your friends, school guidance counselor, teachers, and parents.

Do the Research There is an amazing amount of information on the Internet and in print about choosing the right college.

Create a List Develop a list of conditions you want to use to evaluate and eliminate colleges.

Write It Down Creating a chart of the colleges you are considering and the pros and cons of each can be very helpful.

Visit! If you can, visit some of the colleges you are thinking about. There is nothing like actually seeing the campus and the students.

 Go to this book's Online Learning Center at **glencoe.com** to learn more about college and career readiness.

CHAPTER SUMMARY

Section 12.1
Consumer Rights and Responsibilities

Consumers have an influence on the market-place. All consumers have rights and responsibilities. One right is to collect information, but you have the responsibility of evaluating that information. Before making a consumer complaint, determine what you want to achieve, whom you will contact, and how.

Section 12.2
Consumer Safety

You can help protect your privacy and your identity by being cautious about giving out personal information. Fraud occurs any time people deceive consumers into paying for false or useless products or services. By being courteous and obeying laws, you can help make the marketplace better for all consumers.

Vocabulary Review

1. Create a fill-in-the-blank sentence for each vocabulary term. The sentence should contain enough information to help determine the missing term.

Content Vocabulary
- consumer (p. 225)
- redress (p. 226)
- consumer advocate (p. 230)
- small-claims court (p. 230)
- identity theft (p. 232)
- fraud (p. 234)
- telemarketing (p. 234)
- pyramid scheme (p. 235)
- chain letter (p. 235)
- Ponzi scheme (p. 235)
- return policy (p. 236)
- shoplifting (p. 237)

Academic Vocabulary
- collectively (p. 225)
- vacuum (p. 225)
- recover (p. 234)
- goods (p. 237)

Review Key Concepts

2. **Describe** the importance of teens in the consumer population.
3. **Identify** seven consumer rights and their corresponding responsibilities.
4. **Explain** why the availability of information is important to consumers.
5. **Summarize** two decisions that must be made before making a consumer complaint.
6. **Describe** at least five ways identity theft can happen.
7. **Identify** five common types of fraud.
8. **Summarize** why it is important for consumers to act responsibly.

Critical Thinking

9. **Analyze** Think of an item that you purchased recently. What or who influenced your decision?
10. **Apply** Suppose someone calls you and asks you to donate money to a charity. Would you give that person your credit card information? Describe what you would do.
11. **Hypothesize** Imagine that a friend tells you he is going to steal a jacket because he does not have the money for it. How would you respond to your friend? In your response, explain why shoplifting affects all consumers.

ACTIVE LEARNING

12. Plan a Complaint Suppose that you have returned to the dry cleaner to pick up a shirt you dropped off a few days ago. There is a hole in the shirt that you are certain was not there when you dropped it off. Outline the process you would follow to make a complaint. Decide how you want the problem to be addressed. Specify to whom you would complain. Describe the ways in which you would make contact. Explain what you would say and do. Include a plan for making a second and third complaint in case the first attempt is not successful.

Family & Community Connections

13. Be Proactive One of the best ways to protect yourself from fraud is through education. The more you know, the better chance you have of keeping fraud from happening in the first place. Arrange to speak to a representative from an agency such as the Better Business Bureau or a consumer protection agency. Find out what types of consumer fraud are most common in your community. Ask the representative what steps can be taken to prevent it. Use what you learn to create a brochure that warns citizens of the dangers of fraud. Include the steps they can take to protect themselves. Brochures should be brief, attractive, and easy to read. If possible, make copies to share with the people who live in your neighborhood.

21st Century Skills

Technology Skills

14. Compare Privacy Policies Locate and read the privacy policy for two different online stores. How are they similar? How are they different? What do they say about sharing your personal information? Create a chart to illustrate your findings.

Information Skills

15. Evaluating Information An important consumer responsibility is to evaluate the information you receive about products and services. You learned many sources of information in this chapter. Determine the advantages and disadvantages of each source. Write a paragraph stating which sources of information you are most likely to use for the kinds of products and services you purchase most often.

FCCLA Connections

Financial Literacy Skills

16. Influences on Consumer Spending As part of its mission, FCCLA encourages students to develop money management skills. These are skills that consumers must begin learning and using at a young age. Use the FCCLA Financial Fitness program to conduct online research for money management lessons for children. Prepare a presentation of the information you learn. If possible, share your presentation with students in an elementary class.

Academic Skills

English Language Arts

17. Technology Influences Technology, such as television and the Internet, has created more options for how we find out about products and how we purchase them. With the Internet and other electronic devices, we can instantly access photos, information, and customer reviews for just about anything. Write a brief report describing how online consumer information affects your buying habits.

> **NCTE 12** Use language to accomplish individual purposes.

Social Studies

18. Consumer Actions You learned in this chapter how consumers can affect the economy and the marketplace. Suppose your community began a campaign to encourage people to eat at home instead of dining out. If this campaign gathered a lot of support, how could it affect the local economy? Write a paragraph to explain your evaluation.

> **NCSS VII B Production, Distribution, and Consumption**
> Analyze the role that supply and demand, prices, incentives, and profits play in determining what is produced and distributed in a competitive market system.

Mathematics

19. Graphing Statistics Suppose the statistics below show the annual number of instances of different ways in which identity theft can happen:

- Lost or stolen wallet: 6,615
- Fraudulent address change: 2,577
- Computer hacking: 341
- Stolen financial records: 1,322

Use this information to create a bar graph to show the most common methods of theft.

Math Concept **Bar Graphs** A bar graph represents data using shaded bars or colored lines to show each value. The graph's axes should always be labeled, and the graph should have a title.

Starting Hint Decide what information will go on each axis. Create a legend to show what each color or pattern represents.

 For more math practice, go to the Math Appendix at the back of the book.

> **NCTM Data Analysis and Probability** Select and use appropriate statistical methods to analyze data.

Standardized Test Practice

 CCR College & Career Readiness

SHORT ANSWER

Write two or three sentences to answer each writing prompt.

> **Test-Taking Tip** Put as much information into your answer as possible. Use easy-to-read, short sentences that define key words. Also give an example that explains your answer.

20. Explain why consumers have the responsibility to use information.

21. Describe what the right to redress means.

Chapter 13

Advertising and Shopping

Chapter Objectives

Section 13.1 Facts About Advertising

- **Identify** the common goal of all advertising.
- **Describe** five types of advertising media.
- **List** eight persuasive techniques used in advertising.
- **Explain** four techniques for evaluating advertisements.

Section 13.2 Shopping Skills

- **List** five factors than can affect the choices you make while shopping.
- **Identify** three basic options for shopping.
- **Describe** the best way to get the most for your money.
- **Compare and contrast** shopping for goods and shopping for services.

▶**Explore the Photo**

Companies spend large amounts of money to create ads that will persuade people to buy their products. *Other than billboards and television commercials, what types of advertising can you name?*

Writing Activity

Create an Advertisement

Persuasive Advertising Advertising can be a strong influence on a consumer's decision to buy a product. Suppose you work for a company that is marketing a new cell phone. Write a print advertisement to persuade consumers to purchase your phone. Your ad will appear in magazines. Include a description of the art or photos that would go in your advertisement.

Writing Tips Use these tips to help you write an advertisement:

- Decide which product features you want to emphasize.
- Determine what age group will most likely be influenced by your ad. Use language and factual information that will appeal to that age group.
- Use short, attention-grabbing statements that will allow the consumer to focus on your message.

Facts About Advertising

Wise consumers must be able to evaluate advertisements.

Reading Guide

Before You Read

Compare and Contrast When a section discusses more than one way of performing the same task, try to compare and contrast the different methods.

Read to Learn
Key Concepts
- **Identify** the common goal of all advertising.
- **Describe** five types of advertising media.
- **List** eight persuasive techniques used in advertising.
- **Explain** four techniques for evaluating advertisements.

Main Idea

There are several types of ads, and many persuasive techniques used in advertising. Consumers need to be able to identify and evaluate the information in ads.

Content Vocabulary
◇ campaign
◇ infomercial
◇ direct mail advertising
◇ testimonial
◇ endorse
◇ manipulate

Academic Vocabulary

You will find these words in your reading and on your tests. Use the glossary to look up their definitions if necessary.
■ promote
■ impartial

Academic Standards

English Language Arts
NCTE 6 Apply knowledge of language structure and conventions to discuss texts.

Mathematics
NCTM Problem Solving Solve problems that arise in mathematics and in other contexts.

Social Studies
NCSS X C Civic Ideals and Practices Locate, access, analyze, and evaluate information about selected public issues.

NCTE *National Council of Teachers of English*
NCTM *National Council of Teachers of Mathematics*
NSES *National Science Education Standards*
NCSS *National Council for the Social Studies*

Graphic Organizer

As you read, look for the two basic types of ads and an example of each. Use a graphic organizer like the one shown to help you organize your information.

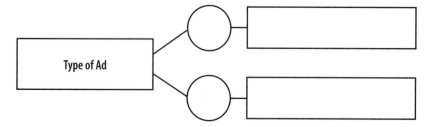

Type of Ad

Graphic Organizer Go to this book's Online Learning Center at **glencoe.com** to print out this graphic organizer.

The Role of Advertising

How do you choose the products you buy? Whether you are aware of it or not, many of your purchasing decisions are influenced by advertising. Every day you are exposed to many advertisements, or ads. Those ads help to determine the products and services you choose. Most advertising is designed to make people want to buy what the advertiser is trying to sell. Businesses spend billions of dollars each year to **promote**, or advertise, their products and services. Not all ads are trying to sell something. Some promote various political, social, and charitable causes. However, all ads have a common goal: to influence people's opinions and behavior.

Most advertising is meant to appeal directly to consumers. Advertisers use a variety of techniques to persuade consumers to choose one product or service over another. When there is little difference in quality between competing brands, the effectiveness of an advertising campaign can help determine whether a product succeeds or fails. A **campaign** ((ˌ)kam-ˈpān) is a series of actions designed to bring about a particular result. You can probably think of several commercials for popular products that use national ad campaigns. For advertisers, an effective ad campaign attracts consumers but usually costs a lot of money. For consumers, too, advertising has both benefits and drawbacks.

Benefits and Drawbacks

Ads can inform you about product features and benefits, make you aware of new or improved products, and tell you about sales and special promotions. Often, you can use ads to compare different products. Advertising also makes it possible for information and entertainment to be provided at little or no cost to the public. Most newspapers, magazines, radio and television stations, and Web sites rely on advertising. Advertisers pay large sums of money to buy space or time for their messages.

Many people find ads annoying, especially when they interrupt entertainment. A more serious consequence is that ads can persuade people to buy goods and services they either cannot afford or do not really need. Some advertising is misleading, suggesting benefits that a product is unlikely to deliver. Advertising also increases the price, sometimes by as much as 75 percent, that consumers pay for goods and services. That is the main reason why unadvertised store brands are usually less expensive than nationally advertised brands.

As You Read

Connect Have you ever tried a new product in response to an online ad? What influenced your decision?

▶ Vocabulary

You can find definitions in the glossary at the back of this book.

Persuasive Advertising

Many stores place weekly ads in the newspaper to highlight certain products and promotions. *How might one of these ads affect your grocery shopping?*

Math For Success

The Power of Advertising

Few people admit to being significantly influenced by ads. However, surveys and sales figures show that well-designed advertising is powerful and persuasive. Examine your family's buying habits to understand the power of advertising. Think about the foods you eat, the places you go, and the movies you watch. Chances are that advertising plays a significant role in your family's consumer choices, as it does for millions of other families. Knowing how powerful advertising is should motivate you to become more aware of how it works.

✓ Reading Check **Recall** Why are store brands often less expensive than name brands?

Types of Ads

Advertisers have created many ways to reach consumers. As new technology develops, new methods of advertising also continue to develop.

Advertising is communicated through numerous forms of media. Remember from Chapter 6 that media are channels of mass communication, such as newspapers, magazines, radio, television, movies, and Web sites. Some of the media that advertisers use to capture consumers' attention and spread their messages are:

- **Newspaper and Magazine Ads** Generally, newspapers carry more local ads than national ads, and magazines carry more national ads than local ads. Some target specific groups of readers, such as teenagers, gardeners, mothers, or cooks, and carry ads designed to appeal to those specific readers.
- **Radio and Television Commercials** Advertisers usually purchase 30 to 60 seconds of air time during or between programs. Ads during major sports events are usually the most expensive because they are seen or heard by such a large audience.
- **Infomercials** An **infomercial**, also called paid programming, is a television or radio ad that lasts 30 minutes or more and is designed to seem like regular programming. A typical infomercial might include a well-known spokesperson, information, product demonstrations, and praise from satisfied customers.
- **Internet Ads** Companies also advertise their products and services on the Internet. They might have their own Web site or purchase ads on other Web sites. E-mail is also a powerful advertising tool.

- **Direct Mail** The practice of delivering ads to consumers' homes by mail is called **direct mail advertising**. The ads may be in the form of letters, brochures, catalogs, or coupon booklets.
- **Outdoor Advertising** Billboards, neon signs, and posters plastered on the sides of buses and buildings are examples of outdoor advertising.
- **Other Advertising Formats** Many other media, from cell phones to blimps floating in the sky, carry ads. You might even be carrying ads yourself! Are you wearing company names or logos on your clothes? If so, this is advertising, and you helped pay for it when you made your purchase.

Information Versus Image

No matter what media they use, ads can be divided into two basic types based on the kind of message they deliver. Information ads supply facts that help you learn about and compare products or services. For example, an ad for athletic shoes might explain how they are designed and constructed to improve performance.

Image ads focus more on the image of the product they are promoting and less on the facts. An image ad for the same athletic shoes might show them being worn by an athlete, with no facts given except the brand name. Image ads are designed to make you associate the product with positive feelings.

✓ **Reading Check** **Define** What is media?

Persuasive Techniques

Advertisers use a variety of techniques to persuade consumers to buy their products. Understanding these techniques can help you analyze ads and your reaction to them. Here are some commonly used persuasive techniques:

- **Positive Images** Advertisers often try to show how happy, healthy, smart, attractive, or popular you will be if you use their product. For example, an ad might suggest that people who wear a certain brand of swimwear get invited to great beach parties.
- **Hidden Fears** Some ads play on consumers' fears. An ad for a cleaning product might suggest that a home will be unsanitary without it.
- **Bandwagon** These ads try to convince you that everyone else has "jumped on the bandwagon" and is enjoying this product, so you should too.

▼ **Implied Promises**

Some ads imply that their products, such as beauty and grooming products, can help improve a person's self-esteem or popularity. *What other types of products might use this technique?*

Health & Wellness TIPS

Read Drugstore Labels

When shopping in the drugstore, pay attention to labels. While labels cannot legally claim that a supplement treats or prevents diseases, labels can often be confusing or misleading. Look for a statement saying whether the Food and Drug Administration (FDA) reviewed the product. Choose supplements based on research, not on label claims.

- **Testimonials** Celebrities, famous athletes, and consumers often make testimonials. A **testimonial** is a positive statement about a product based on personal experience. Keep in mind that in most cases, these people are paid to **endorse**, or approve and support, the product. Paid endorsements are rarely impartial, or unbiased.

- **Demonstrations** Some ads use demonstrations to show the advantages of a product, such as the strength of paper towels or the effectiveness of a razor.

- **Slogans and Jingles** Advertisers hope that clever slogans and jingles, those catchy tunes in some ads stay in your memory and come to mind when you are shopping.

- **Put Downs** Advertisers may make negative statements about a competitor's product to make their own product seem better.

- **Before and After** Advertisers often show photos of a consumer before and after using their product. You have probably seen these types of ads: the overweight man with bad posture (before) transformed into a muscular athlete (after) or the sad-looking teen with acne (before) who becomes clear-skinned and happy (after). Keep in mind that advertisers use all sorts of tricks to exaggerate the differences between the two photos.

✓ **Reading Check** **Identify** What is a testimonial?

Two Views One World

Are Celebrity Endorsements Misleading?

Depending on whom you ask, celebrity endorsements are either a great marketing idea or an abuse of a celebrity's popularity.

Celina: I don't like to see my favorite actors or athletes in ads. I don't think it's fair to use their popularity that way. It abuses their fans' loyalty, and it makes me think less of that celebrity. They are getting paid huge amounts of money to say they like a product. It's misleading because people confuse the fact that they like a celebrity with the idea that they like the product that celebrity endorses.

Huan: Celebrity endorsements have been around for ages, and I don't think there's anything wrong with them. Celebrities work hard for their success, and endorsements are one of their rewards. If celebrity endorsements make people buy the product, that means endorsements work, and if they work, that means consumers want to buy products endorsed by celebrities. So I really don't see the problem.

Seeing Both Sides

What problems might arise when a product and a celebrity are linked? Can you think of a specific celebrity endorsement that caused a problem for either the celebrity or the product?

Figure 13.1

Deceptive Advertising Techniques

Do Not Be Fooled Advertisers sometimes try to trick consumers with lies or omitted information. *In which type of deceptive practice is a bargain-priced item used to attract customers who are then encouraged to purchase a more expensive item?*

DECEPTIVE PRACTICE	DESCRIPTION
False Claims	Advertisers who make specific claims about their products, such as "reduces the risk of skin cancer" or "twice as powerful as other leading brands," must be able to back up their claims with scientific evidence. If they cannot, they are being deceptive.
Hidden Catches	An ad that does not clearly disclose, or make known, important details such as restrictions or extra fees, is deceptive. So is an ad that offers a "free gift" without revealing that you have to purchase something to get it.
Deceptive Pricing	Suppose a store's ad for jeans says, "Sale! $34.99." If the store always sells that brand of jeans for $34.99, then the use of the word "Sale" is deceptive. Items on sale are supposed to have a lower price than usual.
Bait and Switch	Advertisers who use bait and switch lure buyers by advertising an unusually low-priced item that they have only a few to sell. That is the "bait." When shoppers try to buy the advertised item, they might be told, "We just sold the last one." In reality, the bargain item may never have been in the store. The salesperson then tries to "switch" the shopper to a higher-priced item. If the advertised offer is genuine, however, then it is perfectly legal for a salesperson to try to interest you in a higher-priced product.

Evaluating Ads

Once you are aware of the techniques that advertisers use, you can recognize how an ad is trying to manipulate you. To **manipulate** (mə-'ni-pyə-,lāt) is to control or influence someone in a clever or deceptive way. Assume that there may be more to an advertisement than what is on the surface. Use your critical thinking skills to analyze messages in ads and the way they are presented. Here are some suggestions for how to successfully evaluate ads:

- **Look for facts.** Separate emotional appeals, opinions, and persuasive arguments from hard facts. Focus on the facts to make decisions.
- **Check the fine print.** Check the details. For example, if a fitness club is promoting a "special introductory price," it probably means you will pay the advertised price for only a month or two. Look for details that explain if the price goes up and if so, by how much and when.
- **Analyze what is being said.** "Notebook computers from as little as $399" means that $399 is the lowest price at which a notebook computer is being sold. It does not mean that all the store's notebook computers are that price. Often, there is one model at that price, with limited stock. How high do the prices go on the rest of the models? You cannot tell from the ad.
- **Beware of vague claims.** Suppose an ad says, "Doctors agree that … " It is important to ask: Who are these doctors? How many of them were consulted? Are they medical doctors or some other kind? Depending on the answers to these questions, a statement like this may be technically true, yet almost meaningless.

Succeed in SCHOOL and LIFE

Think Critically About Ads

There are questions you can ask yourself to better evaluate an ad's claims. How is the advertiser trying to influence my emotions? Underneath all the distractions like jingles and celebrity spokespeople, what does the ad really say? Is it the product itself that really appeals to me or just the cleverness of the ad? Does the ad provide any actual information that I could verify or use to decide if I want to buy the product?

Deceptive Advertising

A certain amount of exaggeration is expected in ads. However, some ads go too far. They might make false statements or leave out information to try to mislead consumers. That is deception, and it is illegal. See **Figure 13.1** on the previous page for some examples of deceptive practices.

The Federal Trade Commission (FTC) regulates advertising and can require advertisers to prove their claims. If the FTC rules that an ad is deceptive, the advertiser must stop using the ad and may have to pay a fine. Consumers can report suspected cases of deception by calling the FTC or visiting its Web site.

It is up to you to make wise use of advertising. Use critical thinking skills to evaluate ads. Look for facts, analyze information, recognize emotional appeals, and be skeptical of promises that seem too good to be true. Learn to separate the truth from the persuasive techniques. When you know how to evaluate ads, you can benefit from them and enjoy the creativity that goes into an effective advertising campaign.

 Assessing Advertisements

Signs like the ones in this picture are meant to attract people who are looking for bargains. *What information would you look for when entering this store?*

 Podcasts Access the Online Learning Center to download *Managing Life Skills* podcasts.

 Section 13.1 | **After You Read**

Review Key Concepts

1. **Summarize** the benefits of advertising for the consumer.

2. **Contrast** infomercials and commercials.

3. **Paraphrase** why you should be wary of celebrity endorsements.

4. **Describe** what happens when the FTC rules that an ad is deceptive.

Practice Academic Skills

 English Language Arts

5. Consider some ads that you have seen recently either on television or the Internet or in a magazine or newspaper. Based on the information you have learned in this section, do you think most ads are honest or dishonest? Explain your answer in a paragraph.

Social Studies

6. Conduct research to locate at least three examples of political ads. Analyze the ads for the advertising techniques used. Write a brief report to share your findings. Were similar techniques used in all of the ads? Why do you think the techniques used were chosen? Do you think other techniques could be more successful in political ads?

 Check Your Answers Check your answers at this book's Online Learning Center at **glencoe.com**.

> **NCTE 6** Apply knowledge of language structure and conventions to discuss texts.

> **NCSS X C** Locate, access, analyze, and evaluate information about selected public issues.

Shopping Skills

Do you consider yourself to be a smart shopper?

Reading Guide

Before You Read

Use Diagrams As you read, write down the main idea. Then write down any facts, explanations, or examples you find. Start with the main idea, and draw arrows to the information that directly supports it. Then draw arrows from those examples to any information that supports them.

Read to Learn
Key Concepts

- **List** five factors that can affect the choices you make while shopping.
- **Identify** three basic options for shopping.
- **Describe** the best way to get the most for your money.
- **Compare and contrast** shopping for goods and shopping for services.

Main Idea

Smart shoppers know how to plan and research purchases. Shopping for services is not the same as shopping for goods.

Graphic Organizer

As you read, look for three ways that you can shop from home. Use a diagram like the one shown to help you organize your information.

Home Shopping

Graphic Organizer Go to this book's Online Learning Center at **glencoe.com** to print out this graphic organizer.

Content Vocabulary

◇ impulse buying
◇ warranty
◇ rebate
◇ service

Academic Vocabulary

You will find these words in your reading and on your tests. Use the glossary to look up their definitions if necessary.

■ second
■ substantial

Academic Standards

English Language Arts

NCTE 5 Use different writing process elements to communicate effectively.

Social Studies

NCSS III G People, Places, and Environments
Describe and compare how people create places that reflect culture and human needs as they design and build shopping centers.

NCTE *National Council of Teachers of English*
NCTM *National Council of Teachers of Mathematics*
NSES *National Science Education Standards*
NCSS *National Council for the Social Studies*

Plan Purchases

Consumers today have so many choices when it comes to goods and services. Those who plan before they shop usually get better value for their money and are more likely to be satisfied. You do not need to spend a lot of time planning every purchase. However, if you are in the market for a computer, sports gear, a vehicle, or some other expensive or significant purchase, you will want to plan carefully.

As You Read

Connect Do you think Internet shopping sites will replace stores in the future? Why or why not?

Research Products

Your needs, wants, values, goals, and resources affect your choices as you plan purchases and shop. It is important to know which features and options matter most to you, what to look for, and what costs are involved. You may need to do some research to obtain this information.

There are several ways to research products and make an informed choice. Ask people you know who have bought similar items to tell you about their experiences. Study product reviews in consumer magazines. Search online for product and pricing information and customer reviews. Visit stores to gather information. Examine the merchandise, and read labels, tags, and instruction booklets. Ask sales personnel to explain or demonstrate products, and take their recommendations into consideration.

Avoid Impulse Buying

Impulse buying is making unplanned purchases with little or no thought. Retailers have many ways of tempting you to buy more than you intended. They make attractive offers, like "buy one, get one free," or they suggest additional items to go with your purchase. These methods often succeed in getting you to make extra purchases. That is good for the seller, but not necessarily good for you. Impulse buying can drain dollars from your budget. To avoid impulse buying, remember these tips:

- List what you want to buy before you shop, and buy only those items.
- Resolve to not buy anything while waiting in the checkout line.
- Take only as much money as you think you will need for the items on your list.
- If you want something you did not plan to buy, wait and think it over. Return later if you think it is a wise purchase.

✓ Reading Check **Define** What is impulse buying?

◀ **Vocabulary**

You can find definitions in the glossary at the back of this book.

◀ **Resist the Urge**

People are often tempted to buy last-minute items that they do not need. *What can you do to resist this impulse?*

Shopping for Bargains

Garage and yard sales are often a great way to get what you want and save money. *What are some items you would not want to buy secondhand?*

Shopping Options

When it comes to deciding where and how to shop, there are many choices to consider. The basic options for where to shop include stores, secondhand sources, and shopping from home. Each option has advantages and disadvantages to consider.

Stores and Outlets

In stores, you can examine items and compare brands. You can try on clothing, and you can get information and advice from sales clerks. If you want to return an item, you can simply take it back to the store. Here are some of the many available store options:

- **Department stores** carry a wide selection of goods and prices.
- **Discount stores** carry national brands at reduced prices.
- **Specialty stores** sell certain types of merchandise, such as clothing, office supplies, or electronics.
- **Factory outlets** sell discounted goods from one manufacturer. Some products are irregular items that are slightly imperfect. A **second** is an item with more noticeable flaws.
- **Warehouse clubs** offer a wide range of products, from groceries to home furnishings, at discounted prices to customers who pay a membership fee. Many of the products are sold in bulk, or large quantities.

Secondhand Sources

Secondhand items have been owned or used by someone else. At yard and garage sales, swap meets, and flea markets, people sell items they no longer need or want. Secondhand stores buy used items or accept donated items to resell at reduced prices, or sell on consignment, meaning that they act as an agent for the person selling. Auctions are another way to find bargains. Classified ads list everything from furniture to used cars. When buying from any secondhand source, be sure to inspect items carefully since you probably will not be able to return them for a refund or exchange.

Be Smart Be Safe

Stay Safe While Shopping People can be distracted when they shop, making them good targets for criminals. To stay safe, be aware of your surroundings, shop with someone else when possible, avoid carrying large amounts of cash, and park in well-lit areas.

Write About It Picture yourself shopping. Identify any unsafe shopping habits you have. Then write a paragraph about what you could do to make your shopping trips safer.

 Shopping in Comfort

Many people will shop for certain items at home but still prefer to go to the store for other items. *What type of items might be better to purchase in a store rather than online?*

Shopping from Home

You can shop from home, often at any time, using catalogs, television shopping channels, or your computer. Shopping from home allows you to avoid crowded stores and parking lots. You generally have a wider selection from which to choose.

Home shopping is convenient, but it can be easy to buy on impulse and spend more. You cannot see, handle, and compare items directly, so you risk being disappointed when they arrive. You may have to pay a shipping charge, and there may be a cost involved if you return an item. However, if you plan well, home shopping may be a good alternative to visiting stores.

Here are some home shopping options:

- **Catalogs** Retail stores and companies without stores offer catalogs for customers to place orders by phone or mail or through the company's Web site.
- **Television Shopping** Shopping networks on television and informercials are devoted entirely to selling products. Customers usually pay by credit card over the phone.
- **Internet** The Internet makes it easy to compare prices and products from different suppliers. Internet auction sites offer a wide variety of new and used items and can be a good source of bargains. There are independent payment processing services that you may want to consider when making certain online purchases. This limits the number of people who will have access to sensitive financial details, such as your credit card or bank account numbers.

✓ **Reading Check** **Contrast** What is the difference between specialty stores and factory outlets?

Finding Good Buys

The best way to get the most for your money is to comparison shop. Compare similar products to one another, and compare prices offered by different sellers. Visit a variety of stores, look at ads and catalogs, and search the Internet. Consider both quality and price.

Follow these guidelines when making any type of purchase:

- **Evaluate Quality** Low price is not everything. Performance, durability, convenience, maintenance, and safety are important, too. Evaluate quality to help you choose the best products.
- **Evaluate Safety** Consumer magazines and Web sites, product labels, and owner's manuals can help you learn about safety features and how to use products safely.
- **Look for Warranties** A **warranty** is a guarantee that provides protection against faulty products. Read it carefully, and make sure you understand its terms. A full warranty meets certain conditions specified by federal law. A limited warranty does not meet all the conditions of a full warranty, but still gives valuable protection. Some products may have an implied warranty. This kind of protection is provided by state law rather than by the manufacturer or seller. Sometimes you have the option to purchase extended warranties on certain items.
- **Identify Hidden Costs** Hidden costs are not included in the purchase price of the item. These may include accessories, batteries, taxes, fees, maintenance, and shipping costs. Consider your time and energy if you need to assemble an item. Estimate the hidden costs, and include them in your price comparisons.
- **Take Advantage of Sales** You can save a **substantial**, or large, amount of money during a sale. However, do not assume a sale price is the best price. One store's sale price might be higher than another store's regular price. Often, sale items cannot be returned. Sometimes a store manager may be able to give you a discount if you ask. Also, many retailers will honor another store's sale price for the same item. It never hurts to ask.

Succeed in SCHOOL and LIFE

Shop for School Off Season

Have you noticed that when you are shopping for school supplies or new back-to-school clothes, the stores are crowded with others doing the same thing? The stores anticipate this rush, and prices tend to be higher. While you might not be able to anticipate everything that you will need for the upcoming school year, think about buying some of the things you know you will need at the end of the school year, instead of the beginning, to save money.

Life On Your Own

Buyer Beware

You work hard to earn your money, so you want to be satisfied with how you spend it, whether it is on a pair of jeans or a car. Impulse purchasing often does not work out. It is important to think about what you are spending your money on. You are more likely to be happy with your purchases if you spend some time considering the product before purchasing it.

How It Works Before buying a product, be sure to examine it, checking for chips, dents, stains, or tears. Compare prices. You may be able to find a better price elsewhere. Consider the brand. Store brands sometimes offer an equal quality product at a better price, though this is not always the case. Be sure to read the label, which can provide important information. Also, if the product has a warranty, be sure to read the terms and conditions carefully.

Try It Out Think of an item you purchased in the past that you eventually regretted buying. Why did you regret buying this item? Would any of the tips in this feature have helped you avoid this situation? Think about what you learned from that experience. Now, think of another item you are considering buying but have not purchased yet.

Your Turn Conduct online research about this product, finding information about different brands, prices, and warranty information. Use this information to choose the best product and place to purchase it. Summarize your research and decision in a paragraph.

- **Use Coupons and Rebates** Coupons, available in magazines, in newspapers, in the mail, and online, allow you to get a certain amount or percentage off the product price. Use coupons wisely. Do not buy a product just because you have a coupon. A **rebate** is a refund of part of the purchase price of a product. To receive a rebate check, you usually have to fill out a form and send it to the manufacturer with proof of purchase. Rebate instructions may be complex, so follow them carefully.

✓ *Reading Check* **Recall** Name five factors that help determine the quality of an item.

HOW TO... Compare Providers

With services, just like with merchandise, you should compare qualified providers. Make a list of providers who offer the service in your area. Then follow the steps below to help you select the best provider from your list.

Get Recommendations Talk to friends and family who have hired someone to perform similar work. Who did they use? Were they satisfied? Would they recommend that person or company?

Check Qualifications Find out about the providers' experience, skills, and reliability. Ask for samples or pictures of their work. Request names of previous customers. If appropriate, check that they have legitimate and current licenses. Check with the Better Business Bureau to make sure that no complaints have been filed against them.

Get Estimates Ask for a written estimate from each potential provider of how much the work will cost. This will help you to compare prices.

Verify Insurance If the work will be done in your home or on your property, verify that the providers have liability insurance. Workers should also be bonded, which provides protection against financial loss in case of theft.

Read the Contract Some major jobs, such as home repair, require a legally binding agreement called a contract. The contract is signed by the service provider and the customer, and it protects both in the event of a dispute. Read contracts carefully.

Shopping for Services

A **service** is work performed for a fee. Examples range from haircuts to dry cleaning to car repairs to interior decorating. Goods, like shoes or groceries, usually have a set price, but the price charged for a service can vary by provider, making it harder to compare prices from different providers. Hiring someone to provide a service often involves estimates, contracts, and other paperwork. You can often return goods if you are dissatisfied, but you cannot return or undo an unsatisfactory service.

Getting the Most for Your Money

Once you have chosen a provider, do your part to make the experience a good one. Provide any information needed to do the job, and ask questions if you do not understand something. Work with the provider to resolve any difficulties that arise.

After the work is done, evaluate the service you received. Consider efficiency, timeliness, and your satisfaction. Do the same for ongoing service providers, such as cell phone and Internet service providers. If you are dissatisfied with any aspect of the service, discuss the problem with the provider. Service providers want satisfied customers and future clients, so they will generally work with you to resolve problems.

Podcasts Access the Online Learning Center to download *Managing Life Skills* podcasts.

Section 13.2 — After You Read

Review Key Concepts

1. **Identify** three ways to research products.

2. **Describe** two options for shopping from your television.

3. **Summarize** five ways to ensure you find a good buy.

4. **Explain** the steps you should follow to choose a service provider.

Practice Academic Skills

English Language Arts

5. Create an outline for a 30-minute infomercial about your favorite grooming product. Include the main points and details that you will use to help persuade consumers to order the products.

Social Studies

6. As early as the 10th century, people created bazaars, or covered markets, to bring sellers and buyers together. Shopping centers, or malls, were created in the 18th century. Although many people shop from home today, shopping centers function as more than just places to buy goods. Write a one-page report summarizing how shopping centers might continue to evolve to serve people's needs.

Check Your Answers Check your answers at this book's Online Learning Center at **glencoe.com**.

NCTE 5 Use different writing process elements to communicate effectively.

NCSS III G Describe and compare how people create places that reflect culture and human needs as they design and build shopping centers.

Pathway to Your Career

Advertising Manager

What Does an Advertising Manager Do?

Advertising managers oversee the advertising, creative, and media services departments. They are responsible for a company's advertising, marketing, promotions, sales, and public relations. They work to assess the need for advertising and to develop its subject matter and presentation. They also work with their staff to select the type of media, such as radio, television, magazines, or the Internet, used to distribute the advertising.

Career Readiness Skills Advertising managers should be creative, imaginative, flexible, highly motivated, and able to handle stress. The ability to persuade people is very important. Strong verbal and nonverbal communication skills are essential. They also need good judgment and the ability to establish and maintain personal relationships.

Education and Training Most employers prefer a bachelor's degree in a related field, such as business administration or marketing. A master's degree will make the candidate even more competitive. Courses in business, management, economics, accounting, and finance are helpful. Completing an internship in the industry is highly recommended.

Job Outlook Job growth in the industry is projected to increase at an average rate due to domestic and global competition in products and services and increasing activity in television, radio, and outdoor advertising. However, competition for these positions is expected to be intense.

Critical Thinking Find a print advertisement either in a newspaper or in a magazine upon which you think you could improve. Bring in the advertisement or a copy of it, explain why you chose it, and propose a way to improve upon it.

Career Cluster

 **College & Career Readiness**

Marketing Advertising managers work in the Marketing Communications pathway of the Marketing career cluster. Here are some other jobs in this career cluster:

- Promotions Manager
- Product Planner
- Store Manager
- Sales Promotion Manager
- Copywriter
- Manufacturer's Representative

- Analyst
- Creative Director
- Trade Show Manager
- Retail Sales Specialist
- Telemarketer
- Sales Associate
- Media Buyer

Explore Further The Marketing career cluster contains five pathways: Marketing Management, Professional Sales, Merchandising, Marketing Communications, and Marketing Research. Choose one of these pathways to explore further.

 Career Clusters To learn more about career clusters, go to this book's Online Learning Center at **glencoe.com**.

CHAPTER SUMMARY

Section 13.1
Facts About Advertising

Advertising has the power to influence people's opinions and behavior. Advertising has benefits and drawbacks for both advertisers and consumers. Two different kinds of ads are information ads and image ads, and ads are available through different media. Advertisers use many techniques to persuade consumers. Consumers should evaluate ads for the facts. The Federal Trade Commission (FTC) enforces laws against deceptive advertising.

Section 13.2
Shopping Skills

Smart shoppers plan their purchases and avoid impulse buying. You can shop at stores, online, through catalogs, at secondhand sources, and at home. When comparison shopping, consider quality and warranties, as well as price. Shopping at sales and using coupons and rebates can help you save money, but only if you are careful and take time to plan. Shopping for services involves a different process from shopping for goods.

Vocabulary Review

1. Use at least six of these vocabulary terms in a short essay about shopping.

Content Vocabulary
- ◇ campaign (p. 245)
- ◇ infomercial (p. 246)
- ◇ direct mail advertising (p. 247)
- ◇ testimonial (p. 248)
- ◇ endorse (p. 248)
- ◇ manipulate (p. 249)
- ◇ impulse buying (p. 252)
- ◇ warranty (p. 255)
- ◇ rebate (p. 256)
- ◇ service (p. 257)

Academic Vocabulary
- ■ promote (p. 245)
- ■ impartial (p. 248)
- ■ second (p. 253)
- ■ substantial (p. 255)

Review Key Concepts

2. **Identify** the common goal of all advertising.
3. **Describe** five types of advertising media.
4. **List** eight persuasive techniques used in advertising.
5. **Explain** four techniques for evaluating advertisements.
6. **List** five factors that can affect the choices you make while shopping.
7. **Identify** three basic options for shopping.
8. **Describe** the best way to get the most for your money.
9. **Compare and contrast** shopping for goods and shopping for services.

Critical Thinking

10. **Judge** Do you think the benefits advertising provides consumers outweigh the drawbacks? Why or why not? Explain your answer, and defend your position.
11. **Analyze Behavior** Why is it often difficult to resist the temptation of impulse buying? What might make it easier to resist? What can you do to improve your chances of avoiding impulse purchases?

 ACTIVE LEARNING

12. Stage a Debate Follow your teacher's instructions to form into two groups. One group will argue in favor of shopping in stores, and the other will argue in favor of online shopping. Using the information in this chapter and additional research and personal experience, hold a class debate. Follow standard debate rules, allowing each side a chance to speak within a specified time. Be sure to have a strong closing statement for your side. All members should contribute to the research and argument for the team.

Family & Community Connections

13. Consumer Advice The Federal Trade Commission (FTC) works to inform consumers about their rights and to educate the public on how they can be smarter consumers. With your teacher's permission, visit the FTC Web site and research information on consumer protection. Create a brochure that you could share in your community. Your brochure should contain at least five tips related to consumer safety or shopping skills. Advice may include how to evaluate ads or warranties, tips for safe online shopping, or any other topics you think members of the community might find useful. Include appropriate graphics to support your message, and make your brochure appealing.

★ 21st Century Skills

Cross Cultural Skills

14. Persuasion Techniques Culture affects everything we do. With online shopping becoming more popular, it is easier and more common for people to buy and sell products between countries. Because of this, advertisers must design ads to appeal to people of different cultures. Conduct research to discover persuasion techniques used in a country other than the United States. Write a one-page report summarizing your findings.

Technology Skills

15. Online Auctions Visit an online auction site. Conduct research to find out about the rights and responsibilities for consumers using the site. What safeguards are in place to protect buyers from dishonest sellers? What responsibilities do buyers have? Use the information you find to create a presentation for the class.

FCCLA Connections

Financial Literacy Skills

16. Comparison Shopping As part of its mission, FCCLA encourages students to become wise financial managers and smart consumers. Use the Consumer Clout unit of the FCCLA Financial Fitness program to research purchasing decisions. Choose a specific product, and then comparison shop in three places, such as different types of stores, catalogs, and Web sites. Develop a chart to share your findings, and present it to the class.

Academic Skills

 English Language Arts

17. Personal Blog Technology-based products change rapidly. Some people keep up by buying the latest product as soon as it is available. Others are more cautious and wait until the technology is tested and proven. Write a blog entry to share your opinion about when you would buy technology-based products. Would the time differ based on the specific product?

> **NCTE 12** Use language to accomplish individual purposes.

 Science

18. Energy Efficient Products The U.S. Environmental Protection Agency has helped to develop the Energy Star program to help consumers save money while protecting the environment.

Procedure Conduct research to find out how the Energy Star program is helping the environment.

Analysis Write a summary of your findings, including the purpose of the program and its specific impact.

> **NSES F** Develop an understanding of environmental quality and science and technology in local and global challenges.

 Mathematics

19. Compare Prices Comparison shopping allows you to get the best deal for your money. Suppose you found a sweater you want to buy in a department store for $27.99 plus 8.00% sales tax. You found the same sweater in a catalog for $20.99 plus 8.00% sales tax and $4.00 for shipping. Which sweater costs less? Now suppose you need the sweater for a specific event. You can pay an additional $10.00 for rush shipping. Does this change which sweater is the less expensive purchase?

Math Concept **Multi-Step Problems** When solving problems with more than one step, think through the steps before you start.

Starting Hint Begin by calculating the sales tax on each sweater and adding it to the base price. Then add the amount of shipping to the sweater from the catalog.

 For more math practice, go to the Math Appendix at the back of the book.

> **NCTM Problem Solving** Solve problems that arise in mathematics and in other contexts.

 Standardized Test Practice

 College & Career Readiness

MULTIPLE CHOICE
Read the sentence. Then read the question below the sentence. Read the answer choices, and select the best answer to fill in the blank.

> **Test-Taking Tip** In a multiple-choice test, read the question before you read the answer choices. Try to answer the question before you read the answer choices. This way, the answer choices will be less confusing.

Lena's social nature made her biased toward shopping in stores instead of online.

20. In this sentence, the word *biased* means _____.

    a. running diagonally across the weave of a fabric
    b. a distortion of a set of statistical data
    c. voltage applied across an electronic device
    d. having a preference

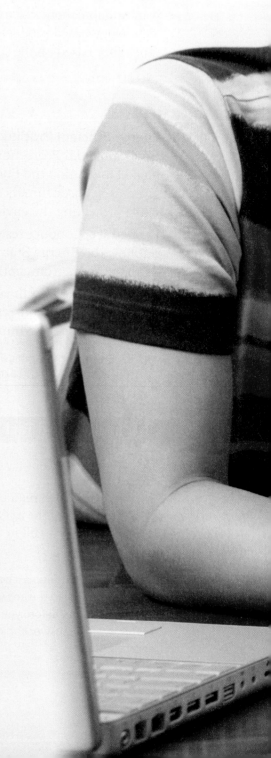

Chapter 14

Manage Your Finances

Chapter Objectives

Section 14.1 Everyday Financial Management

- **Explain** what it means to be financially fit.
- **List** six types of banking transactions.
- **Contrast** the two common ways to prepare for retirement.

Section 14.2 Use Credit Wisely

- **Explain** the different types of credit.
- **Categorize** credit terms and fees.
- **Predict** problems that can stem from irresponsible credit use.

> ➤ **Explore the Photo**
>
> Managing your personal finances will help you make good decisions about how to spend your money. *What are some common ways people keep track of and manage their expenses?*

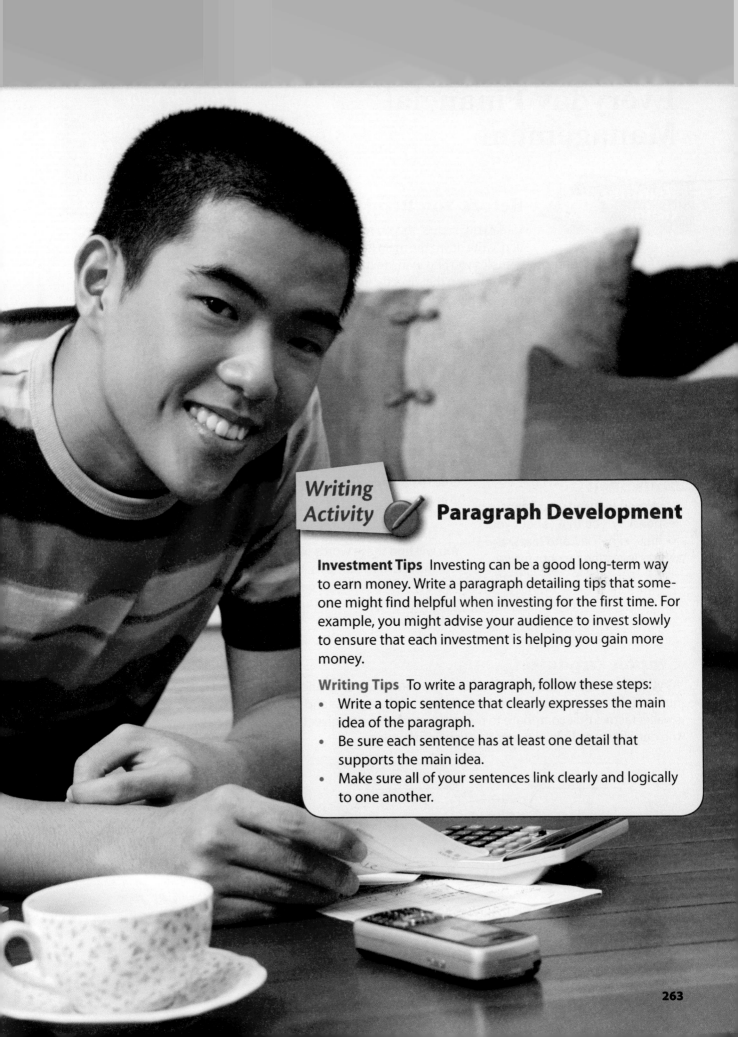

Writing Activity — Paragraph Development

Investment Tips Investing can be a good long-term way to earn money. Write a paragraph detailing tips that some-one might find helpful when investing for the first time. For example, you might advise your audience to invest slowly to ensure that each investment is helping you gain more money.

Writing Tips To write a paragraph, follow these steps:
- Write a topic sentence that clearly expresses the main idea of the paragraph.
- Be sure each sentence has at least one detail that supports the main idea.
- Make sure all of your sentences link clearly and logically to one another.

Everyday Financial Management

Reading Guide

Before You Read

Use Diagrams As you read through this section, write down the main idea. Then write down any facts, explanations, or examples you find in the text. Start at the main idea, and draw arrows to the information that directly supports it. Then draw arrows from these supporting examples to information that supports them.

Read to Learn

Key Concepts
- **Explain** what it means to be financially fit.
- **List** six types of banking transactions.
- **Contrast** the two common ways to prepare for retirement.

Main Idea

When you manage your finances responsibly, you think about your income, expenses, and taxes, as well as investing for your future.

Content Vocabulary
◇ gross pay
◇ net pay
◇ deduction
◇ interest
◇ debit card
◇ reconcile
◇ compound interest
◇ insurance
◇ 401(k) plan
◇ invest

Academic Vocabulary

You will find these words in your reading and on your tests. Use the glossary to look up their definitions if necessary.
■ diversify
■ shares

Academic Standards

English Language Arts

NCTE 7 Conduct research and gather, evaluate, and synthesize data to communicate discoveries.

Social Studies

NCSS VI A Power, Authority, and Governance Examine persistent issues involving the rights, roles, and status of the individual in relation to the general welfare.

Graphic Organizer

As you read, think about the factors that can contribute to financial fitness. Take notes to remind yourself of the main categories and the smaller factors that contribute to them. Use a graphic organizer like the one shown to help you organize your information.

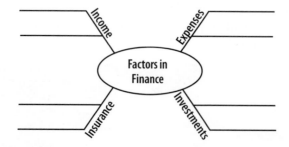

 Graphic Organizer Go to this book's Online Learning Center at **glencoe.com** to print out this graphic organizer.

NCTE *National Council of Teachers of English*
NCTM *National Council of Teachers of Mathematics*
NSES *National Science Education Standards*
NCSS *National Council for the Social Studies*

Financial Fitness

Financial fitness describes your ability to understand your paycheck and bank accounts, identify sources of income, and manage your expenses. It also means paying taxes, buying necessary insurance, and investing in your future. Developing financial knowledge now will help you shape the future you want as an adult.

Understanding Your Income

Many people are shocked when they receive their first paycheck. Before you get a paycheck, the company must deduct, or subtract, some of what you have earned to pay for other things. If you earn $10.00 an hour, for example, you may only receive $7.00 after taxes and other expenses have been taken out of your total earnings.

Paycheck Earnings

Workers are paid at the end of each pay period, which is usually one or two weeks or a month. Some employees receive a paycheck. Others have their pay directly deposited into their bank account. Your pay stub will show your earnings for the pay period. The method for calculating your earnings should be explained to you when you take the job. Possible methods include:

- **Hourly Wages** If you are paid by the hour, you receive your hourly wage multiplied by the number of hours you have worked.
- **Piecework** Often used in manufacturing and assembly work, piecework is based on the number of items you produce.
- **Salary** A salary is a set amount of income for a year. Salaried employees typically receive the same amount each pay period.
- **Commission** Employees involved in sales work may be paid a commission, or a percentage of the amount that they sell. Some receive commission in addition to their salary. Others receive only commission.

On a pay stub, you will see two different listings for pay. **Gross pay** is the total amount you earn, but not how much you will receive. A certain amount will be taken out for taxes and other deductions. The amount you actually receive is your **net pay**. **Figure 14.1** on the next page shows a typical pay stub.

Deductions

A **deduction** (di-'dək-shən) is anything that is subtracted from your gross pay. Some deductions are required by law, while others are optional. Some of the deductions that you may see on your pay stub include:

- **Federal Taxes** Your employer is required to deduct a certain percentage of your gross pay for federal income taxes.

As You Read

Connect What traits do financially responsible people have in common?

Vocabulary

You can find definitions in the glossary at the back of this book.

First Steps

As a young adult, you will be responsible for your own financial decisions. *What money management skills do you think you should learn first?*

Figure 14.1 **Your Paycheck**

Net Pay Your pay stub provides important information about earnings and deductions. *How much did this employee take home after deductions?*

Identification

Earnings	Hours	Current	Year-to-Date	Deductions	Current	Year-to-Date
REGULAR RATE 7.00	54	378.00	4158.00	DENTAL	5.00	55.00
				FEDTAX	23.03	253.33
				STATE TAX	4.29	47.19
				FICAHI	5.45	59.95
				MED INS	16.50	181.50
				SOCSEC	7.20	79.20
Totals	54	378.00	4158.00		61.47	676.17
Net Pay		316.53				

WORKER, PAT L   Period Ending 06/11   Check # 1103503

Employee # 5678   Employee SSN 000-50-1234   Department 425

Earnings   **Net pay**   **Totals**   **Deductions**

- **State and Local Taxes** The amount withheld for state and local income taxes will vary depending on where you live.
- **Social Security** Social Security taxes pay for retirement, disability, and survivors' benefits. They may be listed on your pay stub as FICA (Federal Insurance Contributions Act) or OASDI (Old Age, Survivors, and Disability Insurance).
- **Medicare** Deductions for Medicare pay for the medical expenses of people age 65 or older and of younger people with certain medical conditions.
- **Retirement or Savings Plan** If your company offers a retirement or savings plan, you may choose to have money deducted from your paycheck so that it can be invested in the plan.
- **Benefits** Companies that offer benefits such as health and dental plans may require employees to contribute to the plans.

Income Taxes

The biggest deduction is likely to be for federal income taxes. All workers are required to pay their share. Many state and local governments also collect income taxes. In most cases, employers withhold tax money. This means they keep the amount of money from an employee's paycheck that is to be set aside and sent to the government. The amount depends on how much you earn, how often you get paid, and other factors. Every person must fill out a Form W-4 (Employee's Withholding Allowance Certificate) when a new job begins. The form asks for information about your marital status, number of dependents, and other personal information used to calculate that person's withholdings.

The Internal Revenue Service (IRS) is the agency that collects federal income tax. A tax return can be filled out on paper and sent to the IRS or it can be completed and submitted online. You need certain information and forms to complete your tax return. You can download and print directions and forms from the IRS Web site. Common tax forms include:

- **Form W-2** This form shows your total earnings for the previous year and the total amount of tax that was withheld. Confirm that your Social Security number is correct and that the figures match the year-to-date figures on your last pay stub.
- **Form 1040** You must complete one of three federal tax return forms. Form 1040 is the longest form and can be used by anyone. Form 1040A is a simpler version for taxpayers who fit certain requirements. Form 1040EZ is the simplest form, often used by single people with a small income and no dependents.
- **Form 1099-INT** This form, sent by your bank, shows the amount of interest you earned during the year. **Interest** is a fee the bank pays you for the opportunity to use your money. Interest is income and must be reported on your tax return.

✓ **Reading Check** **Identify** What are the three common types of tax forms?

Character?!
In Action

Plan Ahead
If you have a semester-long assignment, should you start it a week before it is due or at the beginning of the semester? This same principle can be applied to your finances. Even though savings accounts, credit history, and investing may seem like things you do not have to worry about yet, it is important to start thinking about your finances now.

You Decide
Think of a friend or family member who is financially responsible. What does this person do or not do that makes you feel that way?

Bank Accounts

Bank accounts keep your money in a safe, insured place, allowing you to withdraw cash whenever you need it. In a bank account, your money works for you while you are not using it. Some accounts require a minimum balance, charge a monthly service fee, or charge a fee for certain transactions. Consider how much money you will keep in the account. Think about the types of transactions you will make most often, such as writing checks or using a debit card. Choose the account that meets your needs at the lowest cost.

a Control number				
		OMB No. 1545-0008		
b Employer identification number 123456-78		1 Wages, tips, other compensation 9,672.00	2 Federal income tax withheld 745.00	
c Employer's name, address, and ZIP code ABC STORES 2001 RING ROAD LARGETOWN, NY 10001		3 Social security wages 9,672.00	4 Social security tax withheld 599.66	
		5 Medicare wages and tips 9,672.00	6 Medicare tax withheld 140.24	
		7 Social security tips	8 Allocated tips	
d Employee's social security number 000-98-7654		9 Advance EIC payment	10 Dependent care benefits	
e Employee's name, address, and ZIP code JESSE B. STUDENT 4567 LINCOLN ST. LARGETOWN, NY 10001		11 Nonqualified plans	12 Benefits included in box 1	
		13	14 Other	
		15 Statutory employee ☐ Deceased ☐ Pension plan ☐ Legal rep. ☐ Deferred compensation ☐		
16 State NY Employer's state I.D. no. 00-98765	17 State wages, tips, etc. 9,672.00	18 State income tax 345.00	19 Locality name	20 Local wages, tips, etc.	21 Local income tax

Form W-2

Your Form W-2 summarizes your earnings and taxes for the year. *How much federal income tax was withheld from this person's pay?*

Having health insurance promotes health. Heath insurance allows you to see a doctor when necessary and participate in preventive medicine. Health insurance helps people cover health care costs, including doctor visits, hospital stays, surgery, procedures, tests, and home care. Many of these services prevent more serious problems later.

Transactions

Banking used to require a trip to the bank and waiting in line for a bank teller. While that is still an option, there are now many more ways to conduct your banking business:

- **ATMs** Automated teller machines, or ATMs, give bank customers electronic access to their accounts. You can deposit funds, withdraw cash, check balances, and transfer money.
- **Checks** A check is a written order that instructs a bank to pay a specific amount of money to a person or company. It is important to keep an accurate record of all of the checks you write. You can keep track online or in a check register.
- **Debit Cards** A **debit card** is a card that deducts the cost of a purchase from the user's account at the time of purchase. The money is deducted from your account when the receipt reaches the bank. Debit cards are often used in place of checks.
- **Automated Services** Banks can automatically transfer money to and from your accounts with your permission. Direct deposit of your paychecks is an example. You can also arrange to have certain bills paid directly out of your account each month.
- **Telephone Banking** A recorded message will ask you to enter a password or PIN. Typical options include hearing your account balance or recent transactions and transferring money.
- **Online Banking** Using the Internet, you can view current account balances, see a list of previous transactions, and transfer funds between accounts. You may also be able to pay bills, print bank statements, order checks, and request other services.

Life On Your Own

Saving and Investing

People today are living longer and healthier lives than they did in the past, and this is making it more and more important to save and invest your money. It is never too soon to start saving your money. In fact, the choices you make now can impact your lifestyle many years into the future. There are important guidelines that can help you make the most of your money.

How It Works Most people begin by opening a savings account. Before opening a savings account, be sure to find out what fees, if any, are associated with the account. Investments, financial products you can purchase to make your money grow, are another way of planning for your future. Low-risk investments, which include savings bonds and money market accounts, should pay a steady amount of interest over a long period of time.

Try It Out Imagine you have $200 to invest. Research some banks in your area, and find the one that offers the highest interest rates on savings accounts. Next, choose a stock in which to invest. If you need ideas, use the Internet or look in a newspaper. Find out the interest rates for that stock. Assume the interest rate is not going to change for the stock or the savings account.

> **Your Turn** If you were to put your money in a savings account, calculate the interest you would earn over ten years. Next, calculate the profit you would earn over the next ten years if you invested your money in your chosen stock. Which option makes you more money?

Reconcile Your Account

Once a month, your bank sends you a statement of your checking account, either in the mail or online. It tells you the balance at the beginning of the statement period and includes deposits, withdrawals, service fees, and interest payments. When you receive your statement, you should reconcile your account. When you **reconcile** ('re-kən-ˌsī(-ə)l) your account, you check it for accuracy. Check the statement against your check register or online tracker. Record transactions, fees, or interest that you may have forgotten. This will help you manage your account by keeping it accurate and up to date.

Build Your Savings

It is always a good idea to save some of your money for emergencies or future use. Banks use money in savings accounts to make loans and investments, and in return, you earn interest. Two common ways of earning interest are:

- **Compound Interest** Most banks pay **compound interest**. This is interest that is calculated on the deposits you make and on the interest you have already earned. The more frequently interest is compounded, the more you stand to gain, assuming you leave the interest in the account to grow. When you compare interest rates offered by different banks, be sure to pay attention to the annual percentage yield (APY). This figure tells you how much you will earn, including the effect of compound interest.

- **Money Market Account** Once you build up enough savings, you may want to consider a money market account. The financial institution pays a higher interest rate because it invests your deposit. Most money market accounts also allow you to write a limited number of checks each month.

✓ **Reading Check** **Recall** Why is it important to keep your bank account accurate and up to date?

Prepare for the Future

To be financially fit, you must learn to manage your income and expenses. You must have the self-discipline to establish priorities, set goals, and work to meet them. An important part of financial fitness is preparing for your future. That involves much more than simply saving a few dollars.

Insurance

Insurance (in-'shur-ən(t)s) is purchased to provide financial protection in the case of loss or harm. Anyone can experience health problems, accidents, natural disasters, or crime. An insurance policy cannot prevent these problems from happening, but it can give you financial protection if they do.

Succeed in **SCHOOL** and **LIFE**

Planning Ahead

Just like financial planning, academic planning requires foresight and scheduling. No matter how close or distant the goal, be it to complete a homework assignment by the end of the week or improve your grades over the semester, similar principles apply. Try applying some of the tips you learn in this chapter about financial planning to planning for schoolwork.

An insurance policy is a legal contract that spells out the agreement between the insurance company and the consumer. The consumer, or policyholder, agrees to make payments called premiums. In return, the insurance company agrees to compensate, or repay, the policyholder in case of certain events or losses. When buying insurance, be sure you study the policy carefully. Most insurance policies have a deductible, a set amount the policyholder must pay for each loss before the insurance company pays out.

Types of Insurance

People's insurance needs change throughout their life cycles. The four most common types of insurance, considered the basic minimum for most adults, are health, auto, home, and life insurance. Each covers specific types of risks and losses.

- **Health Insurance** This is important because you cannot predict your future medical needs. An illness or accident could result in thousands of dollars in medical bills. Many employers offer health insurance for employees and their families.

- **Auto Insurance** Auto insurance may compensate you if your vehicle is stolen, vandalized, or damaged. Your insurance may cover damage to vehicles and other property caused during an accident. It may also cover injuries to you or others. Insurance requirements and laws vary from state to state.

- **Home Insurance** Property coverage insures against loss resulting from theft, fire, flooding, or other damage. Liability coverage insures against losses caused to others while they are in the home. Homeowners generally purchase policies that cover the building itself as well as the contents. Renters need only to cover their personal property.

- **Life Insurance** Life insurance pays benefits to a specified person or persons in the event of the policyholder's death. Without life insurance, those left behind after the death of a family member may face financial hardship. There is a wide variety of types of life insurance. Some provide insurance protection only. Others combine insurance and investment features.

Accident Insurance

Auto insurance is used for more than just fixing a car that has been in an accident. *In what other ways might you use auto insurance?*

Planning for Retirement

Planning for retirement early gives more time for your investments to grow. Social Security taxes withheld from paychecks go to the Social Security fund, run by the federal government. When people reach retirement age, they start receiving monthly payments from this fund. However, these payments alone are not enough. Most people invest money throughout their working years and draw on that money in retirement. Two common ways to prepare for retirement are 401(k) plans and individual retirement accounts.

- **401(k) Plans** A **401(k) plan** is a retirement plan offered by many companies. Employees who choose to participate have a percentage of their pay withheld from each paycheck. The money is invested in that employee's retirement fund. Many companies that offer this plan make matching contributions.
- **Individual Retirement Accounts** You can also invest in retirement on your own. An individual retirement account (IRA) is a plan that enables workers to set aside money for retirement. Banks and other financial institutions can set up IRAs. Contributions to an IRA cannot exceed a certain amount each year.

Invest for the Future

Banking, budgeting, taxes, and insurance are financial topics that impact your life now or will in the near future. Another piece of the financial puzzle that requires a more long-term view is investing. When you **invest**, you use money to participate in a business enterprise that offers a possible profit. Stocks and bonds are examples of investments. The sooner you begin investing, the more time your money will have to grow. Investing differs from saving. A savings account is the best place for money that you will need in a relatively short time or that you want to have readily available in case of an emergency. Investing is more appropriate for money that you will not need to touch for years. Also, investing is riskier.

Investment Risks

The value of investments can swing up and down in ways that are hard to predict. You might end up with more or less money than you expected, or you could lose the money you started with. You can manage risk by making smart choices. Start by learning a few simple rules:

- **Basics** Do not invest until you have a steady income, a balanced budget, enough money in your savings account for emergencies, and adequate insurance.
- **Knowledge** Many books, Web sites, and courses are available to help beginners learn about investing. You may also want to consider paying for professional financial advice.
- **Diversify and Balance** Have you ever heard the expression, "Don't put all your eggs in one basket"? Putting all your money in a single investment can be risky. It is safer to **diversify**, or spread, your money among several different investments.

Get Involved!

Making Donations

Think about donating to a charity. If your budget supports it, you can always donate money. But keep in mind there are many other things you can donate, including time, blood, blankets, clothing, food, and more. Money is always welcome, but offering to spend time with a lonely elderly person can make a difference, too. If your budget does not support donating money, think about what else you can donate.

Enjoy Life

Retirement should be viewed as an enjoyable part of life. *Why is it important to start saving for retirement early?*

Investment Options

Anyone who decides to invest money should be familiar with the basic types of investments and the risks they carry. Four of the most popular types of investments are:

- **Certificates of Deposit (CD)** When you invest in a CD, you deposit money with a financial institution for a specified period of time and receive an agreed-upon interest rate in return. Early withdrawal, however, will result in substantial penalties.
- **Bonds** Governments or corporations issue bonds, or certificates of debt, as a way of borrowing money. Consumers buy the bonds by paying money to the issuer. The issuer promises to repay the debt, plus an additional amount, by a certain date.
- **Stocks** Corporations raise money by selling stocks, or shares of a company's money or assets held by an individual investor. Corporations do this by making **shares**, or individual units of ownership, available to investors. Investors who purchase stock receive a portion of the profits if the corporation does well, but risk losing money if the company does badly.
- **Mutual Funds** A mutual fund is a group of investments held in common by many individual investors. The fund managers use the money to purchase and manage stocks, bonds, and other types of investments. Earnings are divided among the fund's investors. Mutual funds are usually less risky because they are highly diversified and managed by financial experts.

 Podcasts Access the Online Learning Center to download *Managing Life Skills* podcasts.

Section 14.1 — After You Read

Review Key Concepts

1. **Give** four examples of ways you might be paid.
2. **Identify** two ways to build your savings.
3. **List** the four most common types of insurance adults need.

Practice Academic Skills

 English Language Arts

4. Four types of insurance are mentioned in this chapter, but there are other types. Pick one other type of insurance and research it. How common is it? Do you think getting that type of insurance is a good idea? Write a brief report summarizing your findings and opinion.

 Social Studies

5. Income tax is only one type of tax. Use the Internet and other resources to investigate the taxes in your city and state. What is taxed? How can this affect the way you choose to spend your money? Write a brief report analyzing your findings.

Check Your Answers Check your answers at this book's Online Learning Center at **glencoe.com**.

NCTE 7 Conduct research and gather, evaluate, and synthesize data to communicate discoveries.

NCSS VI A Examine persistent issues involving the rights, roles, and status of the individual in relation to the general welfare.

Use Credit Wisely

Credit is a valuable tool when used wisely.

Reading Guide

Before You Read

Look It Up As you read this section, keep a dictionary close by. If you hear or read a word that you do not know, look it up in the glossary at the back of this book or in the dictionary. Before long, this practice will become a habit. You will be amazed at how many new words you learn.

Read to Learn

Key Concepts

- **Explain** the different types of credit.
- **Categorize** credit terms and fees.
- **Predict** problems that can stem from irresponsible credit use.

Main Idea

There are different types of credit including cash loans, sales credit, and credit cards. Using credit has many financial advantages, but it needs to be used wisely.

Graphic Organizer

As you read, take note of the advantages and disadvantages of using credit. Use a table like the one shown to help you organize your information.

Using Credit	
Pros	Cons

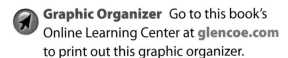
Graphic Organizer Go to this book's Online Learning Center at **glencoe.com** to print out this graphic organizer.

Content Vocabulary

◇ credit
◇ creditor
◇ finance charge
◇ credit report
◇ credit rating
◇ annual percentage rate (APR)

Academic Vocabulary

You will find these words in your reading and on your tests. Use the glossary to look up their definitions if necessary.

■ principal
■ terms

Academic Standards

English Language Arts

NCTE 8 Use information resources to gather information and create and communicate knowledge.

Mathematics

NCTM Problem Solving Apply and adapt a variety of appropriate strategies to solve problems.

Social Studies

NCSS VII K Production, Distribution, and Consumption Distinguish between economics as a field of inquiry and the economy.

NCTE *National Council of Teachers of English*
NCTM *National Council of Teachers of Mathematics*
NSES *National Science Education Standards*
NCSS *National Council for the Social Studies*

Understand Credit

As You Read

Connect Think about the ways your wants and needs can contribute to your credit.

As you consider the credit cards available to you, remember the responsibility that goes with them. You are about to start building your credit history. It is up to you to build a history that reflects how well you can manage your credit.

When you use **credit**, you receive money, goods, or services now and promise to pay for them in the future. The idea of credit is summed up by the phrase "buy now, pay later." It sounds simple, but in fact, buying on credit is serious business. When you buy on credit, you are committing your future resources.

Banks, finance companies, stores, and other organizations that extend credit are creditors. A **creditor** allows consumers to borrow money on the understanding that the consumer will pay back the loan over a specified period of time. During that period, the consumer will pay back the **principal**, which is the original amount borrowed. Customers also have to pay interest which, as you learned in Section 14.1, is the fee paid for the opportunity to use the creditor's money. Because of interest, you pay more when buying on credit than you would if you paid by cash, check, or debit card at the time of the purchase.

Vocabulary

You can find definitions in the glossary at the back of this book.

Types of Credit

There are several types of credit. Each type has advantages and disadvantages and is associated with particular kinds of transactions. The three most common types of credit are:

- **Credit Cards** Businesses, banks, and other financial institutions issue credit cards, the most widely used type of credit. Credit cards offer great ease and convenience, but their downside is that they often carry higher interest rates than other types of credit.

- **Sales Credit** If you buy something now from a store and pay the store for it over time, you are using sales credit. This is also known as an installment plan because the customer makes regularly scheduled payments called installments. Stores hope that by giving you more time to pay for a purchase, you will buy more than you otherwise would. The amount of interest charged for sales credit varies from business to business.

Prepare for the Future

The concept of buying now and paying later may be appealing. *What are some of the risks of using credit?*

- **Cash Loans** If you are in the market for a car or another large purchase, you may decide to take out a cash loan. If you apply for a cash loan, you must prove that you can repay it or offer something of value to secure it. People who buy a home, for example, generally offer the home itself as security. If they fail to repay the loan, the creditor can force the sale of the home to settle the debt.

Pros and Cons of Using Credit

In addition to being convenient, credit offers several other major advantages. It enables you to buy things that you need but cannot yet afford. For example, buying a car on credit allows you to enjoy the benefits of the car while you are still paying for it. Credit also helps you handle unexpected expenses, such as the cost of replacing or repairing a broken appliance or paying for an unplanned medical bill. Credit is also helpful in building proof of your financial responsibility. Using a credit card responsibly and making your payments on time, for example, could help convince a creditor to give you a loan in the future.

The most notable disadvantage of using credit is its potential cost. When you use credit, you incur, or take on, finance charges. A **finance charge** is made up of interest and any additional fees, such as charges for late payments. With most credit cards, unless you pay the balance in full by the stated due date, you will incur additional finance charges every month until you pay off your bill. Over time, these charges can add a significant amount to the cost of your purchase.

Credit also tends to encourage impulse buying. It is much easier to hand over a credit card for something that catches your eye. You would be much more likely to pause and consider your purchase if you had to hand over cash instead. Credit makes it more difficult to understand that you are spending real money. Many people find that credit encourages them to overspend. Developing good consumer skills can help you enjoy the benefits of credit while minimizing the drawbacks.

Becoming Creditworthy

If you want to use credit, you need to convince creditors that you can be trusted to pay back the money. Lenders have several ways of assessing the risk they are taking before they agree to extend credit. One way is to examine the applicant's finances.

Applicants who have used credit in the past have a credit history, which is a pattern of past behavior in paying debts. Creditors are more likely to extend credit to those whose credit history indicates that they paid past debts in full and on time. People who have a record of failing to pay debts or of being repeatedly late with payments are considered a high credit risk. They are less likely to be granted additional credit.

Financial *Literacy*

Find the Best Deal

Susanna, a recent college graduate, is planning to buy her first new car. She has $3,000 saved, but she needs to borrow another $15,000 to purchase the car. The sales manager explained that the $15,000 loan will be offered with a 10 percent interest rate, and there are three different options to pay off the $15,000 loan:

Loan A (three years): 36 payments of $484

Loan B (four years): 48 payments of $480

Loan C (five years): 60 payments of $319

What is the total interest of each loan? Which option is the best deal?

Math Concept **Loan Terms** When borrowing money, the period of the loan matters as much as the interest rate.

Starting Hint To calculate the interest of each loan, subtract the principal amount ($15,000) from the total cost of each option.

 For math help, go to the Math Appendix at the back of the book.

NCTM Problem Solving Apply and adapt a variety of appropriate strategies to solve problems.

Succeed in **SCHOOL** and **LIFE**

Establish First-Time Credit

If you do not have any credit history yet, there are ways to start developing it. Open savings and checking accounts. Make regular deposits, and avoid overdrawing. If possible, put utility bills, such as telephone and Internet service, in your name. Pay those bills on time. Apply to a local store for a credit card. Pay your credit card bills on time.

The questions on a credit application also help creditors determine whether or not they will give you credit. A creditor may verify your answers by calling your employer and other appropriate people. Here are some typical questions:

- **Employment** Where do you work? How long have you worked there? What is your occupation? How much do you earn?
- **Housing** Where do you live? How long have you lived there? Do you own or rent? What is your monthly housing payment?
- **Financial** With which banks do you have accounts? How much is in each account? What loans do you currently have? How much do you owe on those loans? What are your monthly loan payments?

When deciding about loans, lenders also use information from credit bureaus. These agencies gather information about consumers' spending patterns from banks, stores, and other sources. They compile the information into a **credit report**, a record of a particular consumer's transactions and payment patterns. They then sell those reports to lenders who are evaluating a specific person's credit application.

Credit bureaus do not make judgments about whether a person is a good credit risk. They simply provide information. The lenders make the decision based on the credit application and credit report. After considering this information, they come up with a credit rating. A **credit rating** is an evaluation of a consumer's credit history. If the credit rating is positive, the lender will likely approve the credit application.

✓ **Reading Check** **Identify** What types of questions do creditors ask before they give a person credit?

Choosing a Credit Card

Unless you have a bad credit history, you should not find it difficult to obtain a credit card. What you may find difficult, though, is deciding what credit card to use. There are thousands from which to choose. Understanding some basic features can help you choose wisely.

- **General Purpose Cards** Issued by major banks and financial institutions, general purpose cards can be used to purchase goods and services at businesses throughout the country and around the world. Most general purpose cards can also be used to obtain cash from automated teller machines and to make online purchases.

◀ **Prepare for the Future**

One of the advantages of using credit is that you can buy things that you cannot yet afford, such as a major appliance or a car. *What are some other advantages of using credit?*

276   Unit 4 ··· r Skills

- **Private Label Cards** Issued by chain stores and gasoline companies, these cards can be used only for purchasing from the company that issues them. Some stores may offer special discounts to customers who use their cards.
- **Co-Branded Cards** These cards carry the name of the issuing bank and of another company, such as an airline or hotel chain. Users earn rewards for using the card, such as air miles or free nights at hotels.
- **Smart Cards** Online shoppers use smart cards with a computer chip that stores information such as user name, password, and shipping information. To make an online purchase, you insert the card into a special reader, which fills out the Web order form.

Comparing Fees and Terms

You should read carefully and compare the fees and **terms**, or conditions, of each credit card's agreement. These are spelled out in the small print of a credit card agreement and can vary considerably from issuer to issuer. Here are some costs and features to consider:

- **Annual Percentage Rate** The **annual percentage rate (APR)** is the annual rate of interest that the company charges you for using credit. The lower the APR, the less interest you pay.

Two Views One World

Is Credit Helpful or Harmful?

Some people feel that credit expands their horizons, allowing them more freedom, while others feel credit can trap and limit them.

Samantha: I think credit is a great advancement. It allows you to buy things you wouldn't normally be able to buy. I have a part-time job right now, and I'm earning money. I really wanted to go on a trip with my school, so I used my credit card to pay for the trip, and I'll pay off my credit card bill with the money I earn from my job. Without credit, I wouldn't have been able to go on the trip.

Devin: I understand the arguments supporting credit, but I just think its disadvantages outweigh its advantages. For many people, the temptation of credit is too much, and they end up in debt. And credit card companies charge such high interest rates and fees, that the debt is practically impossible to pay off. Once you have bad credit, it's very hard to fix, and bad credit means you'll have trouble buying a car or house or any other big purchase.

Seeing Both Sides
Have you had experience with credit yet? If so, which opinion better reflects your experience? If not, given what you know about credit, which opinion do you agree with? Why?

Prepare for the Future

Credit counselors can help people resolve credit problems and get out of debt.
Why is it important to resolve credit problems as quickly as possible?

- **Credit Limit** Your credit limit is the maximum amount of credit that the creditor will extend to you. If your credit limit is $2,000, for example, you must not run up charges that exceed that amount. As your credit history gets better and better, you can request higher credit limits.
- **Fees** Some issuing companies charge an annual fee for the use of their card. You might also be charged fees for late payments or for going over your credit limit.
- **Grace Period** Most credit card companies allow a grace period after the payment due date. If you pay the balance on your card late but still during the grace period, you will not have to pay any finance charges.
- **Special Features and Incentives** Many credit cards offer incentives or rewards to encourage consumers to choose their credit cards. Common incentives include travel insurance, frequent flyer miles, cash back rewards, points that can be used to buy products, and discounts on car rentals.

When selecting a card, it is a good idea to compare a few different credit cards side by side. You should choose the features that most closely match your needs and spending habits. If you intend to carry over a balance, look for low interest rates. If you plan to pay off the balance every month, you might look for incentives that would be useful to you.

✓ **Reading Check** **Define** What is an annual percentage rate?

Use Credit Responsibly

When using a credit card, set rules for yourself and stick to them. These rules will help you manage your finances, make sure you do not get into significant credit card debt, build good credit history, and protect yourself from fraud. Be realistic and specific, and set your own limit on what you will charge each month. Use your credit card receipts to keep track of your spending and to check that your bill is correct. If possible, pay off the balance on your bill within the grace period. If you cannot pay the full balance, pay the most you can afford.

Credit is a valuable tool when used wisely. However, irresponsible credit card use can lead to serious problems. Warning signs of irresponsible credit use include constant worry about debt, spending more than what is earned, "maxing out" credit cards, and using one credit card to pay off another. Consequences of these actions include harassment by collection agencies that may be called in to claim the unpaid debt and possible repossession of goods. Perhaps the most serious consequence is developing a poor credit history. Bad credit makes it difficult or impossible to get a loan in the future. It can take many years to improve a bad credit rating. If you think you are getting into credit trouble, take action immediately to recover from the situation. Contact your creditors and see if you can work out a payment plan.

Instead of receiving your credit card bills and bank statements in the mail, go paperless. Most banks and credit card companies now offer online, paperless delivery of bills and statements. This option not only reduces paper waste, it can also be more convenient.

 Podcasts Access the Online Learning Center to download *Managing Life Skills* podcasts.

Section 14.2 After You Read

Review Key Concepts

1. **Explain** the impact that interest has on credit.
2. **Compare and contrast** general purpose credit cards and smart cards.
3. **Summarize** ways to use a credit card responsibly.

Practice Academic Skills

 English Language Arts

4. Use the Internet and other resources to research a specific type of loan called a payday loan. Write a paragraph defining what payday loans are and explaining the dangers of this type of credit.

 Social Studies

5. Use the Internet and other resources to research the use of credit cards in the United States. Then write a brief report about the positive and negative effects of the introduction and increased use of credit cards in America.

 Check Your Answers Check your answers at this book's Online Learning Center at **glencoe.com**.

NCTE 8 Use information resources to gather information and create and communicate knowledge.

NCSS VII K Distinguish between economics as a field of inquiry and the economy.

College Entrance Exams

What Are College Entrance Exams?

College entrance exams, required by most colleges, are tests used to measure students' abilities, compare students, and select students for admission. There are two major college entrance exams: the SAT and the ACT. You must check to see which exam each specific college accepts.

What is the difference between the ACT and the SAT?

Both are national standardized tests that help colleges evaluate students. However, they are very different. The ACT has a science section, while the SAT does not. Both the SAT and ACT have essay sections, but the essay is optional on the ACT. The SAT is scored out of 2400, while the ACT is scored out of 36. Also, there is a penalty for wrong answers on the SAT, but not on the ACT.

How do I know which test to take?

If the college you are applying to accepts only one, the decision is easy. However, many accept both, and then you must decide which to take. Generally, if you feel relatively comfortable with vocabulary, grammar, and writing essays, you should take the SAT. If your vocabulary is not as strong or if you are more academic than test savvy, you might want to take the ACT. However, the best way decide is to take a practice test for each and see how you do.

Do I need to study for these tests?

Yes! Even though you might have heard these tests measure only intelligence, studying for them, familiarizing yourself with their formats, and taking practice tests can greatly improve your scores. Since your score could be the difference between getting into the college of your choice or not, it is definitely worth the extra time to study.

Hands-On

College Readiness Think of one college to which you are thinking of applying, and find out whether it accepts the SAT, the ACT, or both. Based on this information and what you learned previously on this page, which test do you think you would take? With permission from your parents or teacher, go online and find out when this test is offered and where. Also, find out if there are any practice tests being offered in the near future.

Path to Success

CCR ☆ **College & Career Readiness**

Set a Goal Different colleges require different college entrance exam test scores. Figure out what your goal score is.

Assess Yourself Take a practice college entrance test to see how close you are to your goal score.

Draft a Study Plan Based on your practice test, create a study plan along with a time frame.

Get Help There are many resources if you need help preparing for the exam, including your teachers, classes, online courses, and test preparation books.

Take Care of Yourself On test day, be sure to get enough sleep, eat breakfast, and wear comfortable clothes.

Stay Positive Believing you can do well on your college entrance exams will pave the way for more successful test taking.

 Go to this book's Online Learning Center at **glencoe.com** to learn more about college and career readiness.

CHAPTER SUMMARY

Section 14.1
Everyday Financial Management

Your financial fitness is determined by your ability to understand and manage your paycheck, bank accounts, income, and expenses. Your income is affected by how you are paid and by the deductions that are taken out of your paycheck. Managing your income is easier with bank accounts. Insurance is a way to protect your income and possessions.

Section 14.2
Use Credit Wisely

Banks and other organizations often extend credit to their customers. There are both advantages and disadvantages to using credit. It is important to choose the right card for your needs and to pay close attention to the terms and fees included in the agreement. Credit should be used responsibly to avoid debt, high fees, bad credit, and other financial problems.

Vocabulary Review

1. Create a fill-in-the-blank sentence for each vocabulary term. The sentence should have enough information to determine the missing word.

Content Vocabulary
- gross pay (p. 265)
- net pay (p. 265)
- deduction (p. 265)
- interest (p. 267)
- debit card (p. 268)
- reconcile (p. 269)
- compound interest (p. 269)
- insurance (p. 269)

- 401(k) plan (p. 271)
- invest (p. 271)
- credit (p. 274)
- creditor (p. 274)
- finance charge (p. 275)
- credit report (p. 276)
- credit rating (p. 276)
- annual percentage rate (APR) (p. 277)

Academic Vocabulary
- diversify (p. 271)
- shares (p. 272)
- principal (p. 274)
- terms (p. 277)

Review Key Concepts

2. **Explain** what it means to be financially fit.
3. **List** six types of banking transactions.
4. **Contrast** the two common ways to prepare for retirement.
5. **Explain** the different types of credit.
6. **Categorize** credit terms and fees.
7. **Predict** problems that can stem from irresponsible credit use.

Critical Thinking

8. **Predict** Imagine you are self employed and want to start saving for retirement. What savings plan do you think makes the most sense?
9. **Draw Conclusions** Suppose you have been given $500 to invest for two years. How would you invest that money? Explain in a paragraph.
10. **Analyze** Why do you think people fall so easily into the credit card trap?
11. **Identify** What interpersonal skills can help resolve financial conflicts?

ACTIVE LEARNING

Family & Community Connections

12. Insurance Options Imagine you are buying one of the four main types of insurance: health, auto, home, or life insurance. Choose one type, and research consumer advice related to that type of insurance. If you were shopping for this type of insurance, what basic choices would you have to make about the kind of coverage you want before you make a purchase? How  would you choose what type of insurance policy to purchase? How would you choose who to buy it from? Summarize your findings in a brief report.

13. Paying Your Taxes There are several options when it comes time to file your tax returns. Some people choose to use the services of a certified tax preparer. Others choose to prepare their returns using financial software that collects your data and calculates your tax information for you. Yet others choose to fill out the forms themselves with no additional assistance. Discuss these options with people in your community who have used these methods. Which method seems to be most common? What are the advantages and disadvantages of each? Write a brief report summarizing what you found out about each method based on your conversations.

21st Century Skills

Technology Skills

14. Desktop Publishing Use desktop publishing software to create a booklet or brochure educating teens about credit cards. Include suggestions for using credit cards wisely, recognizing credit problems, and dealing with problems if they arise.

Media Literacy Skills

15. Financial Magazines There are many words used in finance that are not used in other situations. Use the Internet to find an article in a popular financial magazine. Make a list of the financial terms you do not understand. Use the context to try to define the word on your own. Then look up the terms in a dictionary. How does context help you understand words you have never seen before? How can learning the vocabulary in this article help you in the future?

 Connections

Financial Literacy Skills

16. Basic Banking As part of its mission, FCCLA encourages students to address important financial literacy issues. Understanding personal finances will help you become creditworthy and stay that way. Think about financial costs that are in your future. This may mean buying a car or saving for college. Write a savings plan that will help you reach your savings goal.

Academic Skills

 English Language Arts

17. Advice Column Imagine you are a columnist for a financial magazine for teens. Think about common questions that teens have about financial management, such as saving for a new computer or paying for college. Use what you have learned in this chapter to write a question and its answer as if it will be published. Use humor, and be creative when you offer advice to your readers.

> **NCTE 7** Conduct research and gather, evaluate, and synthesize data to communicate discoveries.

 Social Studies

18. The Cost of Technology Consider a popular technology development, such as GPS or hybrid cars. Research the development and cost of using that technology. What are the short-term and long-term financial effects of buying and using that technology? Is it to your advantage to invest in that technology?

> **NCSS VII C Production, Distribution, and Consumption** Consider the costs and benefits to society of allocating goods and services through private and public sectors.

 Mathematics

19. Calculate Interest Yvette has saved $5,000. She wants to earn as much interest as possible with her checking account. She can open a checking account at First Bank at a two percent interest rate. Her other choice is a checking account at Second Bank at a four percent interest rate. How much more money would she make with the account at Second Bank after a year?

Math Concept **Subtracting Percentages**
To subtract percentages, first convert them to decimals. You can do this by dividing the percent by 100. For example, 2% would be 2 ÷ 100 = .02.

Starting Hint Subtract the interest rate at First Bank (2%) from the interest rate at Second Bank (4%). Then multiply your answer by the total amount Yvette has invested ($5,000).

 For more math practice, go to the Math Appendix at the back of the book.

> **NCTM Problem Solving** Solve problems that arise in mathematics and in other contexts.

Standardized Test Practice

CCR College & Career Readiness

WORD PROBLEMS
Directions Read the problem. Then choose the correct answer.

Test-Taking Tip When attempting a word problem, first find the necessary information. Identify the question being asked and the information necessary to answer that question. You can ignore everything else in the problem.

20. Today, you paid four bills with checks for a total of $89.37. You also used your debit card to purchase a pair of shoes for $58.39 and lunch for $5.72. Lastly, you deposited a $55.00 check that your friend gave you to repay a loan. How much more or less money do you have in your account than you did when the day started?

Prepare Your Résumé

In this project, you will research two types of résumés and use the information to create your own résumé. You and your peers will review one another's résumés, and you will use the feedback to revise your document and prepare it for print and online applications.

My Journal

If you completed the journal entry from page 220, refer to it to see if your thoughts have changed after reading the unit.

Project Assignment

In this project you will:
- Research two kinds of résumés.
- Make a list of your work experience and your specific workplace skills.
- Decide on the best résumé format.
- Use the information to create your résumé.
- Work with a partner to assess your résumé and offer feedback.
- Refine your résumé, and create a text version for online job sites.
- Use what you have learned to create an oral report about the experience.

THE SKILLS BEHIND THE PROJECT

Key personal and relationship skills you will use in this project include:
- Communicating respectfully
- Accepting constructive criticism
- Offering constructive feedback

Academic Skills

 English Language Arts

> **NCTE 5** Use different writing process elements to communicate effectively.
>
> **NCTE 8** Use information resources to gather information and create and communicate knowledge.

STEP 1 Research Different Types of Résumés

Use the information about résumés from Chapter 16, the Career Appendix in the back of this book, and other resources to find two different ways to organize a résumé.
- A chronological résumé organizes information by work experience, from the most recent to the least recent.
- A skills-based résumé focuses on skills that are suitable for the workplace, and examples of how you have used the skills.

STEP 2 Prepare Your Résumé

Make a list of your work experience and related skills. Then decide if a chronological or skills-based résumé is more appropriate for you. Use a word processing program to create your résumé. You may wish to use the résumé builder in the *Career Plan Project Workbook* at this book's Online Learning Center at **glencoe.com**.

Writing Skills
- Describe the duties for work positions held or skills demonstrated.
- Use proper grammar, spelling, and punctuation.
- Edit the information you have written to be concise and professional.

STEP 3 Connect with Your Peers

Follow your teacher's instructions to form pairs. Exchange résumés with your partner. Review the information on your partner's résumé, and prepare three questions about the experience listed. Ask your questions, and take notes about the questions your partner asks you. Give each other constructive feedback about the résumés.

Listening Skills
- Take notes during the discussion.
- Listen attentively.
- Demonstrate understanding of your partner's questions.
- Answer questions fully and directly.

STEP 4 Build Your Portfolio Project

Use the Portfolio Project Checklist to plan and build your portfolio project and give an oral report to share what you have learned with your classmates.

Communication Skills
- Use standard English to communicate.
- Be sensitive to the needs of your audience.

STEP 5 Evaluate Your Project

Your portfolio project will be evaluated based on:

Academic Skills
- Research and self-evaluation skills
- Proper spelling, grammar, and punctuation
- Technology and formatting skills
- Structure and organization of the information on your résumé
- Clarity of your presentation
- Speaking and listening skills

Evaluation Rubric Go to this book's Online Learning Center at **glencoe.com** for a rubric you can use to evaluate your final project.

PORTFOLIO PROJECT CHECKLIST

Plan
- ☑ Incorporate your partner's feedback.
- ☑ Proofread and use spell-check on your résumé.
- ☑ Use professional fonts and design to improve the look of your résumé.
- ☑ Save a copy of your résumé as a text file to paste into online job forms, and fix any spacing issues.

Present
- ☑ Create a five-minute oral report to share what you learned about preparing a résumé with the class.
- ☑ Invite the students to ask questions. Answer any questions. Demonstrate in your answers that you respect their perspectives.
- ☑ Turn in a copy of your résumé and your notes. Place a copy of your formatted résumé in your portfolio.

Portfolio Highlights

Résumé Design and Style

A well-designed résumé can help your search for a career. Potential employers will be able to spot key experience and skills more quickly and will be more likely to keep your information on file. However, a poorly designed résumé can distract employers from noticing your skills.

Highlight Important Information

Use italics and bold type to highlight job titles or important skills. You may want to use graphic elements, such as lines and boxes, to separate the parts of your résumé. Avoid using all capital letters, as this can make the information difficult to read.

Create a Professional Design

Design elements such as fonts, graphics, and templates can be distracting if used too frequently. Your résumé should look eye-catching, but it should also look professional and be easy to read. Give your résumé to two or three different people to get feedback on design format and readability.

Keep It Brief

Try to keep your résumé to a single page. Add new experience and skills as soon as possible to keep your résumé up to date.

UNIT 5

Pathways to Career Success

Unit Portfolio Project Preview

Fill Out a Job Application

In this unit, you will explore ways to develop a plan to meet personal and professional goals. In your portfolio project, you will get the information needed to move your plan forward.

 My Journal

Organizing Information Write a journal entry about one of the topics below. This will help you prepare for the project at the end of this unit.

- Describe the differences between factual and nonfactual information.
- Cite the information someone would need to know in order to understand who you really are.
- Explain how you would go about creating a time line of important events in your life.

Explore the Photo

Your first job can set you on the path to future career opportunities. *How can you make the most of a job, even if it is not exactly what you want to do in the future?*

287

Explore Career Paths

Chapter Objectives

Section 15.1 Understanding Careers

- **Contrast** a job and a career.
- **List** the different types of businesses and employment.
- **Identify** three common areas for change in the workplace.
- **Summarize** eight options for education and training to prepare for a career.

Section 15.2 Evaluate Career Options

- **Identify** five areas to consider when deciding what career to pursue.
- **Explain** how career clusters can help your career search.
- **Describe** how a career ladder is useful in developing a career path.

▶ Explore the Photo

Though there are many reasons for working, it is important for people to enjoy what they do. *How can enjoying what you do help you succeed in your career?*

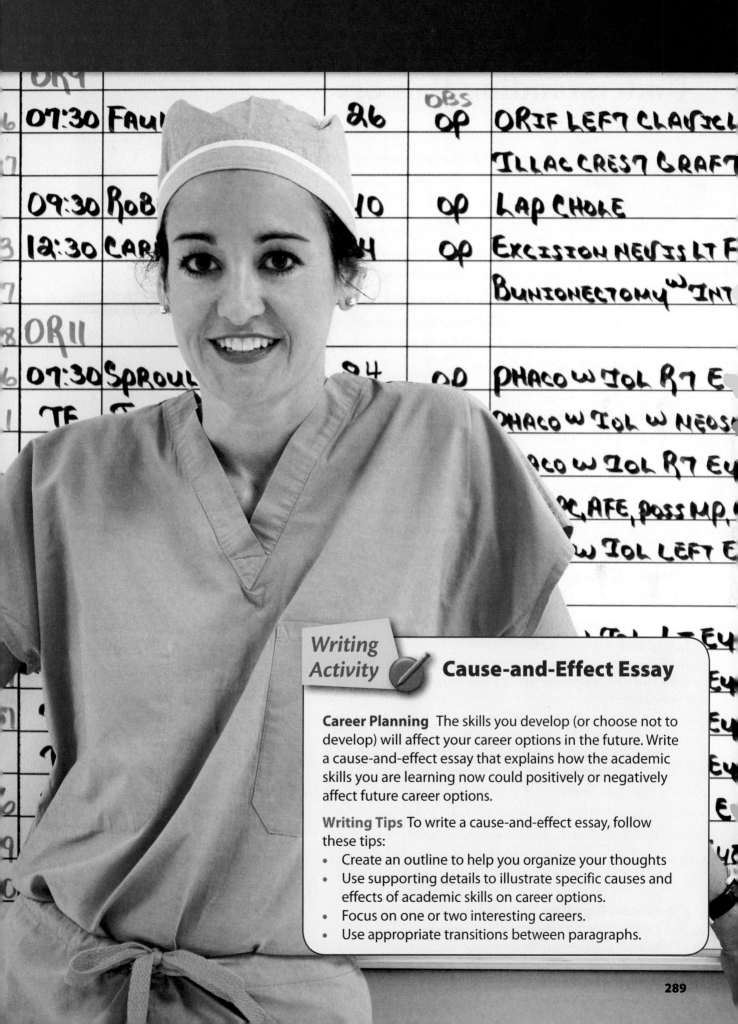

6	07:30	FAUL		26	OBS OP	ORIF LEFT CLAVICL
17						ILIAC CREST GRAFT
	09:30	ROB		10	OP	LAP CHOLE
3	12:30	CAR		4	OP	EXCISION NEVIS LT F
7						BUNIONECTOMY W INT
8	ORI					
6	07:30	SPROUL		24	OP	PHACO W IOL RT E
1	TE					PHACO W IOL W NEOS
						ACO W IOL RT EY
						C AFE, POSS MP,
						W IOL LEFT E

Writing Activity — Cause-and-Effect Essay

Career Planning The skills you develop (or choose not to develop) will affect your career options in the future. Write a cause-and-effect essay that explains how the academic skills you are learning now could positively or negatively affect future career options.

Writing Tips To write a cause-and-effect essay, follow these tips:
- Create an outline to help you organize your thoughts
- Use supporting details to illustrate specific causes and effects of academic skills on career options.
- Focus on one or two interesting careers.
- Use appropriate transitions between paragraphs.

Understanding Careers

Reading Guide

Before You Read

Prior Knowledge Write down what you already know and what you want to find out about each key concept in this section.

Read to Learn
Key Concepts
- **Contrast** a job and a career.
- **List** the different types of businesses and employment.
- **Identify** three common areas for change in the workplace.
- **Summarize** eight options for education and training to prepare for a career.

Main Idea

A person's career can affect his or her lifestyle. There are different types of employers and employment. There are basic skills that will help people in any career.

Content Vocabulary
- ◈ career
- ◈ career path
- ◈ lifestyle
- ◈ entrepreneur
- ◈ global economy
- ◈ downsizing
- ◈ outsourcing
- ◈ apprenticeship
- ◈ internship
- ◈ transferable skill

Academic Vocabulary

You will find these words in your reading and on your tests. Use the glossary to look up their definitions if necessary.

- ■ enlist
- ■ critical

Academic Standards

 English Language Arts

NCTE 8 Use information resources to gather information and create and communicate knowledge.

 Mathematics

NCTM Problem Solving Solve problems that arise in mathematics and in other contexts.

Social Studies

NCSS VII C Production, Distribution, and Consumption Consider the costs and benefits to society of allocating goods and services through private and public sectors.

Graphic Organizer

As you read, look for three ways that your career will affect your lifestyle. Use a house graphic like the one shown to help you organize your information.

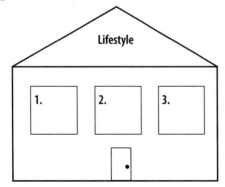

Lifestyle

1.   2.   3.

Graphic Organizer Go to this book's Online Learning Center at **glencoe.com** to print out this graphic organizer.

NCTE *National Council of Teachers of English*
NCTM *National Council of Teachers of Mathematics*
NSES *National Science Education Standards*
NCSS *National Council for the Social Studies*

Career Decisions

Some people seem to know from an early age what kind of work they want to do. Others take a while to decide what is right for them. Whether you have already made a decision or are still exploring your options, it is helpful to think about the impact that your choice of occupation will have on your life. Deciding what work to do is one of the most significant decisions you will make in life.

A career is more than just a job. A job is a specific position with a particular employer. A **career** is a series of related jobs or occupations in a particular field. Most people change jobs in order to gain more experience, earn more money, or just to do something different. Many people also have more than one career in their lifetimes. Often, people start new careers in response to economic conditions or because they seek greater satisfaction from their work.

Why People Work

If you were to ask your classmates why they want a job, most would probably answer, "To make money." Most teens look forward to earning cash for clothes, movie tickets, or gas and car insurance. As you gain independence, you will use your money for things like food and housing. Some day you may need to support a family of your own. Earning a living is important, but it is not the only reason to work. Work can also satisfy certain emotional, intellectual, and social needs. Some additional reasons why people work include

- **Achievement** Supporting yourself helps you feel proud and competent.
- **Fulfillment** Doing well and contributing to society helps you gain a sense of satisfaction.
- **Personal Growth** Working helps you gain knowledge and develop your skills.
- **Sense of Belonging** Being part of a team can be enjoyable.
- **Approval** Doing a job well helps you feel good about yourself and boosts your self-esteem.

Career Paths

Once you have set a career goal, you need to map out the path that will get you to your goal. A **career path** is all of the career moves and knowledge that a person gains as he or she works toward a career goal. Often the steps include education, training, and job experience.

For some careers, you can choose from a variety of paths. You might get a job as soon as you graduate from high school, working up to your chosen occupation by changing jobs and getting promotions. Or you might attend college first, and then start out at a higher level. Another option might be to take college courses at night while working during the day. Whatever path you choose, the main thing is to make sure it leads to your goal. Mapping out a career path is wise, but it is important to keep your plan flexible.

As You Read

Connect How will your life change when you begin working full time?

Vocabulary

You can find definitions in the glossary at the back of this book.

Consider Your Lifestyle

The type of work you choose will shape your lifestyle in many ways. Your **lifestyle** is the way you live, and it reflects your values and attitudes. The career you choose can affect your lifestyle in three important areas:

- **What You Earn** Although pay varies, some career areas and occupations have the potential for higher earnings than others. How much you need and want to earn is something to consider when deciding on a career.

- **Where You Live and Work** Many types of jobs are found everywhere, but others exist only in rural settings or in large cities. Some are more plentiful in specific parts of the country, so it is important to consider location when picking a career.

- **Your Schedule and Free Time** In some jobs, working long hours is expected. Your job might require you to work nights, weekends, and holidays, adjust to a constantly changing schedule, or be on call 24 hours a day. Extensive travel might also limit the amount of time that you can spend at home. Other jobs have shorter and more predictable and regular hours.

Think carefully about your values, and decide what is important to you. Consider these questions: What type of family life do I see in my future? Where do I want to live? What level of material comfort and status will I be happy with? Do I want to take an active role in community life? What kind of balance do I hope to achieve between my work and other areas of my life? With your answers to these questions in mind, you will be able to evaluate career options based on how well their characteristics match your values. Deciding what kind of lifestyle you want will help you narrow down your career choices and eliminate those that are clearly unsuitable.

✓ **Reading Check** **Explain** Why do people change jobs?

Careers and Lifestyle

Your career can affect your lifestyle beyond how much money you make. *Which elements of your lifestyle are most important to you?*

Math For Success

Yearly Salary

Hector is deciding between two job offers. One pays $13.00 an hour for 50 hours a week. The other pays $15.50 an hour for 40 hours a week. Hector wants to spend more time with his family, so he will probably choose the second job. If he does, what will be the difference in his yearly salary?

Math Concept **Multi-Step Problems** When solving problems with more than one step, think through each step before you start.

Starting Hint Calculate how much Hector will make in each job per year (52 weeks). After you have done that, calculate the difference in pay.

 For more math practice, go to the Math Appendix at the back of the book.

> **NCTM Problem Solving** Solve problems that arise in mathematics and in other contexts.

The World of Work

Most career fields include various types of employers and employment. Factors such as pay, benefits, and the work environment vary depending upon the career and employer you choose.

Types of Businesses

The world of work is divided into two broad sectors, or parts of society. The public sector is funded by tax dollars. It consists of local and state governments and federal government agencies. Private sector businesses are not controlled by the government. They produce and sell goods and services to make a profit. Every product you use was produced by a business. Businesses also provide services such as haircuts, dry cleaning, and car insurance.

In the U.S. and countries with similar economic systems, there are three main types of private sector business organizations:

- **Proprietorships** A proprietor is one individual who owns and controls a business. He or she takes all of the profits and risks.
- **Partnerships** Partnerships are owned and controlled by two or more people. All partners share the profits and the risks.
- **Corporations** The owners of corporations are called shareholders because they own shares in the company. Shareholders can make or lose money based on the company's performance.

Two Views One World

Is It Better to Work for a Large or Small Company?

Like small towns and big cities, small businesses and large companies have obvious differences that might be seen as either advantages or disadvantages.

Olivia: Working in a big company is where the action is. All the resources are there. You're surrounded by talented people, and bigger companies have more access to the latest technology. You're assured a steady paycheck, and there is a Human Resources department to help you out with whatever you need. Job descriptions are clearly defined, and you know exactly what you need to do to move up.

Ethan: Working in a smaller company gives you a better idea of what business is all about. Every employee gets to be involved in the company's decisions. Smaller companies are more flexible, and you have more responsibility and a greater sense of power and importance. You also feel more connected with your coworkers and your company. At a smaller company, you'll be a key player instead of just a cog in the wheel.

Seeing Both Sides

Each of these opinions offers advantages for their side of the argument. However, what one person sees as a benefit, another may view as a drawback. Find one point in each of these arguments, and use it to support the other side.

Develop Your Skills

While you have the time and resources that you may not have in the future, commit yourself to improving your talents and skills for future employment needs. This will take time, effort, and self-discipline. Do not be afraid to ask others for help. From time to time, reflect on how you have improved, and celebrate your progress.

You Decide

Your parents have offered to pay for a computer course that you expressed interest in taking. However, with school, homework, and your social life, you are not sure you have time. What should you do?

Types of Employment

Just as there are different types of businesses, there are also different types of employment. You need to be aware of the advantages and disadvantages of each type of employment when considering jobs and careers.

- **Full Time** Working full time generally means spending at least seven or eight hours at work each day, five days a week. You may receive benefits such as paid vacations and health insurance. Full-time work is often the best way to move ahead in your career.
- **Part Time** When working part time, you may work a few days each week or a few hours each day. This allows you more time off to do other things. However, part-time workers earn less than full-time workers and usually do not receive benefits.
- **Contract** Contract workers work on a certain project for a specified period of time. When the project ends, they will need to find another project. Contract work offers flexibility, but it can result in periods of unemployment between projects.
- **Temporary** Temporary workers are hired to help out during busy seasons or to fill in for vacationing employees. Temporary work may be attractive to those who do not want to make a long-term commitment, but it offers no security and often does not include benefits.
- **Freelance** Freelancers are self-employed and usually work for a number of clients. Many freelancers work from home and have flexible work hours. They are also usually their own bosses. However, they may have periods of time without work, and they do not receive benefits.
- **Entrepreneurship** An **entrepreneur** (ˌän-trə-p(r)ə-ˈnər) is someone who sets up and operates a business. Entrepreneurs decide how the business will be run, what hours to work, and who will be hired. This kind of work can be very exciting and rewarding, but entrepreneurs risk losing money if the business fails. More than two-thirds of new businesses fail within their first four years.

✓ **Reading Check**

List Name three types of businesses in the private sector.

◀ **Employment Options**

For some people, freelancing from home is their only source of income, while others do it to add to their income. *What types of jobs could be done as a freelance worker?*

Changes in the Workplace

Today's workplace is constantly changing. Companies have to adapt in order to stay in business. The workers who are best able to anticipate and prepare for change are most likely to be successful.

Economy

The U.S. is part of the global economy. The **global economy** is the way national economies around the world are linked by trade. Goods, services, information, and technology are traded in a global market. In many cases, it is cheaper for the U.S. to import goods than to make them, which has led to a decline in manufacturing jobs. When economic times are hard, companies look for ways to save money. Some resort to **downsizing**, or eliminating jobs to reduce costs. Another cost-saving option is **outsourcing**, or contracting out certain tasks to other companies to save money. Stay informed to help you make wise career choices. Take advantage of new developments, and steer clear of industries in decline.

Health Insurance

At one time, most employees could assume that they would receive health insurance at little or no cost to themselves as one of their benefits. However, rising costs have caused some companies to drop coverage for employees. Companies that continue to offer insurance often require employees to pay a higher share of the costs. When researching jobs, find out about any coverage you can expect and the costs. Factor this into your decision making.

Technology

Technology enables people to work more quickly and efficiently. To compete and do well in today's marketplace, companies must constantly adapt to changing technology. They must invest in equipment and software that will enable their employees to be more productive. They need employees who are flexible and willing to learn new ways of doing things. It is likely that you will need to keep up with changes in technology throughout your working life. Taking the time to learn current technology can be very beneficial.

✓ **Reading Check**   **Recall** What does outsourcing mean?

Career Readiness

Most jobs today require education or training after high school. Depending on the type of work, the education or training period may last from a few weeks to many years. When researching occupations, learn about the time and effort needed to prepare for them. Once you have a clear idea of the requirements, you can explore specific education or training options.

Succeed in **SCHOOL and LIFE**

Cut College Costs

If you can, take honors and advanced placement courses while in high school. You might be able to convert these classes into college credits, which will save tuition costs. Work to get good grades to improve your chances of qualifying for financial aid. Consider the option of an in-state college, because attending college out of state can potentially cost much more.

Education and Training

Further education and training is provided in a variety of schools and colleges throughout the country. Some employers also offer training opportunities. Options to explore include:

- **Apprenticeships** An **apprenticeship** is a training method in which an inexperienced worker learns a trade by working alongside an expert.
- **Internships** Short-term work for little or no pay in exchange for an opportunity to work and learn is called an **internship**.
- **Vocational-Technical Centers** These schools and colleges offer training for skilled occupations in fields such as health care, computer technology, and automotive technology.
- **Trade Schools** Trade schools offer training for specific professions ranging from welding and plumbing to interior design and computer programming.
- **City or Community Colleges** These colleges offer two-year associate's degree programs in a range of occupational areas.
- **Colleges and Universities** These institutions offer four-year courses of academic study leading to a bachelor's degree.
- **Military** The military offers training in more than 1,500 different fields. To receive training, you must **enlist**, or agree to serve, for a specific number of years.
- **Distance Learning** These programs use the Internet, videos, and other forms of communication technology to teach students in their homes or other off-campus locations.

▲ On-the-Job Training

Many careers offer hands-on training through apprenticeships or internships. *What are some of the advantages to learning this way?*

Employability Skills

A **transferable skill** is a general skill that can be used in many situations. Transferable skills, such as honesty, time management, and writing, help you in all aspects of life, including work. Employability skills include both job-specific and transferable skills.

- **Basic Academic Skills** Reading and writing are **critical**, or extremely important, at work. Letters, manuals, reports, schedules, e-mail, and memos require strong reading and writing skills. Math skills are needed for counting change, tallying sales figures, and understanding graphs and charts.
- **Thinking Skills** You will use critical thinking skills to judge the reliability of information. Reasoning skills help you draw conclusions and apply what you learn to new situations. Creative thinking skills help you solve problems and offer ideas.

◀ Get Involved!

Youth Council

Many city councils have a youth council for young people to participate in city council decisions. Not only will participating in such a program get you involved in your community, it will also help you develop transferable skills, such as critical thinking, communication, and problem-solving skills, that will help you in future careers.

- **Interpersonal Skills** You need to know how to work well with others and as part of a team. Teamwork involves working toward a common goal and a willingness to compromise.
- **Technology Skills** You are more likely to get ahead if you know how to use word processing, spreadsheet, database, and scheduling programs, as well as e-mail and the Internet.
- **Management Skills** All workers can use management skills such as planning, prioritizing, organizing, and handling resources to do their work more effectively.
- **Communication Skills** It is important that you know how to actively listen, express yourself clearly, and provide helpful and constructive feedback.

Preparation

The more you prepare for the workplace, the more comfortable you will be when you start your first job. Education, training, and skill development will be a continual part of your career growth in the changing world of work. There is a lot you can do while still in school to build your career readiness. Ask a teacher which transferable skills you can improve, and work on them. Learn the latest technology in your field of interest. Practice your communication skills. Get experience by volunteering or taking a part-time job.

Go Green!

When printing rough drafts, either print on both sides of the paper or print on the back of old documents and scrap papers. Only print in color when absolutely necessary.

 Podcasts Access the Online Learning Center to download *Managing Life Skills* podcasts.

Section 15.1 — After You Read

Review Key Concepts

1. **Clarify** the reasons why people work.
2. **Define** public sector and private sector jobs.
3. **Describe** two ways that companies may cut costs.
4. **Classify** the three basic areas of thinking skills.

Practice Academic Skills

English Language Arts

5. Conduct research and talk to your counselor to find out what kind of financial aid you might receive if you decide to go to college. Contact your state's education department to find out if you might qualify for state funding. Prepare a chart to record and compare your findings.

Social Studies

6. Some services are offered through both the private and public sectors, such as mail delivery. Conduct research to compare the services offered by a private delivery company and by the U.S. Postal Service. Select a specific shape, size, and weight for a package, and compare costs and delivery times, as well as other services offered, such as insurance or tracking. Create a graphic organizer to share your findings.

Check Your Answers Check your answers at this book's Online Learning Center at **glencoe.com**.

NCTE 8 Use information resources to gather information and create and communicate knowledge.

NCSS VII C Consider the costs and benefits to society of allocating goods and services through private and public sectors.

Evaluate Career Options

Many factors will affect the career you choose.

Before You Read

Prepare with a Partner Before you read, work with a partner. Read the titles of the heads, and ask each other questions about the topics that will be discussed. Write down the questions you both have about each section. As you read, write the answers to your questions.

Read to Learn
Key Concepts
- **Identify** five areas to consider when deciding what career to pursue.
- **Explain** how career clusters can help your career search.
- **Describe** how a career ladder is useful in developing a career path.

Main Idea
Before choosing a career, assess your skills, interests, personality, and values, and gather information about possible careers.

Content Vocabulary
◇ aptitude
◇ career cluster
◇ job shadowing
◇ career ladder

Academic Vocabulary
You will find these words in your reading and on your tests. Use the glossary to look up their definitions if necessary.
■ suit
■ prospects

Academic Standards

English Language Arts
NCTE 4 Use written language to communicate effectively.

Science
NSES G Develop an understanding of science as a human endeavor.

Social Studies
NCSS V B Individuals, Groups, and Institutions Analyze influences on people and elements of culture in contemporary settings.

Graphic Organizer
As you read, look for six ways to gain hands-on experience in a career. Use a wheel graphic like the one shown to help you organize your information.

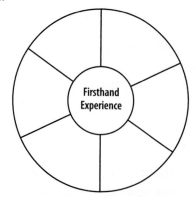

Firsthand Experience

Graphic Organizer Go to this book's Online Learning Center at **glencoe.com** to print out this graphic organizer.

NCTE *National Council of Teachers of English*
NCTM *National Council of Teachers of Mathematics*
NSES *National Science Education Standards*
NCSS *National Council for the Social Studies*

Personal Assessment

How do you know which career field to enter? If you want a satisfying career, you need to examine your options, make the best choice for you, and create a plan to follow your chosen path.

The average person in your generation can expect to work beyond age 67. With all those working years ahead of you, you will want work that is challenging and enjoyable. Start by examining who you are and what is important to you. That means looking at your aptitudes, skills, interests, personality traits, and values.

Your Aptitudes and Skills

An **aptitude** ('ap-tə-ˌtüd) is a natural talent or potential for learning a skill. You were born with certain aptitudes. You also have skills that you have developed through training and practice. For example, being good with numbers is an aptitude, but knowing how to solve a trigonometry problem is a skill. Together, your aptitudes and skills form a valuable package that you can build on and that you can offer an employer.

To identify your aptitudes and skills, consider what school subjects are easiest for you and which skills seemed easiest for you to learn. Think about what you do well and what you could probably learn to do well. Ask teachers, family, and friends what aptitudes and skills they believe you have.

Your Interests

Interests that you enjoy in your free time might suggest a satisfying career direction. Get involved in after-school activities to help you develop current interests and discover new ones. Your school and community probably offer opportunities in sports, music, art, drama, science, and debate. An interest that starts out as a hobby might lead to a fulfilling career.

Your Personality

Consider the kind of person you are when exploring your career options. You will be far happier in a career for which your attitudes, characteristics, and other personality traits are well matched. To learn more about your personality traits, think about such things as whether you like to work alone or with others or if you prefer to lead or to follow. Other things to consider include your level of attention to detail, your ability to work under pressure, and whether you prefer a quiet or a high-energy environment.

Awareness of your personality traits and preferences will be valuable as you research career fields. It will help you focus on the right ones for you and avoid those which do not **suit**, or match, you.

As You Read

Connect If you could choose any job, what would it be? Why?

◆ Vocabulary

You can find definitions in the glossary at the back of this book.

▼ Natural Talents

Everyone has a unique set of aptitudes and skills. *Do you have any skills you worked to achieve despite lacking the aptitude?*

Your Values

Your values are your beliefs, feelings, and ideas about what is important. They will guide you in your career choices. For example, if you care deeply about the environment, look into occupations that focus on protecting natural resources. Other values will also have a bearing on your career choices. For example, is it important that your work hours allow you to spend more time with family? Following a career path that reflects your values will help ensure that you enjoy your work and find it worthwhile.

Self-Assessment Tools

Self-assessment tools include questionnaires, tests, and surveys that help you discover more about your strengths and weaknesses and what is important to you. Books and Web sites also can be helpful. School guidance counselors can tell you more about these tools.

✓ **Reading Check** **Define** What are values?

Research Career Fields

Once you have a clearer understanding of yourself, you can start to identify career fields and occupations that might be a good fit for you. To do that, you will need to do some research.

Career Clusters

When you go to a bookstore, you do not have to look at every book to find the one you want. Instead, you look at signs that direct you to the right section. Similarly, you do not have to research 20,000 occupations to find the best one for you. You can narrow down your search by using career clusters. A **career cluster** is a large grouping of occupations that have certain characteristics in common. Often these occupations require many of the same types of skills. If you have the skills to be successful in one occupation, there are likely to be other occupations in the same career cluster that you might like.

Sources of Information

Many school libraries have a careers section where you can find reference books, magazines, videos, and other information sources, as well as Internet access. Check the publication date of any source you use. Out-of-date sources could give outdated or misleading information.

Print Sources and Online Sources

The Career Guide to Industries describes more than 40 industries, explaining the nature of each industry, working conditions, occupations included, and the outlook for that industry. It also gives information on training, advancement prospects, and earnings. The Occupational Outlook Handbook gives detailed information on thousands of occupations, including the nature of the work, the working conditions, average earnings, and job outlook. Both are updated every two years and are available in print and online. Also available is the Occupational Outlook Quarterly, an online periodical updated every three months. It covers topics such as new and emerging occupations, training opportunities, and salary trends.

The Department of Labor's Occupational Information Network, or O*NET, is an online database that offers information on hundreds of occupations. Use it to research careers and to find out which occupations match your skills and interests.

Interview People

If possible, talk to people who work in careers that interest you. This may not always be possible, but such interviews are worthwhile if you can arrange them. Before meeting with the person, prepare a list of questions. Most people are happy to tell you about their work, and an insider's view will tell you far more than just reading about a job or career.

Get Hands-On Experience

Hands-on work experience is valuable because it helps you learn more about career areas, the drawbacks and rewards of particular jobs, and how businesses operate. On-the-job experience allows you to develop skills and positive work habits, which can help you when you apply for jobs in the future.

Here are some options to consider when looking to gain hands-on experience:

- **Part-Time** Part-time work allows you to work evenings, weekends, or during the summer while you are still in school.
- **Volunteer** Helping out in your community benefits you and others. Although the work is unpaid, the experience is valuable.
- **Youth Employment Programs** Some communities create work opportunities for teens, especially during the summer.
- **Job Shadowing** Spending time in the workplace with someone during a regular workday is called **job shadowing**. You can learn about the work by observing and listening.
- **Work-Study Programs** Schools and businesses work together to provide on-the-job training for teens. Students spend part of their week in school and part at work.
- **Internships** Companies hire interns to work and learn at the same time. Interns are assigned specific tasks and are usually unpaid or receive minimum wage.

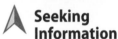

Seeking Information

Libraries are a good resource for finding information on careers. *Other than books, what resources can you find in your library?*

Succeed in SCHOOL and LIFE

Practice Public Speaking

Public speaking is an important workplace skill. It can help you with presentations, meetings, and in conversations with supervisors. Practice public speaking whenever you can. This could involve making a toast at a family dinner, making a speech at a wedding, or simply preparing a speech to give in front of friends or family members.

Information to Gather

Once you have decided to look into career fields or occupations that interest you, what do you need to find out? Here are some topics and questions for you to jump start your research:

- **Nature of the Work** What are the main tasks and responsibilities, and what skills and equipment experience are needed?
- **Working Conditions** What are the number of hours expected? Where is the job located? What is the work environment?
- **Qualifications** What education and training are needed?
- **Employment Patterns** How many people are employed in this line of work? What types of companies employ them?
- **Earnings** What are the average earnings? What accounts for differences in earnings? What kinds of benefits are offered?
- **Outlook** What is the outlook for this occupation or career field? Is it growing fast, slowly, or not at all? What impact might technology have on future **prospects**, or possibilities?

Looking at Trends

Given the rapid pace of change in today's world, it is important to look at issues and trends that may have an impact on your career plans. For example, technology will continue to have a huge impact on career trends. Population patterns, such as the growing number of older Americans, affect the demand for services they need. By anticipating employment and social trends, you can focus on career areas that have a more promising future.

✓ **Reading Check** **Identify** Name four sources of information about careers.

Life On Your Own

Plan for Your Career

Some teens know exactly what career they want. Most teens, however, have not yet decided on their career plans. Although you may not be ready to commit yourself to a career yet, it does not hurt to start thinking about and preparing for career options now.

How It Works Gain a variety of work experience so you can learn which types of work suit your aptitudes and interests. Develop transferable skills, such as time management and communication skills. These skills are useful for all types of jobs. Watch economic trends to see which job markets are growing and which are not.

Try It Out Brainstorm your career options. Jot down some ideas you have about what you might want to do and what you might be good at. Then schedule a meeting with a career expert, such as your school counselor or a job recruiter, to discuss your skills and interests. Also discuss which skills are always in demand and what the market looks like for careers that interest you. With the job expert, pick one career option to focus on.

> *Your Turn* Research this career to find out information such as starting salary, education and training requirements, necessary skills, job outlook, and the typical career path. Summarize your findings in a written description.

Sample Career Ladder

This career ladder represents the steps taken by a counseling department administrator. *Why do you think each step in the ladder is necessary?*

Developing a Career Ladder

At this stage in your life, it is important to get started on the road to success. A good first step is to gather ideas of what you might like to do and learn as much as you can about your options. Focus on one or two career areas that seem to be the best match for you. Use your decision-making skills to evaluate the pros and cons of each option and narrow down your choices. Consider both what you know about yourself and the information you have gathered about career areas and occupations.

When you have an idea about the direction for your career, you can start developing a career ladder, sometimes known as a career plan. A **career ladder** is a visualization of your chosen career path. This helps you see where you currently are in your career path. It also helps you decide what your next career step might be. Each step on the ladder represents another job in your career to get you to your long-term goal.

As you follow your career path, you may discover that your interests or priorities change. Keep an open mind, and be prepared to change course. People tend to change careers more often now than in the past, and that trend is likely to continue.

School Counseling Department Administrator

Counseling Psychologist (with Ph. D.)

Director of Counseling

Head School Counselor

School Counselor

Pupil Services Assistant

Podcasts Access the Online Learning Center to download *Managing Life Skills* podcasts.

Section 15.2 — After You Read

Review Key Concepts

1. **Identify** three types of assessment tools.
2. **Name** six topics you should research about occupations.
3. **Summarize** why it is important to develop a career ladder.

Practice Academic Skills

English Language Arts

4. Develop a list of ten interview questions that you might ask someone to learn more about his or her career. Refer to the list of topics included in the text to help guide your questions. It also might be helpful to have a specific career in mind when you develop your list.

Social Studies

5. Identify a current trend that affects the job market, such as the increase in the number of older adults or rapidly changing technologies. Research ways that the trend could affect careers. Create a brief oral report to share your findings with the class.

Check Your Answers Check your answers at this book's Online Learning Center at **glencoe.com**.

NCTE 4 Use written language to communicate effectively.

NCSS V B Analyze influences on people and elements of culture in contemporary settings.

Pathway to Your Career

Architect

What Does an Architect Do?

Architects design all types of buildings, including schools, skyscrapers, hospitals, museums, hotels, train stations, and houses. Architects are involved in designing, planning, managing, building, and maintaining the structures they craft. They create the overall look of these buildings and ensure that they are functional, safe, and economical. Architects must also work with their clients to make sure their buildings suit the needs of the people who use them.

Career Readiness Skills Architects need to be able communicate their ideas visually to their clients, so artistic and drawing skills are essential. Potential architects must have good visual orientation and the ability to understand spatial relationships. Other important qualities include creativity, the ability to work independently and as part of a team, and computer skills.

Education and Training The three main steps to becoming an architect are to get a professional degree in architecture, gain work experience through an internship, and pass the Architect Registration Exam.

Job Outlook Employment of architects is expected to grow faster than the average for all occupations. Intense competition is expected for positions at top firms. Opportunities will be best for those architects who are able to distinguish themselves.

Critical Thinking Think about how technological changes can influence housing decisions. How is a typical house of today different from a typical house from 100 years ago? Do you think all of the differences are improvements? Why or why not?

Career Cluster

CCR ☆ College & Career Readiness

Architecture and Construction Architects work in the Design/Pre-Construction pathway of this career cluster. Other jobs in this cluster include:

- Painter
- Roofer
- Drywall Installer
- Mason
- Electrician
- Landscape Architect
- Metalworker
- Drafter
- Preservationist
- Code Official
- Cost Estimator
- Pipe Fitter
- Plumber
- Carpenter
- Construction Foreman
- Interior Designer
- Civil Engineer
- Surveyor
- Boilermaker
- Groundskeeper

Explore Further The Architecture and Construction career cluster contains three pathways: Design/Pre-Construction; Construction; and Maintenance/Operations. Choose one of these pathways to explore further.

 Career Clusters To learn more about career clusters, go to this book's Online Learning Center at **glencoe.com**.

CHAPTER SUMMARY

Section 15.1
Understanding Careers

While most people work to make money, a career can also help satisfy physical, emotional, intellectual, and social needs. Your career will affect your lifestyle. There are different sectors and different types of employment. Jobs are constantly changing due to political, economic, and social events. Many jobs require specific education or training. Employability skills can be both job-specific and transferable.

Section 15.2
Evaluate Career Options

A personal assessment can help you choose a career area that is right for you, based on your skills, aptitudes, personality traits, and values. Career clusters make it easier to explore career options. There are a variety of sources with information about careers. There are many ways to gain hands-on work experience. Once you have narrowed down your career options, you should develop a career ladder.

Vocabulary Review

1. Write each of the vocabulary words below on an index card and the definitions on separate index cards. Work in pairs or small groups to match each word to its definition.

Content Vocabulary
- career (p. 291)
- career path (p. 291)
- lifestyle (p. 292)
- entrepreneur (p. 294)
- global economy (p. 295)
- downsizing (p. 295)
- outsourcing (p. 295)
- apprenticeship (p. 296)
- internship (p. 296)
- transferable skill (p. 296)
- aptitude (p. 299)
- career cluster (p. 300)
- job shadowing (p. 301)
- career ladder (p. 303)

Academic Vocabulary
- enlist (p. 296)
- critical (p. 296)
- suit (p. 299)
- prospects (p. 302)

Review Key Concepts

2. **Contrast** a job and a career.
3. **List** the different types of businesses and employment.
4. **Identify** three common areas for change in the workplace.
5. **Summarize** eight options for education and training to prepare for a career.
6. **Identify** five areas to consider when deciding what career to pursue.
7. **Explain** how career clusters can help your career search.
8. **Describe** how a career ladder is useful in developing a career path.

Critical Thinking

9. **Exemplify** Why is it important to consider the lifestyle you would like when planning your career? What are some specific elements of your lifestyle that you plan to consider?
10. **Draw Conclusions** What actions can you take now that will give you a more competitive edge when you start interviewing for jobs?
11. **Compare and Contrast** How might making career choices be different for you from how it was for your parents or grandparents?

ACTIVE LEARNING

12. Education and Training Follow your teacher's instructions to form into small groups. Work with your group to identify five careers that interest you. Using print or online resources, find out how much education or training is required for each career. Categorize each career under one of four headings: high school, post-high school, college degree, or advanced degree. Write the results on the board. As a class, discuss the jobs listed in each category. How are they similar or different?

Family & Community Connections

13. Why People Work Think of three people you know who appear to be happy in their jobs. Arrange a time to interview each of them. If they do not live in your community, you can schedule time for a telephone interview. Prepare your interview questions ahead of time. Ask each person to describe what he or she finds satisfying and rewarding about his or her work. Also ask the people what it was about their career that interested them, and why they chose to pursue it. Take notes during your interview and write a brief report to share your findings. How can you use what you learned in the interviews to help yourself find a job in which you can be happy?

21st Century Skills

Research Skills

14. Economic Systems The United States follows the free enterprise system. People are free to start a company, risking their money in return for the right to keep any profits they earn. Conduct research to learn about a system used in another country, such as the command system or the mixed system. Prepare a chart to compare and contrast the two types of economic systems.

Technology Skills

15. Multimedia Presentation Choose one of the career clusters. Suppose that you have been hired to recruit people into this field. Create a five-minute multimedia presentation that emphasizes the challenges and rewards of this career area. Share your presentation with the class.

FCCLA Connections

Self-Direction Skills

16. Impact of Career Decisions As part of its mission, FCCLA encourages students to discover their strengths and career goals and initiate a plan for achieving the lifestyle they desire. Complete the Career Scan worksheet in the Career Connection program to assess how much of a connection you have already made with choosing a career path. Create an outline of the steps you can take in the next year to continue to work toward a career path.

Academic Skills

English Language Arts

17. Local Job Market Knowing about changes in the job market can help you make good decisions about your career. Sometimes these changes are ongoing trends, and other times they are one-time events. Write a newspaper column about a change in your community that might affect the local job market.

> **NCTE 5** Use different writing process elements to communicate effectively.

Science

18. The Scientific Method The scientific method is a way to answer questions. You must collect information, form a hypothesis, study the results, and draw conclusions that others can evaluate.

Procedure Create a hypothesis about the world of work. Then brainstorm ways to find data to prove your hypothesis.

Analysis Based on your brainstorming results, write a two-paragraph summary of a proposed research project that could prove or disprove your hypothesis.

> **NSES A** Develop abilities necessary to do scientific inquiry, understandings about scientific inquiry.

Mathematics

19. Calculate Work Hours Suppose you work for a company that offers flexible work hours. This company will allow you to work four days a week instead of five, as long as your total hours remain the same. In the five-day work week, employees work nine hours a day, including an hour for lunch. If the total hours must remain the same, how many hours will employees work daily in the four-day schedule, including the lunch break?

Math Concept **Multi-Step Problem** When solving problems with more than one step, think through each of the steps before you start.

Starting Hint Begin by calculating the number of hours worked in a week. To do this, subtract the lunch hour from the total number of hours in a work day. Then multiply that number by five.

 For more math practice, go to the Math Appendix at the back of the book.

> **NCTM Number and Operations** Compute fluently and make reasonable estimates.

 Standardized Test Practice   **CCR** College & Career Readiness

TIMED WRITING
Read the writing prompt. Then write a one-page essay using details and examples to illustrate your points.

Test-Taking Tip Plan out your essay before you begin writing. Jot down the main points or details you want to focus on in the margins of your test. Refer to these points frequently as you write. This can help you stay focused.

20. High school students are faced with many choices upon graduation. Some choose to go to college, while others choose technical schools or apprenticeships. Write an essay explaining what you might do after high school and how it will affect your finances. Be sure to explain how you made your choice, the events or people who influenced your choice, and the impact your choice will have on your finances.

Chapter 16

The Job Search

Chapter Objectives

Section 16.1 Finding Jobs

- **Compare and contrast** a résumé and a portfolio.
- **Describe** six different sources of job leads.

Section 16.2 Getting a Job

- **Explain** how a cover letter and an application form can help you get a job.
- **Review** the steps you can take to prepare for a job interview.
- **List** considerations for evaluating a job offer.

> **Explore the Photo**
>
> Finding a job that is right for you takes preparation and skill. *What preparation do you think you would need to do before looking for a job?*

Writing Activity

Step-by-Step Guide

Interviewing Well A successful interview is a big step toward getting a job. You must be aware of your appearance and be familiar with the company and how your experience and skills fit the job. Write a step-by-step guide explaining how to prepare for an interview. You may use photos or artwork to illustrate your guide, but each step should be clearly written.

Writing Tips To write an effective step-by-step guide:
- Explain terms the reader may not know.
- Write the steps in chronological order.
- Use appropriate transition words.
- Choose precise verbs to make your explanations clear.

Finding Jobs

Finding the right job takes the right kind of preparation.

Reading Guide

Before You Read

Take Guilt-Free Breaks The reason for resting is to refresh yourself. However, if you feel guilty about resting, then your rest period will only create more stress. The brain has a hard time absorbing new data when it is stressed. Your reading skills will be more effective if you are relaxed and ready to learn.

Read to Learn
Key Concepts
- **Compare and contrast** a résumé and a portfolio.
- **Describe** six different sources of job leads.

Main Idea
Create a résumé that will highlight your experience to help you impress prospective employers. A portfolio of work samples can show your skills. You can find job leads in many different places.

Content Vocabulary
◇ résumé
◇ chronological résumé
◇ skills-based résumé
◇ reference
◇ portfolio
◇ job lead
◇ networking

Academic Vocabulary
You will find these words in your reading and on your tests. Use the glossary to look up their definitions if necessary.
■ suitable
■ criteria

Graphic Organizer
As you read, you will discover six categories that are used on a standard résumé. Use a herringbone organizer like the one shown to help you list them.

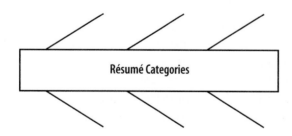

Résumé Categories

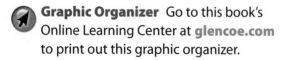

Graphic Organizer Go to this book's Online Learning Center at **glencoe.com** to print out this graphic organizer.

Academic Standards

English Language Arts
NCTE 6 Apply knowledge of language structure and conventions to discuss texts.

Mathematics
NCTM Number and Operations Understand meanings of operations and how they relate to one another.

Social Studies
NCSS IV B Individual Development and Identity Identify, describe, and express appreciation for the influence of various historical and contemporary cultures on an individual's daily life.

NCTE *National Council of Teachers of English*
NCTM *National Council of Teachers of Mathematics*
NSES *National Science Education Standards*
NCSS *National Council for the Social Studies*

Organizing a Job Search

If you were going to make a pizza from scratch, how would you start? You would not just pull random items out of the refrigerator and cabinets and put them in the oven. Instead, you would make sure you had the right ingredients and that you knew what to do with them. The same is true of a job search. Before you start making calls or filling out applications, take time to prepare the documents you will need and to do the necessary research.

Prepare a Résumé

Most employers ask job applicants to provide a résumé. A **résumé** ('re-zə-,mā) is a written summary of a job seeker's work experience, education, skills, and interests. Think of it as a written portrait of your qualifications for a job. This organized list of skills and experience is also helpful for filling out applications and preparing for interviews. Spend quality time on your résumé. It may determine whether or not you will be interviewed for a job. Think carefully about what you will include and how you will organize the information.

There are two basic résumé formats. A **chronological résumé** organizes information by work experience in reverse time order. The feature on the next page shows a sample of a chronological résumé. A **skills-based résumé** focuses on skills that are suitable for the workplace and examples of how you have used the skills. This type of résumé works well for people who do not have extensive work experience. The Unit 4 Portfolio Project on pages 284-285 can help you decide which is the most appropriate format for your résumé.

Many employers also ask for references. A **reference** is the name of a person that an employer can contact to learn more about you. List the names on your résumé, or simply write "References available on request" and provide them later. Ask permission before giving anyone's name as a reference. Choose people such as former employers or teachers. Ask people who know you well and can honestly give a positive view of your abilities and character.

Use a computer to prepare your résumé. Make sure it is neat and that there are no spelling or grammatical errors. Once you are happy with it, print it out and have someone proofread it for you.

Electronic résumés are becoming more and more common. These are computer documents that can be e-mailed to potential employers and posted to job search Web sites. Before you prepare an electronic résumé, find out what guidelines the employer or job search site wants you to follow.

Many companies accept résumés online. Design your résumé so that it can be sent electronically or copied and pasted into a job search or company Web site. Many companies use search techniques to look for certain key words or phrases to help evaluate experience. Other employers read résumés through devices like smart phones.

As You Read

Connect What types of skills do you have that would be valued by an employer?

Vocabulary

You can find definitions in the glossary at the back of this book.

Be Smart Be Safe

Teen Workers There are special rules and restrictions regarding jobs for teenagers. There are rules about how many hours you can work in a week and in a day, and there are age restrictions for some of the more dangerous jobs.

Write About It These rules and restrictions vary from state to state. Check with your state's department of labor for information on some of these rules, and write a summary of what you find out.

HOW TO ..... Write a Résumé

A résumé is a tool for selling yourself to employers or other organizations. It categorizes information in a way that helps employers see how your strengths and accomplishments qualify you for a certain job position. It is important to keep your résumé brief, ideally one page. The résumé below is an example of a chronological résumé.

Name and Contact Information
Write your name, full address, e-mail address, and telephone number (with area code) at the top of your résumé.

Objective Include an objective that fits the job you are applying for. Be sure to change this item if you are using the same résumé when applying for different jobs.

Education List the schools you have attended and diplomas or degrees you have received, beginning with the most recent one. If you are still in school, write the school's name and location, and include the start date. You may also want to include any special subjects or programs.

Emily Nichols
510 Chestnut Street
Springdale, GA 33333
020-555-7890
enichols@xyz.com

OBJECTIVE: To obtain a position as a teacher's aide in a preschool program as a step toward a career as a childcare center director

EDUCATION: *High School Diploma, 2009*
Delany High School, Springdale, Georgia

National Honor Society, 2006-2009
Tutor in a community literacy program, 2006–2008

CONTINUING
EDUCATION: *Springdale Community College, Springdale, Georgia,*
September 2009–present

Courses in child development, sociology, and Spanish.

EXPERIENCE: *Teacher's Aide, Carmine Occupational Center, Springdale, Georgia,*
August 2009–present
Worked with the children of students and faculty in the preschool program for an average of 8 hours per week. Monitored children in the play areas. Read stories to the children. Helped organize game and craft time.

Child Care Assistant, Valley Child Care Center, Springdale, Georgia,
June 2008–August 2009
Worked during the summer as an assistant in the toddler program. Helped prepare meals, test playground equipment, and sanitize indoor toys.

SKILLS: Completed first aid and CPR training at Springdale Valley Medical Center, July 2009. Proven ability to teach young children new skills and lead them in games. Organized the annual Little Brother/Little Sister Day at Delany High School in 2008 and 2009. Ability to read music and play the piano. Ability to speak and write basic Spanish.

REFERENCES: References are available on request.

Work Experience
List your work experience beginning with your most recent job. If you have never been employed, include volunteer work and school activities if they relate to the job for which you are applying.

References You may list the names of your references here, or you can simply write "References are available on request" and provide them later.

Skills Identify any business or other skills and abilities that you have gained in school, on a job, or in other situations.

Create a Portfolio

Depending on the type of job you are seeking, you might want to prepare a career portfolio. A **portfolio** is a collection of work samples that demonstrate your skills. For example, someone who wants to work at a newspaper might have a portfolio of writing samples or artwork. The samples should be placed in a folder that will both protect them and present them attractively.

An electronic portfolio, or e-portfolio, is another way to show your skills. Instead of putting your samples in a folder, you can place your collection on a CD, DVD, or Web page to which you may direct prospective employers. An electronic portfolio helps you demonstrate a variety of skills you have mastered. For example, you might include an audio file documenting your fluency in another language or your debating skills, or you might create a digital video spotlighting your public speaking ability. As with a traditional portfolio, keep your electronic portfolio files up to date. Before submitting a portfolio, ask your potential employer if he or she would prefer a hardcopy or electronic submission.

Whether or not you prepare work samples, you will want to have certain documents with you when you apply for a job or go for an interview. Gather copies of your résumé, a list of references, and letters of recommendation from former employers. It is a good idea to put together a special folder for these items.

✓ Reading Check **Explain** How can you list references on your résumé?

Succeed in **SCHOOL and LIFE**

E-Portfolio Tips

Keep in mind that e-portfolios are not yet universally accepted. Research employers in your field, and inquire about their portfolio expectations. Make sure your digital presentation is well-designed and organized. If it includes links, double check to be sure they are all active and working properly. Avoid photos of yourself, just as you would in a traditional portfolio.

Career Portfolio

The materials you compile for your portfolio can affect your future employment. *What do the materials in your portfolio reveal about you?*

Demonstrate Determination

As with accomplishing any goal in life, getting a job requires resolve and persistence. You might experience setbacks or feel frustrated or disappointed, but it is important to keep trying and not give up. Sticking with it can help you achieve your goals more quickly and more often.

You Decide

Can you think of a time when you almost gave up, but instead you kept at it and eventually accomplished your goal? Describe this scenario and how you found the willpower to keep going.

Finding Job Leads

You have written your résumé and assembled your portfolio. Now you need to identify employers that might want to hire you. A **job lead** is information about a specific job opening. Job leads may come from many sources. Explore different sources of job leads to increase your chances of finding a job that is right for you.

Networking

Networking involves using personal contacts to find a job. Your network may include relatives, friends, neighbors, local business owners, former employers, members of your place of worship, and members of any clubs to which you belong. Let these people know what kind of job you are seeking. One of them might know of a job lead that is **suitable**, or right for the circumstances. Pay particular attention to people who work at companies where you would like to work. They may be able to provide you with job leads and useful information about the company.

Do not feel embarrassed about asking personal contacts for help to find a job. Most people are happy to assist in such an important matter. Networking is an effective way to locate job leads. In fact, sometimes it is the only way to learn about job openings that are not advertised.

School Resources

Take advantage of your school's efforts to help students find jobs. Your school career counselor will have useful information and may also post notices of available jobs. Your school may organize work-study programs that can lead to full-time jobs. Keep your counselors and teachers in mind as potential references.

Job Fairs

You can learn a lot about career opportunities at job fairs. Job fairs feature companies that are knowledgeable about the future opportunities in their field and are looking to hire employees. When talking to company representatives at a job fair, keep these points in mind:

• **Prepare** Find out which companies will be at the job fair, and think about which ones you are specifically interested in and what you want to know about them. Create a list of questions.

◄ **Looking for a Job**

Different job lead sources can help you locate work that might interest you. *Where might you find job leads if you were interested in a specific field of work?*

Internet Advantage

This manager is using the Internet to search for potential employees. *What advantages does the Internet offer to both employers and employees?*

- **Dress Appropriately** Remember that representatives are more likely to take time to talk with you if you look professional.
- **Be Confident and Courteous** Approach a company's booth, smile, and introduce yourself. Ask if the representatives have time to answer your questions. Ask your questions in a courteous manner.
- **Get Names** After learning more about a company, you may decide you want to explore their career offerings further. Make sure to note the names and positions of the representatives you talk to.

Internet Resources

There are many Web sites devoted to helping you find a job. They typically let you search by job title, location, type of work, and other **criteria** (krī-'tir-ē-ə), or characteristics. You can also post your résumé online so that potential employers can access it and contact you if your skills match what they are seeking.

If there is a particular company that you would like to work for, visit its Web site. Job openings may be posted there, and you will also be able to learn more about the company. Knowledge about the company can give you an advantage during an interview. Prospective employers will appreciate the time and effort taken to learn as much as you can about their company.

Financial *Literacy*

Write Equations

Kyle has a job interview next week. Knowing that he needs to make a professional impression, he bought some new clothes that he found on sale at a men's shop. He found a $140 suit at $35 off, a $56 briefcase at 25% off, and two ties for $14 each. How much did he spend?

Math Concept **Order of Operations** To solve an equation you must use the correct order of operations. First, simplify within the parentheses, and then evaluate any exponents. Multiply and divide from left to right, and then add and subtract from left to right.

Starting Hint Before solving this problem, write an expression using the correct symbols. Remember that 25% off means he paid 75% of the price (0.75).

 Math For more math practice, go to the Math Appendix at the back of the book.

NCTM Number and Operations Understand meanings of operations and how they relate to one another.

Printed Ads

Printed newspapers are declining in popularity and circulation due to the convenience of the Internet and other technological advances. However, you can still find job leads in the classified section of most newspapers. The ads are usually organized into different categories, such as "Industrial/Technical," "Medical/Dental," and "Office/Clerical." Certain magazines that focus on specific industries also often carry job leads.

Employment Agencies

Employment agencies bring together job seekers and employers. The job seekers fill out agency applications, and employers describe their openings. It is the goal of the agency to match up the job seekers with the employers.

There are two main types of employment agencies. Public employment agencies, operated by state governments, usually have offices in large cities and towns. They also post job leads on their Web sites. Their services are free. Private employment agencies charge a fee for their services. The employer usually pays the fee. Some agencies specialize in certain career fields, such as health care or technology.

 Podcasts Access the Online Learning Center to download *Managing Life Skills* podcasts.

Section 16.1 After You Read

Review Key Concepts

1. **Explain** how employers use electronic résumés to select job candidates.
2. **List** people you might contact as potential job networking sources.

Practice Academic Skills

 English Language Arts

3. You can demonstrate your skills and interests by creating a job portfolio that will give employers an idea of your personality. Create or gather at least two samples that could be used in a portfolio. Write a letter to an employer describing each of your samples and explaining why they show that you have the ability to handle the job.

 Social Studies

4. Choose a person of historical significance. Use print and Internet resources to research his or her life, occupation, and importance. Use the information you find to create a résumé for this person. Include information on education, experience, and skills.

Check Your Answers Check your answers at this book's Online Learning Center at **glencoe.com**.

NCTE 6 Apply knowledge of language structure and conventions to discuss texts.

NCSS IV B Identify, describe, and express appreciation for the influence of various historical and contemporary cultures on an individual's daily life.

Getting a Job

Making a good impression is an essential part of the interview process.

Reading Guide

Before You Read

How Can You Improve? Before starting the section, think about the last exam you took based on material you had to read. What reading strategies helped you on that test? Make a list of ways to improve your strategies to succeed on your next exam.

Read to Learn

Key Concepts

- **Explain** how a cover letter and an application form can help you get a job.
- **Review** the steps you can take to prepare for a job interview.
- **List** considerations for evaluating a job offer.

Main Idea

Knowing how to write a cover letter and fill out an application form can help you get the right job. Prepare before a job interview, make a positive impression at the interview, and follow up afterward.

Content Vocabulary

◇ cover letter
◇ application form
◇ compensation package

Academic Vocabulary

You will find these words in your reading and on your tests. Use the glossary to look up their definitions if necessary.

■ favorable
■ significant

Academic Standards

English Language Arts

NCTE 4 Use written language to communicate effectively.

Social Studies

NCSS V C Individuals, Groups, and Institutions Describe the various forms institutions take, and explain how they develop and change over time.

NCTE *National Council of Teachers of English*
NCTM *National Council of Teachers of Mathematics*
NSES *National Science Education Standards*
NCSS *National Council for the Social Studies*

Graphic Organizer

As you read, you will discover five ways to create a good impression during an interview. Use a tree diagram like the one shown to help you organize the information.

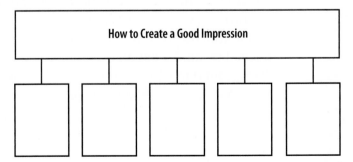

How to Create a Good Impression

Graphic Organizer Go to this book's Online Learning Center at **glencoe.com** to print out this graphic organizer.

You Read

onnect What skills do
ou think would help you
in an interview?

Vocabulary

You can find definitions in
the glossary at the back of
this book.

Applying for a Job

When applying for a job, remember that you may be one of dozens or even hundreds of applicants. To improve your chances of being chosen, you need to "sell yourself" by highlighting your best qualities. Employers will be interested in the skills you have to offer. They will also be influenced by what you write or say, and how you dress, speak, and behave. Whether you apply in writing, in person, or by telephone, making a good impression is essential.

Write a Cover Letter

Generally, a résumé is sent with a cover letter, although some employers do not require a cover letter. A **cover letter** tells the employer that you are applying for a position in the company. The cover letter is the first thing a potential employer sees, and it can make a powerful impression. If you are going to get the great job you want, you need to write a great cover letter. Think of a cover letter as an introduction, a piece of paper that conveys a smile, a confident hello, and a nice, firm handshake. **Figure 16.1** on the next page shows a sample cover letter.

Here are some tips for creating a cover letter that is professional and gets the attention you want.

- **Keep it short.** Potential employers do not have time to read long cover letters. Your cover letter should not be longer than one page.
- **Make it look professional.** Type your letter on a computer, and print it on a laser printer. Use white or off-white paper if you are not submitting the letter online. Type your name, address, phone number, and e-mail address at the top of the page.
- **Explain why you are writing.** Start your letter with one sentence describing where you heard of the opening. For example, "Joan Wright suggested I contact you regarding a position in your marketing department," or, "I am writing to apply for the position you advertised in the *Sun City Journal*."
- **Introduce yourself.** Give a short description of your professional abilities and background. Refer to your attached résumé: "As you will see in the attached résumé, I am an experienced editor with a background in newspapers, magazines, and textbooks." Then highlight one or two specific accomplishments.

◀ **A Good First Impression**

You should have a neat and clean general appearance for a job interview. *What can you do to make sure you look your best when meeting potential employers?*

Figure 16.1 / Cover Letter

A Good Introduction A cover letter is a good opportunity to highlight your strong points. *What qualifications does Emily Nichols point out in her cover letter? How might you change this letter if you were submitting it online?*

Emily Nichols
510 Chestnut Street
Springdale, GA 33333
020-555-7890
enichols@xyz.com

June 11, 20—

Mr. Alex Sanchez, Principal
The Willow Preschool
320 David Road
Springdale, GA 33333

Dear Mr. Sanchez:

Donna Mulvaney, whose daughter Courtney attends your preschool, suggested that I contact you about a position as a teacher's aide at The Willow Preschool. I understand that one of your aides is about to leave and that you plan to replace her.

Please consider me for this position. I worked as a part-time teacher's aide for two years while I was finishing high school. Now that I have graduated, I would like to work with children full time. I believe that I have had enough experience working with children to know that I enjoy this kind of work and that children respond very positively to me.

Please review my enclosed résumé. It provides more details about the skills and experience I can bring to your preschool program.

I am especially interested in working at The Willow Preschool because I have heard many positive things about it from parents in my neighborhood. I hope you will find that I have the necessary skills and background to be considered for the position.

I would be happy to attend an interview at any time. Thank you for your consideration.

Sincerely,

Emily Nichols

Emily Nichols

- **Sell yourself.** Your cover letter should make the reader think you are exactly right for the job. Focus on what you can do for the company. Relate your skills to the skills and responsibilities mentioned in the job listing. If the ad mentions solving problems, relate a problem you solved at school or work. If the ad mentions specific skills or knowledge required, mention your mastery of these in your letter.

Complete an Application Form

Many employers require applicants to complete an application form. An **application form** is a form used to list personal information, such as your address, phone number, and Social Security number. You can also list information about your education.

When you complete an application form, have your résumé and other job search documents handy. That way you will have most of the information you need. Read the instructions before you fill in the form. Write as neatly and as clearly as you can. If a question does not apply to you, write "N/A" for "not applicable." When you are finished, check over the form to make sure it is complete, accurate, and neat. If the application has misspelled words or other errors, an employer might assume that you are careless or sloppy.

✓ **Reading Check** **Explain** What is the goal of a cover letter?

Interviewing for a Job

Many job applicants never get past the initial screening. Being asked to a job interview is a good sign. It means that you have made a strong enough impression to be considered a serious candidate. The interview is one of the most important parts of the job-seeking process. It is well worth spending time to prepare for it.

Prepare for the Interview

A good way to start preparing for an interview is to learn about the company. If the company has a Web site, check it out. If you know someone who already works there, talk with that person. Find out more about what the company does, what is happening in the industry as a whole, and how current market trends may affect the company. Knowing about the company can help you ask intelligent questions and create a good impression.

Another way to prepare is to anticipate the questions you might be asked and plan how you will answer them. It is likely that you will be asked about your education, your work experience, your career goals, and your interest in the job. You might also be asked about your strengths and weaknesses. You might want to arrange for a family member or friend to ask you some typical questions so that you can practice your answers.

Decide ahead of time what you will wear for the interview, and make sure the clothes you want to wear are clean and pressed. Plan to be well groomed, too. Remember that the first thing your interviewer will notice is your general appearance. A clean and neat appearance makes a more **favorable**, or positive, impression.

Make sure you know the exact place and time of the interview and the interviewer's name. If you are not sure how long it will take you to get there, try to do a trial run. On the evening before the interview, gather all the items you will need, including a pen and note pad, and get a good night's sleep.

Make a Positive Impression

During the interview, you will be judged on more than your résumé and your answers to questions. The interviewer will observe the way you conduct yourself. By giving the impression that you are a confident and capable person, you can increase your chances of being hired. To create a good impression:

- Be friendly but businesslike. You want to seem honest and open, but you do not want to seem too informal.
- Speak clearly, and do not mumble. Make sure you do not speak too quickly or use slang or swear words.
- Maintain eye contact.
- Sit up straight with your shoulders back.
- Think positively about yourself.

Ask and Answer Questions

When the interviewer asks questions, listen carefully and be sure not to interrupt. Try to keep your responses brief, focused, and positive. Try to demonstrate an enthusiastic interest in the job and a desire to learn. You want to seem eager, professional, confident, and capable.

After the interviewer has finished asking you questions, he or she will likely ask whether you have any questions. This is the time to bring up the questions that you prepared ahead of time, as well as any others that have come to mind during the interview. It is important that you have questions. It shows the interviewer that you are genuinely interested in the job, and that you paid attention to the conversation. Your questions will help the interviewer judge your interest in the position. They will also help you get the answers you need to make a decision if you are offered the job.

A Successful Interview

Be confident during a job interview. *How can you show confidence to a potential employer?*

Discuss Pay and Benefits

Whether you should discuss pay and benefits at your interview depends on the situation. Some employers provide full details of pay and benefits during the interview. Others prefer to discuss that information only with the person to whom they make an offer.

If the subject does come up, consider the entire compensation package. The **compensation package** includes pay and any additional benefits that the employer offers. You will want a clear understanding of both before making a decision. Information about pay includes how much you will be paid, how often, and how the rate of pay is figured. Benefits vary, but may include paid vacations, paid sick days, health insurance, and other extras. Good benefits can add **significant**, or important, value to the compensation package.

Follow Up

It is courteous to send a follow-up letter shortly after the interview. Thank the interviewer for taking the time to talk with you. If you still want the job, emphasize your continued interest and restate your skills. Use language that expresses enthusiasm and confidence. Your letter will help the interviewer remember you.

If, after the interview, you decide that you really are not interested in the job, you should still send a follow-up letter. Express your appreciation for the interview, and then simply say that you no longer wish to be considered for the job.

✓ **Reading Check** **Determine** When should you ask questions during an interview?

Life On Your Own

Anticipate Interview Questions

Have you ever heard the expression, "Expect the best, but prepare for the worst"? What do you think this expression means? Anticipation can lead to preparation. Anticipating potential problems can help you prepare for them.

How It Works It pays to think ahead. For instance, when driving in heavy traffic, defensive drivers try to anticipate potential problems. What if the car ahead brakes suddenly? Drivers who expect the unexpected will be better prepared to react. This trick can be helpful in many types of situations. By considering what problems might arise, you can take steps to prevent or solve them.

Try It Out Imagine that you have just completed your freshman year at college, and you are preparing for your first interview for a full-time summer job. The position is competitive, and you have heard that there will be some tough questions to test your composure under pressure. You are worried that you might give the wrong answers or draw a blank.

Your Turn Brainstorm a list of five tough questions that an interviewer might ask. Then write down answers that you think would make a good impression. Practice them. How can the process of preparing this list increase your chances of a successful interview?

Evaluating a Job Offer

You may have to go through several interviews before you receive a job offer. Eventually, though, you will hear, "We'd like to hire you." Your first impulse may be to say, "Great! When can I start?" However, a job offer, especially for a full-time position, deserves careful thought. Instead of accepting immediately, politely thank the employer, and ask whether you can take a day or two to decide.

A job offer shows that the employer has decided your skills and abilities are a good match for the company's needs. Now it is your turn to decide how well the job fits you. Consider more than just pay and benefits. Will this job give you the opportunity to learn valuable skills? Do you have the feeling that you will fit in well and enjoy working there? If your answers are yes, those are good reasons to accept the job offer.

Handling Rejection

If an interviewer calls to tell you that you have not been accepted, try to treat it as a learning experience. Ask politely why you were not hired. Some interviewers will take the time to explain. Sometimes you will not hear anything after an interview. Not all employers take the time to make follow-up calls. If this happens, look back at the interview, try to decide what you did and did not do well, and practice so that you will do better next time.

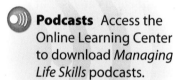

Go Green

When applying for jobs, e-mail your résumé or apply for positions via electronic application whenever possible. If you must print your résumé, try using soy-based inks and recycled paper.

 Podcasts Access the Online Learning Center to download *Managing Life Skills* podcasts.

Section 16.2 — After You Read

Review Key Concepts

1. **Identify** the information that would go on an application form.
2. **Discuss** the importance of your general appearance during an interview.
3. **Summarize** what should go in a follow-up letter.

Practice Academic Skills

 English Language Arts

4. Practice using language effectively to convince an employer to interview you. Write a cover letter that expresses enthusiasm for a job of your choice and details your most important experience and skills. Be sure you use proper grammar and spelling.

Social Studies

5. Look through job leads from a magazine, newspaper, or job Web site. Choose one that interests you, and use print and online resources to find out more information about the company. Prepare a one-page report that describes the history of the company, what the company does, and how any recent trends may have affected the company.

Check Your Answers Check your answers at this book's Online Learning Center at **glencoe.com**.

> **NCTE 4** Use written language to communicate effectively.

> **NCSS V C** Describe the various forms institutions take, and explain how they develop and change over time.

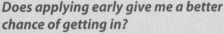
What You Should Know About Applying to College

The only way to get into college is to apply. The college application process is complicated. There are many parts of a college application, including grades, test scores, letters of recommendation, essays, financial aid forms, and interviews. It is important to start early and stay organized.

Does applying early give me a better chance of getting in?

There is no easy answer to this question because this varies from year to year and from school to school. The best way to answer this question is to do research on a school-by-school basis. One advantage to applying early is that you get the process over with sooner. One potential disadvantage is that many schools that accept early admission require you to attend the school if you are admitted, limiting your options.

What is the Common Application?

The Common Application is an application accepted by certain colleges in place of their own application. You fill it out once, and then submit copies of the same application to any school that participates. Some schools have a supplement that must be submitted along with the Common Application. This option can be a great time saver, but not all schools accept it, so be sure to check first.

When will I find out if I got in?

Although it varies from school to school, college applicants usually receive letters informing them if they were accepted, rejected, or put on the waiting list in April of their senior years. Some arrive as early as March. Early decision responses usually arrive in December and January of the applicant's senior year.

Hands-On

College Readiness It is crucial to keep track of all the tasks necessary to complete your college applications. Create a college application checklist. If you need additional information, get permission from a parent or teacher, and go online to research what needs to be done to complete the college application process. Create a checklist with all the tasks that need to be completed down the side and a column for each college you want to apply to. Be sure to include dates and deadlines.

Path to Success

 College & Career Readiness

Talk to Your Counselor He or she will play a big role in the college application process, so be sure to keep your counselor informed.

Start Early You do not want to have to rush through your college applications.

Focus on the Essays Be sure to schedule enough time to write and proofread your college essays.

Get Letters of Recommendation Think carefully about whom you want to ask, and ask early.

Send Applications in Early Mail applications as soon as possible for colleges with rolling deadlines.

Double-Check Review every part of your college applications, and confirm that the colleges received everything they need.

 Go to this book's Online Learning Center at **glencoe.com** to learn more about college and career readiness.

CHAPTER SUMMARY

Section 16.1
Finding Jobs

A carefully prepared résumé with well-chosen references can make the difference between getting a job and not getting a job. Create an electronic résumé, and compile a portfolio of work samples to showcase your skills. You can find job leads by networking, through school resources, in printed ads, through Internet resources, and through employment agencies.

Section 16.2
Getting a Job

When you apply for a job, you must sell yourself through a well-written cover letter and a complete application form. Prepare for a job interview to make a good impression on a potential employer. Be neat and clean in your general appearance, listen carefully, and give short, honest answers to questions. Follow up afterward with a note, and carefully evaluate any offers you receive.

Vocabulary Review

1. Create a multiple-choice test question for each content and academic vocabulary term.

Content Vocabulary
◇ résumé (p. 311)
◇ chronological résumé (p. 311)
◇ skills-based résumé (p. 311)
◇ reference (p. 311)
◇ portfolio (p. 313)

◇ job lead (p. 314)
◇ networking (p. 314)
◇ cover letter (p. 318)
◇ application form (p. 320)
◇ compensation package (p. 322)

Academic Vocabulary
■ suitable (p. 314)
■ criteria (p. 315)
■ favorable (p. 321)
■ significant (p. 322)

Review Key Concepts

2. Compare and contrast a résumé and a portfolio.
3. Describe six different sources of job leads.
4. Explain how a cover letter and an application form can help you get a job.
5. Review the steps you can take to prepare for a job interview.
6. List considerations for evaluating a job offer.

Critical Thinking

7. Review Reread Emily's résumé from page 312. Imagine that you own a preschool. What would you think about Emily's experience and skills? Would you hire her? What questions would you ask her in an interview?
8. Relate Think about the skills you have learned in school. How would these skills be useful to you at a job? Give some specific examples.
9. Predict How would you respond to a friend who says she is not going to prepare for her interview because she does better without rehearsing?
10. Evaluate What are the pros and cons of addressing a cover letter to a specific person versus using the address "To whom it may concern"?
11. Decide Do you think it is better to arrive early or right on time for a job interview? Support your answer.

12. Complete a Job Application Ask a local business for a job application, or use one provided by your teacher. Fill out the application form as if you were applying for a job. Fill in all blanks, but do not reveal any private information. For example, instead of your actual Social Security number, use all zeros. Once you have completed the application, exchange applications with another student. As you examine another student's application, decide by looking at the information whether

you would want to interview him or her and what questions you would ask. Discuss your findings with your partner and with the rest of the class.

13. Interview an Interviewer Conducting a job interview can be a challenge. Employers must find the right candidate for the job. If the candidate is not right, he or she will not do well on the job and will not advance. Search out someone in your community who conducts interviews. This might be a recruiter for an employment agency, a human resources manager at a company, a consultant that works with other businesses, or the manager of a retail business. Set up a time to talk with this person about how he or she conducts job interviews and what traits he or she likes to see in job candidates. Take notes during your interview, paying particular attention to the challenges of finding the right candidate. Give a short oral report to the class, summarizing your findings.

★ 21st Century Skills

Initiative Skills

14. List Job Sources Imagine that you are starting the search for a job tomorrow. Write the title of the job you would like, and then begin listing specific resources for finding job leads. Bring your list with you to class. As a class, discuss which resources seem to be the most popular.

Management Skills

15. Create a Tracking System When you look for a job, you need to keep track of your job search efforts. You could set up a manual tracking system or use a computer to design a tracking system. Choose one of these two methods, and create a tracking system. Write a paragraph to explain why it is important to keep track of your progress.

 Connections

Technology Skills

16. Design a Résumé As part of its mission, FCCLA encourages students to prepare for the future. Use a computer to design two versions of your résumé, one to print and another to send electronically. Use design elements for the first. For the second, do not use fancy formatting as features might become garbled when the résumé is e-mailed.

Academic Skills

 English Language Arts

17. Dialogs Follow your teacher's directions to form pairs. With your partner, write two different dialogs between an interviewer and a job candidate. The first dialog should show the candidate using poor interviewing techniques and skills. The second should show the candidate using good techniques. Role-play your dialogs for the class.

> **NCTE 12** Use language to accomplish individual purposes.

 Social Studies

18. Culture and Interviews Cultures have different expectations for manners and behavior in the workplace. For example, in China, a strong handshake, especially between a female and a male, is not valued. Research a culture that has different expectations and manners from your own, and write a report summarizing those differences and explaining how they could affect an interview.

> **NCSS I B Culture** Predict how data and experiences may be interpreted by people from diverse cultural perspectives and frames of reference.

 Mathematics

19. Calculate Job Sources Imagine you are using your networking contacts to find resources for a job search. You list 10 people as possible contacts for your job search. Each of those 10 people suggests two additional people who might help. Half of those people suggest one more person each. How many people will you have in your job search network?

Math Concept **Multi-Step Problems** When solving multi-step problems, think through each step before starting.

Starting Hint Step 1: Start with 10 people. Step 2: Add two people for each of those 10 people. Step 3: Determine half of the total from step two. Step 4: Add one person for each of the total in step three. Then, add the totals from Steps 1, 2, and 4. (Step 3 gives you an answer you need for Step 4.)

 For more math practice, go to the Math Appendix at the back of the book.

> **NCTM Number and Operations** Understand the meanings of operations and how they relate to one another.

 ## Standardized Test Practice

 CCR College & Career Readiness

MULTIPLE CHOICE
Read the sentences. Then read the question below the sentences. Read the answer choices, and choose the best answer to fill in the blank.

> **Test-Taking Tip** With multiple-choice questions that rely on information given, read the paragraph very carefully to make sure you understand what it is all about. Read the answer choices. Then read the paragraph again before choosing the answer.

Linda set up an appointment with her school counselor to talk about jobs. The counselor told her it would be a good idea to create a network.

20. In the last sentence, the word network means
_____.
  a. a system of computers
  b. a group of people
  c. a group of television stations
  d. a group of wires that cross regularly

Chapter 17

Work and Life Balance

Chapter Objectives

Section 17.1 Success in the Workplace

- **Define** the character traits that employers seek in an employee.
- **Describe** the steps you can take to prepare for a performance evaluation.

Section 17.2 Balancing Multiple Roles

- **List** the three effects that having multiple conflicting roles can have.
- **Summarize** how you can achieve balance in your life.
- **Explain** the help you can get from a support system.
- **Describe** why it is best to not act hastily when considering changing jobs.

> ▶**Explore the Photo**
>
> Learning how to have a successful balance between work and life is an essential life skill. *What do you think might happen if your work and life were out of balance?*

Writing Activity

Unified Paragraph

Work Ethic Having a good work ethic means that you take responsibility for your actions and show pride in your work. You might show a good work ethic on the job, when doing a report for school, or even when taking care of a younger sibling. Write a unified paragraph about a time that you showed a good work ethic. In a unified paragraph, every sentence develops the point made in the topic sentence. Include specific examples in your paragraph.

Writing Tips To write a unified paragraph:
- Make sure the paragraph focuses on one main idea.
- Check that all of the sentences in the paragraph support the main idea.
- Use transition words such as *because*, *in addition*, and *also* to link the ideas in the paragraph.

329

Success in the Workplace

A positive attitude and an understanding of your duties lead to success on the job.

Reading Guide

Before You Read

Look It Up As you read this section, keep a dictionary on hand. If you hear or read a word that you do not know, look it up in the glossary at the back of the book or in the dictionary. You will be amazed at how many new words you learn.

Read to Learn
Key Concepts
- **Define** the character traits that employers seek in an employee.
- **Describe** the steps you can take to prepare for a performance evaluation.

Main Idea

Employers look for employability skills as well as personal qualities that tell them an employee wants to succeed. You must understand your role at work and have a good attitude on the job. Performance evaluations can help you advance in the workplace.

Content Vocabulary
◇ work ethic
◇ initiative
◇ flexibility
◇ workplace culture
◇ enthusiasm
◇ constructive criticism

Academic Vocabulary

You will find these words in your reading and on your tests. Use the glossary to look up their definitions if necessary.

■ entail
■ representative

Academic Standards

English Language Arts

NCTE 5 Use different writing process elements to communicate effectively.

Social Studies

NCSS VI B Power, Authority, and Governance Explain the purpose of government and analyze how its powers are acquired, used, and justified.

Graphic Organizer

As you read, you will discover six ways to show a positive attitude on the job. Use a ladder organizer like the one shown to help you list them.

Show a Positive Attitude
1.
2.
3.
4.
5.
6.

NCTE *National Council of Teachers of English*
NCTM *National Council of Teachers of Mathematics*
NSES *National Science Education Standards*
NCSS *National Council for the Social Studies*

Graphic Organizer Go to this book's Online Learning Center at **glencoe.com** to print out this graphic organizer.

What Employers Want

Succeeding at work means more than simply showing up and doing the job you are paid to do. Employers look for people who have a positive attitude and a willingness to "go the extra mile."

When employers hire employees, they look first for the employ-ability skills that people need to function effectively in the work-place. These include reading, writing, and math skills. Also included are thinking, technology, management, and interpersonal skills.

Employers also look for personal qualities or character traits that demonstrate a desire to succeed. Examples of these traits include:

- **Responsibility** Responsible employees show they can be relied upon. They arrive at work on time, follow directions, and obey workplace rules. They do not waste time, money, or materials. They complete the tasks assigned to them.
- **Professionalism** People show professionalism by being loyal to their company. They promote the company's interests by not saying or doing anything that might reflect negatively on it.
- **Work Ethic** Having a strong **work ethic** means that you rec-ognize that you have an obligation to work hard and complete tasks efficiently and well. You are motivated by a desire to do your best. You do not need constant supervision. You use your initiative. **Initiative** (i-'ni-shə-tiv) is the willingness to do what needs to be done without being asked.
- **Honesty** Honest employees work the hours required of them and do not do personal business on company time. They do not lie or steal company property.
- **Flexibility** Having **flexibility** means being willing to adapt to new or changing requirements. More and more, the work-place is an environment that is changing quickly. Workers today often need to learn new technology and skills. They must also be ready to help others when there is a tight deadline or urgent need.

Your Role at Work

When you start a new job, you want to do well. Your employer wants you to be success-ful, too. You are much more likely to succeed if you understand your role and what is expected of you.

As You Read

Connect How can you show professionalism at work and in school?

Vocabulary

You can find definitions in the glossary at the back of this book.

> ### Working Well with Others
>
> Employees look for many different qualities in work-ers, including responsibility, professionalism, work ethic, honesty, and flexibility. *Why are these personal qualities important?*

Be Smart Be Safe

Workplace Dangers The safety standards for a job in a factory are different from those for a job in an office. Remember that every job has hazards that should be avoided by following certain safety precautions.

Write About It Think about two different jobs you may want to pursue. Research the types of hazards and safety rules for each. Write a summary of what you find.

Some employers provide new workers with a written job description. Others give a spoken description of what the job will **entail**, or involve. Make sure you understand your responsibilities. Do not be afraid to ask about anything that is not clear to you.

In addition to knowing your responsibilities, you need to know how you fit in. Who is your immediate supervisor? With whom will you be working? What are their responsibilities? To whom should you turn if you need help with a minor problem? What about a major problem? To fit in and feel comfortable, you need to understand workplace culture. A **workplace culture** is an atmosphere based on the attitudes, behavior, habits, and expectations of the company's owners and employees. Every workplace is different. For example, some have a casual atmosphere while others have a more rigid atmosphere.

You can figure out your company's workplace culture if you watch, listen, and ask questions. Your coworkers will guide you in appropriate behavior. They will let you know what to expect in specific situations. Once you understand your workplace culture, you will know how best to make your own contributions.

If your job brings you into contact with customers, clients, or suppliers, you will act as a company **representative**, or someone who acts on behalf of someone else. Dress appropriately, and act in ways that reflect positively on the company. Do everything you can to meet or exceed customers' expectations for service.

Friends and family will judge your company by the things you say about it. Show respect in what you say, and you will earn respect for the company and, possibly, more business.

The Importance of Attitude

Your attitude toward your job shows in how you behave and relate to others. You are more likely to succeed if you have a positive attitude. Your attitude should add to a pleasant work environment. A positive attitude will help you handle difficult or uncomfortable situations. Ways you can show a positive attitude at work include:

- **Show Enthusiasm Enthusiasm** (in-'thü-zē-ˌa-zəm) is taking pleasure in what you do and communicating it to others. Enthusiastic employees make teamwork exciting and have a positive effect on others. Of course, it is easy to be enthusiastic when things are going well. It is harder during rough times, but that is when enthusiasm is needed most. Your upbeat attitude may be just what is needed to help people get back on track.
- **Handle Problems Positively** Keeping a positive attitude is more helpful than giving in to feelings of anger or frustration. A positive attitude focuses on what can be done to resolve a problem rather than on the problem itself. Imagine you are printing out letters that need to be mailed today. Suddenly the printer stops working. Someone with a negative attitude would think, "Now I'll never get the job done." Someone with a positive attitude would focus on finding another printer to use.

- **Cope with Pressure** The best approach to pressure is to stay calm and figure out a plan. If you have so many tasks that you do not know where to start, make a list and prioritize. If you have a tight deadline, plan a schedule to see how it can be met. Try to work out your own solutions first. If you still need help, talk to your supervisor.

- **Deal with Mistakes** Everyone makes mistakes from time to time. The key is to know how to handle them. If you make a mistake, try to figure out how to fix it. Then speak to your supervisor. Explain the situation, and suggest your solution. Never try to hide a mistake. Doing so could cause additional problems. It might also cause people to distrust you. Instead, admit what you have done, and accept responsibility for it.

- **Accept Criticism** Nobody likes to be criticized, but in the workplace, you must learn to accept criticism gracefully. Remember that people criticize you because they want to help you do your job better. Your supervisor has the responsibility to offer constructive criticism. **Constructive criticism** is feedback that suggests ways you can learn and improve. Destructive criticism, negative criticism that does not provide helpful suggestions, should always be avoided.

- **Manage Successes and Disappointments** People experience successes and disappointments of all kinds in the workplace. It is fine to express your happiness if you receive a promotion or raise. Remember, however, that other people may be disappointed that they did not receive the same treatment. Likewise, if you experience a great disappointment, try to stay positive.

✓ **Reading Check** **Explain** How can you figure out your company's workplace culture?

Character?!
In Action

Workplace Confidentiality

As an employee, you will learn certain information about your company and the employees. Much of this information is not meant to be known by the public. Show you can be trusted by keeping such information to yourself. Do not discuss company business with people outside the company, and avoid gossip.

You Decide

You accidentally overhear two managers discussing a problem with a coworker with whom you are friendly. They are planning on calling a meeting with her tomorrow to discuss the issue. Would you warn your coworker? Explain your answer.

Life On Your Own

Get Along with Coworkers

Getting along with coworkers can sometimes be a challenge. However, it is an important part of being a productive and efficient employee. Also, knowing how to build and maintain positive relationships at work will make your workday more enjoyable.

How It Works Respect others, and appreciate their differences. If you dislike someone at work, try to separate your personal feelings from the job requirements. Do your best to stay neutral. Try to avoid taking sides in any workplace dispute. Keeping a sense of humor is very helpful. Try to laugh when the joke is on you.

Try It Out Imagine you are working in your first job out of college, and you are trying hard to do your best and get noticed. However, one of your coworkers keeps taking your ideas and presenting them to your mutual manager as her own ideas. You do not want to create conflict, but you also do not think it is fair that she gets credit for your ideas.

Your Turn What would you do in this situation? Would you say something to your manager? Would you confront your coworker? Or would you try to keep the peace and not say anything to anyone?

Evaluating Your Performance

Most companies use performance evaluations to recognize employee accomplishments and point to areas that need improvement. Some companies have a formal process with a written evaluation. Others have a less formal process. In most cases, employees get feedback on their work and on personal qualities such as initiative, attitude, and reliability.

Bear in mind that performance evaluations are important to your future success. Management decisions about promotions, raises, and new responsibilities are often based on these evaluations. Prepare thoroughly for evaluations, and be ready to take seriously any advice you are given.

As part of your evaluation, you might be asked to explain what you think your strengths are and how you might improve. To prepare, think back on your recent job performance. What goals were you given? Did you set any for yourself? What steps did you take to achieve them? What challenges and obstacles did you face, and how did you handle them? Even if you are not asked to evaluate your own performance, thinking about questions like these may help prepare you for what your supervisor has to say. Before the evaluation, jot down questions you want to ask and ideas you want to discuss.

Advancing on the Job

Most people hope and expect to advance in their careers. Employers also want workers whom they can promote and who will continue to grow throughout their careers. It is in a company's best interest to retain good employees and help them develop their potential. Most companies will provide employees with many opportunities to excel, gain new skills, and move up. Some ways that you can advance in your career include:

Succeed in SCHOOL and LIFE

Track Workplace Achievements

To help you prepare for performance evaluations, it is a good idea to keep records throughout the year. Record information about specific tasks and accomplishments, such as your responsibilities on projects, new skills you acquired, new technology you learned, and achievements that you would like to bring to your supervisor's attention.

- **Opportunities to Grow** You are more likely to advance in your career if you take advantage of opportunities to expand your skills and knowledge. Some companies offer seminars and training classes to help employees learn more about their industry, new technology, and effectiveness at work. The company may ask for volunteers to work on special projects. Some companies provide or fund continuing education. Continuing education includes courses geared toward working adults, as well as advanced degrees. Employers may pay tuition fees for courses that will help their employees gain relevant work skills.
- **Mentoring** As you learned in Chapter 2, a mentor is someone who acts as a teacher and guide. A workplace mentor is a person within the company who provides support and advice based on experience. He or she can help you understand workplace culture, suggest ways to improve your skills, and introduce you to people who can help you advance. Some companies have formal mentoring programs. Often, though, a mentoring relationship develops naturally.
- **Leadership** Another way to advance in your career is to demonstrate leadership. Employers are more likely to promote workers who have the ability to guide and motivate others. Demonstrate in your day-to-day work that you know how to make decisions, solve problems, and manage resources. Take advantage of opportunities to organize meetings or other company events. Volunteer to work on committees.

Health & Wellness TIPS

Prevent Computer-Related Injuries

Improper use of computers can lead to injury. Common injuries include shoulder, neck, and wrist pain, and back strain. Use these tips to stay healthy at work:

- ▶ Keep your wrist straight when using the mouse.
- ▶ Stand up and move around at least once an hour.
- ▶ When seated, sit up straight.

 Podcasts Access the Online Learning Center to download *Managing Life Skills* podcasts.

Section 17.1 After You Read

Review Key Concepts

1. **Compare** responsibility and work ethic.
2. **Describe** the benefits of a performance evaluation.

Practice Academic Skills

 English Language Arts

3. Think about the differences in attitude between employees who wish to succeed and those who do not care whether they succeed. Follow your teacher's instructions to form pairs. With your partner, write a skit that shows an example of an employee who wishes to succeed and one who does not care. Perform your skit for the class.

Social Studies

4. The Occupational Safety and Health Administration (OSHA) is an agency that deals with U.S.-based companies. With your teacher's permission, use Internet resources to research OSHA's main tasks. Write two paragraphs about OSHA's responsibilities and its history.

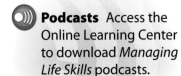 **Check Your Answers** Check your answers at this book's Online Learning Center at **glencoe.com**.

NCTE 5 Use different writing process elements to communicate effectively.

NCSS VI B Explain the purpose of government and analyze how its powers are acquired, used, and justified.

Balancing Multiple Roles

Strike a balance among your responsibilities to minimize stress.

Reading Guide

Before You Read

Two-Column Notes Two-column notes are a useful way to study and organize what you read. Divide a piece of paper into two columns. In the left column, write down main ideas. In the right column, list supporting details.

Read to Learn

Key Concepts

- **List** the three effects that having multiple conflicting roles can have.
- **Summarize** how you can achieve balance in your life.
- **Explain** the help you can get from a support system.
- **Describe** why it is best to not act hastily when considering changing jobs.

Main Idea

The roles in your life may come into conflict with one another. This can have an impact on you and others. A sense of balance will help you feel in control. Support systems at home, in the community, and at work can help you manage multiple roles.

Graphic Organizer

As you read, you will find three factors that can make role conflicts more difficult to manage. Use an arrow chart like the one shown to help you organize the information.

Factors that Complicate Role Conflicts

Graphic Organizer Go to this book's Online Learning Center at **glencoe.com** to print out this graphic organizer.

Content Vocabulary

◇ role conflict
◇ personal boundaries
◇ flextime
◇ job sharing
◇ telecommute

Academic Vocabulary

You will find these words in your reading and on your tests. Use the glossary to look up their definitions if necessary.

■ facilitate
■ perspective

Managing Multiple Roles

Have you ever felt like you were being pulled in a million different directions? Everyone has many different roles. These might include son or daughter, student, part-time worker, friend, hospital volunteer, neighbor, and team member. When you start your career, and perhaps a family of your own, you will take on even more new and expanded roles. Sometimes there are too many demands on your attention, and it seems like you cannot do it all. There are ways to **facilitate** (fē-'si-lə-,tāt), or ease, the management of multiple family, community, and wage-earner roles.

With so many roles in your life, they are bound to conflict with one another at times. A **role conflict** occurs when one role has a significant negative impact on another role. Another word that describes this situation is spillover. One role "spills over" into another, affecting your ability to fulfill it as well as you would like.

Roland was really looking forward to the birthday party for his favorite little cousin, T.J. The weekend of the party, however, Roland was hard at work on a major school project that was due on Tuesday. By Sunday, he realized that unless he skipped the party, he did not have much chance of finishing the project on time.

Roland knew that if he chose to stay home and work on his project, he would miss the fun and disappoint T.J. He decided to go to the party for just a little while. However, he found it hard to relax and enjoy himself because he kept thinking about the unfinished project. His role as student was spilling over into his role as a family member.

The Impact

As Roland's situation shows, role conflicts can affect you in three different ways. These three types of effects are interrelated. You may experience:

- **Internal Effects** When the demands of your roles clash, it is natural for stress to build. You may feel distracted, exhausted, and unable to think clearly.
- **Interpersonal Effects** Relationships are often affected by role conflicts. Spillover affects not only you, but also your family, friends, coworkers, and others.
- **External Effects** Role conflicts can sometimes keep you from participating in activities that are important to you. Clutter is another common external effect. It results when some tasks get pushed aside in the effort to juggle many roles.

As You Read

Connect What different roles do you play in your life?

Vocabulary

You can find definitions in the glossary at the back of this book.

Dealing with Multiple Roles

Balancing multiple roles in life can be challenging. *What can happen if a person has too many roles?*

Math For Success

Like Roland, you probably experience role conflicts. As you age, the challenges become even greater. You must find ways to balance your work life, family life, community involvement, and personal needs.

Role conflicts are an important issue in the workplace. Spillover from family stress is a major cause of absenteeism, tardiness, inefficiency, and distraction at work. The spillover of work stress also negatively affects family life. People under stress at work tend to argue with their spouses more and participate in family activities less.

Adding to the Challenge

Role conflicts can occur under even the best conditions. Certain factors, however, can make them more likely and harder to deal with. These factors include:

- **Difficult Situations** People who have unpredictable work schedules or who hold more than one job may find it very difficult to fulfill their family roles. Even more stress is caused by challenges like finding reliable child care, coping with an extended illness, or caring for an ill or elderly family member.
- **Unrealistic Expectations** A college student who must work long hours to earn money should not expect to also take extra courses and graduate early. New parents trying to function on little sleep should not expect to keep their home spotless.
- **Overcommitment** Many people agree to more obligations than they can handle. This often stems from a desire to please everyone and an inability to say no. It is also easy to underestimate the time and energy needed to fulfill certain roles.

✓ Reading Check **List** What problems can result from role conflicts in the workplace?

The Need for Balance

There is no way to avoid role conflicts completely. Not all roles are equal in their importance to you. You can, however, minimize the negative effects of spillover. Management skills can help you balance your multiple roles effectively. Balancing does not always mean dividing your time and energy in proportion to how much you value each role. Many adults spend most of each workday at their job. This does not necessarily mean they value that time more than the time they spend with their families.

A sense of balance will not eliminate role conflicts, but having balance in your life can help you feel in control. You can enjoy your roles as much as possible rather than feeling overwhelmed by them, and you will be better able to stay focused on your goals.

Achieving Balance

There is no easy way to achieve the balance that will help you manage your many roles. However, there are three strategies that can help: set priorities, handle stress, and manage your time.

Set Priorities

One of the biggest challenges of balancing multiple roles is choosing where to focus your time and energy. To make choices that are right for you, consider your values. Then set priorities based on your values and responsibilities. You may not always be able to do everything you want, but setting priorities can help you put your roles in **perspective**, or in a clearer position. Most people have more than one high-priority role. Setting priorities gives you the flexibility to adjust your roles as needed.

Changing Priorities Your priorities may change over time. David went through a stage of focusing only on his career. To meet the demands of his job, he often worked late or on weekends. He took college courses at night. After he married and had children, however, his priorities changed. His career was still important to him, but he was no longer willing to give up evenings and weekends.

Setting Boundaries Establishing priorities can help you set **personal boundaries**. These are limits you set for yourself based on your values and priorities. They help you to control the number of roles you play and focus on what matters most to you. Whenever you consider another role, ask yourself, "Do I have room in my life for this right now? How will it affect my other roles? Does it fit with my values and priorities?"

Handle Stress

Role conflicts often result in stress. Too much stress can knock you off balance. The more stress you feel, the more difficult it is to manage multiple roles. That can lead to more role conflicts and still more stress. Take steps to reduce stress before it becomes a problem. No matter how busy you are, set aside time to relax and calm your mind. Enjoy fun activities. Take care of yourself by eating right and getting enough sleep. Stay physically active. Something as simple as taking a walk can be a great stress reducer.

✓ **Reading Check** **Define** What are personal boundaries?

> ## Coping with Stress
>
> One way to handle stress is to stay physically active. *What are other ways you can reduce stress that comes from life's imbalances?*

HOW TO... Manage Your Time

The ability to manage your time effectively is a key skill in balancing multiple roles, avoiding stress, and enjoying yourself. Time management helps you focus on your priorities and use your time wisely. Here are some tips for making the best possible use of your time.

Be Realistic Do not overestimate what you can accomplish. Plan for things to take longer than you predict.

Learn to Say No It is better to tell someone you are not able to do something than to say you will and let that person down later.

Write It Down Make a daily or weekly to-do list. Use a calendar to keep track of appointments and special events. Then start each day by checking your to-do list..

Multi-Task You can save time by doing multiple things at once, such as doing homework while riding the bus.

Be Flexible You should be willing and able to make changes to your schedule, if necessary.

Plan for Some Free Time Do not schedule every hour of the day. Be sure you allow time to have fun and relax.

Develop Support Systems

Managing multiple roles is easier with a good support system. A typical support system might include family, friends, community services, and coworkers.

At Home

Many people call on their extended family for support. Working parents, for example, often find that child care and transportation are easier and less expensive with help from grandparents or other relatives. These arrangements also give family members the chance to spend more time with one another.

Good communication helps family members understand one another's roles. If you want your family to support you, be open about any role conflicts you have. Help them understand the demands you face in balancing your life. This not only enhances understanding, but may lead to new solutions. In return, be willing to listen to the concerns of family members and offer your support.

In the Community

Friends and neighbors often come together for mutual support and assistance. For example, neighborhood parents may take turns waiting with young children for the school bus. Julie and Alice, who are neighbors and friends, take turns watching each other's children after school. Neighborhood Watch programs involve organized groups of community members who work with law enforcement officers to prevent crime and vandalism in their neighborhood.

Common social services offered in communities include mental health facilities, free or low-cost medical clinics, drug rehabilitation centers, homeless shelters, and food banks. Those who benefit from community social services most often are the young and the elderly.

Many communities offer programs and facilities to help families balance their multiple roles. Some schools and places of worship offer family-based activities as well as after-school programs for children. Some community service organizations also arrange for supervised after-school programs.

Help with caring for older family members may also be available from the community. Some communities have day care centers for seniors that offer lunches, activities, and outings. Social service agencies can arrange for other needed care, such as Meals on Wheels, a program that provides meals for people who cannot purchase or prepare their own meals.

Succeed in SCHOOL and LIFE

Avoid Overcommitment

It can be hard to say no when people ask you for help, invite you out, or include you in their plans. However, if you want to focus on your priorities, you have to be able to refuse sometimes. Focus on what is best for you. When someone tries to persuade you, stand firm. If you overcommit, you will end up disappointing others as well as yourself.

Two Views One World

How Much Flexibility Is Fair?

When family commitments interfere with your job, how much flexibility and understanding is it fair to expect from a workplace?

Sarah: I think work should come first. Clearly, supervisors should be sympathetic and make allowances when possible if an employee has a problem at home. But it isn't fair for an employee to take time off every time his or her child gets sick. Businesses can't run if employees are always putting their families first. If you cannot balance work and family, maybe you or your spouse needs to stay home or make additional arrangements.

Devin: It's important to take your job seriously, but supporting your family is more important. When your family needs you, you have to figure out a way be there for them. Yes, it is a sacrifice to give an employee time off for family issues, but if that employee is forced to work, he or she will be distracted and not working efficiently anyway. Family comes first, and good supervisors need to figure out a way to deal with that.

Seeing Both Sides

Why do you think people might have different viewpoints about conflicts between work and family?

At Work

Having support at work can make the difference between enjoying a job and feeling stressed. Perhaps you and some coworkers can get together for lunch, share concerns, and encourage one another. Your supervisor may also be willing to help at appropriate times.

Employers know that their employees have personal lives and family obligations. They know about the demands on parents when school is out and the concerns of employees caring for aging relatives. Of course, employers cannot allow workers unlimited time off to deal with personal issues. However, some employers have family-friendly policies that make it easier for wage-earners to balance their lives.

- **Flexible Work Hours** **Flextime** is a system that allows workers to choose when they will begin and end their working day. Some people, for example, start at 7 a.m. and leave at 3 p.m., while others choose to start later and stay later.

- **Compressed Schedules** An employee who works a compressed workweek might work four 10-hour days and then have three days off. This option is often used at hospitals or at schools and universities during summer months.

- **On-Site Child Care** Companies that provide on-site child care facilities make it possible for employees to stay close to their children while they work. Parents can visit their children during their lunch break and are close in case of an emergency.

- **Job Sharing** Under a system called **job sharing**, two part-time workers share one full-time job. They split the hours and the pay. One might work in the mornings and the other in the afternoons, or one might work two days a week and the other three.

- **Telecommuting** To **telecommute** ('te-li-kə-ˌmyüt) means to work from home using technology to link to one's job. Workers link by phone, fax, instant messages, or e-mail, or they may log onto their office computer network from home. This works for people who do not need daily face-to-face contact with coworkers or customers.

- **Family and Medical Leave** Companies with more than 50 employees are required by law to allow workers to take time off to deal with family and medical emergencies. The Family and Medical Leave Act guarantees up to 12 weeks of leave for workers who get sick, need to care for relatives, or need time off for the birth or adoption of a child. Employers are not required to pay employees during their time off, but they are required to have a job for the employee when he or she returns.

If you find that one of your roles is taking too much time and energy and is spilling over into other important roles, try to keep things in perspective. Use your support system. Re-examine your priorities. The more you practice maintaining balance in your life, the easier it will become.

✓ **Reading Check** **Contrast** What is the difference between flextime and telecommuting?

Changing Jobs

Few people stay with the same company all their working life, and as technology further develops, this is becoming the case more and more often. According to the Bureau of Labor Statistics of the U.S. Department of Labor, the average person born in the later years of the baby boom held almost 11 jobs from age 18 to age 42.

Some people move on because they want new opportunities or new challenges with a different employer. Others move on because they are unhappy in their present job or cannot see a way of advancing. Some have a job change forced upon them when they are laid off because their company downsizes, relocates, or goes out of business.

If you are unhappy in your present job and want to look for another one, do not act too hastily. Few people can afford to live without a paycheck. Do not hand in your notice until you have found another position. Usually, it is best not to tell coworkers of your decision to leave until you have another job. Be sure you have your next job lined up before giving up your current job.

When you leave your present job, make a point of leaving on good terms. After all, you may want to ask your employer for a reference. Also, there is always the possibility that you might want to return to your former company in the future. Your former employer and coworkers can remain part of your network as you continue on your career path.

 Podcasts Access the Online Learning Center to download *Managing Life Skills* podcasts.

Section 17.2 After You Read

Review Key Concepts

1. **Give examples** of external effects that come from role conflicts.

2. **Explain** how to set priorities.

3. **Describe** how your family can help you manage multiple roles.

4. **Explain** why people may choose to change jobs.

Practice Academic Skills

 English Language Arts

5. Find a short story about a person who has committed to too many roles. In a one-page essay, write a short summary of the story, identify the role that is out of balance, and then make suggestions about what the character could do to help solve the role conflict.

 Social Studies

6. Many adults must take care of their children as well as their aging family members. Use print and Internet information to find a list of resources that can help people who feel overcommitted because of this situation. Your list should contain an explanation of the resource.

> **Check Your Answers** Check your answers at this book's Online Learning Center at **glencoe.com**.

> **NCTE 2** Read literature to build an understanding of the human experience.

> **NCSS V G** Analyze the extent to which groups and institutions meet individual needs and promote the common good in contemporary and historical settings.

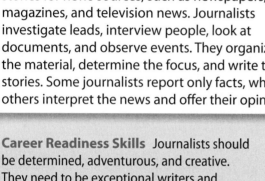

Pathway to Your Career

Journalist

What Does a Journalist Do?

Journalists gather material and write articles and stories for news sources, such as newspapers, magazines, and television news. Journalists investigate leads, interview people, look at documents, and observe events. They organize the material, determine the focus, and write their stories. Some journalists report only facts, while others interpret the news and offer their opinions.

Career Readiness Skills Journalists should be determined, adventurous, and creative. They need to be exceptional writers and should be comfortable with unfamiliar places and people. They should also be able to make people feel comfortable and want to share their stories. They must be able to deal with urgent deadlines and irregular hours.

Education and Training Most employers prefer candidates with bachelor's degrees, preferably in fields such as journalism or mass communications. Some may prefer candidates with degrees in a subject-matter specialty such as business or political science. Employers often look for candidates with experience at school newspapers or internships with news organizations.

Job Outlook Printed newspapers are declining because of the Internet. However, journalists are still needed to write for television and online sources. Competition will be strong for jobs in large cities and national newspapers and magazines.

Critical Thinking Find and read an article in a newspaper or magazine. Recognize what work was done to complete the article. What are the social and psychological implications of working as a journalist? Submit the article along with a written summary of your thoughts.

Career Cluster

CCR ☆ **College & Career Readiness**

Arts, Audio-Video Technology & Communications Journalists work in the Journalism & Broadcasting pathway of this career cluster. Other jobs in this cluster include:

- Costume Designer
- Gallery Manager
- Interior Designer
- Lithographer
- Illustrator
- Fashion Illustrator
- Stagecraft Designer
- Screen Writer
- Sound Effects Engineer
- Textile Designer
- Composer
- Acting Coach
- Video Systems Technician
- Special Effects Designer

Explore Further The Arts, Audio-Video Technology & Communications career cluster contains six pathways: Audio & Video Technology & Film; Printing Technology; Visual Arts; Performing Arts; Journalism & Broadcasting; and Telecommunications. Choose one of these pathways to explore further.

 Career Clusters To learn more about career clusters, go to this book's Online Learning Center at **glencoe.com**.

CHAPTER SUMMARY

Section 17.1
Success in the Workplace

Employers want employees who have character traits that show a desire to succeed. You must understand your role at work and be a good representative of the company. Maintain a positive attitude at work. Performance evaluations help companies recognize employee accomplishments, give constructive criticism, and advance deserving employees. A mentor is someone in the company who acts as a teacher and guide.

Section 17.2
Balancing Multiple Roles

Your many roles will come into conflict with each other at times. This conflict can have an impact on you and your relationships. Difficult situations, unrealistic expectations, and overcommitment can add to the stress. You must set priorities, reduce stress, and manage time to find balance. Support systems at home, in the community, and at work can help you manage multiple roles. There are many reasons to change jobs, but do not change jobs hastily.

Vocabulary Review

1. Arrange the vocabulary words into groups of related words. Explain your decisions.

Content Vocabulary
◇ work ethic (p. 331)
◇ initiative (p. 331)
◇ flexibility (p. 331)
◇ workplace culture (p. 332)
◇ enthusiasm (p. 332)
◇ constructive criticism (p. 333)
◇ role conflict (p. 337)
◇ personal boundaries (p. 339)
◇ flextime (p. 342)
◇ job sharing (p. 342)
◇ telecommute (p. 342)

Academic Vocabulary
■ entail (p. 332)
■ representative (p. 332)
■ facilitate (p. 337)
■ perspective (p. 339)

Review Key Concepts

2. Define the character traits that employers seek in an employee.
3. Describe the steps you can take to prepare for a performance evaluation.
4. List the three effects that having multiple conflicting roles can have.
5. Summarize how you can achieve balance in your life.
6. Explain the help you can get from a support system.
7. Describe why it is best to not act hastily when considering changing jobs.

Critical Thinking

8. Give Examples In what ways could the phrase, "going the extra mile" apply to someone in a workplace?
9. Evaluate "Not every employee will be a manager, but all employees should have management training." Do you agree with this statement?
10. Infer Your friend has a very busy schedule and also volunteers to help a hospital raise money. Why do you think someone so busy would want to do volunteer work? Do you think she will run into role conflicts?
11. Communicate You have a very full schedule. A friend asks you to join a science club, but you think that this will overcommit you. How would you say no to your friend without damaging the friendship?

Family & Community Connections

ACTIVE LEARNING

12. Define Success Follow your teacher's instructions to form groups. As a group, discuss what the concept of "success in the workplace" means. Work together to find a common definition for your group. Then read your definition to the rest of the class. As a class, discuss how the definitions of success in the workplace differ from one another and why you think there might be differences. Is it correct to have one definition of workplace success? Or is there room for more than one correct definition?

13. Balance Family Roles Brainstorm all the chores and jobs that each member of your family must do to keep your household running smoothly. Use this information to develop a family job chart, with space beside each job or chore to write which family member is responsible. If a job can be rotated among different people, show the family members and their rotation turns in the chart as well. Once you have completed the chart, develop rules for how family members can switch responsibilities fairly. For example, family members may swap chores if both family members agree to the switch. If possible, create a computerized version of your chart using spreadsheet software.

⭐ 21st Century Skills

Technology Skills

14. Create a Presentation Use presentation software to create an entertaining visual presentation targeted at teens to describe the negative effects of overcommitment. You may wish to use humorous or exaggerated images to help make your points. Use information you have learned from this chapter. Show your presentation to your class.

Self-Direction Skills

15. Evaluate Yourself Evaluate your performance in school over the past six months. Create an evaluation sheet with at least six categories, such as grades, attendance, and attitude. Then rate yourself in each category on a scale of 1 (poor) to 5 (excellent). Use information from your evaluation to write a summary of suggestions on how you can improve in school. Turn in the summary to your teacher.

 FCCLA Connections

Planning Skills

16. Create a Report Plan As part of its mission, FCCLA encourages students to assume responsibilities and prepare for adult life. This includes managing time wisely. Create a step-by-step plan for writing a report for school. Block out time for researching information, creating an outline, and writing the paper. Do not forget to allow for enough time for you to meet all of your other commitments.

Academic Skills

 ### English Language Arts

17. Write a Customer Service Letter Imagine that you are a customer service representative for a computer company. You have received a letter from a customer complaining about a defective computer. Write a letter responding to the customer's complaint. Make sure your letter is clearly worded, respectful, and free of grammar or spelling errors.

> **NCTE 4** Use written language to communicate effectively.

 ### Social Studies

18. Research FMLA Use print and Internet resources to find out more information about the Family and Medical Leave Act (FMLA) in the United States. Determine how employees become eligible for leave under the terms of the act. Do they continue to receive health benefits while they are on leave? Summarize your findings in a one-page report. Cite your sources.

> **NCSS VI C Power, Authority, and Governance** Analyze and explain ideas and mechanisms to meet needs and wants of citizens.

 ### Mathematics

19. Weekly Expenses Rose spends $42.00 a week on food, $35.00 a week on clothing, and $33.00 a week on entertainment. She takes public transportation to work, which costs an additional $30.00. How many hours per week does Rose need to work if she makes $12.50 per hour, and 12% is taken out for taxes?

Math Concept **Division** In a division problem, the number that is divided is called the dividend. The number by which another number is divided is called the divisor.

Starting Hint First, add up Rose's weekly expenses to learn how much money she spends per week. Then, find out how much money she actually makes per hour after taxes. Divide her weekly expenses by her hourly take-home pay to find out how many hours per week she needs to work.

 For more math practice, go to the Math Appendix at the back of the book.

> **NCTM Problem Solving** Apply and adapt a variety of appropriate strategies to solve problems.

 ## Standardized Test Practice

 CCR College & Career Readiness

READING COMPREHENSION
Read the passage, then answer the question.

Test-Taking Tip Read the passage carefully, identifying key passages as you go. Answer the question based only on what you just read in the passage, not on your previous knowledge.

Many people believe that watching and listening to current employees is the best way to determine a company's workplace culture. Current employees will already know what the company expects.

20. According to this passage, why should new employees listen to current employees?

UNIT 5 — Portfolio Project

Fill Out a Job Application

In this project, you will develop a personal fact sheet that you can use to help fill out job and college applications. You will then practice filling out a job application, working with a guidance counselor to revise your answers and clarify any questions you have.

 My Journal

If you completed the journal entry from page 286, refer to it to see if your thoughts have changed after reading the unit.

Project Assignment

In this project you will:
- Compile information to create a personal fact sheet.
- Obtain job applications from local businesses.
- Use your personal fact sheet to complete the job application.
- Review your application with a trusted adult, and make any necessary revisions.
- Compare multiple job applications for similarities and differences.
- Develop a presentation to share your findings with the class.

THE SKILLS BEHIND THE PROJECT

Key personal and relationship skills you will use in this project include:
- Gathering and consolidating information
- Interacting with adults
- Responding appropriately to information and advice

Academic Skills

 English Language Arts

> **NCTE 8** Use information resources to gather information and create and communicate knowledge.
>
> **NCTE 12** Use language to accomplish individual purposes.

STEP 1 Develop a Personal Fact Sheet

Many jobs require you to fill out an application in addition to submitting a résumé. For this reason, it is important to have a personal fact sheet that you can refer to for all the information that may not be included on your résumé. Your fact sheet will include information such as your current and previous addresses, Social Security number, education details, your driver's license number, and details of current and past work experiences. Conduct research to find out what other information you might want to include. Be sure your fact sheet is legible and organized.

STEP 2 Fill Out a Job Application

Request a job application from a local business. Make a copy of the application before filling it out. Using your fact sheet from Step 1, fill in the copy of the application. If you are not sure what information is needed in a particular space, leave it blank, and come back to it later. If you find yourself looking up information that is not on your fact sheet, consider adding it for future reference.

Information Literacy Skills
- Access information efficiently.
- Use information accurately.
- Manage the flow of information.

STEP 3 Review Your Application

Arrange some time with a trusted adult to review and discuss your completed job application. A trusted adult might include a guidance counselor, parent, or other local professional. Ask for clarification or guidance on completing any spaces that you left blank during Step 2. Then request that the adult review the overall application and offer feedback on ways to improve or more accurately answer any questions.

Interpersonal Skills

• Listen attentively.
• Respond open-mindedly to suggestions and critiques.
• Conduct yourself in a respectable and professional manner.

STEP 4 Build Your Portfolio Project

Use the Portfolio Project Checklist to plan and create an oral report to share your findings with your classmates.

Speaking Skills

• Present your ideas clearly.
• Organize your report by developing an outline.
• Use standard English to communicate.

STEP 5 Evaluate Your Project

Your portfolio project will be evaluated based on:

Academic Skills

• Organization of your report
• Clarity of explanation
• How easy it is to follow your report

 Evaluation Rubric Go to this book's Online Learning Center at **glencoe.com** for a rubric you can use to evaluate your final project.

PORTFOLIO PROJECT CHECKLIST

Plan

☑ Use your updated fact sheet and the feedback from your review to fill out a fresh job application.

☑ Obtain additional job applications from at least two other local businesses.

☑ Compare and contrast the job applications. What information is asked on all the applications? What information is unique?

Present

☑ Prepare an oral report to share the results of your comparison and analysis with the class.

☑ Invite the students to ask questions. Answer any questions. Demonstrate in your answers that you respect their perspectives.

☑ Place your fact sheet and filled-in job application in your portfolio. Share this with your teacher.

Portfolio Highlights

Keep Your Facts Straight

Your personal fact sheet should never be considered complete. It is a document that should be reviewed frequently and updated.

Updated Information

Any time you move, change a phone number, or change jobs, you should update your fact sheet. However, do not delete old data as many applications will ask for this. When you have new information, add it to the fact sheet along with the date.

Not Just Job Applications

Throughout life, you will have to complete many types of applications, including those for jobs, schools, and credit cards. Your updated fact sheet will allow you to have all the necessary information on hand. If you fill in an application that requests information not on your fact sheet, add it!

Security

Your fact sheet will contain a lot of personal information, such as your Social Security number. Whether you keep you personal fact sheet in printed or electronic form, you must ensure the security of the information. Consider saving your file with password protection, if possible.

UNIT 6

Relationships

Unit Portfolio Project Preview

Write a Cover Letter

In this unit, you will explore ways to interact with others and form successful relationships. In your portfolio project, you will connect to potential employers with an effective cover letter.

 My Journal

Making a First Impression Write a journal entry about one of the topics below. This will help you prepare for the project at the end of this unit.

- Cite the first trait that you would like people to notice about you, and how you communicate that quality.
- Write only three paragraphs to represent yourself to a complete stranger.
- Find a letter that you have written to or received from someone, and rewrite it to make it stronger.

Explore the Photo

Most people have different types of relationships at one time that are important to them. *How do you balance numerous relationship responsibilities?*

Chapter 18

Understanding Relationships

Chapter Objectives

Section 18.1 Successful Relationships

- **Distinguish** among different kinds of relationships.
- **Analyze** factors that influence relationships.
- **Describe** ways to build and maintain strong relationships.

Section 18.2 Unhealthy Relationships

- **Identify** characteristics of unhealthy relationships.
- **Examine** the reasons and methods for ending a relationship.

> **Explore the Photo**
>
> Successful relationships can make your life both fun and rewarding. *Why do you think relationships with friends are especially important in your teen years?*

Writing Activity

Personal Letter

Maintain Relationships Writing personal letters shows friends that you care about them and allows you to stay connected. Write a personal letter to a friend with whom you have not talked lately. Include details about the events in your life and what has been on your mind. Ask specific questions about your friend's life as well.

Writing Tips Use these tips to help you write a personal letter:

- For the form of your letter, follow this sequence: heading, greeting, body of the letter, complimentary close, and signature line.
- Re-read your letter when you are finished, proofreading for errors in spelling and grammar.
- Sign typed letters by hand to make them more personal.

Successful Relationships

How important are your relationships to you?

Reading Guide

Before You Read

Predict Before starting this section, browse the content by reading the headings, bold terms, and photo captions. Do they help you predict what this section is about?

Read to Learn
Key Concepts
- **Distinguish** among different kinds of relationships.
- **Analyze** factors that influence relationships.
- **Describe** ways to build and maintain strong relationships.

Main Idea

Relationships are your connection to others. Learning how to make and maintain healthy and successful relationships will enrich your life in many ways.

Content Vocabulary
◇ relationship
◇ expectation
◇ tolerance
◇ discrimination

Academic Vocabulary

You will find these words in your reading and on your tests. Use the glossary to look up their definitions if necessary.

■ casual
■ flavor

Academic Standards

English Language Arts
NCTE 12 Use language to accomplish individual purposes.

Social Studies
NCSS I F Culture Interpret patterns of behavior reflecting values and attitudes that contribute or pose obstacles to cross-cultural understanding.

Graphic Organizer

As you read, list five rewards or benefits of successful relationships. Use a flower graphic like the one shown to help you organize your information.

Relationship Rewards

Graphic Organizer Go to this book's Online Learning Center at **glencoe.com** to print out this graphic organizer.

NCTE *National Council of Teachers of English*
NCTM *National Council of Teachers of Mathematics*
NSES *National Science Education Standards*
NCSS *National Council for the Social Studies*

Kinds of Relationships

How many different people have you interacted with today? How many will you have interacted with before the day is over? Chances are there have been quite a few. Your contacts on a typical day are likely to include family members, classmates, teachers, friends, neighbors, and a variety of other people. Do you find that your interactions with these people are mainly positive, or do you experience difficulty getting along with some of them? Your answer will depend largely on your relationship skills. The better your relationship skills become, the more satisfying and fulfilling your relationships will be.

A **relationship** is the connection you have with another person. Relationships vary in three basic ways: their degree of closeness, their purpose, and their form. For instance, the relationships you have with other teenagers most likely vary in closeness, purpose, and form from the relationships you have with your parents, siblings, and family friends.

Some relationships can be described as close and others as **casual**, or informal, with many variations falling between those two descriptions. Close relationships, such as those with a best friend or relative, are supportive and fulfilling. These relationships give you someone you can confide in and share special times with. Casual relationships, on the other hand, are often linked only to certain activities or behaviors. These might include living in the same apartment building, working the same shift, or going to the same gym. These relationships are given a different level of importance in your life.

Sometimes differences between people in a relationship are valuable because they help each one see things from a fresh point of view. For example, you may have relationships with people whose backgrounds differ from your own. Building relationships with people from a variety of cultures and beliefs can enrich and add **flavor**, or interest, to your life. These relationships may help you see things in new ways and provide opportunities you might otherwise miss.

Many relationships exist for specific purposes. Your relationships with your teachers are based on your need to learn. Members of a soccer team form relationships so they can play well together. Coworkers form relationships that enable them to work together, share ideas, and accomplish goals.

✓ **Reading Check**

Compare What are the differences between a close relationship and a casual relationship?

As You Read

Connect What needs are filled by your relationships with others? How are their needs filled by their relationship with you?

 Vocabulary

You can find definitions in the glossary at the back of this book.

▼ **Coworker Connection**

The relationships that develop between coworkers enable them to work together and share ideas. *How might the way you interact with a coworker be influenced by the purpose of the relationship?*

 Teacher and Student Roles

The teacher-student relationship has well-defined expectations. *What do you expect of your teachers? What do you think they expect of you?*

Influences on Relationships

What is the difference between the way you address an adult and the way you address your friends? When you address an authority figure, you might use Mr., Mrs., or Ms. followed by a last name, or you might call them sir or ma'am. On the other hand, you may use a nickname for a close friend or sibling. There are many factors that influence the ways in which you relate to different people.

Roles and Expectations

Your role in a relationship is one factor that influences your behavior. Everyone has different roles in life. For example, Barry is a son, brother, friend, student, band member, and volunteer. What roles do you play? What roles might you add in the future?

Every role carries with it certain expectations. An **expectation** is a want or need that a person hopes will be met in the relationship. Expectations affect how people act in their different roles. For example, children expect their parents to take care of them. Parents, in turn, expect their children to follow the rules and help around the house. Members of a debate team are expected to practice and follow their coach's instructions. In turn, members expect the coach to provide leadership and treat members fairly.

Sometimes roles and expectations differ. For example, you may expect that a particular friend will call or e-mail you every day, but your friend may not feel that is necessary for your relationship. Younger siblings may expect you to spend more time with them than you can or are willing to spend. Differences in expectations can sometimes cause conflict in a relationship.

Personal Qualities

What draws you to certain people and not to others? Think about the qualities you admire in your friends, and write them down. Do you share these qualities? Then think about the traits in other people that cause you to avoid them. Personal qualities play a key role in choosing relationships. Such qualities include:

- **Values** Personal values about what is right and wrong are major influences on relationships. Friendships with people who have similar values and beliefs are likely to involve less conflict.

Succeed in SCHOOL and LIFE

Meet Teachers' Expectations

Sometimes your performance in the classroom or on a test seems to fall short of your teacher's expectations. When this happens, it is important to make sure you truly understand what is required. Respectfully ask the teacher if he or she can help you identify where changes are needed, and find ways to make that happen. Doing this will show that you really care about your role as a student.

- **Needs** Most people expect relationships to fulfill certain needs, such as the desire for companionship, love, belonging, and acceptance. Consciously or unconsciously, you seek relationships with people who seem most able to meet those needs.
- **Interests and Abilities** Many of your relationships will be with people who share some of your interests. Others will give you the opportunity to develop new interests. If you have certain abilities, such as in music or basketball, you may seek out people who share those interests or can help you develop them.

Self-Esteem

Self-esteem, or the value or importance you place on yourself, also influences your relationships. High self-esteem gives you the confidence to meet new people and have new experiences. When you feel good about yourself, you find it easier to make friends and build worthwhile relationships. High self-esteem also helps you steer clear of relationships that may harm you.

Good relationships, in turn, enhance your self-esteem. How people think of you and the way in which they treat you can strongly affect how you feel about yourself. When people accept you and treat you with respect, it helps reinforce that you are a valuable person. **Figure 18.1** shows some ways in which relationships can be rewarding and beneficial to everyone involved.

When people do not feel accepted, their self-esteem is likely to be low. They find it difficult to be confident about themselves and their abilities. Sometimes people in this situation act like they do not care what others think of them. If that describes you or someone you know, remember that everyone has personal strengths that deserve to be recognized and celebrated. Everyone also has the ability to improve. Make it a habit to give sincere compliments, especially to those who seem to need them most.

✓ **Reading Check** **Identify** What are three personal qualities that influence who people choose to have relationships with?

Character?! In Action

Combat Stereotypes

At times, you may have opportunities to interact with people who are different from you. They may be older or younger, have a disability, or come from different backgrounds. One of the best ways to overcome stereotyping is to be open-minded and get to know people as individuals. Simply starting a conversation could open the door to better understanding.

You Decide

Think about a time when you had an opportunity to interact with someone who is different from you but did not. What kept you from approaching this person?

| Figure 18.1 | **Rewarding Relationships** |

A Two-Way Street Relationships should benefit both people involved. *Can you think of a recent example in which you and a friend both experienced the benefits of a good relationship?*

REWARD	DESCRIPTION
Companionship	Spend time together, and share experiences, feelings, and ideas.
Love and Affection	Know that certain people in your life sincerely care about you.
Support	Know that certain people will be there to cheer you on or help you out when you need them.
Positive Self-Concept	View yourself in a positive light because people you respect also show respect for you.
Expanded Interest	Allow others to expose you to new ideas, which helps you learn and develop new interests.

Be Smart Be Safe

Safe Breakups Ending a dating relationship can be an emotional experience. Should you choose to end a relationship with someone, do it calmly and rationally. If you are at all worried about how the other person might react, end the relationship in a safe place with others around.

Write About It Write a short dialogue between two people whose dating relationship is ending badly. Then rewrite the dialogue so that the breakup goes well. What do you think made the difference between the two outcomes?

Build Positive Relationships

People who enjoy positive relationships are willing to put in the necessary time and effort to build a strong foundation. They find ways to work through problems and disagreements and are committed to the relationship. Some of the qualities found in strong relationships are described in **Figure 18.2**.

Starting Relationships

Think about one of your friendships. Do you remember how it started? Chances are that you became friends because you had something in common. Perhaps you were in the same class, lived in the same neighborhood, or belonged to the same team. Starting a new relationship does not have to be hard. The first step is simply making an effort. School is a good place to start. Whether you are taking photos for the school newspaper or singing in the choir, you will have a chance to meet others who share your interests. Consider getting involved in your community. Part-time paid work and volunteer jobs both provide opportunities to meet new people.

Think about a time when you were at a place where you did not know anyone. Did someone make an effort to talk to you? If so, do you remember how relieved you felt? Now it is your turn. There is always a small chance of rejection, but it is worth the risk to put someone else at ease and possibly make a new friend.

Figure 18.2 **Qualities in a Strong Relationship**

Positive Relationships Just as the pieces of a puzzle fit together to reveal a whole picture, these qualities fit together to build relationships that last. *Which "piece of the puzzle" is the most important to you in a relationship? Why?*

Understanding. Try to see things through other people's eyes.

Honesty. Be honest with others by telling the truth and being trustworthy.

Respect. Be considerate and polite. Be sure to listen to others.

Tolerance. Respect differences. People have a right to their own beliefs.

Acceptance. It is all right for others to be different from you.

Empathy. Show that you understand other people's feelings.

Dependability. Keep your promises. Show people they can count on you.

Patience. Being patient with others shows that you care.

Commitment. Show that you value the relationship and want to make it work.

Communicate. Learn to express yourself effectively and listen attentively.

Flexibility. Be willing to compromise. Do not insist on having your way.

Humor. Learn to laugh at yourself and see the funny side of situations.

Make the First Move

The ability to meet new people and start new relationships is an important life skill. *What are some ways to make introducing yourself to someone new easier?*

Maintaining a Relationship

For some people, starting a new friendship is the easy part. The challenge is to maintain the relationship. This takes time and effort, but the rewards are great. To maintain relationships:

- **Pay Attention** Be sure to keep in touch by telephone and e-mail, and make an effort to schedule face time.
- **Participate** Take time to participate in activities with the important people in your life. Limit your solitary activities.
- **Plan Ahead** Keep your schedule or planner up to date to avoid conflicts with other important activities.
- **Enjoy Meals Together** Eat meals with your family as often as possible. Ask if you can invite friends to join from time to time.

Give and Receive

Both sides must give as well as receive. This principle of giving and receiving applies to all relationships. For example, if your supervisor lets you have the day of the homecoming dance off, you might volunteer to fill in for an absent coworker the next week. In a strong relationship, both people are giving and receiving all of the time. Having something to offer and being appreciated makes you feel good about yourself. When you receive help, you have an opportunity to show your appreciation.

Show Tolerance

Tolerance is essential for getting along with people. **Tolerance** means respecting other people's beliefs and customs. When you show tolerance, you recognize that all people have a right to their values and beliefs. As society becomes more diverse, tolerance becomes even more important. People who lack tolerance may develop prejudice, a biased attitude toward an individual or group. Prejudice is forming opinions about people without knowing them.

Health & Wellness TIPS

Talk Out Problems

Keeping your problems to yourself may seem like a thoughtful thing to do, but it is unhealthy for you. Even when a problem seems minor, talk it out with someone you can trust. Whether a solution is found or not, you will feel better having shared your problem with someone.

The negative attitudes from prejudice can lead to discrimination. **Discrimination** is the unfair treatment of a person or group, often based on race, ethnicity, age, religion, or gender. Discrimination is illegal and destructive to society. Prejudice and discrimination grow out of ignorance. People who have little exposure to other ways of life are more likely to view differences as alarming or negative.

Understanding Authority

Most authority figures are adults, like parents, teachers, and supervisors. As someone who is close to adult age, you probably spend more time with adults than you used to. Those interactions can be rewarding. However, you probably also want to make more of your own decisions. Your desire to have more control over your life is normal, but it might strain your relationships with some adults. Try to strike a balance between asserting your independence and respecting those in authority. These guidelines can help:

- Look at the situation from both sides.
- Be courteous and respectful, and always tell the truth.
- Obey the rules.
- Listen carefully. Ask questions if you do not understand.
- Accept responsibility for your behavior. Admit your mistakes

Having positive relationships with authority figures now will assist in preparation for adulthood and allow you to build positive relationships with authority figures in the future.

 Podcasts Access the Online Learning Center to download *Managing Life Skills* podcasts.

 **Section 18.1** **After You Read**

Review Key Concepts

1. **Describe** the benefits of having relationships with people who are different from you.
2. **Explain** why self-esteem is a major factor in successful relationships.
3. **Define** authority figure.

Practice Academic Skills

 English Language Arts

4. Think of a relationship that you value deeply. Create a visual representation of that relationship, using photos and pictures of people, places, or objects to communicate what the relationship means to you. Write a caption for each photo.

 Social Studies

5. Teens from different parts of the world are the same in some ways and different in others. Research the habits of teens from another country. What does this information say about how their values might differ from yours? Would this difference cause conflict? Point out the effects of cultural patterns on relationships.

Check Your Answers Check your answers at this book's Online Learning Center at **glencoe.com**.

NCTE 12 Use language to accomplish individual purposes.

NCSS I F Interpret patterns of behavior reflecting values and attitudes that contribute or pose obstacles to cross-cultural understanding.

Unhealthy Relationships

How can you tell when you are in an unhealthy relationship?

Reading Guide

Before You Read

Adjust Reading Speed Improve your comprehension by adjusting your reading speed. With more difficult text, slow down and, if needed, reread parts of the text. Reading more slowly will take longer, but you will understand and remember more.

Read to Learn
Key Concepts
- **Identify** characteristics of unhealthy relationships.
- **Examine** the reasons and methods for ending a relationship.

Main Idea

Unhealthy relationships are characterized by mistreatment from one of the participants and negative feelings resulting from the relationship. Ending relationships can be difficult, but sometimes it is necessary.

Graphic Organizer

As you read, think of examples of reasons people choose to end a relationship. Use a three-column chart like the one shown to help you organize your information.

Content Vocabulary
- ◇ stereotype
- ◇ isolated
- ◇ inadequate
- ◇ dependent
- ◇ vulnerable

Academic Vocabulary

You will find these words in your reading and on your tests. Use the glossary to look up their definitions if necessary.
- ■ cue
- ■ function

Academic Standards

English Language Arts
NCTE 4 Use written language to communicate effectively.

Mathematics
NCTM Algebra Represent and analyze mathematical situations and structures using algebraic symbols.

Social Studies
NCSS IV H Individual Development and Identity Work independently and cooperatively within groups and institutions to accomplish goals.

Reasons to End a Relationship		
Mistreatment	Negative Feelings	Practical Reasons

 Graphic Organizer Go to this book's Online Learning Center at **glencoe.com** to print out this graphic organizer.

NCTE *National Council of Teachers of English*
NCTM *National Council of Teachers of Mathematics*
NSES *National Science Education Standards*
NCSS *National Council for the Social Studies*

Harmful Relationships

It is common to think of "romance" when you think of relationships. But relationships affect all aspects of your life, including in your home, at work, at school, and in your community. An unhealthy relationship can poison other parts of your life, so it is important to recognize what can lead to negative situations.

Stereotypical Thinking

Some people make assumptions, or quick decisions, about people before knowing the facts. They may assume, for example, that all teens are irresponsible or that all older people are forgetful. These are examples of stereotypes. A **stereotype** is an expectation that all people in a group have the same qualities or act the same way. Stereotypes are often based on characteristics such as gender, age, race, religion, or nationality. They usually result from limited contact with members of the group about which the assumption is made. Stereotyping people gets in the way of healthy relationships.

Some stereotypes are annoying. Krista, who is six feet tall, is tired of being asked if she plays basketball. Other stereotypes are harmful, like when someone avoids contact with someone else because of a stereotype. Stereotypical thinking can even result in denying people opportunities in life.

Stereotyping interferes with relationships. One way to overcome stereotyping is personal contact with different kinds of people. Another way is to challenge such thinking when it enters your mind or is voiced by someone else.

As You Read

Connect Why would someone choose to stay in an unhealthy relationship?

Vocabulary

You can find definitions in the glossary at the back of this book.

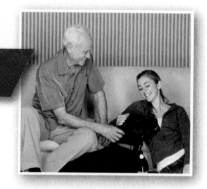

Life On Your Own

Learn from Older Adults

Interacting with a much older person can be challenging for many teens, especially if they have never had a relationships with someone in that age group before. It can be difficult to find common ground on which to base any conversation. Encouraging the older person to share memories is a good strategy.

How It Works Try to create a meaningful connection with an older person by encouraging him or her to talk about the past in a way that relates to your life as well. After all, every older person was a teen once. Talking about that time helps remove age as a barrier to communication.

Try It Out Arrange to spend some time with an older adult. Think in advance about the kinds of questions you would like to ask, such as, "What was it like when you were a teenager?" "What was the toughest choice you ever had to make?" and "How has the world changed since you were young?" Let the older person take the time to remember some specific stories to share. Encourage him or her to continue with additional questions as you think of them. See if you can discover what opinions, traits, and preferences the two of you have in common.

> *Your Turn* How can this kind of conversation be beneficial to both you and the older adult? What can you learn about yourself as a young adult? What can you learn about your past and your future? How do you hope you will be treated when you are an older adult?

Am I in an Unhealthy Relationship?

How do you know if you are in an unhealthy relationship? A person who truly cares about you would never threaten you, pressure you to do something wrong, or ask you to do something that is against your values. Here are some characteristics of unhealthy relationship behavior:

- **Physical Abuse** No one has the right to harm you physically or threaten to. If any relationship includes fear of harm, ask a trusted adult for help now. Physical abuse is never acceptable.

- **Controlling Behavior** It is unhealthy to spend time with a person who wants to control what you do, where you go, and with whom you spend time. Even though that person may claim to do this because he or she cares, do not confuse controlling behavior with caring behavior. In a healthy relationship, you are in control of your own actions.

- **Bullying** If someone tries to boss you around or threaten you, walk away. Such behavior is unacceptable.

- **Irresponsible Behavior** A relationship with someone who encourages you to take unnecessary risks or behave in ways that could get you into trouble can put your health and future at risk.

- **Illegal Activity** If someone pushes you to steal, drink alcohol, use drugs, or participate in other illegal activities, this is your **cue**, or sign, to end the relationship. Look for friends who respect you and the law.

- **Dishonesty** Lies and deceit have no part in a healthy relationship. You cannot be yourself if you feel that you need to lie or if you believe that the other person is being dishonest with you.

Another way to recognize that you are in an unhealthy relationship is to examine how you feel. Healthy relationships build you up and make you feel good about yourself or others. Here are some feelings you might experience if you are in an unhealthy relationship:

- **Isolation** If you feel **isolated**, you feel separated and cut off from everyone but one person. This is a strong sign that the relationship is harmful and headed in the wrong direction. A relationship that isolates you from your other friends and your family will cause you to miss out on activities and the company of others. This is not healthy because no single individual can give you all of the rewards and benefits that come from healthy relationships.

Financial *Literacy*

No More Overtime

Brenda's and Max's relationship has been suffering because of her work hours. Brenda decided to look for a new job that will not require her to work more than 40 hours per week. She needs to earn a weekly take-home pay of at least $600, and she expects 20% of her salary to go to taxes. Create and solve an inequality that represents the minimum hourly wage that Brenda should look for in her job search.

Math Concept **Solving Inequalities** When solving an inequality, you must perform the same operations on each side of the inequality for it to remain valid. For example, if you add 5 to one side of the equation, you must add 5 to the other side.

Starting Hint Using the variable x to represent the hourly wage, write an inequality to solve the problem. The total take-home pay ($600) will be on one side, and the before-tax income (40 hours $\times$ the hourly wage, x) multiplied by 0.8 to find what is left after taxes ($40x \times 0.8$) will be on the other side.

 For math help, go to the Math Appendix at the back of the book.

NCTM Algebra Represent and analyze mathematical situations and structures using algebraic symbols.

Succeed in SCHOOL and LIFE

Think Before Following

When one of your friends wants you to participate in an unsafe, unwise, or illegal activity, stop and think. Do you want to follow along just to please that person? Never let someone else's poor decisions influence your own. Walk away if you have to. In the end, you will be glad you used your own good judgment.

Get Involved!

Decrease School Violence

Ask a school teacher or counselor to help you organize a school-wide campaign against violence and threatening behavior such as bullying. Recruit classmates to spread the word about ways to prevent abusive behavior. Post anti-violence posters around your school, and distribute fliers with advice and contact information for students who are affected by this problem.

- **Low Self-Esteem** A relationship is having a negative effect on your self-esteem if it makes you feel inadequate. **Inadequate** (i-'na-di-kwət) means failing to meet an expectation. If you feel like you are not good enough to be someone's friend, it is time to move on.

- **Dependency** Feeling totally dependent on just one person is unhealthy. A person who feels **dependent** relies too much on someone else for his or her own happiness. Sometimes people become so dependent that they cannot **function**, or manage, without the other person. It is far better to be with someone who encourages you to act independently.

Almost everyone has had to deal with an unhealthy relationship, but some people are more vulnerable to them. People who are especially open to physical or emotional harm or are easily persuaded by pressure are **vulnerable** ('vəl-nə-rə-bəl). Vulnerability may be a personality trait that should be addressed, or it may be a temporary condition caused by certain events or circumstances. Either way, recognizing the signs of an unhealthy relationship is the first step toward dealing with it. In most cases, the best course of action is to end the relationship before the situation worsens.

✓ **Reading Check** **Interpret** How might someone misunderstand the purpose behind controlling behavior?

Two Views One World

How Do You Handle the End of a Relationship?

People have different ideas on the best way to end a relationship that is not working out.

Ethan: I really don't like it when people just let a relationship die out. If you think a relationship has ended for you, you should say so. Otherwise, the other person is left to wonder, "Did I do something wrong?" and wastes time trying to make plans. Then the person who does not want the relationship anymore gets annoyed, and the other person gets hurt or angry. It is kinder to just tell the person it's over.

Olivia: Unless a relationship is really unhealthy, there is no need to "end" it. It is obvious when two people start to have different interests or different feelings. They naturally do not want to spend as much time together. There are no hard feelings on either side. To tell someone your relationship is over makes it sound like you do not want anything to do with the other person ever again. And that is unnecessarily hurtful.

Seeing Both Sides
How do both views show consideration for "the other person"? If you sensed that a relationship was over, how might you try to express that without hurting the other person's feelings?

 Relationships Should Not Harm You

Unhealthy relationships can make you feel isolated, inadequate, or sad. *Why can unhealthy relationships make you feel this way?*

Ending a Relationship

Relationships end for many reasons. You may need to end a relationship because it is unhealthy. You may feel that you have outgrown the other person or no longer have anything in common. Dating relationships often end because one or both people realize they are not well-matched. Some relationships end for practical reasons, like when a person moves.

Ending a relationship is never easy. If you want to explain your reasons for ending a relationship, try not to be accusatory in your explanation. For instance, you might say, "I don't think we have much in common," rather than something hurtful like, "You're boring." Let the other person know that you still value him or her as a person.

No matter who ends the relationship, try not to dwell on the loss. Be grateful for the other valuable relationships in your life, and look ahead to the new ones that are just around the corner.

 Podcasts Access the Online Learning Center to download *Managing Life Skills* podcasts.

 Section 18.2 **After You Read**

Review Key Concepts

1. **Explain** how being isolated in a relationship limits your life.
2. **Summarize** two points of view regarding the best way to end a relationship.

Practice Academic Skills

 English Language Arts

3. Suppose that you have a friend you have known since the first grade. Over the past three years, you have each developed very different values and interests. Now he or she is suggesting you be college roommates. Write your friend a carefully worded letter that declines the invitation to be roommates, yet still communicates that you care about him or her.

 Social Studies

4. Sometimes practicing or acting out a situation can help you find the best solution to a problem, especially when it involves a relationship. Follow your teacher's instructions to form into small groups. Working together, come up with two or three common relationship problems, and take turns acting them out. What pitfalls did you encounter during this exercise? Discuss your conclusions about these situations. Do all of the group members agree?

 Check Your Answers Check your answers at this book's Online Learning Center at **glencoe.com**.

NCTE 4 Use written language to communicate effectively.

NCSS IV H Work independently and cooperatively within groups and institutions to accomplish goals.

Pathway to College

The College Essay

Are College Essays Important?

Like any part of your college application, your college essay can be the difference between acceptance and rejection. It is your chance to show the admissions committee who you are and how you are different from the other applicants. It lets you provide information about yourself besides test scores, grades, and extracurricular activities.

What are typical college essay questions?
Generally, there are three main types of college essay questions The first, sometimes called a personal statement, is an open-ended question looking for information about you. The second requires you to explain or defend your choice of school or career. With this question, colleges are looking for information about your goals and commitment level. The third type explores your creativity and imagination by giving you a specific topic to write about.

Does the topic of my college essay matter?
Absolutely. Your essay topic reveals your interests and preferences. For example, if you are passionate about art, you might choose to write about a painting that inspired you. Also, what you choose to write about reflects your values and what is important to you. Lastly, your essay provides a window into your thought process. Think carefully about your topic, because what you choose to focus on says a lot about you.

What is the point of the college essay?
The college essay has three main purposes. First, it showcases your technical writing skills, including grammar, spelling, and punctuation. Next, it demonstrates your ability to organize your thoughts into structured, logical writing. Finally, and perhaps most importantly, it allows you to paint a clear picture of your unique character and personality.

Hands-On

College Readiness Imagine you are applying to college, and the essay topic on the application is, "Write an essay about a person who has significantly influenced you. Describe that person and how he or she has influenced you and affected your life. Be specific, and give examples." Brainstorm ideas for how you would write this essay. Pick a person, and write a brief outline of your ideas for this essay. Share this with your teacher.

Path to Success

 College & Career Readiness

Answer the Question If you do not answer the essay question, it will not matter how well your essay is written.

Be Specific Avoid predictable, general, or clichéd writing in your college essay.

Make it Short and Sweet Eliminate unnecessary words, and do not go over the word limit.

Proofread Carefully Typos, spelling errors, and grammatical mistakes will count against you.

Do Not Repeat Information Make sure your essay contains new information. It should not be just a summary of the rest of your application.

Be Yourself Write about your unique feelings and thoughts in your college essay.

 Go to this book's Online Learning Center at **glencoe.com** to learn more about college and career readiness.

CHAPTER SUMMARY

Section 18.1
Successful Relationships

Relationships are the connections you have with other people. They vary in three basic ways: their degree of closeness, their purpose, and their form. There are several influences on the ways in which you relate to different people, including expectations, personal qualities, self-esteem, and stereotyping. It is worth the risk to start new relationships. Maintaining relationships requires tolerance, respect for authority, and a willingness to give and receive.

Section 18.2
Unhealthy Relationships

Some relationships are unhealthy. Some of the characteristics of unhealthy behavior in a relationship are physical abuse, controlling behavior, bullying, irresponsible behavior, illegal activity, and dishonesty. Unhealthy relationships can make you experience feelings of isolation, low self-esteem, and dependence. Whether it is due to personal or practical reasons, it is never easy to end a relationship. It is best not to dwell on the loss.

Vocabulary Review

1. Create a fill-in-the-blank sentence for each vocabulary term. The sentence should contain enough information to help determine the missing term.

Content Vocabulary
- relationship (p. 355)
- expectation (p. 356)
- tolerance (p. 359)
- discrimination (p. 360)
- stereotype (p. 362)
- isolated (p. 363)
- inadequate (p. 364)
- dependent (p. 364)
- vulnerable (p. 364)

Academic Vocabulary
- casual (p. 355)
- flavor (p. 355)
- cue (p. 363)
- function (p. 364)

Review Key Concepts

2. Distinguish among different kinds of relationships.
3. Analyze factors that influence relationships.
4. Describe ways to build and maintain strong relationships.
5. Identify characteristics of unhealthy relationships.
6. Examine the reasons and methods for ending a relationship.

Critical Thinking

7. Identify What are some of the ways in which you can show tolerance toward people with customs that are different from your own?
8. Examine Why do people often look to other people who share their same values when it comes to forming relationships?
9. Apply What can a person who is new to a community do to meet people and make new friends?
10. Explain How is stereotypical thinking harmful to individuals and societies?
11. Hypothesize How might having unhealthy relationships as a teen affect someone later in life?

ACTIVE LEARNING

12. Relationship Mobile Create a mobile that represents the qualities that are necessary for a successful relationship. You can use your own photos, pictures from the Internet or magazines, or a combination to depict the qualities. Before starting the project, you must think of examples of what each quality would look in action or how it could be represented visually. Are there some that are harder to depict than others? When you are finished, display your mobile. See whether people can guess which qualities are represented.

Family & Community Connections

13. Interview a Relationship Therapist Therapists and counselors who specialize in improving relationships between spouses, family members, and friends understand a lot about why conflicts occur and how they can be addressed. Interview a therapist about one particular type of relationship. What are the most common types of issues that arise within these relationships? Have they noticed any specific patterns in behavior? What does the therapist do to help people with their relationship problems? Has the therapist ever encountered problems that are unsolvable? If so, what did he or she do then? Write your interview in a question-and-answer format. Be prepared to share your findings.

21st Century Skills

Social Skills

14. Initiate Relationships Many people would like to have new friends but are reluctant to make the first move. However, taking the initiative often results in rewarding relationships. Identify at least two school- or community-related activities that interest you. Find out how you can get involved. Using that information, develop specific, measurable goals that will help you take the initiative and broaden your relationships.

Technology Skills

15. Long-Distance Relationships Research how people use the Internet and other communication technology to maintain relationships with friends and relatives who live far away. What are the most current options available for exchanging information and sharing photos or videos? Summarize your findings in a brief report.

 **Connections**

Communication Skills

16. Promoting Relationship Skills As part of its mission, FCCLA encourages students to effectively manage conflicts. Using the FCCLA STOP the Violence program as a resource, create a presentation that demonstrates how to use active listening and "I" messages to manage conflicts in relationships. You can deliver the presentation to your class or FCCLA chapter and enter it as an Interpersonal Communications STAR Event.

Academic Skills

 ## English Language Arts

17. Friendship in Fiction Fictional books are filled with stories about great friendships. Choose one example of a great friendship from classic or modern literature. Present an oral report about it. Include your reasons for choosing this example and some of the characteristics that made the friendship successful.

> **NCTE 2** Read literature to build an understanding of the human experience.

 ## Social Studies

18. Research Role Changes How different is your role as a teenage boy or girl in today's world different from that of teens generations ago? How have society's expectations changed? Choose an era from at least 50 years ago. Create a Before and After chart listing five examples of changes in roles and expectations for teenage girls and boys. Are your circumstances better or worse?

> **NCSS IV B Individual Development and Identity** Identify and describe appreciation for the influence of various historical and contemporary cultures on an individual's daily life.

 ## Mathematics

19. Demographics Tess is creating an informational pamphlet about international diversity at her office. To ensure that the appropriate information is included, she needs to determine the national and gender percentages in her office. There are 40 employees in Tess's office, and half of them are women. If 30% of the women are European, how many European women work in her office?

Math Concept **Multiplying Percents** To multiply percents, first convert the percents to decimals. Be sure to place the decimal point in the product correctly.

Starting Hint Multiply the percent of employees who are women (50%) by the percent of women who are European (30%). Then multiply that number by the total number of employees.

 For more math practice, go to the Math Appendix at the back of the book.

> **NCTM Problem Solving** Solve problems that arise in mathematics and in other contexts.

 ## Standardized Test Practice   College & Career Readiness

TRUE/FALSE
Read the statement and determine whether it is true or false. Circle your answer.

> **Test-Taking Tip** Read the statement carefully, and make sure that you understand it before responding. For the statement to be true, all parts of it must be correct. If any part of the statement is false, the entire statement is false.

20. Once you become a fully independent adult, you no longer need to deal with authority figures.
   a. True
   b. False

Chapter 19

Your Family

Chapter Objectives

Section 19.1 How Families Work

- **List** the primary functions of families.
- **Define** the traditional family life cycle and its variations.
- **Assess** the effects of current social trends on family life.
- **Identify** ways to strengthen families.

Section 19.2 Family Challenges

- **Give** examples of how common changes can affect a family.
- **Describe** family challenges that can turn into crises.
- **Explain** how sources of help can provide benefits during family challenges.

> ➤ **Explore the Photo**
>
> Families work to meet each member's physical, intellectual, emotional, social, and moral needs. *What is one way in which family support might affect a teen's success later in life?*

Writing Activity

Autobiographical Paragraph

Family Support The support of your family can make all the difference when you are facing a challenge. How does your family help you get through challenging times? Write an autobiographical paragraph about a time in your life when the support of a family member made a difference. What would it have been like without that support?

Writing Tips To write an autobiographical paragraph:
- Include an effective topic sentence to help readers understand your main idea.
- Use first-person words like *I* and *me* to tell your story.
- Use linking words like *then* and *finally* to help your readers follow your logic and the order of events.

How Families Work

How is your family a part of your everyday life?

Reading Guide

Before You Read

Prior Knowledge Write down what you already know and what you want to find out about each key concept in this section.

Read to Learn
Key Concepts
- **List** the primary functions of families.
- **Describe** the traditional family life cycle and its variations.
- **Assess** the effects of current social trends on family life.
- **Identify** ways to strengthen families.

Main Idea
Families are designed to serve certain functions and follow a general cycle of growth. They are affected by societal trends. There are ways to make families stronger.

Content Vocabulary
◇ nurture
◇ socialization
◇ family life cycle
◇ intergenerational
◇ support system

Academic Vocabulary
You will find these words in your reading and on your tests. Use the glossary to look up their definitions if necessary.
■ mobile
■ confidential

Academic Standards

English Language Arts
NCTE 5 Use different writing process elements to communicate effectively.

Science
NSES F Develop an understanding of science and technology in local, national, and global challenges.

Social Studies
NCSS V C Individuals, Groups, and Institutions Describe the various forms institutions take, and explain how they develop and change over time.

Graphic Organizer
As you read, look for possible family structures. Write down four of the structures and their descriptions. Use a cluster web like the one shown to help you organize your information.

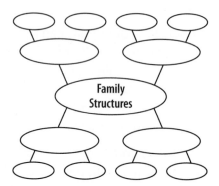

Family Structures

Graphic Organizer Go to this book's Online Learning Center at **glencoe.com** to print out this graphic organizer.

NCTE *National Council of Teachers of English*
NCTM *National Council of Teachers of Mathematics*
NSES *National Science Education Standards*
NCSS *National Council for the Social Studies*

Functions of a Family

Throughout history and in every society, families have served an important purpose. They **nurture** family members by providing the care and attention needed to promote development. That is quite a responsibility, and its impact goes far beyond the family itself. Families provide the structure in which children learn to become independent and live in society. The characteristics and qualities of these new adults influence what society is like as a whole.

Families differ in many ways, but they have certain things in common, such as the responsibility of caring for their members. See **Figure 19.1** for some of the many structures families can take.

Meet Physical Needs

The most basic responsibility of families is to provide for each family member's physical needs, such as food, clothing, and shelter. Infants and young children are entirely dependent on the physical care provided by families. At times, others in the family may also need special physical care due to an illness, accident, or disability.

Physical needs include responsibility for health and safety. Parents must ensure that their children eat nutritious foods and receive appropriate health care. Parents also need to set rules for children to keep them safe and teach them responsible behavior.

Promote Intellectual Development

The family is a child's first teacher. Families share knowledge, stimulate thinking, and encourage creativity. Parents, siblings, and other family members can all help a young child learn. Even after the child is in school, the family needs to remain actively involved in the child's learning. Taking the child to a zoo or planting a garden together are just two examples of teaching and learning opportunities.

As You Read

Connect What can a family do to develop a young family member's intellect?

Vocabulary

You can find definitions in the glossary at the back of this book.

Figure 19.1	**Every Family Is One of a Kind**

Family Structure Families differ in size and in the people they include. *What characteristics do you think all of these forms of families have in common?*

STRUCTURE	DESCRIPTION
Nuclear	Includes two parents and one or more children
Single-Parent	Includes one parent and one or more children
Blended	When two people marry and at least one person has a child or children from a previous marriage
Adoptive	A family with a child or children made a permanent part of the family through legal action
Foster	A family temporarily caring for a child or children; some foster families become adoptive families
Legal Guardian	A person who has financial and legal duties to care for a child or children
Intergenerational	One or two parents, children, and/or other relatives, like grandparents, cousins, aunts, or uncles

Accept Your Emotions

Teen years can be a tough time emotionally. If there is upheaval in your family, it can get even tougher. You must first acknowledge and accept your emotions. You may want to talk with friends and family about your feelings. If you need some time alone, let people know in a nice way. Try doing something that relaxes you or helps you express anger or frustration in a healthy way.

Meet Emotional Needs

Families nurture emotional development by showing love and acceptance. Being loved and accepted by your family helps you develop a positive self-image and high self-esteem. It enables you to show love and affection for others. Families also teach children how to express their emotions in acceptable ways. In a strong family, emotional bonds last a lifetime. Whenever family members face difficulties, they feel confident that their family will be there to listen and help.

Encourage Social Skills

The process of socialization begins in the family. **Socialization** means learning how to interact with other people. The family teaches basic social skills such as communication, cooperation, and respect for others. The social skills that children learn in the family carry over into their other relationships throughout life.

Some social skills are taught directly, like when parents teach children to say "please" and "thank you." More often, children learn social skills by observing and following examples set by others. Even very young children pay attention to how adults in the family interact with one another and with people outside the family. Everything children hear or see, such as tone of voice and body language, helps form their idea of appropriate behavior. That is why being a good role model is such an important parental responsibility.

Instill Moral Values

Families help children develop values that will be the basis for their actions throughout life. Children need to learn the importance of honesty, respect, and fairness. Society benefits when people possess a healthy sense of right and wrong.

Families teach moral values both directly and by example. For very young children, teaching focuses on behavior. The parent of a two-year-old might say, "When we want something, we ask nicely." Two-year-olds follow the rules because it helps them get what they want. When they are older, they learn the reasons for the rules.

✓ **Reading Check** **Explain** What are two different ways that children learn social skills from their families?

◀ Care and Attention

It is the parents' responsibility to provide for a child's physical needs. *Which physical need is being met in this situation?*

➤ The Beginning Stage

Marriage is the traditional start of the family life cycle. *What adjustments might a newly married couple have to make?*

The Family Life Cycle

Family researchers know that families go through a process of growth and change over the years. They have named this process the **family life cycle**. Keep in mind that families vary significantly. The life cycle model does not reflect all variations, but it does give a general picture of how families must adapt to changing situations.

- **Beginning Stage** Traditionally, the family life cycle begins when two people marry. The couple establishes a home and learns to live together. Priorities include building their relationship, working out their respective roles, and setting goals for the future.

- **Parenting Stage** If the couple chooses parenthood, their priorities shift to raising children. As they devote time and effort to caring for children, they have less time for activities as a couple.

- **Launching Stage** This time of transition occurs as the children begin to leave home and become independent. They must adjust to their new responsibilities, just as their parents must learn to relate to them as adults.

- **Middle-Age Stage** After children leave home, parents have more time to focus on being a couple again. They may reassess their careers, take up new hobbies, and become more involved in community activities. Preparing for retirement becomes a more immediate concern.

- **Retirement Stage** Retirement leaves more time for leisure activities. A couple may move to a smaller home or to a retirement community. At this stage, age-related issues involving health and independence are more likely to be major concerns.

These stages are typical, but not universal. Some couples do not have children. Some marry and become parents later in life, when others their age are becoming grandparents. In families with several children, the parenting and launching stages may overlap. Divorce and remarriage cause some families to repeat certain stages. Long after the traditional launching stage, parents may still have adult children living with them or may serve as caregivers for their grandchildren. Some people of retirement age keep working and perhaps even start new careers. Others become unable to care for themselves and move in with their grown children. This can create an **intergenerational** household, which is a household that includes family members from multiple generations.

✓ **Reading Check** **Clarify** Why is the family life cycle only a general model of a family's growth and change process?

Character?! In Action

Make Time for Family

As a busy teen, you may find that your family role sometimes conflicts with your outside activities. You may be expected to help more around the home, take part in family decisions, and accept more responsibility. It is important to plan ahead so that you can be sure to make time for your family.

You Decide

Suppose you have a big math test on a Monday. You have been asked to help clean the house on Sunday for a family party on Sunday evening. How might you handle this?

Family Trends

Every family experiences changes, and many of the changes result from societal trends. Years ago, families followed a traditional model. The father earned the family income, and the mother took care of the home and family. Although that is still true in some families, many couples today opt for different roles. Both may work outside the home and share household and family responsibilities. Some more of the current trends that affect family life include:

- **Smaller Families** In 1800, the average family included seven children. More of the population lived in rural areas, and families needed children to help with farm work. Today, many couples postpone having children or choose to remain child-free, sometimes to establish their careers or to save money.
- **Divorce and Remarriage** The divorce rate is much higher today than it was 50 years ago. When people with children remarry, everyone in the new, blended family must adjust.
- **Single-Parents** Most single-parent households are headed by women, although the percentage headed by men is increasing. Single parents face the challenge of raising their children alone while working to support the family. Having sole responsibility for their children makes it difficult for single parents to spend time with friends or build new relationships.
- **Longer Life Spans** People are living longer. Although many older people are healthy and active, others are not able to live independently. Therefore, an increasing number of adults, referred to as the "sandwich generation," are now the primary caregivers for both their aging parents and their children.
- **Increased Mobility** If your family has moved in the last five years, you are an example of today's highly **mobile**, or movable, society. It is not uncommon for a family to relocate several times. The most common reason is a parental job change. A major disadvantage for families who move a long distance is being separated from members of their extended family.
- **Advances in Technology** Technology makes it easier for families to stay connected, even when they live far apart. However, technology can also isolate families. Spending more time using technology can leave less time for family interaction.

Single-Parent Households

Being a single parent brings unique challenges. *What is one challenge a single parent might face that a married parent would not?*

✓ **Reading Check** **Examine** What impact might today's longer life span have on the typical family?

Qualities of a Strong Family

A strong family is similar to a tree. Both are deeply rooted in a nourishing environment. Both have a solid base with branches going off in various directions. Like a tree, no matter how far a family's branches extend, it stays connected to its roots.

Just as a tree needs soil, water, air, and sunshine to thrive, a family needs certain elements to keep it strong. These elements provide a sense of stability and security and help make family life satisfying and fulfilling. Ask yourself how you can make a greater contribution in your family.

Individual Respect

People in strong families respect one another's abilities, needs, and opinions, even if they do not share them. They accept and appreciate their differences. Guidelines for how family members can show individual respect include:

- Listen to and consider one another's points of view.
- Ask for permission before borrowing someone else's property.
- Give others the privacy they need.
- Be considerate of others' feelings. Avoid negative comments.

Life On Your Own

Appreciate Your Heritage

Each family, no matter how it is formed, has its own heritage, or traditions that are passed from one generation to the next. Traditions may be related to holidays, activities, food, clothing, art, music, games, stories, and more. Wherever you go in life, your heritage goes with you. Appreciate and nurture your heritage to help it survive and thrive.

How It Works When you understand the details of your family's heritage, you feel more connected to who you are and where you come from. These details add color and meaning to your life and can be a source of pride. They also enable you to share the richness of your heritage with others. If you were adopted or fostered, you may have an interesting combination of heritages that contribute to your unique personality.

Try It Out Research your ethnic background and culture. Then interview some of your relatives to see what they might know about your family heritage. See how your online research and personal interviews connect with your own experience in the family. Write down what you learn as a journal entry.

Your Turn Try to incorporate some aspect of your family heritage into your life on a regular basis. Is there a dish you can make, instrument you can learn, or item of clothing you can wear that brings you closer to your heritage?

 **Showing Trust**

Strong family relationships require trust and respect. *What are some ways you can build trust in your family?*

Effective Communication

Effective communication is basic to all relationships, and family relationships are no exception. On a practical level, clear communication is essential for anyone sharing a home because schedules and plans must be coordinated. On a deeper level, it is impossible to develop closeness without open, honest communication. Communication can be simple and informal. Consider posting a family calendar or message board to keep track of everyone's schedule. If you change your plans, call to let others in the family know.

Family meetings can be another useful tool. Some families have regular meetings to keep up with family news and plan their schedules. Others have meetings only when there is a need to solve a specific problem or make decisions that affect the whole family.

Sometimes family members have something on their mind, but are not sure how to bring up the subject. Be sensitive to signs that someone needs to talk, and let that person know you are there to listen. Stay in touch every day. Simple gestures, like asking how someone is doing, help ensure that lines of communication stay open.

Mutual Trust

Family closeness relies largely on trust. When there is trust, you can count on your family's help and support. When you confide in a parent or sibling, you can trust that the information will remain **confidential**, or private. Young children trust their parents to take care of them and meet their needs. As they get older, they trust parents to make decisions that are in the best interests of the family. Parents trust teens to do what they are supposed to do, even when the parents are not around to enforce the rules. Building trust in families is a two-way street. If you want your parents to give you their trust, you must show them that you are trustworthy.

Emotional Support

Emotional support contributes to strong families and is shown in words and actions that are positive and reassuring. When people face challenges that call for extra confidence, knowing that someone believes in them makes a difference. It is important that your family members know you are there for them. You can show emotional support in little ways every day. Here are a few simple suggestions:

- Be supportive of a family member who is facing a challenge.
- Give hugs when appropriate to show love and support.
- Make a habit of giving sincere compliments.
- Find ways to help others without being asked.

Sharing and Tradition

Sharing is one of the first lessons that children learn, and it remains an important tool for strengthening family ties. Dividing responsibilities helps a family function efficiently and lets everyone make a contribution. Family traditions are a form of sharing. They can help create a sense of shared identity and history. Perhaps the most important way of sharing is simply to spend time together as a family. Whether you are doing something special or just telling one another about your days over dinner, sharing helps form strong and lasting bonds.

Outside Support System

Even strong families sometimes need outside help. A **support system** consists of all the people and organizations a family can turn to. The support system often begins with the extended family. A grandparent may be willing to stay with a sick child so a parent can go to work. The support system might also include neighbors and friends. Social service agencies provide help when special problems arise. Libraries are great sources of information. Parks and recreational facilities help families meet their needs. Schools and places of worship may offer after-school programs for young children.

Go Green

You can go green while spending time with your family and developing family traditions. Try planting a tree as a family or working together to start a flower or vegetable garden.

 Podcasts Access the Online Learning Center to download *Managing Life Skills* podcasts.

Section 19.1 After You Read

Review Key Concepts

1. **Explain** how a family meets each member's emotional needs.
2. **Identify** why the middle-age stage can be enjoyable for couples.
3. **Give** an example of why it was helpful to have a large family in the 19th century.
4. **List** some of the typical components of a family support system.

 Check Your Answers Check your answers at this book's Online Learning Center at **glencoe.com**.

Practice Academic Skills

 English Language Arts

5. Think about your family members, their traits, hobbies, likes, and dislikes. Use this information to create a photo essay about your family. Paste photos or insert digital images of your family throughout your writing to help illustrate your descriptions.

NCTE 5 Use different writing process elements to communicate effectively.

 Social Studies

6. The family has changed dramatically in our society, from its average size to the role that each family member plays. Are all of these changes for the better? With your teacher's help, form an even-numbered group. Choose an aspect of family change. Divide into two teams, with one team arguing that the change is positive and the other arguing that it is negative. Have a five-minute debate.

NCSS V C Describe the various forms institutions take, and explain how they develop and change over time.

Family Challenges

Families survive and thrive when they work together.

Reading Guide

Before You Read

Preview Understanding causes and effects can help clarify connections. A cause is an event or action that makes something happen. An effect is a result of a cause. Ask yourself why something happened to help you recognize cause-and-effect relationships in this section.

Read to Learn
Key Concepts
- **Give** examples of how common changes can affect a family.
- **Describe** family challenges that can turn into crises.
- **Explain** how sources of help can provide benefits during family challenges.

Main Idea

Change affects all families. Some changes are commonplace and short-term, while others can be considered crises. There are coping strategies and outside sources to help families deal with both types of changes.

Graphic Organizer

As you read, think about the possible pros and cons of moving to a new neighborhood. Use a T-chart like the one shown to help you organize your information.

Pros of Moving	Cons of Moving

Graphic Organizer Go to this book's Online Learning Center at **glencoe.com** to print out this graphic organizer.

Content Vocabulary
◇ crisis
◇ custody
◇ grief
◇ substance abuse
◇ alcoholism
◇ abuse
◇ neglect

Academic Vocabulary
You will find these words in your reading and on your tests. Use the glossary to look up their definitions if necessary.
■ degree
■ intervene

Academic Standards

English Language Arts
NCTE 6 Apply knowledge of language structure and conventions to discuss texts.

Mathematics
NCTM Problem Solving Monitor and reflect on the process of mathematical problem solving.

Social Studies
NCSS III J People, Places, and Environments Analyze and evaluate social and economic effects of environmental changes and crises resulting from phenomena such as floods, storms, and drought.

NCTE *National Council of Teachers of English*
NCTM *National Council of Teachers of Mathematics*
NSES *National Science Education Standards*
NCSS *National Council for the Social Studies*

Types of Family Changes

Families have a valuable resource in one another. Responding to a change or crisis can bring family members closer together. They can put aside small differences to focus on preserving the family. Change tends to cause stress for families because it requires the family to adapt to a new situation. The **degree**, or amount, of stress varies with the nature of the change. When changes occur in a family, every member of the family is affected. Many changes are planned and fairly commonplace, but they can still result in stress. If you are aware of the adjustments that changes can bring, you will be better able to recognize and respond to problems as they arise.

Moving to a New Home

A move within the same community changes a family's daily life. A move to another community requires a family to adjust to a whole new set of circumstances that includes people, places, and activities. A positive attitude plays a large role in adapting to new circumstances. Moving does not have to mean losing current friends. Keep in touch through e-mail, phone calls, or social networking sites.

Employment Changes

Most people change jobs, and even careers, several times. Even without a simultaneous change of residence, job changes can affect family life. A promotion might mean more income, but also more responsibility. When someone is fired or laid off, he or she may experience feelings of rejection and failure. This is a time when a family needs to gather all of its resources to work through the situation in a positive way.

As You Read

Connect How can you predict whether a change is going to have a big impact on a family?

Vocabulary

You can find definitions in the glossary at the back of this book.

◄ A New Home

Moving to a new home is exciting, but it can also be stressful. *What can be done to ease the transition to a new home and school?*

Math For Success

New Additions

One of the most common changes that families experience is the addition of a new family member. Whether the new arrival is a baby, an older child, stepparents, stepsiblings, or an older relative, the addition changes life for everyone. Family priorities and schedules shift, and family members often have to take on new and different responsibilities. Financial resources may be strained.

Baby A baby is a huge responsibility. Parents get less sleep, and they have less time for themselves and each other. Other children do not get as much time with their parents. Young children must learn to be more independent, and older children must help out. This change can be less stressful if parents and children discuss what will happen before the baby's arrival.

Older Child Some families adopt an older child or open their home to a foster child. These children require an adjustment period. They need plenty of reassurance that they are welcome. Foster children present unique challenges because foster care is usually temporary. That means that families face two adjustments, one when foster children join the family and another when they leave.

Step-Relatives Blended families face many challenges. Adults have to adjust to the marriage and new parenting relationships. Children gain stepparents, and often step-siblings, plus a new extended family. It is not realistic to expect stepparents and stepchildren to love each other immediately, but in time, blended families can build caring, supportive relationships.

A New Baby in the Family

Babies are cute and lovable, but they are a huge responsibility. *What adjustments might siblings need to make when a new baby arrives?*

Moving Back Home

All additions to the family are not necessarily "new." Older children may return home temporarily. Older relatives, not able to care for themselves alone, may move in with their adult children.

Adult Children The responsibilities that come with freedom are sometimes more than young adults can handle. A common reason children go back home is financial hardship. Many young adults find that it is much more expensive than they expected to go to a certain college or to rent an apartment. Another reason is divorce. An adult child, who may even have his or her own children, may move back home to get through a divorce.

Older Relatives Thanks to improvements in health care and the standard of living, people are living longer than ever before. While older adults often stay active and independent for a long time, many eventually need help from their grown children. Dealing with someone who needs constant care is very demanding, and caregivers are at high risk for stress and depression. If an older relative needs special care, every member of the family may need to pitch in. The amount of care that an older adult needs varies. The feature on the next page lists several options available for older adults.

✓ Reading Check **Summarize** Why might an adult child move back home?

Health & Wellness TIPS

Take a Deep Breath

Deep breathing is a simple way to manage the stress that change can cause. Follow these simple steps:

- ▶ Slowly inhale to the count of four.
- ▶ Hold your breath to the count of seven.
- ▶ Slowly exhale to the count of eight.

Two Views One World

How Do You Adjust to Moving Back Home?

Living with parents as a young adult means redefining the roles of parent and child, which can be a challenge for both sides.

Erica: I lived with my parents while I trained to be an electrician. It was hard at first. My parents still treated me like I was a child, but I was eager to lead my own life and did not always want to do things the way my parents wanted me to. So we agreed that instead of rules, we would live by values: respect, responsibility, and courtesy. It was a hard adjustment at first, but we eventually learned how to interact in new ways.

Antonio: To save money, I moved back with my parents after college. After four years on my own, I was looking forward to being looked after and taken care of again. However, my parents expected more from me and treated me like an adult. They insisted that I pay my way and take care of myself. You might say that they pushed me out of the nest. I did not always like it, but I eventually realized it was what I needed.

Seeing Both Sides
Imagine you are either Erica or Antonio. Explain how you grew or what you learned from your experience.

Even with outside help, it is not always possible for older people to live on their own or with family members. If this is the case, a number of residential care options can be explored. Resources like these are especially useful for older people who live alone and do not have family nearby.

Senior Centers Older people who are looking for recreation and companionship may find that their local senior center meets their needs. Consider volunteering at a senior center, even if you do not have a relative living there.

Pickup and Delivery Services Many communities offer services to older adults who are unable to drive. Meals on Wheels is a volunteer program that delivers meals to older people in their homes. Senior transportation services provide rides to doctors' offices and other places.

Home Aides A home care aide can help older adults with bathing, dressing, and other aspects of personal care. A home health aide can give medicines, perform other health care tasks, and provide much-needed support for family caregivers.

Assisted Living Facilities Older adults who need help with meals and personal care but do not require round-the-clock care might benefit from assisted living facilities. These places provide personal care services, social activities, and some health services.

Retirement Communities Older adults who need minimal assistance might benefit from living in a retirement community, where they have their own apartments or houses and generally care for themselves but enjoy transportation services and social activities.

Nursing Homes For individuals with physical or mental disabilities that need round-the-clock care, a nursing home may be necessary. Also called extended care facilities, nursing homes are licensed by the state to provide nursing care, personal care, and medical services.

Crises

A **crisis** is an event or situation that overwhelms the usual coping methods and causes severe stress. Each family responds to a crisis in its own way. Still, it helps to realize that many other families have faced similar problems and gotten through them. Their experiences can help families learn what to expect.

Financial Hardship

All family members need to understand that sacrifices must be made when serious financial problems arise. Wants may have to be put off for awhile so that needs such as food, housing, and health care are met. Each person may need to take on more responsibilities. Patience and support can go a long way.

Divorce

Divorce, the legal end of a marriage, is one of the most painful changes that a family can go through. It is painful for the marriage partners, but if they have children, it is traumatic for the children as well. The effects of divorce are far-reaching and long-term. Children may feel resentment toward one or both parents, or they may fear losing parental love. Although not the case, some children may fear that their behavior caused the divorce. The legally assigned responsibility for the care of children and the decisions that affect them is called **custody**. Parents may be awarded joint custody, in which parents are equally responsible, or primary custody, in which one parent makes the decisions. Children eventually learn to live with the divorce and its effects, but they will always feel a sense of loss.

Teen Pregnancy

Pregnant teens need the support of their parents as they consider their options. Parents can help plan strategies for the future, which may include working to complete school while supporting and caring for the baby. Whether or not they marry, both parents have financial and practical responsibilities for the baby's care. These responsibilities last until the child reaches adulthood and sometimes beyond. The teen parents are not the only people whose lives are affected. Their parents and other family members also face adjustments and, in many cases, must take on added responsibilities.

Health Issues

Some families face the challenge of caring for someone who is mentally or physically ill, injured, or disabled. It is difficult to deal with the uncertainty of health issues and to make medical decisions. Financial difficulties from health care expenses can build up. If a health challenge occurs in your family, find out as much as you can about the condition. Think about joining a support group.

Succeed in SCHOOL and LIFE

Prepare for a New School

Starting out in a new school is especially difficult if you do not know what to expect. Will people be friendly? Will the classes be manageable? Try to find out about the school before your first day. See if you can meet with a teacher or talk to some fellow students ahead of time. This can help you feel more prepared for the adjustment.

Death

Losing a special person to death brings emotional and physical feelings that can be very painful. **Grief** is the sorrow caused by the death of a loved one and the emotional adjustment to that loss. It is important to accept the reality of the situation, express your feelings, share your happy memories, and seek help, if necessary.

Suicide, the taking of one's own life, is an act of desperation and despair. Pay attention if someone close to you experiences depression or mood swings, gives away favorite possessions, or talks about death or suicide. Tell an adult who can **intervene**, or get involved. When a person does commit suicide, family members and friends often feel guilty that they were not able to prevent the tragedy. They need reassurance that they are not to blame. Counseling often helps people work through their feelings after a suicide.

Drug and Alcohol Problems

Substance abuse is the use of illegal drugs or the misuse of legal drugs or substances. Alcohol is the most commonly abused substance. Prolonged use of alcohol can lead to **alcoholism**, which is a physical and mental dependence on alcohol. Substance abuse and addiction leads to physical and mental health problems. Entire families are damaged by the side effects of substance abuse, such as job loss, criminal acts to support addictions, violence, accidents, and suicide. Substance abusers will not stop until they feel ready. Treatment programs are often necessary. People close to substance abusers often need to seek help and support to cope with the situation.

Family Violence

Abuse is never justified. **Abuse** is when a person threatens the physical or mental health of another. Victims of physical abuse may have unexplained injuries, such as bruises in unusual places. Victims of emotional abuse often suffer from low self-esteem. Sexual abuse is any inappropriate sexual behavior, including touching or taking photographs. **Neglect** is the failure to give the proper or required care and attention to somebody. Abusers and their victims can benefit from professional counseling.

Major Disasters

Hurricanes, tornadoes, floods, earthquakes, and fires are just some of the disasters that can strike people's homes or communities. A family's home can be damaged or destroyed. A place of employment could be damaged, affecting work and income. Public agencies and private organizations often provide aid. However, overcoming the emotional effects of a disaster can take a long time. Some people have more difficulty than others.

✓ **Reading Check** **Define** What are neglect and abuse?

Strategies That Can Help

Challenges of any type require families to adapt, make decisions, and learn to cope. Denial does not make a problem go away. It only makes it harder to solve. The first step is to acknowledge the difficulties.

Once a family has recognized and agreed to deal with a specific challenge, there are many possible coping strategies. Talk things over to get to the root of problems and begin to solve them. Be willing to listen or just give a hug to show how much you care. Work together, and take responsibility for things that need to be done without being asked. Follow familiar routines as much as possible. Use the problem-solving strategies from Chapter 9 to help you and your family clarify the situation and evaluate possible solutions. Do not be afraid to ask for help when facing difficult issues.

Sources of Help

Many times people find their own solutions, but sometimes they need outside help. Sources of help include your family, teachers, counselors, religious leaders, friends, support groups, and professional counselors. Many local, state, and national agencies and organizations provide support services. It is a sign of courage and maturity to acknowledge when you cannot handle a problem alone.

 Podcasts Access the Online Learning Center to download *Managing Life Skills* podcasts.

Section 19.2   **After You Read**

Review Key Concepts

1. **Give** an example of how employment changes can cause stress.
2. **Explain** how divorce can be hard on the children involved.
3. **List** some sources of help available to families during crises.

Practice Academic Skills

 English Language Arts

4. Watch a movie about a family that must adjust to a big change. Give an oral presentation reviewing the movie. Talk about the nature of the change the characters endure and how they cope. Describe the ways in which the movie succeeds, or does not succeed, in communicating the struggle of change.

 Social Studies

5. Natural disasters, such as severe storms and earthquakes, can have a devastating effect on families. Research a natural disaster that took place within the past 10 years. Report on its impact on families and their efforts to survive and recover.

Check Your Answers Check your answers at this book's Online Learning Center at **glencoe.com**.

NCTE 6 Apply knowledge of language structure and conventions to discuss texts.

NCSS III J Analyze and evaluate social and economic effects of environmental changes and crises resulting from phenomena such as floods, storms, and drought.

Pathway to Your Career

Child Care Worker

What Does a Child Care Worker Do?

Child care workers look after children when the children's parents are working or away for other reasons. These workers play important roles in children's development. In addition to keeping the children safe, child care workers organize activities to encourage children's physical, intellectual, emotional, and social growth. They help children explore their interests, develop their talents, become more independent, and learn how to get along with others.

Career Readiness Skills Child care workers should be patient and understanding and enjoy spending time with children. They should be enthusiastic and energetic so they can keep up with the children. Knowledge in art, music, and storytelling can be very helpful.

Education and Training Education ranges from a high school diploma to community college courses or a college degree in fields like child development. Child care workers often must pass a background check and get immunizations. Often, they must be certified in first aid and CPR and take part in continuous training in health and safety.

Job Outlook Employment of child care workers is projected to increase faster than the average for all occupations over the next decade. Fewer children will be cared for entirely by parents or other relatives, so the demand for child care workers will increase.

Critical Thinking Assess the interests, characteristics, and skills that make someone a good child care worker. How do your personality and skills compare to those skills? Write a paragraph examining why you think you would or would not be a good fit as a child care worker.

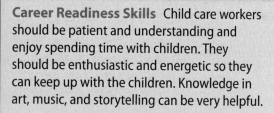

Career Cluster

College & Career Readiness

Education and Training Child care workers work in the Teaching/Training pathway of this career cluster. Other jobs in this cluster include:

- Librarian
- Career Counselor
- Special Education Teacher
- Preschool Teacher
- Language Pathologist
- Child Life Specialist
- Principal
- Clinical Psychologist
- Kindergarten Teacher
- Financial Aid Advisor
- Parent Educator
- Nanny
- Adult Literacy Teacher

Explore Further The Education and Training career cluster contains three pathways: Administration & Administrative Support; Professional Support Services; and Teaching/Training. Choose one of these pathways to explore further.

 Career Clusters To learn more about career clusters, go to this book's Online Learning Center at **glencoe.com**.

CHAPTER SUMMARY

Section 19.1
How Families Work

Although families come in many forms, they all have similar functions. Families are responsible for the physical, intellectual, emotional, social, and moral development of family members. At each stage of the family life cycle, families must adapt to changing situations and priorities. Societal trends create changes that affect families. Families are strengthened by respect, communication, trust, emotional support, sharing, and support systems.

Section 19.2
Family Challenges

Changes in a family affect every member. Common changes include moving to a new home, employment changes, and additions to the family. Serious changes, such as financial hardship, divorce, teen pregnancy, health issues, death, drug and alcohol problems, family violence, and major disasters, may become crises. There are coping methods and outside sources to help families through challenges. Sometimes a crisis can bring a family closer.

Vocabulary Review

1. Use at least five of these vocabulary terms in a short essay about a big family change.

Content Vocabulary
- nurture (p. 373)
- socialization (p. 374)
- family life cycle (p. 375)
- intergenerational (p. 375)
- support system (p. 379)
- crisis (p. 385)
- custody (p. 385)
- grief (p. 386)
- substance abuse (p. 386)
- alcoholism (p. 386)
- abuse (p. 386)
- neglect (p. 386)

Academic Vocabulary
- mobile (p. 376)
- confidential (p. 378)
- degree (p. 381)
- intervene (p. 386)

Review Key Concepts

2. **List** the primary functions of families.
3. **Define** the traditional family life cycle and its variations.
4. **Assess** the effects of current social trends on family life.
5. **Identify** ways to strengthen families.
6. **Give** examples of how common changes can affect a family.
7. **Describe** family challenges that can turn into crises.
8. **Explain** how sources of help can provide benefits during family challenges.

Critical Thinking

9. **Illustrate** How might one family structure change into another family structure?
10. **Examine** What are some challenges and rewards of intergenerational living?
11. **Formulate** What is your theory on how the functioning of families affects society as a whole?

ACTIVE LEARNING

12. Create an Ad Campaign Follow your teacher's instructions to form into groups. Work together to create an advertising campaign on the importance of families. This might include writing a 30-second TV commercial or slogans for T-shirts, billboards, or bumper stickers. What points do you think are most important? What do other members of the group think? Why do you think there might be differences in points of view? As you develop your campaign, consider key words and ideas from this chapter. Present your campaign ideas to the class.

Family & Community Connections

13. Family Interviews Conduct three or more interviews with members of your family or another family who hold a family role that is different from yours. Have each interviewee describe his or her role in the family, including responsibilities and expectations of other family members. Have each interviewee state the pros and cons of his or her particular role and explain which parts he or she enjoys and which he or she finds challenging. Write up each interview in a question-and-answer format. At the end of each interview, sum up in writing what you learned. Were there aspects of these roles that you had never considered? Did any of the answers surprise you? How might these responses affect your behavior in the future?

21st Century Skills

Financial Literacy Skills

14. Financial Strategies When financial hardship reaches a crisis point in a family, every member of the family is affected. What if your family were suddenly faced with a financial crisis? What would you do? Create a list of possible strategies for helping your family survive a financial crisis. Consider both practical and emotional support.

Technology Skills

15. Senior Care Use the Internet to research senior care and services options in your local community. Refer to the chapter to make sure you research all of the categories of care and services. What types of facilities are readily available? What programs and services exist? Is there a type of facility or service that does not seem to be available within your community? Write a report of your findings.

 Connections

Research Skills

16. Disaster Preparedness As part of its mission, FCCLA encourages students to seek opportunities for personal development and preparation for adult life. As an adult, it is important to be prepared for natural disasters, which often come without warning. Do you know what natural disaster poses the greatest risk for your community? Research this disaster, and create a list of tips for being prepared.

Academic Skills

 English Language Arts

17. Family Tradition What is your favorite family tradition? Write a short essay describing this tradition and explaining why it is your favorite. Write about the ways in which you feel this tradition helps make your family stronger.

> **NCTE 12** Use language to accomplish individual purposes.

 Science

18. Hypothesize What do you think the U.S. Census Bureau findings would reveal about family size over the past 20 years? Obtain data from recent census surveys on family size. Is there a trend regarding average family size in the United States?

Procedure Create a point graph using your census research data. Write an analysis of your research findings that begins with your hypothesis. Conclude with a theory explaining your findings.

Analysis Submit your hypothesis, completed graph, and research findings.

> **NSES 1** Develop an understanding of science unifying concepts and processes.

 Mathematics

19. Represent Large Numbers To complete a research project on family structures, Ella needs to know how many households in the U.S. do not have adopted children. The U.S. Census Bureau reported that there are approximately 111,100,000 households in the U.S., and 1,700,000 of those have adopted children. How many households do not have adopted children?

Math Concept **Subtracting Large Numbers** When subtracting large numbers, it is sometimes easier to express the numbers as decimals. Both large numbers in this problem should be changed into decimals.

Starting Hint Rewrite 111,100,000 as 111.1 million and 1,700,000 as 1.7 million. Be sure the decimal points are aligned before subtracting.

 For more math practice, go to the Math Appendix at the back of the book.

> **NCTM Number and Operations** Understand numbers, ways of representing numbers, relationships among numbers, and number systems.

 Standardized Test Practice

 CCR College & Career Readiness

MULTIPLE CHOICE
Choose the phrase that best completes the statement.

> **Test-Taking Tip** In multiple-choice questions, the answers are usually specific and precise. First, read the question carefully. Then read all of the answer choices. Eliminate answers that you know are incorrect.

20. _____ is when divorced parents share legal responsibility for their children.
 a. Controlled custody
 b. Joint custody
 c. Legalized custody
 d. Shared custody

Chapter 20

Your Friends

Chapter Objectives

Section 20.1 Successful Friendships

- **List** the qualities of a successful friendship.
- **Identify** ways to meet people who might become friends.
- **Describe** the benefits of diversity in friendships.

Section 20.2 Friendship Challenges

- **Give** guidelines for handling changes in friendships.
- **Discuss** problems that may occur in peer relationships.

▶ **Explore the Photo**

Good friends function as companions and as support systems. *What are some ways to show friends that you care about them?*

Writing Activity

Write a Poem

"My Friend" Many poems have been written about friendship. Friends are such an important part of our lives, and poetry is an effective way of expressing our most important thoughts and feelings. Think of a close friend, or a good friend from your past. Write a poem describing this friend.

Writing Tips Use these tips to help you write a poem:
- Freewrite as a way to develop and direct your thoughts.
- Choose precise words that develop the meaning and style of your poem.
- Use specific imagery and vivid descriptions to bring your poem to life.
- Remember that poems do not have to rhyme.

Successful Friendships

Good friendships are worth the work required to maintain them.

Reading Guide

Before You Read

Use Color As you read this section, try using different colored pens to take notes. This can help you learn new material and study for tests. You could use red for vocabulary words, blue for explanations, and green for specific examples.

Read to Learn

Key Concepts

- **List** the qualities of a successful friendship.
- **Identify** ways to meet people who might become friends.
- **Describe** the benefits of diversity in friendships.

Main Idea

It is important to know how to develop and maintain quality friendships. Making new friends sometimes involves rejection. Diverse friendships will enrich your life.

Content Vocabulary

◇ empathy
◇ reciprocity
◇ rejection
◇ diversity

Academic Vocabulary

You will find these words in your reading and on your tests. Use the glossary to look up their definitions if necessary.

■ signal
■ alert

Academic Standards

English Language Arts

NCTE 4 Use written language to communicate effectively.

Social Studies

NCSS II D Time, Continuity, and Change Systematically employ processes of critical historical inquiry to reconstruct and reinterpret the past, such as using a variety of sources and checking their credibility, validating and weighing evidence for claims, and searching for causality.

Graphic Organizer

As you read, look for the qualities that are common in strong friendships. Use a describing wheel like the one shown to help you organize your information.

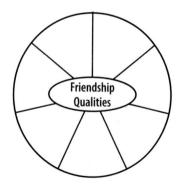

Friendship Qualities

Graphic Organizer Go to this book's Online Learning Center at **glencoe.com** to print out this graphic organizer.

NCTE *National Council of Teachers of English*
NCTM *National Council of Teachers of Mathematics*
NSES *National Science Education Standards*
NCSS *National Council for the Social Studies*

Qualities of Friendship

Friends are an important influence in your life. Your friendships expose you to new ideas and help you develop as a person. While everyone values different traits in friends, certain qualities are present in almost all strong friendships. These qualities include:

- **Common Interests** Whether it is a favorite sports team or a love of music, similar interests encourage communication and provide a basis for spending time together.
- **Caring** Friends care about each other. They are kind, considerate, and concerned about each others' well-being. True friends do not ask each other to do anything wrong or harmful.
- **Empathy** Real friends show empathy. **Empathy** is the ability to identify with and understand someone else's feelings or difficulties. Empathy enables people to share the joy of good times and ease the pain of difficult times.
- **Respect** Friends respect each others' opinions, even if they do not always share those opinions.
- **Dependability** Friends know they can depend on each other to keep their promises and do what they say they will do.
- **Forgiveness** Friends understand that nobody is perfect. They are willing to forgive each other's mistakes, and they apologize when they make mistakes of their own.
- **Reciprocity** Friendships rarely last when one person does most of the giving. **Reciprocity** (ˌre-sə-ˈprä-s(ə-)tē) means there is a mutual exchange. Each person gives and receives.

It takes effort to maintain a friendship. Fortunately, you already know a lot about the qualities that strengthen friendships, because they are the same ones that make any relationship strong. Think back on what you have learned in previous chapters about communicating, cooperating, and resolving conflicts. These and other relationship skills will help you maintain lasting friendships.

As You Read

Connect What qualities do you look for in potential friends?

Vocabulary

You can find definitions in the glossary at the back of this book.

Breaking the Ice

One way to make new friends is to get involved in school activities. *What type of activity or club might you join to meet new people?*

Befriend a New Student

It is tough to start at a new school. When you see a new student, take the initiative to help him or her feel at ease. Go out of your way to be friendly. Introduce the new classmate to your friends and people in other social groups.

You Decide
Can you think of three activities in which you might invite a new student to participate?

Good friends continue to show the qualities that helped them become friends in the first place. They make time for each other, confide in each other, and communicate openly and honestly. They admire each other's strengths and accept each other's weaknesses. When they make mistakes, they forgive each other.

✓ **Reading Check** **Identify** What quality enables two people with different opinions to remain close friends?

Making Friends

It is one thing to know the qualities you want in a friend, but another to find someone who has those qualities. How do you make new friends? The first step is to find opportunities to meet people.

Meeting People

Friendships usually begin because people have something in common. If you want to make new friends, think of ways to meet people who share your interests. Getting involved in school activities is one good way to make new friends while also developing your skills and experience in a particular area.

Volunteering gives you the opportunity to meet people of different ages and backgrounds and help others at the same time. Community participation can help you discover and develop your talents and skills. That makes you more interesting and well-rounded, which are qualities people seek in friends.

Life On Your Own

Make New Friends

When you were a young child, it was probably pretty easy to make new friends. For teens, however, making new friends becomes more complex. The experience can feel awkward and stressful. Fortunately, making friends is a skill that you can acquire with a little courage and some practice.

How It Works What draws you to another person? Let those qualities guide your friend-making strategy. For instance, if you feel most comfortable with someone who is friendly and positive, display those qualities. You might offer to help your potential new friend with a task, or invite him or her to join you in an activity. Do not expect to have everything in common. Instead, focus on the qualities that are most important. Above all, give the friendship time to grow.

Try It Out As a participant in a foreign exchange program, you have just arrived in the home of your host family. You will be with them for two semesters, so you want to establish a friendly relationship with them, especially the two brothers who are close to your age. When you arrive at your new home, you soon discover that the siblings are a tight group and that you are the "odd man out." Even though they are polite, you feel invisible as they chat with each other, sharing jokes and stories that do not mean anything to you. You cannot imagine ever feeling as though you belong there, and you go to sleep on your first night feeling disappointed and worried.

> *Your Turn* What might you do over the next several days to adjust to your new environment? How can you find ways to connect with the family? How might your attitude toward the situation help you?

Taking the Next Step

Meeting people and starting conversations can **signal**, or indicate, the start of a friendship, but it is only a beginning. For a friendship to develop, one person has to take the next step. If you enjoy your first conversation with a person, be the one to take that next step. You might follow up with a phone call or text message, or find a way to talk to the person at school. Suggest doing something together so you can get to know each other better. If you spend time together and discover common interests, the friendship will have a chance to grow. However, it is important not to rush things. Strong friendships cannot be forced and need time and effort to grow.

HOW TO . . . Start Talking

Some people find it naturally easy to start up a conversation with someone they do not know. However, many people find that this feels uncomfortable. If you are in this latter group, you may find that with practice, it can become easier for you to approach and talk to new people. Here are some tips for starting a conversation and keeping it going.

Show Interest Most people like to talk about themselves because it is a topic on which they are experts! If you show interest in a person, he or she will usually be happy to start talking.

Share the Conversation Do not do all of the talking yourself. Good conversation requires a give-and-take pattern of speaking and listening.

Stay on Safe Topics Keep your conversation casual and low-key. It is best to avoid personal or controversial topics when you are getting to know someone. Save the more serious discussions for people you know better.

Ask Questions Ask open-ended questions that require more than a yes or no answer. This encourages the other person to respond in a way that will keep the conversation going.

Be a Good Listener Pay attention to what the other person says, and provide feedback. This shows your interest and may lead to other topics.

Forgive Mistakes

We all make mistakes once in a while. Sometimes a friend's mistake can end up hurting you. However, that does not necessarily mean that you should end the friendship. Some of the most success-ful friendships have lasted because the friends were will-ing to forgive each other and move past their mistakes.

A Variety of Friends

Even though most teens' friends are also teens, having some diversity in friendships can enhance your life experience. *How might a friend who is much older or much younger than you enhance your life?*

Handling Rejection

Whenever you make the effort to reach out to another person in friendship, you risk rejection. **Rejection** is feeling unwelcome or dismissed by others. Everyone experiences rejection at times. After all, not every person you want for a friend will want to be your friend. People have all kinds of reasons for accepting or rejecting others.

Some people are so afraid of rejection that they try to put on an act to get others to like them. This strategy can backfire, because true friends accept you for who you are, not who you pretend to be. On the other hand, rejection can **alert** you to, or make you aware of, the need for a behavior change on your part. Changes made for the right reasons can improve your life and your friendships.

If a friendship ends against your wishes, understand that these are not lifetime commitments and this simply happens sometimes. You may feel sad or angry for a while, and you may even blame yourself. In time, however, these negative feelings will go away, and you will make new friends. Even though being rejected can hurt your feelings and shake your confidence, it is no reason to think less of yourself. The best way to handle the experience is to learn from it, and turn your attention to building relationships with those who want your friendship. If feelings of rejection are difficult to deal with, here are some ideas to consider:

- **Share your feelings.** Talk with one of your other friends or a family member, and be open to advice and suggestions.
- **Be kind to yourself.** Just because you were not the one to end your friendship does not mean you are a bad person or not good enough. The friendship may have simply outgrown itself, and your friend responded first.
- **Appreciate yourself.** On bad days, make a list of your positive points, and refer to your list when you need a boost.
- **Evaluate your actions.** Think about your behavior toward the other person. Did you do something hurtful? If so, learn to behave differently to avoid similar mistakes in the future.
- **Do not spread rumors or gossip.** Avoid making negative comments to peers about the person who hurt you. That kind of behavior only makes you look bad and discourages new friendships.
- **Move on.** Focus on other friend-ships and activities. In time, it will all be just a distant memory.

✓ *Reading Check* **Explain** Why is it important to avoid rushing into friendships?

Diversity in Friendships

Chances are, your friends are similar to you in some ways but different in others. In fact, some of your friends may be quite different from you. That is a plus. **Diversity** is a variety of something, such as ethnicity, culture, age, gender, or opinions. Diversity in your friendships can enrich your life. Some friends may have different cultural backgrounds or belong to different ethnic groups from you. Others may have different religious beliefs or may have grown up under very different circumstances. Diverse friendships help you accept and respect differences and handle conflicts that can arise from lack of understanding.

It is natural that most of your friends are other teens. Among people your own age, you are most likely to find friends who like the same things you do and who face similar problems. Friends of the same age can often help one another gain confidence and develop a positive self-concept. However, when you add friends who are younger or older, your life becomes richer and fuller.

Appreciating the benefits of diverse friendships is a sign of maturity. Through these valuable friendships, people learn to understand themselves and others better. They also discover that people in general are more alike than they are different. This understanding helps us live successfully in a diverse society.

Go Green

Want to save money, spend time with friends, and help the planet all at the same time? Go green by buying in bulk with your buddies. This will not only save money and help the environment, it will give you a chance to spend time with friends.

Podcasts Access the Online Learning Center to download *Managing Life Skills* podcasts.

Section 20.1 — After You Read

Review Key Concepts

1. **Explain** what is meant by the statement, "Never take your friends for granted."
2. **Illustrate** how two people having their first conversation might take the next step toward friendship.
3. **Identify** the various differences that may exist between friends.

Check Your Answers Check your answers at this book's Online Learning Center at **glencoe.com**.

Practice Academic Skills

English Language Arts

4. There are so many old sayings about friendships, and we often say them without really thinking about them. Write a short essay that starts with the saying, "To have a friend, be a friend." Give your own interpretation of the saying. Provide one or two examples to support your ideas.

Social Studies

5. Historical records offer accounts of famous friendships that resulted in significant advances in our society. Research an example of such a friendship. Give a brief oral presentation describing the background story of the friends and their famous achievement.

NCTE 4 Use written language to communicate effectively.

NCSS II D Systematically employ processes of critical historical inquiry to reconstruct and reinterpret the past, such as using a variety of sources and checking their credibility, validating and weighing evidence for claims, and searching for causality.

Friendship Challenges

What do you do when a friend is no longer a friend?

Reading Guide

Before You Read

Stay Engaged One way to stay engaged when reading is to turn the headings into questions, and then read the section to find the answers. For example, *When Friendships End* might become *Why Do Friendships End?*

Read to Learn
Key Concepts
- **Give** guidelines for handling changes in friendships.
- **Discuss** problems that may occur in peer relationships.

Main Idea

Friendships naturally change over time, and sometimes they end. Peer friendships among teens can be complex. It is important to avoid cliques, gangs, and negative peer pressure.

Content Vocabulary
◇ clique
◇ harassment
◇ sexual harassment

Academic Vocabulary

You will find these words in your reading and on your tests. Use the glossary to look up their definitions if necessary.
■ distant
■ engage

Academic Standards

English Language Arts

NCTE 3 Apply strategies to interpret texts.

Mathematics

NCTM Problem Solving Apply and adapt a variety of appropriate strategies to solve problems.

Social Studies

NCSS I G Culture Construct reasoned judgments about specific cultural responses to persistent human issues.

Graphic Organizer

As you read, notice the differences between what some people believe about social cliques and what is actually true about them. Use an opinion-versus-fact chart like the one shown to help you organize your information.

Social Cliques

Opinion	Fact

Graphic Organizer Go to this book's Online Learning Center at **glencoe.com** to print out this graphic organizer.

NCTE *National Council of Teachers of English*
NCTM *National Council of Teachers of Mathematics*
NSES *National Science Education Standards*
NCSS *National Council for the Social Studies*

When Friendships End

Friendships change over time, just as people do. You may feel closest to one friend for a while and then build a closer friendship with someone else. You might remain friends with someone for years, but the nature of your friendship might change. When Diego and Bruce were in high school, they were best friends who spent time together almost every day. Today, ten years later, they are still close, but play a different role in each other's lives. They live in different states but stay in touch through e-mail and IMs, and they make time to visit once a year. Each has new friends for everyday companionship.

As You Read

Connect What would you do if a friend pressured you to do something that felt wrong to you?

Growing Apart

Although some friendships last a lifetime, others grow **distant**, or detached, and eventually end. You may find that you no longer have as much in common with certain friends. If that happens, chances are you will not have to do anything to end the friendship. You will mutually and naturally decide to spend less and less time together.

If you and a friend seem to be drifting apart, try to figure out why. Is this a friendship that you both still value, but that is suffering from neglect? If so, look for ways to strengthen the relationship. However, if it seems that you no longer share common interests, it may be time to let go.

Do not be discouraged when you and a friend grow apart. As you move toward adulthood, you are developing new interests and gaining new experiences. Some of your friendships may not survive these changes. Growing apart from some of your friends is part of growing up. You will have opportunities for new friendships as you move in new directions.

Vocabulary

You can find definitions in the glossary at the back of this book.

Moving On

Entering adulthood means new experiences, new friendships, and sometimes an end to old friendships. *What positive things have you gained from a friendship that eventually ended?*

▲ **Cliques Can Hurt**

Not only can it feel bad to be left out of a clique, it can also be harmful to be a member of one. *What actions can you take to show that you prefer to include, and not exclude, other people?*

Why Do Friendships End?

While friendships sometimes end on their own, there may be other times when you choose to end a friendship. You may realize that you no longer enjoy that person's company, or you may feel that the person does not treat you in a way that you deserve. Do not be afraid to end a friendship that you consider unhealthy or that has simply run its course. It is far better to focus your efforts on mutually rewarding and satisfying friendships.

Not all friendships last forever. People are constantly moving, growing, and changing. Though some friendships last a lifetime, many end abruptly or slowly fade away. Some friendships that seem to have faded may rekindle at another time, sometimes many years later. What exactly causes friendships to end or fade?

- **Distance** Some friendships end because one person moves away. In these cases, remaining emotionally close takes work. Long-distance friendships require effort. Fortunately, ongoing advances in technology make it easier to stay in touch.
- **Conflict** Some friendships end due to conflict or misunder-standings. Most fights can be resolved with communication and an apology, but sometimes the conflict is too big to get over.
- **Jealousy** Feelings of jealousy and possessiveness can end a friendship. Not allowing your friend to spend time with other people may cause him or her to feel smothered.

- **Changing Interests** Friends that used to enjoy the same things may find they have less in common. Changing interests and experiences can cause people to grow apart because they find it harder to relate. Friendships based on core values rather than shared activities are more likely to survive life's changes.
- **Deliberate Action** If a friend is physically or emotionally abusive or is unpleasant to be around, you need to end the friendship. Unhealthy or destructive friendships can prevent you from reaching your potential.

How to End a Friendship

If you must deliberately end a friendship, do it with sensitivity. Ending a friendship is difficult for both parties, but it does not have to create hostility between you. You can still remain cordial if you are tactful in your approach. Below are two possible options for ending a friendship that is not working out:

- **Gradual Approach** One way to end a friendship is to ease out of the relationship. You can distance yourself by finding other activities that gradually take more of your time. Joining an athletic team, volunteering, or spending more time with other friends can be effective ways of stepping back.
- **Direct Approach** If a friendship is unhealthy or destructive, you may need to be more direct. Explain why you must end the friendship. Use the "I" messages you learned about in Chapter 4. Giving reasons rather than blaming the other person takes courage. Doing so can help you end a friendship in as positive a way as possible.

✓ Reading Check **Recall** What should you ask yourself before ending a friendship that seems to be fading?

Peer Relationship Problems

Although peer relationships can be a source of friendships, they can also be a source of problems. You may have already faced situations involving cliques, gangs, harassment, or negative peer pressure. If not, chances are you will. Knowing how to deal with these situations now can help you be better prepared for them.

Cliques

A **clique** ('klik) is a small, exclusive group that restricts who can join. Cliques are formed by people who want to set themselves apart. Belonging to a clique gives its members a sense of identity and importance. Members feel more secure when surrounded by others like themselves. Even though cliques give their members a sense of security, they have obvious downsides. The "us versus them" attitude of many cliques creates barriers to relationships with other people. Cliques may pressure their members to ignore or reject people who do not "fit in." That hurts everyone involved.

Succeed in SCHOOL and LIFE

Brainstorm Ideas

One of the most useful techniques for solving problems is brainstorming. Brainstorming involves getting together as a group to suggest any ideas that come to mind, even ideas that seem silly at first. One idea tends to lead to more ideas, and all ideas are written down. The end result is often a successful solution to the problem. Suggest this technique the next time you are working in a group.

Cliquish attitudes and behaviors are signs of immaturity. Mature people make efforts to include other people, not exclude them. This makes life richer and more satisfying. If you find yourself on the outside of a clique, remember that if a group is so exclusive that it will not take you as a member, it is their loss, not yours. If people cannot accept you for who you are, they are not worth your time.

Gangs

A gang is a clique that goes far beyond excluding people. Gangs not only limit membership, they promote distrust and hatred of outsiders. They engage in antisocial, and often unlawful, behavior. Gang members are more likely to participate in, or become victims of, violence. If you are approached about joining a gang, firmly decline. For more ideas, review the refusal skills in Chapter 6.

Teasing and Harassment

Many teens experience teasing from their peers. Sometimes friends tease one another in a joking way. As long as this type of teasing does not go too far, it is harmless. It helps to have a sense of humor and know how to laugh at yourself.

In other cases, teasing is intended to irritate, anger, or embarrass someone. If teasing stops being funny and starts to bother you, the best response is usually to ignore it. When possible, stay away from people who **engage**, or participate, in this kind of behavior.

Hurtful teasing that continues can be a form of harassment. **Harassment** is a persistent, hostile behavior directed at a specific person. Bullying is another form of harassment that can be particularly harmful. Bullies seek power and attention by being intentionally cruel. The bullying may take the form of pushing, kicking, or other physical harm, or it may involve taunting and intimidation. Bullies want their victims to be afraid of them. In fact, one of the best ways to stand up to a bully is to show that you are not afraid. Review Chapter 7 for more information about bullying and ways to resist it.

Sexual harassment is objectionable behavior of a sexual nature. Sexual remarks, gestures, and touching are considered forms of sexual harassment. Other examples include sexual name-calling, telling sexual jokes, making comments about another person's body, spreading sexual rumors, and pressuring someone to engage in sexual activity.

Harassment in any form should never be tolerated. If you experience or observe such behavior, let the harassers know that their behavior is cruel and offensive. If the harassment continues, talk to your parents and seek help from a teacher, counselor, or other trusted adult. When harassment occurs at school, teachers and school officials have a responsibility to put a stop to it.

Peer Pressure

Pressure from your peers is not necessarily a problem. In fact, some peer pressure from good friends can have a positive influence on you, such as when a friend encourages you to join the debate team or school chorus. However, at times your peers may pressure you to do things that make you uncomfortable.

Negative peer pressure is usually easy to recognize. When someone tries to get you to do something that is illegal or obviously wrong, you know it. However, there may be times when you do not fully realize the consequences of what you are being pressured to do. When you are not sure, stop and think about your values. Doing something that goes against them is never a smart decision. Having a strong self-concept and trusting your own judgment can help you resist negative peer pressure. Make your own decisions, and stand up for what you believe. You are never required to go along with the crowd.

Health & Wellness TIPS

Manage Anger

Anger is a normal human emotion, but if it gets out of control, it can turn destructive. To help control your anger instead of allowing your anger to control you, try these tips:

▶ Breathe deeply while thinking of a relaxing image or phrase.

▶ Try to replace emotional thoughts with logical ones.

▶ Use humor to give yourself perspective.

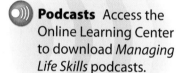

Podcasts Access the Online Learning Center to download *Managing Life Skills* podcasts.

Section 20.2 — **After You Read**

Review Key Concepts

1. **Explain** why it is sometimes necessary and acceptable to end a friendship.

2. **Differentiate** between harmless and harmful teasing.

Practice Academic Skills

 English Language Arts

3. Jargon is language used in a particular activity or profession. Law has its own jargon, or legal terms. Use at least five of these terms to write a law about how friends should settle differences: case, claim, damages, grievance, mediator, parties, settle, testimony, violation, and witness. Look up the terms to make sure you use them correctly.

 Social Studies

4. Differences between friends' cultural backgrounds may occasionally result in misunderstandings. This is because one culture might interpret an act or phrase in a different way from another culture. Write a scenario in which this type of misunderstanding occurs in a friendship, and explain how it might have happened.

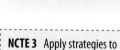

Check Your Answers Check your answers at this book's Online Learning Center at **glencoe.com**.

NCTE 3 Apply strategies to interpret texts.

NCSS I G Construct reasoned judgments about specific cultural responses to persistent human issues.

Pathway to College

The College Interview

What Is the College Interview?

A college interview is an exchange of information during which you learn more about the college, and the college gets to learn more about you. It is your chance to display your personality and unique spirit, things that are sometimes hard to portray on paper. College interviews usually last from 30-60 minutes, and they are often optional.

If they are optional, why should I bother with college interviews?

Think of college interviews as opportunities instead of obstacles. While they are often not required, interviews can be very beneficial to you. They provide you with a chance to convey your charm and personality. They also give you a chance to ask questions and learn more about a college from someone who really knows. Finally, they can provide you with an opportunity to clarify something on your application that you think might need more explanation.

Do I need to practice or prepare?

Practicing and preparing for your college interview is important. Work through any nerves by practicing in front of friends or family members. They might provide you with tips, such as slowing down or speaking up. Also, you should try to anticipate some of the questions you might be asked and brainstorm answers to them.

What are some things relating to college interviews that I should try to avoid?

It is very important not to be late. You only have a short window to make a good impression. Do not memorize and robotically deliver answers; you want to sound natural. Also, avoid mumbling or answering questions with a simple yes or no. Do not swear, chew gum, or use too much slang. Do not brag. You want to be confident but not boastful. Also, be truthful about your academic accomplishments.

Hands-On

College Readiness Work with a partner or a small group to brainstorm potential college interview questions. Come up with a list of questions that you think you might be asked. If you need help, go online to research common college interview questions. Also create a list of questions you might want to ask the college interviewer. Then practice answering the questions on your list with your partner or group. Provide feedback.

Path to Success

College & Career Readiness

Prepare Before your college interview, make notes about why you want to attend the college.

Think Ahead Prepare questions to ask the college interviewer.

Dress Appropriately Choose a suitable college interview outfit.

Share Discuss not only school, but your life outside of the classroom, including activities, community service, and hobbies.

Calm Down Do not over-worry about your college interview. Try breathing techniques to relax.

Follow Up It is important to send a thank-you note to the college interviewer. Make it personal by referring to something you discussed.

 Go to this book's Online Learning Center at **glencoe.com** to learn more about college and career readiness.

CHAPTER SUMMARY

Section 20.1
Successful Friendships

While each friendship is different, qualities such as caring, empathy, and respect are common to strong friendships. To make new friends, look for ways to meet people who share your interests. Start a conversation by showing interest in the other person, listening, and asking open-ended questions. Diversity in friendships often brings many benefits. Good friendships take time and effort to grow and maintain.

Section 20.2
Friendship Challenges

It is natural for some friendships to grow stronger over time and for others to become more distant or to come to an end. Some peer friendships can pose challenges. You can show maturity by avoiding cliques, and you can stay safe by avoiding gangs. Peer harassment is harmful and should never be tolerated. Some peer pressure is positive, but be prepared to recognize and resist negative peer pressure.

Vocabulary Review

1. Write each of these vocabulary words on an index card, and write their definitions on separate index cards. Work in pairs or small groups to match each word to its definition.

Content Vocabulary
- ◇ empathy (p. 395)
- ◇ reciprocity (p. 395)
- ◇ rejection (p. 398)
- ◇ diversity (p. 399)
- ◇ clique (p. 403)
- ◇ harassment (p. 404)
- ◇ sexual harassment (p. 404)

Academic Vocabulary
- ■ signal (p. 397)
- ■ alert (p. 398)
- ■ distant (p. 401)
- ■ engage (p. 404)

Review Key Concepts

2. **List** the qualities of a successful friendship.
3. **Identify** ways to meet people who might become friends.
4. **Describe** the benefits of diversity in friendships.
5. **Give** guidelines for handling changes in friendships.
6. **Discuss** problems that may occur in peer relationships.

Critical Thinking

7. **Differentiate** How do childhood friendships differ from those that develop during the teen years?
8. **Draw Conclusions** Why do you think it often takes many months to build a strong friendship?
9. **Analyze** Why might two friends who seem to be growing apart hesitate to actually end their friendship?
10. **Predict** If one of your friends decided to join a clique, how might it affect your friendship with him or her?
11. **Evaluate** How can you tell when teasing has reached the level of harassment?

ACTIVE LEARNING

12. A Roundtable Discussion Get your teacher's permission to form small groups. Organize a roundtable discussion on the problem of gangs. Choose one person to lead a 15-minute discussion and another to take notes. Sit in a circle to discuss the reasons you think gangs exist and what you think can be done about the problem. Make sure everyone has an opportunity to talk and listens respectfully to everyone else. After, evaluate the results. Did people have differing opinions about causes and solutions? If so, what do you think accounts for the differing points of view?

Family & Community Connections

13. Interview and Research Locate a counselor or mental health professional who is willing to participate in an interview either face-to-face or over the telephone. Ask this expert to describe the most common challenges he or she encounters in peer relationships among teens today. Follow up with questions regarding this challenge. Why do you think this challenge has become so common? How do you think it should be addressed? What advice would you give to teens today regarding their peer relationships? Add your own ideas for questions to this list. After your interview, do some research on the Internet or at the library on the issues that you discussed. Write an essay summarizing what you learned. Make sure that you quote the expert where it is appropriate.

21st Century Skills

Social Skills

14. Show Appreciation It is natural to take good friends for granted. However, keeping friends means showing your appreciation every once in a while. Choose a friend for whom you are especially grateful, and find a creative way to show it. Cook a special dish, create a homemade gift, or treat your friend to a movie. Note your friend's response, how it feels to show appreciation, and the overall effect of your gesture.

Technology Skills

15. Public Service Video Prepare a 60-second public service video that encourages teens to resist giving in to negative peer pressure. Work with your teacher or school administrator to make your video available online.

 Connections

Collaboration Skills

16. Peer Mediation As part of its mission, FCCLA encourages students' individual and group involvement in helping achieve global cooperation. School-wide peer mediation clubs support this mission and foster a safer and happier campus environment. Research peer mediation so you can describe it and discuss its benefits. Use your knowledge to talk to your teacher or school counselor about starting or becoming involved in a peer mediation club at your school.

Academic Skills

 ### English Language Arts

17. Use Adjectives Adjectives help you paint colorful and accurate descriptions of people, places, and things. Create three lists of ten adjectives each. The first list should describe you, and the second and third lists should decribe two of your friends. You can use the same adjective more than once. What are the key similarities and differences between you and your friends? What do the lists say about your choice of friends?

> **NCTE 5** Use different writing process elements to communicate effectively.

 ### Social Studies

18. Cultural Differences In the U.S., people who are meeting someone for the first time often introduce themselves and shake hands. In other cultures, the etiquette for introductions might be different. Find out about three cultures in which a different custom is followed. Be prepared to demonstrate the customs.

> **NCSS I F Culture** Interpret patterns of behavior reflecting values and attitudes that contribute or pose obstacles to cross-cultural understanding.

 ### Mathematics

19. Team Work As part of a school improvement project, Dora has volunteered to lead a landscaping team that will design a garden for the front of the school library. They need to purchase soil, seeds, and fencing to enclose the garden. They do not have a lot of money to spend, so to avoid buying more than they need, the team must determine exactly how much fencing will be necessary to enclose the garden. The garden is in the shape of a right triangle with sides that measure 6 yards, 8 yards, and 10 yards. How much fencing is needed to enclose the garden?

Math Concept **Finding Perimeter** To find the perimeter of an area, add the lengths of all of the sides of the area.

Starting Hint Make an addition problem that includes the length of the three sides of the triangle.

Math For more math practice, go to the Math Appendix at the back of the book.

> **NCTM Measurement** Apply appropriate techniques, tools, and formulas to determine measurements.

 ## Standardized Test Practice

CCR College & Career Readiness

SHORT ANSWER

Short answer questions are not the same as essay questions. These questions call for brief, to-the-point responses. Read the queston carefully, then write a response.

Test-Taking Tip Keep your language simple and direct in short answer questions. Avoid overly elaborate answers. Bulleted or numbered lists can help clarify your response.

20. Although rejection can be a painful experience, it makes sense to not take rejection personally. Why is this true?

Chapter 21

Dating and Marriage

Chapter Objectives

Section 21.1 Responsible Dating

- **Explain** reasons for dating different people before getting married.
- **Provide** guidelines for responsible dating relationships.
- **Identify** the emotional challenges that may arise in a relationship.

Section 21.2 Decisions About Marriage

- **Determine** whether a dating relationship has the potential for commitment.
- **Summarize** the factors that contribute to marital success and failure.
- **List** reasons for choosing to remain single.

➤ Explore the Photo

Dating and learning how to interact as part of a couple is an important life skill and can help prepare you for marriage. *What qualities do you look for in a dating partner?*

Character Analysis

Imagine the Ideal Mate When you think about your future lifelong mate, what qualities come to mind? Your ideal mate is not a perfect person or the person who is most like you. Instead, he or she is someone who is right for you. Write a character analysis of your ideal mate. Make sure to include specific details about the person.

Writing Tips To write a strong character analysis of an ideal mate, follow these steps:

- Describe his or her words and actions.
- Analyze how his or her behavior shows the qualities you believe are ideal.
- Describe the reactions of others to the person.

Responsible Dating

> Set boundaries and practice abstinence when dating.

Reading Guide

Before You Read

Buddy Up for Success One advantage to sharing your notes with a buddy is that you can fill in gaps in each other's information. You can also compare notes before you start quizzing each other.

Read to Learn

Key Concepts

- **Explain** reasons for dating different people before getting married.
- **Provide** guidelines for responsible dating relationships.
- **Identify** the emotional challenges that may arise in a relationship.

Main Idea

It is beneficial to date different people. Dating has rules and carries responsibilities. Dating relationships can bring out emotions that you must learn to handle and express appropriately.

Graphic Organizer

As you read, look for five key questions you should ask before going out on a date. Use a chart like the one shown to help you organize your information.

Questions to Ask Before Leaving for a Date
1.
2.
3.
4.
5.

Graphic Organizer Go to this book's Online Learning Center at **glencoe.com** to print out this graphic organizer.

Content Vocabulary

◇ sexually transmitted infection (STI)
◇ crush
◇ infatuation
◇ jealousy

Academic Vocabulary

You will find these words in your reading and on your tests. Use the glossary to look up their definitions if necessary.

■ compatible
■ boundaries

Academic Standards

English Language Arts

NCTE 12 Use language to accomplish individual purposes.

Social Studies

NCSS IV E Individual Development and Identity Examine the interaction of ethnic, national, or cultural influences in specific situations or events.

NCTE *National Council of Teachers of English*
NCTM *National Council of Teachers of Mathematics*
NSES *National Science Education Standards*
NCSS *National Council for the Social Studies*

Starting a Relationship

Going out with different people has several benefits. It gives you opportunities to improve interpersonal skills, such as making conversation and practicing how to give and take. Through these experiences, you learn to better understand yourself and others. In the long run, going out with a variety of people helps you discover which characteristics you will want in a permanent partner.

Going Out as a Group

Many teens prefer to go out in groups, especially when they begin dating. When you go out with a group, you can have a good time without the pressure that comes with going out as a couple. Group dating makes it easier to feel comfortable with people you may eventually want to date. There are more people to keep the conversation going and make sure the group has a good time.

Going Out as a Couple

Going out on a "couple date" gives you a chance to practice relating to a dating partner one-on-one. It does not necessarily mean that you have a serious relationship with that person. Many teens go out on casual dates with different people with whom they enjoy spending time. This allows them to get to know a variety of people.

After two people been going out together for a time, they may decide to have an exclusive dating relationship. Being a couple helps people to get to know each other well. It also creates a sense of security. It is comfortable to know that you always have a date for the weekend and for special events. However, spending all of your time with one other person has its drawbacks. You might come to rely too much on that relationship and miss opportunities to meet other people with whom you may be **compatible**, or well matched.

Family Rules

Some parents do not allow their teen sons or daughters to date one person exclusively. They may believe that teens need opportunities to socialize with a lot of different people. Or they may be concerned that their son or daughter will get too involved in a relationship and lose sight of important long-term goals, such as getting a good education. Cultural or religious beliefs may also influence a family's rules about dating.

As You Read

Connect What are some reasons you may want to go at your own pace when it comes to dating?

Vocabulary

You can find definitions in the glossary at the back of this book.

Group Activities

Going out as a group can put less pressure on a couple but still allow teens to have fun and get to know one another. *What types of activities would be good choices for group dating?*

Be Smart Be Safe

Dating Safety Tips Dating in groups is the safest choice when you are just getting to know someone. Make sure you know someone well before you go out as a couple. What other guidelines do you know about dating?

Write About It Imagine you are giving advice to another teen who is just starting to date. Write a list of at least five dating safety tips for him or her to remember.

Parents often have rules about where their teens may go and what they can do on a date. Their concerns about drug and alcohol abuse, unsafe driving, and sexual pressures are valid. By setting restrictions, they try to keep teens out of potentially harmful situations. Your parents have been through the dating experience and have gained valuable wisdom. Even if you do not agree with their dating rules, remember that their purpose is to protect you.

✓ **Reading Check** **Explain** Why might a parent not allow a teen to date any one person exclusively?

Responsible Relationships

Dating can be fun, but it has a serious side. When you start going out with someone, you take on new responsibilities. You need to establish **boundaries**, or limits, for your new relationship. It is important to plan ahead so that you are prepared to handle situations that may arise.

Personal Responsibility

In healthy dating relationships, people practice responsibility and respect for themselves and their partners. They follow family and personal rules. They stay true to their values and respect each others' rules and values. If Kyle's curfew is 11 p.m. but Melanie's curfew is 10 p.m., they are both responsible for making sure that the 10 p.m. curfew is kept.

When you go out on a date, your mutual goal is to enjoy each other's company. This can only happen when you accept each other's wishes and feelings. Remember that a person who cares about you will not pressure you to go against your values. Trying to control another person's behavior in a dating situation is a sure sign of an unhealthy relationship.

Communication is an important part of any relationship, and it is especially important to responsible dating. Before you leave for your date, talk with your partner about where you will go, how you will get there and back, what you are going to do, who will pay, when you will be back home, and any other important details. If you agree on these issues ahead of time, there will be no uncertainty, and that can help you both have a good time. Doing this also establishes an understanding of what you expect from the date.

Sexual Responsibility

Media often send the message that sexual activity is an expected part of any dating relationship. That is simply not true. Shelly learned about sexual responsibility the hard way. In her words: "I thought we were in love and that being in love made it okay to have sex. What a mistake! Soon after I said yes, he seemed to lose interest. It really wasn't love at all. I feel like such a fool."

Teen Parenthood

It is important to think about what it means to be a teen parent and how drastically it changes a teen's life. *What are some of the difficulties of teen parenthood?*

As Shelly learned, sexual activity is not to be taken lightly. It can be emotionally damaging, leaving some teens to suffer hurtful feelings of regret and guilt. Although sex would seem to be a private matter, it rarely stays that way. Word gets around, and reputations suffer. Some teens lose the respect of their friends and may have to face parental disappointment. It may be difficult to form new relationships. Perhaps most importantly, they may lose self-respect and peace of mind.

Risks of Sexual Activity

In some ways, Shelly was fortunate. She only had to deal with emotional consequences. Sexual activity, even just one single incident, can result in serious and complex problems that have long-term effects on a teen's life.

Unintended Pregnancy Pregnancy changes teens' lives dramatically. Both parents must assume physical, emotional, and financial responsibility for the baby. Sometimes one or both parents drop out of school. This is a short-sighted solution that severely limits job opportunities and long-term earning potential. The resulting financial problems add stress to the relationship. Teen parents often feel trapped by the responsibilities of parenting. They resent missing out on the normal activities of other teens. You will learn more about the challenges of teen parenting in Chapter 25.

Sexually Transmitted Infections Sexual activity carries the risk of contracting a serious disease. A **sexually transmitted infection (STI)** is a disease spread through sexual contact. Most STIs are treatable but, if left untreated, can cause lifelong health problems. Sadly, many teens with STI symptoms do not get help because they do not want to admit they may have such a disease. In the meantime, they may spread their STI to others.

Acquired immune deficiency syndrome, the STI commonly known as AIDS, is the most devastating because there is no cure. Caused by HIV (human immunodeficiency virus) and often spread by sexual activity, AIDS weakens the body's defense system and eventually causes death. **Figure 21.1** lists and describes common STIs.

Succeed in SCHOOL and LIFE

Practicing Abstinence

Many teens find that abstinence brings them peace of mind and a sense of self-respect. Here are some suggestions to help you stay committed to abstinence:

- Set limits.
- Plan ahead.
- Avoid risky situations.
- Spend time with people who share your beliefs.
- Join a program that encourages abstinence.

Handling Sexual Feelings

The many risks associated with sexual activity make it especially important for you to know how to handle your own sexual feelings. Having such feelings is normal, but it is a mistake to let your feelings control your actions. Think ahead, and make decisions about your behavior before a difficult situation occurs.

Although there are different methods to help prevent pregnancy, the only sure way is to practice abstinence. Abstinence is a deliberate decision to avoid high-risk behaviors, including sexual activity. Unlike many other methods of pregnancy prevention, abstinence also prevents STIs. Some teens reinforce their decision to abstain by joining an abstinence campaign and signing a pledge to avoid sexual activity until they are married.

The choice not to engage in sexual activity is easier when you talk to your dating partner about your decision. Being willing to communicate honestly about avoiding sexual activity is a sign of maturity. Many teens are relieved to learn that the other person agrees. Even if your partner does not agree, you have the right to make your own choices, and your partner must respect your decision.

Figure 21.1 **Sexually Transmitted Infections**

STI Syptoms and Treatments Anyone who experiences any of these symptoms should be tested by a medical professional so that the exact condition can be diagnosed and treated. *Which STIs have no cure?*

STI	SYMPTOMS	EFFECTS	TREATMENT
Chlamydia (klə-'mi-dē-ə)	Painful urination, nausea, low fever, abdominal pain. Sometimes there are no symptoms.	Can cause sterility, the inability to have children.	Can be cured with antibiotics.
Genital herpes	Open sores on sex organs that go away within a few weeks, painful urination, fever.	Can cause brain damage or death if passed to a baby during childbirth.	No cure. Symptoms can be treated.
Genital warts	Small warts on sex organs that cause discomfort and itching.	May become cancerous if left alone.	No cure. A doctor can remove them.
Gonorrhea (ˌgä-nə-'rē-ə)	Burning, itching, and liquid discharge from infected areas.	Can cause sterility in females. A baby born to an infected mother can suffer eye damage.	Can be treated with antibiotics.
Hepatitis B (ˌhe-pə-'tī-təs)	Flu-like symptoms.	Can lead to liver disease or cancer.	No cure. There is a preventive vaccine.
Syphilis ('si-f(ə-)ləs)	Sores on sex organs, fever, rash, hair loss.	Can cause insanity and death.	Can be cured with antibiotics.
HIV/AIDS	No visible symptoms in first stage. Later stages include fever, headache, sore throat, rashes, diarrhea, swollen glands, body aches, diminished appetite, weight loss.	AIDS lessens immunity to other illnesses which may lead to death.	Once HIV develops into AIDS, there is no cure. Some medicines can delay the development of AIDS.

To avoid the pressure to engage in sexual activity, go out in a group and in public rather than spending time alone as a couple. Do not invite a dating partner to your home unless your parents or other trusted adult family members will be there. Do not give in to manipulative arguments such as "Everyone is doing it" and "If you loved me, you would do it." Lines such as these are not only untrue, they show lack of respect.

Effective refusal skills will help you successfully handle the pressure to engage in sexual activity. Refusal skills start with a firm sense of who you are and what is important to you, and this gives you the confidence and assertiveness to communicate your wishes. Here are some refusal tips:

- State your position. Do not apologize or try to justify your decision.
- Avoid mixed messages. Make sure your body language matches your words.
- Keep your values and your long-term goals in mind.
- If someone will not accept "no" for an answer, leave. Call someone to come and get you, if necessary.

As a teen, you are capable of taking sexual responsibility seriously. By doing this, you remain in control of your life and decide for yourself who you want to be.

✓ **Reading Check** **Describe** What are the potential emotional and social effects on a teen who breaks a commitment to abstinence?

Emotional Highs and Lows

By nature, the teen years are a time of emotional confusion. It takes skill to handle your emotions and express them appropriately and, like any skill, it must be learned. Romantic feelings are especially complex and challenging. They are even more so when one person has stronger feelings of attachment than the other, which is often the case.

Crushes and Infatuation

Before they develop a deep, long-term relationship, most people experience less fulfilling ones. These early relationships are sometimes painful, but they provide useful learning experiences.

Many people's first romantic experience involves a crush on someone. A **crush** is a temporary romantic attraction, especially among teens and young people. Crushes are usually directed toward a person with whom a real romantic relationship is not possible. For example, a young teen might have a crush on a celebrity or on a friend's older sibling. Usually the other person is not even aware of the feelings. A crush can be difficult to deal with because the feelings are so strong. Fortunately, crushes are temporary, and the feelings eventually subside.

Character?! In Action

Be Honest but Kind

Honesty is important in dating relationships, but it is also important to be kind. If you need to end a relationship, tell the other person how you feel and why. However, you do not need to share all of your thoughts and feelings, especially if they will be painful to hear. Keep your message simple and truthful, and try to avoid saying anything unnecessarily hurtful.

You Decide

Imagine that you are breaking up with someone because you are no longer having fun in the relationship. What words might you use that would be honest and also kind?

You probably know people who began a relationship based on infatuation. **Infatuation** is an intense, short-lived, and sometimes irrational passion. Like a crush, infatuation tends to be idealistic and unrealistic. Infatuated people are drawn by physical attraction and other surface qualities they find appealing, and they ignore characteristics or behaviors that might cause problems. Infatuation also tends to be self-centered, meaning that infatuated people are more concerned about their own happiness than about the other person's feelings. Infatuation can fool people into thinking they love someone. When people make a commitment based on infatuation, they usually regret it.

Jealousy

People in dating relationships sometimes find themselves feeling jealous. **Jealousy** is the feeling that the person you care about is more interested in something or someone else than in you. For example, Marcelo was upset when his girlfriend Abby started to spend hours working on projects with the other members of the homecoming committee.

When you care about another person, it is normal to feel jealous at times. However, intense or prolonged jealousy is destructive to a relationship. Extremely jealous people are usually insecure. They may resent any situation that seems threatening and become possessive and controlling.

Frequent attacks of jealousy call for self-examination. The jealous person may be expecting too much. Remember, no one relationship can fulfill all of a person's needs. It is best for couples to balance the time they spend together and apart. Having other friends and separate interests helps people develop as individuals and relieves pressure from the relationship.

Ending a Relationship

There are many reasons why a couple might argue, and sometimes these arguments lead to a breakup. *How can you show respect for a person when ending a relationship?*

Breakups

It usually takes considerable time and numerous relationships before you find a person with whom you are truly compatible. Consequently, most relationships have to end. Ending a relationship on a friendly note is ideal, but that does not always happen. Telling someone that you want to end a relationship, or hearing this message from another person, can be painful.

If you decide that it is time to end your relationship, make a "clean break." Do not just drift away or stop calling. Talk to the person, and explain why you want to end the relationship. Be firm but fair. Remember the positive emotions you felt in the past, and be sensitive to the other person's feelings.

If another person decides to end a relationship with you, do not try to prevent the breakup. Clinging to a relationship with an unwilling partner is unhealthy and just postpones what is bound to happen. No matter who ends the relationship, avoid saying negative things to or about each other.

After a breakup, give yourself time to recover. Do not be in a hurry to start a new relationship. Instead, reflect on the one that ended. What was good about it? What went wrong? What you learn may help you develop more fulfilling relationships in the future.

 Podcasts Access the Online Learning Center to download *Managing Life Skills* podcasts.

Section 21.1   After You Read

Review Key Concepts

1. **Summarize** the dating rules parents may set for their teens and the possible reasons for those rules.
2. **Explain** how mutual respect relates to the concept of responsible dating.
3. **Draw** a comparison between infatuation and real love.

Practice Academic Skills

 English Language Arts

4. Create a fictional couple in which one partner is emotionally distressed over something that occurred in their relationship. Write a dialogue between the two people, and include an ending. Does the situation get resolved? Why or why not?

 Social Studies

5. How we use our face, hands, and body are examples of body language. Some types of body language have different meanings in different cultures. In dating situations where people have different cultural backgrounds, this can cause problems. Research and write a paragraph about a common form of body language that may be misinterpreted due to cultural differences.

Check Your Answers Check your answers at this book's Online Learning Center at **glencoe.com**.

NCTE 12 Use language to accomplish individual purposes.

NCSS IV E Examine the interaction of ethnic, national, or cultural influences in specific situations or events.

Decisions About Marriage

When is it time to make a commitment?

Before You Read

What You Want to Know Write a list of what you want to know about marriage and commitment. As you read, write down the heads in this section that provide that information.

Read to Learn
Key Concepts

- **Determine** whether a dating relationship has the potential for commitment.
- **Summarize** the factors that contribute to marital success and failure.
- **List** reasons for choosing to remain single.

Main Idea

Commitment sometimes leads to marriage. Strong marriages are based on caring, respect, and trust. Marriages fail for many different reasons.

Content Vocabulary

◇ commitment
◇ engagement period
◇ monogamy
◇ annulment

Academic Vocabulary

You will find these words in your reading and on your tests. Use the glossary to look up their definitions if necessary.

■ prohibit
■ delay

Academic Standards

English Language Arts

NCTE 5 Use different writing process elements to communicate effectively.

Mathmatics

NCTM Number and Operations Compute fluently and make reasonable estimates.

Social Studies

NCSS I A Culture Analyze and explain the ways groups, societies, and cultures address human needs and concerns.

NCTE *National Council of Teachers of English*
NCTM *National Council of Teachers of Mathematics*
NSES *National Science Education Standards*
NCSS *National Council for the Social Studies*

Graphic Organizer

As you read, think about one- or two-word categories that describe the topics an engaged couple should discuss before they get married. Use a cluster web like the one shown to help you organize your information.

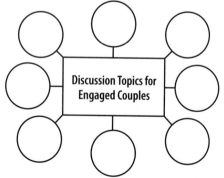

Discussion Topics for Engaged Couples

Graphic Organizer Go to this book's Online Learning Center at **glencoe.com** to print out this graphic organizer.

Love and Commitment

In time, you may find someone with whom you feel ready to make a commitment to a relationship. Making a **commitment** means you both accept that you have an obligation and responsibility to each another. There are different levels of commitment. At first, a couple may simply agree not to go out with others. In time, the commitment may become a plan for marriage.

Is It Love?

People have long struggled with the question, "How can I be sure it is love?" They may have believed that they were in love in the past, only to discover that their feelings changed. Looking at past relationships can help you recognize what kind of relationship will or will not work for you. When you think back, ask these questions: Why did your feelings for someone in a past relationship change? Was there a lack of understanding? Was the emotional connection one-sided? Did you share enough interests, values, and goals?

Caring, respect, and trust are the keys to lasting relationships. Successful couples know how to give and receive. They find things that they have in common, but they know how important it is to maintain individual identities. What do you have in common with your relationship partner? What are the differences that keep things interesting? Do you have similar values and compatible goals for the future? Does your love motivate you to take action to benefit the person you love? Does the relationship make you a better person? It is important to give a relationship enough time to develop. Learn all you can about the other person. One way to tell whether love will last is simply to give it time and find out whether it endures.

✓ **Reading Check** **Explain** What is meant by "different levels of commitment" for couples?

How Marriage Works

When two people determine that their love makes for a lasting relationship, they usually start thinking about marriage. Plans for marriage typically begin with an engagement period.

Getting Engaged

When people get engaged, they make a promise to marry. Getting engaged communicates to family and friends that the two people have made a commitment. The **engagement period**, which may last a few months, a year, or longer, serves an important purpose. It gives the couple time to test their relationship, make sure that marriage is the right decision, and plan for their wedding and married life.

Some of the questions that couples need to ask and answer during their engagement are listed on the next page.

As You Read

Connect What would you like to achieve in your life before getting married?

Vocabulary

You can find definitions in the glossary at the back of this book.

Succeed in SCHOOL and LIFE

Balance Your Priorities

Sometimes, teens who either have or plan to have a committed relationship neglect other priorities such as school and career goals. However, people who continue to work toward their own achievements, whether they are in relationships or not, are usually more fulfilled and prepared for whatever life brings them. Balance between relationships and personal goals and responsibilities is one of the keys to future success.

- Where will we live?
- How will we manage household tasks?
- How will we manage our finances?
- Will we continue our education? If so, how will we pay for it?
- Will we both have careers? What if a career change requires relocation?
- Do we want to have children? If so, how many? How will we raise them?
- Do we agree on religious matters? If not, how will we handle religious differences?

At one time, engagements were considered legal contracts and were rarely broken. Today, broken engagements are not unusual. Why do people change their minds? Some realize that they rushed the decision to get engaged. They decide to slow down and give the relationship more time to develop. Some find that their feelings for their partner have changed over time. Others discover that they are not ready to take on the responsibilities of marriage.

A broken engagement brings a sense of loss, and it can be very painful. However, it is better to call off an engagement than to ignore the warning signs that the marriage will not last. An unhappy marriage or a divorce is much more painful in the long run than a broken engagement.

Every state has laws governing marriage. Marriage laws serve to legalize the couple's agreement, regulate property rights, and provide protection for children. Because marriage laws differ from state to state, engaged couples need to check the laws for the state in which they will marry.

Life On Your Own

Express Your Commitment

Productive communication is a necessary part of a healthy relationship. Whether the person in question is a relative, friend, or romantic interest, the same rule applies: The clearer people can be in communicating their thoughts and feelings, the stronger their bond is likely to become. When people in a relationship do not communicate, misunderstandings and distance can develop between them.

How It Works It is worthwhile to take the time to keep important relationships strong. Use your words and actions to communicate a sense of commitment to the relationship. For instance, a committed relationship partner is a good listener when times are difficult; demonstrates trust by keeping confidences and being honest; acts responsibly and with respect; and uses kind and caring words.

Try It Out You have unintentionally, or accidentally, neglected someone who means a lot to you. Perhaps you forgot to do something that was important to him or her, or you said something hurtful. You need to find a way to show this person that your action was not intentional, and that you are committed to your relationship.

> *Your Turn* Think about the things you might do or say to express your commitment to someone when they feel neglected. Create a two-column chart with the headings "Words" and "Actions." Fill in the chart with at least five suggestions for each column.

Here are examples of marriage laws:

- **Mutual Consent** All states require mutual consent for marriage. If either party is against the idea, the marriage is not valid.
- **Monogamy** All states have laws that require monogamy. **Monogamy** (mə-'nä-gə-mē) is marriage to only one person at a time.
- **Marriage Age** Most states allow people to marry after they reach the age of 18. Parental consent is needed for marriages below that age.
- **Physical Requirements** Most states require a blood test shortly before marriage to establish that the partners do not have certain communicable diseases.
- **Waiting Period** Most states give couples time to think over their decision by requiring a waiting period of one to five days before or after the license is issued.
- **Marriage License** All states require couples to obtain a license in order to marry. The license serves as a legal record of the marriage.
- **Marriage Officials** State laws identify officials who may perform a marriage ceremony. Officials include members of the clergy and civil authorities, such as judges and mayors.
- **Prohibited Marriages** All states prohibit, or forbid, marriage between close blood relatives, such as sisters and brothers, uncles and nieces, and aunts and nephews. Some states prohibit marriage between cousins.
- **Annulment** State laws allow annulment of a marriage if the legal requirements for marriage were not met. An **annulment** means that no valid marriage ever existed.

Math For Success

Dates and Dollars

Developing a budget for a date can help you spend your money wisely. To develop a date budget, follow these steps:

1. Decide how much money you will spend on the date.
2. Make a list of options for the date, such as going to a movie, going bowling, eating pizza, and so on.
3. Write down the costs for the options listed in step 2.
4. Choose the options that will fit within your budget.

Math Concept **Multi-Step Problems** When solving problems with more than one step, think through the steps before you start making your plan for solving the problem.

Starting Hint First decide how much you want to spend. Then decide the costs of your date options. Choose from your options, and add the costs to find the options that fit within your budget. You may have to do some re-calculating to get the costs to fit within your budget.

For more math practice, go to the Math Appendix at the back of the book.

NCTM Number and Operations Compute fluently and make reasonable estimates.

What Makes a Marriage Strong?

Choosing your partner carefully does not guarantee that a marriage will succeed. Life brings constant challenges, such as career changes, the birth of children, illness, financial problems, and other events, that can test a marriage. Dealing with such issues while maintaining a close, caring relationship requires effort. When deciding whether to marry someone, consider how well a potential partner deals with change and difficulty. One of the keys to a strong marriage is communication. Partners who express their feelings, discuss issues, and make decisions together will have a happier relationship.

◀ **A Strong Marriage**
Qualities necessary for a strong marriage include sharing and mutual respect. *What other qualities can you think of that would contribute to marital harmony?*

Another key is sharing. When couples share responsibilities so that neither partner feels overburdened, their marriage will be stronger. Couples also need to be able to resolve conflicts. Even the most devoted partners do not agree on everything. Above all, the couple must be committed to making the marriage work.

When Marriages Fail

Marriages are more likely to end in divorce today than in the past. This does not necessarily mean that there are more unhappy marriages today. In the past, couples often stayed in troubled marriages because society generally disapproved of divorce. Today, couples feel more free to make that decision and are more likely to give up on an unhappy marriage. Marriages fail for many different reasons, including:

- **Lack of Commitment** Some do not take the marriage commitment seriously and walk away when there is trouble.
- **Unrealistic Expectations** If a marriage partner expects everything to go smoothly all of the time, he or she will be disappointed.
- **Individual Changes** In some marriages, the partners change in ways that make them less compatible.
- **Money and Child Rearing** Disagreements about finances and how to raise children are often named as contributing factors.
- **Immaturity** Some people get married before they are emotionally ready to take on adult responsibilities.

Teen Marriage

Even for mature adults, marriage presents enormous challenges. For teens, the problems can be even more difficult. Teen marriages do not have a high rate of success. If the teens marry because of a pregnancy, the pressures increase, and so does the rate of divorce.

Most teens feel it is better to wait until they are older to marry. Delaying marriage gives teens a chance to pursue their education and career goals. It gives them time to learn more about themselves. This helps them make smarter decisions about who they want to marry and what they want in a marriage.

✓ **Reading Check** **Identify** What are some reasons members of a couple may have for breaking their engagement?

Health & Wellness TIPS

Be Your Own Person

At the beginning of a relationship, it is normal to want to be as close as possible. However, do not get into a pattern of ignoring your own needs for the sake of someone else. Healthy relationships consist of two whole people, not two halves.

Remaining Single

In the past, everyone was expected to get married, and most people did. Today, a large percentage of people remain single. Some have always been single, and others are single following a divorce or the death of a spouse.

People stay single for a variety of reasons. Some have not met a person they want to marry. Some prefer the independence and freedom of single living. They may choose to focus on other fulfilling aspects of life, such as a career, travel, or community service. Some people remain single so that they can care for aging family members. Many people **delay**, or put off, marriage in order to complete their education or make progress in their career.

It is important to recognize that marriage is a choice, not something that anyone is required to do. Getting married because your family expects it or because all your friends are getting married is not likely to bring you happiness. The decision to marry should not be based on what others expect of you, but rather, on what you want for yourself.

Go Green

Whether you are going out on a date or just planning to enjoy a movie with a friend, you will need some kind of transportation. If possible, why not make the earth-friendly choice? Walk or ride bicycles to your destination.

 Podcasts Access the Online Learning Center to download *Managing Life Skills* podcasts.

Section 21.2 After You Read

Review Key Concepts

1. **Explain** how a past relationship might help you decide whether a current relationship will work out.
2. **Identify** the primary purposes of marriage laws.
3. **Illustrate** three scenarios in which someone might decide to delay marriage.

Practice Academic Skills

 English Language Arts

4. Imagine you are a newspaper columnist. Your editor's assignment for the paper's Valentine's Day issue is to interview a couple who has been married for 50 years or more. Write a three- to five-paragraph column based on how you imagine the interview would go. Look at a real newspaper columnist's work as a guide to the writing style.

 Social Studies

5. Wedding ceremonies represent a couple's personal choices in everything from wardrobe to vows. These choices are frequently culture-based and have symbolic meaning. Research the wedding ceremonies of different cultures. List some unique aspects that are based on culture and what they are meant to symbolize. Make sure your list represents at least four different cultures.

Check Your Answers Check your answers at this book's Online Learning Center at **glencoe.com**.

NCTE 5 Use different writing process elements to communicate effectively.

NCSS I A Analyze and explain the ways groups, societies, and cultures address human needs and concerns.

Pathway to Your Career

Wedding Planner

What Does a Wedding Planner Do?

A wedding planner organizes and coordinates the many parts of a wedding, including the location, photographer, florist, reception, catering, and musicians. They provide advice on a wide range of decisions, such as wedding colors, flowers, bridal attire and accessories, music, invitations, decorations, and food. Wedding planners reduce the stress that typically accompanies a wedding and ensure the day goes as smoothly as possible.

Career Readiness Skills Wedding planners should be creative, personable, and calm under pressure. They must be organized, good with money, and skilled at negotiating. Networking skills, such as developing and maintaining connections, are important. Wedding planners should stay on top of trends in fashion, colors, flowers, and music. They should be familiar with the customs and traditions related to different types of wedding ceremonies.

Education and Training Having a bachelor's degree, especially in fields like marketing, public relations, business, and hospitality management, provides a competitive edge but is usually not required. Most training is done informally on the job, and most skills are learned through experience.

Job Outlook Employment is expected to grow faster than the average for all occupations over the next decade. As people get married later in life, they often have more money to spend on their weddings, which increases the demand for wedding planners.

Critical Thinking A trend in wedding planning is to have themed weddings. Imagine a theme that would work well for a wedding. Write a paragraph describing the theme, and give details about how you would apply the theme.

Career Cluster

CCR ☆ College & Career Readiness

Human Services Wedding planners work in the Personal Care Services pathway of this career cluster. Other jobs in this cluster include:

- Manicurist
- Soup Kitchen Manager
- Hairdresser
- Childcare Facilities Director
- Mortician
- Personal Trainer
- School Psychologist
- Financial Planner
- Image Consultant
- Parent Educator
- Sales Consultant
- Career Counselor
- Child Counselor

Explore Further The Human Services career cluster contains five pathways: Early Childhood Development & Services; Counseling & Mental Health Services, Family & Community Services; Personal Care Services; and Consumer Services. Choose one of these pathways to explore further.

 Career Clusters To learn more about career clusters, go to this book's Online Learning Center at **glencoe.com**.

CHAPTER SUMMARY

Section 21.1
Responsible Dating

Going out in groups has benefits, especially when you are just beginning to date. When you start going out with someone, you take on new responsibilities for yourself and for your dating partner. Sexual responsibility includes understanding the risks, handling sexual feelings, and resisting sexual pressure. Crushes, infatuation, jealousy, and breakups challenge people to deal with difficult emotions.

Section 21.2
Decisions About Marriage

An engagement period gives a couple time to prepare for marriage. Every state has laws governing marriage. Teen marriages do not have a high rate of success. Even among mature couples, marriage can pose significant challenges. Communication, sharing, and commitment help create a strong marriage. There are many reasons for choosing to remain single. Marriage is a choice, not a requirement.

Vocabulary Review

1. Create multiple-choice test questions for each content and academic vocabulary term.

Content Vocabulary
- ◇ sexually transmitted infection (STI) (p. 415)
- ◇ crush (p. 417)
- ◇ infatuation (p. 418)
- ◇ jealousy (p. 418)
- ◇ commitment (p. 421)
- ◇ engagement period (p. 421)
- ◇ monogamy (p. 423)
- ◇ annulment (p. 423)

Academic Vocabulary
- ■ compatible (p. 413)
- ■ boundaries (p. 414)
- ■ prohibit (p. 423)
- ■ delay (p. 425)

Review Key Concepts

2. **Explain** reasons for dating different people before getting married.
3. **Provide** guidelines for responsible dating relationships.
4. **Identify** the emotional challenges that may arise in a relationship.
5. **Determine** whether a dating relationship has the potential for commitment.
6. **Summarize** the factors that contribute to marital success and failure.
7. **List** reasons for choosing to remain single.

Critical Thinking

8. **Analyze** What would be your main concerns if you were the parent of a teen who was starting to date? What rules would you set for your son or daughter?
9. **Draw Conclusions** How do crushes and infatuation help prepare people for real love?
10. **Examine** How might being in a relationship make someone a better person?
11. **Distinguish** Why do you think some marriages are better able than others to withstand unexpected challenges?

ACTIVE LEARNING

12. Movie Review Watch a movie that features a dating relationship between two teens. How is this couple responsible or irresponsible in their behavior? Do they demonstrate mutual respect? Do they share common goals and values? Do the characters accurately represent real teen relationships? If this couple existed in real life, would they stand a good chance of having a lasting relationship? Write a review of the movie. Include a description of the relationship based on your observations and on what you learned in the text. Conclude your review by explaining whether or not the relationship would succeed over the long term.

Family & Community Connections

13. Form a Support Group When a relationship does not work out, the emotions that result can be hard to handle. The standard advice is to talk about your feelings. However, teens who feel they cannot talk to a parent about something so personal might end up holding their feelings inside. A peer support group can be a big help. Such groups have rules about how to listen without judging and give caring and helpful feedback. Talk to your school counselor about starting such a group at your school. Ask for guidelines regarding group topics, confidentiality of group members, and any special circumstances that might arise. Discuss group size, location, session length, and scheduling. Create a proposal to present to school administrators.

⭐ 21st Century Skills

Communication Skills

14. Practice Assertiveness When you are assertive and express your feelings with confidence, there is no need to shout or force your point of view. Follow your teacher's instructions to form into groups. Create a list of assertive statements to use in response to pressure from a partner to engage in sexual activity.

Decision-Making Skills

15. Make Difficult Choices Nina and Thomas have been dating exclusively for two years and have begun to talk about marriage. Nina was offered a full scholarship to an out-of-state college. Thomas plans to attend the local university so he can stay home and help take care of his brother, who is disabled. What advice would you offer to Nina and Thomas?

 Connections

Technology Skills

16. Desktop Publishing As part of its mission, FCCLA encourages students to make decisions and assume responsibilities. Dating requires making good use of these skills. Use appropriate software to create a brochure that gives teens advice about how to date responsibly and avoid the risks of sexual activity. Include guidelines given in the text, but add your own ideas as well.

Academic Skills

 English Language Arts

17. Divorce Rates Conduct research on the topic of changing divorce rates. Use this chapter and information from the National Center for Health Statistics to write a report. Cite at least two statistics from different decades as evidence of the divorce rate trend. Include at least one reliable explanation for that trend.

> **NCTE 7** Conduct research and gather, evaluate, and synthesize data to communicate discoveries.

Science

18. Research Love Chemistry Have you ever heard the attraction between two people referred to as "chemistry"? According to scientists, there is truth to this. Naturally occurring chemicals are associated with feeling "in love."

Procedure Ask your teacher for reliable Web sites to research the natural chemical involved in the "chemistry" of love.

Analysis Write a summary that includes an explanation of one natural chemical associated with feelings of being in love.

> **NSES C** Develop understanding of the behavior of organisms.

 Mathematics

19. Saving Money Rosa and Jim plan to drive across the country to visit relatives. They each earn $100 a week and estimate that they will need $1,000 to make the trip. If they are going on the trip in seven months, how much do they need to save each month to have the $1,000 in time for the trip? How much will they have left to spend each month?

 Math Concept **Multiple-Step Problems** Decide what you need to know and when you need to know it. In this problem, answer the first question before you answer the second question.

Starting Hint First, decide how much Rosa and Jim will need to save each month ($1,000 ÷ 7). Then calculate how much they make each month ($100 × 2 × 4 weeks). Then subtract the amount they need for the vacation to find what they have left to spend each month.

 For more math practice, go to the Math Appendix at the back of the book.

> **NCTM Problem Solving** Solve problems that arise in mathematics and in other contexts.

 ## Standardized Test Practice

CCR College & Career Readiness

TIMED WRITING
Read the writing prompt. Then write a one-page essay using details and examples to illustrate your points.

Test-Taking Tip Plan out your essay before you begin writing. Jot down the main points or details you want to focus on in the margins of your test. Refer to these points frequently as you write.

20. Most likely you have experienced feelings of infatuation, or you know someone who has had this experience. Based on what you know and on the material in this chapter, write an essay stating what you understand about infatuation and how it differs from real love. Explain how you would use this knowledge in making decisions about future relationships.

Chapter 22

Workplace Relationships

Chapter Objectives

Section 22.1 The Workplace Environment

- **Explain** how workplace relationships differ from other types of relationships.
- **Identify** strategies for getting along with coworkers.
- **List** guidelines for getting along with supervisors.

Section 22.2 Workplace Relationship Challenges

- **Name** common workplace relationship problems and how to address them.
- **Summarize** the reasons for keeping your personal life out of your workplace.

> ➤ **Explore the Photo**
>
> You must learn how to interact positively with your coworkers if you want to succeed and enjoy work. *What individual qualities can help you do this?*

Write Using Details

Initiative A person who shows initiative looks for what needs to be done and does it without waiting to be asked. In the workplace, this is especially useful. Employers value people who are able to recognize a need and who are willing to act upon it. Write a paragraph about a time when you showed initiative at work or at school. Use details in your writing.

Writing Tips Use these tips to help you write using details:
- Use descriptions that will help bring your subject to life.
- Think about the senses of sight, taste, hearing, smell, and touch to help you choose details.
- Make sure that the detailed sentences in your paragraph support your main idea.

The Workplace Environment

Workplace relationships are different from other relationships.

Reading Guide

Before You Read

Look It Up As you read this section, keep a dictionary handy to use in addition to the glossary at the back of the book. If you hear or read a word that you do not know, look it up in the glossary or the dictionary. Before long, this practice will become a habit.

Read to Learn
Key Concepts

- **Explain** how workplace relationships differ from other types of relationships.
- **Identify** strategies for getting along with coworkers.
- **List** guidelines for getting along with supervisors.

Main Idea

Workplace relationships differ from outside friendships. Following guidelines for good relationships with coworkers and supervisors can help create a positive work environment.

Content Vocabulary

◇ etiquette
◇ supervisor

Academic Vocabulary

You will find these words in your reading and on your tests. Use the glossary to look up their definitions if necessary.

■ contribute
■ objective

Academic Standards

English Language Arts

NCTE 4 Use written language to communicate effectively.

Social Studies

NCSS IV F Individual Development and Identity
Analyze the role of perceptions, attitudes, values, and beliefs in the development of personal identity.

NCTE *National Council of Teachers of English*
NCTM *National Council of Teachers of Mathematics*
NSES *National Science Education Standards*
NCSS *National Council for the Social Studies*

Graphic Organizer

As you read, think about the ways in which coworker relationships are similar to and different from outside friendships. List the qualities that are unique to each type of relationship and the qualities that are common to both. Use a Venn diagram like the one shown to help you.

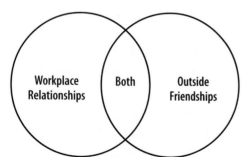

Workplace Relationships | Both | Outside Friendships

 Graphic Organizer Go to this book's Online Learning Center at **glencoe.com** to print out this graphic organizer.

Why the Workplace is Different

Workplace relationships are different from other types of relationships. People work with all different ages and backgrounds, with a wide variety of personalities and attitudes. Building working relationships takes time, but it can be exciting and interesting to be surrounded by so much variety.

Compare working relationships with personal friendships, and you can see some obvious differences:

- **You cannot choose your coworkers.** You may find that you have little in common with some of your coworkers, beyond the fact that you work at the same place.
- **You will not always grow close over time.** Workplace relationships may remain more functional than personal. The focus for everyone in the workplace is to get the job done.
- **You cannot simply end a workplace relationship.** A friendship can be ended by choice if it is not working out. At work, you must find ways to get along with everyone. Also, relationships can end abruptly if you or a coworker leaves a job.

It is important to remember these differences so you can adjust your behavior and your expectations. If you expect a workplace relationship to be like a personal friendship, you will likely encounter problems in the workplace. However, it is also important to remember that you and coworkers have something important in common. You want to have a pleasant, rewarding, and successful work experience. If you base your relationship on this common goal, you are likely to have a positive experience working together.

✓ Reading Check **Clarify** What is meant by "adjust your expectations" when it comes to workplace relationships?

You and Your Coworkers

Good working relationships make any job more enjoyable. Just as important, such relationships **contribute** to, or add to, a positive and productive work environment. Coworkers' attitudes and behaviors in the workplace determine whether or not they are fostering successful working relationships.

Cooperate and Do Your Part

Keep your on-the-job friendships separate from your working relationships. When it comes to job-related matters, such as dividing tasks or coordinating work schedules, everyone needs to be treated equally to maintain a positive workplace environment.

In any job, you have to work cooperatively with others to achieve common goals. You and your coworkers must coordinate your efforts so that everything goes smoothly. Even if you are working independently on an assignment or project, someone else is depending on you.

As You Read

Connect How might positive workplace relationships help make you a more well-rounded person?

▷ Vocabulary

You can find definitions in the glossary at the back of this book.

Your behavior and communications with your coworkers, supervisor, customers, and anyone else with whom you interact on the job depends on you. Know what is expected of you and do it. Doing your part is especially important on a team project. It means putting in extra effort when it is needed. If someone calls in sick, you might have to take on extra work. If your team is behind schedule and facing a crucial deadline, you might have to work late. When you are willing to do what is needed to get the job done, others will notice and appreciate it.

Workplace Etiquette

Good manners are as important in the workplace as in any other area of life. **Etiquette** (ˈe-ti-kət) is a set of behaviors based on showing consideration and respect for others. When you practice workplace etiquette, you demonstrate your ability to get along successfully in a work environment. Here are some standard rules:

- **Respect Ideas** In meetings, give people a chance to be heard without interruption, even if you do not agree with them.
- **Respect Time** Do not disturb others when they are busy, unless it is absolutely necessary. If you need to discuss something with your supervisor or a coworker, ask when it would be convenient to meet. Be on time for meetings, and keep discussions brief and to the point.
- **Respect Space** If you share a work area, keep your part of it tidy. Try not to disturb coworkers with unwanted noise or smells. If a work space neighbor is allergic to roses, do not keep a vase of them right near that person's work space.
- **Respect Privacy** Do not snoop in a coworker's desk, file cabinet, or locker. Try not to listen to coworkers' telephone calls and private conversations or look at their computer screens. Treat other people's computer files the way you would treat personal letters. Do not open them unless they are addressed to you. Remember, respect is a two-way street. When you show respect for your coworkers, you will gain their respect in return.

Being on Time

An important part of workplace etiquette is reliability, which includes being on time. *How might being late for work or a meeting affect your coworkers?*

Communication

When you work as part of a team, speaking, listening, and writing are especially important. You need to be able to provide information that the team needs and receive feedback and information from other team members. Whether you are creating a business letter, memo, report, or an e-mail, clear and concise writing helps you communicate effectively. A poorly written document may cause confusion and misunderstanding.

HOW TO... Work Well with Others

As with any other work-related skill, you can learn how to develop good relationships with your coworkers. The qualities listed here are among those that can help you work effectively with others and avoid friction. No matter where you work, now or in the future, you will find them useful.

Be Sociable You do not have to be friends with everyone on the job, but you do need to be sociable. Behave in a friendly manner, smile, say hello, and be generally pleasant to coworkers.

Use Tact People who have tact know what to do or say in order to avoid offending others. For instance, "You might find it works better if you do it this way" is a more tactful statement than, "You are doing that all wrong."

Be Fair Always treat coworkers fairly. Recognize the efforts of others and give credit where it is due. If you are involved in assigning tasks, do so in a way that distributes the workload as evenly as possible.

Have a Sense of Humor Offering a light-hearted joke during a tense situation can relieve stress and bring people closer together. Make sure, however, that the joke will not offend anyone, or it will have the opposite effect.

Be Patient At some point, you might be asked to teach a coworker a skill or to train a new employee. Have patience with the other person's learning process and mistakes. Remember, you were new on the job once, too.

Communication at work also means asking for help when you need it. Do not be afraid to ask questions or to admit that you do not understand something. To be effective, you need a clear idea of your tasks and responsibilities. Most supervisors are happy to provide guidance. Coworkers can also be a source of advice and tips.

✓ **Reading Check** **Explain** Why is the ability to write effectively such a key skill in most jobs?

▲ Accepting Guidance

Knowing how to ask for help, accept authority, and learn from your supervisor are all important workplace skills. *How might developing such skills affect your future career?*

You and Your Supervisor

The same qualities that enable you to get along with your co workers will help you get along with your supervisor. A **supervisor** is responsible for making sure that people do their work so that projects can be completed and goals can be achieved. Supervisors assign tasks, check progress, and resolve problems.

Accept Authority

Supervisors have knowledge, training, and experience that allows them to oversee the work of others. You are accountable to your supervisor for the quality of your work, and he or she is responsible for evaluating your performance and giving you feedback.

As an employee, you need to recognize your supervisor's position, and respect and accept his or her authority. Follow your supervisor's instructions, and ask for clarification or advice when you need it. Keep your supervisor informed about your work at all times. If any problems arise, discuss them with your supervisor and offer suggestions for solving them.

Take Initiative

Following instructions is important. In addition, supervisors appreciate when employees practice initiative in their work. Initiative is taking action and making decisions without the help or advice of other people. People who show initiative are willing to do what needs to be done without being asked. The key to taking initiative as an employee involves knowing when it is appropriate to move ahead on your own. When faced with a situation in which you can take initiative, ask yourself:

- Is this task within the scope of my job?
- Do I have the knowledge and skills to do this task on my own?
- Have I handled similar tasks successfully in the past?
- Would my supervisor appreciate not being bothered with the details of this task?
- Has my supervisor encouraged me to take initiative?

If the answers to these questions are "yes," this is probably a good situation in which to show initiative. When you use your initiative, you show that you take your work seriously and have your employer's interests in mind. Your supervisor will notice and appreciate your effort.

Respond to Criticism

Your supervisor is responsible for making sure you do your work correctly. If you make mistakes, or if the quality of your work is poor, your supervisor will talk to you about it. Good supervisors will do this in a constructive way. Constructive criticism is feedback that includes suggestions for ways you can learn and improve. The goal of the criticism is not to put you down, but to correct your mistakes and improve your performance. If you receive criticism, you might be tempted to be defensive. However, take a step back and look at the criticism in an **objective**, or detached, manner. In other words, do not take it personally. Remember that your supervisor wants you to succeed.

Many places of business have organized recycling programs to help control the waste that comes with employee use of paper, boxes, cans, and bottles. Ask your supervisor if you can start a recycling program at your workplace, or expand on its current program.

 Podcasts Access the Online Learning Center to download *Managing Life Skills* podcasts.

Section 22.1 — After You Read

Review Key Concepts

1. **Illustrate** how being friends with coworkers can create problems.
2. **Identify** four rules of workplace etiquette.
3. **Compare and contrast** the roles of the supervisor and coworker.

Practice Academic Skills

 English Language Arts

4. Work with a partner to practice writing business e-mails. Assume the roles of a supervisor and an employee. Write one email from the employee to the supervisor regarding a conflict with another worker. Switch roles, then write a second email about a project that is in danger of missing a deadline. Reply to one another's messages for a total of four e-mails.

 Social Studies

5. The qualities that employers seek in employees are often described in the various job opening ads that appear on the Internet or in print media. Examine some of these ads and keep notes on what relationship-oriented qualities are mentioned. Which qualities seem to appear most often? Why do you think employers emphasize them? Share and discuss your findings with the class.

Check Your Answers Check your answers at this book's Online Learning Center at **glencoe.com**.

NCTE 4 Use written language to communicate effectively.

NCSS IV F Analyze the role of perceptions, attitudes, values, and beliefs in the development of personal identity.

Workplace Relationship Challenges

Unique personalities can pose unique challenges.

Reading Guide

Before You Read

Preview Understanding causes and effects can help clarify connections. A cause is an event or action that makes something happen. An effect is a result of a cause. Ask yourself, "Why does this happen?" to help you recognize cause-and-effect relationships in this section.

Read to Learn
Key Concepts
- **Name** common workplace relationship problems and how to address them.
- **Summarize** the reasons for keeping your personal life out of your workplace.

Main Idea
Conflicts, stereotyping, rivalries, and harassment are common problems that impact workplace relationships. It is best to keep personal matters out of the workplace. Sometimes it can be challenging to balance work life and personal life.

Graphic Organizer
As you read, look for ways in which you can solve problems to maintain a work-life balance. Use a problem-solution graphic like the one shown to help you organize your information.

Content Vocabulary
◇ third party
◇ rivalry
◇ resentment

Academic Vocabulary
You will find these words in your reading and on your tests. Use the glossary to look up their definitions if necessary.

■ neutral
■ alternate

Academic Standards

English Language Arts
NCTE 2 Read literature to build an understanding of the human experience.

Mathematics
NCTM Number and Operations Understand the meanings of operations and how they relate to one another.

Social Studies
NCSS VI C Power, Authority, and Governance Analyze and explain ideas and mechanisms to meet needs and wants of citizens, regulate territory, manage conflict, establish order and security, and balance competing conceptions of a just society.

NCTE *National Council of Teachers of English*
NCTM *National Council of Teachers of Mathematics*
NSES *National Science Education Standards*
NCSS *National Council for the Social Studies*

Work-Life Balance Challenges

Problem	Solution
A coworker is too chatty with you during work time.	
You are responsible for the care of a young child or older relative.	
Your friends and relatives tend to call or text you at work just to check in.	
There is an unexpected family matter that needs your attention.	
There is a an issue in your personal life that may affect your job on an ongoing basis.	

 Graphic Organizer Go to this book's Online Learning Center at **glencoe.com** to print out this graphic organizer.

Managing Workplace Personalities

Constance had been on the job for two months. She was learning fast and doing well when Alisha was hired. Due to a lack of office space, Alisha was placed in the same small office with Constance. It did not take long for the two coworkers to realize that, although they were both conscientious workers, they had completely different approaches to their work. Constance liked to listen to music while working. She enjoyed decorating her workspace with photographs and colorful knick-knacks. She also liked when coworkers from other offices would occasionally come by for a brief chat.

Alisha liked to work in a quiet, uncluttered environment. Although she was friendly with her coworkers, she preferred to socialize only during breaks away from her desk. She found Constance's style of working distracting. Constance found Alisha's preferences restrictive. After a few weeks of sharing an office, both found their productivity levels decreasing and their stress levels rising.

When you work full time, you often spend more hours per day with your coworkers than you do with your own family. Occasionally, problems arise in workplace relationships just as they do in other types of relationships. Short of quitting your job, you cannot walk away from a relationship with a coworker. Therefore, you have to confront such relationship challenges and find ways to deal with them. Common problems that impact workplace relationships include conflicts, stereotyping, rivalries, and incidents of harassment. As you read about these problems, consider how you might respond to each problem.

Conflicts

Workplace conflicts may result from personality differences, poor communication, jealousy, and other factors. Conflicts are most likely to occur when people are feeling stress. Sometimes personal problems or distractions can interfere with work. A tight deadline or an especially busy period can make tempers short and lead to ill will. Staff changes, such as layoffs or new management, may make people feel insecure or worried, resulting in irritability or exaggerated responses.

If you become involved in a minor conflict with someone at work, you may be able to resolve it simply by talking things over. Try using the conflict resolution skills explained in Chapter 7. If a conflict is serious or prolonged, talk with your supervisor. Unresolved workplace conflicts can upset the atmosphere for everyone and must be dealt with as quickly as possible.

Some companies have formal policies and procedures for resolving employee conflicts. If a conflict persists, mediation by a third party may be necessary. A **third party** is a person who is not directly involved in or affected by a particular situation. This person is considered **neutral**, or impartial and unbiased.

As You Read

Connect What types of situations might create an atmosphere of stress in the workplace?

◆ Vocabulary

You can find definitions in the glossary at the back of this book.

Be Smart Be Safe

Nighttime Work Safety Working at night comes with its own safety issues. Coworkers can help protect themselves and each other by being aware of and alert to the risks of dark and deserted areas inside and just outside of the workplace.

Write About It Write two or three safety issues that are associated with working a night shift. Then write a list of safety suggestions that might be distributed to nighttime workers.

Practice Sociability

Sociability in the workplace requires being friendly but not intrusive. Sociable people feel comfortable greeting others and making small talk. Why not start sharpening your sociability skills now? In your daily encounters with people, practice making the kinds of conversations you would have with coworkers. Keep a journal of your experiences. If some attempts do not go well, identify ways you can improve next time.

Stereotyping

The American workplace is highly diverse. It presents an opportunity to work alongside people of different ages, genders, ethnicities, cultures, backgrounds, viewpoints, and abilities. These experiences enable us to observe, understand, and appreciate other people's customs, beliefs, and ways of doing things.

For a diverse workplace to succeed, workers must avoid thinking in terms of stereotypes. A stereotype is an expectation that all people in a particular group will have the same qualities or act in the same ways. It is an oversimplified and distorted belief about a person or group. Stereotypes are harmful and unfair because they do not acknowledge individual differences.

The best way to combat stereotyping is to treat people as individuals rather than as part of a group. Do not form an opinion of anyone before you get to know the person. Many businesses and employers sponsor diversity training programs to help employees recognize and overcome stereotyping. Keep an open mind and treat everyone fairly, and you will be able to build good working relationships based on mutual respect.

Showing respect for differences can minimize conflict at work. It shows that you are part of a community of workers with common needs and goals. It is also a good way to broaden your understanding, and perhaps make some exciting discoveries as well.

Life On Your Own

Finding Workplace Solutions

From schools to businesses and from families to friendships, teams are the backbone to success. Your ability to work with others in a team environment makes a major difference in whether you enjoy a fulfilling and successful life. It does not matter whether you are a leader or a follower. What matters is that you can work together with others to achieve a common goal.

How It Works In the workplace, it is not unusual for a team to be assigned a project to complete in a specific amount of time. Sometimes, everything goes as expected and the project is completed without a hitch. At other times, there are unexpected glitches: a team member falls ill; an important piece of equipment breaks down; an unintentional error slows the team's progress. This is when team members must pull together and communicate about solutions, without placing blame on each other.

Try It Out You are the leader of a work team given the task of preparing a 25-page booklet to be used at an important, company-wide meeting. Two hours before the meeting is about to take place, you notice an error on page 12: The term "word processing," which is used four times on the page, reads "worm processing." You call an emergency team meeting to share the news. Some of the team members start blaming the team member who was responsible for proofreading the booklet for the problem.

Your Turn Think of a way to redirect team members' attention away from blaming their teammate and toward working together to solve the problem. How could your attitude toward this challenge affect theirs? Is there humor to be found in the situation? What suggestions might help the team focus on a solution?

Rivalry

Rivalry is a situation in which people compete against each other to gain an advantage. It is natural for people to compete for recognition and advancement, especially in the workplace. Some companies even encourage rivalry by offering rewards and incentives based on specific achievements or overall job performance.

Rivalries among coworkers can have positive and negative effects on the workplace environment. Ideally, rivalries should motivate individuals or teams to do their best, and not cause any hard feelings. However, some workplace rivalries can result in anger and resentment. **Resentment** is ongoing annoyance or anger caused by a sense of having been badly treated.

Some employers work to minimize rivalries by emphasizing cooperation rather than competition. Coworkers who see themselves as members of a team are less likely to compete just to gain an advantage over someone else. Good team players are more concerned about achieving team goals than about who gets the credit.

Working Cooperatively

One way to minimize rivalries in the workplace is to emphasize cooperation over competition. *Why might some employers prefer a competitive working atmosphere?*

Harassment

Workplace harassment can take many forms. Taunting, intimidation, and threats are all examples of harassment. Sexual harassment is unwelcome behavior of a sexual nature, whether physical, verbal, nonverbal, or even written.

Any kind of harassment in the workplace is unacceptable and should not be ignored. Unless someone takes action to stop the harassing behavior, it is likely to continue. If you experience or observe such behavior, report the situation to your supervisor. If the harasser is your supervisor, talk to your supervisor's manager. Workplace harassment is offensive and it violates people's rights. Companies are supposed to adopt and enforce policies to prevent and punish such behavior.

✓ Reading Check) **Recall** What is stereotyping and how can it negatively affect the workplace?

Financial *Literacy*

Hourly Wages

Abby has two part-time job offers. The first pays $15.00 an hour. The second pays $18.00 an hour. Each job is 2 hours a day. She could take the subway, which costs $1.50 each way, to the first job. The second job is further away, and she would have to take the train. A round-trip train ticket costs $6.00. What fraction of her daily pay would she be spending on transportation for each job? Which job should she take?

Math Concept **Fractions** A fraction is part of an entire object. The numerator is the top number of the fraction, and the denominator is the bottom number.

Starting Hint Remember that $6.00 is the total daily transportation cost for the second job, but for the first job, you need to multiply $1.50 by two.

Math For more math practice, go to the Math Appendix at the back of the book.

NCTM Number and Operations Understand the meanings of operations and how they relate to one another.

Eat Breakfast

Find a way to eat breakfast every morning. It may be tempting when you are scrambling to get to work or class to skip it, but your body needs breakfast to replenish your energy supply after you have been sleeping all night. See Chapter 27 for some quick breakfast strategies.

Work Life vs. Personal Life

Have you ever had to wait in a store or other place of business because the person who was supposed to be helping you was chatting on the phone or with a coworker? How did that make you feel? Such situations serve as a good reminder that while you are at work, you should stay focused on the job that you are being paid to do.

A job takes up a lot of your time and energy. In a happy life, however, work is just one part. You need to balance work with personal and family needs. Keeping your personal life out of your workplace is not always easy, but it is important. First, it protects you from the stress of trying to juggle too many things at once. Second, it helps you to be a better employee and coworker.

However, even if you have the best intentions, personal distractions can threaten to take your focus away from your work. Sometimes these distractions come from within the workplace itself. A coworker might come by your work area and start a conversation that is not work-related. It is fine to make small talk with your coworkers occasionally, but keep it brief. After a minute or two, say something like, "I'd like to talk more, but I really need to get back to work now." If you want to continue the conversation, you might offer to meet for lunch or after work.

Two Views One World

Should Coworkers Become Friends?

Some say that if getting along with coworkers is good, then being friends with them is better, but not everyone agrees.

Samantha: I always work better with people when we're friendly, but not friends—not in the way I'm friends with people outside of work. At work, friendships can interfere with your ability to do your job. Suppose you were to get promoted. Could you give orders to a friend? What if you had to report a friend to a supervisor? I think this situation causes too much conflict for everyone, and the whole workplace suffers.

Erica: I don't push it, but I always try to make friends with people at work. I think that work friendships are a bonus. A job can get tough and stressful. When you like and care about your coworkers, it gives the feeling that "we're all in this together." It motivates you. Plus, it is great to find new people with whom to enjoy things outside of work. I mean, you can never have too many friends, right?

Seeing Both Sides
What qualities are common to friendships and good workplace relationships? How might a discussion about these qualities help Samantha and Erica find common ground in this discussion?

More often, distractions come from outside the workplace. Everyone has family responsibilities and personal matters to which they must attend. Responsible workers make the necessary arrangements so that these matters will not disrupt the workplace. For example, working parents arrange for child care or after-school activities. They have an **alternate**, or back-up, plan in case the children cannot go to school or to their regular care provider.

As much as possible, deal with personal and family matters outside working hours. If you must make a personal phone call, do so during your lunch hour or break. Follow any rules about using the company's phones or computers for personal matters. Discourage family members and friends from contacting you at work unless there is an emergency. Help them understand that you have an obligation to your employer and your coworkers.

Although your goal is to keep work life and personal life separate, it is not always possible. If personal or family matters arise that cannot wait, deal with them. However, use as little work time as possible. If there is a continuing concern in your personal life that may impact the job, explain this to your supervisor. Together, try to work out a solution that is fair to both of you.

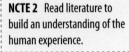

Podcasts Access the Online Learning Center to download *Managing Life Skills* podcasts.

 Section 22.2 **After You Read**

Review Key Concepts

1. **Explain** how rivalry in the workplace can have a positive or a negative effect.

2. **Give** examples of personal distractions that come from within the workplace and those that come from outside of the workplace.

Practice Academic Skills

 English Language Arts

3. Ask for your teacher's help in finding a written scene from a play, movie script, or television script in which characters are together in a place of employment. Read the scene and evaluate the characters' interaction. What does or does not work in their workplace relationship? Write a paragraph with your conclusions.

 Social Studies

4. Use the Internet or library to research the definition of harassment according to the United States Equal Employment Opportunity Commission. Write a summary based upon what you learn. Underline the areas of information that you feel should be highlighted.

Check Your Answers Check your answers at this book's Online Learning Center at **glencoe.com**.

NCTE 2 Read literature to build an understanding of the human experience.

NCSS VI C Analyze and explain ideas and mechanisms to meet needs and wants of citizens, regulate territory, manage conflict, establish order and security, and balance competing conceptions of a just society.

Pathway to College

College Majors

What Is a College Major?

Your college major is the specific academic subject or professional field that you focus on during your time at college. You must demonstrate sustained, high-level work in this particular field. Depending on your college, you might be able to major in two fields, have a major and a minor, or even create your own major.

How do I choose my major?

During the first and second years of college, students often take general education courses, such as English, math, and history, while trying to decide on a major. During this period, you can take different types of classes to figure out which best suit your interests, and which ones you find the most enjoyable. It is also very important to think about the long term. Classes that are fun may not necessarily lead to the career that is right for you, so keep future employment in mind as you start to narrow your major choices.

When do I have to declare a major?

At many colleges, you are not required to declare a major until the end of your sophomore year. If you are attending a two-year program, however, you will likely select your major at the beginning. Keep in mind that not all colleges are the same. It is very important that you are in constant communication with your academic advisor to make sure you are on track.

By choosing my major, am I choosing my profession?

For most students, picking a major is not the same as picking a career. If you major in something very specific, like nursing or accounting, you are learning a specific trade which will likely lead to a specific career. Most majors, however, such as English and history, help prepare you for a variety of careers.

Hands-On College Readiness Pick a college, and go to that school's Web site. Print out a list of all the majors offered. Spend some time looking them over and researching what jobs are associated with specific majors. Then choose a major you think you might be interested in. Write a brief report explaining why you are interested in that specific major.

Path to Success

CCR College & Career Readiness

Get Information When considering a major, talk to students in that major. Meet with professors. Read about the available classes.

Think Ahead If you are interested in a specific career, find out which majors are recommended for that career.

Take It Seriously Choose your major carefully. You are about to invest several years of your life studying a specific subject in detail.

Do the Research Keep an open mind and look into all of your options before deciding.

Take Your Time Choosing a major is not a decision that should be made in an hour, a day, or a week.

Know You Are Not Alone Picking a major is usually done with the help of academic advisors.

 Go to this book's Online Learning Center at **glencoe.com** to learn more about college and career readiness.

CHAPTER SUMMARY

Section 22.1
The Workplace Environment

Workplace relationships differ from friendships in several ways. Do your part, work cooperatively, and communicate clearly to help you get along with coworkers. Workplace etiquette is a matter of being respectful and considerate. To get along with your supervisor, you need to accept authority, take initiative, and respond appropriately to criticism.

Section 22.2
Workplace Relationship Challenges

Problems can arise in workplace relationships just as they can in other types of relationships. Conflicts, stereotyping, rivalries, and harassment are examples of workplace problems that you may encounter on the job. It is important to keep work and personal life separate and maintain a healthy balance of both.

Vocabulary Review

1. Think of an example for each of these vocabulary terms that occurs in everyday work, school, or personal life.

Content Vocabulary
◇ etiquette (p. 434)
◇ supervisor (p. 436)
◇ third party (p. 439)
◇ rivalry (p. 441)
◇ resentment (p. 441)

Academic Vocabulary
■ contribute (p. 433)
■ objective (p. 437)
■ neutral (p. 439)
■ alternate (p. 443)

Review Key Concepts

2. **Explain** how workplace relationships differ from other types of relationships.
3. **Identify** strategies for getting along with coworkers.
4. **List** guidelines for getting along with supervisors.
5. **Name** common workplace relationship problems and how to address them.
6. **Summarize** the reasons for keeping your personal life out of your workplace.

Critical Thinking

7. **Predict** What kinds of situations would be especially difficult to deal with if you became best friends with one of your coworkers? Why?
8. **Conclude** Breaks and lunch hours provide opportunities to be sociable. Why is it a good idea to take advantage of these opportunities?
9. **Apply** Describe one situation that would call for a coworker to take initiative, and one situation in which it would be more appropriate to wait for guidance from a supervisor.
10. **Discriminate** How can you tell the difference between positive and negative rivalry?
11. **Interpret** Does work-life balance mean that you must value your work life and your personal life equally? Explain your answer.

12. Partner Skit Follow your teacher's instructions to form into pairs. Review with your partner the section of the chapter that discusses getting along with supervisors. Together, create a fictional situation in which a supervisor must give constructive criticism to an employee regarding his or her performance on the job. Then present two short skits for your class: one in which the interaction goes well, and one in which the interaction does not go well. Invite classmates to discuss the skits. What made the difference between the two scenarios? How did the participants' behavior affect the outcome?

13. Work vs. Personal Life Interview three different adult friends or family members who work outside of the home. Ask them to describe their experience of trying to keep their work and personal lives separate. Questions to ask may include: What kinds of situations tend to repeat themselves? Which are hardest for you to handle? How do you resolve your challenges? Do you think there are unfair advantages or disadvantages that affect your challenges? What does your employer do to help employees balance their job responsibilites with the demands of a family? Take notes on their responses. Analyze your notes and see if you can find any patterns or themes in your information. Give an oral presentation to the class.

★ 21st Century Skills

Technology Skills

14. Telecommuting Interview an employee or employer who has experience with telecommuting. How does it affect workplace relationships, if at all? Do telecommuting employees feel isolated? Is teamwork affected? What strategies can help? Write a report of your findings.

Interpersonal Skills

15. Resolve a Workplace Conflict Imagine that you have been promoted to assistant manager and are now in charge of the four employees with whom you used to work side by side. Two of these employees do not get along. What strategy would you use to handle this and why?

 Connections

Collaboration Skills

16. Conquer the Generation Gap As part of its mission, FCCLA encourages students to promote greater understanding between youth and adults. People live longer and retire later than ever before. Follow your teacher's instructions to form groups. Brainstorm about ways to bridge the generation gap in the workplace. Create a set of bylaws based on your brainstorming.

Academic Skills

 English Language Arts

17. Write a Song or Rhyme Workplace relationships are the heartbeat of the workplace. When coworkers follow the guidelines of workplace etiquette, the day seems to move to a smooth and pleasant rhythm. Use this concept to write a 3-verse song or rhyme about workplace etiquette. Type up your song or rhyme and make copies to distribute to your class.

> **NCTE 12** Use language to accomplish individual purposes.

 Social Studies

18. FMLA The U.S. Department of Labor's Family and Medical Leave Act (FMLA) of 1993 was enacted to help provide job security to workers who need time off from work for personal reasons. Find an overview of this law on the Internet. Write a brief paragraph stating your point of view about this law. Do you agree with it? Would you change anything about it? Explain your answer.

> **NCSS VI A Power, Authority, and Governance** Examine persistent issues involving the rights, roles, and status of the individual in relation to the general welfare.

 Mathematics

19. Select Data Randomly To analyze time management at work, you are planning to interview members of the community. To obtain an unbiased sample, you need to randomize your choice of interviewees. Should you select interview subjects from a local professional organization, talk to people at a workplace, or pick names out of the phone book?

Math Concept **Randomization**
Randomizing data prevents bias from influencing results. Select a sampling method that involves no prior information about the group being sampled.

Starting Hint Eliminate any group that defines a specific population. For example, selecting interview subjects from only a high school group would mean that your data would not represent the age range, education levels, or other characteristics of the community.

 For more math practice, go to the Math Appendix at the back of the book.

> **NCTM Data Analysis and Probability** Select and use appropriate statistical methods to analyze data.

 Standardized Test Practice

CCR College & Career Readiness

TRUE/FALSE
Read each statement. On a separate piece of paper, write **T** if the statement is true, and **F** if the statement is false.

Test-Taking Tip For true/false questions, look for clue words that usually make a statement false. Some of these words are *always, all, only, none,* and *very.* Words such as *usually* and *generally* are often used with true statements.

20. You can never have a successful workplace relationship with a close friend.

21. It is sometimes challenging to have a workplace relationship with a close friend.

22. Constructive criticism is grounds for dismissal in most cases.

UNIT 6 Portfolio Project

Write a Cover Letter

In this project, you will write a draft cover letter. You will have a local business manager review your letter and provide feedback. You will interview him or her about effective cover letters. You will then make revisions to your cover letter, and create an oral presentation.

My Journal

If you completed the journal entry from page 350, refer to it to see if your thoughts have changed after reading the unit.

Project Assignment

In this project you will:

- Use online and print resources to find and print an appropriate job lead.
- Compare your experience and skills with those required for the job.
- Write a draft cover letter for the job.
- Ask a local business manager to review your cover letter.
- Interview the business manager for information on effective cover letters.
- Make revisions to your cover letter.
- Use the notes from your interview and your cover letter to create an oral presentation for your class.

THE SKILLS BEHIND THE PROJECT

Key personal and relationship skills you will use in this project include:
- Evaluating choices and making decisions
- Communicating respectfully
- Organizing information

Academic Skills

 English Language Arts

> **NCTE 4** Use written language to communicate effectively.
>
> **NCTE 12** Use language to accomplish individual purposes.

STEP 1 Research Job Leads

Use print and online resources to find a written job lead that appeals to you and for which you think you would be well-suited. Ideally, the job should be in a career path in which you are interested. Below are examples of places to find job leads:
- Job listing Web sites
- Newspapers
- Magazines
- Employment agency Web sites
- Company Web sites

STEP 2 Write Your Draft

Compare the job lead you chose with the experience and skills on your résumé. Write a draft of a cover letter introducing yourself and expressing your interest in the job. Check your writing for accuracy and proper grammar and spelling. Your cover letter should "sell" you. It should make you sound like someone a company would want to hire.

Writing Skills

- Remember that your cover letter is making a first impression.
- Use examples that illustrate your points.
- Consider your audience.
- Write in complete sentences.
- Write concisely, meaning your writing is brief but complete.

STEP 3 Connect with Your Community

Locate a manager for a local business who hires employees. Ask him or her to review your cover letter and make suggestions to improve its effectiveness. Interview the manager to find out what information he or she looks for in a good cover letter. Ask what factors can "make or break" a cover letter. Take notes during your interview.

Interview Skills
- Listen attentively.
- Record interview responses, and take notes.
- When you transcribe your notes, write in complete sentences, and use correct spelling and grammar.

STEP 4 Build Your Portfolio Project

Use the Portfolio Project Checklist to plan and build your portfolio project and give an oral report to share what you have learned with your classmates.

Speaking Skills
- Speak clearly and concisely.
- Be sensitive to the needs of your audience.
- Use standard English to communicate.

STEP 5 Evaluate Your Project

Your portfolio project will be evaluated based on:

Academic Skills
- Letter-writing skills
- Interviewing and note-taking skills
- Organization and clarity of your presentation
- Use of technology to create your presentation
- Speaking and listening skills

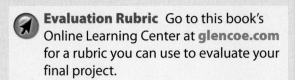

Evaluation Rubric Go to this book's Online Learning Center at **glencoe.com** for a rubric you can use to evaluate your final project.

PORTFOLIO PROJECT CHECKLIST

Plan
- ✔ Using a word processing program, save a copy of your cover letter. Label it "before."
- ✔ Make any recommendations from the manager to the new copy of your cover letter. Save a new version of the cover letter using a word processing program. Label it "after."
- ✔ Transcribe the notes from your interview, and create an oral report about how students can improve cover letters.
- ✔ Illustrate your presentation using the "before" and "after" versions of your cover letter.

Present
- ✔ Give your presentation to the class.
- ✔ Invite the students to ask questions. Answer any questions. Demonstrate in your answers that you respect their perspectives.
- ✔ Turn in your interview notes and copies of your "before" and "after" cover letters to your teacher.

Portfolio Highlights

Cover Letter Technology Tips

A well-written cover letter is an introduction to employers that highlights your skills and experience. You can use technology to help you create even more effective cover letters and to make sure that your letter and résumé get to the right people.

Use Your Research Skills

Use the Internet to search for information on the company to which you are sending the letter. This will help you write a letter that is more personalized, and it will show the company that you took the time to become informed about it.

Contact the Right Person

Avoid simply e-mailing a résumé and cover letter randomly to a company. You should have a reason for choosing a particular contact person, and you should explain that reason in your e-mail. Otherwise the contact person may ignore your e-mail.

Use Words Wisely

Pay careful attention to the words you choose in a cover letter and résumé that you e-mail. Use key words that are important to the job. Employers may keep your e-mail in a database, and these key words can help you get noticed.

Parenting and Caregiving Skills

Unit Portfolio Project Preview

Gather References and Recommendations

In this unit, you will learn about life cycles and the re-sponsibilities and means of support that develop between people throughout their lives. In your portfolio project, you will identify the people who can support you in your future endeavors.

 My Journal

Enlisting Support Write a journal entry about one of the topics below. This will help you prepare for the project at the end of this unit.

- Explain how other people might help you pursue goals.
- Describe the best language to use when asking others for help.
- Tell how you like people to describe you to others whose help you need.

Explore the Photo

From infancy to late adulthood, there are consistent stages of human development. *How do these stages play out in our society's family structure?*

451

Chapter 23

Lifespan Development

Chapter Objectives

Section 23.1 Study of Development

- **Summarize** reasons for studying human development.
- **Identify** the five areas of development.
- **Explain** what makes development unique for each person.

Section 23.2 Patterns of Development

- **Describe** the nine stages of development.
- **Identify** four general categories of disabilities.

> **Explore the Photo**
>
> Development continues throughout a person's life. *How do you think children's development is affected by the people around them?*

Writing Activity Humor

Learning from Mistakes People are constantly learning, and mistakes are a natural part of learning. Being able to laugh at your mistakes shows a sense of humor and makes the learning experience fun. Write a story about a time you or someone else had a humorous learning experience.

Writing Tips To write humorously, follow these steps:
- If you have trouble thinking of a time to write about, try freewriting or brainstorming with a friend.
- Let your natural humor come through in your writing. Do not try to force the humor.
- Be sure to explain what you learned from the experience and how humor helped you get through it.

Study of Development

Learning and developing last a lifetime.

Reading Guide

Before You Read

Guilt-Free Rest If you feel guilty about resting, you are creating more stress. Your reading skills will be more effective if you are relaxed and ready to learn.

Read to Learn
Key Concepts

- **Summarize** reasons for studying human development.
- **Identify** the five areas of development.
- **Explain** what makes development unique for each person.

Main Idea

The five areas of development are physical, intellectual, emotional, social, and moral. Development is unique for everyone.

Content Vocabulary

◇ life-span development
◇ gross motor skills
◇ fine motor skills
◇ temperament
◇ heredity
◇ environment

Academic Vocabulary

You will find these words in your reading and on your tests. Use the glossary to look up their definitions if necessary.

■ interrelated
■ rate

Academic Standards

English Language Arts

NCTE 4 Use written language to communicate effectively.

Mathematics

NCTM Algebra Understand patterns, relations, and functions.

Social Studies

NCSS IV D Individual Development and Identity Apply concepts and theories about the study of human growth and development, such as learning and motivation.

Graphic Organizer

As you read, note the two types of motor skills and examples of each. Use a cluster diagram like the one shown to help you organize your information.

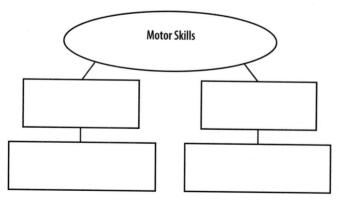

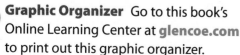

Graphic Organizer Go to this book's Online Learning Center at **glencoe.com** to print out this graphic organizer.

NCTE *National Council of Teachers of English*
NCTM *National Council of Teachers of Mathematics*
NSES *National Science Education Standards*
NCSS *National Council for the Social Studies*

The Journey of Development

Sonia has been away at college for almost a year and has not seen her baby cousin Max since he was a young infant. Last time Sonia saw Max, he was a baby who drank from a bottle, slept a lot, and could barely sit up. Now he is a little dynamo. He can walk across the room, feed himself, play with his toys, and charm his older cousin. Sonia cannot believe what a difference a few months can make.

As You Read

Connect In what ways are you still developing? How are your parents still developing?

Development Throughout Life

What Sonia witnessed was just the beginning of a long journey. Human development is a lifelong process. From the rapid growth of infancy to the more gradual transitions of the later years, change is one of the constant features of life's journey. Consider the many ways that you have changed just in the past few years. This fascinating process will continue throughout the rest of your life.

Life-span development is the growth and change that occurs throughout a person's life. Every aspect of life involves ongoing growth and development. People never finish developing. They are all like works in progress. Every day, people get another chance to work toward becoming who they want to be.

Studying human development will help you better understand yourself and those around you. It helps prepare you to care for children. You influence children even if your contact is not that frequent, perhaps as an older sibling, cousin, babysitter, or even teacher. An understanding of human development also helps you relate to people at other stages, such as your parents or older relatives.

◆ Vocabulary

You can find definitions in the glossary at the back of this book.

Figure 23.1 Human Development Theories

Pioneers in Development Each of these researchers made a major contribution to the study of human development. *What is a common theme among these theories?*

RESEARCHER	MAIN IDEAS OF THEORIES
Sigmund Freud (1856–1939)	Personality develops through a series of stages. Experiences in childhood profoundly affect a person's adult life.
Jean Piaget (1896–1980)	Children go through four stages of learning and must be given learning tasks appropriate to their level of development.
Abraham Maslow (1908–1970)	People have a hierarchy of needs. They can only develop to their fullest if their needs are met. Physical and safety needs must be met before higher needs such as love, esteem, creativity, and morality can be addressed.
Erik Erikson (1902–1994)	There are eight stages of development: infancy, early childhood, preschool, school age, adolescence, young adulthood, middle adulthood, and maturity. In each stage, a crisis or conflict must be solved.
Daniel Levinson (1920–1994)	Focused on adult development. Each person has a life structure, which is the underlying pattern of life at any one time. These patterns change about once a decade as people grow and develop throughout their adult lives.

Development Theories

Many scientists and researchers have studied human development. Some focus on childhood development, when the rate of change is most rapid and the changes are most dramatic. Others study the entire life span of human development. **Figure 23.1** on page 455 shows just a few of these scientists and the main ideas of their development theories. Keep in mind that not everyone agrees on any given theory. Also, not everyone agrees on how people should apply these theories to everyday life. Though development theories differ, most scientists believe that people develop in stages. While this is useful for observing and measuring growth, it suggests a precision that does not really exist. Stages of development do not arrive and depart on a schedule. You may enter a stage earlier than someone else and remain there longer. The stages as defined by each theorist are intended to be used only as general guidelines. Every person will grow and develop in a unique way.

✔ **Reading Check** **Identify** Which development theorist believed we have a hierarchy of needs?

Areas of Development

Human development is an amazing, complex process. Each person develops into a unique individual with his or her own appearance, abilities, and personality. Even so, certain general patterns can be seen in the development process. The changes that take place as you develop can be grouped into five areas: physical, intellectual, emotional, social, and moral. In each area, changes continue throughout life.

Physical Development

Changes in appearance, strength, and coordination are all part of physical growth and development. Physical development involves motor skills, or muscle movements. There are two basic types of motor skills. **Gross motor skills**, also known as large motor skills, are skills that use the large muscles of the body, such as those of the legs and shoulders. You use these skills to walk, run, jump, swim, and lift things. **Fine motor skills**, also called small motor skills, are skills involving the smaller muscles of the body, such as those in the fingers. Fine motor skills are needed for tasks such as writing, playing a musical instrument, and using tools.

Succeed in SCHOOL and LIFE

Mood Swings

Do you ever feel like you are on an emotional roller coaster? To deal with mood swings, start by recognizing that they are a normal part of adolescence. Talk to friends and family members about your feelings. Find time to do things that relax you and help you let off steam. If necessary, find tactful ways to let others know that you need some time alone.

Intellectual Development

This area of development involves your ability to think, understand, reason, and communicate. Young children first experience the world through their senses. Gradually they learn to organize the information their senses give them and put it into words. Intellectual development is not shown only through school work. Intelligence can be seen in many ways, such as musical talent, creative skills, and problem-solving abilities. As people grow older, they begin to learn that actions have consequences. Predicting outcomes helps improve the ability to plan and prepare. People continue to learn through their senses. Some people learn better from one sense than another. This represents their different learning styles. For example, learning by listening is called auditory learning. Learning by seeing is called visual learning. A kinesthetic learner will learn best by actually doing something. Knowing how a person learns best can help develop his or her learning skills. Learning is often reinforced, though, by using more than one style. For example, taking notes in class involves both listening and doing.

Emotional Development

Infants have limited ways of expressing emotion. They cry if they are sad and smile if they are happy. As children mature, they learn to recognize and express more complex emotions and to handle them in socially acceptable ways. Emotional development also involves the development of self-esteem.

Social Development

Social development involves learning to relate to other people. Children start to develop social skills at an early age. They gradually learn to get along with other children, share, and make friends. More complex social skills, such as cooperating, negotiating, and building different kinds of relationships, develop over time.

Everyone has a unique temperament. **Temperament** is an inborn style of reacting to the world and relating to others. Infants reveal their temperaments in how active and persistent they are, how well they adapt to new people and events, and how they respond to their environment. A person's basic temperament is inherited and lasts throughout life. This does not lock you into specific behavior, though. You can always learn new ways to deal with people.

 Building Blocks

The five areas of development build on one another. *Which areas do you think these children are developing by doing this activity?*

Moral Development

Very young children have no concept of right or wrong. Their actions are driven mainly by self-interest. With guidance, children learn what acceptable behavior is and that their actions have effects on others. They learn to understand right from wrong. Once they understand the difference, they develop a conscience that will guide their behavior and help them develop moral standards. Moral development is vital for society as well as for individuals. Society is weakened when people do not consider others.

How Development Works

The five areas of development are interrelated. **Interrelated** means each area is affected by the others. Think of the development required to speak. Physically, children need to have developed good hearing as well as control of the muscles used for speech. Intellectually, they need the mental capacity to communicate. Socially, they need to be able to interact with others and imitate role models.

Most children follow the same basic sequence of development, building on what they learn. For instance, they babble before they speak, and they crawl before they walk. What differs from individual to individual is the **rate**, or speed, of development. Some children develop more rapidly than others. One child may begin to walk at ten months. Another may not walk until 15 months. One child may use ten words at 18 months of age. Another may use 50 words at the same age. Each person develops in his or her own time.

✓ **Reading Check**　**Define**　What is social development?

Influences on Development

What makes development so highly individual? The source of your uniqueness is a complex interplay between the traits that you inherit and the environment you grow up in. The combination of these influences is different for every person.

◀ Made That Way

Heredity plays a large part in how a person looks, but it has an effect on other traits as well. *What are some traits that you inherited from your parents?*

Heredity

Heredity refers to the set of characteristics that you inherit from your parents and ancestors. You inherit these characteristics through genes, the basic units of heredity that are passed from parents to children. The genes determine physical traits such as eye and hair color, height, and build. They may also help to determine your emotional makeup, or temperament. For example, the tendency to be easygoing or shy may be inherited.

Environment

Your environment also has a profound impact on your development. **Environment** is the people, places, and things that surround and influence a person, including family, home, school, and community. Home life, for example, influences children's development. A loving home environment will have positive effects on emotional development. A family's living conditions, economic status, culture, traditions, level of education, access to health care, and community involvement are also environmental aspects that can influence a child's development. Even technology affects development. Technological advances can bring a higher standard of living through better health care and more widespread education. Television and computer technology enable people to expand their knowledge. On the other hand, spending too much time in front of a television or computer could cause people to miss out on social interaction.

 Podcasts Access the Online Learning Center to download *Managing Life Skills* podcasts.

Section 23.1 — After You Read

Review Key Concepts

1. **List** five researchers who have studied human development.
2. **Summarize** how the five areas of development work together.
3. **Describe** what makes up a person's environment.

Practice Academic Skills

 English Language Arts

4. Consider how a person's moral development impacts society as a whole. Think about a recent news story you heard or read. Write a case study in which you describe what happened in the news story, and analyze the impact the action had on the people involved and on society.

 Social Studies

5. Identify a child development researcher, and use print or online resources to learn about his or her theory, as well as how that theory can be used in teaching children. Prepare a presentation to share your findings with the class.

Check Your Answers Check your answers at this book's Online Learning Center at **glencoe.com**.

NCTE 4 Use written language to communicate effectively.

NCSS IV D Apply concepts and theories about the study of human growth and development, such as learning and motivation.

Patterns of Development

People go through many stages between infancy and old age.

Reading Guide

Before You Read

Understanding It is normal to have questions when you read. Write down questions while reading. Many of them will be answered as you continue. If they are not, you will have a list ready for your teacher when you finish.

Read to Learn
Key Concepts
- **Describe** the nine stages of development.
- **Identify** four general categories of disabilities.

Main Idea

There are many stages of human development that people typically go through from conception to late adulthood. Some people have special needs which must be recognized as soon as possible.

Content Vocabulary
◇ developmental tasks
◇ prenatal
◇ embryo
◇ fetus
◇ reflex
◇ hand-eye coordination
◇ bonding
◇ parallel play
◇ cooperative play
◇ puberty

Academic Vocabulary

You will find these words in your reading and on your tests. Use the glossary to look up their definitions if necessary.

■ prone
■ key

Academic Standards

 English Language Arts

NCTE 5 Use different writing process elements to communicate effectively.

Social Studies

NCSS I A Culture Analyze and explain the ways groups address human needs and concerns.

Graphic Organizer

As you read, note at least one characteristic of intellectual development from infancy through adolescence. Use a chart like the one shown to help you organize your information.

Stage	Characteristics of Intellectual Development
Infancy	
Toddler Years	
Preschool Years	
School-Age Years	
Adolescence	

Graphic Organizer Go to this book's Online Learning Center at **glencoe.com** to print out this graphic organizer.

NCTE *National Council of Teachers of English*
NCTM *National Council of Teachers of Mathematics*
NSES *National Science Education Standards*
NCSS *National Council for the Social Studies*

Developmental Stages

Humans develop in distinct stages that correspond roughly to chronological age. During each stage, humans experience changes in the five areas of development you read about in Section 23.1: physical, intellectual, emotional, social, and moral. Each stage of development, from infancy to late adulthood, is marked by certain tasks. **Developmental tasks** are skills and abilities that are mastered as part of the maturing process. Some of these tasks are obvious, such as learning to walk. Others are more subtle, such as learning to reason and think logically.

Prenatal Development

Prenatal means before birth. Prenatal development refers to the process that begins with conception and ends with birth. During the first eight weeks of pregnancy, the developing baby is called an **embryo** ('em-brē-ˌō). During this phase, all major body structures and internal organs form, and the heart begins to beat. From the ninth week until birth, the developing baby is called a **fetus** ('fē-təs). During this phase, bones harden, muscles grow, and body systems reach full development.

Infancy

In their first year of life, infants undergo dramatic changes in all five areas of development. The changes that take place during infancy occur more rapidly than at any other stage of life.

Physical Newborns have many inborn abilities. They use all five senses, although vision is blurred at first. They also have several reflexes. A **reflex** is an instinctive, automatic response, such as grasping and sucking. During infancy, newborns start to develop **hand-eye coordination**, which is the ability to move the hands and fingers precisely in relation to what is seen. As gross motor skills develop, they learn to roll over, sit up, crawl, and stand.

Intellectual Soon after birth, babies can follow the movement of objects with their eyes and turn their heads toward sounds. They learn to communicate by crying to express hunger, anger, and discomfort. They learn to wave bye-bye, play peek-a-boo, and respond to simple requests, such as "Point to your nose."

Emotional Infants develop trust through bonding. **Bonding** is the act of forming emotional ties between parents and child. Through daily contact with parents, babies learn that their basic needs for food, safety, cleanliness, and closeness will be met. This gives them the security to learn and thrive.

Social and Moral Babies learn to smile at about three months. By seven months, they start to recognize faces and voices and respond to their name. Although there is debate among researchers about when moral development begins, as infants get older they begin to understand right and wrong.

As You Read

Connect What factors do you think are affecting your emotional development as a teen?

Vocabulary

You can find definitions in the glossary at the back of this book.

The Toddler Years

Physical growth usually slows as infants become toddlers. During this stage, which lasts from about ages one to three, children master an amazing number of skills.

Physical Most toddlers begin walking by 15 months. By two years, they can usually run, climb, and walk up and down stairs. Parents should encourage them but watch them closely to prevent accidents. As toddlers' fine motor skills develop, they learn to dress themselves and play with more complex toys.

Intellectual Language skills grow from a few simple words to short phrases to complete sentences. Toddlers begin to grasp basic intellectual concepts, such as cause and effect. They learn about size and space. They might also start to enjoy looking at books with colorful pictures and short, repetitive sentences.

Emotional As toddlers learn to do things for themselves, they began to think of themselves as capable individuals, separate from their parents and caregivers. Their self-esteem grows as the people around them encourage them. They often express strong emotions and have many mood changes.

Social Toddlers tend to engage in parallel play. **Parallel play** is when children play near, but not actually with, other children. Around the age of two, toddlers struggle to assert their independence. They want to do everything themselves. Toddlers often experience frustration, which may result in temper tantrums.

Moral Toddlers begin to develop a sense of right and wrong. Through the reactions of caregivers to what they do, toddlers discover that some behaviors are acceptable while others are not. They start to test the limits of what they are allowed to do.

The Preschool Years

Preschoolers are between three and five years old. They are more independent and have better control over their bodies. They are starting to build skills that will help prepare them for school.

Physical Gross motor skills further develop. Preschoolers can hop, run, pedal a tricycle, and throw and catch a ball. Their fine motor skills, too, are better developed. They learn to draw recognizable objects, print their names, and use scissors to cut paper.

Intellectual Most preschoolers start to count, identify colors, and recognize letters. As their vocabulary grows, they learn to express more complex ideas and ask a lot of "how" and "why" questions. They often enjoy playing dress-up and make believe.

Emotional Language skills are improving, so they can express themselves more easily and with less frustration. They are less self-centered. They begin to show understanding for the thoughts and feelings of others. Preschoolers experience a full range of emotions, from anger and anxiety to joy and pride. They may be fearful as they cannot yet distinguish between fantasy and reality.

Social During the preschool years, children move from parallel play to cooperative play. **Cooperative play** is a type of play in which children play and interact with one another. These play activities help children learn to take turns, share, and solve problems together. Around age four or five, a child is likely to choose another child as a best friend.

Moral Preschoolers have a rigid sense of right and wrong. They get upset when someone does not follow the rules set by adults. Some believe that preschoolers behave well to be rewarded or to avoid punishment. Others believe that they are beginning to understand basic moral concepts such as fairness and justice.

The School-Age Years

When children reach school age, they begin to spend large periods of time in a structured setting away from home. Interaction with other adults and with their peers helps them continue to build their skills.

Physical Physical growth slows down. Baby teeth are replaced by permanent ones. School-age children can ride a bicycle and participate in games that involve more skillful running, jumping, and throwing. The continued development of fine motor skills allows them to write and draw more precisely.

Intellectual During the school-age years, curiosity continues. They ask many questions and acquire reasoning skills as they think about why and how things happen. They build on these skills to master more complex tasks. They learn to use symbols such as numbers and letters, which enables them to read and do simple arithmetic.

Emotional School-age children begin to outgrow their preschool fears. However, they are more **prone**, or sensitive, to stress caused by academic pressures or events at home, such as divorce or moving to a new home. Those with high self-esteem and supportive families are more likely to handle stress effectively.

Social School-age children generally have more social opportunities outside the family. They form peer groups that help them learn how to negotiate and compromise in group settings. Children also continue to develop skills that society values, such as sharing and considering the feelings of others.

Moral School-age children begin to understand that some rules are flexible and can be changed. They care about what other people think, and most want to be thought of as good. A child's conscience takes on a stronger role.

Encouraging Skills

School-age children are building a variety of skills, including reasoning skills, math skills, and social skills. *What skills are these children working on?*

Adolescence

Adolescence, or the teen years, is a time of change in all areas of development. It is the period in life when you prepare for adulthood. Responding to the changes in positive ways eases the transition.

Physical Adolescence begins with puberty. **Puberty** is the changes triggered by hormones that result in a physically mature body that is able to reproduce. When puberty begins and ends varies, but it is similar for everyone. One obvious change is the body taking on the characteristics of a man or a woman.

Intellectual New intellectual skills enable teens to imagine consequences of different actions and consider alternatives. They develop the ability to reflect on the results of decisions and to learn from mistakes. Teens are better able to think in abstract terms. They can think things through, test ideas, and form judgments.

Emotional Hormones also affect emotions. Mood swings are common, and many teens experience stress related to the changes. Teens may wrestle with the desire to be treated as an independent adult in some situations and to have someone take care of them in others. Adolescence also brings increased sexual awareness.

Social It is typical for teens to spend more time with peers and less time with family. Family is still important, though, and many teens continue to look to parents for advice. Friendships become deeper and more stable. Though romantic feelings may develop, many teens are not yet ready for one-to-one relationships.

Moral Most teens know the difference between right and wrong, but do not always act accordingly. Because they want to fit in and please others, they may feel pressured to go along with the crowd. One of the responsibilities of becoming an adult is to examine your beliefs and develop a strong value system of your own.

Early Adulthood

Early adulthood stretches from the late teens to the late thirties. This is when individuals determine who they are and what they want to do. For many people, these are some of the busiest years of their lives. They complete or continue their education, establish a career, gain financial independence, and build long-term relationships.

Physically, young adults are at their peak. They have finished growing and have the potential to enjoy a high level of fitness. However, because many work in jobs that do not require physical activity, they must make an effort to stay active and fit.

Intellectually, young adults can enjoy the mental stimulation that comes from establishing a career and working toward career goals. Learning is a lifelong process, and those who recognize this and create opportunities to learn will benefit from it over the years.

This stage is often a very sociable time. Many people enjoy exploring new interests and spending time with a variety of people. It is during this stage, too, that many people marry and start families.

Middle Adulthood

Middle adulthood, from the forties to the mid-sixties, is often a period of reflection and contemplation. Many people at this stage of life evaluate their lives and re-examine their priorities. Some face major life events such as divorce and remarriage, children leaving home, the birth of grandchildren, or the illness or death of loved ones. For many people in middle adulthood, life becomes a balancing act between work, family, and social commitments. Those in the so-called "sandwich generation," who care for both children and aging parents, can be particularly stretched by conflicting demands. However, this can also be a very fulfilling and enjoyable stage in life since people are often more comfortable with themselves and more settled than during earlier life stages.

Adults can remain physically fit during these years if they stay active and eat a healthful balance of nutritious foods. Still, sooner or later, some physical changes associated with aging become noticeable, such as gray hairs or a need for reading glasses. Some respond to the signs of aging with alarm and a flurry of attempts to slow the process down. Others accept that they are growing older and concentrate on enjoying their families, careers, and involvement in their community.

Many adults realize their professional goals during this stage. Some decide to seek fulfillment and intellectual stimulation in a different field of work. Many in middle adulthood take up new hobbies and join clubs or other organizations. Pursuing new challenges and keeping the mind active can help maintain mental fitness.

Life On Your Own

Change Your Perspective

Sometimes a solution seems obvious to you but not to someone else. Different types of people come up with different ideas and see things in different ways. This is why collaborations are often so successful, but it is important to remember that not everyone sees the world the way you do. To agree on the solution to a problem, it can be helpful to look at the situation from a different perspective.

How It Works To appreciate someone else's perspective, try putting yourself in his or her place. What are the other person's concerns and needs? When you change your perspective, you can see why other people's priorities are different from yours. You develop greater empathy and become more willing to compromise. You can start working toward a real solution, one that you can both agree on.

Try It Out Imagine that at the age of 76, your strong-willed great-uncle admits he is starting to feel his age. Arthritis and failing eyesight make working in his kitchen and negotiating the stairs in his home difficult, perhaps even dangerous. Your family wants your great-uncle to move into an assisted living community, but he will not hear of it. "I can still take care of myself," he insists. "I absolutely love my house, and I'll never leave it."

> *Your Turn* Defend the position either of your family or your great-uncle. Write a paragraph explaining your concerns. In small groups, identify differences in the two perspectives. Focus on outcomes both parties want, and suggest possible workable solutions.

Thanks to advances in health care and medicine, many enjoy active and productive lives in their seventies, eighties, and beyond. It is not uncommon for seniors to work beyond retirement age, either because they want to or because they cannot afford to stop working. Whether working or retired, older adults can find these years enjoyable. A lot depends on an individual's health, financial situation, and attitude.

Physical changes may cause older people to slow down. The joints often become less flexible, and muscles may become weaker. Many experience some loss of vision or hearing. Mental abilities often start to decline with age. It may take longer to learn new tasks, it often becomes more difficult to recall facts, and short-term memory loss may occur. Emotionally and socially, late adulthood can be difficult because many older people must deal with the death of a spouse or other loved ones.

In spite of these challenges, the majority of older people are able to lead active, fulfilling lives. A positive attitude is a **key**, or very important, factor. Many seniors choose to stay as physically active as possible, to continue learning new things, and to maintain social relationships. They keep up with current events and stay involved in the community. As older adults tend to have more time on their hands than in previous life stages, many may choose to spend more time with family and friends and to explore activities they enjoy. Older people who feel they are still making a useful contribution are most likely to gain satisfaction from their later years.

✓ **Reading Check** **Contrast** Explain the difference between parallel play and cooperative play.

Special Needs

Some people have needs significantly different from those of the typical person. These people are said to have special needs. Like everyone else, people with special needs want to experience success and feel good about what they do. It is important for special needs to be recognized as soon as possible if people are to reach their full potential.

Most special needs involve a disability of some kind. Disabilities can be present from birth, although they might not be recognized right away. People may also become disabled later in life due to disease, injury, or problems of aging. Here are some examples of special needs:

▲ Active Retirement

Many seniors continue to live active lifestyles after retiring from work. *How are these seniors enriching their lives?*

Succeed in SCHOOL and LIFE

Aging Gracefully

Growing old does not have to mean becoming irrelevant. As in all stages of life, it is important to stay mentally active, but it is even more important for the elderly. You can use these tips in your later life or when interacting with elderly people in your life. To stay mentally active: read and write, do crossword puzzles, attend lectures, go to plays, play board games, remain social, or take classes.

- Physical disabilities include disabilities that limit movement, vision, or hearing.
- Mental disabilities affect intellectual development and everyday life skills.
- Learning disabilities affect the ability to understand or use language. People with learning disabilities often have average or above average intelligence, but have difficulty with certain tasks such as listening, reading, spelling, or doing math problems.
- Emotional problems may be indicated by withdrawal from others, aggressiveness, or violence, especially if these behaviors are extreme or repeated.

Recognizing and meeting special needs is essential at any time of life. However, it is especially important during childhood, since the early years are such a crucial time for development. Fortunately, much is known today about appropriate support for children with special needs. Children with learning disabilities, for example, can learn quite well as long as they have instruction that is tailored to their needs. When a disability is correctly diagnosed and treated, much can be done to help the person reach his or her full potential.

People with special needs are like everyone else in most ways. They have the same basic needs for friendship, respect, and dignity. Children with special needs, like all children, need love and guidance. The greatest desire of most people with disabilities is to fit in with others and be as independent as possible.

Get Involved!

Read for the Visually Impaired

In many communities, there are opportunities for people to volunteer to read aloud to the visually impaired. You may be asked to read letters, novels, the newspaper, or other printed materials. You could read directly to a person or record your voice to be played later.

 Podcasts Access the Online Learning Center to download *Managing Life Skills* podcasts.

Section 23.2 — After You Read

Review Key Concepts

1. **Explain** what a developmental task is.
2. **Describe** why it is important to recognize special needs as soon as possible.

Practice Academic Skills

 English Language Arts

3. This chapter stated that a sense of humor is helpful for dealing with the physical changes of adolescence. Create a comic strip in which you give an example of a situation in which humor could be useful to cope with these changes. Comics can include original art, clip art, or pictures found in magazines or online.

 Social Studies

4. Choose one of the types of disabilities identified in the text, and research groups in your community that help individuals with that type of disability. Create a trifold brochure in which you identify the groups researched and the type of services they offer.

 Check Your Answers Check your answers at this book's Online Learning Center at **glencoe.com**.

> **NCTE 5** Use different writing process elements to communicate effectively.

> **NCSS I A** Analyze and explain the ways groups address human needs and concerns.

Pathway to Your Career

Social Worker

What Does a Social Worker Do?

Social workers help people by teaching them how to deal with everyday issues, improve their relationships, and solve their personal problems. There are many different types of social workers. Some help clients who face disability, disease, unemployment, or substance abuse issues. Others help families with serious conflicts, such as domestic abuse. Social workers conduct research and are often involved in policy development.

Career Readiness Skills Social workers must have a desire to help others and an ability to relate to different types of people. They should be fair and sensitive to people and their problems. They should be emotionally intelligent, strong communicators, and able to refrain from judging others.

Education and Training A bachelor's degree, usually in social work, psychology, or sociology, is the minimum requirement for entry into this occupation. All states have licensing requirements, and although standards vary by state, most place a lot of importance on communication skills, professional ethics, and sensitivity issues.

Job Outlook Employment opportunities for social workers are expected grow faster than the average over the next decade. Due to a growing elderly population, job prospects should be especially favorable for social workers specializing in the aging population.

Critical Thinking There are many types of social workers, including family, school, mental health, and gerontological social workers. Choose one specialty and research it. Theorize about why someone might be drawn to that specialty. Write a paragraph summarizing your findings.

Career Cluster

CCR ☆ College & Career Readiness

Health Science Social workers work in the Therapeutic Services pathway of this career cluster. Other jobs in this cluster include:

- Nurse
- Optometrist
- Pharmacist
- Physician
- Lab Technician
- Acupuncturist
- Paramedic
- Radiation Therapist
- Biochemist
- Pharmacy Manager
- Toxicologist
- Art Therapist
- Physical Therapist
- Patient Advocate
- Veterinarian
- EMT
- Geneticist
- Dentist

Explore Further The Health Science career cluster contains five pathways: Therapeutic Services; Diagnostics Services; Health Informatics; Support Services; and Biotechnology Research & Development. Choose one of these pathways to explore further.

 Career Clusters To learn more about career clusters, go to this book's Online Learning Center at **glencoe.com**.

CHAPTER SUMMARY

Section 23.1
Study of Development

Development is a unique and complex process that follows general stages and patterns. Various theorists have looked at ways to describe human development. The five development areas are physical, intellectual, emotional, social, and moral. These interrelate to create growth and change. Heredity, environment, technology, and other influences also have an impact on how a person develops.

Section 23.2
Patterns of Development

Development is marked by certain tasks in a chronological order. It begins with conception and continues to late adulthood. Infancy, toddlerhood, and adolescence have more dramatic, rapid changes. Preschoolers and school-age children learn to function away from home. Adults focus on balancing responsibilities. Some people also have special needs that influence their development.

Vocabulary Review

1. Arrange the vocabulary words into groups of related words. Explain your choices.

Content Vocabulary
◇ life-span development (p. 455)
◇ gross motor skills (p. 456)
◇ fine motor skills (p. 456)
◇ temperament (p. 457)
◇ heredity (p. 459)
◇ environment (p. 459)
◇ developmental tasks (p. 461)
◇ prenatal (p. 461)

◇ embryo (p. 461)
◇ fetus (p. 461)
◇ reflex (p. 461)
◇ hand-eye coordination (p. 461)
◇ bonding (p. 461)
◇ parallel play (p. 462)
◇ cooperative play (p. 463)
◇ puberty (p. 464)

Academic Vocabulary
■ interrelated (p. 458)
■ rate (p. 458)
■ prone (p. 463)
■ key (p. 466)

Review Key Concepts

2. **Summarize** reasons for studying human development.
3. **Identify** the five areas of development.
4. **Explain** what makes development unique for each person.
5. **Describe** the nine stages of development.
6. **Identify** four general categories of disabilities.

Critical Thinking

7. **Draw Conclusions** Do you think heredity or environment has a stronger influence on a person's development? Explain your answer.
8. **Predict** How does the way a pregnant woman cares for herself affect the development of her baby?
9. **Appraise** If a 7-year-old boy wants to play on the soccer team for 7- to 9-year-olds, what developmental tasks should his parents be sure he has?
10. **Analyze** Identify a risky behavior, and examine how adolescent development plays a part when teens participate in or resist this behavior.
11. **Relate** What suggestions would you give to a friend who has difficulty getting along with his or her 10-year-old sibling?

ACTIVE LEARNING

12. Screen Time Create a survey to determine the approximate amount of time people are using screens on a daily basis. Include activities such as watching TV and movies, using the computer, and texting. Ask ten parents about the average amount of screen time they and their children use daily. As a class, compile and graph your results according to the developmental stage. What conclusions can you draw? Is there a link between age and screen time use? How does screen time use vary among developmental stages? How is screen time positive? How is it negative?

Family & Community Connections

13. Relate to Older Family Members Understanding adult development can help you relate better to older family members. Identify neighbors or other individuals in late adulthood at a local retirement or assisted-living center. Interview several residents about the changes they have experienced in their health and activities since age 55. What changes have they made in their lifestyles? How have their relationships changed? What makes them feel valued and worthwhile? Using the information gathered, describe ways you can interact with an elderly family member or close neighbor to show an understanding of their needs. Create a visual presentation of the information. Share your presentation with the class.

★ 21ˢᵗ Century Skills

Media Literacy Skills

14. TV Programs That Teach Watch an educational television program for preschoolers. Divide a paper into two columns. In the left column, summarize what is taking place in each segment of the show. In the right column, identify the developmental skills each segment is teaching.

Adaptability Skills

15. Interact with Children Imagine you are a child care worker who is moving from working in the toddler room to working in the preschool room. Outline how you will adapt your expectations and interactions with preschoolers. Consider such topics as how you would talk with a preschooler and how you would respond to the ways preschoolers express feelings.

FCCLA Connections

Technology Skills

16. Stages of Development As part of its mission, FCCLA encourages students to develop practical knowledge. Follow your teacher's instructions to form into groups. Research a specific developmental stage. Using presentation software, communicate information about the stage you selected. Deliver the presentation to your class or FCCLA chapter.

Academic Skills

 English Language Arts

17. An Infant's Perspective Imagine you are an infant learning to sit up or say your first words. How do you think you would view your world? What would you be thinking and feeling? How would you develop this skill? Write a letter to your parents sharing your perspective. Express your joys and frustrations in achieving this developmental task.

> **NCTE 4** Use written language to communicate effectively.

 Science

18. Observe Children Learn about human development by watching children play. **Procedure** Create an observational checklist of one area of developmental tasks for a specific age. With a parent's permission, observe a child in the selected age range for at least 20 minutes. Record the child's behaviors.

Analysis Is this child developmentally on target? What behaviors lead to your conclusion?

> **NSES A** Develop understandings of scientific inquiry.

 Mathematics

19. Temper Tantrums Children ages one to three tend to have temper tantrums because they feel frustrated when they cannot put their needs and wants into words. Translate the following verbal statement about tantrums into an algebraic expression: Cathy and Robert's baby has twice as many temper tantrums per day as Scott and Krystal's baby.

Math Concept **Algebraic Expressions** Algebraic expressions use variables as placeholders for changing values. Unlike algebraic equations, algebraic expressions do not have equal signs.

Starting Hint Assign a variable for Cathy and Robert's baby (x) and one for Scott and Krystal's baby (y). Then use those two variables to write your algebraic expression.

 For more math practice, go to the Math Appendix at the back of the book.

> **NCTM Algebra** Represent and analyze mathematical situations and structures using algebraic symbols.

Standardized Test Practice

 CCR College & Career Readiness

READING COMPREHENSION
Read the passage, and then answer the question.

> **Test-Taking Tip** Read the passage carefully, noting key statements as you go. Answer the questions based only on what you just read in the passage, not on your previous knowledge.

A baby is playing at home when a stranger walks by the window and waves. Confused, the baby looks to his mother who waves back at the passerby and smiles. The baby is reassured. This baby has just shown social referencing, the process of assessing other people's facial expressions to decide how to react to a situation.

20. According to the passage, social referencing:
  a. only occurs in babies.
  b. involves facial expressions.
  c. is a self-comforting technique.
  d. happens only when strangers are present.

Chapter 24

Child Care

Chapter Objectives

Section 24.1 **Basic Needs and Safety**

- **Identify** five areas of basic needs for which children depend on their caregivers.
- **Give** examples of three ways to childproof a home.
- **List** eleven common childhood injuries.
- **Describe** four types of substitute child care.

Section 24.2 **Positive Guidance and Nurturing**

- **Identify** four areas in which a child has needs beyond physical needs.
- **Explain** three ways to help guide children's behavior.
- **Summarize** how play promotes a child's development.

➤ Explore the Photo

Raising a happy, healthy child means more than just providing food and diapers. *How is this parent contributing to the child's emotional or intellectual needs?*

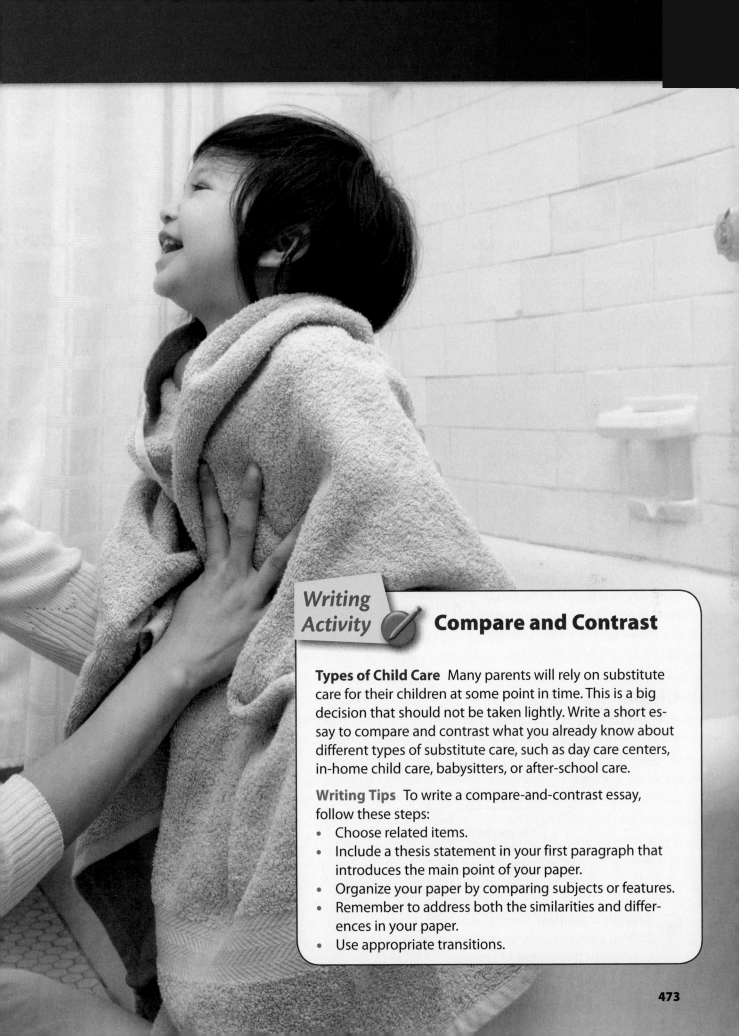

Writing Activity

Compare and Contrast

Types of Child Care Many parents will rely on substitute care for their children at some point in time. This is a big decision that should not be taken lightly. Write a short essay to compare and contrast what you already know about different types of substitute care, such as day care centers, in-home child care, babysitters, or after-school care.

Writing Tips To write a compare-and-contrast essay, follow these steps:

- Choose related items.
- Include a thesis statement in your first paragraph that introduces the main point of your paper.
- Organize your paper by comparing subjects or features.
- Remember to address both the similarities and differences in your paper.
- Use appropriate transitions.

Basic Needs and Safety

Children need love, and much more, to thrive.

Reading Guide

Before You Read

Get Creative Make associations while you read. Think of a rhyme or set a series of short steps to music to help you remember the information. Your memory trick does not have to be beautiful or impressive. It only has to mean something to you and be something you will remember.

Read to Learn

Key Concepts

- **Identify** five areas of basic needs for which children depend on their caregivers.
- **Give** examples of three ways to childproof a home.
- **List** eleven common childhood injuries.
- **Describe** four types of substitute child care.

Main Idea

Caregivers must meet the basic needs of children and keep children safe. It is important to know how to handle emergencies when they occur. Parents must choose child care services carefully.

Content Vocabulary

◇ caregiver
◇ parenting
◇ immunization
◇ vaccine
◇ age-appropriate
◇ childproof
◇ first aid
◇ cardiopulmonary resuscitation (CPR)

Academic Vocabulary

You will find these words in your reading and on your tests. Use the glossary to look up their definitions if necessary.

■ primary
■ promote

Academic Standards

English Language Arts

NCTE 2 Read literature to build an understanding of the human experience.

Mathematics

NCTM Number and Operations Understand numbers, ways of representing numbers, relationships among numbers, and number systems.

Social Studies

NCSS I A Culture Analyze and explain the ways groups, societies, and cultures address human needs and concerns.

NCTE *National Council of Teachers of English*
NCTM *National Council of Teachers of Mathematics*
NSES *National Science Education Standards*
NCSS *National Council for the Social Studies*

Graphic Organizer

As you read, note four things you can do to help prevent injuries to young infants. Use a cluster chart like the one shown to help you organize your information.

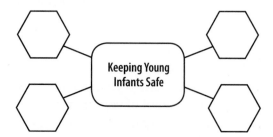

Keeping Young Infants Safe

Graphic Organizer Go to this book's Online Learning Center at **glencoe.com** to print out this graphic organizer.

Meeting Children's Basic Needs

Anyone who takes care of a child is a **caregiver**. Most children have several caregivers. The **primary**, or main, caregivers are usually the parents. This means that they have the main responsibility for raising the children. Since taking care of children is such a big job, parents often need the help of others. Relatives, babysitters, and child care professionals may be among those who provide care, either occasionally or on a regular basis. All of these caregivers need parenting skills. **Parenting** is the process of caring for children and helping them grow and develop. This includes providing care, guidance, and support in order to promote a child's growth and development.

Caring for a child is a serious responsibility. You can prepare yourself by gaining the knowledge and skills you need to be an effective caregiver. This chapter and the next one will help you get started. You can continue to learn more about caregiving by reading other books and articles, observing effective caregivers with children, asking experienced caregivers for advice, and gaining experience of your own.

The most basic responsibility of caring for children is meeting their physical needs. Infants and young children depend on their caregivers for basic needs such as food, sleep, clothing, cleanliness, and health care. If physical needs are not met, overall development may suffer.

- **Food** Children need nutritious foods to **promote**, or encourage, healthy growth and development. Caregivers need to learn about appropriate foods and portion sizes for different ages. Food habits develop early in life, so caregivers play an important role in establishing healthful eating habits. For example, toddlers who are given fresh fruits instead of cookies and sweets may be less likely to have a "sweet tooth" as adults.

As You Read

Connect Think about ways that you could help make your home safer for children.

Vocabulary

You can find definitions in the glossary at the back of this book.

People Need People

Children rely on their parents for basic needs such as health care, clothing, and food. *How do children's needs change as they grow older?*

A big part of keeping a child safe involves childproofing your home, which might include using safety gates around stairs. *What might a parent do to help keep a child safe when visiting someone else's home that is not childproofed?*

- **Sleep** Infants and young children need more sleep than teens and adults. Most infants and toddlers take one or two naps during the day and sleep as long as 12 hours at night. However, getting children to bed can be a challenge! Young children may resist going to bed, and older children often find creative reasons for staying up past their bedtimes.
- **Clothing** Infants need basic garments such as shirts and sleepers and, of course, lots of diapers. Toddlers and preschoolers are active and can get dirty quickly, so their clothes should be comfortable, durable, and easy to care for. Clothes that slip on and off easily encourage young children to learn to dress themselves.
- **Cleanliness** Infants explore their world by touching and putting objects in their mouths. Be sure to keep toys and other favorite objects clean. Infants and children also need frequent baths. Be sure to always check the water temperature before placing or allowing a child in the water, and never leave a young child alone in a bathtub.
- **Health Care** Infants need regular checkups during their first year to make sure they are developing normally. After the first year, children need less frequent checkups. Caregivers should make sure that children get immunizations. An **immunization** is a shot of a small amount of a dead or weakened disease-carrying germ given so that the body may build resistance to the disease. The disease-carrying germ that is injected in the body is called a **vaccine**. Health care providers can tell you what vaccines are recommended at what ages. Many child care centers and schools require proof of immunization before enrollment.

✓ **Reading Check** **Define** What is a caregiver?

Keeping Children Safe

Safety should be a top priority for every caregiver. While accidents and injuries will happen, many can be avoided by taking some simple precautions.

Safety for Young Infants

You might think that a baby who is just a few months old could not get into much trouble. However, even very young infants can wriggle out of your grasp in an instant, and they love to put all sorts of things in their mouths. To prevent injuries, follow these safety rules:

- Keep small objects and all plastic bags away from the baby. They can cause choking or suffocation.

- Never leave a baby alone on a raised surface, such as a bed, dresser, or changing table. It only takes a few seconds for the baby to roll over and fall.
- Choose toys that are age-appropriate and undamaged. **Age-appropriate** means it is suitable for the age and developmental needs of a child. Most toys are labeled with a recommended age. This is often because they might have pieces too small for younger children. Inspect toys regularly for loose pieces and other damage.
- Make sure the baby's crib and other equipment meet current safety standards.

Childproofing the Home

When babies learn to pull themselves up, crawl, and then walk, their world expands and so do the potential hazards. Children this age are very curious and love to explore. They are often unaware of dangers around them. It is up to caregivers to provide a safe environment.

You can start by childproofing the home. To **childproof** means to take steps to protect a child from possible dangers. You can do this by identifying potential hazards and then removing the hazards or keeping children away from them. One good way to identify hazards is to explore on your hands and knees. At that level, it is easier to see potential dangers that you might not otherwise spot. Some basic tips when childproofing include:

- Put covers over electrical outlets.
- Install safety gates at the top and bottom of stairs.
- Keep scissors, matches, lighters, and other dangerous objects out of children's reach. Store poisonous substances, such as cleaning products, chemicals, paints, and medicines, on high shelves or behind doors that lock or have childproof latches.
- Make sure there is no risk of furniture, such as a dresser or television stand, falling over on a climbing child. If necessary, secure the furniture to the wall.
- Make sure all windows that can be opened have secure screens.
- Move small appliances, such as the toaster and iron, out of reach. Unplug them when not in use.
- Teach children that heaters and the range are hot and must not be touched. Keep the handles of pots and pans turned toward the center of the range so that children cannot grab them.

Health & Wellness TIPS

Wash Your Hands

Especially when you are around children, it is important to wash your hands frequently. Keeping your hands clean is one of the best things you can do to avoid getting sick and spreading germs to others. To wash your hands:

► Use warm water.
► Use soap.
► Wash them for at least 20 seconds.

Financial *Literacy*

The Cost of Food

According to the U.S. Department of Agriculture, the average married couple will spend about $200,000 to raise a child to the age of 17. If food is about 18 percent of this total, how much does the average couple spend on food for a child through age 17?

Math Concept **Multiply Decimals by Whole Numbers** Make sure you keep the decimal place in mind when multiplying decimals.

Starting Hint Rewrite the percent as a fraction with a denominator of 100. Then convert the fraction to a decimal. Multiply this decimal by the total amount ($200,000).

Math For more math practice, go to the Math Appendix at the back of the book.

NCTM Number and Operations Understand numbers, ways of representing numbers, relationships among numbers, and number systems.

Safety away from Home

Caregivers need to be equally concerned about children's safety when they are away from home. For any car journey, no matter how short, secure infants and children in approved safety seats that are installed in the back seat.

If you take children to a park or other public place, do not let them out of your sight. Be especially vigilant if you are near a swimming pool or other body of water. Choose playgrounds that have well-maintained equipment and soft ground cover. When children are old enough to understand, teach them about "stranger danger." Tell them that they must never get into a car or agree to go anywhere with someone they do not know.

Preventing Abuse

Keeping children healthy and safe includes protecting them from abuse. Child abuse can take several forms, including physical abuse, emotional abuse, and sexual abuse. Neglect, another form of abuse, occurs when caregivers fail to meet children's basic needs.

No matter what form it takes, abuse is inexcusable and illegal. If you notice signs of possible abuse, such as unexplained injuries, take action to protect the victim from further harm. Every state has a hotline number to report suspected abuse. You do not have to give your name. The people who answer have special training that enables them to assess the situation and determine what to do.

✓ **Reading Check** **Recall** Why should furniture be secured to the wall when childproofing?

Dealing with Emergencies

No matter what precautions are taken, injuries can occur that need prompt action. Some are serious enough to require emergency procedures. The first rule for dealing with any emergency is to stay calm so you can assess the situation and determine what needs to be done.

Providing First Aid

To deal with common injuries, caregivers need to know the basics of first aid. **First aid** is emergency care or treatment given right away to an ill or injured person. Some common first aid procedures are described in **Figure 24.1** on the next page.

If you are with someone who suffers a serious injury, such as a broken bone or severe bleeding, call emergency medical services immediately. In many areas, the number is 911. Stay on the phone until the operator ends the call. The operator will ask you questions about the victim's condition and tell you what to do. Keep the victim warm to prevent shock, and offer reassurance until help arrives. In general, you should not try to move an injured person.

Emergency Procedures

While it is always important to call emergency medical services in an emergency situation, sometimes you do not have time to wait. In some situations, knowing how to preform the right emergency procedures may save a life. Choking is one example of an emergency that needs immediate action. Choking occurs when a piece of food or some other object becomes lodged in a person's airway, preventing the person from breathing. If the victim is one year or older and conscious, but unable to speak, breathe, or cry, you can perform these steps:

1. Stand or kneel behind the victim, and wrap your arms around his or her waist.
2. Make a fist with one of your hands, and grasp it with your other hand.
3. Pull your hands into the victim's abdomen with a quick, upward thrust.
4. Continue to repeat the abdominal thrusts until the object is dislodged.

Figure 24.1 Basic First Aid Procedures

Treatment for Common Injuries A course in first aid gives you knowledge and confidence for dealing with emergencies. *What should you do if someone in your care is stung by a bee?*

PROBLEM	WHAT TO DO
Bites (animal or human)	Wash the wound with water. Cover it with sterile gauze. Call a physician for advice.
Bites (insect)	For minor bites, wash the area, and apply antiseptic. For ticks, use tweezers to pull out the tick, and then treat as a minor bite.
Broken Bone	Seek emergency medical care. Do not try to straighten the limb.
Bruises	Wet a clean washcloth in cold water and wring it out. Gently apply it to the bruise.
Burns	For minor burns, immediately run cold water over the burn for about five minutes. For more serious burns, go to the hospital or call an ambulance. Do not try to treat or remove burned clothing.
Cuts and Scrapes	For minor cuts and scrapes, apply direct pressure to stop bleeding. Wash the wound, and then apply antiseptic and a bandage. For deep cuts, seek medical help.
Foreign Object in Eye	Gently pull the lower lid down while the person looks up. If you can see the object, lightly touch it with the corner of a clean, soft, lintless cloth to remove it. If you cannot remove it, seek medical help.
Nosebleed	Keep the person seated and leaning forward. Do not tilt the head back, as this may cause choking. Apply direct pressure on the bleeding nostril for 10 minutes. If you cannot stop the bleeding, seek medical attention.
Poisoning	Call the poison control center immediately. Report the name of the substance and the amount swallowed. If you are told to go to the hospital, take the container along.
Sprains	Apply ice to reduce any swelling. Wrap the injured limb in an elastic bandage, and keep it elevated. Consult a physician if necessary.
Stings	Scrape against the stinger with a flat object, such as a credit card, until you pull out the venom sac. Wash the area thoroughly, and apply ice to prevent swelling. Some people are highly allergic to stings. If the victim is short of breath, feels faint, or has stomach pain, seek medical help immediately.

Another emergency procedure is used for someone whose heart has stopped beating. **Cardiopulmonary resuscitation (CPR)** is a first-aid procedure that combines rescue breathing with chest compressions. Rescue breathing forces air into the victim's lungs, while chest compressions help keep blood circulating through the body while the heart has stopped. Only people who have been properly trained should perform CPR. If you are interested in learning this lifesaving technique, contact the American Red Cross or the American Heart Association.

✓ Reading Check **Define** What is first aid?

Choosing Child Care Services

If you become a parent, you will have to think about child care arrangements. Parents have many different reasons for using child care services. Some couples decide they will both continue working after their child is born. Many single parents have to arrange for child care so that they can earn a living. Some parents simply want to give their children opportunities to interact with other children.

Parents who decide to use substitute child care have a number of options to choose from. The quality and availability of these options vary greatly, even within a single community. Parents want what is best for their children but must also consider factors such as cost and convenience. Here are some of the options they may consider:

- **In-Home Care** Parents may arrange for a caregiver to come to their home. This allows the child to stay in familiar surroundings.
- **Family Child Care** Some caregivers look after a number of children in their own home. The children can enjoy a homelike setting and develop social skills as they play with one another.

- **Child Care Centers** This type of facility offers programs with carefully planned activities in an environment designed for children. Centers must meet health and safety standards to be licensed. The number of children per caregiver is monitored so that all children receive adequate supervision and care.
- **Before- and After-School Care** Working parents of school-age children may need child care for a few hours before and after school each day. Such programs might be offered by community centers, local agencies, schools, or child care providers.

Many parents spend a good deal of time choosing the right setting and the right caregivers for their children. They might get recommendations, interview caregivers, and ask for references. Parents often ask questions such as:

- How many children are assigned to each caregiver?
- What training and qualifications do the caregivers have?
- What activities are offered? How will they benefit my child?

Parents should visit any child care facility that they are considering. They should observe how the caregivers relate to the children, inspect indoor and outdoor equipment for safety and cleanliness, and generally get a feel for the atmosphere of the place.

Get Involved!

Work with Children

If you enjoy working with children, think about volunteering at a community day care or elementary school. Like many volunteer opportunities, this will be a two-way street. While you are helping the children by shaping and inspiring them, they are helping you by broadening your horizons and allowing you to practice your child care skills.

 Podcasts Access the Online Learning Center to download *Managing Life Skills* podcasts.

Section 24.1 After You Read

Review Key Concepts

1. **Paraphrase** what the term parenting means.
2. **List** three things a caregiver can do to keep a child safe outside of the home.
3. **Identify** which type of emergency procedure requires training to perform.
4. **Contrast** in-home care and family child care.

Practice Academic Skills

 English Language Arts

5. There are many books available on how to care for a baby. Visit your local library to find a book that teaches you how to feed an infant with a bottle, change a baby's diaper, or give a baby a bath. Write an outline of the steps. Practice the skill on a doll, and then demonstrate it to the class.

 Social Studies

6. Providing for the basic needs of children can sometimes be overwhelming for new parents. Research organizations in your community that help meet the nutritional or clothing needs of young children. Combine your findings with those of your classmates to create a directory for parents of young children.

 Check Your Answers Check your answers at this book's Online Learning Center at **glencoe.com**.

NCTE 2 Read literature to build an understanding of the human experience.

NCSS I A Analyze and explain the ways groups, societies, and cultures address human needs and concerns.

Positive Guidance and Nurturing

What did you learn from the games you played as a child?

Reading Guide

Before You Read

Two-Column Notes Two-column notes are a useful way to study and organize what you have read. Divide a piece of paper into two columns. In the left column, write down main ideas. In the right column, list supporting details.

Read to Learn
Key Concepts
- **Identify** four areas in which a child has needs beyond physical needs.
- **Explain** three ways to help guide children's behavior.
- **Summarize** how play promotes a child's development.

Main Idea
Children need guidance and nurturing to reach their potential in all developmental areas. Playing contributes to a child's development.

Graphic Organizer
As you read, note five tips to make reading with a child a more enjoyable learning experience. Use a hand graphic organizer like the one shown to help you organize your information.

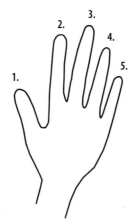

 Graphic Organizer Go to this book's Online Learning Center at **glencoe.com** to print out this graphic organizer.

Content Vocabulary
◇ stimulating environment
◇ guidance
◇ quiet play
◇ active play
◇ free play
◇ attention span

Academic Vocabulary
You will find these words in your reading and on your tests. Use the glossary to look up their definitions if necessary.
- resiliency
- consistency

Academic Standards

 English Language Arts

NCTE 5 Use different writing process elements to communicate effectively.

 Science

NSES A Develop understanding about scientific inquiry.

 Social Studies

NCSS IV A Individual Development and Identity Articulate personal connections to time, place, and social/cultural system.

NCTE *National Council of Teachers of English*
NCTM *National Council of Teachers of Mathematics*
NSES *National Science Education Standards*
NCSS *National Council for the Social Studies*

Nurturing Children

When you nurture children, you provide the care and attention needed to promote development. Previously, you learned about the physical needs of infants and children. However, those needs are just the beginning. For children to develop to their full potential, they also need a loving, stimulating environment and caregivers who provide for their intellectual, emotional, social, and moral needs. A **stimulating environment** is an environment in which one has a wide variety of things to see, taste, smell, hear, and touch.

- **Intellectual** Research about how the brain develops shows the importance of an environment that stimulates all five senses. Even more important, children need interaction with others. When you talk with children, read to them, play with them, and share interesting activities with them, you are helping to stimulate their intellectual development.
- **Emotional** All young children need to feel loved and valued. They need people in their lives who will listen to them, give them smiles and hugs, cheer their accomplishments, and comfort them when they are upset or afraid. Children who feel successful and loved have greater confidence and higher self-esteem. These qualities provide strength and **resiliency**, or the ability to overcome disappointment and stress.
- **Social** Children need to learn how to make friends, get along with others, and express their thoughts, feelings, and desires in socially acceptable ways. To develop these social skills, they need both opportunities to be around other children and guidance from caregivers. As they learn to play with others, share, and take turns, children gain valuable skills that will help them get along with people throughout their lives.
- **Moral** Children also need to develop a sense of right and wrong. Consistent, loving guidance helps them do so. Basic values such as fairness and empathy are best taught by example.

✓ **Reading Check** **Recall** What is more important to a child's intellectual needs than toys and experiences?

Guide Behavior

Children are not born knowing how to behave. Children need guidance so they can learn what behavior is expected of them. **Guidance** means using firmness and understanding to help children learn how to behave. Caregivers need to be patient, understanding, and gentle as they guide children toward appropriate behavior. Another important quality is **consistency**, or reliability and stability. If the rules for good behavior constantly change, children will not know what is expected of them. If you respond to misbehavior one day but overlook it another day, the child will be confused.

As You Read

Connect Think of specific examples of how your caregivers nurtured you as a child.

Vocabulary

You can find definitions in the glossary at the back of this book.

Provide Stimulation

Children absorb information from everything in their environment. *How is this father helping and teaching his daughter?*

Look Ahead

An important life skill is being able to think in the long term and anticipate consequences. Having a baby might seem like a fun adventure, but are you ready for that lifelong responsibility? Inviting an elderly relative to move in with you might be the right thing to do, but have you considered the financial, social, and emotional consequences?

Promote Good Behavior

Modeling appropriate behavior is the best way to promote it in children. Children imitate what they see and hear. Responding positively to children's good behavior encourages them to repeat it. When a child does something well, offer specific praise.

Set Limits

Children need to know what they may and may not do. Although they will sometimes complain about rules, they actually feel more secure when they know what is expected of them. Reasonable limits protect children from harm and prevent them from hurting others, while still allowing them to explore and learn. State limits clearly and positively. Telling children what they may do is often more effective than telling them what they may not do.

Handling Misbehavior

Occasionally, most children do things they should not do. Sometimes they have not been told that an action is wrong. It is not fair to punish children in that situation. Nor should they be punished for actions that they cannot help. Sometimes children know the rules but forget to follow them.

HOW TO... Read to a Child

Taking time to read with children is rewarding. Young children love to cuddle up and listen to a story. They enjoy asking questions and sharing the funny, happy, scary, or sad feelings the story describes. Such experiences fulfill many of their developmental needs. Here are some tips for how best to read to a child.

Choose Age-Appropriate Books Stories should be suitable for the child's age and interests.

Read it Again Be prepared to read the same story many times. Children love to hear stories over and over.

Let Them Read When children are old enough, let them read along, help them with tough words, and praise them.

Discuss the Story Talk about the pictures, how the characters are feeling, what might happen next, and how the story connects to the child's own life.

Have the Child Participate Children love to choose the books, turn the pages, and point at pictures.

Other times, they may challenge their limits to see what will happen. In such situations, caregivers need to respond appropriately. Effective options for dealing with misbehavior include:

- **Redirect behavior.** With infants and toddlers, misbehavior can often be avoided or stopped by redirecting the child's attention. For example, if a toddler is trying to reach for a breakable object, offer a safe toy instead.
- **Give reminders.** All children make mistakes. Reminding the child of the desired behavior may be all that is needed in some cases, such as "Use your quiet voice in the house, please."
- **Remove the child from the situation.** Often just putting a child in a time out situation gives the child a chance to calm down and regain his or her self-control.
- **Make the punishment appropriate.** If a child will not pick up his toys, it is appropriate to not allow him to play with them for an hour. It would not be appropriate to cancel a trip planned for next week. Such punishment is too far removed from the present time and is unrelated to the misbehavior.
- **Enforce consequences.** This is sometimes hard for a parent to do. However, it teaches the child that you mean what you say.

✓ **Reading Check** **Explain** Why do children need limits?

Learning Through Play

When children play, they are doing much more than just having fun. Play has as much purpose for children as work does for adults. Play provides opportunities for children to explore and learn about the world around them.

Play and Development

When children play, they learn about the world, themselves, and others. This begins with infants playing peek-a-boo and continues throughout life, in such activities as sports and board games. Play can promote progress in all areas of development.

Character?!
In Action

Respect Children
Some people think you need to talk down to children and treat them very differently than you would adults. However, just like adults, children feel valued when they are treated with respect. When children are talking to you, give them your full attention and do not interrupt. Whenever possible, offer children appropriate choices, and accept what they choose.

You Decide
Your sister is trying to get your little brother to stop asking so many questions. She tells him if he does not stop, a monster will eat him tonight. Do you think this is a fair way to deal with your brother?

How Organized Should Children's Activities Be?

Some people feel that the more instruction children have, the more they will learn, but others think that too much structure represses creativity.

Ryan: Activities for young kids should be structured. My little brother attends a school that offers all kinds of organized activities that have been proven effective with children. He gets to meet other kids his age, and the atmosphere is more enriching than if he were just left to his own devices. These people have studied and read and tried different things, so when they say they know what activities are good for kids, I believe them.

Sarah: I think kids should have as much freedom as possible. I love watching my little cousin play with her friends. They learn so much on their own, just using their imaginations. I think they learn more when they have to make their own fun without a lot of direction from adults. There's no pressure, no schedule, no pre-planned activities. I think if they have to entertain themselves, it challenges them more and encourages creativity.

Seeing Both Sides
Which point of view do you agree with more? Which type of experience did you have more often as a child?

- **Physical** Physical activities, like playing tag, help develop motor skills, strengthen muscles, and improve coordination.
- **Intellectual** Reading to children teaches them about letters, words, and ideas. Storytelling, puzzles, pretend play, and drawing encourage creativity.
- **Emotional** Play can be a way to build bonds. Playing with children lets them know that they deserve your time and attention. This boosts their self-esteem.
- **Social** Playing group games promotes social skills like sharing, taking turns, resolving conflicts, and compromising.
- **Moral** Playing with others also helps children understand how their actions affect those around them.

Types of Play

Different types of play have different benefits, so it is important to encourage all of them. Types of play include:
- **Quiet play** involves activities that engage the mind and use small motor skills. Examples include using clay or puzzles. Quiet play helps children learn to sit still and focus.
- **Active play** involves physical activities that use large motor skills. Examples include climbing a jungle gym and riding a tricycle. Active play provides exercise and an energy release.
- **Free play**, also called creative play, is a time when children can choose any safe activity they want.

Promoting Children's Play

Caregivers should encourage play that is age appropriate. Activities that are within a child's skill and interest level are more fun, safer, and more stimulating.

Infants and Play

Because infants explore the world through their senses, they need toys that stimulate the senses with different textures, shapes, sounds, and colors. Mobiles, rattles, and teething rings are examples of toys that infants enjoy playing with. The best plaything for infants, however, is an interested adult. Babies want attention. They love to be held, see faces, and hear voices. Since infants are somewhat limited in how they can play with toys, they get more out of playtime when an adult interacts with them.

Toddlers and Play

Toddlers enjoy running, jumping, climbing, and dancing. They love to explore the physical world by filling and emptying containers and stacking blocks. These activities help them learn about size, space, and balance. Sensory activities, like painting or playing with water or sand, encourage creativity and motor skill development. Toddlers like to imitate adults by "helping" with simple household chores. Toddlers tend to have short attention spans. **Attention span** is the length of time a person can concentrate on a task without getting distracted. To keep play stimulating, offer a new activity as soon as the child appears to lose interest. Individual activities are best, since toddlers have not yet learned to take turns or share.

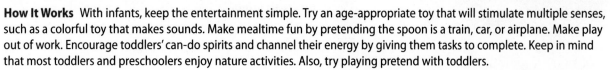

Life On Your Own

Keep Children Entertained

Children like to be kept active and entertained. Yet if you ask a child what he or she wants to do, often that child does not have any ideas. With young children, it is usually the responsibility of the caretaker to come up with ideas for activities. Simple, low-cost activities can help you keep a child's hands and mind active.

How It Works With infants, keep the entertainment simple. Try an age-appropriate toy that will stimulate multiple senses, such as a colorful toy that makes sounds. Make mealtime fun by pretending the spoon is a train, car, or airplane. Make play out of work. Encourage toddlers' can-do spirits and channel their energy by giving them tasks to complete. Keep in mind that most toddlers and preschoolers enjoy nature activities. Also, try playing pretend with toddlers.

Try It Out Imagine you are a guest at a wedding, and you have been asked to watch one of the other guest's three children, a 5 year old, a 2 year old, and an infant. You do not have any toys, children's books, or anything else specifically made to entertain children. However, the children are bored and becoming restless, and you need to figure out something to do to keep them occupied.

> *Your Turn* Come up with one activity or game for each child that does not require any special toys or equipment. Keep in mind the age of each child. Explain why you picked that activity for each child.

Preschoolers and Play

Play becomes more complex in the preschool years. Children's gross and fine motor skills are becoming more developed. Their artwork begins to look more realistic. They can build more complicated block towers. They can put together smaller puzzle pieces. They are also getting better at sharing and playing together. Preschoolers are developing their imaginations, too. Pretend play helps them express their feelings and practice the behavior they see in adults. At this age, children often look to caregivers for approval. You will hear them say "Watch me!" and "Look at what I made!" Show genuine interest and appreciation for children's efforts to encourage them and build their self-esteem.

Provide Opportunities

You can make everyday events, such as a trip to the supermarket or the bank, into fun learning experiences. At the supermarket, for example, you might talk about why the freezer section is cold or encourage a child to count the cans of soup in the cart. Play materials do not have to be fancy or expensive. A large empty box, an empty margarine tub, clean paintbrushes and water, and old clothes to dress up in all provide opportunities for play.

The role of the caregiver is to encourage play, not control it. Offer play materials and suggest activities when needed, but avoid telling the child what to do. Give a child paper and a crayon and say, "Would you like to make something with these?" rather than, "Draw a horse for me." This gives the child the power to choose.

As children grow older, they need less guidance and encouragement to play. Still, they benefit when caregivers become involved in their play from time to time. Look for appropriate opportunities to suggest ideas, provide materials, and join in the fun. Children who spend time with interested, creative caregivers gain much from the experience.

 Everyday Opportunities

Even simple activities like cooking can be great learning opportunities for children. *What can the parent teach the child during this experience?*

Electronic Entertainment

Children love to be entertained, and some caregivers are happy to let television do the entertaining. Many child care experts believe, however, that too much television can be harmful to children's development. Watching television requires very little interaction or thought and does not promote physical activity. Additionally, many programs and commercials are inappropriate for young children. Computer and video games are more interactive than television, and some can stimulate learning. Still, playing these games is an inactive and often solitary pastime, as is surfing the Internet.

Here are suggestions of how parents and caregivers can make the most of what television and electronic games have to offer:

- Balance electronic entertainment with active and social play. Limiting your own TV and computer use will set a good example.
- Choose appropriate programs and games. Most have ratings or age recommendations to help you decide.
- Keep televisions and computers in areas used by the entire family, not in children's rooms.
- Monitor children's computer activities.
- Watch television programs with the child, and talk about what is happening. If the child loses interest, turn it off.
- Consider using filtering software to prevent access to inappropriate Web sites.
- Teach children not to give out personal information to strangers online.

Want a truly carbon-neutral activity for kids? Play tag or hide and seek outside. Getting children outside provides them with the opportunity to run around, get exercise, have fun, and learn about the environment.

 Podcasts Access the Online Learning Center to download *Managing Life Skills* podcasts.

Section 24.2 — After You Read

Review Key Concepts

1. **Describe** a child's social needs and how a caregiver can meet them.
2. **Explain** five options for dealing with misbehavior.
3. **Summarize** three different types of play.

Practice Academic Skills

 English Language Arts

4. Reading to a child provides an opportunity for a caregiver to bond with the child and encourages intellectual development. Create a picture book appropriate for 1- to 3-year-olds. Your book might teach a basic concept like colors or animals or it might be a simple story.

 Social Studies

5. Interview older relatives or family friends to learn what kinds of toys and games they played with as children. Ask how the toys were used and what children learned from them. Write a brief report comparing what children learn with the toys they play with today versus what they learned from the toys they played with in the past. What is similar and different about the two time periods?

 Check Your Answers Check your answers at this book's Online Learning Center at **glencoe.com**.

NCTE 5 Use different writing process elements to communicate effectively.

NCSS IV A Articulate personal connections to time, place, and social/cultural system.

Pathway to College

Letters of Recommendation

What Are Letters of Recommendation?

Most colleges require two or three letters of recommendation from people who know you well. The purpose of these letters is for the admissions committee to learn more about you. They have data on your test scores, classes, and grades. Now they want to know how others see you.

Whom should I ask to write my letters of recommendation?

First of all, read the application carefully. Colleges sometimes request letters from specific people, like your teacher in a certain subject, so be sure to follow instructions. If the choice is left up to you, think about using teachers from your junior year or your current year. Do not go back too far, since colleges want someone who knows you now to write the letters of recommendation.

When should I ask people to write my letters of recommendation?

You do not want your recommendation writers to feel rushed. You need to give people at least a month to complete and send your letters of recommendation. However, as with most of the college application process, the earlier the better. Be sure to ask even earlier if you are applying to early decision or early action plans.

How do I make sure my recommendations are good?

The idea is that you know your teachers well enough to know who will provide favorable recommendations. However, if you have any doubt, just ask if they would feel comfortable writing you a recommendation. Be sure to spend time talking to your recommendation writers about what you remember about taking their class. If you can, highlight a particular accomplishment.

Hands-On

College Readiness When requesting that someone write you a letter of recommendation, it is often a good idea to provide that person with a brief overview of your high school involvement and contributions. Imagine you are asking a teacher to write you a letter of recommendation. Write a summary of your high school experience, highlighting what you view as your positive contributions.

Path to Success

 College & Career Readiness

Do Not Be Shy To get letters of recommendation, you have to ask people to write them.

Make it Easy Always provide your teachers with an addressed and stamped envelop for each letter.

Provide Deadlines Make sure your teachers and counselors know when the letters are due.

Trust Your Teachers Waive your right to view recommendation letters. This gives more credibility to the recommendations.

Follow Up Check in with your teachers a week or so prior to the deadline to make sure they have mailed the letters.

Thank Them Be sure to write thank-you notes to everyone who provided you with a letter of recommendation.

 Go to this book's Online Learning Center at **glencoe.com** to learn more about college and career readiness.

CHAPTER SUMMARY

Section 24.1
Basic Needs and Safety

Children depend on caregivers to meet their basic physical needs, including food, sleep, clothing, cleanliness, and health care. Taking steps such as childproofing the home will help keep children safe. Caregivers need to know what to do in emergency situations, so it is helpful to be familiar with first aid and CPR. If abuse is suspected, it should be reported. Parents should explore child care options carefully.

Section 24.2
Positive Guidance and Nurturing

Caregivers must meet children's intellectual, emotional, social, and moral needs. Guiding behavior involves promoting good behavior, setting reasonable limits, and handling misbehavior. Children's play is purposeful and promotes progress in all areas of development. Children need a balance of different types of play activities. Caregivers should provide a variety of opportunities for play and learning.

Vocabulary Review

1. Use these vocabulary terms to create a crossword puzzle, using the definitions as clues.

Content Vocabulary

◇ caregiver (p. 475)
◇ parenting (p. 475)
◇ immunization (p. 476)
◇ vaccine (p. 476)
◇ age-appropriate (p. 477)
◇ childproof (p. 477)
◇ first aid (p. 478)
◇ cardiopulmonary resuscitation (CPR) (p. 480)

◇ stimulating environment (p. 483)
◇ guidance (p. 483)
◇ quiet play (p. 486)
◇ active play (p. 486)
◇ free play (p. 486)
◇ attention span (p. 487)

Academic Vocabulary

■ primary (p. 475)
■ promote (p. 475)
■ resiliency (p. 483)
■ consistency (p. 483)

Review Key Concepts

2. **Identify** five areas of basic needs for which children depend on their caregivers.
3. **Give** examples of three ways to childproof a home.
4. **List** eleven common childhood injuries.
5. **Describe** four types of substitute child care.
6. **Identify** four areas in which a child has needs beyond physical needs.
7. **Explain** three ways to help guide children's behavior.
8. **Summarize** how play promotes a child's development.

Critical Thinking

9. **Evaluate** Do you think parents and other caregivers should be required by law to learn first aid techniques? Why or why not?
10. **Compare** Children need different types of play to fully develop. Compare the possible benefits of quiet play to active play.
11. **Hypothesize** Many parents feel that offering a child choices rather than telling the child what to do helps reduce misbehavior. Do you agree?

ACTIVE LEARNING

Family & Community Connections

12. Technology Presentation Technology has made an impact on many areas of our lives in recent years. This includes the area of child care. Follow your teacher's instructions to form into groups. As a team, research examples of technology that can be used to enhance the safety and security of children. Use your findings to prepare a presentation for your class. Presentations should include information on when the product was developed, how it works, and how it promotes the safety of children. If possible, give a demonstration of the products.

13. Interview a Caregiver Interview a person who provides child care for one or more toddlers. This could be a parent, a babysitter, or a professional child care provider. It could be in a home or in a child care center. Ask the caregiver to describe what he or she does to help stimulate and entertain the toddlers. How does he or she encourage the toddler to learn and be creative? Does he or she use the suggestions provided in this chapter? Does the caregiver offer a variety of types of play? Does he or she use everyday opportunities as learning experiences? Write a brief report to share your findings with the class, and compare those findings to what you learned in this chapter.

21st Century Skills

Research Skills

14. Child Care Options Conduct research to find available child care options in your community or a nearby area. Create a chart to compare the cost and features of the options you find. Features might include the age of children, the number of children, the hours of operation, whether food is provided, and the number of caregivers on staff.

Technology Skills

15. Evaluate Children's Web Sites Locate and evaluate three different Web sites that offer games or activities for preschool or school-age children. Rate the sites on education and entertainment value. Write a review to summarize your evaluations, and state whether you would recommend any of the sites.

 FCCLA Connections

Responsibility Skills

16. Providing Opportunities As part of its mission, FCCLA encourages students to become strong family members. Use the Parent Practice unit of FCCLA's Families First program to develop monthly play days for children. Your program should provide a safe environment, organized activities, and ways to help children learn through play. Use a graphic organizer to show dates, locations, and activities.

Academic Skills

English Language Arts

17. Role Models The best way to promote good behavior in children is by modeling it. Children tend to mimic the actions of adults around them more often than listening to them. For example, you can tell a child to eat his or her vegetables but if he or she sees you consistently eating sweets, the child is more likely to choose sweets over vegetables as well. Develop a list of ten actions that you think are most important for adults to model.

> **NCTE 12** Use language to accomplish individual purposes.

Social Studies

18. Compare Child Care Choose a country other than the United States. Conduct research to learn how child care is usually handled in that country. How is it similar or different from in the U.S.? Write a report with your findings, including a summary of what you feel the pros and cons are for that country's approach.

> **NCSS I A Culture** Analyze and explain the ways groups, societies, and cultures address human needs and concerns.

Mathematics

19. Childproofing In order to childproof her kitchen, a mother wants to move all cleaning products from under the sink to a cabinet that is out of reach for her three-year-old. She needs to make sure the new cabinet is large enough. The cabinet under the sink has dimensions of 1 foot, six inches by 2 feet by 16 inches. What is the volume of this cabinet in cubic inches?

Math Concept **Compute Volume** Volume is the measure of space occupied by a solid region. The volume of a rectangular solid equals its length times its width times its height.

Starting Hint First, convert all three dimensions to inches. Then multiply all three values together to find the total volume.

 For more math practice, go to the Math Appendix at the back of the book.

> **NCTM Measurement** Understand measurable attributes of objects and the units, systems, and processes of measurement.

Standardized Test Practice

CCR College & Career Readiness

ANALOGIES
Some objective tests contain questions that test your ability to recognize analogies. You determine the relationship between two or more words and then apply that relationship to another set of words.

Test-Taking Tip To solve an analogy, begin by determining the relationship between the first two terms. Then choose the term that has the same relationship to complete the second pair.

20. Toy is to play as book is to _____.
a. paper
b. draw
c. read
d. word

Responsibilities of Parenting

Chapter Objectives

Section 25.1 Preparing for Parenthood

- **List** six things that parents are responsible for providing to their children.
- **Name** four characteristics that indicate personal readiness for becoming a parent.
- **Summarize** why parents might have a hard time adjusting to their new roles as parents.

Section 25.2 Teen Parenthood

- **Identify** four basic problems that teen parents will face.
- **List** three options available to teen parents.

> ▶ **Explore the Photo**
>
> Parenting has many rewards as well as many responsibilities. *What are some of the rewards that you think might come from being a parent?*

Fiction Writing

The Rewards of Parenting Fiction is an invented story. When you write a story, you are answering the question, "What happened?" Think about some of the rewards that being a parent might bring. Then write a short story about a parent experiencing the rewards of parenting. The characters and events in your story may be based on people you know, but remember this is fiction so you should make up the details and dialogue.

Writing Tips To write a fiction story, follow these steps:
- Make sure your story has a beginning, middle, and end.
- Plan out your plot, characters, and setting before you begin writing your story.
- Introduce the plot in the opening paragraph to help grab your reader's interest.
- Have your characters use realistic dialogue.

Preparing for Parenthood

Parenting is so much more than having children.

Reading Guide

Before You Read

Be Organized A messy environment can be distracting. To lessen distractions, organize an area where you can read this section comfortably.

Read to Learn
Key Concepts

- **List** six things that parents are responsible for providing to their children.
- **Name** four characteristics that indicate personal readiness for becoming a parent.
- **Summarize** why parents might have a hard time adjusting to their new roles as parents.

Main Idea

Parenting has both rewards and responsibilities. Prospective parents should examine their reasons for wanting a child and their readiness to have a child.

Content Vocabulary
◇ parenting readiness
◇ emotional maturity

Academic Vocabulary
You will find these words in your reading and on your tests. Use the glossary to look up their definitions if necessary.
- pride
- prospective

Graphic Organizer

As you read, note realistic and unrealistic reasons for becoming a parent. Use a graphic organizer like the one shown to help you organize your information.

Academic Standards

English Language Arts

NCTE 8 Use information resources to gather information and create and communicate knowledge.

Social Studies

NCSS I C Culture Apply an understanding of culture as an integrated whole that explains the functions and interactions of language.

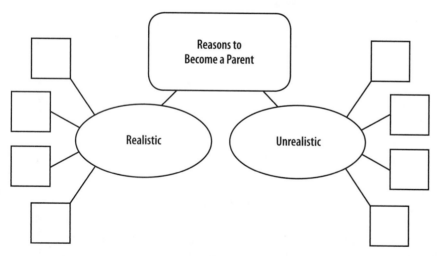

Graphic Organizer Go to this book's Online Learning Center at **glencoe.com** to print out this graphic organizer.

NCTE *National Council of Teachers of English*
NCTM *National Council of Teachers of Mathematics*
NSES *National Science Education Standards*
NCSS *National Council for the Social Studies*

Rewards and Responsibilities

As Jamie cradled her newborn son in her arms, she felt a mixture of joy, apprehension, and awe. She knew that her life had changed forever. She looked up at Dave, her husband, who was gazing intently at the baby's face. "I cannot wait to start teaching him how to catch a ball and ride a bike," Dave said.

Jamie laughed. "Well, I'm afraid you are going to have to wait. Our little boy has a lot to learn first."

"You're right," said Dave, "and so do we." Jamie and Dave looked at their son in wonder. They were excited and nervous about being parents. They knew it was going to be one of the most rewarding experiences of their life, but also one of the most challenging. They looked forward to sharing the joys and responsibilities of their new roles.

Rewards of Parenting

Welcoming a child into the world can bring great joy. It is just one of the many rewards of parenting. Raising children gives parents a chance to experience the world through the wonder of a child's eyes. Parents develop new skills, strengths, and understanding of their child, their spouses, and themselves. They experience a sense of accomplishment, pass on family traditions, and forge deep bonds of love.

There is nothing quite like seeing a baby's first smile or hearing a toddler say, "I love you." Parents often feel happiness and love that they have never felt before. Having children can also enrich an already strong marriage. Parents watch with **pride**, or pleasure and satisfaction, as their children grow into independent adults. But along with all of these rewards come a lot of work and responsibility.

Responsibilities of Parenting

Most new parents do not realize how hard parenting is. Parents are responsible for providing constant care, love, security, shelter, guidance, and financial support. Moreover, parenting is a responsibility that continues for many years. Each stage of childhood is different, requiring parents to constantly meet new challenges. Also, for parents who have more than one child, each child brings different challenges to the parents.

As You Read

Connect When do you think parents' responsibility for their children ends?

◆ Vocabulary

You can find definitions in the glossary at the back of this book.

> **Share the Joy**
>
> Many parents share in their child's successes and accomplishments. *How might this parent be sharing in her child's sense of accomplishment?*

Parenting Roles

As discussed in Chapter 24, parents must meet the physical, emotional, intellectual, social, and moral needs of their children. Providing love, attention, and guidance are just as essential as providing food, clothing, and shelter. Parents often play the roles of housekeeper, cook, chauffeur, friend, playmate, coach, tutor, and counselor to their children.

Caring for a child is a 24-hour-a-day job. Parents cannot just set the responsibilities aside for a while. Somebody has to be responsible for a young child at all times. Parents who have an outside job must make arrangements for substitute child care while they are at work.

Parents also have the responsibility of being good role models. Whether parents realize it or not, children are constantly observing the values, character traits, and skills that the parents demonstrate in their everyday actions. For better or worse, children will pattern themselves after the examples set by their parents, so it is very important that parents are constantly thinking about and assessing their actions.

The Cost of Parenting

The cost of raising a child begins even before the baby is born. As soon as a woman knows or suspects she is pregnant, she should see a doctor. Regular medical care is needed throughout the pregnancy to monitor the health of both the mother and baby. It gives the baby the best possible start in life. A healthy start is something that every child deserves.

Life On Your Own

Be a Positive Example

Children naturally imitate the speech, actions, and attitudes of older children and teens. By setting a positive example, you can have a positive influence on the development of children. Setting a good example benefits both you and the child, and it is good practice for when you start your own family as an adult.

How It Works It is important to be consistent around children and ensure that your words match your actions. You should also give reasons for your actions. Examples are most effective when a child connects your behavior with your values. If you make a mistake, admit it. It is important to be honest with children, and it will also show them that no one is perfect. Respect children's limitations. Be realistic about what you can expect from them.

Try It Out You spend a lot of time with your younger cousin, and she really looks up to you. Lately you have noticed her being negative, talking back to her parents a lot, and not doing what they tell her to do. When you start to think about it, you realize she might have picked some of this behavior up from you. You have not been getting along that well with your parents, and she has probably seen you behaving this way and started to mimic it.

> *Your Turn* What would you do in this situation? What would you say to your cousin? What might happen if you talked to her about her behavior without changing your own?

Figure 25.1 **Ideas About Parenthood**

Fact Versus Fiction Many people who consider becoming parents do so for the wrong reasons. *Why do you think the reasons on the left are unrealistic?*

UNREALISTIC IDEAS	REALISTIC REASONS
I'm lonely. A child will love me.	• Our marriage is strong, and we're ready to become parents.
I feel unimportant. A baby will attract attention, and I'll be noticed.	• I am willing to put someone else's needs ahead of my own.
My parents (or in-laws or friends) want us to have a child.	• I'm secure in who I am and will work hard to be a good parent.
My relationship with my spouse is shaky. A child will make it stronger.	• We know what we're taking on, and we accept the responsibility.
I'm afraid of the future. A child will care for me when I'm old.	• We are emotionally and financially ready to have a family of our own.

A new baby brings many expenses. Parents may need to buy equipment such as a car seat and crib. The baby will need food, diapers, and clothes, which are quickly outgrown. Even parents with health insurance usually have to pay for routine medical exams and immunizations. Child care can be another major expense.

As children get older, the costs of food and clothing increases. School, sports, and other activities add still more expenses to the list. Parents' financial responsibilities continue until the child earns a living and becomes independent.

✓ **Reading Check** **Recall** How is parenting a growth experience for adults?

Readiness for Parenting

Despite all the responsibilities, many people still want to have children. Just the sight of an adorable baby can bring out these desires. Sometimes, however, the motives behind the desires do not make sense. Some people have unrealistic ideas about what having a child might mean to them. Compare the different ideas about parenthood shown in **Figure 25.1**. Which show more maturity?

Parenting is a lifelong, life-changing commitment. The decision to have a child needs to be backed up by sound reasoning. No one should have a child just to make someone else happy. A child cannot fix other problems or weaknesses in your life or strengthen a weak relationship. Making a careful decision to have a child benefits both the parents and the child. Children deserve to be born to parents who are ready for parenthood.

How do people know when they are ready to become parents? They need to analyze their **parenting readiness**. This is their level of preparation. They can start by recognizing that parenthood is a serious decision that requires serious effort. Then they need to honestly analyze their emotional, financial, and personal readiness.

Emotional Readiness

Prospective, or likely, parents need to be emotionally mature. **Emotional maturity** means being responsible enough to consistently put someone else's needs before your own needs. With emotional maturity comes the ability to understand one's feelings and to act on them appropriately. Emotionally mature parents have the inner resources to put the needs of their child before their own needs. They have patience, sensitivity, self-control, and self-confidence. Their expectations about raising a child are realistic, not idealistic. They know that their lives will change the moment they become parents, and they truthfully believe they can handle the demands and responsibilities of parenting. Part of handling the demands of children includes understanding and coping with a child's changing emotions as well. If parents cannot cope with their own emotions, they will have difficulty coping with a child's emotions.

Money Management

Raising a child can be very expensive. *What are some of the costs parents-to-be should consider?*

Be Smart Be Safe

Shaken Baby Syndrome
Shaken baby syndrome is the term for the internal head injuries a baby or young child can get from being shaken violently. Possible results include blindness, hearing loss, learning disabilities, and death.

Write About It Research situations that could lead parents or caregivers to shake infants. What solutions or advice can you come up with to help parents and protect infants. Summarize your findings and ideas in a brief report.

Financial Readiness

Because raising a child is expensive, couples should assess their financial readiness to become parents. They need to determine how they will manage the immediate and long-term costs of raising a child. That means examining their current income and expenses.

There are many important questions that people thinking about having a child need to ask themselves. Are spending cuts needed to increase savings or to meet additional expenses? Will a larger living space be needed? If so, how much will housing costs increase? If both parents have jobs, will one stay at home to care for the child? Can the family manage on one income? If both parents continue working, how much will quality child care cost? Such questions help couples review the financial realities of raising a child so they can make a decision that is right for them.

Personal Readiness

A child gives a family a new and different focus. Couples must be ready to put the needs of their child first, delaying some of their personal needs and wants. They must also assess whether they have the skills and qualities they will need for raising a child. While much of parenting is learned "on the job," some parenting skills can be developed ahead of time. Couples with the following characteristics are more likely to be successful parents:

- **Management Skills** Parents need to know how to use their money, time, and energy wisely. They must be able to manage the family budget, juggle tasks and schedules, and care for themselves and their children.

- **Flexibility** Parents who are flexible are better able to meet daily challenges. At a moment's notice, parents may have to clean up a spill or take care of a sick baby. A child's ever-changing emotions and desire for independence often do not fit in with a parent's schedule, and parents must be able to adapt.
- **Willingness to Sacrifice** Parents often need to sacrifice their time, money, and personal interests for the sake of their children. This creates a healthy, nurturing family environment.
- **Consistency** Parents need the maturity to behave consistently. Establishing and enforcing routines, rules, and limits help children feel secure and understand their boundaries.

✓ **Reading Check** **Paraphrase** What does the term emotional maturity mean?

HOW TO... Cope with Emotions

Along with the necessary emotional and financial readiness required to be a good parent, you also need to be personally ready. One aspect of this is being able to deal with a child's constantly changing emotions. It is helpful and important to be aware that most young children go through predictable stages in their emotional development.

Eighteen Months Eighteen-month-old children are often defiant, trying to establish control in their life. Give them choices. Instead of saying, "Pick up your toys and books" ask them, "Which do you want to pick up first? Your toys or your books?"

Two and One-Half Years Two-and-one-half-year-olds may feel overwhelmed and frustrated. Being consistent and offering them the comfort of routines will make them feel more secure.

Three Years Three-year-olds are generally happy and eager to please. Keep them occupied by engaging them, asking them a lot of questions, and requesting their help, when appropriate.

Three and One-Half Years Three-and-one-half-year-olds may become fearful and insecure. Be comforting and patient as they work through their fears and security issues.

Two Years Two-year-olds are usually very affectionate and can often get in their caregiver's way. They are constantly seeking approval and praise, so be sure to give them positive feedback and attention.

Adjusting to Parenthood

No matter how ready they are or how much they have prepared, new parents face major adjustments. Months after a baby is born, new parents are still getting used to their new roles. Newborns tend to sleep just a few hours at a time, and parents need to adjust their schedules around this. Newborns also need to be fed and have their diapers changed 10 to 12 times a day, around the clock. All of this occurs at a time when the mother is still recovering from delivery and both parents are likely to be tired. This can make adjusting to the new responsibilities difficult.

The Mother's Recovery

A mother's recovery from giving birth may take longer than expected. Not only are there many physical issues that a new mother needs to adjust to and recover from, it is also not uncommon for new mothers to experience periods of depression and anxiety. New mothers have many new hormones flowing through their bodies, and while these help them to care for and nurture their new child, they can also make the new mother feel emotional. New mothers also often spend all of their time and energy focusing on and taking care of their new baby, and they sometimes forget that they also have to spend some time and energy taking care of themselves.

Two Views One World

Can Readiness for Parenthood Be Evaluated?

Does evaluating readiness before becoming a parent make parenting any easier or is there no way to know until you try?

Alex: Becoming a parent is a huge commitment, and getting ready for it is all about thinking things through and preparing. Before I was born, my parents weighed all the factors, including their finances, careers, and relationship, to see if they were ready and willing to be good parents. Because of this, when I was born, they felt more confident and prepared. They knew they had what it took to take care of me.

Rachel: Preparation is all well and good, but first time parents can't truly know what they're in for until they actually have a baby to take care of. Some people talk about parenting readiness like it's a math equation: a good income plus maturity plus a good marriage equals good parents. But those things really just scratch the surface. Even if a couple thinks things through and feels ready, they have no idea how demanding the job actually is.

Seeing Both Sides
What role do the readiness factors mentioned in this chapter play in good parenting? How do they relate to other considerations and qualities that are important to good parenting?

Adjusting as a Couple

A father may feel like an outsider when the mother and baby get a lot of attention. Both parents often worry about finances and how to cope with their new responsibilities. Studies show that marital satisfaction often decreases after the birth of a baby. Spouses tend to argue more and to show less affection to one another.

All of these possible results are normal adjustments to parenthood and family life. It is how the couple handles them that makes the difference. Couples who can acknowledge and deal with the challenges are more likely to experience a stronger marriage. New parents should not hesitate to accept offers of assistance. Help from family and friends can be a real boost during this time.

Planning Ahead

The decision to become parents deserves careful thought and discussion. Serious planning involves a healthy pregnancy. The healthiest pregnancies begin even before the woman becomes pregnant. The couple should discuss how they will handle the demands of parenting along with their other responsibilities and goals. Above all, they should remember that the happiest and healthiest children are born to parents who are ready for them.

Go Green

Expecting parents might want to consider cloth diapers. Millions of disposables diapers go into landfills in the U.S. each year. Using cloth diapers helps the environment, but since cloth diapers are reusable, it also helps parents save money,

 Podcasts Access the Online Learning Center to download *Managing Life Skills* podcasts.

Section 25.1 **After You Read**

Review Key Concepts

1. **Identify** three rewards of parenting.

2. **Summarize** the emotional changes a child experiences between the ages of eighteen months and three-and-a-half years.

3. **Describe** why new parents tend to be very tired.

Practice Academic Skills

 English Language Arts

4. Use print or online resources to find ways that a couple can keep their relationship strong after children are born. Use your findings to create a trifold brochure with at least five ideas for new parents.

Social Studies

5. Conduct research to discover what children call their mothers and fathers in other countries around the world. Make a list of the country names and corresponding terms. How are these terms similar or different? What are mothers and fathers called in your region of the country? Summarize your analysis in a paragraph.

Check Your Answers Check your answers at this book's Online Learning Center at **glencoe.com**.

> **NCTE 8** Use information resources to gather information and create and communicate knowledge.

> **NCSS I C** Apply an understanding of culture as an integrated whole that explains the functions and interactions of language.

Teen Parenthood

Parenting is one of the most difficult jobs in the world, especially for teens.

Reading Guide

Before You Read

Understanding It is normal to have questions when you read. Write down questions while reading. Many of them will be answered as you continue. If they are not, you will have a list ready for your teacher when you finish.

Read to Learn
Key Concepts
- **Identify** four basic problems that teen parents will face.
- **List** three options available to teen parents.

Main Idea
Teen pregnancy can pose many challenges and risks for both the child and the parents. Options for pregnant teens include marriage, single parenthood, and adoption.

Content Vocabulary
◇ premature
◇ low birth weight
◇ paternity
◇ adoption
◇ closed adoption
◇ open adoption

Academic Vocabulary
You will find these words in your reading and on your tests. Use the glossary to look up their definitions if necessary.
■ deficiency
■ support

Academic Standards

 English Language Arts

NCTE 5 Use different writing process elements to communicate effectively.

 Mathematics

NCTM Data Analysis and Probability Formulate questions that can be addressed with data and collect, organize, and display relevant data to answer them.

 Social Studies

NCSS I A Culture Analyze and explain the ways groups, societies, and cultures address human needs and concerns.

NCTE *National Council of Teachers of English*
NCTM *National Council of Teachers of Mathematics*
NSES *National Science Education Standards*
NCSS *National Council for the Social Studies*

Graphic Organizer

As you read, look for two types of adoption. Write a description of each. Use a chart like the one shown to help you organize your information.

Type of Adoption	Description
1.	
2.	

 Graphic Organizer Go to this book's Online Learning Center at **glencoe.com** to print out this graphic organizer.

Consequences of Teen Pregnancy

Adjusting to parenthood is difficult for anyone, but it can be especially hard for teens. Teen parents face difficulties that parents in their twenties and thirties often do not. Most teens are not mature enough, physically, emotionally, or financially, to take on the responsibility of caring for a child.

Pregnancy causes many problems that affect both the teen mother and father. When Tracy became pregnant, she and Parker married. Parker took a job, planning to finish high school after a year. Before that could happen, their car broke down and he needed to work overtime to pay for the repairs. Soon after, Tracy became pregnant again. By the time their second child was a year old, Parker had been out of high school almost three years. He did not feel like going back, even though he knew he could earn more with a high school diploma or a General Equivalency Diploma (GED).

Teen parenthood has predictable consequences. The four basic types of problems include health risks, education challenges, financial issues, and emotional and social stress. These problems also affect the teens' families and society.

Health Risks

Pregnancy presents special health risks for both a teen mother and her baby. A teen is not yet physically or emotionally mature and may not be ready for the extra demands of pregnancy. As a result, teens are at greater risk than adult women for experiencing serious medical complications from a pregnancy. One such complication is significant iron **deficiency** (di-ʼfi-shən-sē), or shortage, which can deprive the baby and mother of oxygen.

Babies born to teen mothers are more likely to be premature. **Premature** means born before 37 weeks of development. They are also more likely to have **low birth weight**, which means weighing less than 5 pounds, 8 ounces at birth. Babies who are premature or have low birth weight are at risk for serious health problems, such as vision and hearing loss, respiratory problems, mental retardation, learning disabilities, and cerebral palsy. A significant percentage of these babies die before their first birthday.

As You Read

Connect How might being a teen parent affect your future career plans?

Vocabulary

You can find definitions in the glossary at the back of this book.

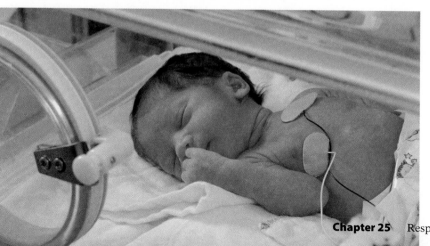

Newborns in Need

Children born to teen mothers face more risks than other children. *What are some of the health problems facing premature babies?*

Good prenatal care is essential for teen mothers because of the increased risks. A female teen has high nutritional needs. If she becomes pregnant and there is no extra emphasis on nutrition, her body may not be able to provide the nutrients that she and her growing baby need. In addition, a critical period of development occurs before most mothers are even aware they are pregnant. Many teens put off getting medical care because they do not want to face the fact that they are pregnant. However, those who take proper care of themselves greatly increase the chances of having a healthy baby.

Babies born to teen parents often have less supportive and stimulating home environments than those born to older parents. They tend to have higher rates of behavioral problems. They are more likely to be neglected or abused because their parents do not know how to deal with stress. Years later, they are more likely to be teen parents themselves. All of these effects have long-term consequences for the children, their families, and society as a whole.

Education Challenges

It is important for pregnant teens to complete their schooling, at least through high school. Unfortunately, many drop out to support themselves or care for their child. Nearly half of the teen mothers who leave school never finish their education. This is true even for those who plan to return. Without a high school diploma, it is hard to find a job, especially one with a salary to **support**, or pay the costs of, a family. This puts a strain on society to help support the family.

Pregnant and parenting teens can work with school counselors and social service agencies to find solutions to such problems. These resources can help find ways to provide care for the babies while their parents take classes. Graduating should be a high-priority goal for young mothers and fathers.

Financial Issues

Most teen parents experience financial problems. Teen mothers need good medical care. That care costs money, as does childbirth. Teen parents who keep their child must provide food, clothing, housing, and health care. This continues for at least 18 years.

Even when teen parents do not marry, both are legally responsible for providing for their child. If the father chooses not to stay involved with the child, it is especially important to establish paternity. **Paternity** is the legal identification of a man as the biological father of a child. Paternity will legally ensure the father's responsibilities toward the child. A medical test can prove paternity.

For many teen couples, the burden of child care expenses becomes overwhelming. To meet financial needs, a young couple's goals and plans for the future must be changed. This tension can lead to arguments. The stress from financial issues can affect other family members and even the baby. Sometimes society must help care for the child through government and welfare programs.

Emotional and Social Stress

Adolescence can be an anxious, confusing time, and it is made more difficult when pregnancy occurs. Pregnancy increases concerns about the future, forcing teens into decisions they are not ready to make. Teen fathers may react to a partner's pregnancy with feelings of shock, anger, or guilt. They may feel anxious about what to do and have the urge to run from the responsibility. Teen mothers who are left to care for their children without the father's support feel abandoned, hurt, and upset.

Adjusting to new relationships can cause great stress. Changes to old relationships can also cause stress. Teens who must put time and energy into caring for a child have fewer resources for other pursuits and interests. They also do not have the freedom or the money to go out and have fun with friends, as their peers are doing.

Teen parents may miss their old friends, but find they no longer have much in common with them. Teens who enjoyed sports or other after-school activities may have to cut back or give them up completely. Teen parents quickly realize that their lives have changed in profound ways. Teen parents who succeed do so against great odds. Usually they have support systems that help them complete their education and earn a living while caring for their child.

✓ **Reading Check** **Explain** Why is it important to prove paternity?

Teen Parenting Options

Teens can and do get pregnant. Many, though, have trouble believing and acknowledging the symptoms when it happens. A girl who fears she might be pregnant may try to ignore the possibility. However, for her health and the baby's health, it is essential that she confirm the pregnancy and get good care as soon as possible.

A teen who suspects she is pregnant should talk to someone close. This could be her boyfriend, a parent or other family member, a trusted friend, a teacher, or a counselor. She should also see a doctor as soon as possible to confirm the pregnancy.

Once her pregnancy has been confirmed, a teen can begin to make plans. The father should be involved, too. After all, the father has rights and responsibilities. The pregnancy will have a long-lasting effect on the lives of both parents.

Math For Success

The Cost of Having a Baby

Most people know that having a child is expensive. However, many people forget that the costs actually start before the child is born. Talk to someone you know who has a child, and do research to find an average cost of giving birth. Present your findings in a table.

Math Concept **Present Data in a Table** Create a three-column table in which you present your data. The first column should list different costs, such as medical costs, hospital costs, and so on. In the second column, list the costs you get from your interview. In the third column, list the costs you find during your research. Add the items in the second and third columns, and compare the answers.

Starting Hint Give your table a title, and label each column so that anyone who looks at your data will know what it represents.

 For more math practice, go to the Math Appendix at the back of the book.

NCTM Data Analysis and Probability Formulate questions that can be addressed with data and collect, organize, and display relevant data to answer them.

To make responsible plans, both teens will have to carefully consider the options and their consequences. Family can be a good resource for support and guidance at this time. When faced with pregnancy, teens have several options. Each one must be considered seriously. There are several factors that must be considered for each option.

Marriage

Most people would agree that a strong and successful marriage benefits parents and their children. At any age, however, marriage is not easy. This is especially true for teens. It takes a special commitment, responsibility, and hard work.

Married teens face a special set of problems. As the initial excitement of marriage wears off, the strains of responsibility and the new social situation set in. Teens who marry because of a pregnancy face an additional problem. They have to adjust to parenthood at the same time they are adjusting to being married. Married teens often feel isolated from friends, but do not fit into the adult world yet either.

Married teens who are able to meet these challenges can find themselves with a rewarding relationship. Having two people share the child care lessens the work of each. With hard work and commitment, married teens can build a caring home for a child.

Adoption

Teens facing pregnancy and parenthood may consider the option of having another family adopt their child. **Adoption** is a legal process by which people acquire the rights and responsibilities of parenthood for children who are not biologically their own. An adopted child becomes a member of the adoptive parents' family, just as if he or she were born into that family.

The decision to place a baby for adoption is not easy. Teens considering adoption need to think it through carefully, because it is a permanent decision. Some teens choose adoption because they feel they are giving their child an opportunity for more care, guidance, and love than they are able to provide at this stage of their lives. Placing a baby for adoption for these reasons is an act of love. However, even when the decision is made with careful thought and consideration, it is an emotional decision. Agencies that specialize in adoptions help with this decision.

There are two different types of adoption. A **closed adoption**, or confidential adoption, is an adoption in which the birth parents do not know the names of the adoptive parents. There is no exchange of information after the adoption.

▼ **An Act of Love**

Adoption can be a very positive experience for everyone involved. *Why might this 30-year-old married woman be better able to provide for a child than a teen couple?*

An **open adoption** is an adoption in which the birth parents and adoptive parents know something about one other. There are different levels of open adoption based on how much information is shared with both sets of parents, and this level of knowledge and communication should be worked out between the birth parents, adoptive parents, and adoption agency.

Single Parenthood

Having a tiny baby to cuddle and love can seem very appealing. Indeed, it can be rewarding to care for someone who is so small, helpless, and dependent. However, caring for a newborn is a huge responsibility, and becoming a parent is a lifelong commitment.

All these responsibilities can be draining for an adult. They can be even harder for a teen. Not surprisingly, many teen parents suffer from burnout or depression. They need to find support.

Teens considering single parenthood need to be realistic and ask a lot of questions. How much emotional and financial help can one teen parent expect from the other or from his or her own parents and other family members? A teen considering single parenthood must guard against romanticizing the situation. For example, a teen who is not interested in marriage during the pregnancy is unlikely to change his or her mind after the birth. Parents, counselors, and other trusted adults can help teens develop realistic expectations for their own situations as single parents. It is possible to be a successful single parent, but it is not an easy road for anyone.

Health & Wellness TIPS

Spend Time with Loved Ones

Relationships are an important part of your health. Strong bonds with others mean you will have help when you need it. Additionally, being connected provides protection from loneliness and depression. Spend time building and maintaining your relationships with friends and family to stay healthy.

 Podcasts Access the Online Learning Center to download *Managing Life Skills* podcasts.

Section 25.2 — After You Read

Review Key Concepts

1. **Explain** why teen parents are less likely than other teens to finish school.

2. **Predict** why teen parents might consider adoption.

Practice Academic Skills

 English Language Arts

3. Suppose that you write an advice column for a local newspaper. A seventeen-year-old has written to you saying that she is unmarried and thinks she is pregnant. Write a response to the teen advising her on steps she might take.

 Social Studies

4. One major problem teen parents face is a lack of financial resources. The federal government offers some programs that help women and children in need. Conduct research to create a list of government-sponsored resources, including what services they provide.

Check Your Answers Check your answers at this book's Online Learning Center at glencoe.com.

> **NCTE 5** Use different writing process elements to communicate effectively.

> **NCSS I A** Analyze and explain the ways groups, societies, and cultures address human needs and concerns.

Pathway to Your Career

Secondary School Teacher

What Does a Secondary School Teacher Do?

Secondary school teachers help students build on what they learned in elementary school and teach them additional information that they will need to succeed in life. They usually specialize in a specific subject, such as mathematics, biology, or German. Additional responsibilities can include providing career guidance, overseeing study halls, supervising extracurricular activities, and accompanying students on field trips.

Career Readiness Skills Teachers should be able to communicate well, inspire trust, and motivate students. They should be organized, reliable, patient, and creative. They must be able to work well with other teachers and parents.

Education and Training Secondary school teachers usually have a degree in the subject they plan to teach and also from a teacher education program. Most of these programs require participation in a student-teaching internship and classes in computers and other technologies. All states require public school teachers to be licensed, though this is not always required for private schools.

Job Outlook Job prospects for secondary school teachers are expected to grow about as fast as the average job growth. There will be more demand for teachers in the faster growing fields like math, science, and bilingual education and for those willing to work in less desirable school districts.

Critical Thinking Think about a secondary school teacher who took an interest in you or inspired you in some way. Write a paragraph identifying why that teacher was special to you and what qualities made him or her a good teacher.

Career Cluster

CCR ☆ College & Career Readiness

Education and Training Secondary school teachers work in the Teaching/Training pathway of this career cluster. Other jobs in this cluster include:

- Child Care Program Director
- Professional Coach
- Elementary School Teacher
- Education Researcher
- College Lecturer
- Preschool Teacher
- Museum Coordinator
- Human Resources Manager
- Early Childhood Teacher
- Media Coordinator

Explore Further The Education and Training career cluster contains three pathways: Administration and Administrative Support, Professional Support Services, and Teaching/Training. Choose one of these pathways to explore further.

 Career Clusters To learn more about career clusters, go to this book's Online Learning Center at **glencoe.com**.

CHAPTER SUMMARY

Section 25.1
Preparing for Parenthood

The rewards of parenting are significant, but require hard work and sacrifice. Parents have great responsibilities, including playing different roles and finding financial resources. The decision to have a child should be based on sound reasoning. Prospective parents should consider their emotional, financial, and personal readiness.

Section 25.2
Teen Parenthood

Teen pregnancy poses health risks to both the mother and the child. Teen parents face many challenges, including education, financial, and emotional and social stress. Both the father and the mother are legally and financially responsible for their child. Options for teen parents include marriage, adoption, and single parenting.

Vocabulary Review

1. Create a multiple-choice test question for each content and academic vocabulary term.

Content Vocabulary
◇ parenting readiness (p. 499)
◇ emotional maturity (p. 500)
◇ premature (p. 505)
◇ low birth weight (p. 505)
◇ paternity (p. 506)
◇ adoption (p. 508)
◇ closed adoption (p. 508)
◇ open adoption (p. 509)

Academic Vocabulary
■ pride (p. 497)
■ prospective (p. 500)
■ deficiency (p. 505)
■ support (p. 506)

Review Key Concepts

2. **List** six things that parents are responsible for providing to their children.
3. **Name** four characteristics that indicate personal readiness for becoming a parent.
4. **Summarize** why parents might have a hard time adjusting to their new roles as parents.
5. **Identify** four basic problems that teen parents will face.
6. **List** three options available to teen parents.

Critical Thinking

7. **Examine** Look at the list of unrealistic ideas about parenthood shown in Figure 25.1. What assumptions are being made in each case? Are they valid assumptions? Why or why not?
8. **Hypothesize** What do you think might be done to reduce the number of teen pregnancies?
9. **Distinguish** It is important to be able to tell the difference between fact and opinion. Is the statement, "Teen parents are not capable of being good parents" fact or opinion? Explain your answer.
10. **Draw Conclusions** This chapter discusses the qualities that indicate readiness for parenting. What qualities might interfere with being a successful parent? How could these qualities be changed?
11. **Judge** People are required to have a license for many activities, such as driving a car or practicing medicine. Do you think a parenting license should be required to have children? Why or why not?

12. Write a Radio Show

Follow your teacher's directions to form into small groups. Imagine you are presenting a radio show about books and magazines for new parents available at the public library. Visit the library to learn about the parenting materials it offers. Then write a 15-minute script describing the materials available. For books, include the focus and author's name. For magazines, include the titles and frequency. Indicate at what stage the materials would be helpful to read. Present your show to the class.

13. Explore Parenting Decisions

Talk with several adults about their decision to become parents or not to become parents. What influenced their decision? How has the choice they made affected their lives? If they have children, did they feel they were ready? How did they prepare once the decision was made? Summarize your findings in a brief report. Be sure to change names to protect people's privacy. Did you notice a difference in answers based on the age group of the people you interviewed? Did answers vary based on the number of children the people have? You also might want to create a chart to help you organize and review the information you collect.

✦ 21st Century Skills

Technology Skills

14. Write a Scene Use word-processing software to write a scene for a play in which a young couple discusses whether to start a family. You can end the scene with either decision, but be sure both characters show good communication skills as they talk about the issue and discuss their personal readiness.

Media Literacy Skills

15. Portrayal of Parenthood Select a book or movie about a couple having a new baby. Read the book or watch the movie, and write a review of how parenting is portrayed. Based on the information in the text, did the parents seem ready to have a child? Did they have the child for realistic reasons? Did the parents seem to show a realistic level or responsibility or did they "make it look easy"?

 Connections

Financial Literacy Skills

16. Financial Preparation As part of its mission, FCCLA encourages students to develop their practical knowledge skills. Conduct research and create a list of supplies that a newborn baby would need. Then research prices for those items using stores, catalogs, or Web sites. Based on your findings, develop a list of money-saving tips for new parents.

Academic Skills

 English Language Arts

17. Earn Your Rewards Many of the rewards of parenthood are sharing the child's "firsts," such as first words. Think of a time when you experienced something for the first time. Create a list of the steps you had to take to accomplish the task. Write a paragraph describing some of the challenges you faced and some of the rewards you received.

> **NCTE 12** Use language to accomplish individual purposes.

 Science

18. Investigate a Research Claim Research reveals that pregnant teens are less likely to receive adequate medical care while pregnant. One reason for this is that medical care can be expensive, and teens have no way to pay for that care.

Procedure Conduct research to learn how these findings can be useful.

Analysis Use the information from your research to write a one-page report.

> **NSES C** Develop understanding of the interdependence of organisms and behavior of organisms.

 Mathematics

19. Child Care Costs Jake and Mina have a four-year-old daughter, Maddy. They did some research and discovered that early care and education for a four-year-old in a child care center in an urban area averages about $5,790 per year. They are working on their finances and budget for the upcoming year, and they need to figure out how much they need to save weekly to pay for child care?

Math Concept **Multistep Problem** When solving problems with more than one step, read through all the steps. Then think through each step before beginning.

Starting Hint First, convert one year into weeks (52). Then divide the total cost by the number of weeks. Be sure the decimal point is in the correct place in your answer.

 For more math practice, go to the Math Appendix at the back of the book.

> **NCTM Number and Operations** Compute fluently and make reasonable estimates.

 **Standardized Test Practice**

CCR College & Career Readiness

TRUE/FALSE
Read the passage. Then determine whether the statement is true or false.

Test-Taking Tip Statements that contain extreme words, such as all, none, never, or always, or that have unsupported opinions, are often false. Look for less extreme words, such as sometimes, often, and usually. These statements are more likely to be true.

Many teen mothers are unable to continue attending high school once they have a baby to care for. Statistics show that the dropout rate is higher for teen mothers than for other female teens. There are some programs that help teen mothers stay in school while they raise their child.

20. According to the passage, teen mothers never finish high school.
   a. True
   b. False

Gather References and Recommendations

In this project, you will create a list of people you would like to use as references and ask their permission to do so. You will then request letters of recommendation to include in your portfolio.

 My Journal

If you completed the journal entry from page 450, refer to it to see if your thoughts have changed after reading the unit.

Project Assignment

In this project you will:

- Determine who you would like to use as references.
- Obtain permission to include these people on your reference list.
- Develop a list of your references along with their contact information.
- Request letters of recommendation.
- Compile and organize your letters of recommendation for easy accessibility.
- Follow up with requests as necessary.

THE SKILLS BEHIND THE PROJECT

Key personal and relationship skills you will use in this project include:

- Interacting with adults
- Communicating respectively
- Gathering and consolidating information

Academic Skills

 English Language Arts

> **NCTE 4** Use written language to communicate effectively.
>
> **NCTE 12** Use language to accomplish individual purposes.

STEP 1 Choose Your References

Many interviewers and job applications will request references. These may be professional or character references. Think about people you know who might be willing to vouch for your strengths and skills such as:

- Teachers or counselors
- Employers
- A committee chairperson
- Team leaders

STEP 2 Compile Your Reference List

Obtain permission from your references and get their accurate contact information. This information should include their name, address, phone numbers, and e-mail address. For professional references, also include the person's title and company. Find out if the person prefers to be contacted at his or her business, home or cell phone number, e-mail, or address.

Interpersonal Skills

- Be polite and confident when you contact the adult.
- Wait until the adult finishes answering a question before asking the next question.
- Repeat the information as needed to ensure you have written it down correctly.

STEP 3 Request Letters of Recommendation

Refer to your list of references. The next step is to obtain a few letters of recommendation that you can have ready to provide upon request. Choose and contact four people from your reference list to request letters of recommendation. Ask for recommendations reflecting your character as well as your academic or employability skills. Be aware of nonverbal communication. If someone seems uncomfortable providing the letter, you should thank him or her for their time and seek a letter from someone else.

Communication Skills
- Thank the person for his or her time and assistance.
- Reach a verbal agreement on when you can expect the letter.
- Be very clear on dates and expectations.

STEP 4 Build Your Portfolio Project

Use the Portfolio Project Checklist to organize and share your references with your classmates.

Information Literacy Skills
- Acquire and use information.
- Organize and maintain information.
- Use technology to process information.

STEP 5 Evaluate Your Project

Your portfolio project will be evaluated based on:

Academic Skills
- How concisely you gathered and consolidated your information into a document
- Logical organization

 Evaluation Rubric Go to this book's Online Learning Center at **glencoe.com** for a rubric you can use to evaluate your final project.

PORTFOLIO PROJECT CHECKLIST

Plan
- ☑ Using an appropriate computer software program, create a spreadsheet or database to help you organize and track your information. Include fields for the person's name, contact information, the date of the request, and if or when you received the recommendation.
- ☑ Fill in the spreadsheet with all your information from Steps 2 and 3.
- ☑ Save your file, and update it as necessary.

Present
- ☑ Make a presentation to your class to share your spreadsheet or database. Include your reasons for selecting the people you chose.
- ☑ Invite the students to ask questions. Answer any questions. Demonstrate in your answers that you respect their perspectives.
- ☑ Place your spreadsheet and letters of recommendation in your portfolio. Share this with your teacher.

Portfolio Highlights

Letters of Recommendation

Strong recommendation letters are an essential element of your portfolio. Letters of recommendation can take some time to gather, so you should plan ahead and request them as soon as possible.

Whom Should You Ask?
Request letters from people who will vouch for your strengths and skills. Supervisors and coworkers can write about your work ethic and employability skills. Teachers and counselors can write about your academic skills and character strengths.

How Should You Ask?
Requests should be made in person whenever possible. If asking in person is not possible, a phone call is appropriate. Do not ask, "Will you write me a letter of recommendation?" Rather, consider something like, "Do you know my work well enough to write me a good recommendation letter?"

How Can I Make It Easier?
Be prepared to offer any information that the person might want to include, such as your GPA. You might also want to print out sample letters from reliable Internet sources to have available in case the person is not sure how to format the letter.

Wellness, Nutrition, and Food Choices

Unit Portfolio Project Preview

Showcase Your Skills

In this unit, you will use information and judgment to plan, shop for, and prepare healthful foods. In your portfolio project you will examine how using your skills can accomplish many tasks.

 My Journal

Taking a Personal Inventory Write a journal entry about one of the topics below. This will help you prepare for the project at the end of this unit.

- Discuss how a skill that is learned and used in one area can be adapted for a completely different area.
- Tell why other people in your life might be able to identify your skills more accurately than you might.
- Some people think it is egotistical to communicate your own abilities and talents. Give your point of view.

Explore the Photo

The way we eat, shop for food, and prepare meals and snacks has a great impact on our well-being. *What are some habits that will allow you to enjoy food and maintain good health?*

Chapter 26

Health and Wellness

Chapter Objectives

Section 26.1 Wellness for Life

- **Summarize** wellness and fitness.
- **Outline** factors that influence body weight.
- **Describe** three common health risks among teens.

Section 26.2 Taking Care of Yourself

- **Identify** four areas of health for which you can take personal responsibility.
- **Explain** the causes and effects of stress.
- **Describe** how you can take charge of your health care.

➤ Explore the Photo

Staying active helps you stay physically fit. *What other benefits are related to physical activity?*

Writing Activity

Persuasive Essay

Too Good to Be True Some companies use advertising to convince people that they have the miracle product to make customers the healthiest they can be. These advertisements are usually misleading, and some products have been known to cause harm. Write a persuasive essay that convinces other teens to find out the facts about a product before they purchase and use it.

Writing Tips To write a successful persuasive essay:
- Write an opening that will capture the reader's attention.
- Clearly express your view on the topic.
- Provide specific reasons why the reader should agree with your view.

Wellness for Life

Reading Guide

Before You Read

Study with a Buddy It can be difficult to review your own notes and quiz yourself on what you have just read. According to research, studying with a partner for as little as twelve minutes can help you study better.

Read to Learn
Key Concepts
- **Summarize** wellness and fitness.
- **Outline** factors that influence body weight.
- **Describe** three common health risks among teens.

Main Idea

You are responsible for your health and well-being. Being informed and making smart decisions about your health and safety can improve the quality of your life now and in the future.

Content Vocabulary
◇ wellness
◇ fitness
◇ endurance
◇ aerobic activities
◇ flexibility
◇ body image
◇ Body Mass Index (BMI)
◇ anorexia nervosa
◇ bulimia
◇ binge eating
◇ substance abuse

Academic Vocabulary

You will find these words in your reading and on your tests. Use the glossary to look up their definitions if necessary.
■ credit
■ composition

Academic Standards

English Language Arts

NCTE 12 Use language to accomplish individual purposes.

Social Studies

NCSS IV A Individual Development and Identity Articulate personal connections to time, place, and social/cultural system.

Graphic Organizer

As you read, look for healthful ways to lose or gain weight. Use a chart like the one shown to help you organize your information.

Weight Management	
Healthful Ways to Lose Weight	**Healthful Ways to Gain Weight**
1.	1.
2.	2.
3.	3.
4.	4.

 Graphic Organizer Go to this book's Online Learning Center at **glencoe.com** to print out this graphic organizer.

Your Well-Being

Wellness is an approach to life that emphasizes taking positive steps toward overall good health and well-being. Wellness has two primary goals: to promote health and to prevent disease. Wellness encompasses physical, mental and emotional, and social health.

To promote wellness, set realistic goals and break big goals into smaller goals. Write down your goals, using specific language. Keep track of your progress in a calendar or notebook. Lose the excuses, and stick to your plan. If you need help, ask for support from family and friends. Be sure you celebrate your successes. If you reach a goal, give yourself **credit**, or praise. Stay positive if you do not reach your goals right away or if they take longer than expected.

As You Read

Connect What are three ways you can make sure you are as healthy as you can be?

Aim for Fitness

Fitness is when your body works at its peak, you look your best, and you are healthy and strong. Regular physical activity promotes overall physical health. It also helps you look and feel better. Getting enough physical activity each day strengthens your heart and lungs, improves your muscle tone, and helps you maintain a healthy weight. Leading an active life also helps improve balance, coordination, and flexibility, and manage stress.

Vocabulary

You can find definitions in the glossary at the back of this book.

The Elements of Fitness

To be fit, you need an active lifestyle that promotes the three main elements of fitness: strength, endurance, and flexibility.

- Strength is the ability of your muscles to exert force. Build muscle strength with activities involving lifting and carrying.
- **Endurance** is your ability to use energy over a period of time without getting tired. Build endurance with **aerobic activities** (ˌer-ˈō-bik), which are continuous, rhythmic activities that help improve heart, lung, and muscle function.
- **Flexibility** is the ability of your joints to make the full range of movements available to them. Improve flexibility with bending and stretching activities.

Look at the Results

Making healthful choices in one area of your life can motivate you to improve your health in other ways. *Why do you suppose this is true?*

Avoid Injury

Avoid injury by warming up and cooling down before and after vigorous activity. Warming up gradually increases your heartbeat and temperature, making muscles more flexible. Cooling down helps your body recover from activity. Always drink plenty of water to prevent dehydration, the excessive loss of body fluids that can lead to muscle cramps, dizziness, and nausea.

✓ **Reading Check** **Recall** What are the two primary goals of wellness?

Get Involved!

Help Your Neighbors

You can stay active while helping others. Volunteer to help neighbors out with yard work or shoveling snow. Offer to help elderly people with their household chores or to run errands for them. You will be giving back to your community while staying active.

A Healthy Weight

The mental concept you have of your physical appearance is your **body image**. It is normal for people to be different sizes and shapes. It is important to have a realistic body image. Accept the characteristics that you cannot change. Focus instead on maintaining a weight that is healthy for your body. Regular physical activity and sensible eating can help you maintain a healthy weight. You also need to know your individual healthy weight range. Weight is a complex issue that involves a number of factors:

- **Height** The taller a person is, the more he or she can expect to weigh.
- **Age** Adults typically weigh more than teens of the same height.
- **Gender** Males generally weigh more than females of the same height.
- **Bone Structure** People with larger body frames usually weigh more than those with smaller body frames.
- **Body Build** People who are muscular tend to weigh more than those who are not.
- **Growth Pattern** Teenagers mature at different ages and progress at different rates.

HOW TO...

There are many ways to increase your activity level. Some are organized activities, such as playing on a sports team or taking a yoga class. Others can be less structured. Walking the dog, choosing to take the stairs, and playing catch are all also great forms of exercise.

Power Your Own Wheels Bicycling, rollerblading, and skating are great ways to exercise while getting around or spending time with friends.

Use Your Feet Walk instead of getting a ride whenever you can. Park farther away from the entrance to places.

Take a Class Try something you have never done before, such as yoga, Pilates, karate, or a dance class.

Take the Stairs Forget the elevator and escalator. Climb the stairs whenever you can.

Work Out at Chore Time Vacuuming, raking leaves, and taking out the trash all get you moving.

Play! Be a kid again. Make a snowman, fly a kite, jump rope, shoot hoops, or take your dog for a walk.

Body Mass Index

You cannot tell whether your weight is right for you just by looking in a mirror or getting on a scale. The **Body Mass Index (BMI)** in **Figure 26.1** uses weight, height, and age to help determine an appropriate weight range. It can help you determine if you are underweight, overweight, or at risk of becoming overweight. There is a wide range of appropriate weights for someone of your height and age. BMI charts are good for general information, but they do not take into account muscle mass and body **composition**, which is the ratio of fat to lean tissue in your body.

Smart Weight Management

Being overweight and underweight are both unhealthy. Being overweight contributes to heart disease and diabetes, and it puts a strain on muscles and joints. Being underweight contributes to anemia, low energy, and other disorders associated with poor nutrition.

Weight management is a matter of energy balance. Food supplies your body with energy, and physical activity uses energy. This energy is measured in units called calories. When the energy you take in is balanced with the energy you use, your body weight remains stable. Using more energy than you take in results in weight loss. Taking in more energy than you use results in weight gain. If you think you might be overweight or underweight, ask your doctor for advice before making any decisions or taking action.

Health & Wellness TIPS

Lose Weight the Right Way

Not all methods of losing weight are healthy, and not all of them are realistic and maintainable. For safe weight loss, try these tips:

- ▶ Eat real food, not special liquids or powders.
- ▶ Include foods from all the food groups.
- ▶ Stick to a regular exercise program.
- ▶ Avoid all extremes.

| **Figure 26.1** | **Body Mass Index (BMI)** |

Calculate Your BMI BMI is a number that indicates a measurement of the relative percentages of fat and muscle mass in the human body. *How can determining your BMI be useful to you?*

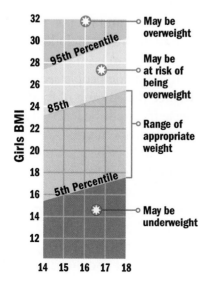

Divide your weight in pounds by your height in inches. Divide again by your height in inches. Multiply by 703 to get your BMI. Find the point on the chart where your age and BMI intersect to determine if you are at an appropriate weight for your age and height.

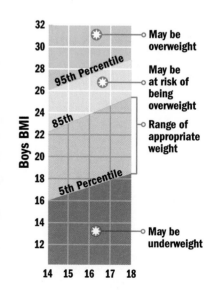

Losing Weight

Weight gain is a natural and healthy part of teen growth. If your doctor advises you to lose weight, you need to do it safely. Weight loss should be gradual, no more than 1 to 2 pounds a week. Most successful weight loss combines sensible eating with increased physical activity. To lose weight safely, increase physical activity, choose nutritious foods that are lower in fat and calories, cut back on foods that are high in calories but low in nutrition, and avoid diets that severely restrict food choices.

Gaining Weight

Some of these same cautions apply to weight gain. Weight should be gained slowly and steadily, and foods should be nutritious and balanced. Add a moderate amount of good fat sources to your meals, such as avocado and olives. Drinking juices is a good way to increase your calorie intake. Eat more frequently, and eat larger portions. Snack on hearty, nutritious foods, such as yogurt and fruit.

▲ Smart Snacking

Whether you are underweight or overweight, it is smart to keep chips, ice cream, sugary snacks, and other low-nutrient foods to a minimum. *What are some more healthful options for snacking that you enjoy?*

✓ **Reading Check** **Explain** Why should you know your BMI?

Health Risks

Health risks can be linked to emotional factors such as low self-esteem, unrealistic body image, or depression. Some result from immature decision making. Knowing the risks and knowing how to avoid them can help protect you from serious health problems.

Eating Disorders

Eating disorders are extremely dangerous and can be life-threatening if untreated. People with eating disorders need professional help. They may need a combination of medical, nutritional, and psychological counseling. The support of family and friends is key during the recovery process. Types of eating disorders include:

- **Anorexia nervosa** (ˌa-nə-ˈrek-sē-ə (ˌ)nər-ˈvō-sə) is an extreme urge to lose weight by starving oneself. Anorexic people see themselves as fat. They drastically reduce the amount of food they eat and often dangerously increase their physical activity. Anorexia damages the bones, muscles, skin, and organs.
- **Bulimia** (bü-ˈlē-mē-ə) involves extreme and often secret overeating followed by attempts to get rid of the food by using laxatives or vomiting. These practices severely damage the body.
- **Binge eating** is compulsive overeating. Binge eaters consume large amounts of food at one time, even if they are not hungry. They often feel shame, guilt, and depression after overeating. This disorder can lead to obesity, heart disease, and diabetes.

Substance Abuse

The use of illegal drugs and the misuse of legal drugs is called **substance abuse**. It is linked to violence, suicide, disease, and death. Many abused substances are addictive, meaning they cause a mental or physical dependence that leads users to crave them. Substance abuse is a serious problem with serious consequences.

- Alcohol is a depressant that produces mental and physical impairment. People who drive after drinking even a small amount of alcohol risk injuring or killing themselves and others. Binge drinking, when a person drinks large quantities in a short period of time, can lead to alcohol poisoning and death.

- Tobacco contains nicotine, a powerful and addictive drug that interferes with brain function and causes users to want more and more tobacco. Cigarette smoking leads to heart disease, emphysema, and lung cancer. Smokeless tobacco can lead to tooth loss from gum recession and mouth and throat cancer.

- Drug abuse is the use of illegal drugs, such as marijuana, cocaine, and heroin, and the misuse of legal medicines. Taking a prescription medicine without a doctor's orders or taking someone else's prescription medicine is drug abuse.

Drugs interfere with a user's ability to think clearly and make sound judgments. Drug addicts risk their health and face a painful withdrawal process. Abstain from the use of alcohol, tobacco, and other drugs to avoid these problems.

Succeed in SCHOOL and LIFE

Exercise in Small Bits

It can be difficult to find the time to exercise for the recommended 60 minutes every day. Do not think all of your exercise needs to be done at once. Small bits of fitness add up. Multiple short spurts of exercise and longer continuous workouts have been shown to have similar benefits.

Two Views One World

Does the Media Affect Body Image?

How much influence do images of models and movie stars in the media have? Do they cause any harm?

Alex: Everyone knows those models and actors on TV and in movies don't look like real people. They are fun to look at, but no reasonable person expects to be as thin as models and celebrities. I don't think those images affect us that much because we all know that movies, TV shows, and magazine ads are a fantasy land where everyone is thin and good-looking. Those people don't reflect reality.

Olivia: We are constantly exposed to ultra-thin celebrities, and it definitely affects our body images. When really thin and beautiful models and actors are held up as the ideal of what we should all look like, people start to feel bad about the way they look. Unless you have all the time in the world, a personal chef, and a personal trainer, you can't expect to look like them, and yet we all feel guilty because we don't.

Seeing Both Sides
Do you think models and movie stars affect the way you and your peers view body image? Explain your answer.

Sexually Transmitted Infections

As you learned in Chapter 21, sexually transmitted infections (STIs) are diseases that are transmitted from one person to another as a result of sexual contact. The only certain way to avoid contracting an STI is to practice abstinence. STIs vary in severity and symptoms. Some STIs have no symptoms in their early stages, while others have painful symptoms. Different diseases need different treatment, so diagnosis is essential. Left untreated, STIs can have serious long-term effects including sterility, brain damage, and heart disease. Most STIs, if caught early, can be treated with antibiotics. However, some STIs cannot be cured. In those cases, treatment can help manage the symptoms, but the person has the disease for life.

Abstinence

Teens who choose to abstain from high-risk behaviors show that they care about their health, their families, and their future. When you say no to high-risk behaviors, you are demonstrating that you are capable of making mature decisions and resisting pressure to do something that is not in your best interest. Millions of teens choose abstinence and the peace of mind that goes with it. Act according to positive values and take control of your life.

 **Podcasts** Access the Online Learning Center to download *Managing Life Skills* podcasts.

Section 26.1 After You Read

Review Key Concepts

1. **Outline** the benefits of regular physical activity.

2. **Explain** why it is important to have a realistic body image.

3. **Identify** factors that contribute to taking health risks.

Practice Academic Skills

 English Language Arts

4. It often helps to write down the reasons you have made a particular decision. Write a paragraph that describes why it is important for you to make wise choices for your health. Use complete sentences and correct grammar.

 Social Studies

5. Your own positive changes toward a healthier you can be shared with your community. Create a realistic plan that would bring people together to build a healthier community. This may include posters, sports teams, or another activity that builds relationships in your community.

Check Your Answers Check your answers at this book's Online Learning Center at **glencoe.com**.

NCTE 12 Use language to accomplish individual purposes.

NCSS IV A Articulate personal connections to time, place, and social/cultural system.

Taking Care of Yourself

Positive change comes from a desire to be the best you can be.

Reading Guide

Before You Read

Check for Understanding If you have questions as you are reading, that means you are checking your understanding of the material. To get the most out of the text, try to answer those questions.

Read to Learn

Key Concepts

- **Identify** four areas of health for which you can take personal responsibility.
- **Explain** the causes and effects of stress.
- **Describe** how you can take charge of your health care.

Main Idea

Your overall health is determined by your physical, emotional and mental, and social wellness. You can improve your health by learning to cope with stress. Work with your doctor to manage your health care.

Graphic Organizer

As you read, identify and describe four guidelines you can use in everyday life to stay safe. Use a table like the one shown to help you organize your information.

Staying Safe	
What to Do	**How to Do It**
1.	1.
2.	2.
3.	3.
4.	4.

 Graphic Organizer Go to this book's Online Learning Center at **glencoe.com** to print out this graphic organizer.

Content Vocabulary

◇ stress
◇ adrenaline
◇ primary care physician
◇ specialist

Academic Vocabulary

You will find these words in your reading and on your tests. Use the glossary to look up their definitions if necessary.

■ adequate
■ assume

Academic Standards

English Language Arts

NCTE 8 Use information resources to gather information and create and communicate knowledge.

Mathematics

NCTM Problem Solving Solve problems that arise in mathematics and in other contexts.

Social Studies

NCSS V B Individuals, Groups, and Institutions Analyze group and institutional influences on people, events, and elements of culture in both historical and contemporary settings.

NCTE *National Council of Teachers of English*
NCTM *National Council of Teachers of Mathematics*
NSES *National Science Education Standards*
NCSS *National Council for the Social Studies*

Take Charge of Your Health

As You Read

Connect How can decisions about your health affect other areas of your life?

Health and wellness require balance in your life, and as a young adult on the verge of independence, you are the one in charge of your health and safety. Good health includes physical health, mental and emotional health, and social health. Safety is also part of good health.

Physical Health

You are responsible for your own physical health. You make choices about what to eat and when to work, relax, and sleep. It is you who must pay attention to any symptoms of illness. Some of the decisions you make can have long-term effects on your life. For example, using sunscreen during outdoor activities helps protect your skin against damage and the possibility of cancer later in life. Understanding developments and issues in physical health will help you make informed decisions about your health.

Nutrition

Every meal and snack is an opportunity to choose foods rich in the nutrients you need for physical and mental energy. Healthful eating can also reduce the risks of weight problems, heart disease, diabetes, and some forms of cancer. Eating wisely helps you look and feel your best. Eating a wide variety of nutritious foods, including plenty of fruits and vegetables, helps you achieve wellness.

Vocabulary

You can find definitions in the glossary at the back of this book.

Physical Activity

The body is designed for movement and needs regular physical activity. It should not be hard to find ways to be active. Exercising and playing sports are obvious examples, but everyday movements, including climbing stairs and walking your dog, also count. Regular physical activity benefits not only your physical health but also your mental, emotional, and social health. Exercise gives you greater strength and endurance, helps you maintain an appropriate weight, and enables you to manage stress effectively.

Get Moving

There are plenty of fun ways to get moving. *How is the teen in this photo benefitting from walking her dog?*

Rest

When you stay up late, how do you feel the next day? You probably feel tired and maybe a little irritable. You may have trouble concentrating or feel less coordinated than usual. Along with good nutrition and regular physical activity, your body needs **adequate**, or enough, rest. During a good night's sleep, your body systems are able to repair and energize themselves. On average, most people need eight hours of sleep each night. How you feel can tell you whether you need more or less rest.

Hygiene

Good hygiene, or cleanliness, is also basic to overall wellness. It helps you manage acne, oily skin and hair, increased perspiration, body odor, and other common hygiene problems. Maintaining a good level of hygiene is really a matter of just a few simple habits, such as a daily bath or shower, regularly brushing and flossing your teeth, and keeping your hair, hands, and nails clean.

Mental and Emotional Health

People who are mentally and emotionally healthy think clearly, feel good about themselves, and are able to cope with the demands of life. They welcome change and enjoy developing new skills. They learn from their mistakes and deal with frustrations without feeling overwhelmed.

While some aspects of mental and emotional health may be linked to heredity, you control many others. When you have problems in this area, it can affect your physical and social health as well. Here are some suggestions for maximizing your mental and emotional health:

- Challenge yourself to learn new skills and information.
- Put your talents and abilities to good use.
- Learn from your mistakes.
- Focus on your strengths, not on your weaknesses.
- Take responsibility for your choices and actions.
- Be open-minded and flexible.
- Develop positive ways to handle your emotions.

Talk to an adult, school counselor, or mental health professional to help you cope with mental or emotional health issues. It is important to ask for help when you need it.

Social Health

Your social health is all about the relationships you have with the people around you. People with good social health have positive, supportive relationships. They treat others with kindness and respect. They have good communication skills that enable them to make and keep friends and to give and ask for support when it is needed. Social health also includes your role within society as a whole. By getting involved in your community, you make it a better place for everyone.

Financial *Literacy*

Health Care Costs

Spencer has a serious but treatable health issue. He wants to calculate how much money he will spend on doctor's appointments and medicines. He has a health insurance plan with a $250 deductible. Spencer's doctor's appointment cost $120. His prescription will cost him $20 each time he gets it filled. How many times will he need to get his prescription filled before he reaches his deductible?

Math Concept **Deductible** The deductible in an insurance policy is the portion of any claim that is not covered by the insurance provider. It is usually a fixed amount that must be paid by the insured before the full benefits of a policy can apply. Adding each out-of-pocket expense the insured makes will indicate how close he or she is to reaching the deductible.

Starting Hint Begin with $250 and subtract the cost of the doctor's appointment ($120). Divide that answer by the cost for each prescription ($20).

 For more math practice, go to the Math Appendix at the back of the book.

NCTM Problem Solving Solve problems that arise in mathematics and in other contexts.

All Work and No Play

Studying and doing homework are important, but it is equally important to maintain balance in your life. If you are overworked and overwhelmed, you may not be as healthy and happy as you could be. You also need to be sure you are not constantly sitting and focusing. You need to relax and be active, too. Make sure you mix in fun with responsibility.

Character In Action

Know When to Get Help

Friends sometimes trap themselves in lifestyles that will have devastating effects and could even be life-threatening. If friends confide in you about serious problems, such as an eating disorder or a substance abuse problem, ask a trusted adult or community agency how you can help. Encourage your friends to seek treatment, and support them when they do.

You Decide

A friend has told you she thinks she might be anorexic. She made you promise not to tell anyone, but you are really worried about her. What would you do?

Safety

Being responsible for your health means that you also **assume**, or take on, responsibility for your safety. Many teens feel invincible or indestructible, as if they cannot or will not get hurt. It takes only reading a news story or watching a newscast to know that this is completely untrue. These guidelines can help keep you safe:

- **Be aware of the risks.** Whatever the situation, stay aware of your surroundings, and be on the lookout for any possible safety risks.
- **Be prepared.** When you know what risks you face, you can plan how to avoid or minimize many of them. In any situation, think of what might go wrong and mentally rehearse how you would react. The situations you imagine might never occur, but thinking through the possibilities keeps you alert, aware, and ready to act.
- **Stay within your limits.** Be realistic about your abilities and be firm about your values. When it comes to your safety, resist pressure from others and make your own decisions. Remember, you will be the one who must deal with the consequences of your actions.
- **Follow the rules.** Safety rules are based on analyzing years of accident and injury information. Know the rules and follow them. They are designed to protect you.

✓ **Reading Check** **Examine** What is social health?

Stress

You will experience many stressful situations in life. **Stress** is your body's response when you feel overwhelmed by responsibilities and demands. It makes you feel tense and can affect all aspects of your health. The key to dealing with stress is to learn how to manage it effectively and in a healthy way. Some stress, when handled well, can actually be helpful, but stress can have negative effects for your health as well.

Responding to Stress

Stress is a good example of the mind-body connection. Stress is an emotional response that can cause many physical reactions. A body experiencing stress releases a hormone called **adrenaline** (ə-'dre-nə-lən) into the bloodstream, where it increases the heartbeat and breathing rate. This is part of the "fight-or-flight" response, which allows the body to react quickly in an emergency by supplying it with a boost of strength and energy to either fight back or flee from danger. Negative or prolonged stress can cause more severe symptoms, like upset stomach, difficulty sleeping, loss of appetite, overeating, and headaches. These physical effects remain until the danger passes.

You experience stress when pressures seem to go beyond your ability to cope with them. Family and friends may make demands that produce stress. Sometimes you are the one who puts pressure on yourself. Major life events, such as a death or divorce in the family or a serious illness or injury, cause significant stress. When stresses build up, they can affect all aspects of your health. Physically, you might lose your appetite, develop headaches, or have trouble sleeping. Emotionally, you might feel nervous or drained. Stress can cause tension in your relationships with others.

Sometimes stress has a positive effect. For example, the stress of a gymnastics meet or a dance recital can motivate you to do your best. Positive events, such as a wedding, the birth of a baby, and even traveling, can create stress. Stress can make your mind and body become more focused.

Multiple Roles

One potential cause of stress is the challenge of managing your various roles in life. A role is the part you play when you interact with others. People have multiple roles. For example, you might be a son or daughter, sister or brother, friend, student, team member, and community volunteer. Each role brings its own responsibilities. At times, they can make you feel like you are being pulled in too many different directions. Good management skills can help you juggle your roles. For example, learning to manage your time can help you fulfill your obligations and still have time for yourself. Relationship skills, such as communication and negotiation, can help you work with others to find solutions.

Life On Your Own

Cope with Stress

Being a teen can be stressful. Teens are often juggling homework, family, friends, dating, and after-school activities. They may also be handling other stressful situations, such as parental divorce and peer pressure. Too much stress can take a toll on your emotional and physical health. Luckily, there are some guidelines you can follow to help you manage your stress.

How It Works Exercise regularly, with the goal of being physically active for at least 60 minutes each day. Be sure to eat regular, healthful meals instead of eating on the run and indulging in junk food. Get plenty of sleep. When you are well rested, you are better able to tackle what life throws at you. Release stress with activities such as reading a book, listening to music, or going for a walk.

Try It Out It is college application time, and lately, you have been feeling overwhelmed. You think almost constantly about your grades and what you are going to be doing next year. You have noticed some changes in yourself. You have not been sleeping well, and you are finding it harder to concentrate and focus. You have also been irritable.

> *Your Turn* What symptoms in this situation indicate that you are feeling stressed? What are some things you could do to relieve your stress? At what point might you decide to talk to somebody about how you are feeling?

Coping Strategies

It is important to recognize and manage the negative effects of stress before they become too troublesome. When you feel stressed, do you have an emotional reaction, physical symptoms, or both? Depending on your answer, try some of these coping strategies:

- **Get moving.** If you start to feel overwhelmed, find a physical activity that will help you unwind.
- **Make time for yourself.** Schedule some time to relax and do something you enjoy.
- **Talk to someone.** Share your thoughts and feelings with someone you trust.
- **Plan ahead.** If you are nervous about an upcoming event, take time to prepare for it and rehearse.
- **Be realistic.** Accept that most things are not perfect.
- **Learn from experience.** If something goes wrong, decide what you can do better next time.
- **Learn to say no.** It is better to say no to commitments than to make promises you cannot keep.

✔ **Reading Check** **Interpret** What does it mean to have multiple roles?

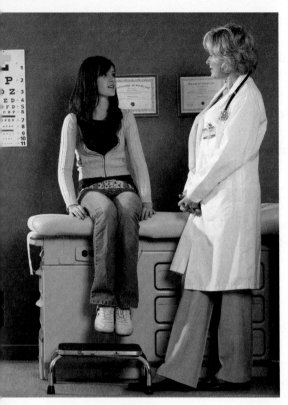

Preventive Medicine

Taking responsibility for your health includes practicing prevention and getting regular checkups. *What does "prevention is the best medicine" mean?*

Health Care

You probably see a doctor when you are sick, but it is also important to have checkups when you feel fine. Regular checkups help keep unseen or minor problems from turning into serious problems. Checkups are also a good time to discuss any questions you have about health. Experts recommend that you have a physical and an eye exam every year, and that you visit your dentist twice a year. Wellness means taking positive steps toward overall good health. One of those steps is to seek the advice of health care professionals. Doctors, nurses, dentists, and dental hygienists are some of the health care professionals who can help you make informed decisions.

The Health Care System

The United States has the most advanced health care system in the world. It is also the most expensive. Many people have some form of health insurance to help them pay for medical expenses. When you start working, your employer may offer health insurance. Because insurance plans vary widely, you should study your plan carefully. For routine medical care, a **primary care physician** provides general care and performs checkups. A doctor trained to treat specific diseases or medical conditions is called a **specialist**. For example, you would be referred to an orthopedic surgeon for a broken leg.

Health Care Responsibilities

Health care professionals can do only so much. They need your cooperation. You need to schedule checkups, ask questions, make appointments if you have a problem, and follow doctors' advice. You are also responsible for maintaining healthy habits and protecting yourself from disease. Perform recommended self-exams, be alert for signs of disease, and use health care products wisely. Accepting responsibility for your health is an important part of wellness.

Resources for Health

To make responsible decisions about your health, you need reliable information. Some questions can be answered by a parent or other trusted adult, such as a school nurse. For further information, check your school or public library for books, newspapers, magazine articles, and other print sources. The Internet can also be useful, but keep in mind that not all Web sites give accurate information. Generally, the Web sites of government agencies and professional health groups are the most reliable places to start.

Most communities have agencies that help individuals and families with health issues. Find out what your community does to promote wellness. Take advantage of programs that will help you reach your goals. If you need help or support, do not be afraid to ask.

Go Green

Exercise machines powered by electricity at fitness centers and home gyms require a lot of energy to operate. Walking, hiking, biking and jogging are all great cardiovascular activities, and the only energy required is yours.

 Podcasts Access the Online Learning Center to download *Managing Life Skills* podcasts.

Section 26.2   After You Read

Review Key Concepts

1. **Name** four steps you can take to maintain or improve your physical health.

2. **Define** the "fight-or-flight" response.

3. **Describe** how you can help your doctor when managing your health care.

 Check Your Answers Check your answers at this book's Online Learning Center at **glencoe.com**.

Practice Academic Skills

 English Language Arts

4. Use the Internet and other resources to research a topic about health that relates to this section. How can what you have learned help you to make positive changes in your own life? Write a short report about your findings, and present it to the class.

NCTE 8 Use information resources to gather information and create and communicate knowledge.

Social Studies

5. Restaurants have a variety of menu selections, some more healthful than others. Research a variety of restaurant menus in your community. How does the food they offer fit into a healthful lifestyle? How do restaurants tempt you to eat more food? What can you do to eat healthfully in restaurants?

NCSS V B Analyze group and institutional influences on people, events, and elements of culture in both historical and contemporary settings.

Pathway to College

The Waiting List

What Is the Waiting List?

Being put on a waiting list means you are neither accepted nor rejected from a school. Colleges put students on the waiting list when the students meet the admissions requirements but the college has already accepted its maximum number of applicants. You will be offered a spot only if space becomes available.

What do I do if I get wait-listed?

If you get wait-listed, the first thing you should do is decide whether or not you really want to go to that school. If you do, you should let the school know you wish to remain on the list. If you plan on attending another school or do not want to take the chance, simply let the school know you do not want to remain on the waiting list.

How can I improve my chances of being accepted?

First, be sure to express your desire to remain on the waiting list by returning the waiting list card. Then write a letter to the school's admissions office trying to persuade them to let you in. You do not want to seem pushy, but if you have accomplished something since you sent your application in, be sure to highlight that. Emphasize your strong desire to attend the college, and make a case for why you would be a good addition to their student body.

Can I get a sense of my chances of being admitted?

While not all schools do this, some colleges rank their waiting lists. Do not be afraid to contact a school's admissions office and ask if it ranks its waiting list. Many admissions officers will be willing to tell you your status or chances of getting accepted off the waiting list. During this phone call, it is very important to indicate your desire to stay on the waiting list. If not, the school might remove you.

Hands-On   **College Readiness** Imagine you have been wait-listed at the school that is your first choice. Write a letter to the school's admissions office listing the reasons why you think they should accept you. Think about highlighting things that may not have been obvious or included in your application. How can you make yourself stand out from the rest of the waiting list and convince the school to accept you?

Path to Success   **CCR** ⭐ **College & Career Readiness**

Stay Involved If you are put on a waiting list, show the admissions board you are dedicated to activities, such as sports and clubs.

Keep Studying If you are wait-listed, you may be reevaluated based on your third or fourth quarter grades.

Be Assertive Call or write the admissions office and ask teachers and coaches to do the same. Resubmit your grades if it makes sense.

Request an Interview If you have already been interviewed, request a second interview.

Stay Positive Realize that being wait-listed is an accomplishment in and of itself.

Consider Your Options Think about whether you will be just as happy at a college that accepted you outright.

 Go to this book's Online Learning Center at **glencoe.com** to learn more about college and career readiness.

CHAPTER SUMMARY

Section 26.1
Wellness for Life

Wellness involves taking positive steps toward overall health. Regular physical activity improves physical, mental and emotional, and social health. Aim for an active lifestyle that promotes strength, endurance, and flexibility. Maintain a weight that is healthy for you. Eating disorders are serious mental health conditions that require professional help. Teens who avoid high-risk behaviors show that they care about their health.

Section 26.2
Taking Care of Yourself

You are responsible for your own health and safety. You make decisions every day that affect your physical health, mental and emotional health, social health, and your safety. Stress is part of everyone's life and can be negative or positive. You need to learn to manage your stress. Regular doctor and dental visits are important, and it is up to you to participate in your own health care management with your care providers.

Vocabulary Review

1. Use each of these content and vocabulary terms in a sentence.

Content Vocabulary
◇ wellness (p. 521)
◇ fitness (p. 521)
◇ endurance (p. 521)
◇ aerobic activities (p. 521)
◇ flexibility (p. 521)
◇ body image (p. 522)
◇ Body Mass Index (BMI) (p. 523)
◇ anorexia nervosa (p. 524)
◇ bulimia (p. 524)
◇ binge eating (p. 524)
◇ substance abuse (p. 525)
◇ stress (p. 530)
◇ adrenaline (p. 530)
◇ primary care physician (p. 532)
◇ specialist (p. 532)

Academic Vocabulary
■ credit (p. 521)
■ composition (p. 523)
■ adequate (p. 528)
■ assume (p. 530)

Review Key Concepts

2. **Summarize** wellness and fitness.
3. **Outline** factors that influence body weight.
4. **Describe** three common health risks among teens.
5. **Identify** four areas of health for which you can take personal responsibility.
6. **Explain** the causes and effects of stress.
7. **Describe** how you can take charge of your health care.

Critical Thinking

8. **Judge** What contributes to the negative body image many teens have?
9. **Draw Conclusions** What do you consider to be the main causes of stress in people your age? Why?
10. **Cause and Effect** Describe a situation that shows how the physical, mental and emotional, and social health influence one another.
11. **Distinguish** Find an article about nutrition, body image, stress, or other health issue. Distinguish between fact and opinion in the article.

ACTIVE LEARNING

Family & Community Connections

12. Developing an Activity Plan You are more likely to reach your goals if you have a plan in place that you can check in on and follow. Develop a personal schedule for the busiest day during your week that includes at least 60 minutes of physical activity a day. What activities do you enjoy that you might add to your schedule? Be sure to include activities that promote the three elements of fitness. You can break up the activities into smaller parts. Be sure also to include all of the other things you will need to get done that day.

13. Youth Fitness Research youth fitness programs in your area to determine if there is a program that accepts volunteers to coach younger children in a sport or other fitness activity. Then contact the office or person in charge of the volunteer program. What benefits do they find in coaching children? What benefits do they see in the children as they participate in sports? Would you think about volunteering in this way? Why or why not? What do you think you might get out of an experience like that? Summarize your findings and opinions in a report, and be prepared to share your report with the rest of the class.

21st Century Skills

Technology Skills

14. Video Presentation With a partner, use reliable sources of information to learn about effective warm-up and cool-down exercises. Choose several of the exercises to practice. Make a video demonstrating the exercises and explaining what each one achieves. Be prepared to show your video to the class.

Self-Management Skills

15. Healthy Choices Assess the tools you will need in your life to maintain a healthy lifestyle. Explain three things that you find challenging that you could do to improve your health. Suggest ways you can set realistic goals, track your progress, and stay motivated.

FCCLA Connections

Communication Skills

16. Student Body As part of its mission, FCCLA encourages students to establish healthy attitudes and habits. Make Healthy Choices is a unit in FCCLA's Student Body program. Much of this unit focuses on choosing a positive lifestyle by avoiding alcohol, tobacco, and other drugs. Research this unit, and then write a how-to guide to instruct and motivate peers who want to choose a drug-free lifestyle.

Academic Skills

English Language Arts

17. Literature Connections There are many examples of characters in literature who do not take the proper steps toward personal wellness. Choose a character from a short story or novel. Identify ways this character did or did not take responsibility for his or her own health. What health-related choices did the character make and why? What were the results?

> **NCTE 12** Use language to accomplish individual purposes.

Science

18. Long-Term Stress Chronic, or long-term, stress can have a negative impact on your physical health.

Procedure Conduct research to find out what people can do to prevent long-term stress. What recommendations can you find for managing stress?

Analysis Prepare a short presentation to share with the class.

> **NSES F** Develop understanding of personal and community health.

Mathematics

19. Find a Healthy Weight Range Body Mass Index (BMI) is a measure of body weight relative to height. Felipe wants to know if his weight falls into the healthy weight range. He is a 16-year-old male who weighs 182 pounds and is 6 feet tall. A healthy BMI for boys in this age range is about 17 to 24. What is Felipe's BMI? Is he in the healthy range for his age group?

Math Concept **Multi-Step Problems**
When solving problems with more than one step, think through the steps before you start. Be sure you understand the entire problem and the order of steps before starting.

Starting Hint Use this formula to determine Felipe's Body Mass Index: BMI = (weight in pounds/(height in inches)^2) × 703.

 For more math practice, go to the Math Appendix at the back of the book.

> **NCTM Measurement** Apply appropriate techniques, tools, and formulas to determine measurements.

Standardized Test Practice

 CCR College & Career Readiness

ANALOGIES
Select the pair of words that best expresses a relationship similar to the one expressed in the capitalized pair.

Test-Taking Tip Analogies are relationships between two words or concepts. Common relationships in analogy questions include cause and effect, part to whole, general classification and specific example, and synonym/antonym pairings.

20. NUTRIENTS : HEALTH
  a. safety : injury
  b. physical activity : running
  c. stretching : flexibility
  d. hygiene : stress

Chapter 27

Nutrition and Meal Planning

Chapter Objectives

Section 27.1 Nutrition and Food Choices

- **Summarize** the basic nutrient needs.
- **Compare and contrast** nutrient needs throughout the life cycle.
- **Name** the main influences on personal food choices.
- **Describe** the purposes of the Dietary Guidelines for Americans and MyPyramid.

Section 27.2 Meal Planning

- **Explain** how planning helps you make wise food choices.
- **Identify** strategies for eating healthfully when away from home.
- **Evaluate** how individual needs affect food choices.

> **Explore the Photo**
>
> What we like to eat is influenced by our family from the beginning. *How does your family influence your food choices?*

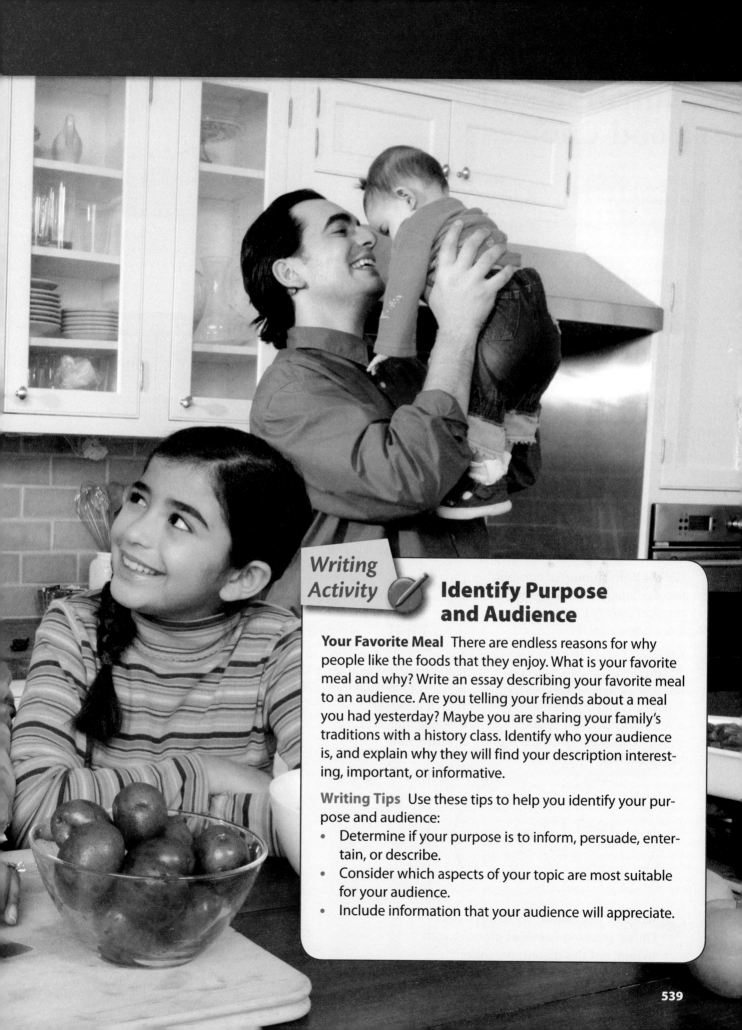

Writing Activity

Identify Purpose and Audience

Your Favorite Meal There are endless reasons for why people like the foods that they enjoy. What is your favorite meal and why? Write an essay describing your favorite meal to an audience. Are you telling your friends about a meal you had yesterday? Maybe you are sharing your family's traditions with a history class. Identify who your audience is, and explain why they will find your description interesting, important, or informative.

Writing Tips Use these tips to help you identify your purpose and audience:

- Determine if your purpose is to inform, persuade, entertain, or describe.
- Consider which aspects of your topic are most suitable for your audience.
- Include information that your audience will appreciate.

Nutrition and Food Choices

Today's food habits affect tomorrow's health.

Reading Guide

Before You Read

Think of an Example Look over the Key Concepts for this section. Think of an example of how or when you could use one of the skills listed. Thinking of how you might apply a skill can help motivate your learning by showing you why the skill is important.

Read to Learn

Key Concepts

- **Summarize** the basic nutrient needs.
- **Compare and contrast** nutrient needs throughout the life cycle.
- **Name** the main influences on personal food choices.
- **Describe** the purposes of the Dietary Guidelines for Americans and MyPyramid.

Main Idea

Get the right amount of nutrients for your age, gender, and level of physical activity to help you live a longer, healthier life.

Graphic Organizer

As you read, compare and contrast the Dietary Guidelines for Americans and MyPyramid. Use a Venn diagram like the one shown to help you organize your information.

The Dietary Guidlines / MyPyramid (Venn diagram)

 Graphic Organizer Go to this book's Online Learning Center at **glencoe.com** to print out this graphic organizer.

Content Vocabulary

◇ nutrient
◇ carbohydrate
◇ fiber
◇ proteins
◇ saturated fats
◇ unsaturated fats
◇ trans fats
◇ cholesterol
◇ vitamin
◇ minerals
◇ osteoporosis
◇ dietary supplement
◇ Dietary Guidelines for Americans
◇ MyPyramid
◇ fortified

Academic Vocabulary

You will find these words in your reading and on your tests. Use the glossary to look up their definitions if necessary.

- concentrated
- inadequate

Academic Standards

 English Language Arts

NCTE 12 Use language to accomplish individual purposes.

 Mathematics

NCTM Number and Operations Understand numbers, ways of representing numbers, relationships among numbers, and number systems.

 Science

NSES A Develop understandings about scientific inquiry.

 Social Studies

NCSS IV E Individual Development and Identity Examine the interaction of ethnic, national, or cultural influences in specific situations or events.

NCTE *National Council of Teachers of English*
NCTM *National Council of Teachers of Mathematics*
NSES *National Science Education Standards*
NCSS *National Council for the Social Studies*

Nutrients

Scientists who study food and its effects on the body have identified more than 40 key nutrients. A **nutrient** is a chemical in foods that helps the body work properly. Nutrients maintain good health and fight disease. Each nutrient performs different functions. No single nutrient can do the work of another. The nutrients work as a team to provide energy and help your body systems run smoothly.

Carbohydrates

A **carbohydrate** ('kär-(,)bō-'hī-,drāt) is a nutrient that provides your body with energy. Grains, vegetables, fruits, and dry beans and peas are high in carbohydrates. They are your body's most efficient fuel. Many foods that supply carbohydrates are sources of fiber.

- **Starches** Starches are called complex carbohydrates. Complex means there is more than one part that makes up the whole carbohydrate. Your body digests starches and breaks them down into glucose, which is the major source of energy for your body. Rice, potatoes, bread, and pasta are high in starch.
- **Sugars** Sugars are simple carbohydrates. Fruits, grain products, and milk provide natural sugars. Sugar that has been removed from its natural source and processed is called refined sugar. Table sugar, molasses, lactose, honey, and corn syrup are refined sugars. Refined sugars are added during the preparation of cakes, candy, cookies, soft drinks, and many processed foods. The amount of added sugar per serving is listed on food labels. Limit the amounts of refined sugar for your best health.
- **Fiber** Certain carbohydrate foods contain threadlike cells called fiber. **Fiber** is a plant material that cannot be digested, but is necessary for moving food through the digestive system. Fiber is not an actual nutrient since the body does not digest it, but it may reduce the risk of heart disease and cancer. Fruits and vegetables, especially the peels and seeds, are good sources of fiber. Whole-grain cereals and breads are excellent sources of fiber.

Proteins

Proteins are the nutrients your body uses to build and repair body tissues. They are the basis of all your body's cells and form the major part of your hair, nails, and skin. Proteins are especially important for children and teens because they are still growing.

Your body breaks down proteins into chemical building blocks called amino acids. Amino acids recombine to make up body tissues. Foods like meat, poultry, fish, eggs, and milk provide all of the essential amino acids and are called complete proteins. Foods that provide some but not all of the essential amino acids are called incomplete proteins, such as grains, vegetables, nuts, and seeds. Incomplete proteins can be combined to provide complete protein. Beans and rice provide the essential amino acids. Dry beans or peas plus grains, nuts, or seeds are other options. These foods need to be eaten on the same day, although not necessarily in the same meal.

Fats

Fats are your body's most **concentrated**, or intense, sources of energy. Fats allow your body to transport and store other nutrients, and help regulate body temperature and growth. After the body has used the fat it needs, it stores the rest as body fat. Body fat insulates the body, cushions vital organs, and serves as a reserve supply of energy. Fat is naturally present in some foods, such as meat, fish, dairy products, and nuts. It is also used as an ingredient in salad dressings, cakes, cookies, and many other prepared foods.

Usually in solid form at room temperature, **saturated fats** are found mostly in animal products. Tropical oils, such as coconut and palm oil, are also high in saturated fats. Usually in liquid form at room temperature, **unsaturated fats** are found mainly in oils from vegetables, nuts, and seeds. Trans fatty acids, also called **trans fats**, are formed when food manufacturers turn liquid oils into solid fats in a process known as hydrogenation. Saturated and trans fats can be found in vegetable shortenings and stick margarines.

Cholesterol (kə-ˈles-tə-ˌrōl) is a white, wax-like substance that plays a part in transporting and digesting fat. High blood cholesterol levels can lead to heart disease, high blood pressure, and other health problems. Most cholesterol is produced in the liver. It is also found in certain foods, including egg yolks and dairy products.

Vitamins

A **Vitamin** is a nutrient that helps your body function properly and process other nutrients. See **Figure 27.1** on page 543 for a list of vitamins. You need to get enough vitamins to avoid problems such as diseases of the eyes, skin, and bones.

Water-soluble vitamins, such as Vitamin C and the B vitamins, are easily absorbed and can move through the body when dissolved in water. Water is constantly lost through urine and perspiration, so you need fresh supplies of these vitamins every day.

Vitamins A, D, E, and K are fat-soluble vitamins. They dissolve and travel through the bloodstream in droplets of fat. They can be stored in body fat until your body needs them. However, getting too many vitamins can be harmful. The body can get rid of some of the unneeded vitamins, but others can build up to dangerous levels.

Figure 27.1 **Vitamins at a Glance**

Getting Your Vitamins Eating a variety of foods provides the many different vitamins your body needs. *What vitamins did you get from your breakfast today?*

VITAMIN	FUNCTION	SOURCES
Vitamin A	Builds good vision, healthy teeth and gums, and strong bones; helps the immune system resist infection.	Eggs, liver, milk products; foods that contain beta-carotene, which the body uses to make vitamin A, including yellow-orange fruits and vegetables, such as cantaloupes, apricots, carrots, and sweet potatoes; dark green leafy vegetables, such as broccoli and spinach.
B Vitamins	Help nerve and brain tissues work well; aid digestion.	Milk products, meat, breads and cereals, dry beans and peas, dark green leafy vegetables, enriched cereals, fortified juices.
Vitamin C	Helps the body build cells; aids in healing cuts and bruises; helps form healthy teeth and gums and strong bones.	Citrus fruits (such as oranges and grapefruits), strawberries, kiwi, cantaloupe, tomatoes, potatoes, broccoli, raw cabbage, bell peppers, plantains.
Vitamin D	Helps the body use minerals, such as calcium and phosphorus; helps form strong bones and teeth.	Your body makes vitamin D if your skin is exposed to enough sunlight; added to many milk products; fatty fish such as salmon and mackerel.
Vitamin E	Helps keep red blood cells healthy.	Vegetable oils, grains, nuts, dark green leafy vegetables.
Vitamin K	Helps the blood to clot.	Broccoli and other dark green leafy vegetables, cauliflower, egg yolks, liver, wheat bran, wheat germ.

Minerals

Minerals are nutrients that regulate body processes and that form parts of many tissues. Your body contains large amounts of some minerals and tiny quantities of others. For example, calcium is the mineral that is present in the body in the largest quantities. Iron is present in only very small, or trace, amounts. Maintaining the proper levels of these minerals, as well as quantities of other essential minerals, is vital to good health.

It is particularly important to get enough calcium during adolescence. Maintaining healthy bones is an ongoing process. People who do not get enough calcium are more likely to develop a condition called osteoporosis. **Osteoporosis** (ˌäs-tē-ō-pə-ˈrō-səs) is a condition in which bones are weakened because they lose the calcium that keeps them strong.

Iron is vital for building red blood cells. People who do not get enough iron may develop iron-deficiency anemia. Anemia is a condition that results in lack of energy and low resistance to infections. **Figure 27.2** on the next page shows the functions and food sources for some of the minerals you need.

Figure 27.2

Minerals at a Glance

The Minerals You Use Calcium helps keep your heartbeat regular. *What are some other functions that minerals perform in your body?*

MINERAL	FUNCTIONS	SOURCES
Calcium	Builds and maintains healthy bones, teeth, and muscles; keeps the heartbeat regular; helps the blood clot normally.	Dairy products, dark green leafy vegetables, canned fish with soft bones (such as sardines, salmon, and mackerel), fortified orange juice, fortified soy milk.
Iron	Builds red blood cells, which transport oxygen through the body.	Liver, spinach, meat, eggs, raisins, dry beans and peas, nuts, enriched grain products.
Phosphorus	Works with calcium to help build and maintain strong bones and teeth; helps the body obtain energy from other nutrients.	Dairy products, meat, fish, poultry, dry beans and peas, whole-grain breads and cereals.
Potassium	Regulates muscle contractions and transmission of nerve signals; helps regulate fluid in cells; works with sodium to regulate blood pressure.	Oranges, bananas, dairy products, meat, poultry, fish.
Sodium	Helps regulate blood pressure; helps regulate fluid balance in the body.	Table salt.
Magnesium	Helps the body build strong bones; regulates the nervous system and body temperature.	Whole-grain cereals and breads, dry beans and peas, dark green leafy vegetables, nuts, seeds.
Zinc	Necesary for proper growth, affects senses of taste and smell; helps wounds heal.	Shellfish, meat, eggs, dairy products, whole-grain breads.
Iodine	Necessary for proper functioning of the thyroid gland, which produces substances that help the body obtain energy from nutrients.	Iodized salt, seafood.

Water

Nearly 70 percent of your body weight is made up of water. Water is found in every cell and is the basic material of your blood. It transports nutrients throughout the body and carries away waste products. Water also helps move food through the digestive system and helps regulate the temperature of your body.

Your body loses two to three quarts of water a day, and you need to replace it. Water, juices, milk, and soups are healthful choices. Foods such as fruits and vegetables also provide small amounts of water. You need additional fluids in hot weather and when you exercise or do physical work.

✓ **Reading Check** **Define** What are proteins?

Life Cycle Nutrients

When a person does not get an adequate supply of needed nutrients over a long period of time, he or she can develop a nutrient deficiency, or shortage of a nutrient. The symptoms vary depending on the nutrient that has been in short supply. Tooth decay, skin disorders, and fatigue are just a few examples. Getting too much of some nutrients can also cause health problems.

Nutrition experts have studied the nutrient needs of males and females at different ages. They have developed reference values for each nutrient. Collectively, the reference values are called Dietary Reference Intakes, or DRIs.

One of the DRIs is the Recommended Dietary Allowance (RDA). An RDA is the amount of a specific nutrient needed daily by the majority of healthy people of a specific age and gender. Adequate Intake (AI) is the measure used for nutrients for which there is not yet enough scientific knowledge to establish an RDA. An AI is an amount believed to be sufficient to meet daily needs.

The U.S. government uses and updates the DRIs to shape national nutrition policies. The U.S. Food and Drug Administration uses DRIs as the basis for the Daily Values used in food labeling.

Specific Nutrient Needs

People of all ages need the same basic nutrients. Understanding the benefits of nutrition and knowing what is appropriate at specific life stages are keys to nutritional health throughout life.

- **Children** Children grow rapidly, and activity levels are high. Infants, toddlers, and preschoolers need an increasing amount of food energy from calories to build body tissue and provide fuel for physical activity. **Inadequate**, or not enough, nutrients can result in poor growth and decreased resistance to infection.
- **Teens** Like children, teens grow rapidly. Depending on their level of activity, teen males may need up to 2,800 calories a day, and teen females may need 2,200 calories a day. Teens need more iron as they grow and build muscle. Once girls begin to menstruate, their need for iron increases. Teens need up to 1,300 milligrams of calcium a day to build strong bones.
- **Adults** When people are no longer growing and become less active, they need fewer calories to maintain an appropriate weight. Those who eat the same amounts of food as they did when they were younger are likely to gain weight. Adults continue to need the same nutrients, but in smaller amounts.

 Stay Active

Adults who eat well and stay active earlier in life are more likely to be healthy and active later. *What would you say to someone who thinks it is too late to increase physical activity?*

Positive Attitude

When you become discouraged about a goal, do you give up or remind yourself about the result? Reminding yourself about what you would like to accomplish and seeing how far you have already come is a good way to remain positive when you are working toward a goal. Even though it can be easier to give up, reaching even the smallest goals can inspire you to reach your larger goals.

You Decide

Think of a friend or family member whom you consider goal-oriented. What does this person do or not do that makes you think this way?

- **Pregnant and Nursing Women** In general, pregnant women need an extra 300 calories per day for the last six months of pregnancy to supply enough energy for mother and fetus. They also need extra protein, vitamins, and minerals. Poor nutrition during pregnancy, as well as the use of tobacco, alcohol, or other drugs, can harm the health of both mother and child. Nursing mothers need an extra 500 calories a day from nutrient-rich foods. They also need additional vitamins and protein, as well as calcium. The higher the intake of nutrients, the more nutritious the breast milk will be, and the healthier the mother and baby.

- **Athletes** Athletes who are actively training need the same nutrients as other people, but they need extra calories. Physical activity requires carbohydrates for energy. They should also get plenty of extra fluids, especially during hot weather to help prevent dehydration and heatstroke.

There are many misconceptions about the nutritional needs of athletes. Normal eating patterns meet athletes' protein needs. Most people, including athletes, do not need dietary supplements. A **dietary supplement** is an extra vitamin, mineral, or other nutrient in the form of pills, capsules, or powders. These substances should be taken only under the advice of a medical professional.

Athletes should eat a meal three to four hours before competition to allow time for digestion. It should contain a variety of foods and should be high in complex carbohydrates and low in fats.

✓ **Reading Check** **Recognize** Why should nursing mothers increase their calorie intake?

Influences on Food Choices

People's food choices are affected by both social and personal influences. Humans do not just eat to live. Food has many purposes. Besides meeting basic physical needs and helping you stay healthy, food also helps to meet emotional and social needs.

Physical Needs

Hunger is your body's physical signal that it is short of energy and needs food. Hunger is different from appetite. Appetite is a desire, rather than a need, to eat. Having a good appetite is healthy.

Eating the right foods helps your body perform vital functions. What you eat and drink helps regulate, or maintain, your bodily functions, such as your heartbeat, your temperature, and your ability to heal. Food also supplies the energy you need for automatic actions such as breathing and digesting and more demanding activities such as sports. Food habits can affect your long-term health. A well-nourished body is better equipped to heal properly and combat disease than a poorly nourished body.

Outside Influences

Of course people need food to survive, but many food choices are made based on other factors as well. Think of some of your favorite foods. Why do you enjoy them? It may be because of one of these influences:

- **Family** The foods that a family eats are influenced by the family's food budget and by how much time the family has for preparing and eating meals.
- **Cultural and Ethnic Background** The foods that grow in each region of the world influence the eating patterns of the people who live there. Every culture on earth has developed its own unique way to prepare food.
- **Religious Customs** Religious customs form the way many people in the world prepare, serve, and eat their food. Some religious food customs are thousands of years old.
- **Regional Traditions** Food served in different regions of the country is influenced by the food that is harvested in that area.
- **Friends** Your friends may eat different foods in their home than you do in yours. Sharing meals and foods with each other is a good way to learn about traditions that are different from your own.
- **The Media** Magazines, newspapers, and television programs offer many suggestions for preparing food and eating for good health. Cooking shows are a fun way to get ideas for new dishes and for variations on traditional favorites.

Personal Influences

Personal influences on your food choices are unique to you. They have to do with the way you live, your personal preferences, and your eating habits.

- **Lifestyle** The patterns of your daily life influence what and when you eat. You may have to plan quick meals or order food at a restaurant. Your food choices may also depend on the time you are able to spend on food preparation.
- **Individual Preferences** You already know that you enjoy some foods more than others. You may discover new foods to add to your list of favorites.
- **Habits** It is a good idea to become aware of the eating habits that you have. If you develop good habits now and make them part of your lifestyle, you could gain health benefits for years to come.

Math For Success

How Much Calcium?

An 8-ounce glass of milk provides 300 milligrams of calcium. That amount provides 23 percent of what you need as a teenager for the day. What is the total amount of calcium recommended for you for the day?

Math Concept **Percents** A percentage such as 23% represents part of a whole. A whole is represented by 100%. Percentages can be shown as a decimal or as a fraction. For example, 23% = 0.23 = 23/100.

Starting Hint To determine the numerical value of 100% of something, set up a proportion, a statement of equality in which each member is a fraction, with x representing the unknown quantity. Solve for x.

 For more math practice, go to the Math Appendix at the back of the book.

NCTM Number and Operations Understand numbers, ways of representing numbers, relationships among numbers, and number systems.

Make Informed Food Choices

When you evaluate, or judge, food and nutrition information, the most important point to keep in mind is the source of your information. The most reliable sources include government agencies such as the Food and Drug Administration, and nonprofit organizations such as the American Heart Association. If organizations or companies provide information to try to sell a product, the information may be biased or unreliable. Always check your sources and use critical thinking skills to determine which sources are trustworthy.

Recognize Myths and Fads

To make informed food choices, you need to be able to separate food facts from food myths. Some fad diets exclude one or more of the major nutrients or allow a person to eat very few calories per day. These plans do not provide enough vital nutrients. Diet pills may lead to death or permanent damage to your health.

✓ **Reading Check** **Contrast** What is the difference between hunger and appetite?

Healthful Choices

Nutrition experts have worked with the United States government to create guidelines. The Dietary Guidelines for Americans and MyPyramid are two resources you can use to evaluate your food, nutrition, and wellness decision making skills.

The Dietary Guidelines for Americans

The **Dietary Guidelines for Americans** offer science-based advice for making smart choices for healthful living. These guidelines are developed jointly by the U.S. Department of Agriculture (USDA) and the Department of Health and Human Services. These guidelines are revised every five years and are designed to help you reach your best level of health. The Dietary Guidelines have suggestions about nutrition, physical activity, and wellness. There are nine Dietary Guidelines for healthful living:

- **Get enough nutrients within your calorie needs.** You need a certain amount of calories in a day. Choose a variety of nutrient-rich foods from each food group every day, such as whole-grain foods, vegetables, fruits, low-fat and fat-free milk and milk products, and lean meats and beans. Choose foods low in saturated fat, trans fats, cholesterol, added sugars, and salt.
- **Maintain a healthy weight.** Overweight is a condition that can lead to health problems, including diabetes, heart disease, high blood pressure, some types of cancer, and arthritis. Underweight is also a health concern. The key to weight management is energy balance. Consume only the amount of calories that you will use each day in order to maintain your weight.

Succeed in **SCHOOL and LIFE**

Respect Viewpoints

Many people you meet throughout your life will have different views of the world from your own. It is important to recognize the differences in others and respect their opinions. Disagreements over food, beliefs, and other aspects of life will always occur. It is important to recognize and be tolerant of other people's views. When you show that you respect their views, they will be more likely to respect yours. This can help you build positive relationships beyond school, as you begin your career and life on your own.

- **Be physically active every day.** Physical fitness is about physical activity and healthful eating. Build 60 minutes or more of moderate or more strenuous activity into your daily routine.
- **Choose whole grains, fruits, vegetables, and milk.** Enjoy these foods as the main ingredients of your meals. Choose low-fat milk and milk products, lean meats and beans, and limit desserts with a lot of added sugar.
- **Limit fats and cholesterol.** You need only a small amount of fat in your diet. Cut back on saturated fats, including butter and deep-fat fried foods, to help lower your cholesterol. Choose low-fat or fat-free varieties of the foods you like. Include unsaturated fats, such as vegetable or olive oil, in your meals.
- **Be choosy about carbohydrates** Limit your intake of sugary foods. Eat fiber-rich vegetables, fruits, and whole grains for nutrition without added sugar.
- **Reduce sodium and increase potassium.** Too much sodium is linked to high blood pressure, heart attack, and stroke. Many fruits and vegetables are good sources of potassium. Flavor your foods with herbs and spices instead of salt.
- **Avoid alcoholic beverages.** Alcohol can affect your ability to make sound decisions, which can increase the chance of injury and death. Alcohol has calories, but almost no nutrients.
- **Keep food safe.** Store and prepare food properly to avoid bacteria, viruses, and other germs that cause foodborne illness.

Science For Success

Compare Fat Content

Knowing how much fat a food contains is helpful in determining how healthful that food is.

Procedure Collect three potato chips and three cubes each of fruit, vegetables, and cheese. Place each food on a piece of brown paper bag, labeling each with the name of the corresponding food. Allow the food to sit for 30 minutes, and then remove the food. Dispose of the food without tasting.

Analysis Which items left greasy marks on the paper? Which left wet marks? How are the foods that left greasy marks alike? How are the foods that left wet marks alike?

NSES A Develop understandings about scientific inquiry.

MyPyramid

Good health involves making smart food choices and getting at least 60 minutes of physical activity each day. **MyPyramid** is a system developed by the USDA to help individuals make wise decisions about food and physical activity. MyPyramid breaks foods into five groups, plus the Oil Category. See **Figure 27.3** on page 550.

- **Grain Group** Grains are the richest source of carbohydrates, and they provide B vitamins, vitamin E, iron, fats, incomplete proteins, and fiber. For the most nutrition, select whole-grain, enriched, or fortified grain products. **Fortified** foods have added vitamins or minerals not naturally present in the foods.
- **Vegetable Group** Vegetables are valuable sources of carbohydrates and are high in fiber. They provide many important vitamins and minerals, including vitamins A and C, iron, and calcium. Choose fresh, frozen, canned, or dried vegetables, eaten raw or cooked, and vegetable juices.

- **Fruit Group** Fruits and 100 percent fruit juice contain many of the same nutrients as vegetables. They are good sources of fiber and carbohydrates and provide essential vitamins and minerals, especially vitamin A, vitamin C, and potassium. Choose fresh, frozen, canned, or dried fruits, eaten raw or cooked, and fruit juices.
- **Milk Group** Milk is a source of carbohydrates, fat, and protein. It is rich in riboflavin, phosphorus, calcium, and vitamin A, and is often fortified with vitamin D to help you absorb the calcium. Yogurt and cheese are also nutritious choices.
- **Meat & Beans Group** All foods from meat, poultry, fish, dry beans or peas, eggs, nuts, and seeds are considered part of this group. They are all sources of protein and B vitamins. These foods also provide vitamins A and E, iron, and other minerals. Many foods in this group contain saturated fats, though excess fat can be removed.
- **Oils** The narrowest color band in MyPyramid represents oils. Although oils are needed for good health and help the body absorb some nutrients, they are high in calories. Eat them in very small amounts. Healthful oils are generally liquid at room temperature and include olive oil and vegetable oil.

Figure 27.3 ## MyPyramid

Stay Healthy and Active MyPyramid advises making small changes to eat healthier and be more active. *Why is it smart to take smaller steps when improving your eating and physical activity habits?*

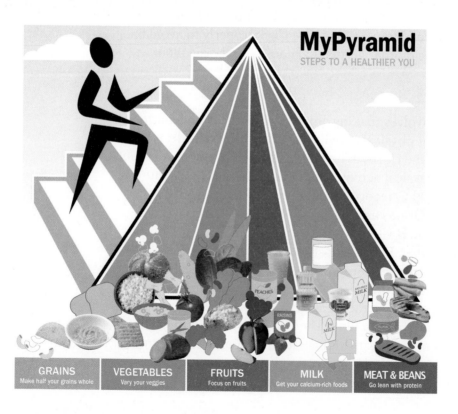

Figure 27.4 | **Portion Sizes**

How Much do You Eat? You can use common objects to help you determine the correct portion size. The information here is based on a 2,000 calorie diet. *How do these objects compare to your usual portion size?*

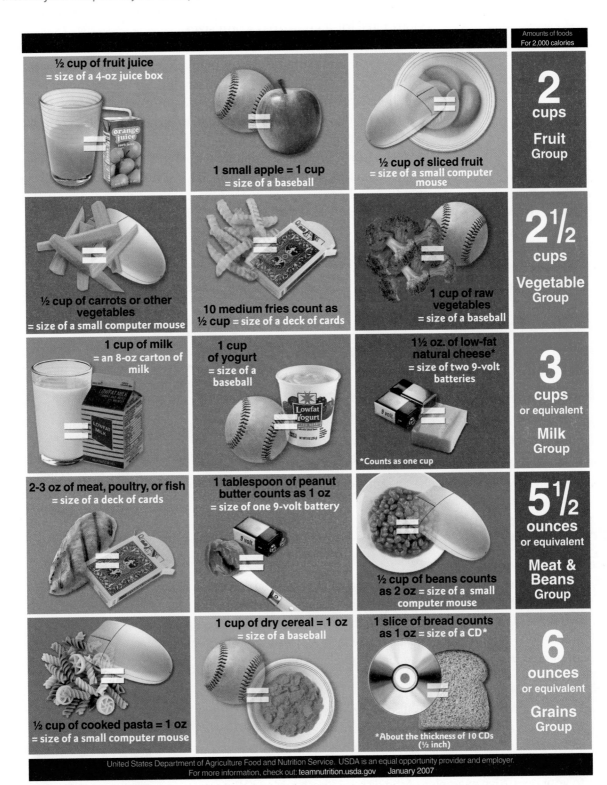

Amounts of foods
For 2,000 calories

½ cup of fruit juice = size of a 4-oz juice box

1 small apple = 1 cup = size of a baseball

½ cup of sliced fruit = size of a small computer mouse

2 cups Fruit Group

½ cup of carrots or other vegetables = size of a small computer mouse

10 medium fries count as ½ cup = size of a deck of cards

1 cup of raw vegetables = size of a baseball

2½ cups Vegetable Group

1 cup of milk = an 8-oz carton of milk

1 cup of yogurt = size of a baseball

1½ oz. of low-fat natural cheese* = size of two 9-volt batteries

*Counts as one cup

3 cups or equivalent Milk Group

2-3 oz of meat, poultry, or fish = size of a deck of cards

1 tablespoon of peanut butter counts as 1 oz = size of one 9-volt battery

½ cup of beans counts as 2 oz = size of a small computer mouse

5½ ounces or equivalent Meat & Beans Group

½ cup of cooked pasta = 1 oz = size of a small computer mouse

1 cup of dry cereal = 1 oz = size of a baseball

1 slice of bread counts as 1 oz = size of a CD*

*About the thickness of 10 CDs (½ inch)

6 ounces or equivalent Grains Group

United States Department of Agriculture Food and Nutrition Service. USDA is an equal opportunity provider and employer.
For more information, check out: teamnutrition.usda.gov   January 2007

MyPyramid gives a range of recommended food amounts from each group. This is because people's calorie needs vary, depending on their age, gender, body type, and activity level. The number of calories that a person requires is directly related to how many calories he or she burns through physical activity. MyPyramid offers a personalized, interactive way to identify the foods you need to eat and how much you need to eat of each. See **Figure 27.4** on the previous page for a guide to portion sizes.

When using MyPyramid, be sure to vary your choices within each food group. For example, enjoy many different types of vegetables rather than choosing the same two or three kinds all the time.

Choose plenty of low-fat, high-fiber, nutrient-rich foods. Nutrient-rich foods are low or moderate in calories and rich in important nutrients. In general, nutrient-rich foods are also low in fats and added sugars. Such foods include whole-grain products; fresh fruits and vegetables; legumes; lean meats, poultry, and fish; and dairy products. Choose low-fat or fat-free milk and milk products. Limit your intake of foods that are not nutrient rich.

 Podcasts Access the Online Learning Center to download *Managing Life Skills* podcasts.

Section 27.1 — After You Read

Review Key Concepts

1. **Explain** why it is important to eat a variety of foods.
2. **Define** the Recommended Dietary Allowance (RDA).
3. **Identify** the reasons people eat.
4. **Explain** why MyPyramid gives a range of recommended food amounts from each food group.

Practice Academic Skills

English Language Arts

5. Your life experiences have helped shape what you enjoy eating. Think of a pleasant memory you have that includes food. Use your five senses to describe the memory and how it influenced your preference for a certain food or meal. Use what you have learned about influences on food from this section to explain your preference.

Social Studies

6. Every region in the world has its own unique style of preparing the food that is available to its people. Research a region of the world different from your own. Compare and contrast the foods that are typically served at breakfast, lunch, or dinner in the selected region to your own. Give examples of the dishes in both regions. Write your findings in an essay.

 Check Your Answers Check your answers at this book's Online Learning Center at **glencoe.com**.

NCTE 12 Use language to accomplish individual purposes.

NCSS IV E Examine the interaction of ethnic, national, or cultural influences in specific situations or events.

Section 27.2

Meal Planning

Improve your health and save time and money with thoughtful meal planning.

Reading Guide

Before You Read

Look It Up As you read this section, keep a dictionary nearby in addition to the glossary at the back of the book. If you hear or read a word that you do not know, look it up in the glossary or the dictionary. Before long, this practice will become a habit. You will be amazed at how many new words you learn.

Read to Learn

Key Concepts

- **Explain** how planning helps you make wise food choices.
- **Identify** strategies for eating healthfully when away from home.
- **Evaluate** how individual needs affect food choices.

Main Idea

The food choices you make are influenced by how you plan your meals, the options that are available, and any health concerns you have for yourself or others.

Graphic Organizer

As you read, think about what you have to consider when you prepare a meal for others. Use a web diagram like the one shown to help you organize your information.

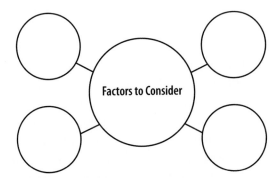

Factors to Consider

 Graphic Organizer Go to this book's Online Learning Center at **glencoe.com** to print out this graphic organizer.

Content Vocabulary

◇ vegetarian
◇ food allergy
◇ food intolerance
◇ lactose intolerance
◇ diabetes

Academic Vocabulary

You will find these words in your reading and on your tests. Use the glossary to look up their definitions if necessary.

■ accommodate
■ scratch

Academic Standards

🔖 **English Language Arts**

NCTE 12 Use language to accomplish individual purposes.

🌐 **Social Studies**

NCSS IV D Individual Development and Identity Apply concepts, methods, and theories about the study of human growth and development, such as physical endowment, learning, motivation, behavior, perception, and personality.

NCTE *National Council of Teachers of English*
NCTM *National Council of Teachers of Mathematics*
NSES *National Science Education Standards*
NCSS *National Council for the Social Studies*

Nutrition Through the Day

As You Read

Connect How do your daily activities and commitments affect your food choices?

It is important to eat meals and snacks at regular intervals. Skipping meals is not healthy and often leads to overeating and poor food choices later in the day. The Dietary Guidelines and MyPyramid give you goals for your food choices and physical activity level. Planning meals ahead of time can help you make smart decisions about your food choices. If your plans change during the day, it is important to understand how to be flexible with your food choices while still receiving the nutrients you need.

Snacking is a good way to refuel when you need extra energy. For good nutrition, snack on a variety of low-fat, low-sugar, nutrient-rich foods. Remember that snacks count as part of your daily food total, along with breakfast, lunch, and dinner.

✓ **Reading Check** **Describe** What is important to remember about snacking during your day?

Family Meals at Home

Families that plan ahead are more likely to enjoy well-balanced, nutritious meals that are appetizing and attractive. Planning also enables families to satisfy everyone's needs and schedules while staying within their food budget.

Menu Planning Considerations

Meal planning begins with deciding on a menu, which is a list of foods that will be included in the meal. A common strategy is to first select an entrée ('än-,trā), or main dish. Then you can select side dishes that work well with the main dish.

When planning meals for your family, you need to know how many people will be eating at each meal. Will everyone be eating at the same time, or will food have to be kept warm or reheated later? What foods do family members especially like or dislike? Does anyone have dietary restrictions or other special food needs? If so, you will need to **accommodate** them, or find ways to help them.

◆ Vocabulary

You can find definitions in the glossary at the back of this book.

As you plan meals, be realistic about your resources:

- **Time** If you do not have much time, plan simple meals that involve few preparation steps and short cooking times.
- **Preparation Skills** Plan meals that are easy to prepare using basic cooking skills. As you gain experience and confidence, expand your skills by preparing more complicated dishes.
- **Money** Plan your meals within the family food budget.
- **Supplies and Equipment** Make sure you have or can get the foods and equipment you need before you start preparing a menu. Check to see if you need any special tools and equipment, or if you have something you can use as a substitute.
- **Nutrition** Include nutrient-rich foods from several food groups as you plan meals.

When you plan meals, keep these characteristics in mind:

- **Meal Appeal** Plan and prepare attractive and appetizing food.
- **Color** Plan meals that include colorful fruits and vegetables.
- **Shape and Size** Vary the shapes and sizes of foods for an appetizing look. Try using a variety of cutting techniques.
- **Texture** A variety of textures adds interest to a meal. Combine a soft pasta with chewy vegetables and a crisp salad.
- **Flavor** The right combination of flavors makes a meal more enjoyable. Combine the mild flavors of rice or pasta with the hotter and spicier flavors of curry or spaghetti sauce.
- **Temperature** Vary the temperature of foods in a meal. A chilled salad and warm bread would go well with hot chili.

Preparation Options

Consider your options for purchasing and preparing the foods in your planned menu. For example, if you plan to have burritos, you could order them from a restaurant, heat up frozen burritos, or make them yourself. Each option has benefits and drawbacks. Ordering burritos is the easiest option, but also the most expensive. Frozen burritos would save time, but might not be as tasty or nutritious as those you make yourself. What are the pros and cons of making homemade burritos?

Two Views One World

How Helpful Is Nutrition News?

On the subject of nutrition, the news about what is good for you and what is not seems to change every day. How can you act on information like that?

Huan: I try to use the latest findings to plan what I eat, but sometimes I get confused. Every day, some new study seems to contradict an older one. First margarine was better for you because butter had cholesterol. Now butter is better because margarine has trans fat. Some people say you should eat a low-carbohydrate diet, while others say you should just worry about cutting back on fat. I'm starting to wonder who I can trust.

Rachel: Scientists are learning so much about nutrition. Every piece of information helps us make better decisions. You have to expect that the guidelines of good nutrition will keep changing as people learn more about the human body and the roles of different nutrients. A lot of things we accept now probably sounded unbelievable at first. It's great and helpful that people keep making new discoveries about food.

Seeing Both Sides
How would you describe Huan's and Rachel's individual attitudes toward nutrition news? Identify points on which the two might agree.

Many preparation options involve convenience foods, which are foods that are partly prepared or ready to eat. Convenience foods can save you time and effort, but they are not always the best choice. Using them usually costs more than making a meal from **scratch**, or using basic ingredients instead of a prepared mix. Many convenience foods are high in sodium. Some are high in fat or sugar.

Choosing Recipes

A recipe gives you detailed instructions for preparing a particular dish. You can find recipes on the Internet, cookbooks and other print resources, and from family and friends. You might enjoy learning family recipes that you can pass on to future generations.

When choosing a recipe, be sure to read it carefully. As when planning a menu, you need to consider your resources. Nutrition is also a consideration when choosing recipes. Some recipes include nutrition information about the amount of calories and nutrients per serving. Often, you can modify a recipe to make it more healthful. For example, you can substitute fat-free sour cream for regular sour cream in a recipe for beef stroganoff.

✓ Reading Check **Recall** What are two of the biggest advantages of planned family meal times?

Dining Out

When you eat away from home, it can sometimes be challenging to make healthful food choices. Your selections may be limited, and you may not be able to find out the fat, sugar, or sodium content of a particular food. If you choose carefully, however, you will be able to enjoy tasty, healthful meals and snacks when you dine out.

Restaurant Meals

Look for restaurants that have a large selection of menu items. The more choices you have, the easier it is to find healthful foods. Choose a main dish that is broiled, grilled, steamed, or baked instead of fried to avoid excess fat. If possible, ask to have your entrée prepared without added fat. Consider having soup and a dinner salad instead of an entrée. Broth- or tomato-based soups are lower in fat than cream-based soups. Many restaurants serve very large portions, so you may want to share a dish with a friend, or take some of the meal home for later. Drink water or milk instead of soda. Choose fresh fruit for dessert. If you do not see fruit on the menu, ask whether it is available.

▲ Plan What to Pack

If you make packed lunches for school, enjoy experimenting with healthful combinations of foods that you like. *Why is it important to like the foods that you choose for your lunch?*

Eating at School

When you select your lunch from the offerings in the school cafeteria, keep in mind your daily nutrition requirements and other meals and snacks you will be having that day. For snacks, choose fresh, dried, or canned vegetables and fruits as lower-fat alternatives to foods high in added sugar.

If you bring food from home, choose whole-grain breads such as whole wheat, multigrain, rye, pumpernickel, or oatmeal. Use sandwich fillings with less fat and sodium. Try water-packed tuna, lean meat or poultry, or chopped or shredded vegetables. Mashed, cooked dry beans mixed with chili powder and dry mustard, or low-fat cottage cheese mixed with chopped fruit or vegetables are also good options. Enjoy your meal with low-fat milk or 100 percent fruit juice and fresh fruit, plain popcorn, fig bars, or yogurt.

Vending Machines

Making healthful choices at a vending machine may be easy or impossible, depending on what the machine offers. Although some machines sell only candy and chips or soda, larger vending machines may provide more nutritious options.

If the vending machine is refrigerated, you might find an apple or yogurt. An apple is high in fiber and has no fat. Yogurt is low in fat and sodium and provides calcium and riboflavin. Raisins are low in calories and have only a trace of fat and sodium.

✓ **Reading Check** **Identify** What should you look for in restaurants if you want low-fat, nutrient-rich foods?

Life On Your Own

Choose Nutritious Restaurant Meals

Calories tend to add up when you dine out regularly. It is much harder to control what you eat when you are dining out. However, you can make healthful selections almost anywhere. Your choices, not the restaurant type, determine the nutrition in your meal.

How It Works Learn about the type of food the restaurant serves. Include nutrition and variety in your order. Try ordering sandwiches on whole wheat bread, or choose salad or vegetables as side dishes instead of French fries. Pay attention to how foods are prepared. Do not hesitate to order dressings and sauces on the side or ask for foods to be prepared in different ways. Keep portions small. Ask for half-portions or split with a friend. Think about ordering an appetizer as an entrée.

Try It Out Imagine you are out to eat at one of your favorite restaurants. You are trying to eat more healthfully while dining out, but you really want to order the special, which is pasta with Alfredo sauce, broccoli, and pan-fried chicken. It comes with your choice of two sides, selecting from a side salad, baked potato, rice pilaf, French fries, creamed spinach, or mixed steamed vegetables.

> *Your Turn* How could you change this order to make it more healthful? Which two sides might you select if you were trying to eat healthfully? What else could you do while eating out to cut down on calories?

Health & Wellness

TIPS

Protein for Vegetarians

Quinoa ('kēn-ˌwä) is a grain that provides a complete protein. Use it in main dish recipes to replace meat in a meal. Other suggestions for vegetarians:

▶ Eat a variety of plant-based foods.

▶ Eat dried foods and nuts for energy.

▶ Choose fortified cereals and soy beverages.

Meeting Individual Needs

Planning meals and snacks requires extra consideration when you, a family member, or a guest has special needs. Understanding these individual needs makes it possible to plan nutritious, appealing meals and snacks for anyone.

Vegetarian Food Choices

People may be vegetarians for religious, cultural, ethical, or health reasons. A **vegetarian** is a person who avoids eating meat, poultry, and fish. A well-planned vegetarian eating plan can be low in fat and cholesterol and high in fiber. Vegetarian eating plans vary. Vegans, for example, eat only foods from plant sources. Lacto-vegetarians eat foods from plant sources as well as milk products. Ovo-vegetarians eat foods from plant sources plus eggs. Lacto-ovo vegetarians eat foods from plant sources plus milk products and eggs. Semi-vegetarians occasionally eat meat, poultry, or fish.

Vegetarians need to ensure that they get enough protein, vitamins, and minerals from other foods:

- **Protein** Vegetarians can get complete protein by eating a variety of grain products, legumes, vegetables, and nuts each day.
- **Iron** Enriched cereals and breads, dried fruits, dry beans, and dark green leafy vegetables are sources of iron. Foods rich in vitamin C help the body absorb iron.
- **Calcium** Legumes, green leafy vegetables, and fortified soy milk and orange juice provide calcium.
- **Vitamin D** Vegetarians who do not drink milk can get vitamin D from fortified breakfast cereals and some soy beverages.
- **Vitamin B12** Fortified cereals and fortified soy products can supply this nutrient.
- **Zinc** Good sources include whole-grain foods, legumes, nuts, wheat germ, and tofu.

Food-Related Medical Conditions

A **food allergy** occurs when the body's immune system reacts to a particular food substance as though it were a foreign invader. Reactions include stomach pain, diarrhea, rashes, itching, swelling, or nasal congestion. In extreme cases, the reaction can be life-threatening. Common triggers are nuts, eggs, milk, wheat, shellfish, and soybeans. Once a food allergy is identified, the food can be eliminated from the diet. Nutrients found in the elimated foods can be provided by other foods.

A **food intolerance** occurs when the body has trouble digesting a food or food component. A gluten intolerance can cause diarrhea, anemia, bone pain, and muscle cramps if wheat products are consumed. **Lactose intolerance** is an inability to digest lactose, the form of sugar that is found in milk. This can lead to gas, bloating, abdominal pain, or diarrhea. To avoid these issues, they may need to limit their milk intake, or use special lactose-free milk products.

Diabetes (ˌdī-ə-'bē-tēz) is caused by inadequate production or use of the hormone insulin. Insulin is used to control blood sugar levels. Some people with diabetes need regular insulin injections. Diabetes is a lifelong condition for those who develop it early in life. Overweight and inactivity can increase a person's chances of developing it later in life. People with diabetes need to make careful food selections and get the right balance of food.

Go Green

Carry water, fruit juice, or other healthful beverages in a reusable container to stay hydrated during your day and save space in the landfills.

Food for Children

Infants get most of the energy and nutrients they need from formula or breast milk. Between four and six months, most infants can eat semisolid food such as rice cereal. Then caregivers can introduce solid foods to check for allergic reactions. Strained, pureed vegetables come first, followed by fruits, and then cooked and pureed meats. At eight or ten months, babies are ready for finger foods, such as soft toast, pieces of fruit, cooked vegetables, and cheese.

During the toddler, preschool, and elementary school years, children develop eating habits they are likely to carry into adulthood. Growth slows but activity levels increase, so nutrient and calorie needs are still high. Children should be given a variety of nutrient-rich foods and regular, consistent meal patterns. Allowing children to help in the kitchen or doing simple cooking activities with them helps make learning about food and nutrition fun.

 Podcasts Access the Online Learning Center to download *Managing Life Skills* podcasts.

 Section 27.2 — **After You Read**

After You Read

1. **Predict** what might happen if you skip meals during the day.
2. **List** three choices you can make to eat more healthfully when eating away from home.
3. **Identify** reasons for which some people may require special foods.

Practice Academic Skills

 English Language Arts

4. You can organize your meals for a single day, a week, or however long you wish. Practice planning for your meal needs by creating a plan for one day. Include breakfast, lunch, dinner, a snack, and a dessert. Organize your plan in an outline.

 Social Studies

5. Obesity is a very serious health concern. It can damage your heart as well as almost every other part of your body. With your teacher's permission, go online to find out the causes of obesity. Collect your research in a short essay that explores the issue and ways you think it should be addressed.

Check Your Answers Check your answers at this book's Online Learning Center at **glencoe.com**.

NCTE 12 Use language to accomplish individual purposes.

NCSS IV D Apply concepts, methods, and theories about the study of human growth and development.

Pathway to Your Career

Registered Dietitian

What Does a Registered Dietitian Do?

Registered dietitians help people eat better by planning food programs and supervising meal preparation. They advise people on dietary matters relating to health, well-being, and nutrition. They also prevent and treat illnesses by encouraging healthful eating habits and suggesting changes in diet. They may consult with individuals, but most jobs are in hospitals, nursing care facilities, and doctors' offices.

Career Readiness Skills Registered dietitians should be knowledgeable about relationships among science, diseases, and food. They must be good at communicating and at encouraging people to make changes in their lives. They must think independently to plan various dietary programs, and they must understand the national food guidelines and recommendations.

Education and Training A bachelor's degree is usually required in dietetics, food service systems management, foods and nutrition, or a related area. Graduate degrees also are available and usually expand job opportunities. Licensing requirements vary from state to state. Registered dietitians can also receive a credential, which can make them more competitive in the job market.

Job Outlook Average employment growth is projected over the next decade. This job growth will result from increasing emphasis on disease prevention through improved dietary habits, and a growing and aging population.

> **Critical Thinking** Research one health problem for which a person might see a registered dietitian. Write a summary describing the health problem and why a person with this problem might choose to see a registered dietitian.

Career Cluster

CCR ☆ **College & Career Readiness**

Agriculture, Food, and Natural Resources Registered dietitians work in the Food Products & Processing Systems pathway of this career cluster. Other jobs in this cluster include:

- Food Inspector
- Ecologist
- Rancher
- Geologist
- Veterinarian
- Wildlife Biologist
- Pet Shop Operator
- Livestock Seller
- Greenhouse Manager
- Plant Pathologist
- Cartographer

Explore Further The Agriculture, Food, & Natural Resources career cluster contains seven pathways: Food Products & Processing Systems; Plant Systems; Animal Systems; Power, Structural & Technical Systems; Natural Resources Systems; Environmental Systems; and Agribusiness Systems. Choose one of these pathways to explore further.

 Career Clusters To learn more about career clusters, go to this book's Online Learning Center at **glencoe.com**.

CHAPTER SUMMARY

Section 27.1
Nutrition and Food Choices

Nutrient needs vary through the life span. Food meets physical, emotional, and social needs. The Dietary Guidelines for Americans and MyPyramid offer recommendations and guidelines for better health through nutrition and physical activity.

Section 27.2
Meal Planning

Consider your resources as you plan meals. Recipe sources include cookbooks, newspapers and magazines, the Internet, and family and friends. Select healthful meals and snacks when dining out. Some people have special food requirements.

Vocabulary Review

1. Create a fill-in-the-blank sentence for each vocabulary term. The sentence should contain enough information to help determine the missing term.

Content Vocabulary

- ◇ nutrient (p. 541)
- ◇ carbohydrate (p. 541)
- ◇ fiber (p. 541)
- ◇ proteins (p. 541)
- ◇ saturated fats (p. 542)
- ◇ unsaturated fats (p. 542)
- ◇ trans fats (p. 542)
- ◇ cholesterol (p. 542)
- ◇ vitamin (p. 542)
- ◇ minerals (p. 543)
- ◇ osteoporosis (p. 543)
- ◇ dietary supplement (p. 546)
- ◇ Dietary Guidelines for Americans (p. 548)
- ◇ MyPyramid (p. 549)
- ◇ fortified (p. 549)
- ◇ vegetarian (p. 558)
- ◇ food allergy (p. 558)
- ◇ food intolerance (p. 558)
- ◇ lactose intolerance (p. 558)
- ◇ diabetes (p. 559)

Academic Vocabulary

- ■ concentrated (p. 542)
- ■ inadequate (p. 545)
- ■ accommodate (p. 554)
- ■ scratch (p. 556)

Review Key Concepts

2. Summarize the basic nutrient needs.

3. Compare and contrast nutrient needs throughout the life cycle.

4. Name the main influences on personal food choices.

5. Describe the purposes of the Dietary Guidelines for Americans and MyPyramid.

6. Explain how planning helps you make wise food choices.

7. Identify strategies for eating healthfully when away from home.

8. Evaluate how individual needs affect food choices.

Critical Thinking

9. Analyze Behavior Think about when and why you snack. What situations or feelings, other than hunger, tend to trigger your snacking behavior? How can you improve your response to these behaviors?

10. Cause and Effect During some years, the number of meals eaten in restaurants increases. In others, restaurants see a decline in their business. What factors might explain these trends?

11. Create Imagine your sister is allergic to peanuts, your brother is a vegetarian, and your dad has diabetes. Your mom wants a well-balanced meal. Create a menu for you and your family that everyone can enjoy.

ACTIVE LEARNING

Family & Community Connections

12. Create a Vitamin Mural Vitamins regulate many different processes in your body. Vitamins are found in many foods you eat every day, yet few people know which foods are the best sources of certain vitamins. As a class, create a mural showing different foods classified according to vitamin content. For example, carrots would be grouped  with other foods labeled as vitamin A. Include groups for vitamins A, D, E, K, B, and C. Be sure your mural includes colorful, informative, and attractive art.

13. Food Allergies A food allergy is a reaction of the body's immune system to ingested food. Peanuts, eggs, milk, wheat, strawberries, fish, and shellfish are some foods that commonly cause allergic reactions. Interview two people you know, such as family members, friends, teachers, neighbors, or coaches, who have allergies to certain foods. Ask them to discuss their allergies. How do their bodies react when eating certain foods? When they have a bad reaction, how do they deal with it? Have they ever received medical treatment for their allergies? Do their allergies pose a problem when dining out? Share your information with the class.

21st Century Skills

Stress Reduction Skills

14. Make a Plan MyPyramid recommends at least 60 minutes of physical activity every day for better health. Create a plan to use this advice when you become stressed. In what types of activities would you participate? Write a brief essay that explains your plan and how it can help you reduce your stress level.

Self-Management Skills

15. Nutrition Resources New discoveries are constantly being made about nutrition. How can you stay up to date? Good management means knowing how to make the best use of the resources available to you. Make a list of resources that could help you obtain accurate, timely information about nutrition. Include human, material, and community resources. Explain why each resource would be helpful.

 Connections

Technology Skills

16. MyPyramid As part of its mission, FCCLA encourages students to eat right and explore good nutrition. Go online to **MyPyramid.gov** and use the MyPyramid Plan to create a personalized daily food plan. Consider how challenging you think it would be to follow the plan. Does the plan you have created differ much from the way you eat currently? If so, in what ways? What would be the most challenging part of the new plan for you to follow?

Academic Skills

 English Language Arts

17. Type 2 Diabetes Use reliable Internet sources to learn about the causes, incidence, and treatment of Type 2 diabetes. Prepare a report of your findings. Include information about healthful behaviors that could reduce a person's risk of diabetes.

> **NCTE 8** Use information resources to gather information and create and communicate knowledge.

 Science

18. Vegetarianism A vegetarian diet is typically low in sodium, cholesterol, and fat, especially saturated fat. Generally, a vegetarian diet is high in fiber and high in potassium.

Procedure Use the Internet to research the health benefits and drawbacks of a vegetarian diet.

Analysis Use a word processing program to write a summary of your findings.

> **NSES 1** Develop abilities necessary to do scientific inquiry.

 Mathematics

19. Healthier Baby Food on a Budget Instead of buying 4-ounce jars of baby food for 50¢ each, Karen buys frozen peas for 99¢. Observing all safety rules, Karen makes baby food by putting the peas in a blender. Each bag makes 31 ounces. About how much money is she saving?

 Estimation by Rounding When rounding numbers, look at the digit to the right of the place to which you are rounding. If the digit is 5 or greater, round up. If it is 4 or less, round down.

Starting Hint First, find out how many jars Karen would have to buy to equal the amount of homemade blended peas. Then subtract the costs to show savings.

 For more math practice, go to the Math Appendix at the back of the book.

> **NCTM Number and Operations** Compute fluently and make reasonable estimates.

Standardized Test Practice

CCR College & Career Readiness

ANALOGIES
Read the pairs of terms. Then choose the best word to fill in the blank.

> **Test-Taking Tip** Analogies establish relationships between terms. Identify the relationship that is common to each of the pairs. Think of a sentence that would tie the pairs together. For example, *A daisy is a type of flower.* When you find a sentence format that fits all of the pairs, apply the multiple-choice options to the blank to see which fits the format.

20. GOLDEN RETRIEVER : DOG

DAISY : FLOWER

CARROT : VEGETABLE

_____ : VEGETARIAN

    a. lettuce

    b. meat

    c. vegan

    d. hearty

Chapter 28

Shopping for Food

Chapter Objectives

Section 28.1 Cost Effective Meal Management Practices

- **Identify** six money-saving strategies to help maintain your food budget.
- **Explain** how a shopping list can be a food budget management tool.

Section 28.2 Food Choices that Promote Good Health

- **List** six pieces of information found on food labels.
- **Describe** how to get better quality for your money when grocery shopping.
- **Identify** which food items should be stored as soon as possible to avoid spoilage.

> **Explore the Photo**
>
> The ingredients you buy can make the difference between a healthful meal and a less healthful meal. *Why might some people prefer to buy produce from a farmers' market instead of a grocery store?*

Writing Activity

How-To Essay

Shopping Lists Some people plan their meals for the week and create a list of needed ingredients. You might create a list from the sale items in the weekly advertisements or based on coupons you have collected. Write a how-to essay explaining the method or combination of methods you use to create a shopping list.

Writing Tips To write a how-to essay, follow these steps:
- List, in order, the steps you would take to create a shopping list.
- Include an introduction and a conclusion.
- Use transitional words and phrases.
- Be sure your instructions are clear and easy to follow.

Cost Effective Meal Management Practices

A good shopping list can be an effective cost-management tool.

Before You Read

Prior Knowledge Write down what you already know and what you want to find out about each key concept in this section.

Read to Learn

Key Concepts

- **Identify** six money-saving strategies to help maintain your food budget.
- **Explain** how a shopping list can be a food budget management tool.

Main Idea

Many factors affect the cost of food and a family's food budget. Planning ahead and using a shopping list can help you stick to your food budget.

Graphic Organizer

As you read, look for seven examples of places to shop for food. Use a fishbone diagram like the one shown to help you organize your information.

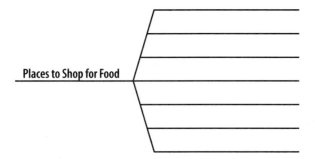

Places to Shop for Food

 Graphic Organizer Go to this book's Online Learning Center at **glencoe.com** to print out this graphic organizer.

Content Vocabulary

◇ store brand
◇ generic brand
◇ national brand
◇ comparison shopping
◇ unit price
◇ staple

Academic Vocabulary

You will find these words in your reading and on your tests. Use the glossary to look up their definitions if necessary.

■ economic
■ estimate

Academic Standards

 English Language Arts

NCTE 4 Use written language to communicate effectively.

Mathematics

NCTM Number and Operations Understand the meanings of operations and how they relate to one another.

Social Studies

NCSS VIII B Science, Technology, and Society Make judgments about how technology has transformed human society and our understanding of human-environment interactions.

NCTE *National Council of Teachers of English*
NCTM *National Council of Teachers of Mathematics*
NSES *National Science Education Standards*
NCSS *National Council for the Social Studies*

Food Budget Considerations

You have probably been food shopping dozens of times, either alone or with someone in your household. Whether you are buying a week's worth of groceries or just picking up a few items, food shopping requires decision making at every step. You make some of the decisions ahead of time by determining what items you need. You make other decisions in the store. Do the salad greens look fresh? Should I buy fresh, frozen, or canned green beans? Which brand should I buy? The more knowledge you have, the easier and more successful your decision making will be. Smart shoppers know how to get the highest quality foods at the best prices.

Food is a significant expense in the family budget. Have you ever wondered why some foods cost more than others or why food prices go up and down? To understand food prices, it helps to know something about how food gets to the store.

Food Costs

Most food begins at a farm, in the form of crops or livestock. From there it may be shipped to a processing center. After it is processed and packaged, it is shipped to the supermarket. Along the way, many people are involved in preparing, inspecting, advertising, manufacturing, packaging, storing, and selling the food.

All the businesses involved in this process have to make money. When you buy a carton of yogurt or a box of cereal, you are paying not only for the raw materials but also for all the work that went into getting the food into your shopping cart.

Food costs depend on many **economic**, or cost-related, factors, like processing, packaging, and transportation. Food costs also vary depending on supply and demand. When supplies are plentiful, prices tend to be lower, and prices go up when supplies are short. Fresh fruit and vegetables can cost more when they are out of season or when weather conditions results in smaller crop yields. Other factors that can affect food costs are brand, product form and variety, packaging, and store type. Partly prepared or ready-to-eat foods often cost more.

Dining out can add even more to your food costs. You pay for not only the food but also the costs of preparing it, serving it, and cleaning up afterwards. Eating at home costs less because you do these tasks yourself. Many families limit the number of times they dine out to stay within their budget. They save restaurant meals for special occasions.

As You Read

Connect What strategies does your family use to save money on groceries?

Vocabulary

You can find definitions in the glossary at the back of this book.

> ### Smart Food Shopping
>
> Clipping coupons from the weekly paper is just one way to be a savvy shopper and save money. *What are some other ways to make grocery shopping more affordable?*

Succeed in SCHOOL and LIFE

Eat Healthy on a Budget

A great way to save money on food and eat more nutritiously is to plan your lunch and snacks before you go to school. You can quickly and easily prepare a healthful lunch the night before. Also be sure to carry some fresh fruit or granola bars in your backpack for snacks instead of hitting the vending machine.

Food Budget

Most families expect to spend a certain amount on food each week, which is their food budget. A family's food budget will depend on the family's income and the size of the family. The age of the family members is also a factor. Growing teens tend to need more food than older family members. Available time and food preparation skills also affect the food budget. A family with the time, skill, and desire to prepare home-cooked meals will spend less on food than one that relies more on convenience foods or dines out often.

Strategies to Save Money

Do you consider yourself a skilled grocery shopper or do you think you still have a lot to learn? Some people spend significantly less on groceries than other people because they are aware of tips on how to save money. They also take the time to follow those tips. Some of the tips that can help you make the most of your food budget include:

- Take advantage of sales. Stores often have weekly specials on selected items.
- Use coupons for items that you buy regularly. You can find coupons in newspapers and fliers and on product packages or the Internet. Look for stores that double or triple coupons.
- Buy store or generic brands when you have no preference. A **store brand** is used for a supermarket's own product. A **generic brand** usually has a plain label and no brand name. Both store and generic brands are generally less expensive than national brands, and often equal in quality. A **national brand** is sold by major food companies. National brands are generally more expensive because they include the cost of promotions and advertising.
- Plan meals around low-cost main dishes. For example, a main dish made with beans and rice can cost much less than one made with meat, fish, or poultry.
- **Comparison shopping** is comparing prices of different forms, container sizes, and brands to get the best value for your dollar. Comparison shop to find the best prices of different available forms of food, such as fresh, frozen, and canned.
- Use frequent-customer cards, or reward cards, that give discounts at the checkout counter.

Compare the Cost of Foods

You can often use newspaper advertisements or store Web sites to compare products and prices between different stores before you go shopping. When you are in the supermarket, you should comparison shop different brands or forms of food. For example, is it a better deal for you to buy fresh fruit or frozen fruit? Is the generic brand of cereal as nutritious and tasty as the national brand? Be sure to check the lower and higher shelves, since the shelves at eye level tend to contain the more expensive products.

When comparison shopping, you cannot just look at the sticker price of the different options. You need to check unit prices. The **unit price** is the price per ounce, pound, or other unit of measure. This information makes it easy to compare the cost of products in different-size packages to find the best buy. Unit prices are often displayed on labels attached to the front of the shelf where the item is found. If the shelf tag has no unit price, **estimate**, or use your knowledge to guess, what the unit price is. Simply divide the total price by the number of ounces or other unit.

Items in larger packages often have a lower unit price. However, do not buy more than you can use. Buy a large size only if you can store it properly and use it all before it spoils. If not, you will waste food and money.

✓ **Reading Check** **Contrast** What is the difference between store brands and generic brands?

Life On Your Own

Curb Your Cravings

We all crave certain types of food occasionally. No one is completely sure what causes these cravings. However, many people believe that you can shift your cravings toward more healthful foods. Completely depriving yourself can often backfire though, so you might want to indulge in moderation every once in a while.

How It Works Cravings are not just limited to snacks and sweet foods. They can occur at breakfast, lunch, dinner, or anytime in between. With a little thought, though, you can usually satisfy your craving with a more healthful option. For example, rather than grabbing that strawberry pastry in the morning, try tossing a handful of strawberries on your cereal. When you crave chocolate ice cream, try a low-fat chocolate sorbet instead.

Try It Out Suppose you had a family meeting last night to discuss the overall health of your family. It was agreed that you would all like to try eating more healthfully in order to have more energy and feel better in general. You left the meeting with the task of coming up with ideas for easy ways to practice more healthful eating. You are having a follow-up family meeting next week to present your ideas and decide on a plan with which the whole family can live.

> *Your Turn* Keep a journal of your family's meals for one week. At the end of the week, review everyone's food choices, and look for anything you can substitute for overly fattening or unhealthful foods. Keep a journal for one more week, trying to make the healthy substitutions. At the end of the week, compare your two journals. How did your family do?

Plan for Food Shopping

Any project goes better if you plan ahead, and that is certainly true of food shopping. By planning ahead, you can make sure you get everything you need. That way you will not discover that you are out of a vital ingredient when you are preparing a meal. Planning also helps you save time and money.

Making a Shopping List

The most important step in preparing to shop is creating a shopping list. A shopping list is an important food budget management tool. Having a list helps ensure that you do not forget something. It also helps you avoid impulse buying.

Begin your list by reviewing the ingredients you need for the menus you have planned. Also check your supplies of staples. A **staple** is a basic food item you keep on hand, such as rice and flour. Since these items do not spoil easily, many people keep them on hand at all times. Complete your list with any other item you need, such as paper products, detergent, and perhaps frozen dishes to have for last minute-meals. If you have coupons, match them to the items on your list.

You will save time in the store if you organize your shopping list. Group similar types of food together. Take a pen with you, and check off each item as you place it in your cart. That way you will be less likely to overlook something on the list.

Where to Shop

You have many choices when shopping for food. Some people buy all their groceries at a supermarket for the convenience of "one-stop shopping." Others buy different kinds of items in different places. Here are some of the options when shopping for food:

- Supermarkets sell all kinds of foods. They might also offer specials, samples, and coupons. Many will include services, such as a pharmacy, florist, or bank.
- Warehouse, or discount, stores are similar to supermarkets, but food is often sold in larger quantities and at lower prices.
- Specialty stores carry certain types of foods. Examples include fish markets, butchers, bakeries, cheese shops, or ethnic food stores.
- Convenience stores are small stores with limited selections. Prices are generally higher than at other types of food stores because you pay a price for the convenience.
- Food cooperatives, or co-ops, are worker- or customer-owned stores that buy food in large quantities and sell to members at lower prices. Variety may be limited.

Benefits of Planning

Using a shopping list can help you save time and money. *How can you save money by planning ahead and shopping for a week or two in one trip instead of going to the supermarket daily?*

- Farmers' markets sell locally grown and produced foods. While most are open during growing or harvest seasons, some are open year-round. Produce will vary based on what is in season.
- Online stores can be more expensive because you are paying for someone else to select and deliver the food to you. Many supermarkets now offer an online shopping option.

Where you shop will depend on your priorities. Remember that prices, quality, selection, and service can vary widely. To get the best deals, you may need to shop around. Whatever type of store you choose, evaluate cleanliness as well prices. Dirt, unpleasant odors, and evidence of pests are signs that you should shop elsewhere.

When to Shop

How often should you go food shopping? Some families prefer to make one large shopping trip every week, with a few quick trips in between to pick up items like milk. Others prefer to make several small shopping trips every week so that they always have fresh ingredients. How often you shop for food will vary based on your schedule, storage space, and personal preferences. Planning ahead and making fewer shopping trips will likely save you money.

No matter how often you shop, it is smart to go food shopping after you have eaten rather than before. If you shop for food when you are hungry, you may be tempted to buy items that look good but that you do not really need.

Get Involved!

Grocery Shopping for the Elderly

Many communities have organizations that provide shopping services for the elderly. Should you decide to volunteer for one, there are some things to keep in mind. Buy smaller sizes as these are easier for the elderly to lift and less likely to perish before use. Also, look for easy-to-open bottles and pop-top cans. What other things should you keep in mind when shopping for the elderly?

 Podcasts Access the Online Learning Center to download *Managing Life Skills* podcasts.

Section 28.1 **After You Read**

Review Key Concepts

1. **Summarize** factors that can affect a family's food budget.
2. **List** the items that should be included on your shopping list.

Practice Academic Skills

 English Language Arts

3. Different families have different methods and styles of shopping for food. Write a journal entry describing how you plan to shop for food when you live on your own. What types of food will you buy? Where will you shop? What steps will you take to save money?

 Social Studies

4. Technology impacts every aspect of our lives, including grocery shopping. Many people use computer software to create and organize their shopping lists. Some people use online shopping to buy their groceries. Write a brief report describing some of the advantages and disadvantages of online grocery shopping. Do you think you might try it? Why or why not?

 Check Your Answers Check your answers at this book's Online Learning Center at **glencoe.com**.

NCTE 4 Use written language to communicate effectively.

NCSS VIII B Make judgments about how technology has transformed human society and our understanding of human-environment interactions.

Food Choices that Promote Good Health

How can you use food labels to make more healthful choices?

Reading Guide

Before You Read

Self-Checking As you read, stop when you come to a new heading. Ask yourself questions about what you have just read. If you cannot remember the answers, go back and find them. This is called self-checking.

Read to Learn

Key Concepts

- **List** six pieces of information found on food labels.
- **Describe** how to get better quality for your money when grocery shopping.
- **Identify** which food items should be stored as soon as possible to avoid spoilage.

Main Idea

It is important to understand and use the information supplied on food labels. You should always use care in selecting quality food products.

Content Vocabulary

◇ allergen
◇ Daily Values
◇ sell-by date
◇ perishable
◇ use-by date
◇ expiration date
◇ pasteurized

Academic Vocabulary

You will find these words in your reading and on your tests. Use the glossary to look up their definitions if necessary.

■ enable
■ regulates

Academic Standards

English Language Arts

NCTE 4 Use written language to communicate effectively.

Social Studies

NCSS IV E Individual Development and Identity Examine the interaction of ethnic, national, or cultural influences in specific situations or events.

NCTE *National Council of Teachers of English*
NCTM *National Council of Teachers of Mathematics*
NSES *National Science Education Standards*
NCSS *National Council for the Social Studies*

Graphic Organizer

As you read, note three types of dates found on food packages and a description of each. Use a flow chart like the one shown to help you organize your information.

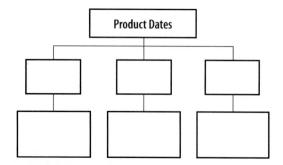

Product Dates

Graphic Organizer Go to this book's Online Learning Center at **glencoe.com** to print out this graphic organizer.

Analyze Food Labels

Get into the habit of reading food labels when you are shopping. They provide valuable information to help you analyze foods. They **enable**, or allow, you to judge the nutritional value of food items so you can make informed decisions and healthful choices.

Required Label Information

The federal government requires full ingredient labeling on all processed, packaged foods. The U.S. Food and Drug Administration **regulates**, or controls, labels for all food except meat and poultry. The U.S. Department of Agriculture regulates the labels on meat and poultry. By law, food labels must contain the name of the food and its description; amount of the food, by weight or by volume; ingredients listed by weight; nutrition facts; name and address of the manufacturer or distributor; and allergen labeling. An **allergen** is a protein substance in food that triggers an allergic reaction.

Nutrition Information on Food Labels

Labels for many foods are legally required to provide nutrition information. **Figure 28.1** shows a sample of a Nutrition Facts panel. Notice that the panel gives the "% Daily Value" for many of the nutrients. **Daily Values** are the recommended amounts of nutrients in an eating plan. Daily Values help you judge whether a food is high or low in a specific nutrient.

As You Read

Connect How do you make decisions when you go food shopping?

Vocabulary

You can find definitions in the glossary at the back of this book.

Figure 28.1 ## Nutrition Facts Panel

Analyze Information The nutritional data on food labels can help you make better food choices to promote health. *Why is it important to read the serving size?*

Calories The total calories and calories from fat in one serving

Nutrients The metric amounts of fats, cholesterol, sodium, carbohydrate, fiber, and protein in one label serving; sometimes other nutrients are included

Vitamins and Minerals The % Daily Value of the vitamins and minerals

Serving Size and Number How big a serving size is and how many servings are included; the Nutrition Facts are for one serving

% Daily Value The % that one serving provides of the Daily Value for some nutrients; the % Daily Value helps you judge how much of a nutrient a serving provides

% Daily Values Explanation Daily Values are based on a 2,000-calorie diet; your Daily Value may be higher or lower depending on your calorie needs

Nutrition Facts
Serving Size 3/4 cup (50g)
Servings Per Container 30

Amount Per Serving	
Calories 200	Calories from Fat **35**

	% Daily Value*
Total Fat 3.5g	**6%**
Saturated Fat 0.5g	**3%**
Trans Fat 0g	
Polyunsaturated Fat 2g	
Monounsaturated Fat 1g	
Cholesterol 0mg	**0%**
Sodium 65mg	**13%**
Total Carbohydrate 37g	**12%**
Dietary Fiber 6g	**22%**
Soluble Fiber less than 1g	
Insoluble Fiber 2g	
Sugars 9g	
Protein 6g	**12%**

Vitamin A	0%	• Vitamin C	60%
Calcium	4%	• Iron	15%
Thiamin	20%	• Riboflavin	15%
Niacin	20%	• Vitamin B6	20%
Folate	20%	• Vitamin B12	15%

* Percent Daily Values are based on a 2,000 calorie diet. Your daily values may be higher or lower depending on your calorie needs:

		Calories	2,000	2,500
Total Fat	Less than		65g	80g
Sat Fat	Less than		20g	25g
Cholesterol	Less than		300mg	300mg
Sodium	Less than		2,400mg	2,400mg
Total Carbohydrate			300g	375g
Dietary Fiber			25g	30g
Protein			50g	65g

Label Terms

Some product labels make claims about the food's nutrient content with terms such as free, reduced, or light. By law, these claims must follow strict guidelines. See **Figure 28.2** for a list of these terms and how they are defined by the government. Labels may also contain terms such as organic, natural, or fresh. These terms are also regulated by the government. A food may only be labeled as organic if it is produced with at least 95 percent organic ingredients. If a food is labeled as natural, it has little processing and must explain why it is natural. The term fresh may only be used on raw food that has not been frozen, heated, or treated with preservatives.

Product Dating

Some foods have dates stamped or printed on their packages. These dates can help you judge the food's freshness. You may see different types of dates on different types of products.

- **Sell-By Date** This indicates the last day a product may be sold. Sell-by dates are usually found on products that are perishable, such as dairy products and meats. **Perishable** ('per-i-shə-bəl) means easily spoiled. The date allows a reasonable amount of time for you to store and use the product at home.
- **Use-By Date** This gives the last day a product is considered fresh. A food may still be safe to eat after this date, but its taste and nutritional quality may have suffered.
- **Expiration Date** This indicates the last day a product should be eaten. After this date, the product may not be safe and should be discarded.

✓ **Reading Check** **Define** What are Daily Values?

Figure 28.2 Nutrient Content Claims

Know the Lingo Consumers look to food labels to help them make more healthful choices. *Would a reduced-fat food or a light food be the better choice?*

COMMON TERM	DESCRIPTION
Free	None or an amount so small it probably has no effect
Low	An amount defined as low for each nutrient or substance, or for calories
Reduced	Food with at least 25 percent less calories, fat, saturated fat, cholesterol, sugars, or sodium than the original version of the food
Light	Food with one third fewer calories, 50 percent less fat, or 50 percent less sodium than the traditional food
High	An amount that is 20 percent or more of the Daily Value for a nutrient
Good Source	An amount that is 10 to 19 percent or more of the Daily Value for a nutrient
More	An amount that is 10 percent or more of the Daily Value for a nutrient
Lean	Fewer than 10 grams of fat, 4.5 grams or fewer of saturated fat, and fewer than 95 milligrams of cholesterol per 3-ounce cooked serving

Selecting Quality Foods

Have you noticed that some shoppers take time to choose food carefully whereas others just grab the nearest item? Those who choose carefully are more likely to be satisfied with their purchases.

Fresh Fruits and Vegetables

You can find many types of fresh fruits and vegetables in the produce department. Some of the vitamins in fresh produce start to deteriorate after harvest, so choose produce that looks fresh with a healthy color and no bruises, spots, or sticky areas.

Choose fruit that is heavy for its size, as this indicates the fruit will be juicy and ripe. Fruit that is very soft to the touch, however, may be overripe. Since produce keeps its quality for a short time, buy only what you need. You can buy most produce year round because it can be shipped from all over the world. However, when produce is in season, it is higher in quality and lower in price because it does not have to be shipped far.

Meat, Poultry, Fish, and Eggs

When shopping for meat, it helps to know how you will cook it. If you are using dry heat, you need a tender cut, like cuts with loin, rib, or round in the name. Less tender, and usually less expensive, cuts include the shoulder, chuck, flank, and brisket. They are better suited to moist cooking methods. This long, slow cooking method helps tenderize the meat. Poultry and fish can generally be cooked in dry or moist heat. Here are some guidelines for judging the quality of meat, poultry, and fish:

- Check the color of the meat. Beef should be bright red, pork grayish-pink, and lamb light or dark pink.
- Poultry should look plump and meaty. The skin should be creamy white to yellow with no bruises or discoloration.
- Fresh fish should have a mild smell. The flesh should be firm.
- Tap the shells of live shellfish such as mussels, oysters, and clams. They should close tightly when tapped.
- Before putting raw meat, poultry, or fish in your cart, place it inside a plastic bag so it will not leak or drip on other food.

Eggs come in different sizes and may be white or brown. Though brown eggs may cost more, the two varieties are actually identical in terms of quality, taste, and nutritional value. Be sure to open the carton to make sure the eggs are not cracked or broken.

Looking for Quality

Meat can be one of the most expensive items in your food budget, so you need to choose carefully to get the most for your money. *Why should you look at the color of the meat before buying it?*

Succeed in SCHOOL and LIFE

Read Food Labels

Learn to read the Nutrition Facts on food labels. This is an easy way to help support a healthful lifestyle. You may be surprised at some of the information you find. For example, many people think that fruit juice is a good way to fit fruit into their diet. When you read the label, though, you will notice that juice is often very high in calories.

Supermarket Courtesy

When you are food shopping, be considerate of your fellow shoppers. As you ponder your choices, do not block the aisle with your cart. Handle produce gently to avoid damaging it. If you decide not to buy an item, return it to its place. Use the express checkout lane only if you have the correct number of items.

You Decide

The express checkout lane specifies 10 items or less. You have only seven items, but the person in front of you has a full shopping cart. What would you do?

Grain Products

There is a wide variety of grain products from which to choose, including breads, cereals, rice, and pasta. Whole-grain products, made from the entire grain kernel, retain the grain's original nutrients and fiber. Examples include whole wheat bread and brown rice. If you want whole-grain bread, check the ingredients list.

In contrast, when making grain products such as white bread, parts of the grain kernel are removed, causing some nutrient loss. Enriched grain products have had some of these nutrients replaced, but the nutrients are not replaced to the original levels. Some grain products are fortified, meaning that additional nutrients not in the original grain have been added. In general, it is best to choose whole grains or grains that have been minimally processed.

Dairy Foods

When shopping for milk and other dairy foods, check the labels for fat content. If you want to restrict your fat intake, choose fat-free or low-fat milk instead of whole milk. Be sure you buy pasteurized milk. **Pasteurized** ('pas-chə-,rīzd) means heat-treated to kill bacteria that could cause disease or spoiled milk.

Reading labels is essential when choosing yogurt and ice cream, too. Like milk, these products may be fat-free or low-fat, but may still be high in calories because of added fruits and sugar. If you are concerned about calories, you might want to choose a fat-free yogurt with less sugar and add your own fresh fruit.

There are many varieties of cheese. They range from firm, aged cheeses, such as cheddar, to soft, unripened types, such as cream cheese. Although most regular cheeses are high in fat, lower-fat versions are available. Always check that packaging is airtight.

Canned and Packaged Foods

Canned and packaged foods are convenient, but many are high in sodium, sugar, or fat. Use the Nutrition Facts panel to help you make healthful choices. Avoid buying cans that are bulging, dented, or rusty as these may contain dangerous bacteria. Also avoid any food packages that have been opened or damaged.

Frozen Foods

When selecting frozen foods, avoid soft or soggy packages because they may be thawing. Also, avoid packages that are stained, covered with ice, or irregularly shaped. They may have been thawed and refrozen, and the safety and quality of the food may have suffered. Wait until the end of your shopping trip to pick up frozen foods so they will not start to thaw in your cart.

✓ Reading Check **Explain** Why should you buy fruits in season whenever possible?

Be Smart Be Safe

Check the Date Always look for the sell-by date when purchasing milk. If kept in the refrigerator at the proper temperature, milk is generally good for several days after the sell-by date. Do not buy more milk than you think you will use before that date.

Write About It Why do you think milk has a sell-by date instead of a use-by date? Write a paragraph explaining your answer.

Finishing Your Shopping

Once you have made all your selections, it is time to enter the checkout line. Be aware that products in the checkout lines, such as magazines, gum, and candy, have been specifically selected to tempt you. Try to avoid purchasing these items on a whim. If they were not on your shopping list, chances are you do not need them. If you realize you have forgotten something, it is polite to take your cart out of line so that you will not keep others waiting.

Be sure to pay attention to the signs posted. Express lanes may allow only a limited number of items and no checks. Some supermarkets have self-scan lanes, where customers scan, bag, and pay for their items without the help of a cashier. Be sure to have your coupons and payment ready for the cashier.

Once you have loaded your purchases into your car, take the shopping cart to the cart return. Shopping carts left in the parking lot could damage cars or get in the way of traffic.

After you have loaded your purchases, return home as quickly as possible. Store perishable items, including frozen foods, meats, and dairy products, as soon as you get home to avoid spoilage. If you planned well and selected items carefully when shopping, you will have a kitchen stocked with healthful, tasty foods for enjoyable meals and snacks.

Plan meals and make a shopping list that includes enough food and other products to sustain your family for the longest possible time. This will cut frequent grocery shopping trips that use extra fuel.

 Podcasts Access the Online Learning Center to download *Managing Life Skills* podcasts.

Section 28.2 After You Read

Review Key Concepts

1. **Describe** three categories of information found on the Nutrition Facts panel.
2. **Summarize** how to judge the quality of poultry.
3. **Identify** two special types of checkout lanes.

 Check Your Answers Check your answers at this book's Online Learning Center at **glencoe.com**.

Practice Academic Skills

 English Language Arts

4. Many people prefer to buy organic fruits and vegetables, when available. According to the U.S. government, food can be labeled as organic only if it is grown without the use of artificial fertilizers, pesticides, irradiation, or genetic engineering. Organic foods tend to be more expensive. Write a brief essay explaining why you would or would not prefer to buy organic produce.

> **NCTE 4** Use written language to communicate effectively.

 Social Studies

5. Many food choices are influenced by the cultures that surround us. Many specialty supermarkets today specialize in specific ethnic cuisines. Visit an ethnic supermarket or conduct research on the Internet, and make a list of food items available that are new to you.

> **NCSS IV E** Examine the interaction of ethnic, national, or cultural influences in specific situations or events.

Pathway to College

Scholarships

What Is a Scholarship?

A scholarship is a form of financial aid given to students to help cover education expenses. Most scholarships are limited to paying for the cost of tuition, but there are some that may be applied to housing costs as well. You are not required to pay back scholarship funds, and there are many different types available.

Who qualifies for scholarships?
Some scholarships require that you prove financial hardship, but most do not. Scholarships are generally given to students who show promise in specific courses of study or to students with impressive academic, athletic, or artistic talents. Some scholarships are awarded for outstanding leadership and community service. You may also be eligible for some scholarships if you are a member of a group or organization.

How can I learn more about scholarships?
There are many scholarships available through private organizations. Scholarships are available from the colleges and universities to which you apply, and more are available through the government. In addition to online searches, talk to your guidance counselor. He or she may know about local awards and other scholarships that fit your unique situation.

When should I start searching for potential scholarships?
While most scholarship application deadlines fall sometime during your senior year, it is best to start your research as early as sophomore or junior year. Identify awards early to make sure you are qualified before you apply. You might even start focusing more on a specific area for which you hope to get a scholarship. For example, participating in certain after-school activities for multiple years may qualify you for some awards.

Hands-On

College Readiness With permission from your parents or teacher, go to the FCCLA Web site and find out about what scholarships can be won through the organization. Describe the project or activity required to earn the scholarship. What monetary awards are offered? Who is eligible? What can you do now to prepare for earning such a scholarship? Write a summary of the information you learned.

Path to Success

 College & Career Readiness

Get a Head Start Scholarship funding is often limited, so start early in the year.

Ask for Help Guidance counselors can help you get started with scholarship research.

Use Every Source The government, private organizations, and the colleges in which you are interested have many scholarship opportunities.

Look out for Deadlines Late scholarship applications will not be considered.

Apply! Never assume that you are not qualified.

Beware of Scams Legitimate organizations do not require that you pay money to get a scholarship.

Do Not Give Up There are scholarships for almost every interest and ability.

 Go to this book's Online Learning Center at **glencoe.com** to learn more about college and career readiness.

CHAPTER SUMMARY

Section 28.1
Cost Effective Meal Management Practices

Many factors affect the price of food, including shipping, processing, marketing, and supply and demand. Families can use money-saving strategies to stay within their food budget. A well-planned shopping list helps ensure that you get all the items you need. Where and how often you shop will depend on your priorities.

Section 28.2
Food Choices that Promote Good Health

Food labels provide information to help you judge the nutritional value and freshness of food products. Much of the information on food labels is regulated by the government. Learning how to select quality foods will help ensure that you get the most value for your money. There are different checkout lanes available to help save you time.

Vocabulary Review

1. Write your own definition for each content and academic vocabulary term.

Content Vocabulary
- ◇ store brand (p. 568)
- ◇ generic brand (p. 568)
- ◇ national brand (p. 568)
- ◇ comparison shopping (p. 568)
- ◇ unit price (p. 569)
- ◇ staple (p. 570)
- ◇ allergen (p. 573)
- ◇ Daily Values (p. 573)
- ◇ sell-by date (p. 574)
- ◇ perishable (p. 574)
- ◇ use-by date (p. 574)
- ◇ expiration date (p. 574)
- ◇ pasteurized (p. 576)

Academic Vocabulary
- ■ economic (p. 567)
- ■ estimate (p. 569)
- ■ enable (p. 573)
- ■ regulates (p. 573)

Review Key Concepts

2. **Identify** six money-saving strategies to help maintain your food budget.
3. **Explain** how a shopping list can be a food budget management tool.
4. **List** six pieces of information found on food labels.
5. **Describe** how to get better quality for your money when grocery shopping.
6. **Identify** which food items should be stored as soon as possible to avoid spoilage.

Critical Thinking

7. **Generalize** How does advertising make it more difficult to stick to your food budget? How does it make it easier?
8. **Predict** What might happen if there were no guidelines for the use of label terms such as *free* and *reduced*?
9. **Contrast** What is the difference between a food cooperative and a warehouse store?
10. **Explain** How can the weather influence the price of certain foods?
11. **Infer** Stores sometimes offer a "Buy one, get one free" deal to attract customers. When might this not be a good deal?

ACTIVE LEARNING

12. Comparison Shop Choose any six food items that your family buys regularly. For example, you might select a certain brand of peanut butter or a specific type of fruit. Compare the prices for these six items from at least two different grocery stores. Both stores can be supermarkets or they can be two different types of stores, such as a supermarket and a warehouse store. Be sure to calculate the unit prices when doing your comparisons. Record your findings in a chart, and write a paragraph to analyze your findings.

Family & Community Connections

13. Family Shopping List A shopping list can be an effective time management tool when used properly. Help your family get organized by creating a generic shopping list. Interview other family members to find out what staples you keep on hand and what other items you regularly purchase when grocery shopping. Compile these items into a list organized by the department or aisle of the store where your family does most of its food shopping. Leave space under each heading for additional items. Identify a space where the list can be posted in your kitchen, and encourage family members to circle or write in items needed. Submit a finalized copy of your shopping list to your teacher.

⭐ 21st Century Skills

Technology Skills

14. Food Budget Use spreadsheet software to track your weekly food expenses in two categories: food from the grocery store and food from restaurants. If possible, save receipts for any food purchases, and enter that information in your spreadsheet for two weeks. Create graphs to compare what is spent each week in each category. Where does the bigger percentage of your food budget go?

Research Skills

15. Seasonal Produce Fruits and vegetables are fresher and generally less expensive when purchased in season. Conduct research from at least two different sources to create a table showing when different fruits and vegetables are in season. Be sure to include some for each season.

 Connections

Financial Literacy Skills

16. Plan Within a Budget As part of its mission, FCCLA encourages students to sharpen their skills in financial planning. Suppose a family of four has a weekly food budget of $200. Plan a nutritious breakfast, lunch, dinner, and snack menu for the family for one week that would stay within the budget. Create a chart to show each menu item and its price.

Academic Skills

English Language Arts

17. Food Packaging Imagine you work for a food company that is developing a new healthful convenience food. Think up a name for the product, write the text for the package, and sketch a design for the package. Be sure to include Nutrition Facts and, if appropriate, nutrient content claims. Be sure to include only appropriate factual claims that would promote the product.

> **NCTE 5** Use different writing process elements to communicate effectively.

Social Studies

18. Shopping Frequency Factors like finances and time affect shopping habits. For some people, there are more physical limitations. In some parts of the world, kitchens have small refrigerators. In other places, electricity is not readily available. Research how these factors affect food shopping habits. Present your results in a report.

> **NCSS IX D Global Connections** Analyze the causes, consequences, and possible solutions to persistent, contemporary, and emerging global issues.

Mathematics

19. Food Budget Bailey is concerned about how her family is spending its food budget, so she wants to create a chart that will show how her family spends money on food. Create a pie chart to show Bailey's weekly food budget. The family of four spends $250 per week, with $25 spent in restaurants, $20 on fast food, $10 on school meals, and $195 on groceries. Organize the pie chart by category.

Math Concept **Putting Statistics into Graphs** Statistics involves collecting, analyzing, and presenting data. The data can then be shown in tables and graphs.

Starting Hint Determine the percentage of each amount by dividing the category amount by the total amount. Use the percentages to create a pie chart.

 For more math practice, go to the Math Appendix at the back of the book.

> **NCTM Data Analysis and Probability** Formulate questions that can be addressed with data and collect, organize, and display relevant data to answer them.

 Standardized Test Practice

CCR College & Career Readiness

MULTIPLE CHOICE
Read the sentence, and choose the best term to fill in the blank.

> **Test-Taking Tip** When answering a fill-in-the-blank question, silently read the sentence with each of the possible answers in the blank space. This will help you eliminate wrong answers. The best term results in a sentence that is both factual and grammatically correct.

20. The _____ is the cost per ounce, quart, pound, or other unit of an item.
  a. cost per serving
  b. unit price
  c. serving unit cost
  d. base cost

Chapter 29

Safe Kitchen, Safe Food

Chapter Objectives

Section 29.1 Kitchen Organization and Safety

- **Paraphrase** how to organize a kitchen for efficiency.
- **Identify** three steps for preventing kitchen accidents.

Section 29.2 Food Sanitation and Safety

- **Describe** three ways to prevent foodborne illness.
- **Summarize** proper freezer storage procedures for food.

▶ **Explore the Photo**

It is important to always keep safety in mind when you are working in the kitchen. *What are some safe practices that you use in the kitchen?*

Writing Activity

Instructional Writing

Prevent Electrical Shocks Many injuries occur in the kitchen due to electrical shock. There are some basic safety guidelines you can observe to prevent this, such as never using appliances when your hands are wet. Conduct research to find more guidelines for preventing electrical shock in the kitchen, and write an instructional brochure.

Writing Tips Use these tips to help you write a successful instructional brochure:
- Think of a catchy title for your brochure to capture the reader's attention.
- Use a bulleted or numbered list to make the information easy-to-follow.
- Keep your bullets short so they are easy to remember.
- Use simple language and instructions that anyone can understand and follow.

Kitchen Organization and Safety

Is your kitchen organized to promote efficiency?

Reading Guide

Before You Read

Take Breaks It is important to take frequent study breaks. They give your brain time to process what you have already covered and get ready to remember new information.

Read to Learn

Key Concepts

- **Paraphrase** how to organize a kitchen for efficiency.
- **Identify** three steps for preventing kitchen accidents.

Main Idea

Kitchens are organized around major appliances and specific tasks. There are simple guidelines to help prevent kitchen accidents.

Content Vocabulary

◇ major appliance
◇ work center
◇ work triangle

Academic Vocabulary

You will find these words in your reading and on your tests. Use the glossary to look up their definitions if necessary.

■ range
■ bare

Academic Standards

English Language Arts

NCTE 12 Use language to accomplish individual purposes.

Science

NSES B Develop an understanding of the structure and properties of matter and chemical reactions.

Social Studies

NCSS VIII B Science, Technology, and Society Make judgments about how science and technology have transformed the physical world and human society.

NCTE *National Council of Teachers of English*
NCTM *National Council of Teachers of Mathematics*
NSES *National Science Education Standards*
NCSS *National Council for the Social Studies*

Graphic Organizer

As you read, look for six common types of kitchen accidents and at least one way to help prevent each. Use a chart like the one shown to help you organize your information.

Kitchen Safety Guidelines	
Accident	Prevention
1.	
2.	
3.	
4.	
5.	
6.	

Graphic Organizer Go to this book's Online Learning Center at **glencoe.com** to print out this graphic organizer.

Kitchen Equipment and Organization

Many consider the kitchen the heart of the home. To keep the kitchen an enjoyable place, people must follow some basic safety rules. You need to know how to use equipment and store and prepare food properly. By learning and practicing safe habits, you can help prevent kitchen accidents and ensure that food is safe to eat.

Working efficiently and safely in the kitchen starts with knowing something about how kitchens are equipped and organized. Meal preparation is much easier when a kitchen includes the basic equipment you need and is arranged efficiently.

Major Appliances

A **major appliance** is a large appliance, such as a refrigerator, stove, or dishwasher. Major appliances are large, tend to be expensive, and perform important tasks. Kitchens are organized around major appliances. Almost all kitchens include a refrigerator and a **range**, or stove, or else a separate cooktop and oven. These are generally considered to be the **bare**, or minimum, essentials. Many kitchens also have a dishwasher and a microwave oven. Before using any major appliance, read the instruction manual. Follow the directions for proper use and care. They will help you make the best possible use of the appliance while being safe and energy efficient.

Small Appliances

Small appliances are portable, or easily moved, and less expensive than major appliances. There is a small appliance for almost every food preparation task. Electric mixers, food processors, blenders, and slow cookers are just a few examples. Before purchasing a small appliance, though, think carefully. How often would you use it? How much time and energy would it save? Are those savings worth the money you would spend on the appliance, the space needed to store it, and the time needed to maintain it?

Other Kitchen Equipment

A well-equipped kitchen also includes a variety of utensils. These tools include such items as knives, cutting boards, measuring cups, pots, and pans. As with small appliances, consider your needs when buying utensils. While many specialized tools are available, you can accomplish most tasks using basic items. If you do not have a cheese slicer, you can just use a knife.

As You Read

Connect What equipment and appliances do you use in the kitchen?

◆**Vocabulary**

You can find definitions in the glossary at the back of this book.

Organization Means Efficiency

Having an organized kitchen will save you time and energy. *Which work center is this person working in?*

> **Kitchen Safety**

Using pot holders is a simple way to help prevent accidents from happening in the kitchen. *What are some other habits you can develop to avoid accidents in the kitchen?*

Kitchen Organization

A well-organized kitchen helps you manage the tasks of storage, preparation, and cleanup. It allows you to move around the kitchen quickly and easily, finding what you need when you need it, and preparing meals efficiently. Good management can help you save time and energy.

An efficient kitchen has organized work centers. A **work center** is an area devoted to a certain type of task. The idea is to place all the items and supplies needed for a certain task in one area. That way, you will not need to stop in the middle of your food preparation to look for something. Work centers should have a clutter-free surface for working.

Most kitchens have three basic work centers. There should be a storage center near the refrigerator and cabinets. There you might keep storage containers, plastic storage bags, and other items you use for storing foods. A cooking center would be located near the microwave and the range. The cooking center should be equipped with such items as pots and pans, cooking tools, pot holders, and wooden spoons. The cleanup center should be near the sink and dishwasher. It often contains items such as cutting boards, soaps, vegetable brushes, and dish towels. When everything you need for a task is close at hand, you can work more efficiently.

To prepare food efficiently, you need a clear path from one work center to another. The imaginary lines connecting the three work centers form the **work triangle**. Think about your kitchen at home. If you drew a diagram of your kitchen and connected these three points, would the resulting triangle be long and skinny, or more evenly balanced? In an efficient kitchen, the distance between any two points of the triangle is not so long as to waste steps.

✓ *Reading Check* **Contrast** What is the difference between major appliances and small appliances?

Succeed in SCHOOL and LIFE

Organize Your Pantry

Keeping an organized pantry can save you time and make your kitchen safer. Store newer food in the back. When you go shopping, rotate the older items to the front so you will use them first. This helps prevent foods from expiring. Purge your pantry at least once a year, looking for expired foods.

Kitchen Accident Prevention

Knowledge is one of the most useful resources for working in a kitchen. Knowing what dangers might occur will help you avoid them. If you pay close attention to your work, develop careful work habits, and follow safety rules consistently, you can prevent most kitchen accidents.

Sources of Danger

There are quite a few hazards in a typical kitchen. Knives are sharp, and an oven or range gets hot rapidly when it is turned on. Grease on the floor can cause you to slip and fall. Metal pots, pans, tools, and even food can get so hot that they can burn.

Many electric appliances can shock you if they have frayed cords, are used incorrectly, or are used near water. Leaks from gas appliances, such as ranges, can cause explosions and fires.

Cleaning products stored in the kitchen can cause serious injuries. Many common cleaning agents are poisonous if they are swallowed. They can also cause irritation or injury if they splash into a person's eyes. These products can be particularly dangerous to young children, who are naturally curious.

Safety Precautions

There are basic safety rules that can help prevent cuts, burns, falls, fires, electric shocks, poisoning, and other serious injuries that can occur in the kitchen. The list is long, but learning and following these rules can help everyone prevent kitchen accidents.

Cuts

Always hold a knife by its handle. Use a cutting board, and make a cut by moving the knife blade away from your fingers. Wash knives separately. Insert beaters or cutting blades into an appliance before plugging it in. Unplug the appliance before removing or cleaning the beaters or blades. Watch out for sharp edges on the lids and rims of opened cans.

Burns and Scalding

Use pot holders when handling hot items. Lift the far side of a pan's cover first so that the steam will not burn you. Keep handles turned inward so that the pans will not get knocked off the range.

Falls

Wipe up spills immediately. Use a step stool to reach high shelves. Never leave anything on the floor where someone might trip over it.

Science For Success

Fighting Fires

Fire requires three elements to start and survive: heat, fuel, and oxygen. Removing any one of these elements can extinguish a fire.

Procedure Choose one type of kitchen fire to analyze. Conduct research to identify what might cause this type of fire and safe ways to put it out.

Analysis Write a report to share your findings. In your report, describe the type of fire, typical causes, and safe ways to put out that type of fire.

NSES B Develop an understanding of the structure and properties of matter and chemical reactions.

Fires

Keep all flammable materials, including your sleeves and clothing, away from the range. Tie back long hair. Clean all grease from the oven, cooktop, and vent above the burners. Turn off all range or appliance controls when you have finished cooking. Always keep a fire extinguisher in or near the kitchen in case a fire occurs. Smother a grease fire by turning off the heat source and covering the pan, but never use water. If you smell gas, leave the building, call your gas company immediately, and follow their instructions.

Electric Shocks

Never overload an electrical outlet. Plug only one electric appliance in at a time. Unplug appliances when they are not in use. Be sure to pull on the plug, not on the cord. Keep electric appliances away from water. Do not use appliances with frayed cords. Never drape cords over the edge of a counter. Never stick metal objects, such as knives or forks, inside a toaster or other electric appliance.

Poisoning

Store household chemicals well out of the reach of children. If necessary, secure cabinet doors with childproof latches or locks. Be sure all household chemicals are properly labeled.

 Podcasts Access the Online Learning Center to download *Managing Life Skills* podcasts.

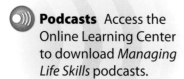 **Section 29.1**

After You Read

Review Key Concepts

1. **Summarize** factors to consider before buying a small appliance.
2. **Describe** the steps you can take to prevent burns and scalding in the kitchen.

Practice Academic Skills

 English Language Arts

3. Brainstorm a list of ten small kitchen appliances. Decide which of these three categories you would put each appliance in: Basic Necessity, Nice to Have, or Waste of Money. Write a brief explanation of how you decided which category to place each appliance in.

Social Studies

4. Your home's smoke alarm can alert you to a kitchen fire with loud beeps. Inventors have created a new smoke detector that uses wasabi, a Japanese horseradish with a strong odor and taste, to alert the deaf to a fire. The Wasabi Smoke Detector sprays potent wasabi extract into a room to alert deaf people to a fire. Research other types of alarms that can alert the hearing impaired to a kitchen fire. Write a brief summary to share your findings.

 **Check Your Answers** Check your answers at this book's Online Learning Center at **glencoe.com**.

NCTE 12 Use language to accomplish individual purposes.

NCSS VIII B Make judgments about how science and technology have transformed the physical world and human society.

Food Sanitation and Safety

Food preparation is more than just washing your hands.

Reading Guide

Before You Read

Preview List two things you know and two questions you have about foodborne illness and storing food safely. As you read, confirm your knowledge and find answers to your questions.

Read to Learn
Key Concepts
- **Describe** three ways to prevent foodborne illness.
- **Summarize** proper freezer storage procedures for food.

Main Idea
There are safety guidelines everyone should follow to help prevent foodborne illness. It is important to know and follow basic food storage procedures.

Content Vocabulary
◇ foodborne illness
◇ cross-contamination
◇ danger zone
◇ rotation
◇ freezer burn

Academic Vocabulary
You will find these words in your reading and on your tests. Use the glossary to look up their definitions if necessary.
■ contact
■ transfer

Graphic Organizer
As you read, look for three safe methods to use when thawing frozen foods. Use a graphic organizer like the one shown to help you organize your information.

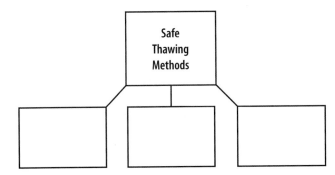

Safe Thawing Methods

 Graphic Organizer Go to this book's Online Learning Center at **glencoe.com** to print out this graphic organizer.

Academic Standards

 English Language Arts
NCTE 12 Use language to accomplish individual purposes.

Mathematics
NCTM Measurement Understand measurable attributes of objects and the units, systems, and processes of measurement.

Social Studies
NCSS I A Culture Analyze and explain the ways groups, societies, and cultures address human needs and concerns.

NCTE *National Council of Teachers of English*
NCTM *National Council of Teachers of Mathematics*
NSES *National Science Education Standards*
NCSS *National Council for the Social Studies*

Preventing Foodborne Illness

As You Read

Connect In what ways have you practiced safe food handling at home?

Foodborne illness, also known as food poisoning, is sickness caused by eating food that contains a contaminant, or harmful substance. Most foodborne illness occurs when food is contaminated with harmful bacteria. Bacteria are carried by people, animals, insects, and objects. In small amounts, they usually cause no harm. When they are allowed to multiply, though, they become a health hazard. In general, bacteria are more likely to multiply in food that is not kept at the right temperature. Three basic guidelines for preventing foodborne illness are to avoid cross-contamination, control the temperature of food, and practice cleanliness.

Many different kinds of bacteria can cause foodborne illness. E. coli bacteria are generally found in raw or undercooked ground meat, contaminated water, and unpasteurized milk. Salmonella bacteria are found in raw or undercooked poultry and eggs.

One of the most serious foodborne illnesses is botulism, which can be fatal. Improperly canned foods are the most common source. Never eat food from a can that is bulging, swollen, or leaking.

Avoid Cross-Contamination

 **Vocabulary**

You can find definitions in the glossary at the back of this book.

Cross-contamination is the spreading of harmful bacteria from one food to another. Cross-contamination most commonly occurs when raw meat, poultry, or fish or their juices come in **contact** with, or touch, other foods. For example, you could cause cross-contamination if you used the same knife to cut raw meat and vegetables without washing it in between. Guidelines for preventing cross-contamination include:

- Make sure that raw meat, poultry, and fish are kept away from other foods at all times, including in the shopping cart and refrigerator and on countertops.
- Wash everything that touches raw meat, poultry, and fish in hot, soapy water before using it again, including cutting boards, utensils, countertops, and hands.
- Place cooked food on a clean plate. Never use the same plate that held the raw food unless it has been washed thoroughly.
- Use a paper towel to wipe up food scraps, spills, or meat juices. Then wash the counter and your hands right away.

Control Temperatures

You can also help prevent foodborne illness by keeping foods at the proper temperature when thawing, cooking, and serving them. A general rule to follow is, "Keep hot foods hot and cold foods cold." Bacteria grow to dangerous levels most rapidly when they are exposed to temperatures between 40°F (4°C) and 140°F (60°C). This is known as the **danger zone**. Figure 29.1 on the next page shows safe and unsafe temperatures for handling food.

➤ Avoid Contamination

It is important to keep raw meat away from other foods to avoid cross-contamination. *What other steps can you take to help prevent cross-contamination?*

Thaw Foods Safely

Freezing food does not kill bacteria. It simply keeps bacteria from growing. When thawing frozen foods, take care to avoid the danger zone. The bacteria may still be alive and could grow to harmful levels. Never leave frozen meat, poultry, or fish on the countertop to thaw at room temperature. Bacteria can grow on the outside of the food before the inside thaws. When done properly, you can thaw frozen foods safely using the refrigerator, cold water, or a microwave oven.

Refrigerator To thaw in the refrigerator, allow plenty of time. Many foods require a day or more. For example, a turkey may take several days. Always place frozen foods on the lowest shelf in a plastic bag so they do not drip on other foods. Once you defrost the food in a refrigerator, use it as soon as possible.

| Figure 29.1 | **Danger Zones** |

Safe Food Temperatures Bacteria die when food are thoroughly cooked at high temperatures. *Why should you use a meat thermometer to check the inside temperature of a hamburger?*

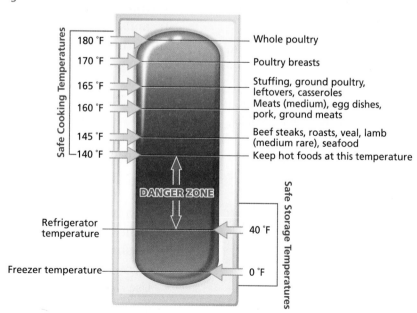

Safe Cooking Temperatures

- 180 °F — Whole poultry
- 170 °F — Poultry breasts
- 165 °F — Stuffing, ground poultry, leftovers, casseroles
- 160 °F — Meats (medium), egg dishes, pork, ground meats
- 145 °F — Beef steaks, roasts, veal, lamb (medium rare), seafood
- 140 °F — Keep hot foods at this temperature

DANGER ZONE

Refrigerator temperature — 40 °F

Freezer temperature — 0 °F

Safe Storage Temperatures

Cold Water When defrosting food in cold water, keep the frozen food in a leak proof plastic bag so that water will not come in contact with the food. If water touches the food, you risk the development of bacteria. Change the water approximately every 30 minutes. It requires about 30 minutes for every pound of food to defrost.

Microwave You can use the defrost or low setting on the microwave oven. If you use the microwave method, be sure to cook the food immediately after you thaw it. Place the food on a plate before placing it in the microwave to avoid cross-contamination.

Cook Foods Thoroughly

Proper cooking ensures that foods reach a high enough temperature to kill harmful bacteria. You cannot always tell whether food is done by looking at it. The best way to ensure that foods are cooked thoroughly is to check the internal temperature. You can use an oven-proof thermometer designed to stay in food while it is cooking or an instant-read thermometer used after cooking.

Serve Foods Safely

Once food is cooked, keep it hot until it is served. If the air is 90°F (32°C) or higher, do not keep food out for longer than one hour. If the air is below 90°F (32°C), you can generally keep food out for up to two hours. If the food will not be eaten immediately, keep foods above 140°F (60°C) in a slow cooker or oven. Cold foods that spoil easily, such as milk, custard pies, or mixtures containing mayonnaise, should be kept cold. If you take food on a picnic, use insulated containers. Always cover and refrigerate leftovers right away.

Practice Cleanliness

You can prevent bacteria from spreading and multiplying by following basic food safety rules. One rule is to keep the kitchen, food, equipment, and yourself clean. To do this, follow these simple guidelines:

- Wash your hands before working with food and after using the restroom.
- Use hot, soapy water to wash tools, utensils, cutting boards, and other surfaces every time you prepare food.
- Use only clean dishcloths, sponges, and towels. Use separate towels for wiping dishes and drying your hands.
- Wash the tops of cans before you open them.
- Use a spoon, not your fingers, for tasting food. If the spoon has been used for tasting once, wash it before reusing it.

- Use a tissue when you sneeze or cough, and turn away from the food. Then wash your hands.
- Keep your hair out of the food. If your hair is long, tie it back.
- Wash fresh fruits and vegetables under cold, running water.
- Keep pets out of food preparation areas. Never allow cats to jump on countertops.
- Avoid touching the eating surfaces of plates, flatware, and glassware when you set the table.

Pests, such as flies, ants, and mice, carry dirt and bacteria that can contaminate foods and surfaces. Keep the kitchen clean to help keep pests away. If pests are a problem, choose a pest-control method that is effective and safe. Do not allow insecticides to come in contact with food or with surfaces, utensils, or containers that will touch food. If the pest problem persists, call a professional exterminator to deal with it.

✓ Reading Check **Recall** What is the danger zone, and what can happen to food in the danger zone?

Store Food Safely

Storing food properly keeps it safe. It also saves money because less food is wasted. A general principle to follow with all food storage is "first in, first out." Set up a system of **rotation**, in which food items are stored so that older supplies are used before newer ones. For example, when you purchase a new carton of milk, place it behind the carton that is already in the refrigerator so that you will be sure to use the older milk first.

Health & Wellness TIPS

Pack a Safe Lunch

Packed lunches that cannot be refrigerated need special handling. Follow these tips:

- ▶ Use an insulated lunch bag or tote to maintain temperatures.
- ▶ Freeze cold foods before you pack them. They will thaw by lunchtime and will help keep other foods cool.

Life On Your Own

Make Produce Appealing

Fruits and vegetables are healthy and versatile foods. They can be used as entrées, side dishes, desserts, or snacks. You can make your fruits and vegetables more appealing by varying the color and shapes of the vegetables on a plate. Some produce will discolor once cut or peeled, but there are some things you can do to help your produce stay appealing longer.

How It Works Tossing sliced fruit in lemon juice or another citrus fruit juice will keep the fruit from turning brown. Similarly, rub lemon juice on the cut edges of vegetables to prevent discoloration. Also, cooking vegetables al dente, or tender but firm, will help them maintain a bright and appealing color.

Try It Out You are attending a party with some friends and have volunteered to bring some snacks. The host has already planned on serving some chips and dips and cookies. You would like to offer a more healthful snack and are considering bringing something made with fruit. Another friend then asks you to work together to prepare a tray with a variety of fruits and vegetables.

> **Your Turn** Come up with a list of fruits and vegetables to include on your tray, and suggest ways to prepare them to make them appealing. How would you slice them? Would you cook them or offer them raw?

Clean Up After Yourself

Keeping a clean kitchen shows that you value your safety and the safety of others. If you spill something, clean it up immediately. Spills on the floor can cause people to slip and fall. Spills on the counter could cause cross-contamination. After cooking, wash the dishes or put them in the dishwasher.

You Decide

You are preparing a meal with a friend. How can you divide the cleaning duties to ensure that the kitchen stays safe and clean?

Also look for sell-by and use-by dates on food containers. Be sure to use food before the use-by date has passed or within a reasonable time after the sell-by date. If a food is expired, throw it away. Be sure to read labels and packages for storage instructions too. The three main types of food storage are refrigerator, freezer, and dry storage.

Refrigerator Storage

Most perishable foods, like dairy products, eggs, meat, poultry, and fish, should be stored in the refrigerator. Some fresh fruits and vegetables are also usually stored in the refrigerator. Canned, bottled, and packaged foods may need to be refrigerated after opening. Foods can dry out quickly in the refrigerator, so use airtight covered containers or wrap foods in foil or plastic. The refrigerator temperature should be between 32°F (0°C) and 40°F (4°C). **Figure 29.2** lists the refrigerator storage times for some common foods.

Freezer Storage

Perishable foods that require long-term storage should be kept in the freezer. The freezer temperature should be 0°F (-18°C) or below. Foods that are bought frozen should be kept in their original containers. Foods that are frozen at home need special packaging to prevent freezer burn. **Freezer burn** is a condition caused by moisture loss due to improper packaging before freezing. It can cause unappealing, dried-up white areas on food, as well as loss of flavor.

Figure 29.2 **Refrigerator Storage Times**

Is the Food Fresh? Some foods stay safe in the refrigerator longer than others.
How can you be sure you do not leave leftovers in the refrigerator too long?

SAFE STORAGE TIME	FOODS
1 to 2 days	Poultry; fish and shellfish; ground meat; store-cooked convenience meals; cream pies
3 to 5 days	Cold cuts (opened); fresh meats (not ground); leftover cooked meats and meat dishes; fully cooked ham slices; store-prepared salads
Up to 7 days	Milk; cream; cottage cheese; bacon; whole fully cooked ham; hard-cooked eggs; hot dogs (opened); smoked sausage; cakes and pies
Up to 3 weeks	Eggs; sour cream; hard cheese (opened); hard sausage
Up to 3 months	Butter; margarine; salsa (opened); salad dressing (opened)
Up to 6 months	Ham (unopened can); hard cheese (unopened)

Prevent freezer burn by using airtight plastic containers, plastic freezer bags, heavy-duty foil, or freezer paper. Include a label listing the contents, number of servings, and date. Most meats can be stored for 12 months. Dairy products should be used within 6 months. Use a rotation system to ensure that you use older supplies first. Some foods do not freeze well, such as cooked egg whites, lettuce, and dishes with mayonnaise or salad dressing.

Dry Storage

Dry storage consists of kitchen cabinets, shelves, or a pantry where food remains at room temperature. It is suitable for many canned, bottled, and packaged goods. Some perishables, such as potatoes, onions, oils, and dry herbs, are also best kept in a cool, dry place. Dry storage should be kept below 85°F (29°C).

Avoid using shelves near heat sources, such as the range or a radiator. Do not store food above the refrigerator because its motor can heat this space. Avoid areas that might get damp, such as under the sink, and do not store food near cleaning products or trash.

Unopened packages can be stored for weeks or even months. Once opened, though, you may have to **transfer**, or move, leftover canned foods to a storage container and refrigerate them. Read labels to learn which foods need refrigeration after opening. Foods like cereals and crackers can remain at room temperature but should be placed in airtight storage containers.

 Podcasts Access the Online Learning Center to download *Managing Life Skills* podcasts.

Section 29.2   After You Read

Review Key Concepts

1. **Summarize** what you can do to avoid cross-contamination between foods.
2. **Explain** safe storage procedures for refrigerated foods.

Practice Academic Skills

 English Language Arts

3. Write a 30-second public service announcement about food safety. Choose one area of food safety to focus on. Your announcement should capture listeners' attention and inform them about one important aspect of food safety. Read your announcement to the class, if possible.

 Social Studies

4. Using print or Internet resources, research how people in Colonial times kept food from spoiling during hot weather. What other techniques did they have for preserving and storing food? Write a brief essay to share your findings.

Check Your Answers Check your answers at this book's Online Learning Center at **glencoe.com**.

NCTE 12 Use language to accomplish individual purposes.

NCSS I A Analyze and explain the ways groups, societies, and cultures address human needs and concerns.

What Does a Chef Do?

Chefs prepare, season, and cook a wide range of foods, including soups, salads, entrées, side dishes, and desserts. They also create new recipes. They perform many tasks, such as cutting vegetables, trimming meat, preparing poultry, and monitoring temperatures. Chefs are ultimately responsible for the food that comes out of the kitchen. They work in many types of restaurants and other food services establishments, such as cafeterias.

Career Readiness Skills Chefs should have a strong interest in food and related culinary arts. They need to be efficient, quick, and work well as part of a team. They must have good coordination skills for cutting and chopping. They need to be creative and have good senses of taste and smell. Personal cleanliness is essential.

Education and Training While a college degree is not necessarily required, chefs often attend cooking school, which can be anything from 2 years at a vocational school to a 4-year college degree in hospitality or culinary arts. Some high schools offer courses in basic culinary skills. There is often mandatory on-the-job training.

Job Outlook Job opportunities for chefs are expected to grow at about the same pace as the average for other occupations. This will be due to a continued growth in food services and a high turnover rate in the industry.

> **Critical Thinking** Chefs work in many different situations. You could be a chef in a big restaurant or a personal chef who cooks for private clients. Find out more about each type, and write a paragraph summarizing your findings and explaining which type you would rather be and why.

Career Cluster

CCR ☆ College & Career Readiness

Hospitality and Tourism Chefs work in the Restaurants and Food/Beverage Services pathway of this career cluster. Other jobs in this cluster include:

- Architectural Guide
- Museum Docent
- Animal Trainer
- Pastry Chef
- Caterer
- Theme Park Manager
- Tour Guide

- Hotel Manager
- Interpreter
- Restaurant Owner
- Meeting Planner
- Wine Steward
- Parks Ranger
- Travel Agent
- Concierge
- Baker

> **Explore Further** The Hospitality and Tourism career cluster contains four pathways: Restaurants & Food/Beverage Services; Lodging; Travel & Tourism; and Recreation, Amusements & Attractions. Choose one of these pathways to explore further.

 Go to this book's Online Learning Center at **glencoe.com** to learn more about college and career readiness.

CHAPTER SUMMARY

Section 29.1
Kitchen Organization and Safety

Kitchens are organized around major appliances. Before purchasing small appliances or utensils, consider whether you really need them. Kitchens with an efficient work triangle and well-organized work centers are easier to use. Following safety precautions can help prevent kitchen accidents and injuries such as cuts, burns, fires, and electric shocks.

Section 29.2
Food Sanitation and Safety

You can prevent foodborne illness by practicing cleanliness, avoiding cross-contamination, and carefully controlling food temperatures. It is very important to learn proper techniques for thawing, cooking, storing, and serving food. The three types of food storage areas are the refrigerator, freezer, and dry storage. Use the "first in, first out" principle to help prevent waste and spoilage.

Vocabulary Review

1. Create a fill-in-the-blank sentence for each of these vocabulary terms. The sentence should contain enough information to help determine the missing word.

Content Vocabulary
- ◇ major appliance (p. 585)
- ◇ work center (p. 586)
- ◇ work triangle (p. 586)
- ◇ foodborne illness (p. 590)
- ◇ cross-contamination (p. 590)
- ◇ danger zone (p. 590)
- ◇ rotation (p. 593)
- ◇ freezer burn (p. 594)

Academic Vocabulary
- ■ range (p. 585)
- ■ bare (p. 585)
- ■ contact (p. 590)
- ■ transfer (p. 595)

Review Key Concepts

2. **Paraphrase** how to organize a kitchen for efficiency.
3. **Identify** three steps for preventing kitchen accidents.
4. **Describe** three ways to prevent foodborne illness.
5. **Summarize** proper freezer storage procedures for food.

Critical Thinking

6. **Draw Conclusions** Why is it important to design the layout of a kitchen for efficiency? How might this contribute to safety?
7. **Hypothesize** Incidents of foodborne illnesses are often associated with outdoor meals and with meals for large numbers of people. What might explain this?
8. **Apply** Why do workers who bag groceries in supermarkets generally put meat in separate bags from the other groceries?
9. **Analyze** Why is it unsafe to drape cords over the edge of a counter?
10. **Judge** Is a sandwich maker practicing food safety if he touches cooked chicken, his face, and a cutting board while wearing gloves? Explain.
11. **Infer** Why is it unsafe to thaw food on a counter at room temperature?

ACTIVE LEARNING

12. Health Inspection Follow your teacher's direction to form into small groups. Use the information learned in this chapter to develop a checklist of things that a health inspector might look for in a professional kitchen. Compare your checklist with those that the other groups created. Is there anything they included in theirs that you should add to yours? Once your group has agreed on the final checklist, each group member should take a copy and play the role of health inspector to inspect their kitchen at home. Then write a brief summary of actions you could take to improve the safety and sanitation of your kitchen at home.

Family & Community Connections

13. Create an Advertisement There are hundreds of small kitchen appliances available for consumers. For example, many people buy toasters, blenders, crock pots, coffee makers, and food processors. Visit a local store that sells kitchen appliances. Speak to a manager or knowledgeable salesman in the appliance department. Find out which type of small appliance does not sell very well. Ask the manager or salesman if they know why it does not sell as well as some of the other appliances. Is it too expensive? Is it too hard to use? Does another appliance do the same task? Is the task it preforms too specific? Then conduct research on the appliance to find out what positive features it has. Create a magazine ad for that appliance to help increase sales by showcasing the appliance's use and features.

⭐ 21ˢᵗ Century Skills

Problem-Solving Skills

14. Kitchen Efficiency Evaluate the way foods and utensils are stored in your kitchen. Are there clearly defined work centers with the appropriate items? Think of ways you might rearrange the food and utensils in your kitchen to create more efficient work centers. Prepare a brief presentation to share your analysis and suggestions with your family.

Technology Skills

15. Build a Web Site Create a Food Safety Guide in Web browser format (XHTML). On the main page, outline the topics you will cover. Provide links to pages on which you give more information about each topic.

 **Connections**

Leadership Skills

16. Design a Kitchen As part of its mission, FCCLA encourages students to strengthen leadership skills that will contribute to success in a broad range of career fields. Design a functional kitchen by taking on a Designer's Assistant role, as specified in the Housing, Interiors, and Furnishings section of FCCLA's Leaders at Work national program. Use the information learned in this chapter, as well as information you find on the Internet, to help design your kitchen.

Academic Skills

 English Language Arts

17. Investigate a News Story Locate a recent news story in a newspaper or online about an incident of foodborne illness. Identify the cause of the illness, and learn where the incident occurred. Write a one-page report summarizing the incident, and include an analysis of how you feel the incident could have been avoided.

> **NCTE 7** Conduct research and gather, evaluate, and synthesize data to communicate discoveries.

 Science

18. Foodborne Illness Choose a specific foodborne illness microorganism to learn more about.

Procedure Research the microorganism you have chosen. You might answer questions like: Where can it be found? What symptoms of illness does it cause? How can the illness be prevented?

Analysis Using what you have learned, create a presentation, and share your findings with the class.

> **NSES C** Develop understanding of the interdependence of organisms and behavior of organisms.

 Mathematics

19. Comparing Costs Many major appliances carry an EnergyGuide label. This label indicates how the appliance's energy use compares to that of other similar models. Suppose refrigerator A costs $800 and uses $65 of electricity a year. Refrigerator B costs $750 and uses $75 of electricity per year. Which refrigerator would be more economical if you plan to use the refrigerator steadily for 10 years?

 Math Concept   **Multi-Step Problem** When solving problems with more than one step, think through the steps before you start.

Starting Hint Begin by calculating the cost of using refrigerator A for 10 years. Add that cost to the purchase price. Repeat these steps for refrigerator B. Then compare the two totals to determine which is more economical.

 For more math practice, go to the Math Appendix at the back of the book.

> **NCTM Problem Solving** Apply and adapt a variety of appropriate strategies to solve problems.

 ## Standardized Test Practice

CCR College & Career Readiness

ANALOGIES
Read the pairs of terms. Then choose the best word to complete the final pair.

Test-Taking Tip When you look at the two pairs of terms listed here, identify the relationship that is common to all of them. The answer that establishes the same type of relationship as the other terms is correct.

20. dishwasher : large appliance
knife : utensil
_____ : small appliance

a. refrigerator
b. blender
c. kitchen
d. portable

Chapter 30

Prepare and Serve Meals

Chapter Objectives

Section 30.1 Food Preparation Techniques

- **Describe** the four basic pieces of information included in recipes.
- **List** four preparation skills that will help ensure success in the kitchen.
- **Identify** three categories of cooking techniques.

Section 30.2 Table Service and Proper Etiquette

- **Summarize** three benefits of family mealtimes.
- **Describe** how to properly set the table.
- **Explain** the purpose of mealtime etiquette.

> **Explore the Photo**
>
> Preparing a complete meal can be a challenging and rewarding experience. *What are some of the advantages of preparing a meal yourself over dining out?*

Explain a Viewpoint

Your Favorite Cooking Technique Stewed chicken and baked chicken are very different dishes. The cooking technique used severely affects the resulting dish. Do you have a favorite cooking technique? What types of food do you cook using this technique? Why is it your favorite? Write a descriptive paragraph to explain your viewpoint about your favorite cooking technique.

Writing Tips To effectively explain your viewpoint:
- Come up with a strong topic sentence.
- Orient the reader by presenting details in a logical order.
- Select precise transition words.

Food Preparation Techniques

What techniques have you used to prepare food?

Reading Guide

Before You Read

Compare and Contrast When a chapter discusses more than one way of performing the same task, try comparing and contrasting the different methods.

Read to Learn

Key Concepts

- **Describe** the four basic pieces of information included in recipes.
- **List** four preparation skills that will help ensure success in the kitchen.
- **Identify** three categories of cooking techniques.

Main Idea

Most recipes contain the same basic information. There are many techniques to learn for preparing and cooking food.

Content Vocabulary

◇ recipe
◇ yield
◇ convenience food
◇ customary measurement system
◇ metric system
◇ volume
◇ equivalent measurement
◇ moist-heat cooking
◇ dry-heat cooking
◇ standing time

Academic Vocabulary

You will find these words in your reading and on your tests. Use the glossary to look up their definitions if necessary.

■ sequence
■ dovetail

Graphic Organizer

As you read, note four different methods for measuring ingredients. Use a measuring cup graphic organizer like the one shown to help you organize your information.

 Graphic Organizer Go to this book's Online Learning Center at **glencoe.com** to print out this graphic organizer.

Academic Standards

 English Language Arts

NCTE 12 Use language to accomplish individual purposes.

 Mathematics

NCTM Number and Operations Understand the meanings of operations and how they relate to one another.

 Social Studies

NCSS IV B Individual Development and Identity Identify the influence of various historical and contemporary cultures on an individual's daily life.

NCTE *National Council of Teachers of English*
NCTM *National Council of Teachers of Mathematics*
NSES *National Science Education Standards*
NCSS *National Council for the Social Studies*

Recipes for Success

The first step to success in the kitchen is a good recipe. A **recipe** is a list of ingredients and instructions for making a food or beverage. Think of recipes as road maps to successful food preparation. They provide you with all the information you need to make an array of tempting dishes, from apple crisp to zucchini soup. Following recipe directions carefully will help ensure that the meals you prepare are tasty and appealing.

As You Read

Connect What is your attitude toward cooking?

What a Recipe Tells You

The information provided in a recipe may be arranged in several ways. In the most commonly used format, the ingredients are listed first, followed by the assembly directions. Another less common format combines the ingredients and directions. No matter how recipes are organized, most include the same basic information.

- The ingredients are listed with exact amounts needed and in the order that they should be used. The list of ingredients also generally includes any pre-preparation steps that need to be done before measuring, such as chopping vegetables or marinating meat.
- The directions are step-by-step instructions for preparing the dish. The directions will tell you what equipment you need, the cooking method to use, the temperature for the cooking equipment, and the times for cooking, chilling, and setting.
- **Yield** is the number of servings the recipe makes.
- The nutrition information lists the calorie and nutrient content for the recipe. This is optional information that is not always included. However, it can be useful in helping you choose healthful options that support your eating plan.

Vocabulary

You can find definitions in the glossary at the back of this book.

Recipe for Success

Following a recipe enables anyone to be a successful cook. *What could happen if you did not read through the entire recipe before beginning?*

Using Recipes

Before using a recipe, read it carefully. Make sure you have all the ingredients on hand and that you understand the directions. For best results, follow the recipe directions exactly. This is especially good advice when you are a beginning cook or when you are using a new recipe for the first time.

Once you gain more experience, you can be creative by varying recipes to suit your taste. Some types of recipes are more flexible than others. Recipes for certain baked products, such as breads and cakes, depend on exact proportions of ingredients. If you make changes, the dish could end up with an unpleasant texture or other problems. It is easier to make creative changes to dishes with more flexible recipes, such as stews, salads, or casseroles.

Occasionally, you may want to prepare more or fewer servings of a recipe. You can use your math skills to change the yield of the recipe. For example, suppose a recipe for pasta salad makes four servings, but you have six people to feed. Since you want to make 1½ times as much salad, multiply the amount of each ingredient by 1½. Of course, you might choose to multiply all the ingredients by two and have leftovers.

Using Convenience Foods

Sometimes you might choose to save time by preparing mixes and other convenience foods rather than following a recipe, which takes more time and effort. A **convenience food** is a food that has been partially or fully prepared or processed to make it easier and faster to use. Examples include canned soup, hot dogs, hamburger patties, frozen dinners, frozen vegetables, or boxed macaroni and cheese. Read and follow the directions on the package carefully. Sometimes they will suggest variations for a touch of creativity. You might want to combine convenience foods and fresh foods in some recipes. For example, you could use a ready-made pie crust combined with a homemade filling to make an apple pie. You might use a combination of canned and fresh vegetables in vegetable soup. Or you could add fresh vegetables to the top of a frozen cheese pizza. Combinations like these allow you to enjoy the benefits of convenience foods and home cooking and also often add nutritional value to the convenience food meal.

✓ **Reading Check** **Define** What is a convenience food?

Life On Your Own

Plan Ahead in the Kitchen

To solve most problems, you have to choose a course of action and plan the details of carrying out that plan. The more details there are to think about, the more overwhelming the process can be. A good approach can be to work backward.

How It Works Start by visualizing the end of the process. Then work back step by step to figure out how to get there. For example, suppose you are making a booklet for your club. The last step in the process is to pick up the booklets from the copy shop. The step before that would be to drop off the pages at the copier. Continue the process by deciding what steps would be needed to prepare the pages.

Try It Out To prepare the meal, first choose the recipes you will use. Then list the steps in each recipe and the time needed to complete each one. Use these steps to figure out what time you need to start cooking. Use these steps and times to make a schedule, working backwards to put the tasks in order and find your start time. Then follow your schedule, checking off tasks as they are done.

> **Your Turn** Use the steps described to plan and prepare a three-course meal of simple recipes to share with someone important in your life for a special event, such as for a birthday or Mother's day. How can the habit of scheduling help you make larger, more complicated meals?

Prepare and Organize

Cooking a meal involves many different preparation skills, including organization, measuring, cutting, and mixing. These are skills that take knowledge and practice to master. Timing and efficiency are just as important to meal preparation as cooking skills are. When you are preparing a whole meal, you must decide what needs to be done in what **sequence**, or order, so that all the food is ready at the same time. With careful planning, you can put together a meal that everyone, including the cook, can enjoy.

Make a Schedule

Preparing several dishes so they are ready at the same time can be tricky, but it gets easier with practice. Start by reading the recipe or package directions for each food on the menu. Make a list of all the tasks needed to prepare each dish. Then estimate how much time each task will take. Once you have decided on the sequence of tasks, determine when you will need to start each task so that it is completed on time. It is best to allow a little more time than you think you will need. To make a schedule, figure out the best sequence for doing all the tasks on your list. Try these suggestions:

- **Dovetail tasks.** Look for ways to **dovetail**, or overlap, tasks to save time. Perhaps you can make a salad while rice is cooking.
- **Group similar tasks.** For example, you might decide to chop all the vegetables for several different dishes at one time.
- **Prepare some items ahead of time.** Could you prepare and refrigerate a gelatin dessert the day before? Make things easier on yourself by getting a head start.

Working Efficiently

Once you have your schedule, you are ready to prepare the meal. The process will go more smoothly if you start by clearing the kitchen counters to give yourself room to work. Then, assemble all the ingredients, utensils, and appliances you will need before you start. Check off each task as you complete it. Clean up as you work. Rinse bowls, utensils, and pans immediately, and soak them in hot, soapy water until you can wash them. If you are working with another person, take care not to get in each other's way. Use separate work areas, or alternate tasks at the sink or range. As you gain experience in the kitchen, cooking will become easier.

Measuring Techniques

Do you know the difference between a teaspoon and a table-spoon? Do you know the right way to measure flour and the right way to measure oil? Are you familiar with the different types of measuring cups? If you do not know how to measure ingredients accurately, recipes will not turn out the way you expect. Too much or too little of an ingredient can make a big difference.

Units of Measure

There are two different systems of measurement which are used to give the ingredient amounts in a recipe. The first is called the **customary measurement system**, which is the system of measurement used in the United States. The other is called the **metric system**, which is a system of measurement based on multiples of ten. The metric system is used in most countries outside of the U.S. The metric system is also used by American scientists and health professionals. Remember that the two measurement systems are just different ways of expressing the same amounts. Both systems include units for measuring volume and weight. **Volume** is the amount of space taken up by an ingredient.

Figure 30.1 — Equivalent Measurements

Customary and Metric Equivalents let you measure ingredients in more than one way. *If a recipe called for 1½ pints of milk, how many cups would you measure?*

CUSTOMARY UNIT	CUSTOMARY EQUIVALENT	APPROXIMATE METRIC EQUIVALENT
VOLUME		
¼ tsp.	—	1 mL
½ tsp.	—	2 or 3 mL
1 tsp.	—	5 mL
1 Tbsp.	3 tsp.	15 mL
1 fl. oz.	2 Tbsp.	30 mL
¼ c.	4 Tbsp.	60 mL
⅓ c.	5⅓ Tbsp.	80 mL
½ c.	8 Tbsp.	120 mL
¾ c.	12 Tbsp.	180 mL
1 c.	16 Tbsp. or 8 fl. oz.	250 mL
1 pt.	2 c. or 16 fl. oz.	500 mL
1 qt.	2 pt. or 4 c. or 32 fl. oz.	1,000 mL or 1 L
1 gal.	4 qt. or 8 pt. or 128 fl. oz.	4 L
WEIGHT		
1 oz.	—	28 g
1 lb.	16 oz.	500 g
2 lb.	32 oz.	1,000 g or 1 kg

Customary units for measuring volume include teaspoon (tsp.), tablespoon (Tbsp.), fluid ounce (fl. oz.), cup (C. or c.), pint (pt.), quart (qt.), and gallon (gal.). Metric units for measuring volume include milliliter (mL) and liter (L). Customary units for measuring weight include ounce (oz.) and pound (lb.). The metric units used for measuring weight are gram (g) and kilogram (kg).

Notice that in the customary system, the term ounce is used as a measure of weight as well as volume. Remember that these two kinds of ounces are not the same. Generally, if an ingredient is a liquid or if the measurement specifies fluid ounces, you can assume that ounces refer to volume. With solid foods, the same term most often refers to weight.

When working with recipes, it is helpful to understand equivalents. This is especially true if you are changing the yield. An **equivalent measurement** is the same amount expressed using a different unit of measure. For example, 16 ounces is the same amount as 1 pound or about 500 grams. **Figure 30.1** on the previous page lists some common equivalents used in cooking.

Equipment for Measuring

To measure ingredients correctly, you need to use the right equipment in the right way. Basic equipment for measuring includes:

- A liquid measuring cup made of clear glass or plastic with markings on the side. It has a spout so you can measure and pour liquid ingredients without spilling them.
- A set of dry measuring cups in different sizes used for dry or solid ingredients.
- A set of measuring spoons used for measuring small amounts.

Methods for Measuring

For accurate measurements, you need to follow the right procedures. Different measuring methods are used for different kinds of ingredients.

Dry Ingredients To measure dry ingredients like flour, sugar, baking powder, and spices, select the correct size of dry measuring cup or measuring spoon. Hold it over waxed paper or over the ingredient's container to catch any spills. Fill the cup or spoon slightly higher than the brim. Then use a knife or spatula to level off, or scrape the top off, so that it is even with the brim of the cup or spoon. Always spoon flour gently into the measuring cup. If you dip the cup into the flour, the flour could pack down, giving you more flour than you need. When measuring brown sugar, spoon the sugar into a measuring cup, and press it down firmly. Continue to add and pack down the sugar until the cup is full.

Accuracy Counts

To have a successful recipe, you must measure accurately. *Why should you put a measuring cup on a flat surface instead of holding it in your hand?*

Solid Fats You can measure solid fats, such as butter, margarine, and shortening, by spooning the fat into a dry measuring cup and packing the solid fat firmly. Level off the top, and then scrape the fat out with a spatula. If you buy butter or similar fats in quarter-pound sticks, use the tablespoon markings on the wrappers to cut off the amount you need.

Liquid Ingredients For small amounts of liquids, select the correct sized measuring spoon. Hold the spoon away from the bowl of other ingredients so that if any of the liquid spills, it will not fall into what you are making. Fill the spoon just to the brim. For larger amounts, use a liquid measuring cup. Place it on a level surface, and add the liquid. Check the measurement at eye level by crouching down and looking through the side of the cup. If necessary, pour some liquid out or add more until the liquid reaches the right mark on the cup.

Measuring by Weight If a recipe specifies an amount by weight, you should use a kitchen scale. First place an appropriate empty container on the scale. Adjust the scale to read zero so that the scale is not weighing the container. Then add the ingredient to the container until the scale shows the correct amount. In some cases, you may not need a scale to measure by weight. Many packaged foods give the weight on the label.

Cutting Techniques

Many food preparation tasks involve cutting food into smaller pieces. There are many different techniques for cutting food, ranging from slicing and dicing to peeling and shredding. By learning the terminology and practicing your skills, you can become an expert at cutting techniques. **Figure 30.2** defines different techniques for cutting foods.

| Figure 30.2 | **Techniques for Cutting** |

Make the Cut! Different cutting tools and techniques let you cut food into different shapes and sizes. *Why might recipes tell you to chop or dice vegetables?*

Pare Use a paring knife or a peeler to cut away the skin of a fruit or vegetable. A peeler cuts a thinner layer than a paring knife.

Slice Cut food into thin, flat pieces using a sharp knife and a cutting board. Steady the food with your other hand or with a fork. A food processor may be used to slice some foods.

Chop and Mince To chop food, cut it into small, irregular pieces. To mince food, keep cutting until the pieces are as small as you can make them. A food processor may also be used for chopping and mincing.

Cube and Dice To cube or dice foods, cut them in three directions. First, slice the food. Then stack the slices and cut them in two directions to make small squares. To cube, the squares should be about ½-inch wide. Diced squares are about ¼-inch wide.

Purée Use a food processor or blender to mash food until it is smooth. Vegetables are usually cooked before being puréed.

Shred and Grate Use a grater to shred foods such as carrots and cheese. Use a knife to shred foods such as lettuce and cabbage. A food processor can also be used to shred or grate food.

Figure 30.3 **Techniques for Mixing**

Mix It Up Using the proper mixing techniques will help ensure that your recipe turns out right. *Why would you fold a mixture rather than beat it?*

Blend Thoroughly combine ingredients until the mixture has a uniform appearance. Use a spoon, wire whisk, egg beater, electric mixer, or electric blender.	**Stir** Mix ingredients with a spoon or wire whisk in a circular or figure-8 motion.	**Beat** Mix ingredients vigorously to introduce air into them. Beat by hand with a spoon or wire whisk using a quick, over-and-over motion. Use a rotary motion with an electric mixer or beater.
Whip Beat very rapidly with a beater, wire whisk, or electric mixer to incorporate as much air as possible and increase the volume of the food.	**Cream** Use a spoon, beater, or electric mixer to beat a solid fat with sugar until the mixture is smooth and creamy.	**Fold** Use a wooden spoon or rubber scraper to add a delicate ingredient, such as beaten egg whites, to a mixture. Begin by gently cutting straight down through the mixture and across the bottom. Then, without lifting the utensil out, bring some of the mixture up and over. Rotate the bowl by a quarter turn, and repeat until the ingredients are combined.
Cut In Mix a solid fat with dry ingredients using a cutting motion with a pastry blender, a fork, or two knives.	**Toss** Tumble ingredients lightly together using a fork and spoon.	**Knead** Work dough with the hands to blend the ingredients, and make it smooth and springy by repeatedly folding, pressing, and turning it.

Mixing Techniques

To mix means to combine ingredients evenly. A good recipe should clearly explain how and in what order to mix ingredients. You may think that it does not matter how ingredients are combined, but actually, the technique used can really affect the results. See **Figure 30.3** for common mixing technique descriptions.

✓ Reading Check **Contrast** What is the difference between cubing and dicing?

Cooking Techniques

Cooking is applying heat to food. Most cooking techniques fall into one of three categories: cooking with moist heat, dry heat, or fat. The method used depends on the type of food and the results you want.

Cooking with Moist Heat

Moist-heat cooking uses hot liquid, steam, or both. Foods such as rice and dry beans are cooked in moist heat so that they can absorb water and soften. This method is also a good choice for making meats, vegetables, and other foods tender. Moist heat helps flavors to blend, as when you make sauces and soups. Some examples of moist-heat cooking methods are:

Steam Boil a small amount of water in a pan, and put the food in a steamer basket that holds it above the water. Cover the pan, and let the water continue to boil while the steam cooks the food. When done properly, steaming retains most of the food's nutrients.

Boil Heat liquid at a high temperature so that bubbles rise continuously to the surface and break. The boiling point of water is 212°F (100°C). A recipe might tell you to bring sauce to a boil or to cook noodles in boiling water. Most foods, however, should not be cooked in boiling liquid. Boiling can rob most foods of nutrients and cause them to overcook.

Simmer Heat liquid to a temperature just below the boiling point. Small bubbles should form, with some bubbles rising slowly to the surface. Vegetables are often cooked in simmering liquid. Fewer nutrients are lost than with boiling.

Poach Cook whole foods in a small amount of liquid at temperatures just below simmering so that they keep their original shape. Poaching is used for tender foods such as fish, fruit, and eggs.

Braise Cook food in simmering liquid and steam, using a pan with a tight-fitting lid. This method is often used to help tough cuts of meat become more tender. Meats are usually browned before braising.

Stew Cook small pieces of food by covering them completely with a liquid and simmering slowly in a covered pan. Stewing is used for less tender cuts of meat and for poultry, vegetables, and some fruits.

Pressure-cooking This method requires a special airtight pot in which the food cooks quickly in very high temperatures. This method is used for foods that normally take a long time to cook.

Cooking with Dry Heat

Dry-heat cooking is a method used to cook food uncovered without adding liquid or fat. Foods cooked with dry heat get brown and crisp on the outside but remain moist and tender on the inside.

Roast and Bake To roast and bake, you cook food uncovered in the oven. Many foods can be baked, such as breads, fruits and vegetables, cakes, cookies, pies, and casseroles. Fish, tender meat and poultry, and some fruits and vegetables can be baked or roasted. Foods that are roasted or baked often have a crisp, brown crust and are soft and flavorful inside.

Broil To broil, you cook food with direct heat from above. When you use the broiler unit of an oven, you place the food on a broiler pan, which has slots that allow fat to drain away during cooking. Broiling is often used for tender meats, such as steaks and hamburgers, and for poultry, fish, and some vegetables.

Grill To grill, you cook food on a grate over an open flame. Grilling is like broiling, but with the heat coming from below the food rather than from above it. You can generally grill the same foods that you can broil.

 The Art of Grilling

Grilling gives food an interesting look and a rich flavor. *What other foods besides meat have you eaten that were grilled?*

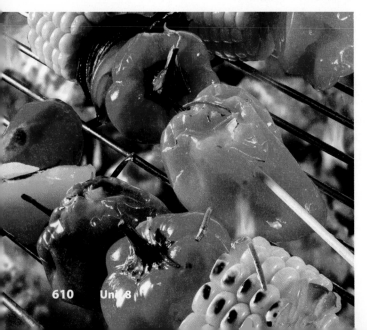

Cooking with Fat

Cooking with fat is a quick method that produces flavorful foods. However, it has the disadvantage of adding fat and calories to the food. When cooking with fat, choose oils that are low in saturated fats. Olive oil and canola oil are healthful cooking oils. Nonstick cooking spray is also a good choice. There are several methods for cooking with fat.

Sauté (sȯ-ˈtā) Cook small pieces of food in a small amount of fat over low to medium heat. For example, a recipe might tell you to sauté chopped onions until they become soft and transparent. Stir the food occasionally as it sautés.

Pan-fry This method is similar to sautéing and is used for larger pieces of food, such as tender meats, fish, or eggs. While pan-frying, you may need to turn the food so it cooks evenly.

Deep-fat Frying Cook food by immersing it in hot fat. Be sure to follow the recipe directions carefully so you do not overheat the fat. Also be sure food is dry before deep-fat frying it. French fries and doughnuts are examples of deep-fat fried foods. This method of frying adds the most fat.

Stir-frying Stir and cook small pieces of food very quickly at high heat in very little fat. This method can be used for vegetables, meat, poultry, and fish. Because it uses less fat, stir-frying is a more healthful way to cook with fat than the other methods.

Microwave Cooking

The microwave oven performs many cooking tasks faster than a conventional oven, so you can cook a meal in minutes. Microwave ovens are also cleaner and more economical to operate than conventional ovens. Most microwave ovens are best suited for cooking relatively small amounts of food, and they are ideal for reheating cooked foods and defrosting frozen foods.

Microwave Cookware

Not all cookware is suitable for microwave cooking. Ceramic, glass, plastic, and paper containers are usually appropriate, but look for a label indicating that they are microwave-safe. Microwave-safe ceramic, glass, and plastic containers are unaffected by microwaves. They are also heat-resistant, so they do not crack, melt, or shatter when the food becomes hot.

Metal pans and bowls should never be used in a microwave oven. They may cause arcing, or electrical sparks, that can damage the oven and start a fire. Some dishes have metallic trim or a metallic glaze, and they, too, should not be used. Avoid using recycled paper in a microwave oven, since it may include metal fragments.

Round, oval, or ring-shaped pans work better than square or rectangle containers. The round pans allow the microwave energy to strike the food from all angles. Food in the corners of a rectangular container tends to overcook.

Be Smart Be Safe

Microwave Safety Be careful not to burn yourself when using a microwave. Use pot holders when you remove food, just as you would with a conventional oven. Watch out for steam when removing covers from cooking containers.

Write About It Research other general safety rules to keep in mind when using a microwave. Write a summary of the tips you learn.

Microwave Techniques

Food heats up quickly in a microwave oven, so moisture also builds up rapidly. This may cause some foods to burst. Another concern is the possibility of uneven cooking. Special techniques can help prevent these problems.

Stirring and Rotating Microwaves penetrate food to a depth of about 1½ inches. The heat generated by the vibrating food molecules is then conducted toward the center of the food. That is why the center of food takes longer to cook than the outer edges. Soups, stews, and other foods containing liquids heat evenly if you stir them occasionally. For best results, stir from the outer edge toward the center. When a food cannot be stirred, it needs to be rotated. Most microwave ovens have a turntable that will do the job for you. If your microwave oven does not have a turntable, rotate the dish a quarter- or a half-turn part-way through the cooking. This allows the microwaves to penetrate the food on all sides. In some cases, you might also need to rearrange food pieces or turn them over.

Covering Most foods should be covered to hold in moisture and prevent spattering. Paper towels or napkins work well for covering bacon, sandwiches, and appetizers. Wrapping breads in paper towels prevents them from becoming soggy. Use towels that are marked "microwave-safe." Some paper towels may contain synthetic fibers that could melt. Wax paper is often used on casseroles to hold in some moisture while letting steam escape. Microwave-safe dishes with covers are ideal for vegetables and casseroles because they hold in more steam. Microwave-safe plastic wrap also holds in steam. To keep it from bursting, pierce the wrap or turn it back at one corner before starting to cook.

Puncturing Foods that are sealed in plastic or encased in a skin should always be pierced before they are placed in a microwave oven. Otherwise, steam will build up inside the food and cause it to burst. Piercing foods with a fork or making a small knife slit will prevent pressure buildup. Puncture whole potatoes, sausages, hot dogs, tomatoes, egg yolks and apples, as well as vegetables that are to be cooked in plastic pouches.

▼ Microwave Magic

Microwaves can be convenient since they cook faster than conventional ovens. *What types of food do you cook in the microwave?*

Defrosting Defrosting cuts down on meal preparation time and allows you to create and change menus easily. Also, you can prepare individual servings or whole meals ahead of time, freeze them, and then thaw and reheat them when you are ready. The length of time it takes a food to defrost depends on the size and density of the food and on the temperature at which it was frozen. Most microwave cookbooks provide a defrosting chart. Some models of microwave ovens have automatic defrosting features that set the defrosting time and power level based on the food weight.

Standing Time A mistake that many people make is to ignore the standing time called for in a recipe. **Standing time** is a period of time when food continues to cook after microwaving. As the food stands, the molecules inside it continue to vibrate and to cook it. Standing time is almost as important as cooking time to ensure that the food turns out properly.

To prevent burns when using a microwave oven, always use pot holders to remove food from the oven. Do not use containers with tight-fitting covers as steam could build up. Watch out for steam when you remove covers from containers or open bags of microwave popcorn. Be sure to let food stand before eating it.

 Podcasts Access the Online Learning Center to download *Managing Life Skills* podcasts.

Section 30.1 — After You Read

Review Key Concepts

1. **Explain** how to change the yield of a recipe.

2. **List** nine different mixing techniques.

3. **Identify** five different techniques that can be used when cooking food in a microwave.

 Check Your Answers Check your answers at this book's Online Learning Center at **glencoe.com**.

Practice Academic Skills

 English Language Arts

4. Organization in the kitchen means organizing your workflow as well as keeping a clean and organized kitchen. Suppose you and two friends are preparing a meal for a dinner party. Decide on a menu which includes an appetizer, salad, main course, and dessert. Using the techniques discussed in this section, develop a flow chart to show who would do each task in the meal preparation.

 Social Studies

5. Many family's meal traditions are influenced by a family's ancestors or cultural heritage. Conduct research to find out the origin of a favorite dish and how it became a favorite for you or your family. What culture did it originate in? Was it recently introduced to you by a friend or is it a family recipe that has been handed down through the generations? Write a brief summary to share your findings.

Table Service and Proper Etiquette

Good mealtime etiquette can help make a meal relaxing and enjoyable.

Reading Guide

Before You Read

Use Diagrams As you are reading through this section, write down the main idea. Write down any facts, explanations, or examples you find. Start at the main idea and draw arrows to the information that directly supports it. Then draw arrows from these examples to any information that supports them.

Read to Learn
Key Concepts
- **Summarize** three benefits of family mealtimes.
- **Describe** how to properly set the table.
- **Explain** the purpose of mealtime etiquette.

Main Idea

There are many benefits to sharing a meal. Meals can be served in different ways. It is important to set the table properly and observe mealtime etiquette.

Content Vocabulary
◇ family style
◇ plate service
◇ buffet service
◇ place setting
◇ flatware

Academic Vocabulary

You will find these words in your reading and on your tests. Use the glossary to look up their definitions if necessary.

■ asset
■ advance

Academic Standards

English Language Arts

NCTE 5 Use different writing process elements to communicate effectively.

Social Studies

NCSS I F Culture Interpret patterns of behavior reflecting values and attitudes that contribute or pose obstacles to cross-cultural understanding.

Graphic Organizer

As you read, look for five special touches that can make table settings stand out. Use a graphic organizer like the one shown to help you organize your information. The first one has been completed for you.

Napkins

Special Touches for Table Settings

Graphic Organizer Go to this book's Online Learning Center at **glencoe.com** to print out this graphic organizer.

NCTE *National Council of Teachers of English*
NCTM *National Council of Teachers of Mathematics*
NSES *National Science Education Standards*
NCSS *National Council for the Social Studies*

Table Service

A well-prepared meal does more than satisfy hunger and contribute to good nutrition. It should also be an enjoyable experience. While the flavor of the food is certainly part of that enjoyment, so is the pleasure of good company. Whether you are dining with family or friends, at home or away, look for ways to make meals more pleasant for everyone.

Family Mealtime

For many families, mealtime provides a valued opportunity to be together. People can relax, talk about the day's events, share ideas, and enjoy one another's company. Family mealtimes help teach you how to act in social situations. It is not always possible to share a meal together every day. That makes it all the more important to enjoy meals when the family does have time to eat together. It is also an opportunity to establish healthful lifetime eating patterns. Studies show that being relaxed while eating helps the digestive process. The pleasant atmosphere of a family meal can help you associate healthful food with enjoyment.

Serving Styles

Every family has its own customs for serving and eating meals. They may be influenced by the family's lifestyle, ethnic background, religious beliefs, or family traditions. Some serving styles may depend on the situation. As you read about some mealtime customs that are common in the United States, remember that it is important to respect other customs too. There are three serving styles that are most common in the United States:

- With **family style**, the food is brought to the table in serving dishes, which are then passed from person to person. People can serve themselves the amount they want and can avoid any foods that they dislike. One disadvantage is that people may be tempted to overeat.
- With **plate service**, the food is placed on each person's plate in the kitchen, and the plates are brought to the table. Food that has not been served is kept hot in the kitchen until second helpings are offered. Plate service, often used for formal meals, saves cleanup time because no serving dishes are used. It is also easier to control portion sizes.

As You Read

Connect What do you enjoy most about family meals?

Vocabulary

You can find definitions in the glossary at the back of this book.

Food and Fun

Mealtime is a great way to spend time together as a family. *What could you do to make family mealtimes more enjoyable?*

- In **buffet service** ((ˌ)bə-ˈfā), bowls and platters of food are arranged on a serving table, with dinner plates at one end, and people serve themselves as they walk along the table. Then they find a place to sit down and eat. This style is generally used for large gatherings when there is not enough seating for everyone at one table.

✓ **Reading Check** **Recall** What are four things that can influence a family's serving style?

Setting the Table

Most families set the table in similar ways. Traditional rules for setting the table make it easy for you to know what to expect, no matter where you eat. You also can add special touches for variety or to create a certain atmosphere.

HOW TO... Set a Place

A table should be set before people sit down to eat. Even a simple table setting can make a meal feel special. The arrangement of a place setting is based on both tradition and function. When arranged properly, tableware looks better and is more convenient to use. If possible, allow 20 inches (50 cm) in width for each place setting. Align the bottom of the utensils with the bottom edge of the dinner plate.

1. Dinner Plate Place in the center of each place setting, about 1 inch (2.5 cm) from the edge of the table.

2. Forks Place the dinner fork just to the left of the dinner plate, with the tines up. Place the salad fork to the left of the dinner fork.

3. Knife Place immediately to the right of the dinner plate. The blade should face the plate.

4. Spoons Place to the right of the knife. If there is more than one spoon, the one used first goes on the outside.

5. Salad Plate Place above the forks. If there is a bread plate, it goes to the left of the salad plate.

6. Water Glass Place just above the tip of the knife.

7. Beverage Glass Place to the right of the water glass and slightly farther forward.

8. Cup and Saucer Place to the right of the spoons, with the cup's handle facing the right.

9. Napkin Place to the left of the forks. You may want to use a napkin ring, or you can fold the napkin in a rectangle and place it with the folded edge away from the forks.

Place Settings

Sit-down meals should have individual place settings. A **place setting** is the arrangement of tableware for one person. Tableware for a simple place setting includes a plate, glass, napkin, and flatware. **Flatware** includes the knives, forks, and spoons for eating. Depending on the foods served, a place setting might include more forks or spoons, a bread plate, a salad plate, another glass, or a cup and saucer.

Special Touches

Many people like to add special touches to table settings to make special occasion meals stand out. Even everyday meals can be made more special with a few touches that show you care. Try the following tips to make your table settings stand out:

- **Table Covering** A tablecloth adds elegance to a meal when it is clean, pressed, and hanging evenly around the table. Another option is to use place mats. Place mats and tablecloths are available in different materials, colors, and patterns for every occasion.
- **Napkins** Colorful napkins add a cheery touch to a table setting. Choose colors that go well with the table covering. Cloth napkins can make a meal seem more special, while paper napkins add a more casual feel.
- **Table Decoration** A simple flower arrangement, or even a single cut flower in a bud vase, can make a meal feel unique. You may also want to try silk flowers, a bowl of fresh fruit, a plant, or a decorative vase.
- **Lighting** For special occasions, you may want to place several candles in candleholders or try floating votive candles in a bowl of water.
- **Music** Soft background music can set a pleasant mood for dining. Make sure the volume is set on low so that everyone can hear the conversation.

✓ **Reading Check** **Identify** What does tableware for a simple place setting include?

▲ **Restaurant Rules**

Good manners are important whether eating at home or in a restaurant. *Why do you think it is important to keep your voice level down in a restaurant?*

Proper Mealtime Etiquette

Etiquette is polite behavior that shows respect and consideration for others. Mealtime etiquette is designed to make meals comfortable and enjoyable for everyone. You show respect for others at mealtime through the way you look, the way you eat, and the way you talk. The good manners you practice at home will be an **asset**, or advantage, as you enjoy meals in social settings away from home.

Keep It Simple

When entertaining, keep it simple so that you can enjoy yourself too. Choose recipes that you know and are confident with. If you have one complicated recipe, keep the rest of the menu simple. Also, choose dishes that can be prepared in advance, and set the table ahead of time.

Table Manners

For the most part, good table manners are just common-sense courtesy. Here are some basic guidelines to keep in mind:

- Sit up straight at the table. Avoid resting your elbows on the table while you eat.
- Place your napkin on your lap. Keep it there except when you are using it.
- If a serving dish is not within easy reach, ask for it to be passed to you. Do not reach in front of someone or across the table.
- Use the serving forks and spoons, not your own flatware, to serve yourself.
- Do not start eating until everyone has been served, unless a host urges you to start.
- If there are several forks or spoons and you are not sure which to use, start with the outermost one. Flatware for the first course is always farthest from the plate.
- Take small bites and chew quietly and with your mouth closed. Do not speak or drink with food in your mouth.
- Break bread or rolls into small pieces with your hands.
- If you are having trouble getting food onto your fork or spoon, push it with a small piece of bread or with your knife.
- Sip rather than gulp your drink.
- Rest your flatware on the plate, not the table.
- If you need to cough or sneeze, cover your mouth or nose with a handkerchief or napkin and turn away from the table. If the coughing or sneezing continues, excuse yourself from the table.
- If you are eating at someone's home and are not sure how to eat a particular food, watch to see what the host does.
- Signal that you have finished by placing your flatware across the center of your plate, with the handles in the 4 o'clock position and your napkin to the left of the plate.

Conversation

Conversation is an important part of dining. Meals are a time for warmth and friendship, not for arguments or disputes. Discuss topics of interest to everyone, and avoid discussing unpleasant experiences. Try to include everyone in conversations. When you are a guest in someone's home, thank your hosts before you leave. A special word of thanks for the food and hospitality is always appreciated. For some occasions, you might want to bring a simple gift for the hosts and send a note of thanks afterwards.

Restaurant Etiquette

When you enter a restaurant, look to see if it is an informal restaurant where guests seat themselves. Often a sign indicates whether someone will lead you to a seat. When you are seated, review the menu. Ask the server any questions that you have about the food. If there are any specials, servers will inform you of them.

If you need to get the attention of a server during the meal, speak in an ordinary voice as he or she passes your table. If the server is across the room, raise your hand to catch his or her eye. After receiving the bill, review the list of items ordered and make sure the total is correct. If there has been a mistake, politely and quietly bring the error to the server's attention.

Tipping is the practice of giving extra money to servers in appreciation of good service. Tipping is customary in all restaurants that offer table service. Usually, 15 percent of the cost of the food before taxes is an acceptable tip. Many customers tip 20 percent in more expensive restaurants. Some restaurants automatically add a 15 or 18 percent tip to any check when there are six or more people at a table. A cash tip is often left on the table. If you use a credit card, you can add the tip to the total on the receipt if you prefer.

If you are with a group in a restaurant, try to decide in **advance**, or ahead of time, how you will handle the bill. If you want separate bills at the end of the meal, let the server know ahead of time. If you get one bill, decide how it will be divided. The easiest way may be to divide the total between the number of people at the table. This arrangement could be unfair, though, if some people ordered more expensive meals than others. Either way, one person should take responsibility for collecting the money, adding it up, and making sure the server receives the correct amount, including the tip.

Consider investing in cloth napkins and using these instead of disposable paper napkins. You could even look for used cloth napkins at secondhand stores, flea markets, or online auction sites. They make mealtime special and show that you care for the environment!

 Podcasts Access the Online Learning Center to download *Managing Life Skills* podcasts.

Section 30.2 — After You Read

Review Key Concepts

1. **Describe** the three most common serving styles.

2. **Summarize** how to properly set a table.

3. **Explain** why hygiene is an important part of mealtime etiquette.

Practice Academic Skills

 English Language Arts

4. Write a scene for a play portraying an enjoyable family meal. The focus of the scene should be friendly, family conversation. You might also include descriptions of the setting and the food itself and how these contribute to the experience. Your scene should include family members from at least two generations.

 Social Studies

5. Conduct research to learn about mealtime etiquette in another culture. Find out about serving customs, eating customs, and polite behavior. Be sure to include information that would be helpful for a tourist to know when visiting that culture. Create an oral report to share your findings with the class.

 Check Your Answers Check your answers at this book's Online Learning Center at **glencoe.com**.

NCTE 5 Use different writing process elements to communicate effectively.

NCSS I F Interpret patterns of behavior reflecting values and attitudes that contribute or pose obstacles to cross-cultural understanding.

Pathway to College

Paying for College

How Do I Pay for College?

It is one thing to decide what kind of education or training you need, but another to figure out how you are going to pay for it. Educational costs can be expensive. You may have to pay for tuition, books and supplies, room and board, and transportation. It is important to think about where the money is going to come from.

When should I start thinking about paying for college?

It is a good idea to face this question as soon as possible and start saving money now. Consider taking a part-time job after school and a full-time job during school breaks. Start a savings account for college expenses, and do not use this money for any other purpose. Talk to your family. Depending on their income, they may be able to set money aside for your education in a special, tax-free account.

What are the possible sources of money for college?

Many students receive financial aid in the form of scholarships, grants, or loans. You learned about scholarships in the Pathway to College feature in Chapter 28. Grants are usually given on the basis of need and do not have to be repaid. Loans, which are offered by colleges and banks, must be repaid over a period of time. Education loans are usually offered at a lower interest rate than most other loans.

What can I do to learn more?

Each college has its own financial aid policy, and this information may or may not appear in materials sent to you. It is a good idea to schedule a face-to-face or phone interview with a member of the financial aid staff who will be able to answer specific questions about costs, the financial aid process, and options for financing your education. You should come up with a list of questions before this meeting.

Hands-On

College Readiness Imagine you have picked the school where you are going to continue your education after high school. You have called the school and scheduled a meeting with someone in the financial aid office. To prepare for this meeting, come up with a list of questions you want to ask the financial aid officer who you are going to be meeting with to find out all you need to know.

Path to Success

College & Career Readiness

Start Early The sooner you start saving your money for college and doing research, the better prepared you will be.

Consider All Options High tuition is not a requirement for a good education.

Grades Are Not Everything The majority of federal aid is based on financial need and not on grades.

Over-Apply The more grants, scholarships, and loans you apply for, the higher the chances are you will get the money you need.

Get Help There are many sources of assistance including college financial aid offices, your guidance counselor, your parents, books, and Web sites.

Invest in Your Future Generally, the more education and training you receive, the more money you will be able to earn in the future.

 Go to this book's Online Learning Center at **glencoe.com** to learn more about college and career readiness.

CHAPTER SUMMARY

Section 30.1
Food Preparation Techniques

A recipe provides the information you need to prepare a dish. A good schedule and efficient work methods will help you organize meal preparation. Accurate measuring is a key to recipe success. A variety of techniques are used for cutting and mixing. Different cooking methods affect food in different ways. To cook successfully in a microwave, select the right cookware, and use recommended techniques.

Section 30.2
Table Service and Proper Etiquette

Sharing meals as a family has several benefits. Common serving styles for family meals include family style, plate style, and buffet style. Each item in a place setting goes in a specific place. Special touches help make a table attractive and a meal memorable. Using good manners at mealtime allows everyone to have an enjoyable dining experience.

Vocabulary Review

1. Find a visual example of each content vocabulary term.

Content Vocabulary

- recipe (p. 603)
- yield (p. 603)
- convenience food (p. 604)
- customary measurement system (p. 606)
- metric system (p. 606)
- volume (p. 606)
- equivalent measurement (p. 607)
- moist-heat cooking (p. 609)
- dry-heat cooking (p. 610)
- standing time (p. 613)
- family style (p. 615)
- plate service (p. 615)
- buffet service (p. 616)
- place setting (p. 617)
- flatware (p. 617)

Academic Vocabulary

- sequence (p. 605)
- dovetail (p. 605)
- asset (p. 617)
- advance (p. 619)

Review Key Concepts

2. **Describe** the four basic pieces of information included in recipes.
3. **List** four preparation skills that will help ensure success in the kitchen.
4. **Identify** three categories of cooking techniques.
5. **Summarize** three benefits of family mealtimes.
6. **Describe** how to properly set the table.
7. **Explain** the purpose of mealtime etiquette.

Critical Thinking

8. **Determine** If you had to choose between a microwave oven and a conventional oven for all your cooking, which would you choose? Why?
9. **Analyze** Why do you adjust a kitchen scale to zero before measuring?
10. **Give Examples** What are some possible topics of conversation that should be avoided when dining with someone you do not know well?
11. **Compare and Contrast** How are etiquette rules the same for a fast food restaurant and a fine dining restaurant? How are they different?

ACTIVE LEARNING

12. Analyze TV Cooking Show Follow your teacher's directions to form into pairs. Choose a cooking show to watch on TV. You and your partner should each take notes while watching the show. Write down a simple recipe that is demonstrated. Then use your notes and work with your partner to prepare the dish that was shown. If possible, share your dish with other classmates or family members, and ask for their opinions as well. Write an analysis of the cooking show. Were the ingredients and directions given easy to follow? Did your dish turn out as expected?

Family & Community Connections

13. Planning Family Meals Do busy schedules often get in the way of family meals? Arrange to meet with the other members of your family to discuss making mealtime more special. Talk about ways you can adjust your schedules so that you can eat together as a family more often. If you already eat as a family regularly, discuss ideas for improving the mealtime atmosphere. For example, perhaps you could take turns adding special touches to the table setting. Based on your discussion, make a plan for one week. Then meet with your family again to evaluate how well the plan worked. Make any necessary changes to continue to have more enjoyable family mealtimes. Summarize your plan and evaluation, and share your results.

21st Century Skills

Technology Skills

14. Make a Training Video Ask an experienced cook to work with you to create a video that demonstrates five of the cutting and mixing techniques from the chapter. Ask the person to explain and demonstrate each technique. Use video editing software to edit the video.

Social Skills

15. Design a Table Setting Prepare a special table setting at home to demonstrate what you have learned about special touches. When the meal is served, ask the family to give you feedback. What did they notice in particular? How did your table setting affect the mood of the meal? Write two paragraphs to describe your setting and the feedback received.

FCCLA Connections

Planning Skills

16. Cultural Food Fair As part of its mission, FCCLA encourages students to strengthen family ties. One way to do this is by acknowledging your cultural traditions. Use the FCCLA planning process to organize a cultural food fair that will exhibit diversity in the school. Food fairs should include demonstrations of cultural food preparation techniques as well as samples of traditional foods. Write a brief report summarizing the steps and evaluating how it went.

Academic Skills

 English Language Arts

17. Recipes from Old to New Use print or online resources to locate a recipe that is at least 100 years old. How does it differ from today's recipes? Rewrite the recipe to follow today's style. Use the information in this chapter to help guide you in your update. Write a summary that explains the differences on your updated recipe.

> **NCTE 8** Use information resources to gather information and create and communicate knowledge.

 Social Studies

18. Utensils May Vary Just as food differs from one culture to another, so too do the utensils used to prepare, serve, and eat the food. Conduct research on utensils used in another culture to prepare, serve, or eat food. Develop a presentation with photos or art, if available, to describe some of these utensils to your classmates.

> **NCSS I A Culture** Analyze and explain the ways groups, societies, and cultures address human needs and concerns.

 Mathematics

19. Change Recipe Yield A chili recipe lists the ingredients for four servings, but you need to make six. How much would you need of each ingredient?

1 lb. ground beef
16 oz. red beans
8 oz. whole, peeled plum tomatoes
2 cloves garlic, diced
½ c. diced onion and green pepper
¼ c. diced celery
1 tsp. chili powder
½ tsp. salt

Math Concept **Multiplying Fractions** To multiply fractions, multiply the numerators and multiply the denominators.

Starting Hint Begin by dividing the desired yield by the recipe's yield to determine the amount of change. Then multiply each ingredient by that amount.

 For more math practice, go to the Math Appendix at the back of the book.

> **NCTM Problem Solving** Solve problems that arise in mathematics and in other contexts.

 Standardized Test Practice

 CCR College & Career Readiness

TRUE/FALSE
Read each of the statements, and determine whether it is true or false.

Test-Taking Tip When trying to assess whether a statement is true or false, make sure you understand the full statement. All parts of a statement must be correct for the statement to be true. If any part of the statement is false, the entire statement is false.

20. Indicate if each of these statements is true or false.
a. Butter should be measured as a dry ingredient.
b. Melted butter should be measured as a liquid ingredient.
c. You should pack down flour in the measuring cup for an accurate measurement.

Showcase Your Skills

In this project, you will create and organize a complete list of your skills, interests, awards, honors, and certifications. You will get input from a trusted adult on how you organized your list and what you chose to include. You will also get feedback on which of your skills best reflects your personality and interests. Then you will revise your list and create a new section for your job portfolio to showcase this information about you.

My Journal

If you completed the journal entry from page 516, refer to it to see if your thoughts have changed after reading the unit.

Project Assignment

In this project you will:
- Brainstorm your skills, and put them into a list.
- Add any awards, honors, or certifications to your list.
- Organize your list into categories.
- Get feedback on your list.
- Revise your list based on the feedback.
- Create a sample project from one skill on your list, and present it to the class.

THE SKILLS BEHIND THE PROJECT

Key personal and relationship skills you will use in this project include:
- Assessing your skills
- Organizing information
- Listening respectfully

Academic Skills

 English Language Arts

> **NCTE 4** Use written language to communicate effectively.
>
> **NCTE 12** Use language to accomplish individual purposes.

STEP 1 — List Your Skills

Think about the skills that you have developed through school, your hobbies, and your interests. Brainstorm a list of all of these skills. They may include:
- Hobbies such as photography, crafting, or sewing
- Talents such as playing a musical instrument or drawing
- Technology skills such as using presentation or spreadsheet software
- Achievements and awards, such as being part of a sports team or winning an academic award

STEP 2 — Organize Your List

Read through the brainstorming list you created. Organize the items from your brainstorming list into categories (for example, hobbies, creative skills, technology, and athletics). Once you have organized your list, use word processing software to create a presentable copy of your categories of skills, honors, awards, and achievements.

Organization Skills
- Create appropriate categories.
- Change or combine categories, if necessary.
- Take a break, and then review your organization for accuracy.

STEP 3 Connect with Your Community

Ask a trusted adult, such as a parent, teacher, or school counselor, if he or she would be willing to look over your list. Have the adult review your list's organization, and make suggestions. Ask if he or she thinks any skills are missing. Ask which skill you have listed best reflects your personality as he or she knows it and why. Think of a sample project you can create for your portfolio using that skill. For example, if the skill is art, draw a picture to demonstrate your skill.

Interpersonal Skills

- Be polite, and do not interrupt the adult while he or she is speaking.
- Listen attentively.
- Ask questions to better understand the adult's point of view.

STEP 4 Build Your Portfolio Project

Use the Portfolio Project Checklist to create your sample project, and share your sample project with the class.

Communication Skills

- Use standard English to communicate.
- Be sensitive to the needs of your audience.

STEP 5 Evaluate Your Project

Your portfolio project will be evaluated based on:

Academic Skills

- Organization skills
- Note-taking and revision skills
- Speaking and listening skills
- Creativity, presentation, and neatness

 Evaluation Rubric Go to this book's Online Learning Center at **glencoe.com** for a rubric you can use to evaluate your final project.

PORTFOLIO PROJECT CHECKLIST

Plan

☑ Create and organize a complete list of your skills, interests, awards, honors, and certifications.

☑ Reorganize your skills list based on feedback from the adult you interviewed.

☑ Make copies of your revised skills list and your sample project.

Present

☑ Create a presentation to share your skills list and sample project with your class.

☑ Invite the students to ask questions. Answer any questions. Demonstrate in your answers that you respect their perspectives.

☑ Place a copy of your skills list and sample project in your job portfolio.

☑ Turn in a copy of your skills list and a copy of your sample project to your teacher.

Portfolio Highlights

Update Your Skills List

Your skills list is not a fixed document. It should change as you add and improve your skills. Constantly think about the skills you have gained in school, through volunteering, and at work, and update your list frequently.

Track Accomplishments, Not Duties

Potential employers want to know what you can do for their company. Keep track of accomplishments in school and on the job. Do not simply list day-to-day activities. Instead, keep a list of special projects you finish. Use specific information whenever possible.

Include Special Training

If you attend a conference, workshop, or special class, add it to your skills list. Add the specific skills that you learned or improved while you were at the event.

Create Electronic Samples

Whenever you update your skills list, create a new electronic list that can be e-mailed to potential employers. Scan any sample projects you have created for your portfolio so that they can be e-mailed, too.

UNIT 9

Clothing and Fashion Choices

Unit Portfolio Project Preview

Community Service Project

In this unit, you will explore ways to communicate your unique statement through clothing. In your portfolio project, you will lend your time and experience to assist your own community.

My Journal

Give and Receive Write a journal entry about one of the topics below. This will help you prepare for the project at the end of this unit.

• Discuss an area of your community that you wish to support and explain why.

• Describe the traits and abilities you might be able to lend to a worthwhile cause.

• Reflect on what you would like to gain from a community service experience.

Chapter 31

Design Your Look

Chapter Objectives

Section 31.1 Fashion and Design Basics

- **Describe** how the fashion industry and fashion designers influence consumers.
- **Identify** the elements and principles of design.
- **Summarize** the components of color.

Section 31.2 Your Fashion Statement

- **Identify** the functions of clothing.
- **Define** essential clothing.
- **Explain** how to evaluate your wardrobe.
- **List** ways you can expand your wardrobe.

➤**Explore the Photo**

Your personal style can affect how others view you and relate to you. *What message about yourself do you want to communicate with your clothing style?*

Writing Activity

Objective Description

Personal Style How much can you determine from a person's choice of clothing? Observe someone who has a distinct style. Write an objective paragraph about that person and his or her clothes. Do not criticize or praise the choices. Simply use objective details to describe what you see.

Writing Tips Use these tips to help you write an objective description:

- Start with a sentence that gives an overall description of what you see.
- Give details that paint a picture in your readers' minds.
- Sum up your description with a conclusion that supports your opening sentence.

Fashion and Design Basics

How does the fashion world influence you?

Reading Guide

Before You Read

Use Color As you read this section, try using different colored pens to take notes. This can help you learn new material and study for tests. You could use red for vocabulary words, blue for explanations, and green for examples.

Read to Learn

Key Concepts

- **Describe** how the fashion industry and fashion designers influence consumers.
- **Identify** the elements and principles of design.
- **Summarize** the components of color.

Main Idea

The fashion industry and fashion designers have a strong influence on our lives. The elements and principles of design make it possible to create a countless variety of looks.

Graphic Organizer

As you read, identify specific primary, secondary, and intermediate colors. Use a table like the one shown to help you organize your information.

Primary Colors	Secondary Colors	Intermediate Colors

 Graphic Organizer Go to this book's Online Learning Center at **glencoe.com** to print out this graphic organizer.

Content Vocabulary

- ◇ fashion
- ◇ style
- ◇ target market
- ◇ status symbol
- ◇ illusion
- ◇ silhouette
- ◇ emphasis
- ◇ proportion
- ◇ hue
- ◇ value
- ◇ shade
- ◇ tint
- ◇ intensity

Academic Vocabulary

You will find these words in your reading and on your tests. Use the glossary to look up their definitions if necessary.

- ◼ anonymous
- ◼ dictate

Academic Standards

English Language Arts

NCTE 12 Use language to accomplish individual purposes.

Science

NSES E Develop abilities of technological design, understanding about science and technology.

Social Studies

NCSS II B Time, Continuity, and Change Apply key concepts such as time, chronology, causality, change, conflict, and complexity to explain, analyze, and show connections among patterns of historical change and continuity.

NCTE *National Council of Teachers of English*
NCTM *National Council of Teachers of Mathematics*
NSES *National Science Education Standards*
NCSS *National Council for the Social Studies*

Fashion Influences

Fashion refers to design characteristics that are popular at a particular point in time. A **style** is a distinctive form of a clothing item. Different styles have characteristics that distinguish them from one another. Polo, rugby, and T-shirt are all styles of knit shirts. A style of clothing may or may not be considered fashionable at any given time.

Fashion Designers

Ideas for clothing designs and styles begin with the work of professional fashion designers. Some designers are well known and specialize in unique, often costly garments that are mainly sold to a small number of people who can afford them. These fashions probably do not look much like the clothes worn by people you know.

There are also thousands of **anonymous**, or unidentified, designers who are employed by clothing manufacturers. They pay attention to trends set by known designers, and then produce their own creations using shapes, fabrics, or details inspired by the designers. These creations are what most people are likely to buy. Some designers are hired to create knock-offs, which are lower-cost imitations of famous fashion designers' creations.

All fashion designers, whether famous or anonymous, must pay attention to their target market. A **target market** is a group of consumers to whom a company is trying to appeal with their products. Their designs may be inspired by movies, television, magazines, news events, travel, art exhibits, or ethnic or historical clothing.

Segments of the Fashion Industry

Designers and the companies they work for make up the fashion industry. Most of them fall into these segments:

- **Textile Companies** These companies produce fibers and fabrics from which clothing is made.
- **Apparel Manufacturers** Apparel, or clothing, manufacturers employ the designers who produce their brand. They buy the fabric and mass produce the clothing. This industry is sometimes known as the rag trade or garment industry.
- **Fashion Merchandisers** This segment sells apparel and accessories. Department stores, online merchants, and catalog companies fall into this segment. Some retail employees decide what fashions to offer for sale, and others keep track of merchandise or assist customers.
- **Fashion Promoters** Experts in fashion promotion may work for trade publications, ad agencies, and public relations firms. They specialize in the use of advertisements and images to influence consumers.

As You Read

Connect How much does the fashion industry affect your choice of clothing and why?

◆ Vocabulary

You can find definitions in the glossary at the back of this book.

▼ High Fashion

The word "fashion" has different meanings. One meaning refers to the high fashion collections that debut in cities like New York and Milan every season. *What comes to mind when you hear the word "fashion"?*

Public Influence

Many consumers like to wear fashions that carry a designer label and are willing to pay more for them. Manufacturers place their logos in visible places on clothes and accessories to appeal to these consumers. For such consumers, designer clothing is a **status symbol**, which is a sign of a high position or rank.

The fashion industry can also affect people's self-image. Advertisers use certain types of models to send a message about which characteristics are the most desirable. This type of advertising is especially powerful because physical appearance is a major factor in clothes-buying decisions. However, you do not need to let advertising **dictate**, or determine, your fashion decisions. Let your own values be your guide.

✓ **Reading Check** **Define** What is the rag trade?

The Use of Line

Lines in the construction of a garment may have different effects on the look of its wearer. *What effect is created by the lines in this teen's shirt?*

Understand Design

Whether you acquire new garments or create outfits with clothing you already have, you can use the elements and principles of design to help you look your best. Create subtle illusions and bold statements to boost your confidence and help make a good impression. The right outfit for a job interview can reinforce a professional image. Experimentation can be fun, but remember the elements and principles of design to get the most from your wardrobe.

Design Elements

An **illusion** is an image that fools the eye. Illusions can minimize or hide certain physical features by leading the eye in a specific direction. If you study almost any garment carefully, you can pick out these elements: line, shape, space, texture, and color.

Line The stripes on a sweater, a scoop neckline on a T-shirt, and the seams on jeans are examples of line. As you look at a line, your eye tends to follow its direction. A vertical line leads your eye up and down, communicating a sense of strength. An unbroken vertical line can give the illusion of more height and less width. Vertical lines spaced far apart give the illusion of added width. Horizontal lines lead your eye from side to side, creating an illusion of width. Diagonal, or slanted, lines suggest excitement and movement. Straight lines suggest a crisp, more formal look, while curved lines create a softer effect. Zigzag lines cause the eyes to keep changing direction, creating drama.

Shape The shape or form created when lines are combined is called a **silhouette** (ˌsi-lə-ˈwet). A garment may have more than one shape, but most can be categorized in one of these four shapes:

- A natural shape follows the body's outline and emphasizes the natural waistline.
- In the bell shape, vertical and horizontal lines are combined. This can add curves and make the wearer appear shorter.
- A tubular shape is rectangular. This shape can make the wearer appear taller and slimmer.
- A full shape makes the body appear larger because it has more horizontal and curved lines than the other shapes.

Space The area within the outline of a garment or outfit is called space. Space can be divided by seams, buttons, pockets, trim, or accessories. Imagine a simple black dress with a high neckline and no waistband. Now imagine the same dress with large patch pockets and a white belt. These features would divide the space into different areas, resulting in a different look.

Texture The way a fabric looks and feels is its texture. Casual clothing often uses denim, corduroy, and bulky wools, which differ from the smooth feel of the silk, satin, and fine wools used in formal wear. Like line, fabrics can be used to create illusions. In general, nubby and bulky fabrics make a person look larger. Fabrics with a dull finish, such as denim and flannel, usually make the figure look smaller. Shiny fabrics draw attention.

Color Of the five design elements, the one that people usually notice first when they look at a garment is color. Most people have a favorite color, and it is often one that is flattering to them. Learning more about color can help you select clothes in colors that suit you and put outfits together in new ways.

Design Principles

Fashion designers use a set of artistic guidelines that are the principles of design. These are emphasis, proportion, balance, harmony, and rhythm. Paying attention to design principles can help you achieve a wardrobe that works well for you.

Emphasis **Emphasis** (ˈem(p)-fə-səs) is the technique of drawing attention where you want it. In clothing, there is usually a focal point, the part of the outfit that catches your eye first. By choosing the right focal point, you can draw attention away from areas that you want to minimize and toward areas that you want to emphasize. For instance, a contrasting collar draws attention to the face.

Science For Success

Tricking the Eye

In fashion, design elements can be used to create optical illusions, or visual perceptions that trick the eye into seeing something in a specific way.

Procedure Look for examples of the optical illusions in nature, at home, in magazines, or on a person. Note how design elements such as line and color contribute to the illusion.

Analysis Give a presentation describing your examples of optical illusions. Offer ideas on how these illusions might be applied to serve people's purposes.

NSES E Develop abilities of technological design, understanding about science and technology.

Figure 31.1

The Color Wheel

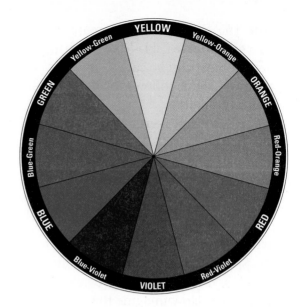

Relationships in Color The color wheel shows the relationship between primary, secondary, and intermediate colors. *What color is produced by mixing equal parts of red and blue?*

Fashion designers add emphasis using color, line, texture, design details, and trims. When you are putting together an outfit, you can use accessories to add your own emphasis. For example, a belt in a bright, contrasting color can draw attention to the waist.

Proportion In clothing, **proportion** refers to the relationship in size of one part of a design to another part, and to the whole design in general. Proportion in a suit is the length of the jacket in relation to the length of the skirt or pants.

Designers know that unequal proportions are the most pleasing to the eye. A longer jacket and shorter skirt, or a shorter jacket and longer skirt, would be more visually appealing than a suit in which the skirt and jacket are the same length.

Choose clothing that is in proportion to your own size. If you have a small frame, avoid clothes with large features such as pockets and jacket lapels. If your body frame is large, clothes with very small details or accessories would look out of proportion.

Balance Balance in clothing design involves giving equal weight to the spaces on both sides of an imaginary center line. The two sides do not have to be identical for the design to appear balanced. Balance helps create a feeling of stability.

Harmony Harmony occurs when all of the aspects of a design work together. The individual items do not have to match, but rather have some elements in common that bring the look together.

Rhythm Rhythm carries the eye through a regular pattern of design elements. For instance, on a blazer, the bottom of a pocket might have the same curve as the bottom of the front opening. Sometimes when outfits do not look "right," it is because they lack rhythm. For example, when plaids do not match at a visible seam, the rhythm of the pattern is broken.

✓ **Reading Check** **Give an Example** How might a fashion designer use the principle of emphasis when creating a garment?

Succeed in SCHOOL and LIFE

Choose Your Best Colors

How do you know which colors are most flattering to you? Stand in front of a mirror in natural daylight. Hold colored paper, fabric, or clothing under your chin. Try a wide variety of colors, shades, and tints. See which ones work best with your eyes, skin, and hair. Also, think about compliments you tend to receive when you wear certain colors. If you are still not sure, find a book or store that offers information on color analysis.

Figure 31.2 — Color Schemes

Use Color to Your Advantage Color scheme principles can help you gain confidence in choosing color combinations for clothing. *Can you imagine an outfit for each of the color schemes described below?*

Monochromatic
Tints and shades of a single color

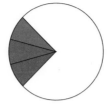

Analogous
Two or more colors positioned next to each other on the color wheel

Complementary
Colors positioned directly across from one another on the color wheel

Split-complementary
One color, plus the two colors positioned on either side of its complementary color

Triadic
Any three colors positioned an equal distance apart on the color wheel

Understand Color

Do you know the difference between a hue and a shade? Such terms can help you better understand and discuss the role of color and color combinations in fashion. These same terms are also used in art and interior design. A diagram referred to as the color wheel (**Figure 31.1**) shows how different colors are related.

Components of Color

A **hue** ('hyü) is a specific color that can be identified by name, such as green, red, or blue-violet. Study the color wheel on the previous page to find these colors:

- **Primary Colors** Red, yellow, and blue are called primary colors because they are used to create all other hues.
- **Secondary Colors** Orange, green, and violet are called secondary colors because they are formed by mixing equal amounts of two primary colors. Orange, for example, is an equal mixture of red and yellow.
- **Intermediate Colors** Yellow-green, yellow-orange, red-orange, red-violet, blue-violet, and blue-green are called intermediate colors because they are formed by mixing a primary color and a secondary color.

Be Smart Be Safe

Fabric Allergies Any type of clothing fabric has the potential to trigger an allergic reaction in some people. Fabric allergies can cause mild to severe symptoms that affect the skin, eyes, nose, or throat. On rare occasions, they require immediate medical help.

Write About It Write a brief report about a fabric that has been known to cause allergic reactions in some people. Include a list of common symptoms and advice on how to handle a reaction.

Black and white are neutral colors used to change the value of a color. **Value** refers to the lightness or darkness of a hue. Adding black to a hue darkens that hue. The darker value is called a **shade**. Adding white to a hue lightens that hue. The lighter value is called a **tint**. Pastel colors, like lavender and sky blue, are tints.

Intensity is the brightness or dullness of a color. Neon orange and lime green are bright, high-intensity colors. Navy blue and rust are subdued, low-intensity colors. The color wheel can help you choose color combinations, or color schemes, that look good together. See **Figure 31.2** on the previous page to create outfits with visually appealing color schemes.

Effects of Color

Like the other elements, color can create illusions. Black and dark shades are generally more slimming than light tints or bright colors. Colors are often classified as "cool" or "warm." Coolness and warmth can also create illusions. A one-color outfit gives the illusion of added height. On the other hand, separate clothing items that have sharp contrasts in hue, value, or intensity might make the wearer look shorter.

You skin, hair, and eye color affects the way a color looks on you. You have probably noticed that some colors look better on you than others do. Your best colors will make your complexion look healthier and your eyes sparkle. Less flattering colors can make your face look tired or your eyes appear dull.

 Podcasts Access the Online Learning Center to download *Managing Life Skills* podcasts.

Section 31.1   After You Read

Review Key Concepts

1. **Differentiate** between a fashion and a style.
2. **Identify** the five basic elements of design.
3. **Give** examples of warm and cool colors.

Practice Academic Skills

 English Language Arts

4. Write a short, descriptive essay identifying your favorite color and explaining your choice. How does this color make you feel? How do you incorporate it into your life? Why do you think favorite colors are so individual?

 Social Studies

5. There is an expression that goes, "Everything old is new again." This is often true when it comes to fashion. Use the Internet or library to find a particular clothing style from another decade that went out of fashion and came back into fashion more than 30 years later. Why do you think that this style returned to popularity?

Check Your Answers Check your answers at this book's Online Learning Center at **glencoe.com**.

NCTE 12 Use language to accomplish individual purposes.

NCSS II B Apply key concepts such as time, chronology, causality, change, conflict, and complexity to explain, analyze and show connections among patterns of historical change and continuity.

Section 31.2

Your Fashion Statement

What do your clothes say about you?

Reading Guide

Before You Read

Understanding It is normal to have questions when you read. Write down questions while reading. Many of them will be answered as you continue. If they are not, you will have a list ready for your teacher when you finish.

Read to Learn
Key Concepts
- **Identify** the functions of clothing.
- **Define** essential clothing.
- **Explain** how to evaluate your wardrobe.
- **List** ways you can expand your wardrobe.

Main Idea
Clothing fulfills many functions in our lives. There are simple ways to evaluate your wardrobe and expand it.

Graphic Organizer
As you read, look for an explanation of the difference between clothes that you need and clothes that you want. Think of at least four examples of each. Use a T-chart like the one shown to help you organize your information.

Clothes I Need	Clothes I Want

 Graphic Organizer Go to this book's Online Learning Center at **glencoe.com** to print out this graphic organizer.

Content Vocabulary
◇ dress code
◇ wardrobe
◇ clothing inventory

Academic Vocabulary
You will find these words in your reading and on your tests. Use the glossary to look up their definitions if necessary.
■ customary
■ prohibit

Academic Standards

English Language Arts
NCTE 8 Use information resources to gather information and create and communicate knowledge.

Mathematics
NCTM Problem Solving Understand the meanings of operations and how they relate to one another.

Social Studies
NCSS I A Culture Analyze and explain the ways groups, societies, and cultures address human needs and concerns.

NCTE *National Council of Teachers of English*
NCTM *National Council of Teachers of Mathematics*
NSES *National Science Education Standards*
NCSS *National Council for the Social Studies*

As You Read

Connect How do you know when it is time to do a wardrobe evaluation?

◈ Vocabulary

You can find definitions in the glossary at the back of this book.

▽ Protective Clothing

This teen's helmet helps protect her head and face. *What other protective clothing and gear are required in different types of sports?*

The Impact of Clothing

No matter how much we think or do not think about our clothing, it can have a major impact on how we act and feel. It is not surprising that clothing is available in so many different forms and styles. Think about the many functions that clothing fulfills in our lives, from physical to emotional to social.

Comfort and Protection

Dressing appropriately for the climate and weather is essential for your comfort and health. In hot weather, loose-fitting, loosely woven clothes help your body to cool by letting perspiration evaporate. In cold weather, layers of warm garments, a head covering, and gloves or mittens help you maintain a safe body temperature. Certain occupations and sports activities require special safety apparel. Whether it is steel-toed shoes, safety glasses, or a hockey helmet, you need to wear the appropriate items for your own protection.

Self-Expression

Clothing choices can express your personality, interests, attitude, and cultural pride. Other qualities revealed by clothing include:

- **Values** A T-shirt from a volunteer effort, a sweatshirt from a religious retreat, or even a souvenir ball cap from the last place you went on vacation can reveal things that matter to you.
- **Mood** Certain clothing choices can reveal your mood, either cheerful and confident or down and uninterested.
- **Status** Some people feel it is important to wear expensive, designer clothes to impress others. While there is no harm in wearing designer brands, designer clothes are not a solid foundation on which to base self-esteem. Judging people on the basis of their clothes alone is unfair and often inaccurate.

Meeting Expectations

When choosing what to wear, most people consider their own preferences, as well as expectations about what is appropriate and **customary**, or traditional. These expectations vary depending on a number of factors:

Societal Standards and Trends Ideas about appropriate clothing change over time. For example, prior to the early 20th century in America and other Western societies, it was considered improper for women to wear pants.

Culture Clothing customs vary in different cultures. Designers often look to other cultures for inspiration, but every culture retains unique, traditional clothing styles.

Dress Code At some time in your life you may be required to follow an official **dress code**, a set of rules describing required or appropriate clothing. Many schools and workplaces use dress codes to promote a desired atmosphere. A dress code describes what should be worn or should not be worn. For example, a school might **prohibit**, or ban, shirts with inappropriate slogans or images, tank tops, and clothes that may be too revealing. Dress codes may include other aspects of appearance. For example, employees might be required to shave facial hair, cover tattoos, and remove certain jewelry as a condition of employment.

Situation or Occasion Dressing appropriately for an event can make you feel confident and at ease. A job interview requires different attire from what you might wear to your friend's barbecue. Perhaps you prefer unconventional clothing, but you may decide to choose conservative clothes to attend your grandmother's 80th birthday party.

Peer Influence Pressures and judgements can sometimes arise when your values differ from those of your friends. Some people are so determined to become part of a certain crowd that they lose sight of who they are and what is important to them. If you feel such pressure, ask yourself whether being part of a group is worth putting aside your beliefs and standards. With clothing, as with all choices, establish your priorities and act on your values.

Roles Whether a particular outfit is considered appropriate also depends on an individual's role. The president of a company might wish to perform her job wearing jeans, but her colleagues and clients might consider such casual clothing inappropriate for her role. Therefore, she chooses to wear business suits to enhance her professional image. On the other hand, jeans worn by a warehouse worker at the same company are perfectly acceptable.

Group Identity Clothes can identify people as belonging to a certain group. Military uniforms are an obvious example, but there are also more subtle ones. Your peer group has adopted certain clothing styles that are seldom worn by people from your grandparents' generation. People use clothing to express membership in social groups of all kinds, both positive and negative.

✓ **Reading Check** **Explain** How can a person's clothing affect his or her professional image?

Uniformity

Some businesses and institutions, such as workplaces, schools, and even fancy restaurants, enforce dress codes. *What are some advantages of this approach?*

Succeed in SCHOOL and LIFE

Dress for the Occasion

Not sure how to dress for an occasion? Here are some guidelines: It is customary to dress up for ceremonies such as graduations and weddings. The attire for evening wedding is often more formal than for those held earlier in the day. Clothing for religious services varies considerably, so if you are uncertain, ask about appropriate attire ahead of time. Funeral customs vary, but wearing conservative clothes in subdued colors shows respect.

Clothing Essentials

Families must manage their clothing expenses carefully and consider their resources, set priorities, and establish a budget. In most families, the clothing budget is limited and must be shared by everyone. If one person overspends, the others have to get by with less. You can show responsibility when you take care of the clothes you already have, keep your spending within agreed-upon limits, and make wise clothing purchases. Even if you have your own money to spend on clothes, careful management will leave more money in your pocket to spend another day or to put into savings.

The clothing needs of individuals and families change throughout the life span. Children need clothing that allows for safe and free play and is easy for them to put on and take off. Children's rapid growth also requires that their clothing be replaced frequently. For adults, clothing needs depend on the kind of work they do and their other activities. People of any age who have physical limitations may need clothing with special features for comfort and convenience.

Clothing for Special Needs

A person's limited mobility may call for specific clothing needs. Someone might have an arm or leg in a cast for a while. Perhaps an older family member uses a scooter to get around. Someone with arthritis may have difficulty with small buttons. Whatever a person's circumstances, he or she will want to look nice, feel comfortable, and be as independent as possible.

When choosing clothes for people with limited mobility, choose garments that are easy to put on and take off. Garments that open in the front or have a large neck opening are helpful. Choose clothes that fit loosely enough for comfort but are not baggy. Avoid long, loose clothes that might cause a fall or become tangled in equipment. To help prevent falls, select flat shoes with nonslip soles. Clothes that must fit over a cast need to be wider. For garments that fit under a brace or cast, select a soft knit. If crutches will be used, choose longer shirts. Pockets make it easier to carry items. Slippery or smooth fabrics allow for easier transfer to and from a wheelchair or scooter.

Assess Your Wardrobe

To dress well and shop wisely, it is best to evaluate your current wardrobe and take an inventory of your clothing. *Which of your clothing items are most likely to stand the test of time?*

✓ **Reading Check**

Identify What qualities should you look for in children's clothing?

Evaluate Your Wardrobe

A person's **wardrobe** is his or her personal collection of clothes. Take the time to evaluate your wardrobe to help prevent feeling like you have nothing to wear.

Needs Versus Wants

Part of good wardrobe management is knowing the difference between your needs and wants. Clothing needs are those basic garments required for your daily routines for school, work, and activities. Clothing wants are more likely to be based on emotion. You will probably be happiest if your wardrobe reflects some of your wants as well as your needs. Remember, however, that needs come first.

To identify your clothing needs, think about your daily life. Where do you go? What do you do? The types of clothes that you wear most often should account for most of your wardrobe. Consider not only your current needs and wants, but also your plans. Perhaps you will go on job interviews, or take a special vacation. Planning ahead makes it easier to find the right outfit for the right circumstances at a reasonable price.

Clothing Inventory

A **clothing inventory** is an organized list of the garments you own. Such a list can help you get your wardrobe in shape. For sweaters, shirts, pants, and so on, create three columns labeled "Description," "Evaluation," and "Action."

Suppose you have a pair of brown corduroy pants. On the "pants" sheet, jot down in the first column "brown corduroy." In the next column, write an evaluation of the pants. If you wear the pants often, find them comfortable, and they are in good condition, write that down. If not, write the appropriate remarks, such as "too loose" or "needs repair." Based upon your evaluation in the second column, decide on your action plan for the pants. Options may include "keep as is," "have fixed," "redesign," and so on. Update your inventory list as your actions are completed. If an item cannot be repaired or redesigned, write "recycle" as your action plan, and set the garment aside. Clearing out items that just are not right for you will make room for pieces that work better.

✓ Reading Check **Differentiate** When it comes to items of clothing, what is the difference between a need and a want?

Math For Success

Price Versus Cost

Collin bought a new sports jacket for $75, which he felt was a good price, especially for the camel hair fabric. It was even less pricy than the plain wool jacket, which was $120. However, Collin soon found himself using the camel hair jacket for work twice a week. He realized that the jacket needed to be dry-cleaned twice a month to keep it wearable. Because of the fragile fabric, the cost for dry cleaning the jacket was $25, whereas the cost to clean the plain wool jacket would have been $12. Five months later, did Collin still feel he had made the less expensive choice? What is the difference in overall cost after five months?

Math Concept **Order of Operations** Do all operations within grouping symbols first. Multiply and divide in order from left to right, and then add and subtract in order from left to right.

Starting Hint Calculate the relative costs of the dry cleaning fees. Add each fee to the price of the jackets, before subtracting the lower figure from the higher figure. This will give you the difference in overall cost.

 For more math practice, go to the Math Appendix at the back of the book.

NCTM Number and Operations Understand the meanings of operations and how they relate to one another.

Health & Wellness TIPS

Buying Baby Clothes

It can be fun to shop for baby clothes for a friend's or relative's newborn. Follow these tips when buying baby clothes:

► Look for the legally required flame-retardant tag.
► Make sure closures are firmly connected to the fabric.
► Check that there are no elastic bands on the item.

Character In Action

Respecting Others' Property

Sharing and borrowing clothing can be a great way to expand your wardrobe options. When you do wear someone else's garment, return it promptly and in good condition. Treating borrowed clothing even more carefully than your own shows respect and builds trust. Remember, too, to return the favor when the lender asks to borrow an item of clothing from you.

You Decide

Imagine that a friend or sibling borrowed an item of your clothing and returned it in damaged condition. What would you say? Might the event change your attitude about lending out clothing? What factors would influence your reaction?

Expand Your Wardrobe

After you have completed your clothing inventory, take a look at what items are left. How well does your collection of clothes fit the needs and wants you identified earlier? If you are like most people, you will discover some gaps in your wardrobe. Clothes are expensive, so you may not be able to buy everything right away. Fortunately, there are resources other than money that can help. Time, skills, creativity, friends, family members, and even the clothes you already own, can be resources for expanding your wardrobe.

- **New Combinations** Experiment with new looks by mixing and matching different items. Combining clothes in new ways gives you a greater variety of outfits from which to choose.
- **Accessories** Accessories, such as a belts, ties, scarves, hats, and jewelry, are used to enhance an outfit. By adding, removing, or changing accessories, you can give an outfit a different look.
- **Redesign** With creativity and a few supplies, you can convert old jeans, shirts, or jackets into truly unique garments. Fabric and craft stores sell decorative buttons, beads, trims, iron-on and sew-on appliqués, fabric paints, and dyes.
- **Sewing** Sewing skills can be used not only to update older outfits but to create new garments as well. In some cases, sewing your own clothes costs less than buying them.
- **Trade and Borrow** Some families consider this an acceptable practice, and others do not. Make sure you ask what items are acceptable to trade or borrow and for how long.
- **Rent** Renting may be an option. Costumes, uniforms, tuxedos, and some gowns are often available to rent.

Life On Your Own

Resolve Clothing Conflicts

Conflicts between teens and adults over clothing choices are nothing new. As you approach adulthood, you have a greater say in deciding what clothes to buy and wear, especially if you pay for them yourself. At the same time, you are also developing greater respect for other people's points of view. Being able to compromise at times about what you wear can pave the way for more harmonious relationships.

How It Works To reach a fair compromise, you first need to understand the other person's concerns over your choice of clothing. What aspects of the outfit bother the other person most? See if you can adjust your choices and still maintain your individuality. Sometimes it is simply a matter of switching out a pair of shoes or adding an accessory. Use your creativity to reach a happy compromise.

Try It Out Your family has been invited to an anniversary party at the home of a relative. You slip on a pair of jeans, ironed shirt, and clean sneakers. However, the moment your father sees you, he tells you to go back into your room and put on a more formal outfit. You object because it is just not your style, but your father insists that you change.

Your Turn Think about how you might strike a compromise regarding your clothes for the evening. What is your father's objection to your outfit? Is there a way you can modify it and still feel comfortable with what you are wearing?

Buying Clothes

Taking a clothing inventory and practicing the options discussed in this chapter can help reduce your need to buy new clothes. However, after you review your clothing inventory and consider your options, you may still decide to purchase some items. If that is the case, start with a plan. What items of clothing should you buy? What items do you need, and what items do you want? Set priorities, ranking the garments that you need by importance. Your list should include important details about the items you need.

Suppose you know that you need two or three pairs of pants to replace ones that you have outgrown. Instead of just writing "pants" on your shopping list, think about which styles, colors, and fabrics would most enhance your wardrobe. Some garments are versatile, or flexible, enough to be used for more than one occasion. These types of items are very useful additions to a wardrobe. Perhaps the right outfit could be worn for family gatherings, graduation ceremonies, and job interviews.

Keep in mind that your wardrobe will go further if items can be mixed and matched. Review your wardrobe inventory for recurring colors and styles. What items might you wear more often if you had something to go with them? To get the most from your wardrobe additions, shop for items that coordinate with the clothes you already own.

Go Green

Instead of throwing away clothing items that you no longer use, recycle them. Sell, give, or donate items that are in good condition. Reuse pieces of fabric, trim, or buttons for new sewing or craft projects. You might even cut up soft and absorbent items to use as cleaning cloths.

 Podcasts Access the Online Learning Center to download *Managing Life Skills* podcasts.

Section 31.2 — After You Read

Review Key Concepts

1. **Identify** the types of expectations that influence what we wear.
2. **List** some of the possible requirements of clothing for someone who is disabled.
3. **Explain** the benefits of evaluating your wardrobe.
4. **List** three ways, other than buying clothes, to expand your wardrobe.

 Check Your Answers Check your answers at this book's Online Learning Center at **glencoe.com**.

Practice Academic Skills

 English Language Arts

5. Prepare a presentation to be entitled, "How to Dress for Success." Research your information on the Internet, at the library, and/or by interviewing a career counselor or other expert. Give an oral report based on your findings.

NCTE 8 Use information resources to gather information and create and communicate knowledge.

Social Studies

6. Hats and other forms of head coverings have great significance in many cultures around the world. Research head coverings that are commonly associated with different cultures, and make a list of your findings.

NCSS I A Analyze and explain the ways groups, societies, and cultures address human needs and concerns.

Pathway to Your Career

Graphic Designer

What Does a Graphic Designer Do?

Graphic designers, or graphic artists, communicate a message using words, graphics, animation, and sound. They work to create anything from a layout of a magazine to producing marketing brochures to designing video games. Their creations may be in the form of print, Web page interactive media, and even movies. Graphic designers may also be called information designers.

Career Readiness Skills To be a graphic designer, you will need to be a skilled visual and verbal communicator. Most graphic designers work with different types of software programs, so you will need strong computer skills as well. This career is one that depends on your creativity, attention to detail, and your ability to follow instructions and work well with others.

Education and Training Most entry-level jobs require a bachelor's degree, but you can study graphic design at two-year colleges, four-year colleges, technical schools, and art schools. Most of these locations will offer the courses you need in fine arts, graphic design, Web design, and art history.

Job Outlook Jobs are expected to grow at an average rate for the next ten years. About a quarter of all graphic designers are self-employed. Gaining experience can lead to management positions in the field.

Critical Thinking Search your school or community for an example of graphic design such as your school paper, yearbook, or literary journal. How has the designer communicated the message? How has the use of color and graphics helped relay the information to the reader?

Career Cluster

CCR ☆ College & Career Readiness

Arts, Audio-Video Technology & Communications Graphic designers work in the Visual Arts pathway of this career cluster. Other jobs in this cluster include:

- Audio Technician
- Web Site Designer
- TV Producer
- Movie Director
- Cinematographer
- Actor
- Fashion Designer
- Museum Curator
- Publicist
- Dancer Artist
- Author
- Editor
- Graphic Designer
- Publisher

Explore Further The Arts, Audio-Video, Technology & Communications career cluster contains six pathways: Audio & Video Technology & Film; Printing Technology; Visual Arts; Performing Arts; Journalism & Broadcasting; and Telecommunications. Choose one of these pathways to explore further.

 Career Clusters To learn more about career clusters, go to this book's Online Learning Center at **glencoe.com**.

CHAPTER SUMMARY

Section 31.1
Fashion and Design Basics

Working with designers, the fashion industry has a strong influence on consumers, both individually and as a group. The elements of fashion design include line, shape, space, texture, and color. The principles of design include emphasis, proportion, balance, harmony, and rhythm. The color wheel can help you understand color and choose pleasing and flattering color combinations.

Section 31.2
Your Fashion Statement

You may choose clothes for comfort and protection, to express yourself, or to meet the expectations of others. Families must adjust to meet changing clothing needs. A clothing inventory can help you evaluate how well your current wardrobe meets your needs and wants. Look for ways to recycle garments that you no longer want. Buying new clothes is not the only way to expand your wardrobe.

Vocabulary Review

1. Write a short essay that describes your personal style. Use at least ten of the following vocabulary terms.

Content Vocabulary
- fashion (p. 631)
- style (p. 631)
- target market (p. 631)
- status symbol (p. 632)
- illusion (p. 632)
- silhouette (p. 633)
- emphasis (p. 633)
- proportion (p. 634)
- hue (p. 635)
- value (p. 636)
- shade (p. 636)
- tint (p. 636)
- intensity (p. 636)
- dress code (p. 639)
- wardrobe (p. 641)
- clothing inventory (p. 641)

Academic Vocabulary
- anonymous (p. 631)
- dictate (p. 632)
- customary (p. 638)
- prohibit (p. 639)

Review Key Concepts

2. **Describe** how the fashion industry and fashion designers influence consumers.
3. **Identify** the elements and principles of design.
4. **Summarize** the components of color.
5. **Identify** the functions of clothing.
6. **Define** essential clothing.
7. **Explain** how to evaluate your wardrobe.
8. **List** ways you can expand your wardrobe.

Critical Thinking

9. **Analyze** How might clothing ads affect the self-concept and self-esteem of those who do not look like the models or wear the trendiest brands?
10. **Predict** If you owned a clothing boutique, would you enforce a dress code on your employees? Why or why not? Explain your answer.
11. **Compare** How would you describe the difference between being stylish and being trendy? Which would you rather be? Why?

ACTIVE LEARNING

Family & Community Connections

12. Fashion Demonstration Choose a day to give a demonstration on how accessories can dramatically change an outfit. Ask classmates to bring in one accessory of clothing, such as a belt, scarf, jewelry, or hat. Choose two classmates to come to class wearing a plain, basic outfit such as a solid dress or jeans and a shirt. Have your "models"

stand in front of the class while you have them add on the various accessories brought in by the class in different combinations. Have the class vote on their favorite looks.

13. Interview a Merchandiser A merchandiser, sometimes called a buyer, is someone who is hired by a store or store chain to shop for and select merchandise from a manufacturer or designer for future sale by that store or store chain. For small stores, the merchandiser is often also the owner. Ask for your teacher's help to find and interview a local merchandiser. Where does he or she find merchandise? How does the merchandiser make decisions? What is involved with the merchandising process (establishing price, determining quantity, arranging shipping, and so on)? Write an outline that illustrates all of the steps involved, from looking for merchandise to displaying it in a store.

21st Century Skills

Technology Skills

14. Haute Couture Haute couture (ˌōt-kü-ˈtür) is a French term used to describe the high fashion seen on runways in cities such as New York and Paris. Use the Internet to research haute couture images and information. Do you think that haute couture should be considered a form of art? Write an essay expressing your opinion.

Media Literacy Skills

15. Onscreen Influence Sometimes a fashion trend debuts in a movie or on television. Then, as quickly as it arrived, it disappears. Are you in tune to how media influences popular fashion trends? Examine a current movie or television show, and note a distinctive fashion worn by one or more characters. Write a paragraph evaluating the fashion. Will it catch on or not? Explain your answer.

 **Connections**

Cross-Cultural Skills

16. Dressing with Modesty As part of its mission, FCCLA encourages individual and group involvement in helping achieve global cooperation and harmony. In many parts of the world and in many cultures, people are taught and encouraged to dress with modesty. Invite classmates of different backgrounds to share their knowledge, experiences, and opinions on the subject of modest dress in a class discussion. Set ground rules for listening without judging.

Academic Skills

 English Language Arts

17. Fashion Writing The language used in fashion advertisements is designed to spark consumers' imaginations and create excitement about new fashions. Study some of these ads. Note the types of words and writing patterns used. Then find three fashion photos in a magazine or catalog, and write your own ad-like descriptions of the outfits.

> **NCTE 4** Use written language to communicate effectively.

 Social Studies

18. Clothing Copies Counterfeit and knock-off versions of fashion items are both copies of original items. However, there are some important differences between the two. Create a poster that is divided into two parts. On one side, define counterfeit versions, and on the other side, define knock-off versions. Illustrate your poster with images of popular fashions and accessories.

> **NCSS VI C Power, Authority, and Governance** Analyze and explain ideas and mechanisms to meet needs and wants of citizens, regulate territory, manage conflict, establish order and security, and balance competing conceptions of a just society.

 Mathematics

19. Clothing Budget Heidi recently accepted a job as a fashion consultant, and she needs to create a budget for her growing expenses. She will be bringing home $200 a week. She figures that 10% of that money will pay her prepaid cell phone bill, 25% will go into her savings account, and 30% will go toward movies, lunches, and gifts. How much money per week will Heidi have left to spend on a new wardrobe? What if she earned $100 a week? Or $300 a week?

Math Concept **Calculate Percentages** A percent is a ratio that compares a number to 100.

Starting Hint First, calculate the percentage that is left over each week for Heidi's clothing budget. Convert the percentage to a dollar amount. Use the same function for alternative amounts of income.

 For more math practice, go to the Math Appendix at the back of the book.

> **NCTM Number and Operations** Understand numbers, ways of representing numbers, relationships among numbers, and number systems.

 Standardized Test Practice

 College & Career Readiness

SHORT ANSWER
Read the questions carefully. Write down a short response for each.

Test-Taking Tip Try not to leave an answer blank on a short-answer test. Although you may not get the exact answer, the work you provide may result in partial credit. You can ask your instructor if partial credit will be given.

20. What do fashion promoters do?

21. How might some people see clothing as a status symbol?

22. What is a dress code?

Chapter 32

Choosing and Caring for Clothes

Chapter Objectives

Section 32.1 Shopping for Clothes

- **Identify** ways to manage clothing costs.
- **Construct** a checklist for evaluating clothing.

Section 32.2 Fabrics and Their Care

- **Name** the common categories of fibers and yarns.
- **Describe** types of fabric construction and finishes.
- **Summarize** guidelines for routine clothing care.
- **List** methods for storing clothing.

> ▶**Explore the Photo**
>
> How you choose and care for your clothing affects how you view yourself and how others view you. *What would you like your clothing to say about you?*

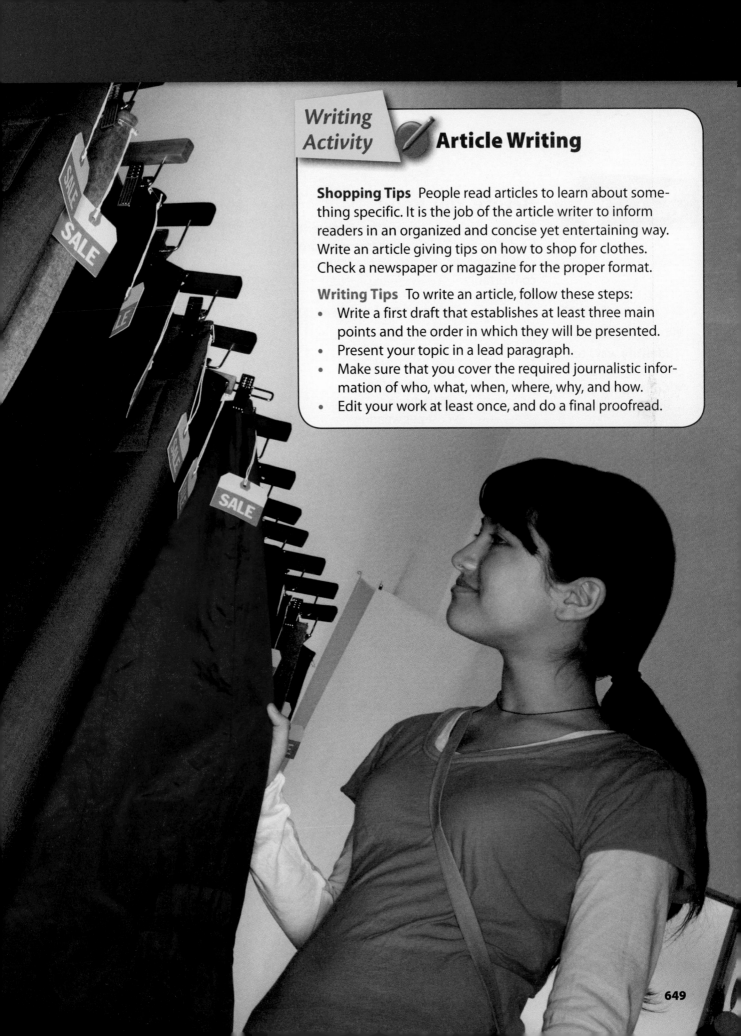

Writing Activity

Article Writing

Shopping Tips People read articles to learn about something specific. It is the job of the article writer to inform readers in an organized and concise yet entertaining way. Write an article giving tips on how to shop for clothes. Check a newspaper or magazine for the proper format.

Writing Tips To write an article, follow these steps:
- Write a first draft that establishes at least three main points and the order in which they will be presented.
- Present your topic in a lead paragraph.
- Make sure that you cover the required journalistic information of who, what, when, where, why, and how.
- Edit your work at least once, and do a final proofread.

Shopping for Clothes

You can achieve a great wardrobe on a budget.

Reading Guide

Before You Read

Be Organized A messy environment can be distracting. To lessen distractions, organize an area where you can read this section comfortably.

Read to Learn
Key Concepts
- **Identify** ways to manage clothing costs.
- **Construct** a checklist for evaluating clothing.

Main Idea

Knowing your shopping options is one way to manage the cost of buying clothing. It is also important to evaluate the value of your purchases when you shop for clothes. Keep in mind how long something will be in style and what the cost per wearing will be.

Content Vocabulary
◇ private-label
◇ irregular
◇ second
◇ vintage clothes
◇ markdown
◇ cost per wearing
◇ classic
◇ fad
◇ hang tag
◇ sewn-in label
◇ fiber content

Academic Vocabulary

You will find these words in your reading and on your tests. Use the glossary to look up their definitions if necessary.
■ distributor
■ consideration

Academic Standards

English Language Arts

NCTE 12 Use language to accomplish individual purposes.

Social Studies

NCSS II B Time, Continuity, and Change Apply key concepts such as time, chronology, causality, change, conflict, and complexity to explain, analyze, and show connections among patterns of historical change and continuity.

Graphic Organizer

As you read, think about different shopping resources for both new and pre-owned clothes. Use a checkerboard graphic like the one shown to help you organize your information. Write new clothing sources in the shaded boxes and pre-owned clothing sources in the white boxes.

Shopping Resources

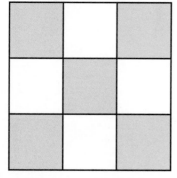

 Graphic Organizer Go to this book's Online Learning Center at **glencoe.com** to print out this graphic organizer.

NCTE *National Council of Teachers of English*
NCTM *National Council of Teachers of Mathematics*
NSES *National Science Education Standards*
NCSS *National Council for the Social Studies*

Managing Clothing Costs

Looking your best does not have to be expensive. You might be surprised at how little some well-dressed people spend on clothes. Instead of spending a lot of money, many people use good taste and sharp shopping skills to achieve their special look.

Where to Shop for Clothes

A variety of shopping options can help you achieve a great wardrobe on a budget. Make a point to compare clothing prices from different stores in your area. Once you become familiar with those prices, you can apply your price comparing skills to recognize bargains. Bargains can be found when shopping at locations away from home, through catalogs, or on the Internet. You will soon get to know which sources offer the best selection and prices. Some of the most commonly available shopping sources for new clothing include:

- **Department Stores** These stores offer less expensive, private-label clothes. **Private-label** means made by an unnamed manufacturer especially for the **distributor**, or store. Most department stores have frequent sales, too.
- **Discount Stores** Although there can be great deals on clothing at discount stores, it pays to check items carefully. Garment quality and condition can vary greatly.
- **Off-Price Retailers** You can find brand-name and designer merchandise at reduced prices at off-price retail stores, but they may not offer the latest styles.
- **Factory Outlets** Items that cannot be sold at regular stores are available at factory outlets. If the items are labeled **irregular**, that means the clothes have slight imperfections that are generally not noticeable and do not affect use or wear. For example, the color of a sweater might not be the exact shade that the manufacturer intended. If the items are labeled **second**, that means they have more noticeable flaws, such as a small hole.
- **Catalog and Online Stores** The convenience of catalog and online shopping has made it popular. However, it is important to remember that shipping charges are usually added to the price. Always read the company's return policy, because you never know how an item is going to fit. If you need to return it, you might not get a refund of the shipping charges. You might even have to pay additional charges for return shipping.

Many people appreciate finding quality pre-owned clothes at bargain prices. These items have usually had some wear, but it is also possible to find "like-new" clothes that have been owned but not worn. Sources of pre-owned clothes include:

- **Consignment Stores** These stores operate by selling other people's used clothes and sharing the profits with the garments' owners. Most consignment stores carefully screen merchandise, resulting in fairly high quality.

As You Read

Connect Think about where you do most of your clothes shopping. Is it time for a change?

▶ Vocabulary

You can find definitions in the glossary at the back of this book.

Character In Action ?!

Honest Shopping

Have you ever been tempted to buy an outfit, wear it once, and then return it? Some shoppers think this practice is harmless, but garments that show signs of having been worn cannot be resold at their original price, so the store loses money. Buying a garment with the intent of wearing it once and returning it is actually a form of theft.

You Decide

You have a party coming up, and you have found the perfect outfit, but it is out of your price range. What options do you have if you cannot afford the outfit you want?

▼ Other Ways to Shop

Catalogs and Web sites offer expanded options and the convenience of shopping from home. *What drawbacks to these sources should you keep in mind?*

- **Thrift Stores** Some nonprofit organizations sell donated clothes and other goods to the public through thrift stores. The proceeds of these stores are used for charitable projects.
- **Garage, Yard, and Rummage Sales** All of these private-party events can be sources of used clothes. However, the quality of these garments can range from good to very poor.
- **Vintage Clothing Stores** Vintage clothes are garments from a previous era, generally representing decades from the 1930s to the not-so-distant past. Vintage clothing stores can be found in many cities and on the Internet, though you might also find vintage clothing at thrift stores or yard sales. Vintage clothing prices can be low, comparable to new clothes, or higher.

Check pre-owned clothes carefully before you buy them. Look for stains, tears, faded areas, missing buttons, and broken zippers. If you can make minor repairs yourself, the item may still be well worth the price.

How to Save When Shopping

Store sales are an important key to stretching your shopping budget. This includes paying attention to sales and patiently waiting for them. Cherise's attitude about sales is simple. "If I see a sweater or something I really want, I just wait for it to go on sale," she says. "If someone else buys it before me, I just figure it wasn't meant to be and save that money for something else."

Store advertisements notify you of many types of sales strategies. To help you save on your clothing expenses, consider these tips:

- If you know you will need a new winter coat, look for one at preseason or during a holiday sale.
- Take advantage of clearance sales designed to move the current season's clothes and make room for the next season's clothes.
- Coupon sales can also provide excellent savings.
- While shopping, look for **markdown** items. These items have permanent price reductions on specific items. The longer an item takes up space on a rack, the more it is marked down.

Managing Wear and Care Costs

As long as you own a garment, you will need to care for it. If the garment can be washed along with other items, the cost of care is minimal. Washing an item separately might cost just a few dollars a year. However, fees for professional dry cleaning can add up quickly. When shopping, look for care instructions on garment labels and consider the impact on your budget.

Cost Per Wearing

The amount of wear you are going to get from a clothing item can be an important **consideration**, or factor. The more times you wear an outfit, the more cost efficient it becomes. **Cost per wearing** is an estimate of how much money you actually pay per use. To calculate cost per wearing, divide the total cost of the garment, including any cleaning costs, by the estimated number of wearings.

Most of the time, you will not actually make these calculations. Still, it is helpful to keep the principle of cost per wearing in mind. It reminds you that buying a garment that you will wear often is money well spent. This means that quality counts. An item that falls apart the first time you wash it is no bargain. A more expensive item may be a better buy if its higher quality means it will last longer.

Classics Versus Fads

Before spending money on clothing, consider how long it will remain in style. **Classic** items, like sweaters and traditional jeans, will likely stay popular for a long time. A **fad** is a style that remains popular for only a short time. Pants with very narrow or very wide legs may be in style one year and not the next. Fads can be fun, but because they come and go quickly, their cost per wearing is higher.

Both classics and fads can have a place in your wardrobe. The key is to find ways to be in style without breaking your budget. When you see a new style that you like, try to recognize whether it is a fad, and make your buying decisions accordingly.

✓ **Reading Check** **Explain** When is a good time to buy a winter coat and why?

Life On Your Own

Shop Responsibly

Consumers expect certain things when they shop, including clean dressing rooms and friendly and fair treatment from employees. As a shopper, you have responsibilities too. Shopping involves handling merchandise that does not belong to you. It is the property of the store until you pay for it. If you choose not to buy an item, the item should be left in good condition for other potential buyers.

How It Works Before trying on clothes, remove jewelry that could catch on clothing. Be careful with buttons, zippers, and hangers. Do not transfer any dirt or makeup onto clothing items. If you notice an issue with a piece of clothing, let a salesperson know. Leave the dressing room in good condition, putting clothing items back on hangers and either giving them to a salesperson or returning them to the correct racks.

Try It Out You are shopping with a friend. Your friend brings about 15 clothing items into the dressing room. After he has finished trying them all on, you notice them in a pile on the dressing room floor, with hangers strewn about them. You ask your friend if he is planning on picking up the clothes, and he replies, "That is what the salespeople are for. Why should I have to do something that other people are paid to do?"

> **Your Turn** Think about what you might say or do in this situation to avoid leaving a mess in the dressing room. Might you be able to change your friend's point of view?

Evaluate Your Selection

When you are trying to decide whether or not to buy a piece of clothing, you do not simply pick the clothing item off the rack and take it directly to the cash register. So how do you decide whether an item of clothing would be a wise addition to your wardrobe? You should start by reading the clothing item's labels, noting what type of clothing care is required. You should then check the item's fit and quality. Once you have done these things, you will know more about the garment and will be able to evaluate the purchase and reach an informed decision.

HOW TO .... Evaluate Quality

To get the most for your money, look at details on clothing that indicate whether it is well made. If you find an inexpensive item of clothing that is only made well enough to last for two months, it is not actually a good buy. Areas of a garment that you should check before buying are:

Care Information Check the label for fiber content and care information. Make sure you are willing to follow the care instructions.

Wearing Quality The tighter the knit or weave, the better the garment will hold its shape.

Seam Stitching should be straight, smooth, and secured at each end.

Trim Any decoration should be attached neatly and smoothly.

Pattern If the fabric has a pattern such as stripes or plaid, make sure the design is straight and even all around.

Wrinkling Grasp a handful of the fabric, crush it in your hand, and release it. If the wrinkles stay, the garment is likely to wrinkle easily.

Fasteners Do zippers slide smoothly? Do snaps work properly? Are there any buttons missing?

Corners and Edges Are the corners of collars smooth and flat? Do all edges on the garment lie flat? Avoid bunched edges or irregular corners.

Hem Hemmed edges should be smooth. Unless decorative stitching is used, the hem should be almost invisible.

Figure 32.1 **Checking for a Good Fit**

Does This Garment Fit? Pay attention to specific areas of each garment you try on. *Are there any areas that you regularly tend to overlook?*

HOW TO CHECK IF A GARMENT FITS:

- **Collar or Neckline** A collar or neckline that is too tight may restrict breathing or cause irritation. Collars that are too large feel uncomfortable and do not look good.
- **Chest and Back** A garment should feel comfortable across your chest and back as you walk, sit, bend, and move your arms.
- **Waistband or Waistline** Clothes that are tight in the waist are uncomfortable. You should be able to slip your finger easily inside the waistband. Waistbands should be about 1 inch (2.5 cm) larger than your waist measurement.
- **Pant Legs** The bottom edge of pant legs should break at the top of your shoes or feet.
- **Hemline** A garment's length should be appropriate for the item's proportions and its intended use. Garments that are too long or short restrict movement.
- **Hip Area** Pants and skirts should fit smoothly but allow the wearer to bend and sit comfortably.
- **Sleeves** Sleeves that are too short or too long can restrict movement or get in the way. Long sleeves should come to your wrists.
- **Fasteners** Zippers and buttons should not gap or pull as you move.
- **Shoulders** Most sleeves start at the edge of the shoulder. If sleeves are too tight, they restrict arm movement.

Read Tags and Labels

If you usually just check clothing tags for size and price, take a closer look. The tags and labels attached to clothes contain other valuable information about the garments. A **hang tag** carries the brand name, the size, warranty information, and a bar code. This tag is meant to be removed after purchase. A **sewn-in label** gives information such as manufacturer name, country of manufacture, fiber content, and care instructions. This label information must, by law, be provided by clothing manufacturers. **Fiber content** is given as the percentage of each fiber by weight. This information can help you predict how well a garment will wear, whether it will wrinkle easily, and other qualities.

Before you purchase an item, consider how likely you are to follow the care instructions on the sewn-in label. If you are not willing to hand wash a shirt in cold water and hang it to dry or to pay the extra costs that result from a "Dry Clean Only" garment, do not buy that garment. Choose one that can be machine washed and dried with similar clothes.

Check the Size and Fit

A trip to the store dressing room is time well spent. If you are not sure what size to try on, ask a sales clerk for advice. Clothing sizes for females are often given in numbers within size categories, such as juniors, misses, women's, and petites. Each category is designed for different body proportions. For males, sizes are often given in measurements. For example, pants labeled 30 x 32 have a 30-inch waist and a 32-inch inseam (inside leg length).

For both males and females, clothing sizes may be given as letters, such as "M" for medium or "XL" for extra large. However, these sizes are not necessarily consistent.

In addition to size, the style of a garment can greatly affect its fit. If a garment does not fit right, you probably will not wear it often. That means you will lose money or have to return the item. Move around in the dressing room when you try on a garment. Sit down, reach up, and bend over. If you cannot do any of these things easily or if the garment sags, pulls, or gaps anywhere, it does not fit properly. Even when snug-fitting clothes are popular, avoid garments that are too tight. Clothes with a little breathing room look better, wear longer, and are more comfortable. See **Figure 32.1** on the previous page for fitting guidelines.

Catalogs and online clothing sources usually provide detailed information about how to choose the correct size based on body measurements. Still, individual garments vary, so be sure to check the return policy.

Check Quality

Some clothes shoppers are convinced that higher prices indicate higher quality. This may be true some of the time, but it is definitely not always true. To know whether you are getting your money's worth, be careful to check the quality of the garment.

 Podcasts Access the Online Learning Center to download *Managing Life Skills* podcasts.

Section 32.1 After You Read

Review Key Concepts

1. **Give** an example of a high cost-per-wearing item and a low cost-per-wearing item.
2. **Identify** the different ways in which size information is given on a clothing tag.

Practice Academic Skills

 English Language Arts

3. Write a three-paragraph essay describing your favorite clothes shopping place. Include details describing what you like about this place and a description of a positive experience or purchase supporting your choice. Make sure to use proper essay style.

 Social Studies

4. Department stores have served as a major source for clothes buying in the United States for many years. Research the development of one American department store chain, from its first store to more recent developments. Create a list of these milestones. Try to draw connections between milestones and major historical events.

Check Your Answers Check your answers at this book's Online Learning Center at **glencoe.com.**

NCTE 12 Use language to accomplish individual purposes.

NCSS II B Apply key concepts such as time, chronology, causality, change, conflict, and complexity to explain, analyze, and show connections among patterns of historical change and continuity.

Fabrics and Their Care

Take care of your clothes, and they will take care of you.

Reading Guide

Before You Read

Look It Up As you read this section, keep a dictionary near you to use in addition to the glossary at the back of the book. If you hear or read a word that you do not know, look it up in the glossary or the dictionary. Before long, this practice will become a habit.

Read to Learn

Key Concepts
- **Name** the common categories of fibers and yarns.
- **Describe** types of fabric construction and finishes.
- **Summarize** guidelines for routine clothing care.
- **List** methods for storing clothing.

Main Idea
There are several types of fabrics that are used to make clothes. Each has its own characteristics and care needs.

Content Vocabulary
◇ fiber
◇ natural fiber
◇ manufactured fiber
◇ yarn
◇ blend
◇ fabric finish
◇ colorfast
◇ mildew

Academic Vocabulary
You will find these words in your reading and on your tests. Use the glossary to look up their definitions if necessary.
■ comprise
■ true

Academic Standards

English Language Arts
NCTE 8 Use information resources to gather information and create and communicate knowledge.

Mathematics
NCTM Number and Operations Compute fluently and make reasonable estimates.

Social Studies
NCSS IX B Global Connections Explain conditions and motivations that contribute to conflict, cooperation, and interdependence among groups, societies, and nations.

NCTE *National Council of Teachers of English*
NCTM *National Council of Teachers of Mathematics*
NSES *National Science Education Standards*
NCSS *National Council for the Social Studies*

Graphic Organizer

As you read, take note of the different types of natural fibers and manufactured fibers. Use a T-chart like the one shown to help you organize your information.

Natural Fibers	Manufactured Fibers

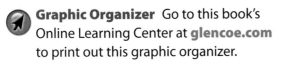

Graphic Organizer Go to this book's Online Learning Center at **glencoe.com** to print out this graphic organizer.

As You Read

Connect Is there a particular type of fabric that is more commonplace in your wardrobe?

Vocabulary

You can find definitions in the glossary at the back of this book.

Understanding Fibers and Yarns

The fabric in your clothing starts with fibers. A **fiber** is a very fine, hair-like strand. Grouped together, fibers **comprise**, or make up, the yarns that are made into fabrics used to create clothing, towels, and other textiles.

Natural Fibers

Although there are many types of fibers, they can be grouped into two categories: natural and manufactured. A **natural fiber** is a strand that comes from plants or animals. In clothing, natural fibers absorb moisture and allow air to reach the skin. Clothing made from natural fibers is comfortable, keeping the wearer cool in warm weather and warm in cold weather. However, it also often requires more care than clothing made from manufactured fibers. Each natural fiber has its own characteristics:

- **Cotton** Made from the seedpod of the cotton plant, cotton fabric is strong, absorbent, and comfortable in hot weather. Although it is capable of shrinking and wrinkling, it can be treated with finishes to prevent these problems.
- **Linen** Made from the stalk of the flax plant, linen is absorbent, comfortable, and even stronger than cotton. However, it wrinkles easily and must be pressed with a very hot iron. Linen is sometimes used for fashions that have an unpressed look.
- **Wool** Made from sheep fleece, wool is warm because its fibers trap air. Wool wears well, resists wrinkles and abrasion, and repels water. A favorite target of moths, wool shrinks easily and usually must be dry cleaned. However, special fabric finishes can make wool garments both washable and moth resistant.
- **Silk** Made from fibers in the cocoon that the silkworm spins, silk is lightweight, flexible, and naturally lustrous. Although they resist wrinkling, silk fabrics can be easily damaged by perspiration, deodorant, and high ironing temperatures.
- **Ramie** Made from the stems of China grass, ramie has a natural luster and is especially strong. It is absorbent and washable and resists mildew and insects. Because of its stiff texture, ramie is usually blended with other fibers.

Manufactured Fibers

Many of today's fabrics are made from manufactured fibers. A **manufactured fiber** is a strand formed either completely or in part by chemicals. For instance, rayon and acetate are made from a combination of natural wood chips and chemicals. Like natural fibers, manufactured fibers have their own characteristics:

- **Rayon** Absorbent, soft, and comfortable, rayon drapes easily but also wrinkles easily. It may shrink, so dry cleaning is usually recommended.

- **Polyester** Washable, fast-drying, and not absorbent, polyester resists wrinkling and shrinking. It tends to attract oily stains and might pill, or form tiny balls of fiber on the surface.
- **Nylon** Strong and lightweight, nylon holds its shape well. It is washable, fast-drying, and not absorbent. It tends to collect static electricity and is sensitive to heat.
- **Acrylic** Soft and warm, acrylic resists fading and wrinkling. Some acrylics tend to pill or attract static electricity. Acrylic fabrics should not be dried at high temperature.
- **Acetate** With the look of silk and an easy drape, acetate is sensitive to heat, must be dry cleaned, and may wrinkle and fade.
- **Spandex** This elastic fiber, often combined with other fibers, should not be bleached or laundered at high temperatures.

Yarns

Yarn is the thread-thin product of fibers that have been twisted or grouped together. Various types of yarns can be formed from fibers. Long, straight fibers usually create smooth, silky yarns. Short, curly fibers tend to make softer, fluffier yarns. The thickness of the yarn also depends on how tightly the fibers are spun together. The qualities of the fiber and yarn affect a fabric's wear and care.

A **blend** is a yarn made from two or more different fibers. Blends are created to take advantage of the best features of each type of fiber. One blend commonly found in shirts is 60% polyester and 40% cotton. It has the comfort and look of cotton, but often does not require ironing because of the polyester.

✓ **Reading Check** **Clarify** What is the advantage of clothes made from blended fibers?

Fabric Construction and Finishes

Textile mills use several methods to make yarns into fabric. The two most common methods are weaving and knitting.

Woven Fabrics

Weaving involves interlacing two sets of yarns together at right angles. Woven fabrics generally hold their shape well and are stronger than knits. The type of weave, along with the characteristics of the fiber and yarn, helps determine whether the fabric is soft, smooth, or textured. The three basic types of weaves are:
- **Plain Weave** The most common weave, plain weave is often used for shirts and sheets.
- **Twill Weave** Strong fabrics, like denim, are usually produced using twill weave.
- **Satin Weave** Smooth, less durable fabrics with a sheen are produced using satin weave.

 Fibers, Yarns, and Fabrics

Fibers are twisted together to make yarn, which is then turned into fabric. *Do you think most people today are aware of how fabrics are made?*

659

Financial *Literacy*

Compare Clothing Costs

You are moving to a cold, snowy climate. You want to buy a new scarf and hat set, but it costs $35.00 plus tax. You have knitting needles and the pattern seems simple, so you decide to try to make the set. The yarn you need costs $8 per skein, and you will need two skeins. For the tassels, you will need a crochet hook that costs $7.95 and a tapestry needle that costs $2.50. You will also have to pay 8 percent sales tax on all of these items. Is it worth it to make the set?

Math Concept **Price Comparison** When deciding between two options, such as a store-bought item and a homemade item, be sure to include all of the associated costs, including tools and supplies.

Starting Hint Calculate how much you will spend on all the items you need to purchase, and multiply that amount by 0.08 to determine the tax. Add the two amounts, then decide if it is more cost effective to purchase the set or to make it yourself.

Math For more math practice, go to the Math Appendix at the back of the book.

NCTM Number and Operations Compute fluently and make reasonable estimates.

Knit Fabrics

Knit fabrics are constructed by pulling loops of yarn through other loops of yarn, creating interlocking rows. Many workout garments are made from knit fabrics because knits stretch with movement and return to their original shape. Knit clothes are comfortable and do not wrinkle easily.

Other Fabric Construction Methods

Some manufacturers produce fabrics in ways other than weaving and knitting. Nonwoven fabrics, such as felt, are made by matting or bonding fibers with heat, moisture, or adhesives. Bonded fabrics, such as those used for water-repellent rainwear, are created by fusing one fabric to another, making two layers. Quilted fabrics are produced by putting a fluffy layer of batting between two layers of fabric. The layers are held together by decorative stitching or a special heat treatment.

Fabric Finishes

A **fabric finish** is any special treatment that improves the appearance, feel, or performance of a fabric. Color or design can be a finishing treatment added at various stages of the production process, from fiber to finished garment. Manufacturers use computers to achieve the exact colors they want. Some fabrics and garments are **colorfast**, which means that their color will remain the same over time. If a garment is not colorfast, its color may fade after repeated washings. The care label may say, "Wash with like colors." Doing so will help prevent the dye that comes out of a non-colorfast garment from staining other clothes.

Some finishes make fabric look more appealing or feel especially pleasant. Flannel is brushed to raise fiber ends, creating a softer texture. Some finishes make a fabric shinier or crisper. Others add a practical property such as wrinkle resistance or soil release. These finishes may be permanent or temporary. Some children's clothing and sleepwear are treated to make them flame-resistant, an important safety feature.

✓ Reading Check **Differentiate** Discuss differences between woven and knit fabrics.

Caring for Your Clothes

Taking the time to care for your clothes on a regular basis protects your investment in your wardrobe, helps your family's clothing budget go further, and guarantees that what you need is available when you need it.

At the end of each day, or whenever you change clothes, take a few moments to inspect the garments you have worn. If you see any stains, treat them promptly using the methods described later in this chapter. The sooner you treat stains, the greater your chances are of removing them. Also, look for any minor repairs that are needed, and take care of them as soon as possible.

If you do not need to take care of stains or repairs, decide what other care is needed. Put garments that need washing in a hamper until you are ready to do laundry. However, remember that clothes do not always need to be washed or cleaned after every wearing. Sometimes you can just air out garments by hanging them outside the closet or draping them over a chair. You might also need to brush off lint or press out wrinkles.

Once clothes are ready to wear again, put them where they belong. If you just heap them in a pile, they can easily become wrinkled, dirty, or damaged.

Cleaning Your Clothes

Shrunken shorts, pink T-shirts that used to be white, and stiff blue jeans are all problems that can be avoided by learning the few simple steps to doing laundry.

Sorting Laundry

As you prepare to do your own laundry or the family laundry, separate clothes into groups according to:

- **Care Instructions** Read the sewn-in care labels. Separate items that can be washed in warm water from those that need cold water, hand washing, or dry cleaning. Look for special instructions, such as "wash separately."
- **Color** To keep colors **true**, or unchanged, separate whites and light colors from bright or dark colors.
- **Weight of Items** Separate heavy-weight items from more delicate items.
- **Linting** Items such as towels and rugs often produce a lot of lint. Separate them from items to which lint might cling, such as a pair of black slacks.

The Sorting Process

The sorting process ensures that clothes with similar characteristics are washed together. *Why is the sorting process important?*

- **Amount of Soil** If an item is heavily soiled, such as a mud-stained sports uniform, wash it separately from lightly soiled clothes. As you sort, prepare clothes for washing. Check pockets and remove all items. Close zippers and hook-and-loop fasteners, which can snag other garments.

Once you have sorted the laundry, you will have several piles of clothing. If a load has only a few items, try to delay laundering it. Large loads are more efficient than small ones, saving detergent, water, and energy. Also remember to balance loads to prevent tangling. Laundering four sheets in one load could result in tangling. Instead, launder fewer sheets with some pillowcases.

Removing Stains

Stains on clothes are a very common problem. Removing most of them is not difficult, especially when you act promptly. You have three opportunities to deal with stains:

Step 1 Treat the stain as soon as you notice it. Immediately rinsing the stain in cold water will often remove most of the spot. A stain removal product in the form of a moist towelette made for such situations is another option.

Step 2 You can also wait to treat the garment when you check it at the end of the day. Soaking garments in plain cold water, or water mixed with detergent, eliminates many stains.

Step 3 Your last chance is to treat the stain just before you wash the garment. Pre-treating stains just before laundering can be done in several ways. You might rub a little detergent directly onto the stain. Or you might apply a prewash stain removal product to the soiled area, especially if it is oily or greasy. The package should tell you what types of stains the product is designed to remove and how to remove them. You typically need to wait a few minutes to allow the product to soak in and work before laundering.

Often the worst thing you can do with a stained garment is wash it in hot water and then dry it in a dryer. Heat sets many stains, making later removal difficult or impossible. If a stain remains after washing, air dry the garment, and then after it is dry, try to treat the stain again.

Machine Washing

Once you have sorted laundry and pretreated stains, you can begin the wash cycle. If you are using a particular washer for the first time, ask for a quick lesson. Front-loading machines, for example, operate differently from standard top-loading machines. Here are general directions for a standard top loading machine:

Step 1 Select the water temperature appropriate for the items in the load. When two temperatures are listed, such as "warm/cold," the wash cycle will be warm and the rinse water will be cold.

Step 2 Set the washer cycle for the type of load, such as regular, permanent press, or delicate. You also need to choose the length of the wash cycle. Lightly soiled clothes require less time to wash than dirtier clothes.

Step 3 As the machine starts to fill with water, add detergent and any other laundry products according to package directions. Some machines have special dispensers for bleach and liquid fabric softener.

Step 4 When the detergent is mixed with the water, add the items being washed. Pile them in the washer loosely so they can move freely during the wash cycle.

Hand Washing

Some delicate garments are labeled "hand wash." You might also want to use this method when you have just one or two items to launder. Start by soaking the item in sudsy water. Then gently squeeze the suds through the garment. Drain the sink or basin and refill it with fresh water to rinse the garment. Repeat the rinse step until the water is free of suds.

Drying Your Clothes

Labels usually tell how to dry garments. "Tumble dry" means the item can be dried by machine, but you can use a different method if you prefer. Some clothes must be line dried, dried flat, drip dried, or dried in the shade.

- **Machine Drying** Select the temperature setting that best matches instructions on clothes' care labels. Some dryers have sensors to determine when clothes are dry. For others, you must set the drying time. Clean the lint filter before every load. Not only does this help clothes dry faster, but it is also essential for safety because lint is very flammable. Remove dry clothes promptly so they do not wrinkle. Fold or hang them, smoothing areas such as collars and cuffs with your fingers.
- **Line Drying** Hanging laundry outside on a breezy day helps wrinkles disappear and clothes smell fresh. You can also air-dry clothes indoors on hangers, a clothesline, or a drying rack. Air drying saves energy.
- **Drying Flat** Use this method when the care label recommends it. Such items may shrink or be damaged by the dryer, and they may stretch out of shape if line dried. For fastest drying, use a mesh drying rack that allows air to circulate. If you do not have a drying rack, place the item on a thick towel and gently reshape it. Turn the garment over every few hours, replacing the damp towel with a dry one.

Hand Washing Clothes

Avoid twisting or wringing garments when hand washing. After rinsing, roll the garment in a towel to remove excess water. *Why should you avoid twisting or wringing hand-washed clothes?*

Succeed in SCHOOL and LIFE

Store School Clothes

Do you feel as though you never have enough storage space for your school clothes? To maximize storage space, use hangers designed to hold more than one garment. Install hooks or over-the-door racks for belts and other accessories. Store out-of-season and seldom used items in less convenient places, like under your bed or in empty suitcases.

Ironing Clothes

An iron uses heat and pressure to remove wrinkles. *What temperature would you use for a synthetic fiber, such as polyester?*

Be Smart Be Safe

Safe Ironing Ironing helps you look well-dressed and professional. But it is important to keep some safety tips in mind. Never leave a hot iron unattended. Always keep the iron moving over the clothing to prevent burns. Make sure the iron is completely cool before putting it away.

Write About It Different types of fabric have different safe ironing temperatures. These are often indicated on an iron. Use an iron or the Internet to list these fabrics from lowest to highest ironing temperatures: cotton, linen, nylon, polyester, silk, and wool.

Whatever method you use, it is important to dry clothes promptly. Wrinkles set when wet clothes are left in the washer. If left long enough, wet or damp clothes may develop mildew. **Mildew** is a fungus that shows up as small black dots. Damp clothing may also develop a sour odor. As you remove items from the washer, shake out each garment to help minimize wrinkling.

Removing Wrinkles

No matter how carefully you wash and dry your clothes, some items will get wrinkled. You can remove wrinkles by using an iron. An iron is used for two different wrinkle-fighting techniques: ironing and pressing. Ironing involves sliding the iron over the fabric in a back and forth motion to smooth out wrinkles. It is used on sturdy fabrics, such as cotton. Pressing involves lifting the iron and setting it back down on the fabric. This technique does not incorporate the back and forth motion so it is used on fabrics that may stretch, such as knits and wools.

Select the iron's heat setting based on the garment's fabric and care label. There are also often temperature guides on the iron itself, indicating safe temperatures for different fabric types. For a blend, choose the lowest suggested setting. An iron that is too hot can scorch, or even melt, clothes. Allow a few minutes for the iron to preheat to the chosen temperature.

When ironing a garment, start with small areas such as collar, cuffs, and then sleeves. Then iron the large flat areas, such as the back and front of a shirt. Make sure to keep the iron moving when it is touching the clothing to avoid burning or melting the fabric.

Dry Cleaning

Most people own some garments that must be dry cleaned. The dry cleaning process uses special chemicals to get clothes clean.

When you take garments to be commercially dry cleaned, point out any stains and try to identify what caused them. That will help the dry cleaner determine how to remove them.

There are two alternatives to commercial dry cleaning: dry cleaning machines that are provided in some coin-operated laundries and dry cleaning kits to use with a regular dryer. The kits contain pre-moistened cloths to place in a special bag with a few garments. After the garments tumble in the dryer for a specified time, you remove them promptly and hang them on hangers. The process works best with wool, rayon, silk, linen, and cotton knits. As with all laundry products, it is important to follow directions carefully.

✓ **Reading Check** **Describe** What are three opportunities to take care of stains on an item of clothing?

Storing Your Clothes

Organized storage can save valuable space in your closets and drawers. It can also save time, especially when you are rushing to get dressed. Storage methods also affect how clothes look and how long they last. Follow these tips to keep clothes looking fresh and wrinkle-free:

- Use plastic or padded hangers for items of clothing you need to hang.
- Store knits and other delicate clothing folded rather than on hangers to prevent stretching.
- Keep your closet and drawers organized by keeping like items together.
- Avoid overcrowding in your closet. It can cause clothes to wrinkle and lose shape.
- Be sure clothes are stain-free before putting them away. Stains set with time, and some can attract damaging insects.
- To prevent mildew from forming, make sure clothes are completely dry before you store them. Avoid storing clothing in damp, humid areas, such as a basement.

Following these simple storage strategies can protect your clothes and prolong their wearability, allowing you to enjoy them for as long as possible.

Podcasts Access the Online Learning Center to download *Managing Life Skills* podcasts.

Section 32.2 — After You Read

Review Key Concepts

1. **Distinguish** between 100 percent cotton and 100 percent polyester when choosing an outfit for a summertime hike.
2. **Give** examples of fabric finishes.
3. **Categorize** the factors to consider about clothing items when sorting your laundry.
4. **Explain** the reason for having an organized clothing storing system.

Check Your Answers Check your answers at this book's Online Learning Center at **glencoe.com**.

English Language Arts

5. A brochure is a small booklet containing descriptive or informational material. Look at several examples of brochures from your school or places of businesses. Then, using your textbook and the Internet as information sources, create a brochure about doing laundry. Target young people who are moving out on their own for the first time.

Social Studies

6. A quick glance at a sewn-in label on a garment will tell you where that item was manufactured. In many cases, the item is made overseas. This is because many clothing manufacturers have moved their factories to other countries. Research this issue on the Internet. Then give a short oral presentation stating what you learned and how it might affect your own clothes-buying decisions.

Pathway to College

The Transition to College

What Can I Do to Make the College Transition Easier?

The jump to college is exciting, but it can also be quite stressful. You are leaving behind what you are comfortable with and going off to explore a new place. Many students overlook the stress involved in making so many changes so quickly. The more prepared you are, the easier the transition will be.

What is the biggest change?

The biggest change between high school and college is more independence and increased responsibility. These can be exciting and enjoyable things, but they need to be handled carefully. You likely will not have as strong a support system as you do now. For example, you will probably have to start managing your own money. You need to start learning how to make smart decisions and think in the long-term.

How do I deal with the academic challenges of college?

College courses will be more difficult, and you will probably have more reading, writing, and problem sets than you are used to. Most first-year college students experience an adjustment period, so if you are struggling at first, do not think you are not going to make it. Give yourself a chance to adjust gradually by choosing a course load that includes some challenging classes and some less intense ones.

How can I learn to manage my time at college?

In high school, you probably had a lot of help with time management, but at college, the responsibility of managing your schedule will largely be your own. If you cut classes or do not do assignments, no one will nag you. Write down when and where your classes meet, when assignments are due, and when tests will take place. Give yourself time to study rather than waiting until the last minute.

Hands-On

College Readiness One of the biggest transitional problems that new college students experience is learning how to stay organized. Between living on their own for the first time, choosing and taking classes, developing a new social life, joining clubs and activities, learning a new place, and figuring out housing and food, students have their hands full. They can easily get overwhelmed. Think of some things new college students can do to get and stay organized. Put these suggestions into a list.

Path to Success

☆ College & Career Readiness

Set Up a Schedule Find a daily routine that works for you, and stick to it.

Go to Class Skipping class can be tempting, but it is a sure way to fall behind.

Be Patient Remember that making new friends takes time and will not happen immediately.

Go to Office Hours Professors will post the hours they are available outside of class. Take advantage of these opportunities.

Get Enough Rest You may feel so busy that you start cutting back on sleep, but this is not a good idea.

Ask for Help If you are falling behind, seek help from your college's resources, including tutors, academic advisors, and writing centers.

 Go to this book's Online Learning Center at **glencoe.com** to learn more about college and career readiness.

CHAPTER SUMMARY

Section 32.1
Shopping for Clothes

You can save money on clothes by comparing different shopping resources and considering the cost of wear and care. Hang tags and care labels provide useful information. Trying on a garment is the only sure way to know whether it fits properly. Check a garment's quality by examining its fabric and construction. You have a responsibility to treat merchandise carefully as you shop.

Section 32.2
Fabrics and Their Care

Fibers are either natural or manufactured. Fabrics can be woven, knit, or constructed in other ways. Fabric finishes are designed to improve fabric in some way. Inspect clothing after wear. Stains can usually be removed if treated promptly. Pay attention to care label information when laundering clothes. Some clothes must be dry cleaned. Storing clothes correctly keeps them in good condition.

Vocabulary Review

1. Use at least 12 of these terms to create a crossword puzzle. Use definitions as clues.

Content Vocabulary
- private-label (p. 651)
- irregular (p. 651)
- second (p. 651)
- vintage clothes (p. 652)
- markdown (p. 652)
- cost per wearing (p. 653)
- classic (p. 653)
- fad (p. 653)
- hang tag (p. 655)
- sewn-in label (p. 655)
- fiber content (p. 655)
- fiber (p. 658)
- natural fiber (p. 658)
- manufactured fiber (p. 658)
- yarn (p. 659)
- blend (p. 659)
- fabric finish (p. 660)
- colorfast (p. 660)
- mildew (p. 664)

Academic Vocabulary
- distributor (p. 651)
- consideration (p. 653)
- comprise (p. 658)
- true (p. 661)

Review Key Concepts

2. Identify ways to manage clothing costs.
3. Construct a checklist for evaluating clothing.
4. Name the common categories of fibers and yarns.
5. Describe types of fabric construction and finishes.
6. Summarize guidelines for routine clothing care.
7. List methods for storing clothing.

Critical Thinking

8. Generalize Which general categories in an average teen's wardrobe would you expect to have the highest and lowest cost per wearing?
9. Evaluate What assumptions might consumers make about high-priced clothes with designer logos? Are these assumptions justified?
10. Analyze What types of fabrics would you choose for a travel wardrobe?
11. Predict What might happen if you tried to iron or press clothes without knowing the fiber content of the fabric?

ACTIVE LEARNING

12. Be a Label Reader The next time you go shopping for clothes, make a point of reading the labels of every garment that you bring to the dressing room. Make sure that you know what an item is made of, where it was made, and how to care for it. Think about how this information affects your purchase decision. Is the care involved worth the cost of the garment? Are you comfortable with the manufacturing information? After your shopping trip, write a brief report on what you read, what you decided, and why.

Family & Community Connections

13. Fad Report Clothing fads are a part of our lives, and they were a part of our parents' and grandparents' lives too. Ask some of your older relatives, such as siblings, cousins, parents, aunts, uncles, and grandparents, to share their memories of clothing fads that were once popular. Did they buy or wear the fad? Who else was wearing it? How long did the fad stay in style? How do they feel about the fad now? Create a pictorial report using quotes from your relatives and pictures that illustrate the fads. You can use photographs of your relatives or pictures from magazines or the Internet. View your classmates' reports to see if the same fads were discussed.

21st Century Skills

Technology Skills

14. Analyze Technology Energy Star and EnergyGuide labels are part of a federal effort designed to help consumers choose laundry appliances that save energy. Go online to research Energy Star and EnergyGuide. How do they work? What is your opinion of these programs? Is there anything you would do to change them?

Self-Management Skills

15. Dressing Well for Less Use your management skills to devise a plan that would allow you to dress well on a modest budget. Consider your clothing needs, your resources, and your shopping options. Write a paragraph describing your overall goal, and then identify at least four specific actions you can take to reach it.

 **Connections**

Information Literacy Skills

16. Research Storage Options As part of its mission, FCCLA encourages students to take advantage of opportunities for personal development and preparation for adult life. As your life expands to include a career and other activities, your wardrobe is likely to expand as well. Search the term "closet organization" on the Internet to learn about products to reorganize your closet system. List the items that you think you could use.

Academic Skills

 English Language Arts

17. Budget-Stretching Strategies Imagine you write a newsletter on money-saving tips for families with young children. Write an article suggesting strategies to help stretch clothing budgets.

> **NCTE 5** Use different writing process elements to communicate effectively.

 Science

18. Chemicals in Detergent Chemicals called phosphates used to be in laundry detergents, but by the 1950s, most detergent companies had replaced phosphates with alternative ingredients with similar cleaning power.

Procedure Research the cleaning action and environmental impact of phosphates to find out why they are no longer widely used in detergent products.

Analysis Write a brief summary of your findings.

> **NSES F** Develop understanding of personal and community health; natural resources; environmental quality; and natural and human-induced hazards.

 Mathematics

19. Generic or Brand Name? Jackie needs to buy 15 wristbands for her bowling team. At the store, she sees a display of white wristbands with tags bearing a popular trade name. The bands cost $6.95 each or two for $9.99. Jackie sees another display of blue generic wristbands made of the same fabric. They cost $5.01 each. Every penny counts. What should she do?

Math Concept **Multiplying Decimals**
When multiplying numbers with decimals, remember to count the number of decimal places. If the numbers you are multiplying have a total of 3 decimal places, place the decimal in your answer after the third number from the right.

Starting Hint Remember that the 15th brand-name wristband will be full-price.

 For more math practice, go to the Math Appendix at the back of the book.

> **NCTM Number and Operations** Understand numbers, ways of representing numbers, relationships among numbers and number systems.

 Standardized Test Practice   **CCR** College & Career Readiness

FILL IN THE BLANK
Read the sentence, and choose the best word to fill in the blank.

Test-Taking Tip When answering a fill-in-the-blank question, silently read the sentence with each of the possible answers in the blank space. This will help you eliminate wrong answers. The best word results in a sentence that is both factual and grammatically correct.

20. The fiber content information on a clothing label is given as the percentage of each fiber by _____.
   a. weight
   b. estimation
   c. volume
   d. wearability

Chapter 33

Sewing Basics

Chapter Objectives

Section 33.1 Sewing Essentials

- **Identify** the uses of basic sewing equipment and tools.
- **Provide** guidelines for selecting a pattern and fabric.

Section 33.2 Sewing Methods

- **List** the key skills involved in machine sewing.
- **Describe** the tasks commonly accomplished by hand sewing.
- **Give** examples of simple clothing repairs and alterations.

➤ Explore the Photo

Sewing is an important skill that can allow you to expand your wardrobe, change the look of your home, personalize your clothes, and make unique gifts. *What is your idea of a dream sewing project?*

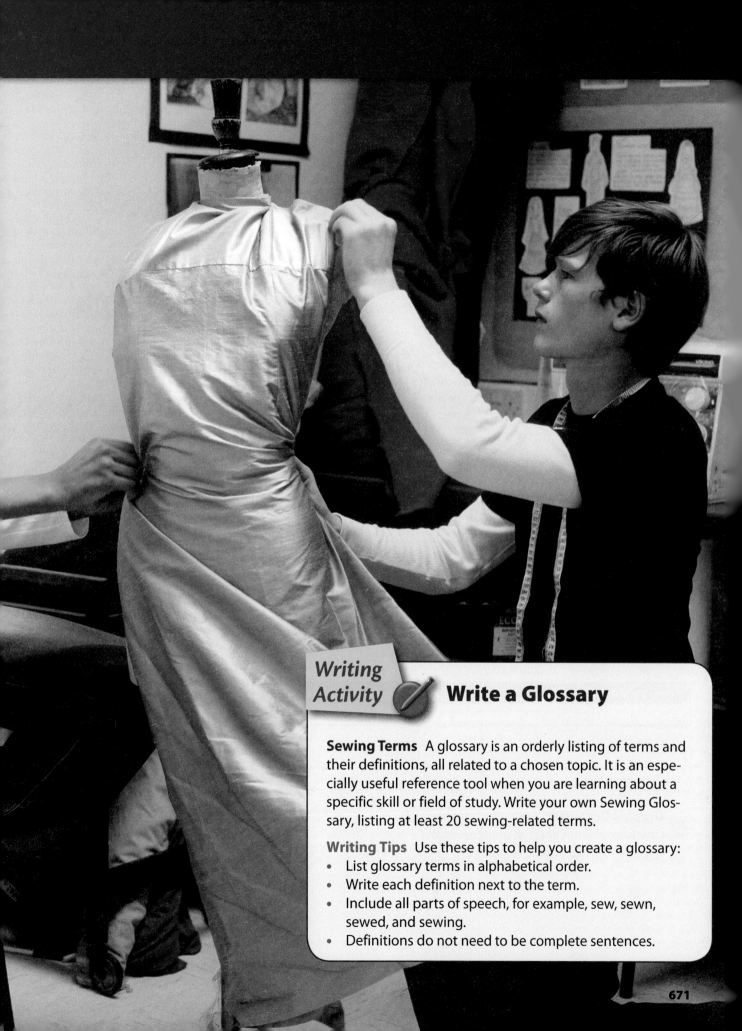

Writing Activity

Write a Glossary

Sewing Terms A glossary is an orderly listing of terms and their definitions, all related to a chosen topic. It is an especially useful reference tool when you are learning about a specific skill or field of study. Write your own Sewing Glossary, listing at least 20 sewing-related terms.

Writing Tips Use these tips to help you create a glossary:

- List glossary terms in alphabetical order.
- Write each definition next to the term.
- Include all parts of speech, for example, sew, sewn, sewed, and sewing.
- Definitions do not need to be complete sentences.

Sewing Essentials

Do you know how to use a sewing machine?

Reading Guide

Before You Read

What You Want to Know Write a list of what you want to know about sewing essentials. As you read, write down the heads in this section that provide that information.

Read to Learn
Key Concepts
- **Identify** the uses of basic sewing equipment and tools.
- **Provide** guidelines for selecting a pattern and fabric.

Main Idea
Know and learn how to use basic equipment and tools to help you complete almost any sewing project. Sewing is a step-by-step process, from choosing supplies to completing each task.

Content Vocabulary
◇ bobbin
◇ serger
◇ notions
◇ selvage
◇ grain
◇ pattern guide sheet

Academic Vocabulary
You will find these words in your reading and on your tests. Use the glossary to look up their definitions if necessary.
■ baste
■ alter

Graphic Organizer
As you read, think about what you need to know about a sewing project before you can start buying fabric and other supplies. Then think about why you need to know it. Use a what and why chart like the one shown to help you organize your information.

What I Need to Know	Why I Need to Know It

 Graphic Organizer Go to this book's Online Learning Center at **glencoe.com** to print out this graphic organizer.

Academic Standards

English Language Arts
NCTE 4 Use written language to communicate effectively.

Social Studies
NCSS IV E Individual Development and Identity Examine the interaction of ethnic, national, or cultural influences in specific situations or events.

NCTE *National Council of Teachers of English*
NCTM *National Council of Teachers of Mathematics*
NSES *National Science Education Standards*
NCSS *National Council for the Social Studies*

Sewing Equipment and Tools

Have you ever wanted to try a new fashion, but could not find the exact item that you wanted? Maybe you were able to find the item, but you did not like the way it fit or you could not afford the price. Or have you ever just wanted some new curtains or a cozy pillow for your bedroom? Creating them on your own can be the answer. Sewing is a great way to expand your wardrobe, change the look of your home, and create unique gifts for others. You can personalize clothes to fit any taste, shape, and size. By developing some basic sewing skills, you can also keep your clothes in good repair so you look your best.

Sewing is a step-by-step process. The more you sew, the more skillful you will become. With basic equipment such as a sewing machine or a serger, and a few essential tools, any project is at a sewer's fingertips. However, it is important to first understand exactly how and when to use each specific item.

As You Read

Connect Which of these items are familiar or unfamiliar to you?

The Sewing Machine

The sewing machine's main purpose is to sew together fabric to create clothes and other items. Various manufacturers make sewing machines, and many of their models are equipped with impressive extra features. Some machines are computerized and programmed to perform some tasks, such as embroidery, automatically. Many experienced sewers appreciate these high-end machines. However, a more basic and less expensive machine is easier for most people to learn. A basic machine works well for most sewing projects.

Most sewing machines have the same basic parts and controls, as seen in **Figure 33.1** on the next page. If you have access to a machine, see if you can identify these parts on it. Check the owner's manual for specific information about that machine's use and regular maintenance care.

Machine Skills

As with most skills, you need to start with the basics. Before using a sewing machine, there are several skills you need to learn and practice.

Wind the Bobbin Machine sewing requires two sets of thread. The top thread comes from a spool on top of the machine. The bottom thread comes from a **bobbin**, which is a small metal or plastic spool positioned beneath the needle. In many machines, the sewer is required to wind thread from the top spool onto the bobbin at the beginning of every project.

◆Vocabulary

You can find definitions in the glossary at the back of this book.

Thread the Machine A sewing machine will not form stitches unless it has been threaded correctly. The spool of thread is placed on the spool pin, then the thread is run through a series of thread guides and finally through the needle. Threading patterns differ by machine. Learn to correctly thread the machine you will use.

Choose Machine Needles Select the needle according to the fabric. Universal needles have a sharp point and are suitable for any fabric. Ballpoint needles have a rounded point and are designed for knit and stretch fabrics. Needle size is designated by two different systems. A larger number indicates a heavier needle. Use a size 9 or 11 (70 or 75) for lightweight fabric, a size 14 (90) for a medium-weight fabric, and a size 16 or 18 (100 or 110) for heavy or thick fabrics. Experts recommend using a new needle for every major sewing project.

Machine Stitching

In machine sewing, the fabric is moved from front to back by two small rows of metal teeth, called feed dogs, located in the needle plate. A stitch is formed when the upper thread and needle pass through the fabric, catching the bobbin thread from below. When repeated, the process creates a row of stitching.

Figure 33.1 Parts of a Sewing Machine

A Place for Everything Although sewing machine models vary, they all have the same basic parts. *Why does a sewing machine require so many parts?*

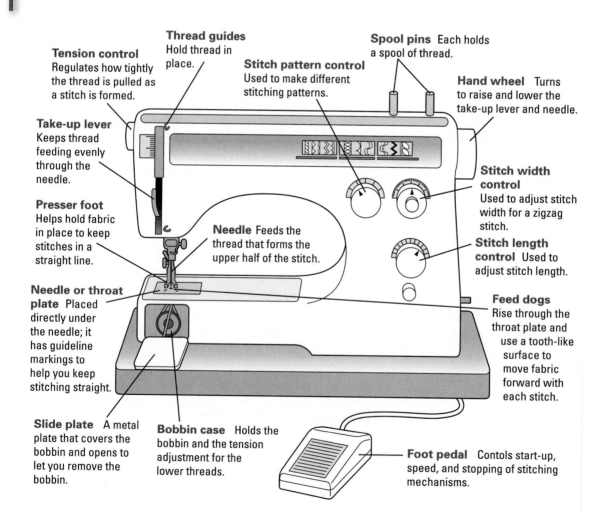

Tension control Regulates how tightly the thread is pulled as a stitch is formed.

Thread guides Hold thread in place.

Stitch pattern control Used to make different stitching patterns.

Spool pins Each holds a spool of thread.

Hand wheel Turns to raise and lower the take-up lever and needle.

Take-up lever Keeps thread feeding evenly through the needle.

Presser foot Helps hold fabric in place to keep stitches in a straight line.

Needle Feeds the thread that forms the upper half of the stitch.

Stitch width control Used to adjust stitch width for a zigzag stitch.

Stitch length control Used to adjust stitch length.

Needle or throat plate Placed directly under the needle; it has guideline markings to help you keep stitching straight.

Feed dogs Rise through the throat plate and use a tooth-like surface to move fabric forward with each stitch.

Slide plate A metal plate that covers the bobbin and opens to let you remove the bobbin.

Bobbin case Holds the bobbin and the tension adjustment for the lower threads.

Foot pedal Contols start-up, speed, and stopping of stitching mechanisms.

Use the machine controls to select the type and length of the stitch. Depending on the machine, stitch length is measured in millimeters or as the number of stitches per inch. Some machines offer specialty stitches, but the four basic stitches are explained below.

Regular Stitch This stitch is used mainly to make the seams that join pieces of fabric together, and is therefore used most often. Set the stitch length control at 10 to 12 stitches per inch, or 2.5 to 2 millimeters. For heavy fabrics, lengthen the stitch slightly.

Basting Stitch Use this long stitch to gather and to **baste**, or hold pieces of fabric together temporarily. Set the length at 6 to 8 stitches per inch, or 3.3 to 4 millimeters.

Reinforcement Stitch This very short stitch helps prevent stretching and strengthens corners or points. Set the control at 16 stitches per inch, or 1.5 millimeters.

Zigzag Stitch Use this Z-shaped stitch to finish seams and edges, make buttonholes, and sew special seams. You can adjust both the width and length of stitches.

The Serger

A **serger** is a machine that sews, trims, and finishes an edge in one step. It is ideal for creating finished seams and narrow, rolled hems. A serger uses two to five threads to make each stitch. Its cutting knives trim seams to just the width of the stitches. It is also often used to create stretchable seams. Some simple garments are made by a serger alone, but generally, a serger is used for specialized tasks, and the rest of the project is done with a sewing machine.

Life On Your Own

Handle with Care

A sewing machine, like any complex and valuable piece of equipment, requires special attention to run properly and to last for a long time. Routine care should be directed at protecting the machine from dirt and damage.

How It Works To protect the machine and your own safety, unplug your sewing machine before doing any maintenance on it. Use a soft cloth to wipe down the machine, taking care to remove any lint from the needle bar and the base of the machine. Use a soft brush to clean the bobbin case and bobbin. Follow the manufacturer's directions to oil the machine, using only high-grade sewing machine oil. To remove excess oil, plug in the machine and stitch on a scrap of fabric.

Try It Out Your sister has given you permission to use her sewing machine for your first major sewing project. You are going to be solely responsible for the care of the machine for two months. It is going to be a busy time, and you will have a lot of things on your mind. How will you make sure that the sewing machine is in top condition when you return it to your sister?

> *Your Turn* A sewing machine cannot tell you when it needs to be cleaned and protected. What would you do to remind yourself to cover it and clean it at all of the appropriate times?

Sergers make two basic types of stitches: the overlock stitch and the overedge stitch. The overlock stitch sews the fabric layers together, creates a finished edge, and trims away the excess fabric. The overedge stitch finishes the edge of a single layer of fabric. Many clothes you buy have serged seams or edges.

Basic Sewing Tools

In addition to sewing equipment, you will need a few tools of the trade to complete your sewing project. These include tools for measuring, cutting, and marking. You will also need pins, hand sewing needles, and a pincushion. See **Figure 33.2** on the next page for commonly used sewing tools.

✓ **Reading Check** **Identify** What are the two types of sewing machine needles?

Finding Your Size and Pattern

Most sewing projects start with choosing your pattern. The instructions and paper shapes contained in a pattern package guide you through your project step by step. Before you select your pattern, you must take body measurements to make sure that you purchase the correct pattern size. Your pattern size usually differs from the clothing size you normally buy. Pattern catalogs, which are available where fabric is sold and on the Internet, provide size charts and measuring instructions. For accuracy, have someone help take your measurements.

When choosing a pattern, read the front and back of the envelope for important information. The skill level indicates what skills are required for the project. "Quick and Easy" is a good choice for a beginner. There should be an illustration or photo of the finished garment or project. Most patterns show more than one view. A written description of pattern details and a drawing of each view should be provided. Also, look for fabric information. The pattern envelope recommends certain types of fabric and advises against others. A yardage chart lists how much fabric to buy, depending on the view, the size, and the fabric width. Finally, see if any notions are needed. **Notions** are the small supplies necessary to complete the sewing project. For example, you may need snaps, thread, a zipper, buttons, and elastic.

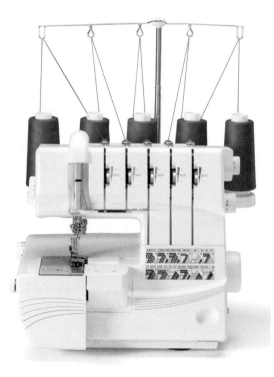

◄ Using a Serger

A serger performs a few specific tasks quickly and efficiently. *For what type of project might you use a serger instead of a sewing machine?*

Figure 33.2

Basic Sewing Tools

Tools of the Trade The proper tools make sewing easier and the results more professional. *Which of these tools are frequently used for non-sewing tasks?*

Shears Used to cut fabric. Shears have long blades and two handles with different shapes. Bent handles allow fabric to remain flat on the table while you cut.

Small Scissors Smaller than shears. Both handles are the same shape. Used for trimming and clipping.

Pinking Shears Used to cut a zigzag edge to help prevent fraying.

Seam Ripper Used to remove stitches. Has a sharp pointed end and a small blade to cut through stitches.

Yardstick Used to measure fabric, mark grainlines, mark hems, and draw long lines.

Sewing/Seam Gauge A 6-inch ruler with an adjustable sliding marker. Handy for measuring hems and seams.

Tracing Wheel Wheel resembles a small, saw-toothed pizza cutter. Used with tracing paper to transfer pattern marks to the fabric. One side of tracing paper is colored.

Fabric Marker Has ink that evaporates or can be washed away with cold water. Do not apply heat to marks before removing them.

Tailor's Chalk Available in squares, pencils, or powdered chalk form. Can be used to mark most fabrics. The residue brushes off.

Needles Carry the thread through fabric to form stitches. Different types are used for hand sewing and sewing machines. Sizes are identified by number, with smaller numbers being finer.

Pin Cushion Holds pins and needles when not in use, keeping them safe and sharp.

Thimble When sewing by hand, protects the finger as it pushes the needle through the fabric.

Thread Forms the stitches that hold together fabric. Should be used in a color that matches the fabric.

Choosing and Preparing Fabric

Always follow the fabric recommendations on a pattern when choosing fabric for your project. Keep in mind that medium-weight fabric with a small, all-over print is a good choice for first projects. Until you have mastered basic skills, avoid slippery fabrics, stripes, plaids, and one-direction designs.

When fabric is laid on a cutting table and folded lengthwise, the selvages should line up. A **selvage** is the finished side edge of the fabric. If they are not lined up, the grain of the fabric may not be at right angles. The **grain** of a fabric refers to the directions in which the lengthwise and crosswise yarns run. A garment made from off-grain fabric will not hang evenly and may twist to one side. If you need help checking the grain or have other questions, ask a staff member at the fabric store. Washable fabric should be washed and dried before it is used. That way, any shrinkage will occur before the garment has been constructed.

Using a Pattern

A typical pattern contains paper pattern pieces and a **pattern guide sheet**. This sheet gives specific instructions for cutting out and sewing the project. On the guide sheet, find the cutting layout information for the particular item or view you are making. This will show the best way to lay out the pattern pieces on your fabric. Cutting layouts often differ depending on the width of the fabric. For easy reference, circle the layout you will use. The guide sheet also provides step-by-step directions for each project and view on the pattern. Circle or highlight the steps you will need to complete.

Jonathan was making a pair of shorts with an elastic waist. The guide sheet indicated that pattern pieces C and D were needed for this view. He unfolded the tissue pieces, cut those two pattern pieces apart from the others, and smoothed them out. The pattern he chose was designed for both men and women and had unisex sizes. When it was time to cut out the pattern pieces, Jonathan realized he would have to cut carefully on the cutting line designated for size Large. Just to be sure, he used a marker to highlight that solid line.

To follow his chosen pattern correctly, Jonathan knew he had to pay close attention to the symbols and lines used on the pattern. For instance, some lines indicate where to fold the fabric and others indicate where to cut the fabric. Other markings indicate places for buttonholes and pockets. See **Figure 33.3** on page 679 for pattern symbols. Commonly used symbols and lines are:

- **Adjustment Line** Double line showing where the pattern may be lengthened or shortened.
- **Buttonhole Lines** Lines that show the exact location and length of buttonholes.
- **Center Front and Center Back Lines** Solid lines that show the center of the garment.

- **Cutting Line** The heavy outer line along which you cut.
- **Dart Markings** Fold line, stitch lines, and dots for matching.
- **Dots, Squares, and Triangles** Markings used for matching seams and construction details.
- **Fold Line** Solid line showing where the fabric is to be folded.
- **Grainline** Heavy, straight line with arrows at each end to indicate how the pattern should be placed on the fabric grain.
- **Hemline** Solid line showing the finished edge of the garment.
- **Notches** Diamond-shaped symbols along the cutting line that are used for matching fabric pieces that will be joined.
- **Placement Line** Line showing the exact location of a pocket, fastener, zipper, or trim.
- **Place-on-Fold Bracket** Arrow with bent ends, indicating that the pattern piece is to be placed along a fold of fabric.
- **Seam Line or Stitching Line** Broken line usually ⅝ inch inside the cutting line.

Getting a Great Fit

If your body measurements are identical to the ones that apply to your pattern size, you are fortunate. For most people, at least one of these measurements is slightly larger or smaller than the other. A small difference probably will not matter much in a loose-fitting garment. However, for more fitted styles, you may need to **alter**, or change, your pattern to match your measurements.

Figure 33.3 **Pattern Symbols**

Look Carefully Pattern symbols are your guide for assembling a project. *What could happen if you mistake the seam line for the cutting line?*

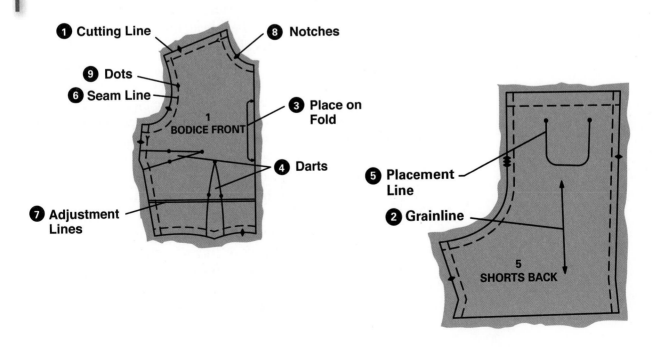

Altering Length

Many garment patterns have length adjustment lines printed on the main pattern pieces. The double lines going across the pattern can be used as guides to either lengthen or shorten a pattern. To lengthen, cut the pattern apart at the adjustment line and spread. To shorten, make a fold on the adjustment line. The depth of the fold should be one-half the amount of excess length. You can also adjust the bottom edge.

Altering Width

Most patterns allow you to alter width up to 2 inches. Suppose you are making pants and want to widen the legs, making each 1 inch bigger around. A pants leg has two seams, the inseam and the side seam, and each of these seams joins two pieces of fabric. This makes four places at which width will be added to each leg. Therefore, divide the total adjustment of 1 inch by four. The result, which is ¼ inch, is the amount of adjustment to make at each seam. On the pattern pieces, draw a new cutting line along each seam, ¼ inch outward from the original cutting line. To decrease width, draw the new line inside the original cutting line.

Pattern Layout and Cutting

Use a large, flat surface to lay pattern pieces out on your fabric. Refer to the pattern guide sheet for directions. Fold the fabric as shown on the cutting diagram. Note how the guide sheet indicates the right (exterior) and wrong (interior) sides of the fabric. Usually, you fold the fabric lengthwise with the right sides together. This brings the lengthwise finished edges together. Position the pattern pieces, pin the pattern to the fabric, and cut out the pattern:

- **Position** Place the pattern pieces on the fabric as shown on the guide sheet. If pattern pieces are shaded on the cutting layout, place them printed side down. Start with pattern pieces to be placed along the fold line of the fabric. Look for the "place on fold" symbol. Pin the pieces along the fold line. Lay out the remaining pattern pieces. Check that each pattern piece is on grain by measuring the distance from each end of the grainline arrow to the selvage. If necessary, adjust the piece and remeasure. Pin on the grainline arrow to hold the piece in place.
- **Pin** Smooth out the pattern pieces. Pin the corners of each piece diagonally. Then insert pins about every 6 inches along the edge of the pattern piece. Insert pins at right angles to the edge, keeping the tips of the pins within the cutting lines.
- **Cut** Carefully check the pattern layout again before you cut. Using sharp shears, cut along the cutting line in the direction indicated by small arrows or tiny scissors. Use long, even strokes, holding the fabric flat with your free hand. Use the points of your shears to cut corners, curves, and notches. Always cut notches outward from the cutting line. Cut double and triple notches together as one long notch.

Marking Pattern Symbols

Before removing the pattern pieces from the fabric, you must transfer key construction symbols from the pattern to the wrong side of the fabric pieces. Darts, dots, placement lines, buttonholes, and other key locations are marked. There are several methods of transferring pattern markings to the fabric. One of the most common methods uses a tracing wheel and special tracing paper. However, fabric-marking pens, tailor's chalk, pins, or thread may be used instead.

To mark pattern symbols using a tracing wheel and tracing paper, follow these steps:

Step 1 Choose a color of tracing paper that will make visible marks, but will not show through to the other side of the fabric.

Step 2 Slide the tracing paper under the pattern so the waxy, colored side is against the wrong side of the fabric. For two layers of fabric, use two pieces of tracing paper or fold one in half.

Step 3 Using a ruler as a guide, roll the tracing wheel once along the line that you want to mark. Mark dots with an *X*.

On multisize patterns, in which different sizes are needed for different parts of the garment, blend sizes by marking a gradual change from the cutting line of one size to another.

 Podcasts Access the Online Learning Center to download *Managing Life Skills* podcasts.

Section 33.1 — After You Read

Review Key Concepts

1. **Describe** the type of sewing machine that is suitable for most people.

2. **Explain** why it is important to pay attention to the symbols and lines printed on a clothing pattern.

 Check Your Answers Check your answers at this book's Online Learning Center at **glencoe.com**.

Practice Academic Skills

 English Language Arts

3. Sewing success relies greatly upon how well the sewer can understand illustrated, step-by-step instructions. Use poster board to create your own pictorial "how-to." Choose a simple, sewing-related task to describe. Include step-by-step instructions and pictures, either drawn or cut from a magazine, to illustrate each step.

> **NCTE 4** Use written language to communicate effectively.

 Social Studies

4. Quilting bees were a popular means of social interaction among women in the mid-19th century in America, and they still exist in our era. Use the Internet to research the topic of quilting bees. Based on what you learn, write a list of at least three reasons why you think that quilting bees are still enjoyed today.

> **NCSS IV E** Examine the interaction of ethnic, national, or cultural influences in specific situations or events.

Sewing Methods

Why buy clothes when you can sew them yourself?

Reading Guide

Before You Read

Visualizing As you read, visualize yourself actually performing some of the sewing tasks described in the section. This can help you remember the necessary steps.

Read to Learn
Key Concepts

- **List** the key skills involved in machine sewing.
- **Describe** the tasks commonly accomplished by hand sewing.
- **Give** examples of simple clothing repairs and alterations.

Main Idea

It is typical to use a basic sewing machine for most sewing projects, then use hand stitching for the finishing steps. You can use basic machine- or hand-sewing skills to make repairs and alterations on clothing.

Graphic Organizer

As you read, look for the five most commonly used types of hand stitches. Use a "hand" graphic like the one shown to help you organize your information.

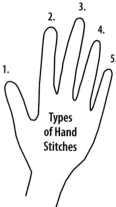

Types of Hand Stitches

 Graphic Organizer Go to this book's Online Learning Center at **glencoe.com** to print out this graphic organizer.

Content Vocabulary
◇ staystitching
◇ facing
◇ dart
◇ sew-through button
◇ shank button

Academic Vocabulary
You will find these words in your reading and on your tests. Use the glossary to look up their definitions if necessary.

■ gauge
■ refurbish

Academic Standards

English Language Arts
NCTE 12 Use language to accomplish individual purposes.

Mathematics
NCTM Measurement Apply appropriate techniques, tools, and formulas to determine measurements.

Social Studies
NCSS VIII A Science, Technology, and Society Identify and describe both current and historical examples of the interaction and interdependence of science, technology, and society in a variety of cultural settings.

NCTE *National Council of Teachers of English*
NCTM *National Council of Teachers of Mathematics*
NSES *National Science Education Standards*
NCSS *National Council for the Social Studies*

Machine Sewing

Using a sewing machine is the most common method for completing major sewing projects. Most sewing patterns include step-by-step machine sewing directions. The directions will call for some basic machine sewing techniques that you are likely to use on many projects.

These basic techniques are used for the following functions:

- **Staystitching** Often, a first step is to staystitch curved areas to prevent them from stretching during the construction process. **Staystitching** is a row of regular machine stitches through a single layer of fabric. The stitching is placed $\frac{1}{2}$ inch from the fabric edge. The staystitching on curved areas does not show in the finished garment.
- **Directional Stitching** Throughout the sewing process, sew in the direction indicated by the small arrows on the pattern, usually from the wide to the narrow end.
- **Stitching Seams** Position the fabric in the machine with the edge on the $\frac{5}{8}$-inch mark. Secure the ends of seams by backstitching them to keep the seams from pulling apart. Start with the needle about $\frac{1}{2}$ inch forward of the seam end. Sew in reverse to the fabric edge, then forward the length of the seam. Remove each pin before sewing over it. Backstitch again at the other end of the seam.
- **Seam Treatments** After stitching, seams may need additional treatment to help them lie flat and smooth before pressing. Techniques such as trimming, clipping, grading, and notching are used for this purpose. The pattern directions will indicate when such techniques are needed.
- **Facings** A **facing** is a shaped piece of fabric used to finish the raw edge of a garment. Facings are typically found at necklines and armholes. On facings that have an inward curve, the seam allowance is clipped up to the staystitching so the seam will lie flat.
- **Darts** A **dart** is a triangular fold used to give shape to a garment. The pattern markings indicate where to fold the fabric to make the dart. Simply match the pattern markings and pin in place. Stitch from the wide end to the narrow end. Leave about 3 inches of extra thread at the end of the dart and tie a knot to secure the stitching.

✔ **Reading Check** **Explain** How do you prevent the ends of seams from coming apart?

As You Read

Connect Think of specific ways in which you might be able to improve upon your current sewing skills.

Vocabulary

You can find definitions in the glossary at the back of this book.

Math For Success

Stitch Count

Suppose you want to make a shirt as a birthday gift for your sister. You need to stitch a 14-inch side seam. The pattern tells you to use a stitch length of 2.5 mm. How many total stitches will you sew to complete the side seam?

Math Concept **Multi-Step Problems** When solving problems with more than one step, think through each step first.

Starting Hint First convert both numbers to the same units of measurement, using the conversion formula: 1 inch = 25.4 mm. Then divide the total length of the seam by the length of a single stitch. Round your answer to the nearest whole number.

Math For more math practice, go to the Math Appendix at the back of the book.

NCTM Measurment Apply appropriate techniques, tools, and formulas to determine measurements.

Hand Sewing

Most project construction can be handled by a sewing machine. However, hand stitching is used for finishing steps on many projects. A variety of repairs can also be made by hand. **Figure 33.4** on the next page shows the five most common hand stitches.

Hand sewing begins by threading a hand-sewing needle and knotting one end of the thread. Choose a needle with a smaller number for lightweight fabric and a larger number for heavy fabric. Secure the knotted end to the fabric where it will not be visible, such as in a seam allowance.

Hemming by Hand

Some sewing projects call for hand hemming the bottom of a garment. For projects like a shirt, the pattern usually indicates where to fold up an edge to form a hem, or bottom seam. For pants and skirts, the person who will wear the garment should try it on while a helper measures, marks, and pins the garment. The helper's steps vary with the type of garment to be hemmed.

- **Hemming Pants** Fold the fabric under so that the hem touches the top of the shoe in front and is about ½ inch longer in back. Pin the folded fabric in place.

Two Views One World

Are All Clothes Worth Fixing?

Everyone needs a wardrobe, yet not everyone agrees about when to fix and when to replace a garment.

Rachel: I'm more than willing to sew up a rip on a favorite piece of clothing, but since I don't buy expensive clothes, or even a lot of clothes, making a lot of repairs seems like a waste of time. There are so many other more valuable things I can do with my time than sit at a table and sew. As long as I have enough clothes in my wardrobe, what's the difference?

Antonio: I guess I just can't stand the idea of waste. Even if I lose a button on a shirt that isn't my favorite, I want to sew it back on right away. What's the point of having a shirt you can't wear? It doesn't take long to fix, and I get a sense of satisfaction when I'm done. Plus, I may have kids someday, and this can help me save money on kids' clothes.

Seeing Both Sides

How might making a distinction between quick and easy sewing repairs and more time-consuming and difficult repairs help Antonio and Rachel find common ground? Might they be able to agree upon a list of "worthwhile" clothing repairs?

Figure 33.4 | Common Hand Stitches

Choose the Right Stitch These stitches are frequently used for hand sewing.
Why are there so many different types of stitches?

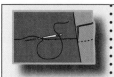

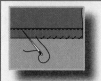
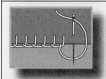

Basting Stitch The basting stitch is a temporary stitch used to hold together fabric for fittings and piece matchings. Pin fabric layers together first and use long, even stitches.

Slipstitch This nearly invisible stitch is used on patch pockets, hems, linings, and trims. Slide the needle in one folded edge and out, picking up a thread of the under-layer.

Hem Stitch As the name indicates, this stitch finishes different hems, especially those with seam binding or a folded edge. Take a tiny stitch in the garment and bring the needle diagonally through the hem edge.

Blanket Stitch The blanket stitch is used to create a decorative edge finish and as thread loops, eyes, belt carriers, bar tacks, and French tacks. Stitch first through the right side of the fabric then pull out the needle at the bottom edge, keeping the thread from the previous stitch under the needle point.

Backstitch The backstitch is used to repair machine-stitched seams and fasten thread ends securely. It is made by carrying the thread back half the length of the preceding stitch, creating strong reinforcement.

- **Hemming a Skirt or Dress** After the desired length of the garment is determined, use a yardstick to **gauge** (ˈgāj), or measure the distance from that length to the floor. Mark the hem line at that spot with chalk or a pin. Repeat the process every few inches around the skirt, making sure to measure the same distance from the floor each time. Fold the fabric under along the markings and pin in place. Check and adjust the length if necessary.

Once the hem has been pinned and the garment removed, decide on the desired depth of the turned-up fabric. Measure and mark that distance from the folded edge. Trim away extra fabric. On woven fabrics, the cut edge of the turned-up fabric is finished in some way before the hem is hand stitched in place. If finishing is needed, options include:
- Zigzagging the edge with a sewing machine.
- Finishing the edge with a serger.
- Attaching seam tape or lace to the edge.
- Turning under the edge of lightweight fabric ¼ inch and pressing or stitching that fold.

Be Smart Be Safe

Sew Safely Many hobbies require that you take safety precautions, and sewing is no exception. This is especially true when you consider the number of sharp objects and tools required for a typical sewing project.

Write About It Write a list of tips that could help prevent sewing-related injuries. The list should be easy to read and suitable for posting in a sewing classroom.

Beat Procrastination

You have probably heard the phrase, "Don't put off for tomorrow what you can do today." Procrastination can be a trap that keeps you from accomplishing the tiniest tasks to the biggest goals. If you find yourself getting into the habit of procrastinating, make a list of what needs to be accomplished. Then begin by tackling the easiest tasks first.

Attaching Fasteners

Most fasteners or closures, such as buttons, snaps, and hooks and eyes, are attached by hand. Hook-and-loop tape is usually attached with machine stitching. For instructions for applying fasteners, check your pattern package.

Everyone needs to be able to sew buttons. There are two types of buttons: sew-through and shank. A **sew-through button** has two or four visible holes. A **shank button**, instead of holes, has a built-in loop, or shank, on the back. Heavy fabrics may require shank buttons.

If a button were sewn flat against a garment, there would not be room to put it through a buttonhole. On a sew-through button, you must form a thread shank, similar to a stem, between the button and fabric to allow space for buttoning. This space is built in on a shank button. The feature below shows how to attach the two main types of buttons.

✓ **Reading Check** **Identify** Which stitch can be used to make a decorative edge finish?

HOW TO .... Attach Buttons

Attaching and reattaching buttons to clothing is one of the most common sewing tasks. Even people who generally do not sew, usually learn how to sew on a button. Fortunately, it is a simple task that requires only a needle and thread, a few minutes, and a little bit of practice. Build your skill by practicing on different types of buttons.

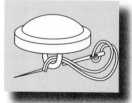

Sew-Through Buttons

Step 1 Start on the underside of the fabric, and bring the needle and thread to the right side.

Step 2 Stick the needle and thread through one hole in the button. Place a toothpick across the top of or underneath the button to allow for a thread shank. Stitch in and out several times through the fabric and buttonholes and over the toothpick. Finish stitching so that your needle and thread are under the button.

Step 3 Remove the toothpick. Pull the button to the top of the thread loop. Wind the thread several times around the stitches under the button to make a thread shank.

Step 4 Bring the needle back to the wrong side of the fabric.

Step 5 Secure the thread by taking several small stitches in the fabric and knot it.

Shank Buttons

Step 1 Sew a feature shank button in place using five or six small stitches through the shank and into the fabric.

Step 2 Fasten the thread securely.

Step 3 Insert an eye fastener and sew the eye in place.

Repairs and Alterations

You can use your basic machine-sewing and hand-sewing skills on clothes you already own. You can **refurbish**, or repair, simple tears and loosenings caused by normal wear. You may also want to make simple alterations to your clothes so they look different or fit better. Check your clothes after wearing for any needed repairs. It is best to fix garments before you launder them. Sewing on buttons or other fasteners is one common repair. Others include:

- **Repairing Snags** Knit fabric can easily develop a snag, which is a loop of yarn that has caught on something and been pulled to the outside. Gently stretch the fabric on each side to ease the snag back into place.

- **Mending Seams** When a seam comes apart, stitch it closed by machine or by hand.

- **Patching Holes** Fabric stores sell iron-on mending tape and patches.

- **Alterations** Just as you can alter a pattern, your existing clothes can be altered to change their fit or style. You can use the basic skills learned in this chapter to change a hemline, take in a seam, or move a button for a roomier waistline. Complicated alterations are better left to professionals or experienced sewers.

Repairing and altering clothing is not only good for your wardrobe, it is good for the environment. The longer we keep our clothes, the fewer we need to buy. The fewer clothes we buy the fewer that need to be made from natural resources and with the use of our energy reserves.

 Podcasts Access the Online Learning Center to download *Managing Life Skills* podcasts.

Section 33.2 — After You Read

Review Key Concepts

1. **Identify** the types of treatments you can use to make a newly made seam lie flat.
2. **Explain** why it takes two people to measure for a hem.
3. **Illustrate** how you would repair a snag in a knit fabric.

Practice Academic Skills

 English Language Arts

4. Prepare to present a short oral account describing your first sewing project. It may have been a pillow you made in the second grade or something you are working on right now. Be sure to include the ups and downs of the project, as well as the results. Jot down a few notes in advance to help you during the presentation.

 Social Studies

5. Use the Internet or library to learn about the history of the sewing machine. Research information on who invented it, and when it was invented. What has been the impact of this invention on individuals and our society as a whole? Write a five-paragraph essay about your findings.

 Check Your Answers Check your answers at this book's Online Learning Center at **glencoe.com**.

NCTE 12 Use language to accomplish individual purposes.

NCSS VIII A Identify and describe both current and historical examples of the interaction and interdependence of science, technology, and society in a variety of cultural settings.

Pathway to Your Career

Merchandise Buyer

What Does a Merchandise Buyer Do?

Merchandise buyers purchase goods, such as clothing, furniture, and electronics, for resale. In other words, they shop for a living. Merchandise buyers consider price, quality, availability, reliability, and trends when choosing goods. They try to get the best deals for their companies. They study sales records, look at inventory levels, and stay informed of any changes affecting the supply and demand for their goods.

Career Readiness Skills Merchandise buyers must have good planning and decision-making skills. They should be resourceful and have good judgment and self-confidence. Marketing skills, leadership skills, and mathematical skills are also important. Communication and negotiation skills are crucial, and they need to predict trends and identify which products will sell.

Education and Training A bachelor's degree with a business emphasis is preferable. Applicants should be familiar with the merchandise they will be selling. On-the-job training is very common. Most trainees begin by selling goods, managing sales workers, checking bills, and keeping track of stock.

Job Outlook Employment is expected to be very competitive because there will be little job growth over the next 10 years. As companies merge, individual buying departments will be cut. Some responsibilities of merchandise buyers are now being done by computers.

Critical Thinking Many different types of companies hire merchandise buyers. Identify one type that interests you. Write a paragraph explaining why you would make a good merchandise buyer for that type of company.

Career Cluster

 **College & Career Readiness**

Marketing A merchandise buyer works in the Merchandising pathway of this career cluster. Other jobs in this cluster include:

- Entrepreneur
- Advertising Manager
- Art Director
- Marketing Associate
- Sales Executive
- Clerk
- Customer Service Representative
- Research Associate
- Sales Manager
- Broker
- Operations Manager

Explore Further The Marketing career cluster contains five pathways: Marketing Management; Professional Sales; Merchandising; Marketing Communications; and Marketing Research. Choose one of these pathways to explore.

 Career Clusters To learn more about career clusters, go to this book's Online Learning Center at **glencoe.com**.

CHAPTER SUMMARY

Section 33.1
Sewing Essentials

Learning to sew begins with learning to use equipment and tools safely and appropriately. Two major tools are the sewing machine and the serger. Before sewing, you must choose and prepare both a pattern and fabric. Patterns can be altered to customize the fit.

Section 33.2
Sewing Methods

Basic machine sewing techniques include directional stitching, staystitching, and making seams, facings, and darts. Hand stitches are used for finishing steps, such as hems and fasteners. With basic sewing skills, you can make many simple repairs. Garments can be altered to change their fit or style.

Vocabulary Review

1. Label each of these content and vocabulary terms as a noun, verb, or adjective. Note that some words may function as more than one part of speech.

Content Vocabulary
- ◇ bobbin (p. 673)
- ◇ serger (p. 675)
- ◇ notions (p. 676)
- ◇ selvage (p. 678)
- ◇ grain (p. 678)
- ◇ pattern guide sheet (p. 678)
- ◇ staystitching (p. 683)
- ◇ facing (p. 683)
- ◇ dart (p. 683)
- ◇ sew-through button (p. 686)
- ◇ shank button (p. 686)

Academic Vocabulary
- ■ baste (p. 675)
- ■ alter (p. 679)
- ■ gauge (p. 685)
- ■ refurbish (p. 687)

Review Key Concepts

2. **Identify** the uses of basic sewing equipment and tools.
3. **Provide** guidelines for selecting a pattern and fabric.
4. **List** the key skills involved in machine sewing.
5. **Describe** the tasks commonly accomplished by hand sewing.
6. **Give** examples of simple clothing repairs and alterations.

Critical Thinking

7. **Recognize** Suppose a friend told you, "There's no reason I should learn how to sew." What assumptions might your friend have made to come to that conclusion? How would you respond?
8. **Evaluate** Do you think that an enthusiastic beginning sewer should buy a serger to go along with his or her sewing machine? Why or why not?
9. **Predict** Think about one of the recommendations given in this chapter. What would happen if a beginning sewer ignored that recommendation?
10. **Give Examples** What would be an ideal sewing project for a sewing beginner, a semi-experienced sewer, and a sewer with advanced skills? Explain your choices.
11. **Conclude** When might a clothing alteration not be a good idea?

ACTIVE LEARNING

Family & Community Connections

12. Sewing Circle Follow your teacher's instruction to form into small groups. Sitting in a circle, each person in the group should work on his or her own sewing project. Every 10 or 15 minutes, group members will hand their projects to whoever is on their left. What is it like to see someone else take over your project? What is it like to work on someone else's project? Is it clear what needs to be done, or do you need to ask or answer questions? After each person has had a turn at each project, look at the results. Discuss your findings with the class.

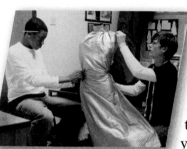

13. Charitable Sewing Project Use an Internet search engine to look for the phrase *charitable sewing projects*. Choose a project that interests you, such as blankets for premature babies, wheelchair totes, or teddy bears kept in ambulances to give to injured children. Contact someone associated with the project to request information and share it with your classmates. Tell your class why you chose this project. What appealed to you about it? Why do you think it is important? Talk to your teacher about how your class can participate in this project. Would it be better to spread the word about the project, or to actually contribute sewing skills? Does learning about such projects change your feelings about sewing? If so, how?

21st Century Skills

Financial Literacy Skills

14. Comparison Shopping Take a list of basic sewing supplies with you to a fabric or discount store. Write down the prices of these items and total their cost. Then see how much a sewing kit containing these items, or a kit with most of the items plus the excluded ones sold separately, would cost. Which do you think is the better deal and why?

Technology Skills

15. Creativity Skills Use the Internet to find sewing ideas for updating the look of a shirt. Apply one or more of the ideas that you find to update a shirt in your own wardrobe. See if you can use supplies and materials to which you already have access at home or in the classroom.

 Connections

Collaboration Skills

16. Family Sewing Co-Op As part of its mission, FCCLA encourages students to help strengthen the function of the family as a basic unit of society. Suggest to your family that you start a sewing cooperative. Have each family member take on the responsibility of doing everyone's simple clothing repairs for an agreed-upon period of time, then switch to the next family member, and so on. After a month or two, report on the success of the plan.

Academic Skills

 English Language Arts

17. Design a Quiz Use your textbook to create a 10-question, sewing knowledge quiz. Use a variety of multiple-choice, true/false, fill-in-the-blank, and short answer questions. Write down your answers on a separate sheet of paper. Then trade your quiz with one of your classmates. Compare scores. How did you do? How did your classmate do? What did you find out about writing quizzes?

> **NCTE 3** Apply strategies to interpret texts.

 Social Studies

18. Wearing a Culture It is possible to represent a culture through the wearing of a special weave, design, emblem, or shape adorning an item of clothing. Find or take a picture of an example of such cultural representation in clothing. Research your example and write a paragraph to accompany the picture.

> **NCSS I D** Compare and analyze societal patterns for preserving and transmitting culture while adapting to environmental or social change.

 Mathematics

19. Calculate Average Project Time Ramon, Ellie, and Angelle have spent a total of 12 hours so far working on an assigned sewing project together. Each must keep track of the time he or she spends on the project. What is the average number of minutes each of them has spent working on the project?

Math Concept **Variables and Operations** Translating words into algebraic expressions requires knowing what the verbal descriptions mean. A variable is a symbol used to represent a number. Operations include addition, subtraction, multiplication, and division.

Starting Hint First convert the hours into minutes. If x = the average number of hours each worker spends on the project, the algebraic expression for the problem is $3x = (12 \times 60)$. Solve for x.

 For more math practice, go to the Math Appendix at the back of the book.

> **NCTM Algebra** Represent and analyze mathematical situations and structures using algebraic symbols.

 Standardized Test Practice   **College & Career Readiness**

MULTIPLE CHOICE
Choose the answer to the question.

> **Test-Taking Tip** In a multiple-choice test, the answers are usually specific and precise. Read the question carefully first. Then read all of the answer choices. Eliminate answers that you know are incorrect.

20. How many sets of thread does machine sewing require?
   a. One
   b. Two
   c. Three
   d. Answer can be a. or c., depending on the machine

Community Service Project

In this project, you will volunteer to participate in a community service project. You will use the experience to create an illustrated story that shows how you helped your community and what skills you gained from the project that can transfer to a future career.

My Journal

If you completed the journal entry from page 626, refer to it to see if your thoughts have changed after reading the unit.

Project Assignment

In this project you will:
- Choose an area of community service that interests you.
- Research and make a list of opportunities for volunteering.
- Call organizations, if appropriate, to find out about types of volunteer opportunities.
- Organize a time and date to volunteer.
- Bring a camera or sketchbook and a notebook to record your experience.
- Use what you learned during the community service to create an illustrated story.

THE SKILLS BEHIND THE PROJECT

Key personal and relationship skills you will use in this project include:
- Motivating team members
- Communicating respectfully
- Taking responsibility

Academic Skills

English Language Arts

> **NCTE 5** Use different writing process elements to communicate effectively.
>
> **NCTE 7** Conduct research and gather, evaluate, and synthesize data to communicate discoveries.

STEP 1 — Choose a Community Service that Interests You

Below are examples of organizations or places that may need volunteers. Choose two groups. You can use these suggestions, or you can research your own area of interest.
- Food banks
- Animal shelters
- Literacy programs
- Public radio stations
- Nursing homes

STEP 2 — Research Your Choices

Contact the organizations you selected, and ask specific questions about details, dates, and locations of volunteer opportunities. Get as many details as you can. Record their answers in a notebook. You can refer to these notes when you write your story. Decide which opportunity works with your interests and schedule.

Research Skills
- Conduct research using a variety of resources.
- Gather specific information through interpersonal communication.
- Take notes on your research, and write a summary of your findings.
- Use the information you gathered to narrow down your choices.

STEP 3 Connect with Your Community

Select one of the volunteer opportunities. Contact the organization to schedule the service. You might consider asking a friend to join you. If you do so, you should act as the leader of the team since you are organizing the activity. Ask the organization for permission to bring a camera to document your experience. Continue to take notes for your story.

Leadership Skills

- Take initiative to complete tasks.
- Ask questions if you do not understand instructions.
- Use teamwork skills to get the job done.
- Be enthusiastic and help motivate others.
- Manage your time successfully.

STEP 4 Build Your Portfolio Project

Use the Portfolio Project Checklist to plan and create an illustrated story to share what you have learned with your classmates.

Communication Skills

- Use standard English to communicate.
- Be sensitive to the needs of your audience.

STEP 5 Evaluate Your Project

Your portfolio project will be evaluated based on:

Academic Skills

- Extent of the research you conducted
- Clarity of your presentation
- Speaking and listening skills
- Structure, organization, and depth of your story
- Creativity, presentation, and neatness

 Evaluation Rubric Go to this book's Online Learning Center at **glencoe.com** for a rubric you can use to evaluate your final project.

PORTFOLIO PROJECT CHECKLIST

Plan

- ✔ Write a story about your day of community service.
- ✔ Illustrate your story with photographs or drawings.
- ✔ Show what you learned from performing the service. Include any skills that you demonstrated, such as leadership and teamwork.
- ✔ Organize your story so it has a beginning, middle, and end. Discuss the volunteer work and describe the skills you learned or practiced. Then conclude by explaining how those skills will be transferable to a future career.

Present

- ✔ Create a presentation to share your story with the class.
- ✔ Invite the students to ask questions. Answer any questions. Demonstrate in your answers that you respect their perspectives.
- ✔ Place your notes and illustrated story in your portfolio. Share your portfolio with your teacher.

Portfolio Highlights

Academic Skills and Achievements

A good portfolio includes samples of coursework in your field of interest. It should also include samples that highlight other aspects of your life, such as hobbies, interests, and special skills.

Communication Skills

Potential employers want to hire people with strong communication skills. Include written reports or projects you completed for classes that showcase your writing ability.

Leadership Skills

Leadership skills are developed in many ways. You may have been an elected leader on a school project, or perhaps you are a role model for someone. If you have demonstrated leadership skills in a school club or committee, athletic team, or volunteer activity, include evidence of your participation.

Awards and Citations

Include any awards or citations for sports, community activities, volunteer work, or academic achievement. If you have already been employed, also include any recognition received in that job.

UNIT 10

Housing, Transportation, and the Environment

Unit Portfolio Project Preview

Prepare for an Interview

In this unit, you will prepare for the outside world by using care and judgment at and away from home. In your portfolio project, you will research and prepare for a mock job interview.

 My Journal

Creating Opportunities Write a journal entry about one of the topics below. This will help you prepare for the project at the end of this unit.

- Describe a time when you used a long-term, step-by-step method to get something you wanted.
- Explain what is meant by the statement, "We all create our own opportunities."
- Discuss how interactions with others play an important role in making the most of opportunities.

Explore the Photo

Our environment is where we live, work, and travel every day. *In what ways are caring for our homes and caring for our environment the same?*

Chapter 34

Homes and Decorating

Chapter Objectives

Section 34.1 Choosing Your Home

- **Summarize** the main priorities for finding the right housing.
- **Describe** six common types of housing structures.
- **List** the advantages and disadvantages of renting.
- **Identify** the advantages and disadvantages of buying a home.

Section 34.2 Designing Your Living Space

- **Describe** a floor plan and its uses.
- **Summarize** the five elements of design.
- **Compare** the three possible types of furniture options.

▶ Explore the Photo

Knowing how to choose a place to live and how to design and decorate that space are very important life skills. *What skills do you think you might need to successfully design and decorate a living space?*

Writing Activity

Write a Personal Narrative

Making a Space Yours Write a personal narrative about decorating your room. Describe what your room looked like before you began, how you gathered ideas for decorating, what your room looked like afterward, and anything else that you remember.

Writing Tips To write a good personal narrative:
- Test your ideas by freewriting or talking them through.
- Be as descriptive as you can.
- Ask yourself questions to fill out details of the narrative.
- Construct a time line or other graphic organizer as a visual map for your narrative.

Choosing Your Home

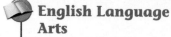

There are many factors to consider before you decide on a type of home.

Reading Guide

Before You Read

Prior Knowledge Look over each of the Key Concepts at the beginning of the section. Write down what you already know about each concept and what you want to find out by reading the lesson. As you read, find examples for both categories.

Read to Learn
Key Concepts
- **Summarize** the main priorities for finding the right housing.
- **Describe** six common types of housing structures.
- **List** the advantages and disadvantages of renting.
- **Identify** the advantages and disadvantages of buying a home.

Main Idea
You must understand your priorities before choosing a type of housing. You may rent or buy, live alone or with a roommate, and choose from a variety of housing types. Both renting and buying have pros and cons.

Graphic Organizer
As you read, you will discover three main types of housing locations. Use a tree organizer like the one shown to help you organize your information.

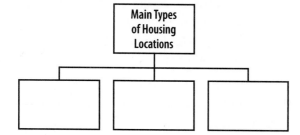

Main Types of Housing Locations

Graphic Organizer Go to this book's Online Learning Center at **glencoe.com** to print out this graphic organizer.

Content Vocabulary
◇ security deposit
◇ mortgage
◇ landlord
◇ tenant
◇ lease
◇ down payment
◇ closing cost

Academic Vocabulary
You will find these words in your reading and on your tests. Use the glossary to look up their definitions if necessary.
■ insure
■ practical

Academic Standards

English Language Arts
NCTE 9 Develop an understanding of diversity in language use across cultures.

Mathematics
NCTM Number and Operations Understand numbers, ways of representing numbers, relationships among numbers, and number systems.

Social Studies
NCSS VI C Power, Authority, and Governance Analyze and explain ideas and mechanisms to meet needs and wants of citizens, regulate territory, manage conflict, establish order and security, and balance competing conceptions of a just society.

NCTE *National Council of Teachers of English*
NCTM *National Council of Teachers of Mathematics*
NSES *National Science Education Standards*
NCSS *National Council for the Social Studies*

Housing Priorities

Housing meets physical needs by giving shelter and a place for belonging and personal activities. It meets emotional needs by offering privacy and a place for personal expression. It meets social needs by providing a place to gather with family and friends.

Housing also fulfills individual needs. People who have disabilities have specific housing needs. Features such as wide doorways and hallways, adjustable-height shelves, and easy-to-operate fixtures make a home accessible and welcoming to all.

Housing needs change across the life span. Human needs, such as space for a growing family, and environmental influences, such as a desire to live close to a good school, can affect housing needs.

Housing Expenses

Most people spend more money on housing than on any other single living expense. Several factors influence the cost of housing, including the size of the home and its location. Housing tends to cost more in rapidly growing areas than in less popular regions.

Before you begin looking for housing, determine what you can afford. If you plan to rent, know that rent is only part of what you will spend. You will have to pay a **security deposit**, a fee paid in advance to cover any damage you might cause to the property. If you cause no damage, you should get the security deposit back when you move out. You will also probably have to pay for utilities such as gas, electricity, water, and cable, unless these are included in the rent. You may need to buy furniture and appliances. You will also likely choose to **insure**, or cover through an insurance policy, your belongings against theft or damage.

People who buy a home pay a monthly mortgage payment instead of rent. A **mortgage** ('mȯr-gij) is a long-term home loan. Like renters, homeowners must pay for utilities, furniture, and appliances. They also pay property taxes, maintenance costs, and sometimes homeowners' association fees. Homeowner's insurance costs more than renters insurance because it covers the building as well as everything inside it.

Renting or Buying

Your first decision is whether to rent or buy. For most young people who are just starting out, buying is not yet an option. To determine how much you can spend on housing, you will need to know your income. A good general rule is to spend no more than one-third of your gross pay on housing. If you spend more, you may not have enough money left for food, clothing, and other necessities.

The decision to rent or buy is not simply a financial one, however. Many young people are not ready to accept the responsibilities of home ownership. People who expect to move frequently may prefer the freedom of renting. Many renters view renting as a temporary arrangement as they save toward buying a home.

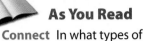

As You Read

Connect In what types of homes have you lived?

Vocabulary

You can find definitions in the glossary at the back of this book.

Character ?!
In Action

Sharing Space

Sharing housing means not only sharing financial obligations, but also sharing space. Some people enjoy the companionship of roommates. Others find that sharing is challenging. If you decide to share, think carefully about the person and the situation. Be willing to compromise as you work out the details of your living arrangement.

You Decide

Imagine you are sharing an apartment with a roommate. How can you make sure that disagreements about sharing space will not turn into major arguments? What skills would be especially helpful?

Sharing Housing

To save money, many decide to share rented housing. The best way to make a shared living arrangement work is to agree on the ground rules beforehand. Important topics to discuss with a potential roommate include how bills will be paid and whether you will share food and cleaning supplies. You should discuss how cleaning tasks will be divided. It is also important to discuss whether overnight and weekend guests are allowed.

Returning Home

Recently, more adult children are returning home to live with their parents. Sometimes it is a matter of economic necessity, and sometimes the arrangement is simply **practical**, or useful. It can be difficult for both parents and children to adjust to this arrangement. Cooperation and communication are essential. Financial arrangements and ground rules should be agreed upon ahead of time.

Choosing a Location

Where do you want to live? The three main types of locations are cities, suburbs, and rural areas, and each have pros and cons.

- **Cities** City life can be exciting, as it offers culture, entertainment, and shopping. However, cities can also be crowded and noisy. Housing in major cities is often very expensive.
- **Suburbs** People wanting access to a city often live in the suburbs, or the residential regions surrounding the city.
- **Rural Areas** People wanting to live away from city life may choose a rural area. Rural areas can lack the excitement and conveniences of city life, but there is less noise and pollution and access to outdoor activities.

Factors to Consider

Choosing a housing location is not as simple as deciding between city, suburb, or rural area. You also need to consider other factors. Do you want to stay in a location that is familiar and where you have family and friends? Or do you desire the challenge of living in a new, unfamiliar place? You should also consider job availability, climate, and cost of living. You might want to consider transportation and what your commute to work would be like.

✓ Reading Check **Explain** What is the best way to make a shared living arrangement work?

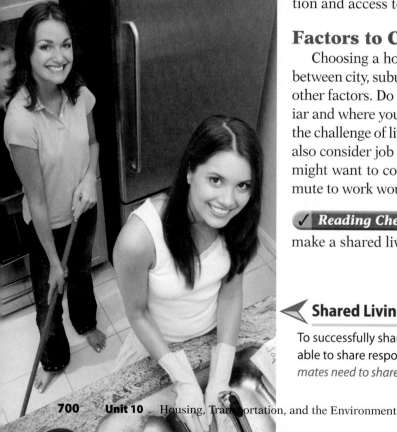

◀ **Shared Living Arrangements**

To successfully share housing with a roommate, you need to be able to share responsibilities. *What types of responsibilities do roommates need to share?*

Types of Housing

When you choose a type of housing, you need to consider both the structure and the type of ownership. People choose different types of housing at different stages in their lives. Young adults often have a limited income and usually start by renting an apartment. After a few years, they may buy a small home. Married couples usually have more options and may choose a larger home where they can raise a family. Older adults whose children have left home may decide to buy a smaller home that they can manage more easily.

Types of Structures

Structures range from single units to large high-rise apartment buildings. Six of the most common types of structures include:

- **Single-Family House** Designed for one person or one family, this type of home offers the greatest privacy because it is not attached to another unit.
- **Loft** In urban areas, old warehouses or factories are sometimes converted into living units called lofts. A typical loft has high ceilings and few interior walls to divide the space.
- **Town House** Single-family houses that are side by side and share walls are called town houses, or row houses. They often have basements and small yards or patios.
- **Apartment** Some apartment buildings contain hundreds of units and others only a few. Units may be beside, above, or below one another. Apartments can drastically range in size.
- **Manufactured Home** A manufactured home is built at a factory and then moved by truck to a permanent site. Manufactured homes are less expensive than other single-family homes, and most come with appliances and floor coverings.
- **Duplex, Triplex, or Fourplex** A duplex is divided into living spaces for two families. There are also buildings designed for three families (triplex) and four families (fourplex).

Types of Ownership

All of the types of housing can be rented or owned. Ownership takes different forms, depending on the home's structure. If you buy a single-family detached home set on its own lot, you own the building and the land. Ownership of a multiple-family complex, such as an apartment or a town house, can take one of two forms:

- **Condominium Ownership** In this form, you own your unit, and you share ownership of common areas such as hallways and grounds. In addition to your mortgage, you pay a monthly fee to cover the cost of maintaining the common areas.

Choosing Where to Live

One thing to consider when choosing housing is where you want to live. *What factors would you consider when choosing an area in which to live?*

Be Smart Be Safe

Smoke Alarms Regardless of the type of housing structure, a properly installed and maintained smoke alarm can prevent damage and injury if there is a fire. Smoke alarms should be placed on every level of a home, including the attic and basement.

Write About It Research how to properly maintain a fire alarm in a home. Take notes, cite your sources, and summarize your findings.

- **Cooperative Ownership** In this form, you own stock in a corporation that owns the property and its grounds. The amount of stock you buy is in proportion to the size of your unit. When you purchase stock, you buy the right to occupy a particular unit, but you do not own that unit. You pay a monthly fee that covers your share of all mortgage payments, maintenance expenses, and property taxes for the whole building.

✓ **Reading Check** **Describe** What is a town house?

Renting a Home

It is likely that the first place you live away from your family will be rented. When you rent a unit, you enter into an agreement with the **landlord**, or the owner of the rental property, and through this agreement, you become the **tenant**, or renter. Before you become a tenant, you should be aware of the pros and cons of renting.

Pros and Cons of Renting

Rental housing comes in all shapes and sizes and may be furnished or unfurnished. Some key advantages of renting rather than owning a home include fixed expenses, or knowing how much you will owe every month. There is also greater flexibility, as you do not have to worry about selling your home. You will have more free time since you are not responsible for repairs and maintenance. Renters insurance is also lower than homeowner's insurance.

However, there are also drawbacks to renting. Renters are restricted in the changes they can make to the property, and some landlords do not allow pets. There are also financial drawbacks, because unlike mortgage payments, the money you spend on rent is simply gone. There are no tax advantages to renting. Renters have little control over how the building is maintained and managed. Those who live in multiple-family buildings may be bothered by other tenants' noise and clutter.

The Benefits of Renting

One of the benefits of renting is that you spend less time on upkeep and repairs and have more time for leisure activities. *What are some other benefits of renting?*

Selecting a Rental

Before you choose a rental home, walk or drive around the neighborhood. Is the unit located in a safe area? Is it close to your work or school? Is public transportation close by? Do the windows provide enough light? Listen for noises, and check for odors. Ask the landlord if utilities are included. Find out about laundry facilities, parking, and security. The more you learn before you choose a rental home, the less likely you are to be disappointed.

Signing a Lease

When you find a place you want to rent, you must fill out an application. Landlords want to know that you can pay the rent. They will check your credit history and verify your employment. You will probably then have to sign a **lease**, a legal document specifying the rights and responsibilities of the landlord and tenant. Read the lease carefully, and clarify anything you do not understand.

✓ Reading Check) **Recall** Why will you likely have more free time if you rent instead of buy a home?

Buying a Home

It may seem far in the future, but you may eventually decide to buy a home of your own. Like renting, buying a home has both advantages and disadvantages.

Some key advantages of being a homeowner include stability, because you will likely participate more in the community and local government. Homeowners have the freedom to adapt their homes and yards as they want. Also, a home is an investment. Unlike with rent, when you pay mortgage, you are actually investing your money. If a home is well cared for, the owner can typically sell it for more than he or she paid for it. There are also tax advantages to owning a home, because homeowners can deduct their property taxes and the interest on their mortgage from their federal income taxes.

However, there are also disadvantages of owning rather than renting. Unexpected expenses can occur without warning. You will have to spend time on home maintenance. Also, homeowners have reduced mobility. Selling a house can be stressful and also quite expensive and time consuming.

Buying Procedures

If you want to buy a home, first determine your needs, wants, and price range. Be sure to evaluate the safety and convenience of any neighborhoods you consider. You can look at available homes with a real estate agent. Real estate agents find homes that meet potential buyer's needs and handle any paperwork. When you find a home you want, you make an offer, or a price you are willing to pay for the home. Buyers often offer less than the asking price. The seller and buyer then negotiate until they agree on a price. The sale is completed at a meeting called a closing.

Succeed in SCHOOL and LIFE

Understand Credit Scores

A credit score results from a mathematical model that uses factors about your spending and repayment habits to create a score. A credit score is used by most home lenders to determine whether you are eligible for a mortgage or other type of loan. The score represents the likelihood that you will repay a loan. Generally, the higher your credit score, the lower the chance you will default on a loan.

Financial Considerations

Go Green!

When you are looking for a house, you may want to consider going green. Green houses use renewable building materials and are designed to be energy efficient. For example, a green house may have solar panels or be made of a clay mixture instead of cement.

Most people do not have enough to buy a home outright, so they take out a mortgage and pay back the loan in monthly installments. They also need enough money to pay the initial **down payment**, or the portion of the purchase price, usually 5 to 20 percent, that a buyer pays up front in cash. Buyers must also pay a **closing cost**, a cost that includes all the various fees due at the time of purchase.

The closing cost may include:

- Title insurance and fees, to make sure the property does not have any previous claims of ownership on it.
- Recording fees, to record the change of ownership with the government.
- Inspection fees, to make sure the home is structurally sound and free of pests.
- Mortgage application fees, to cover the cost of the loan processing paperwork.
- A brokerage commission, to pay the real estate agent for his or her time and services.

Buying a home is usually the biggest purchase that anyone makes. Those who understand and prepare for the process are more likely to find the home they want at a price they can afford.

Podcasts Access the Online Learning Center to download *Managing Life Skills* podcasts.

Section 34.1 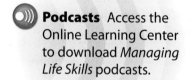 After You Read

Review Key Concepts

1. **Describe** the factors that can affect housing costs.
2. **Contrast** condominium ownership with cooperative ownership.
3. **Analyze** factors you should consider when choosing a rental home.
4. **Name** the steps in buying a home.

Practice Academic Skills

 English Language Arts

5. Different parts of the world have different names for types of housing. For example, the Inuit culture has igloos, while many dachas, or summer homes, can be found in Russia. Use Internet and print resources to find out more about housing types from other cultures, and write a one-page report on your findings. Cite your sources.

 Social Studies

6. The U.S. Department of Housing and Urban Development (HUD) helps increase home ownership, support community development and increase access to affordable housing. With your teacher's permission, visit HUD's Web site and find out what information potential renters and buyers can get from the site. Create a chart that lists and describes some of the resources you found.

> **Check Your Answers** Check your answers at this book's Online Learning Center at **glencoe.com**.

> **NCTE 9** Develop an understanding of diversity in language use across cultures.

> **NCSS VI C** Analyze and explain ideas and mechanisms to meet needs and wants of citizens, regulate territory, manage conflict, establish order and security, and balance competing conceptions of a just society.

Designing Your Living Space

Reading Guide

Before You Read

Use Notes When you are reading, keep a notebook handy. When you come upon a term or concept with which you are unfamiliar, write the word or a question on the paper. After you have finished the section, look up the terms and try to answer your questions based on what you read.

Read to Learn
Key Concepts

- **Describe** a floor plan and its uses.
- **Summarize** the five elements of design.
- **Compare** the three possible types of furniture options.

Main Idea

Use floor plans, traffic flow, and defined areas to organize your space. Design elements and principles can help you personalize your space. Determine your priorities to choose the right furniture, accessories, and appliances.

Content Vocabulary

◇ floor plan
◇ scale drawing
◇ traffic pattern
◇ proportion
◇ emphasis
◇ EnergyGuide label
◇ Energy Star label

Academic Vocabulary

You will find these words in your reading and on your tests. Use the glossary to look up their definitions if necessary.

■ improvise
■ seldom

Academic Standards

English Language Arts

NCTE 12 Use language to accomplish individual purposes.

Social Studies

NCSS I E Culture Demonstrate the value of cultural diversity, as well as cohesion, within and across groups.

Graphic Organizer

As you read, you will discover six design principles. Use a chain organizer like the one shown to help you organize your information.

Six Design Principles

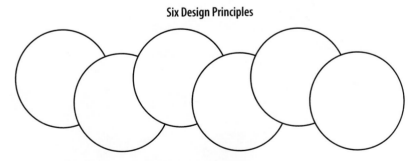

Graphic Organizer Go to this book's Online Learning Center at **glencoe.com** to print out this graphic organizer.

NCTE *National Council of Teachers of English*
NCTM *National Council of Teachers of Mathematics*
NSES *National Science Education Standards*
NCSS *National Council for the Social Studies*

Organizing Your Space

Designing a living space is challenging. How much space do you have? How do you want to use the space? Look through magazines that show different approaches to room design. Notice what you like and dislike when you visit friends' homes. Gradually, you will gain ideas of what you want to accomplish with your own space.

Make a Floor Plan

A **floor plan** is a diagram showing the main structural elements of a home or room. To make a floor plan, sketch the outline of the room's shape, as if you were looking down from the ceiling. Include walls, doors, and windows. Next, measure the room, including the width of doorways and windows. Write down the measurements.

To plan furniture placement, you need to draw to scale. In a **scale drawing**, a given number of inches represents a given number of feet. Use the scale from the floor plan to make furniture templates. Draw, label, and cut out the outlines of the furniture so you can arrange it on the floor plan. Leave clearance space around furniture. For example, you need to leave space for doors to be opened.

Consider Traffic Patterns

As you design your living space, you also need to consider traffic patterns. A **traffic pattern** is the route people use to move through a room or from one part of a home to another.

Create Different Areas

An effective way to organize space is to create different areas for different purposes. Group together furnishings and other items that you would use at the same time.

✓ **Reading Check** **Explain** Why is a floor plan important?

As You Read

Connect Think of your favorite color. How have you used it in your room?

◀▷ Vocabulary

You can find definitions in the glossary at the back of this book.

Organize Your Space

One way to organize living space is to create different areas in a room for different activities. *What kinds of areas could be set up in a common living space, such as a living room?*

Using Design Elements and Principles

No matter how good a floor plan is, paying attention to space alone will not achieve a good design. When designers plan a room, they also consider line, form, texture, and color. These five elements bring harmony to a room's design. Remember, though, that if you share your space with roommates, you need to take everyone's needs and wishes into account before making design decisions about common areas.

Space

The two aspects of space to consider are the space's size and the arrangement of objects within that space. Spaces of different sizes convey different feelings. Large spaces give a sense of freedom. Too much open space, however, can seem empty. Well-designed small spaces can seem cozy, but too little space can feel confining.

The furniture you choose and how you arrange it also change the effect of a room. When space is tight, limiting the number of furnishings will keep the room from looking cramped. Use pieces that serve more than one purpose, such as a storage unit with a pull-down desk. If you have a large space, try using a sofa or long tables to divide the space into smaller areas. You can also try arranging furniture into small clusters or using different wall coverings.

Life On Your Own

Make It Your Own

Getting a new place, whether it is with a roommate or by yourself, can be a lot of fun. Use your new home and your furnishings to reflect your personality. There are endless possibilities for home accessories. No matter what you choose, these small touches give a room personality and tell your guests something about you. It does not matter whether the objects are sophisticated, simple, elegant, or rustic. What matters is that they mean something to you.

How It Works Think about the space you have. If it is small, limit the amount of items you buy. If it is a large, open space, you may need screens or room dividers. If it has no overhead light, you will need floor and table lamps. Furniture is usually accumulated gradually since it is expensive, so prioritize and invest wisely. To stretch your budget, you can buy pieces that serve more than one need. For instance, you can put a sofa bed in the living room for overnight guests or use your kitchen table as a desk. Keep in mind how the rooms will be used, and create a pleasant, practical, and welcoming environment for guests.

Try It Out Create a book of decoration tips and ideas for yourself. Research information on interior design. Write down five to eight rules of thumb for decorating, based on what you have learned. Cut out pictures from interior design magazines or print pictures from the Internet of room designs you like. Paste them in your book for future reference.

Your Turn Have ever walked into a room and felt immediately at ease? Is making a living space comfortable, functional, and stylish important? Why or why not?

Line

Every room has vertical and horizontal lines. These include the lines of windows and doorways and the lines that mark the edges of a wall, floor, and ceiling. Shaped windows and arches have curved lines, while the slant of a staircase has diagonal lines. Each type of line helps create a certain mood. Horizontal lines create restful feelings and an illusion of width. Vertical lines create action and the illusion of height. Curved lines suggest grace and softness, while diagonal and zigzag lines convey excitement and movement.

Form

Form refers to the shape and structure of solid objects. Some objects, such as beds and sofas, are large and bulky. Others, such as benches and end tables, may be small and delicate. When combining furniture, choose forms that are in harmony with one another.

Texture

Texture refers to the appearance or feel of a surface, such as rough, nubby, or smooth, and it influences a room's mood. Plush, soft fabrics suggest richness and comfort, while nubby, rough materials suggest ruggedness and stability. Metal, stone, and glass seem cold. An object's texture affects the way its color and size are perceived because texture affects the way light is reflected.

Color

Color is the most significant design element. In general, warm colors such as yellows, oranges, and reds create a positive, energetic mood. Cool colors such as blues and greens create a feeling of calm. Like texture, color can fool the eye. At the same distance, cool-colored objects appear farther away than warm-colored ones.

Choosing Colors

Color allows you to express your personality and create a mood in a living space. *Why do you think it is important to look at color samples in different lighting before choosing one for your home?*

Using Design Principles

Design principles are a set of guidelines for making the design elements work together in pleasing ways. Design principles include:

- **Proportion** The way one part of a design relates in size to another part and to the whole design is known as **proportion**. A massive oak desk paired with a small wicker chair would be out of proportion. A high-backed leather desk chair would probably work better.
- **Balance** This design principle involves giving equal importance to the spaces on both sides of an imaginary center line. In symmetrical balance, objects on each side of that line are mirror images of one another. In asymmetrical balance, the objects are unmatched but appear to be equal visually.

- **Rhythm** The regular repetition of line, shape, color, or texture is called rhythm. Pictures hung at regular intervals, for example, create a rhythm that directs you to look naturally from one object to the next.
- **Emphasis** As a design principle, **emphasis** is the technique of drawing attention to where you want it. For example, a large, colorful poster hung over a fireplace would draw attention to that part of the room.
- **Unity** When a design has unity, it creates the feeling that all the objects in the room belong together.
- **Variety** Although rooms need unity, not all items in a room should match. You must also have variety. Combining different, but compatible, styles keeps the design from being boring.

✓ **Reading Check** **Define** What is proportion?

Furnishing Your Home

The elements and principles of design can help you choose furniture and accessories. You will need to be patient, though. Most young adults have a limited amount of money to spend on furnishing their first home. With a little planning and creativity, you can create a comfortable living space on a limited budget.

Determine Priorities

First, examine your needs and wants to determine your priorities. Beyond that, it depends on what is important to you. For example, if you love to cook and entertain, a large, welcoming dining table might be a priority to you.

Choose Furniture

You have many options when you choose furniture. With a limited budget, you may need to decide between buying lots of inexpensive items or just a few good quality pieces. There are pros and cons to both choices. Inexpensive items let you furnish your home more quickly, but they may need to be replaced sooner. Options to consider when choosing furniture include:

- **New Furniture** The cost of new furniture depends on the materials used and the construction quality. Materials such as particleboard and plywood are less expensive than solid wood. You can also save money by buying furniture that you assemble yourself. Keep in mind that the sturdier and better constructed the furniture is, the longer it will last.

▲ Multipurpose Furniture

When choosing furniture, consider the option of multipurpose furniture, which can save you money and space. *What types of multipurpose furniture can you name?*

- **Used Furniture** Used furniture that is well made may be a better quality than inexpensive new furniture. Even pieces that are in poor condition might be made usable with minor repairs. You can find used furniture in secondhand stores or you may be able to get hand-me-downs from relatives.

- **Unfinished Furniture** Unfinished furniture is wood furniture that has not been stained or painted. It is usually less expensive than finished furniture. Finishing furniture yourself lets you save money and customize the items to suit your taste.

If your furniture budget is limited, you can always improvise, or make the best of what you have. You can place an old door on two filing cabinets to make a desk. Inexpensive outdoor furniture, such as a picnic table, can work fine indoors until you can afford something better.

Use Accessories

Just as accessories like belts and jewelry add visual interest to an outfit, accessories in the home add visual appeal to a room. Some accessories, such as clocks, lamps, and books, serve a function. Others, such as pillows, candles, and wall hangings, are usually just for decoration. Accessories do not have to cost a lot, and you can change them whenever you wish. Posters, for example, are inexpensive and can reflect interests such as music, art, or sports.

Choose Appliances

If you need to buy a washer, dryer, refrigerator, or other major appliance, shop carefully. These items are expensive, so think about your needs and priorities before you buy. Also, consider your possible future needs. To make informed purchasing decisions, follow these tips:

- Read unbiased reports and reviews that compare and rate various brands and models.
- Avoid models that are larger than you need or that have features you will not use.
- Examine the warranty, and find out how you would get the item repaired, if needed.
- Compare new items with good quality used items. For example, a new washer could cost more than $500, while a used one might cost $100.
- When comparing prices, take into account the cost to operate the appliance.

Most appliances are required by law to have an **EnergyGuide label**. This black and yellow label shows the estimated annual energy consumption of that model. The label also shows the range of energy use for similar models and the estimated yearly operating cost. Also, look for an **Energy Star label** on appliances. This blue and green label shows that a product meets government standards for energy efficiency.

Storage Solutions

Use your creativity to meet your storage needs as you design your living space. The best designs have storage space that is convenient, accessible, and attractive. Before you assess your storage needs, go through the items you plan to store. Discard, recycle, or give away items you no longer need or want. Once you have eliminated unwanted items, follow these guidelines:

- Store similar items together in the same area so they will be easy to find. For example, place towels and bed linens together in a closet or storage unit.
- Store often-used items within easy reach. Avoid keeping something you use often on a high shelf or in a low drawer. Store items that are **seldom**, or not often, used in less accessible places, such as in a box under the bed or at the top of a closet.
- Keep some items visible. Store objects in clear plastic containers or on open shelves so you can locate them easily.
- Take advantage of unused space. Install hooks or pegs on walls and doors to hang belts, ties, scarves, and other items. Hang a shoe rack on the back of a closet door. You could even hang baskets and other lightweight items from hooks in the ceiling.
- Look for furniture with built-in storage. You might find a bench with a seat that lifts up, for example, or a bed with drawers built into the base.

 **Podcasts** Access the Online Learning Center to download *Managing Life Skills* podcasts.

 Section 34.2   **After You Read**

Review Key Concepts

1. **Explain** how a floor plan and scale drawing can help you decide how to arrange your furniture.
2. **Describe** the ways that color can affect the feeling of a room.
3. **Differentiate** between the EnergyGuide label and the Energy Star label.

Check Your Answers Check your answers at this book's Online Learning Center at **glencoe.com**.

Practice Academic Skills

 English Language Arts

4. Write down each of the elements of design. Beside each element, list descriptive words that come to mind as you imagine how you might redesign your bedroom. After you complete your lists, put your thoughts together, and write an overall description of the room.

NCTE 12 Use language to accomplish individual purposes.

Social Studies

5. Certain color schemes have been inspired by cultures and countries around the world. For example, earth tones are often found in Southwest color schemes. Find five different examples of color schemes inspired by cultures, and create a design board to show the schemes.

NCSS I E Demonstrate the value of cultural diversity, as well as cohesion, within and across groups.

Pathway to College

Money Management

How Can I Learn to Manage Money?

While you might have had to manage your own money in some ways in high school, your parents were probably still involved in your finances. In college, you will most likely be on your own. One of the most important skills you will need is knowing how to manage your finances wisely.

What do I need to consider when creating my budget?

List all sources of income including job earnings, savings, and parental support. Then list what you think you might spend in a month. Consider the cost of books and school supplies, meals not covered by a meal plan, entertainment, personal care items, laundry, telephone and Internet service, cab rides or car expenses, and clothes. If expenses are higher than income, you need to either increase income or reduce spending.

Should I get a credit card?

Building credit is an important step in adult life, and it is also a good idea to have a credit card for emergencies. However, credit cards can also be major pitfalls for college students. For some, access to credit results in overspending. You need to weigh the pros and cons and be honest with yourself about how you will respond to having credit. If you decide to get a credit card, never charge more than the amount you can comfortably afford to pay each month.

Do I need a checking account?

It is a good idea to open a checking account in the area where your school is located. Find a bank that offers free or low-fee checking for students and has convenient ATM locations. This reduces out-of-network ATM fees. You should know how to balance a checkbook. It is a dull job, but it is much better than bouncing checks.

Hands-On

College Readiness After your first few months in college, you start to realize you are going through your money much more quickly than you planned. When you sit down and come up with a budget, you recognize that you are spending too much. You do not want to cut out your social life all together, but you are worried about your rate of spending. Come up with at least five small things you could do or changes you could make that would save you money.

Path to Success

CCR College & Career Readiness

Practice Discipline Demonstrate self-control with shopping and spending money.

Be Organized One of the best things you can do to save money is to keep track of how you spend it and what you are spending it on.

Save Saving in college is difficult, but saving even a small portion helps make it a habit and will ensure you have a little something in case of an emergency.

Avoid Big Spenders Some students might spend money recklessly. Avoid spending too much time with these types of students.

Be Careful with Credit Have only one major credit card, and use it sparingly.

Be Car-Free Most college campuses are pedestrian and bike friendly, and cars can be really expensive.

Try Cooking Dining out can be expensive. If you have access to a kitchen, try cooking sometimes.

 Go to this book's Online Learning Center at **glencoe.com** to learn more about college and career readiness.

CHAPTER SUMMARY

Section 34.1
Choosing Your Home

Housing is most people's single biggest expense. You must decide whether you want to rent or buy housing and whether or not you want to share housing with another person. You must also choose a location that suits your needs. There are different types of housing and ownership. Your first home may be rented, although you may decide later to buy a home of your own.

Section 34.2
Designing Your Living Space

Make a floor plan, and consider traffic patterns to make your space more organized. Design elements can bring harmony to a room's design. Design principles are a set of guidelines that help the design elements work together in pleasing ways. There are tips for making smart choices for furniture, accessories, and appliances for your home. Storage needs can be addressed as you design your home.

Vocabulary Review

1. Arrange the vocabulary words below into groups of related words. Explain why you put the words together.

Content Vocabulary
- security deposit (p. 699)
- mortgage (p. 699)
- landlord (p.702)
- tenant (p. 702)
- lease (p. 703)
- down payment (p. 704)
- closing cost (p. 704)
- floor plan (p. 706)
- scale drawing (p. 706)
- traffic pattern (p. 706)
- proportion (p. 708)
- emphasis (p. 709)
- EnergyGuide label (p. 710)
- Energy Star label (p. 710)

Academic Vocabulary
- insure (p. 699)
- practical (p. 700)
- improvise (p. 710)
- seldom (p. 711)

Review Key Concepts

2. **Summarize** the main priorities for finding the right housing.
3. **Describe** six common types of housing structures.
4. **List** the advantages and disadvantages of renting.
5. **Identify** the advantages and disadvantages of buying a home.
6. **Describe** a floor plan and its uses.
7. **Summarize** the five elements of design.
8. **Compare** the three possible types of furniture options.

Critical Thinking

9. **Assess** What types of housing concerns do you think that people with children would have that people without children would not have?
10. **Decide** Imagine a friend asks to stay at your apartment for four months while student teaching. Should your friend share expenses while staying with you? Why or why not?
11. **Predict** What might happen if you tried to design a room without knowing about the elements and principles of design?

ACTIVE LEARNING

Family & Community Connections

12. **Find Double-Duty Furniture** Look through catalogs, magazines, and online furniture Web sites to find examples of furniture that serves more than one purpose. For example, a sleeper sofa also serves as a bed, and a coffee table might have extra room for storage. Create a display board to show at least five images of furniture that does double duty, and explain the dual purposes of each piece of furniture. Present your display board to your class. As a class, discuss whether the furniture pictured would work best in a small or large space.

13. **Interview a Real Estate Agent** Create a list of questions to find out how a real estate agent finds the right home for his or her clients. Questions might include: What factors do you take into consideration? Do those factors change based on each client's needs? What sources do you use to find homes that are for sale or rent? What questions do you ask potential buyers to find out what they are looking for? Find a real estate agent in your community, and set up an interview. During the interview, ask your questions and take notes. After the interview, transcribe your notes. Write a two-page report on your findings. Use proper grammar and spelling in your report, and include direct quotes from your interview.

21st Century Skills

Technology Skills

14. **Search the Internet** Search the Internet by entering the keywords *moving expenses*. Look for a relocation calculator that lets you determine the cost of moving from one city to another. What factors does the calculator take into account? Summarize your findings.

Planning Skills

15. **Determine Furniture Priorities** Imagine that you have rented an apartment, and you need to furnish it. Determine what your furniture priorities are likely to be based on your current activities and tastes. List the items that you consider absolute necessities. Then follow your teacher's instructions to form groups, and share your list with the group. As a group, discuss why different people may have different or similar lists.

 **Connections**

Communication Skills

16. **Discuss Concerns** As part of its mission, FCCLA encourages students to promote greater understanding between generations. Follow your teacher's instructions to form small groups. Create two lists, one listing concerns parents might have about living with their adult children, the other listing concerns adult children might have about living with their parents. Discuss how parents and adult children might communicate to resolve these concerns.

Academic Skills

 English Language Arts

17. Design Elements in Literature Search stories or novels for a detailed description of a room. Assess the design elements that are described in the passage. Using information from this chapter and the literary description, write a one-page summary of how the design elements contribute to or affect the mood of the plot of the story or novel.

> **NCTE 3** Apply strategies to interpret texts.

 Social Studies

18. Identify Japanese Design Use online and print resources to find information about the elements and principles of traditional Japanese interior design. How do the furnishings, accessories, room arrangements, and other features of a traditionally designed home in Japan differ from typical homes in the United States? Use presentation software to create an oral report to share with the class.

> **NCSS I A Culture** Analyze and explain the ways groups, societies, and cultures address human needs and concerns.

Mathematics

19. Housing Cost Percentages Housing expenses should be no more than $\frac{1}{3}$ of your income. Sarah earns $2,100 a month. She wants to rent an apartment for $625 per month. She estimates utilities will be $80 per month. Renter's insurance costs $15 per month. Calculate her monthly expenses, and decide if she can afford this apartment.

 Convert Fractions to Decimals A fraction can be converted to a decimal by dividing the numerator by the denominator.

Starting Hint Convert $\frac{1}{3}$ to a decimal, and round out to two decimal places. Then multiply that decimal by Sarah's monthly income to determine her ideal housing cost total. Add her proposed housing expenses, and compare the total to the ideal housing cost total.

 For more math practice, go to the Math Appendix at the back of the book.

> **NCTM Number and Operations** Understand numbers, ways of representing numbers, relationships among numbers, and number systems.

 Standardized Test Practice

CCR College & Career Readiness

MULTIPLE CHOICE
Read the question. Then read each answer choice. Choose the best answer.

Test-Taking Tip When answering a multiple-choice question, scan the possible answers, eliminating the ones you know are incorrect. Then, if you still do not know the answer, make an educated guess among the choices that remain.

20. Which principle of design is used to draw a viewer's attention to a specific area of a room?
   a. emphasis
   b. proportion
   c. balance
   d. unity

Chapter 35

Transportation

Chapter Objectives

Section 35.1 Transportation Options

- **List** the five most common transportation options for traveling to work or school.
- **Identify** the five factors that make up the cost of a vehicle.

Section 35.2 Vehicle Ownership

- **Describe** the main steps in the process of buying a vehicle.
- **Summarize** the five main types of auto insurance coverage.
- **Identify** five auto maintenance tasks that owners should be able to perform.

> ➤ **Explore the Photo**
>
> As an adult, you will probably use some form of transportation on a daily basis. *In your community, what options are available for traveling between work and home?*

Writing Activity

Question-and-Answer Essay

Safe Driving There are many rules of the road you should follow to stay safe when driving. Use your knowledge of teen drivers to write a question-and-answer essay. The question should focus on how a driver can avoid accidents. Answer the question in a detailed essay.

Writing Tips To write a good question-and-answer essay:

- Develop a question that is challenging but realistic.
- Introduce the question your essay will answer in your first sentence.
- Be sure your essay has an introduction, a body, and a conclusion.
- Make sure each body paragraph supports your answer.

Transportation Options

Cars are only one of many options for getting to a destination.

Reading Guide

Before You Read

Prior Knowledge Look over the Key Concepts at the beginning of the section. Write down what you already know about each concept and what you want to find out by reading the lesson. As you read, find examples for both categories.

Read to Learn
Key Concepts
- **List** the five most common transportation options for traveling to work or school.
- **Identify** the five factors that make up the cost of a vehicle.

Main Idea

There are many different transportation options. Owning a vehicle involves more costs than just the price of the car.

Content Vocabulary
◇ mass transit
◇ commute
◇ carpool
◇ title
◇ lease

Academic Vocabulary

You will find these words in your reading and on your tests. Use the glossary to look up their definitions if necessary.
■ congestion
■ market

Graphic Organizer

As you read, look for six reasons to use public transportation. The first reason has been filled in for you. Use a bus graphic organizer like the one shown to help you organize your information.

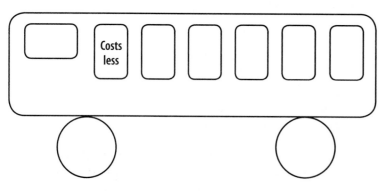

Costs less

 Graphic Organizer Go to this book's Online Learning Center at **glencoe.com** to print out this graphic organizer.

Academic Standards

 English Language Arts

NCTE 12 Use language to accomplish individual purposes.

 **Mathematics**

NCTM Number and Operations Compute fluently and make reasonable estimates.

Social Studies

NCSS I A Culture Analyze and explain the ways groups, societies, and cultures address human needs and concerns.

NCTE *National Council of Teachers of English*
NCTM *National Council of Teachers of Mathematics*
NSES *National Science Education Standards*
NCSS *National Council for the Social Studies*

Transportation Options

How do you get to school, to your friends' places, or to shopping centers? After you graduate, how will you get to work or classes? Depending on where you need to go, you might walk, ride a bike, drive a car, or get a ride with a friend or family member. Perhaps taking a bus, commuter train, or subway is a transportation option where you live.

When deciding how you will get to work or school, compare the cost and convenience of different options. Using a bus may be less convenient than having a car, but it is a lot less expensive. The most common options include owning your own vehicle, using mass transit, sharing a ride, riding a bicycle, or even walking.

Using Mass Transit

People who live in or near a large city often use mass transit. **Mass transit**, sometimes called public transportation, is a system designed to carry large numbers of people. Every day millions of Americans use buses, subways, trains, and even boats to get from place to place.

Mass transit systems serve both the people who use them and society as a whole in numerous ways. Compared to using your own vehicle, mass transit offers these benefits:

- **Costs Less** Mass transit fares are often lower than the cost of gas, parking, tolls, and maintenance for a personal car.
- **Saves Time** Trains and subways can often get passengers to their destination faster than cars because they do not get held up in traffic jams. Passengers can use the time to read, write, or even take a nap.
- **Reduces Stress** Passengers do not experience the stress associated with driving, especially in heavy traffic or bad weather.
- **Reduces Congestion** Using mass transit reduces the number of vehicles that are on the roads, which can help prevent traffic **congestion**, or clogs.
- **Saves Energy** Mass transit uses much less energy per passenger than individual cars.
- **Reduces Pollution** Fewer vehicles means less air pollution from exhaust systems.

Even though mass transit offers these benefits, many people still use their own vehicles instead. They may prefer the greater flexibility that their own transportation provides, or they may dislike the crowded conditions of public transportation.

As You Read

Connect What methods of transportation do you use in a typical week?

Vocabulary

You can find definitions in the glossary at the back of this book.

Public Transportation

Many people think of public transportation as buses, but there are many other forms of mass transit. *What forms of mass transit have you used?*

Apply Academic Knowledge

How many times have you sat in a class and thought, "Why do I need to know this?" Well, academic skills really do help with common life situations, such as transportation options. For example, your math skills will help you calculate how much mileage your car will get on a tank of gas and how much a road trip will cost. Think about how other skills you are learning can help in your transportation decisions.

Some people live in communities that have no mass transit, so they need their own transportation to get anywhere. Overall, the number of Americans who use mass transit is very small compared with the number who drive alone or with others.

Using Your Own Vehicle

The main advantage of driving alone in your own vehicle is convenience. You can leave when you are ready, and you have the flexibility to change your route or your schedule as you wish. The main disadvantage is that driving probably costs more than other options. It may also be more time consuming and stressful. The disadvantage for society is that every car on the road adds to traffic congestion, air pollution, and the consumption of scarce fuels.

Other Transportation Options

There are other options besides driving your own car and using mass transit. For example, sharing a vehicle with others is another option for commuting. A **commute** means to travel regularly from one place to another, especially between home and work. A **carpool** is an arrangement in which a group of people commute together by car. Carpools help save money on fuel and reduce the number of vehicles on the roads. In some carpools, the same person drives every day, and the passengers help pay expenses. In others, the participants take turns driving their vehicles. Some communities encourage carpooling by reserving express lanes on highways for vehicles carrying two or more people. Often, vanpools can be arranged for larger groups of people.

Life On Your Own

Restate the Problem

If you cannot find a solution to a problem, maybe the difficulty lies in how you defined the problem to begin with. Restating the problem in a different way can help you approach it from a new angle. This will often help you find an answer to your challenge.

How It Works When a problem does not seem solvable, take another look at it. Ask yourself what needs, wants, goals, and priorities lie behind the situation. Then see if you can restate the problem in a way that is solvable. For example, suppose you have not been able to find a part-time job. First ask yourself why it is a problem. If you need money, then you can restate the problem as, "How can I earn extra money?"

Try It Out You are looking for a new car. As you go from one auto dealer to another, you begin to wonder why all the cars you like cost so much. You have already done the math and know that with maintenance and insurance costs, your limited budget cannot afford more than a basic model.

> *Your Turn* How can you restate the problem in a way that focuses on solvable aspects? What new options does this generate?

The Cost of Ownership

Costs such as fuel, parking, maintenance, and insurance are often overlooked when considering the cost of a vehicle. *What are some strategies to cut down fuel costs?*

If bicycling is a practical and safe option for you, it is certainly worth considering. It provides exercise, is inexpensive, and does not harm the environment. Some communities have created special bike paths to keep bikers safe and encourage bicycle use. Similarly, some people have the option of walking to school, work, or certain stores.

✓ Reading Check **Conclude** How does reduced congestion result in less pollution?

Getting Your Own Vehicle

If, after considering your options, you decide to get a vehicle of your own, you need to do some careful research. Buying a vehicle is a major step that involves a lot of money. There are many more factors than just the retail price of the car. It is worth taking the time to understand all the factors that are involved so you can make an informed decision.

What Will It Cost?

Not everyone can afford a brand new car when they buy their first vehicle. Many start out by buying a used car. Used cars range in price from a few hundred to many thousands of dollars. When figuring out what your vehicle will cost you, though, you need to consider more than the price of the vehicle itself. This is true whether you are buying used or new. Additional expenses include:

- **Insurance** Auto insurance rates for young drivers can be high, even if you buy an inexpensive car. Insurance is discussed in detail later in this chapter.
- **Fuel** The amount you spend on fuel will depend on the miles you drive and on the fuel efficiency of your vehicle.
- **Parking and Tolls** Daily tolls and parking fees can add up to significant amounts over time.
- **Maintenance and Repairs** Regular maintenance keeps a vehicle working properly. In general, the older the vehicle, the more repairs it will need.

 **Math For Success**

Calculate Weekly Fuel Costs

Tosha owns a car that has a 15-gallon tank and averages 22 miles to the gallon. She drives 25 miles each way to work five days a week, and an additional 150 miles a week for errands and social activities. If gas costs $2.95 per gallon, how much would Tosha's weekly fuel costs be?

Math Concept **Multi-Step Problems** When solving problems with more than one step, think through the steps before you start making your plan for solving the problem.

Starting Hint Begin by calculating the total number of miles Tosha travels each week. Divide this total by the number of miles per gallon her car gets. Then multiply that number by the cost of the fuel.

 For more math practice, go to the Math Appendix at the back of the book.

NCTM Number and Operations Compute fluently and make reasonable estimates.

Podcasts Access the Online Learning Center to download *Managing Life Skills* podcasts.

How Will You Pay?

Unless you can afford to pay cash for a vehicle, you will need to arrange financing terms through a loan or lease. Most people make a down payment by paying a portion of the purchase price up front in cash. They then take out a loan for the remaining amount and pay it back in monthly installments. Loans can be arranged through a bank, credit union, or auto dealership. Typical auto loan periods range from 36 to 60 months. After you make your final payment, you receive the title for the car. A **title** is a legal document showing who owns the vehicle.

Leasing is for new vehicles only. When you **lease**, you pay a monthly fee in exchange for exclusive use of a vehicle for a specific length of time. When the lease period is over, you must return the vehicle or make other financing arrangements. Some leases specify the number of miles you may drive and charge a penalty for additional miles.

If you are in the **market** for, or interested in buying, a new car, look into the pros and cons of buying versus leasing. Lease payments may be lower than monthly loan payments, but at the end of the lease period you will have nothing to show for the money you have paid out.

Section 35.1  After You Read

Review Key Concepts

1. **Paraphrase** the main reasons that more people do not use mass transit.

2. **Compare and contrast** the two financing options available to pay for a car.

Practice Academic Skills

 English Language Arts

3. Write a script for a 60-second radio advertisement to promote using public transportation. Consider the reasons that some people might avoid mass transit and address those concerns in your advertisement to try and change their views.

 Social Studies

4. Many cultures have adapted unique modes of transportation. For example, some rural communities in the United States use horseback or horse-drawn carriage as a regular means of transportation. Choose a country other than the United States and learn about its modes of transportation, other than cars and buses. Write a brief report to share your findings.

Check Your Answers Check your answers at this book's Online Learning Center at **glencoe.com**.

NCTE 12 Use language to accomplish individual purposes.

NCSS I A Analyze and explain the ways groups, societies, and cultures address human needs and concerns.

Vehicle Ownership

If you could have any type of car, what car would you choose?

Reading Guide

Before You Read

Find Answers Before reading this section, write down what you would like to learn about purchasing and owning a car. When you are done reading the section, determine whether your questions were answered.

Read to Learn

Key Concepts

- **Describe** the main steps in the process of buying a vehicle.
- **Summarize** the five main types of auto insurance coverage.
- **Identify** five auto maintenance tasks that owners should be able to perform.

Main Idea

To get the best deal on a car, you must first do research. Auto insurance and car maintenance are two ownership responsibilities.

Content Vocabulary

◇ make
◇ model
◇ book value
◇ sticker price
◇ invoice price

Academic Vocabulary

You will find these words in your reading and on your tests. Use the glossary to look up their definitions if necessary.

■ condition
■ inflate

Academic Standards

English Language Arts

NCTE 7 Conduct research and gather, evaluate, and synthesize data to communicate discoveries.

Science

NSES E Develop understandings about science and technology.

Social Studies

NCSS X B Civic Ideals and Practices Identify, analyze, interpret, and evaluate sources and examples of citizens' rights and responsibilities.

NCTE *National Council of Teachers of English*
NCTM *National Council of Teachers of Mathematics*
NSES *National Science Education Standards*
NCSS *National Council for the Social Studies*

Graphic Organizer

As you read, look for five factors that affect auto insurance costs. Use a web diagram like the one shown to help you organize your information.

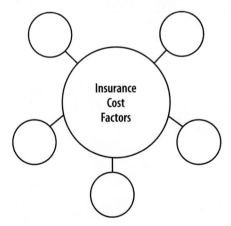

Insurance Cost Factors

 Graphic Organizer Go to this book's Online Learning Center at **glencoe.com** to print out this graphic organizer.

The Purchasing Process

Buying your first vehicle is a major step. It is probably the biggest financial decision you have made in your life up to this point. Start by figuring out what you can afford to pay, taking into account all the costs of vehicle ownership. That will help you determine whether to shop for a new or a used vehicle. Then do your research. Whether you buy new or used, you need to do your homework. Learning all that you can before you start shopping will help you get the right vehicle at the right price.

Once you have determined what you can afford and you have completed your research, you are ready to shop for your vehicle. The process is not complete though until you have negotiated the best price.

If you are like a lot of people, you would prefer a new vehicle. Consider, however, that even the smallest, most basic new car tends to be very expensive. A similar vehicle that is just two or three years old and in good condition can be nearly as nice and cost thousands less. Many dealers offer used vehicles that have been checked over thoroughly and come with a warranty for added peace of mind.

Do Your Research

Once you know about how much you can afford to pay, think about what you need in a vehicle. How much driving do you expect to do? In what road and traffic conditions will most of your driving be? Will you use your vehicle for long trips? For carpooling? Do you need space for tools, sports equipment, or other bulky items? Your answers will help you identify vehicles that meet your needs.

As You Read

Connect What is most important to you in a car?

◆ Vocabulary

You can find definitions in the glossary at the back of this book.

◀ Get Involved!

Volunteer Drivers

Because some senior citizens and people with disabilities are unable to drive themselves, many communities have volunteer drivers that take people to and from medical appointments or to run errands. Some organizations provide cars while others allow you to drive your own vehicle. Why do you think this type of service might be preferable to public transportation for some people?

Car Considerations

There are many things to think about when buying a car in addition to the purchase price. *What car features do you feel are absolutely essential?*

Makes and Models

Car buyers' magazines and online sites provide plenty of information about different vehicles. A car's brand name is called the **make**. The **model** is a particular type or design of the car. By learning about the reliability, safety features, fuel economy, and performance of makes and models in your price range, you will be able to narrow down your choices and identify vehicles that interest you. At that point, you might want to visit some dealerships to find and inspect the vehicles on your list.

Prices

How do you know whether the price a seller is asking for a used vehicle is reasonable? You can check the vehicle's book value. The **book value** is the estimated value of a specific make, model, and year. Book values are available in the Kelley *Blue Book*, which you can buy in a bookstore or borrow from the library. You can also visit the Kelley *Blue Book* Web site. Different prices are given based on factors such as the mileage and overall **condition**, or state of readiness for use, of the vehicle. You might also check the classified ads in your local paper to see what prices are being asked for vehicles that interest you.

If you are shopping for a new vehicle, magazines and online sources can tell you the manufacturer's suggested retail price (MSRP) of specific models. Note that this is not necessarily the price you will pay. For one thing, there are likely to be additional charges for options and other extras. It is also often possible to negotiate a lower price. Still, the MSRP will give you an idea of the vehicle's price in comparison to others.

Shop for the Best Vehicle

Once you have done your research, look for specific vehicles for sale. Look in classified ads, on the Internet, and at dealerships. Prepare a list of questions to ask when you call about an advertised vehicle. If a vehicle sounds promising, arrange to see it. Inspect the exterior and interior carefully. Be especially observant when inspecting a used vehicle. Look for signs of damage or previous repairs. You may want to arrange for a mechanic to check the vehicle.

If you are still interested, take the vehicle for a test drive. You may need to inspect and test drive several vehicles before you find one that you want to buy. Do not let anyone pressure you into buying before you are ready. It is worth waiting until you find the best vehicle for you.

Get the Best Price

Many sellers **inflate**, or raise, their asking price because they expect buyers to negotiate. Classified ads for used cars often state "or best offer." This means the seller will consider taking less than the asking price. Dealerships, too, will often accept less than the sticker price. The **sticker price** is the dealer's initial asking price as shown on the sticker attached to the vehicle. You could save a lot of money by offering a lower price and then negotiating with the seller until you reach an agreement. You can also often negotiate on other things as well, such as the loan term, interest rate, and the cost of extras such as premium paint colors, spoilers, rustproofing, and upgraded sound systems.

You will be able to negotiate more confidently if you have done your research and gathered information ahead of time. Use sources such as the Kelley *Blue Book* or *Consumer Reports* to determine what you can realistically expect to pay. If you are buying a new vehicle, find out the dealer's invoice price. The **invoice price** is roughly the price the dealer paid the manufacturer for the vehicle. The difference between this amount and the sticker price is your negotiating room.

Whether you are buying a new or used vehicle, decide ahead of time on the highest price you are willing and able to pay. Do not let anyone pressure you into buying until you are comfortable with the price. Remember, you can always walk away. If you do not feel comfortable with a specific dealer or dealership, do not be afraid to leave and go to another one.

✓ Reading Check **Contrast** What is the difference between MSRP and the invoice price?

Figure 35.1 Auto Insurance Coverage

Protect Yourself Different types of insurance coverage focus on different needs. *Why do you think most states require drivers to have auto insurance?*

TYPE	DESCRIPTION
Collision	Covers repairs to your vehicle if you have a traffic accident. Will not pay out more than the value of your vehicle.
Comprehensive	Covers damage caused by events other than a traffic accident, such as fire, theft, vandalism, flood, and hail.
Liability	Property damage liability covers damage that your vehicle causes to someone else's vehicle or property. Bodily injury liability covers medical expenses related to injuries suffered by others.
Medical Payments or Personal Injury	Covers medical expenses if you or your passengers are injured in an auto accident.
Uninsured/Underinsured Motorists	Covers damage or injury to you, your passengers, or your vehicle caused by a driver who has no insurance or insufficient insurance.

Understanding Auto Insurance

If you drive a vehicle, you need auto insurance. Most auto insurance policies combine several types of coverage. **Figure 35.1** on the previous page lists the main types of coverage that are available and provides a brief explanation of each.

Liability coverage is required by law in most states. Collision and comprehensive coverage are not required by law, but are sometimes required for a new car loan. The other types of coverage are required in some, but not all, states. An insurance agent can advise you on the amount and types of coverage that you should have and your various options.

HOW TO... Maintain Your Vehicle

When you own your own vehicle, it is your responsibility to maintain it. Though it may seem like these costs are unnecessary, they can actually save you money by preventing breakdowns which could mean costly repairs. You can take your car to a service center for regular maintenance or you could save some money by learning to do a few routine items yourself.

Windshield Washer Fluid Check the level of the fluid regularly. Always be sure that the engine is turned off first. If the fluid is below the fill line or the jug is less than ½ full, add fluid to fill the jug.

Engine Oil Check the oil level each time you refuel. Keeping the oil at the correct level protects the engine. Replace the oil at the recommended intervals. Once every 3,000 to 5,000 miles is typical.

Tire Pressure Use a tire pressure gauge to check tires each month. If they are below the level recommended in your manual, add air. Underinflated tires wear out faster and reduce fuel efficiency.

Lights Ask someone to help you make sure that your lights and signals work when you turn them on and off. Refer to your user manual for directions on how to replace lights that are out.

Fluid Levels Check the transmission fluid and brake fluid when you change the oil. Refer to your user manual to help locate these fluids and to ensure you fill them with the correct type of fluid.

Considerate Driving

Being a considerate driver can help prevent road rage and can help you avoid repair costs. For example, when parking your car, be sure to take only one spot. When you cross the line, others may try and squeeze in next to you and scratch or dent your car. Be aware of others if they are waiting for a spot in a crowded lot. Trying to get there first can lead to an accident.

Buying auto insurance can be complicated. You have a wide range of options from which to choose, and each option has a price. If you think you will be buying a vehicle, do your insurance homework ahead of time. Once you determine your insurance needs and wants, you will be able to compare the rates offered by different insurance companies. It is important that you do your own research and do not simply follow the insurance company's recommendation. Sometimes these recommendations are good, but sometimes they simply want to sell you more insurance that you do not necessarily need.

The most important aspect of auto insurance is liability coverage. If you have an accident and cause injury or damage to other people or their property, your liability insurance will cover the claims against you. You may be tempted to buy the minimum required coverage. Remember, though, that medical expenses resulting from an accident can be very high. Ask an insurance agent to suggest suitable liability coverage.

Choosing Coverage Options

Should you pay for collision and comprehensive coverage, which would compensate you for damage to your own vehicle? A lot depends on the value and age of your vehicle. For a new or relatively new vehicle, this insurance is usually a good idea. For an older vehicle, though, it may not be worth it. The insurance company will not pay more than the vehicle is worth, and repair bills, even to an old car, can be costly. You could end up paying more for the insurance than you would ever receive if you filed a claim. This is why you need to do careful research to make sure you have all the information you need and understand all of your options.

How Rates Are Assessed

Insurance companies base their rates on statistics. They try to predict what the risk is that a specific individual will file a claim. If the company determines that the risk is high, it will charge more for coverage. Drivers under age 25, for example, are responsible for more accidents than older drivers, so young drivers are charged higher rates for auto insurance. Other factors that influence auto insurance costs include your gender, marital status, where you live, and the age and type of vehicle you drive.

As you get older, your driving record will also be considered. Drivers who have had no accidents often have lower insurance rates. Traffic tickets can also negatively affect your insurance rate. If you have gotten multiple speeding tickets or any reckless driving tickets, your rates will likely go up. Also, some insurance companies offer lower rates to people who carry other types of insurance, such as renter's insurance, through the same insurance company.

✓ **Reading Check** **Paraphrase** Why might you be advised not to buy collision and comprehensive coverage on an older car?

Maintaining Your Vehicle

Your vehicle will last longer and will cost you less in repairs if you maintain it properly. Every new vehicle comes with an owner's manual that explains its features and provides a maintenance schedule. If you buy a used car, you may receive the owner's manual. If not, contact the manufacturer and ask for one.

Following the manufacturer's recommendations for maintenance is a good way to keep your vehicle running smoothly. Some people think they can save money by skipping some of the scheduled maintenance, but in the long run it can cost you more in repairs.

You will need a reliable service facility to perform at least some of the maintenance tasks for your vehicle. Ask other drivers for recommendations. Since service can be costly, you may want to perform some maintenance tasks yourself. See the How To feature on page 727 for some basic maintenance tasks.

Always pay attention to your car's warning lights. If the check engine light comes on, take your car to a service station as soon as possible. Watch for any leaks or drips, listen for strange noises, and pay attention to changes in how your car performs. Generally, the longer you wait to address a problem, the more costly it will be.

Health & Wellness TIPS

Avoid Motion Sickness

If you suffer from motion sickness, or car sickness, try to choose the most direct route to your destination. Curved roads often make it worse. Other tips include:

- ▶ Sit in the front seat.
- ▶ Do not read in the car.
- ▶ Open a window for fresh air.

Podcasts Access the Online Learning Center to download *Managing Life Skills* podcasts.

Section 35.2   After You Read

Review Key Concepts

1. **Explain** what the book value of a car is and how you can use it.
2. **Conclude** why liability coverage is required by law in most states.
3. **Give examples** of which basic car maintenance tasks can be learned.

Practice Academic Skills

English Language Arts

4. Obtain the owner's manual for a vehicle. Read the section on vehicle maintenance. Make a chart that shows the items recommended for regular maintenance and how often each task should be done. Also indicate whether the manual gives instruction on how to perform the task. If any tasks are not explained in the manual, write a brief note explaining why you think this is and what actions you could take to ensure the task was done.

Social Studies

5. It is every driver's responsibility to follow the laws regarding auto insurance coverage. Auto insurance laws differ from state to state and country to country. Conduct research to learn what travelers would need to do if they were planning a vacation in which they would drive through more than one country.

Check Your Answers Check your answers at this book's Online Learning Center at **glencoe.com**.

> **NCTE 7** Conduct research and gather, evaluate, and synthesize data to communicate discoveries.

> **NCSS X B** Identify, analyze, interpret, and evaluate sources and examples of citizens' rights and responsibilities.

Pathway to Your Career

Logistics Manager

What Does a Logistics Manager Do?

Logistics managers handle the flow of goods, information, and other resources. Logistics involves working with information, transportation, inventory, packaging, warehousing, and sometimes security. A logistics manager needs to communicate with a variety of parties including suppliers of raw materials, manufacturers, retailers, and consumers.

Career Readiness Skills Logistics managers need to be able to multitask. Because the job requires the ability to compromise, persuade, and negotiate, successful logistics managers must have excellent communication skills. Strong computer and mathematics skills are also essential. Logistics managers should have good problem solving and organizational skills.

Education and Training Because of the diversity of the types of jobs in this field, there is no standard preparation for this occupation. Most employers prefer to hire workers with a college degree. Degrees in business administration, project management, industrial technology, logistics, or transportation are preferred. However, some companies will hire well-rounded liberal arts graduates.

Job Outlook Employment in this industry is expected to increase moderately over the next decade. Most of the decision-making work of logistics managers cannot be automated.

Critical Thinking Many types of companies require logistics managers, from sports gear retailers to shipping companies to food distributors. Research what types of companies hire logistics managers. Pick the company that interests you most, and explain why.

Career Cluster

 College & Career Readiness

Transportation, Distribution & Logistics
Logistics managers work in the Logistics Planning & Management Services pathway of this career cluster. Other jobs in this cluster include:

- Traffic Manager
- Freight Inspector
- Ship Mechanic
- Truck Driver
- Airplane Pilot
- Travel Agent
- Flight Attendant
- Chauffeur
- Subway Operator
- Taxi Driver

Explore Further The Transportation, Distribution & Logistics career cluster contains seven pathways: Transportation Operations; Logistics Planning & Management Services; Warehousing & Distribution Center Operations; Facility & Mobile Equipment Maintenance; Transportation Systems/Infrastructure Planning, Management & Regulation; Health, Safety & Environmental Management; and Sales & Service. Choose one of these pathways to explore further.

 Career Clusters To learn more about career clusters, go to this book's Online Learning Center at **glencoe.com**.

CHAPTER SUMMARY

Section 35.1
Transportation Options

Transportation options are determined by where you live and where you want to go. Using mass transit benefits individuals and society. Owning a vehicle involves many expenses in addition to the purchase price. To pay for a vehicle, you might take out a loan or lease the vehicle, if it is new.

Section 35.2
Vehicle Ownership

Learning all that you can before shopping for a vehicle will help you get the right vehicle at the right price. Before buying auto insurance, examine the options, and decide on the types and amounts of coverage you want. You can save on maintenance costs by doing some basic tasks yourself.

Vocabulary Review

1. Write your own definition for each content and academic vocabulary term.

Content Vocabulary
- ◇ mass transit (p. 719)
- ◇ commute (p. 720)
- ◇ carpool (p. 720)
- ◇ title (p. 722)
- ◇ lease (p. 722)
- ◇ make (p. 725)
- ◇ model (p. 725)
- ◇ book value (p. 725)
- ◇ sticker price (p. 726)
- ◇ invoice price (p. 726)

Academic Vocabulary
- ■ congestion (p. 719)
- ■ market (p. 722)
- ■ condition (p. 725)
- ■ inflate (p. 726)

Review Key Concepts

2. **List** the five most common transportation options for traveling to work or school.
3. **Identify** the five factors that make up the cost of a vehicle.
4. **Describe** the main steps in the process of buying a vehicle.
5. **Summarize** the five main types of auto insurance coverage.
6. **Identify** five auto maintenance tasks that owners should be able to perform.

Critical Thinking

7. **Compare and Contrast** What are some of the pros and cons of different types of vehicles, such as sedans, compact cars, or trucks? Why might some types of vehicles be more practical for certain people?
8. **Analyze** Choose one make and model of car that you might be interested in owning. Find out what the cost is for that model new and used. Remember to consider taxes and other dealer charges. How significant is the price difference?
9. **Predict** Do you think more people would use public transportation if the price of gasoline were to rise significantly?
10. **Infer** Who would be more likely to pay more for auto insurance: a 26-year-old female teacher living in a small town or a 24-year-old male engineer living in a major city?
11. **Determine** Suppose you are considering buying a new car but you cannot afford collision coverage as well as the car payments. What is the risk? What are some alternative strategies you could look into?

ACTIVE LEARNING

12. Practice Car Maintenance Find someone who owns a vehicle and performs basic maintenance tasks described in the text. Arrange for a time that you could meet this person and practice checking tire pressure and fluid levels. Develop a checklist ahead of time with the items you intend to check. Ask the owner to supervise you and offer tips or suggestions if you do anything incorrectly. Mark each item once it is completed. Write a brief summary of your experience to share what you learned. Were some tasks easier than you expected? Were some more difficult than you expected?

Family & Community Connections

13. Mass Transit Survey Develop a survey to find out how people in your neighborhood get to work each day. Do they drive themselves? Ride in a carpool? Take the bus? Ride a bike? Also, ask what the top reason is for their choice. Convenience? Cost? Health? For those people who do not use public transportation, ask them why and what the community could do that would make them more likely to consider using a means other than driving a personal vehicle. For example, would they take the bus if there were more convenient times offered? Would they be more likely to walk if there were more sidewalks? Distribute your survey to 10 adults in your neighborhood. Compile the results and write a one-page report summarizing and analyzing your findings.

21st Century Skills

Financial Literacy Skills

14. Public Transportation Investigate the availability and cost of using mass transit in your community. Pick a destination, and compare the cost of a single ride versus a pass for a certain time frame. If you visit the destination weekly, which option is more cost effective?

Technology Skills

15. Internet Car Shopping Visit a Web site devoted to helping consumers who are shopping for new or used vehicles. Make a list of at least six helpful tools found on the Web site. Experiment with the interactive tools and calculators. Give an example of what you learned from each.

FCCLA Connections

Collaboration Skills

16. Traffic Safety As part of its mission, FCCLA encourages students to develop responsible character traits. Develop and implement a traffic safety program as a Families Acting for Community Traffic Safety (FACTS) or Community Service project. You might focus on safety belts or school speed zones. Write a description of how your program was implemented and an evaluation of how it worked.

Academic Skills

 English Language Arts

17. Analyze Insurance Obtain a copy of an auto insurance policy. Read through it, underlining the most important phrases. Circle any unfamiliar terms. Look up the definitions for those terms, and re-read the policy to see if you understand it better.

> **NCTE 3** Apply strategies to interpret texts.

 Science

18. Video Driving Games Some research studies report that playing video racing games cause people to drive more recklessly. Others argue that playing video games improves a person's peripheral vision, improving his or her driving.

Procedure Research the correlation between video games and driving abilities.

Analysis Write a report concluding whether you think video games have a positive or negative impact on real-life driving skills.

> **NSES 1** Develop an understanding of science unifying concepts and processes.

Mathematics

19. Calculate Percentage Mia works at a bank that has 40 total employees. She is conducting a survey on how her colleagues get to work each day. Half of the employees use public transportation to get to work. If 30% of the people using public transportation take the train, how many people in Mia's office ride the train to work?

Math Concept **Multiplying Percents** To multiply percents, first change the percents to decimals. Be sure to place the decimal point in the product correctly.

Starting Hint First multiply the percent of employees who use public transportation (50%) by the percent of employees who ride the train (30%). Then multiply your answer by the total number of employees.

 For more math practice, go to the Math Appendix at the back of the book.

> **NCTM Number and Operations** Understand numbers, ways of representing numbers, relationships among numbers, and number systems.

 Standardized Test Practice

 CCR College & Career Readiness

READING COMPREHENSION
Read the passage, and then answer the question.

Test-Taking Tip When answering reading comprehension questions, be sure to read the entire passage before you try to answer the question. If you have any questions or doubts, refer back to the passage when answering the question.

A liability coverage expressed as 100/300/50 means $100,000 is the amount the insurance company pays for the injuries of any one person in any one accident; $300,000 is the amount the company pays for all injured parties, if there is more than one; and $50,000 is the limit for damage to the property of others.

20. If Sean buys 25/50/10 coverage, what is the maximum that could be paid for another's car repairs if Sean caused the accident?
    a. $25,000   **c.** $10,000
    b. $50,000   **d.** $5,000

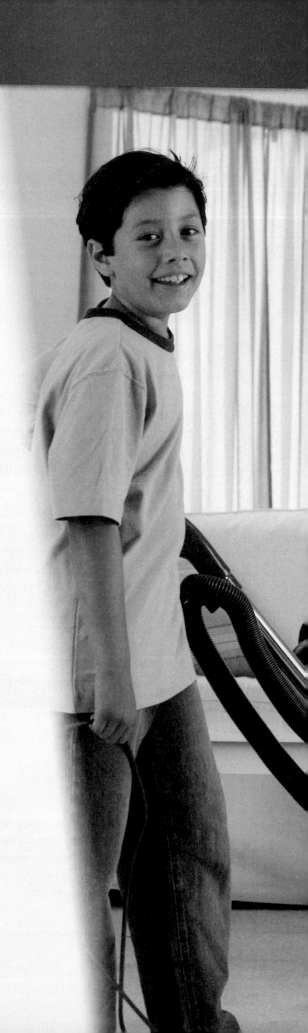

Chapter 36

Home Care and Personal Safety

> **Explore the Photo**
>
> To keep your home clean and safe, there are many tasks you must do daily, weekly, monthly, and yearly. *What tasks are being done in this photo, and how often do you think they need to be done?*

Writing Activity

Expository Writing

Familiar Chores Expository writing explains and informs. Think about an appliance or tool that you use often to perform a regular chore around your home. Write an essay that explains your topic to your audience. Explain clearly how to use the appliance or tool, and support your explanation with facts and details.

Writing Tips To write an expository essay, follow these steps:

- Define your purpose and audience.
- Explain your main idea in a clear thesis statement.
- List facts as supporting details.

Caring for Your Home

Maintaining your home on a regular basis can save you time, money, and effort.

Reading Guide

Before You Read

Restating Definitions Knowing the meanings of vocabulary words is vital to understanding what you are reading. For this section, read each content vocabulary word's definition, and then restate the definition in your own words.

Read to Learn
Key Concepts
- **List** some of the benefits of home care.
- **Describe** how establishing a routine can help with cleaning.
- **Name** seasonal and annual preventive maintenance tasks.

Main Idea

Taking care of your home can save you time and money. It is important to establish a routine to keep a home clean. Assign daily and weekly cleaning tasks. Perform preventive maintenance to keep the home running right.

Content Vocabulary
◇ home care
◇ preventive maintenance

Academic Vocabulary

You will find these words in your reading and on your tests. Use the glossary to look up their definitions if necessary.
■ routine
■ slew

Academic Standards

English Language Arts
NCTE 1 Read texts to acquire new information.

Social Studies
NCSS V G Individuals, Groups, and Institutions Analyze the extent to which groups and institutions meet individual needs and promote the common good in contemporary and historical settings.

Graphic Organizer

As you read, you will find procedures for cleaning five areas inside your home. Use a matrix like the one shown to help you describe them.

Area	Procedure
Windows	
Furniture	
Floors	
Bathroom	
Walls/Cabinets	

Graphic Organizer Go to this book's Online Learning Center at **glencoe.com** to print out this graphic organizer.

NCTE *National Council of Teachers of English*
NCTM *National Council of Teachers of Mathematics*
NSES *National Science Education Standards*
NCSS *National Council for the Social Studies*

Benefits of Home Care

Caring for a home means more than simply keeping things tidy. **Home care** means keeping the home clean, doing routine maintenance tasks, and taking action to prevent home accidents. While some people claim to be too busy to care for their homes, keeping your home in order can actually save you time by allowing you to find items more easily. Would you prefer to spend time doing something you enjoy or hunting for something that is misplaced?

Home care saves money, too. Caring for possessions makes them last longer and stay in better condition. It lowers the risk that you will damage something or throw it out by mistake.

Yet another benefit of home care is that it improves your state of mind, your health, and your safety. A messy, disorganized home can make you feel anxious or depressed and may actually be dangerous. A clean and organized home, on the other hand, offers a more pleasant, more healthful, and safer environment. It also makes your home a nice place to invite guests.

✓ **Reading Check** **Explain** How does home care save time?

Neatness and Cleanliness

Keeping a home neat and clean can become a habit. By taking some simple steps each day, you can keep tasks manageable. You may need to work at it for a while, but if you try to make neatness a habit, it will eventually become second nature. Make a point of noticing current messy habits, such as flinging a coat over a chair when you come home. Get into the habit of hanging up your coat and doing other things that keep a home tidy. Some suggestions for keeping your home neat and clean include:

- Make your bed after you get up in the morning.
- Have a place for everything, and put things away as soon as you finish using them. Inexpensive storage boxes, crates, or shelves might be helpful.
- Sort mail the first time you look at it. Throw away junk mail, and place items that need your attention in a designated place.
- Put newspapers and magazines in a recycling bin as soon as you finish reading them.
- Unload grocery bags as soon as you get home.

◇ **Vocabulary**

You can find definitions in the glossary at the back of this book.

Keeping Your Home Clean

To keep your living space nice, comfortable, and clean, it is important to do some tasks daily and weekly. *What kind of task is pictured here?*

How Do You Organize Your Space?

"A place for everything and everything in its place" is a main rule of organization. However, there are many possible variations to this rule.

Alex: I find it's easier to get things done if projects and supplies are out where I can see them. If I try to be neat by hiding everything away, I tend to put things off or forget. If I need to fill out an application form, for example, I put it on the desk in my room. I keep tools right where I use them most often. The broom and a mop are behind the kitchen door. It's faster and easier to grab them that way.

Celina: To me, part of keeping a home looking nice is putting things away when you aren't using them. Leaving school papers, cleaning supplies, and other stuff sitting out would be like leaving dishes on the counter after they've been washed. Besides, if things are left out, they usually get moved or misplaced. Then it's more work to track them down when I need them.

Seeing Both Sides

Does everyone need to follow the same set of rules for organization? Why or why not? If Alex and Celina shared a common space, what advice would you give them on organizing so that they are both happy?

- When you change clothes, hang up items that do not need to be laundered. Use a hamper or laundry bag for laundry and a separate basket for dry cleaning.
- Keep clutter to a minimum by getting rid of things you do not really need or want.

Establish a Routine

Cleaning goes much faster if you establish a routine for doing tasks. Decide what needs to be done, who will do it, and how often each different task needs to be done. For example, your **routine**, or regular procedure, for cleaning your bedroom each Saturday might be to put away clothes, change sheets, dust furniture, clean the floor, and polish the mirror. Create a routine for every room. This will simplify home care and ensure that no part of the home is neglected.

A routine for cleaning is particularly important for people who share a home. Whether you live with a roommate or other family members, you need a system for sharing home care. Some people like to volunteer for a particular job because it is something they are good at or enjoy. Another approach is to divide the work on a room-by-room basis. Regardless, everybody should participate in cleaning, but individual abilities and health limits need to be taken into account.

Daily and Weekly Tasks

Households run more smoothly when chores are done regularly. Some should be done daily, some weekly, and some only occasionally. Set up a schedule for household chores based on your home, the time you have to spend cleaning, and the help you get from family members and roommates. Some suggestions for daily household chores are:

- Wash the dishes.
- Wipe kitchen counters, the range, and the sink. This may be done more than once per day.
- Sweep the kitchen floor.
- Take out the garbage as needed.

When it comes to weekly chores, you may choose to perform one job each day or do them all at one time. Some suggestions for weekly household chores are:

- Vacuum or sweep the floors, and shake out small rugs.
- Clean bathroom fixtures.
- Wash kitchen and bathroom floors.
- Dust the furniture and other objects.
- Change the bed linens.
- Do the laundry.

There are many other tasks that must be done to maintain a home. Certain jobs need to be done only occasionally, however. You might wash windows, wax floors, clean the refrigerator and oven, and clean ceiling fans and window blinds occasionally. In addition, many families do a thorough cleaning every spring and fall.

Character?! In Action

Take Responsibility

Jeanna goes to the park with a friend for a picnic lunch. When they arrive, they find that the people who used the tables before them did not clean up their trash. Jeanna starts to pick up the trash, but her friend says it is not their job to clean up other people's messes.

You Decide

Do you agree with Jeanna's friend? What do you think Jeanna and her friend's responsibilities are in this situation?

Life On Your Own

Keep the Outdoors Clean

Maintaining the area outside your home is important. Not only will it help your home's curbside appeal, it can also help to keep you safe. It may help you get more money for your home if you own it and choose to sell it. There are several steps you can take to make sure the outside of your home is well cared for.

How It Works To keep the outside of your home clean, keep the porch, patio and deck areas swept and free of clutter and debris. Keep pathways clear of fallen debris and snow or ice. Use a broom to sweep away cobwebs and dirt from outside walls. Wash windows and screens once a year. Mow the lawn, rake fallen leaves, and prune overgrown trees and shrubs. Be sure to put away bikes and other sports equipment immediately after use.

Try It Out If you live in a multifamily complex, some of these tasks might be done by maintenance staff. Even so, you share some of the responsibility for keeping outdoor areas tidy. You must be sure you do your part to keep the area free of clutter and litter. Imagine that you live in a multifamily complex. The common patio is not always kept free of litter and toys, and some neighbors are becoming upset.

Your Turn How can you help with the situation without causing bad feelings between neighbors? What types of outdoor cleaning suggestions and solutions would you give to management and the other neighbors? How would you set an example?

Save Cleaning Time

There are many things you can do to cut back on the time you spend cleaning. Keep out dirt by placing doormats outside and inside every entrance. Remove outdoor shoes as soon as you arrive home. Clean up spills as they occur. Prevent soap scum from building up by wiping the tub, shower stall, and sink after each use. Wash dirty hands as soon as possible to avoid leaving fingerprints on surfaces.

Cleaning Indoors

Television commercials might lead you to believe that you need a **slew**, or a large number, of products to keep a home clean. In fact, you need just a few basic items, like a vacuum, broom, cleaning cloths, sponge, bucket, and cleaning products. Follow these procedures for cleaning different areas inside your home:

- **Windows** Apply a glass-cleaning product. Then dry the windows with a clean cloth or with paper towels.
- **Furniture** Use a soft cloth or duster. Use furniture polish or wax occasionally to protect the wood. Vacuum upholstered furniture, and turn the cushions occasionally.
- **Floors** Blot spills immediately. Clean smooth floors with a broom or mop. Then wash them using an appropriate cleaning product for the floor material. Vacuum carpeted floors.
- **Bathrooms** Use a sponge or brush and cleanser to scrub the tub, shower, toilet, and counters. Rinse all surfaces thoroughly. Use a toilet brush and disinfecting cleaner on the toilet bowl.
- **Walls and Cabinets** Use a cloth and cleanser to wipe fingerprints and spots from walls, doors, switch plates, and cabinets.

✓ **Reading Check** **Identify** What are some daily chores?

Preventive Maintenance

As in the rest of life, it is better to prevent a problem in your home than to have to fix it. **Preventive maintenance** means taking action to prevent problems or keep minor problems from becoming major ones. Certain basic preventive maintenance tasks should be done to keep a home in good condition.

Seasonal Tasks

▼ Keep Your Home Safe

One very important task to keep your home safe is to test smoke detectors and replace batteries as needed. *How often do you think you should test smoke detectors?*

In most situations, these items need attention at least twice a year:

- **Furnace and Air Conditioner** Clean or replace filters at the end of the heating or cooling seasons.
- **Smoke Detectors** Test smoke detectors to make sure they are working properly, and replace batteries as needed. Choose a regular time to do this.
- **Water Heater** Turn off the power source, and drain water from the valve until it runs clear. Sediment buildup shortens a water heater's life and efficiency.
- **Refrigerator** Vacuum the condenser coils to prevent overheating. Check the owner's manual for additional maintenance tips.
- **Garage** Lubricate tracks of automatic garage door openers for smooth operation.
- **Gutters** Clean leaves from gutters and downspouts in the spring and fall.

Annual Tasks

The following maintenance jobs should be done at least once a year. If you rent your home, find out if you or your landlord is responsible for doing them.

- **Exterior** In the spring, inspect the siding, paint, roof, and foundation for any problems.
- **Furnace and Air Conditioner** Have a professional check the furnace in the fall. If you have air-conditioning, have it inspected before periods of heavy use.
- **Fireplaces and Wood-Burning Stoves** To reduce the risk of fire, hire an expert to clean your chimney at least once a year, or twice a year if you use your fireplace often.

Other Tasks

Other maintenance tasks can be performed on an as-needed basis. Prevent drains from clogging by using drain cleaner. Listen to the sounds of your home. If the refrigerator or water heater becomes noisy, have it checked. If a toilet starts to run continually, replace the flush mechanism. Every time you take action to fix a minor problem, you prevent a major problem from developing.

 Podcasts Access the Online Learning Center to download *Managing Life Skills* podcasts.

Section 36.1 — After You Read

Review Key Concepts

1. **Describe** how home care can affect your state of mind.
2. **List** daily and weekly tasks that can help keep a home clean.
3. **Explain** why regular maintenance tasks are important.

 Check Your Answers Check your answers at this book's Online Learning Center at **glencoe.com**.

Practice Academic Skills

 English Language Arts

4. Think of a regular cleaning task, such as vacuuming or doing laundry. Perform research using magazines, books, and Web sites to find tips to make the cleaning task easier. Summarize the information into tips that can be followed by another person. Compile these tips into a brochure on the cleaning task that can be distributed to others. Be sure to cite your sources.

NCTE 1 Read texts to acquire new information.

 Social Studies

5. Mold in homes can rot surfaces and cause allergic reactions in people and animals. With your teacher's permission, search the Internet for information from the Environmental Protection Agency on the cleanup of mold. What safety gear does the agency recommend wearing when cleaning mold from interior surfaces? Create a visual presentation showing images or drawings of each type of safety gear and explaining why that piece of safety gear is important.

NCSS V G Analyze the extent to which groups and institutions meet individual needs and promote the common good in contemporary and historical settings.

Staying Safe

Do you know how to stay safe in your home, in your community, and on the road?

Reading Guide

Before You Read

Explaining as You Read As you read, pause each time you come to a new heading. Explain what you have just read to an imaginary person who is unfamiliar with the information. This will help you monitor your comprehension.

Read to Learn
Key Concepts
- **Describe** where falls, cuts, and poisonings are most likely to happen.
- **List** general measures you can take to prepare for emergencies.
- **Identify** ways to help keep your community safe.
- **Discuss** ways to stay safe on the road.

Main Idea
Taking responsibility for home safety helps to prevent accidents. Be prepared to deal with emergencies in the home. Take steps to help keep your community safe and to stay safe while driving.

Content Vocabulary
◇ ground fault circuit interrupter (GFCI)
◇ carbon monoxide detector
◇ Neighborhood Watch program

Academic Vocabulary
You will find these words in your reading and on your tests. Use the glossary to look up their definitions if necessary.
- leading
- region

Graphic Organizer
As you read, you will discover eight ways to prevent falls. Use a tree organizer like the one shown to help you organize your information.

Academic Standards

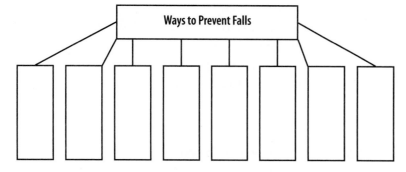

English Language Arts

NCTE 12 Use language to accomplish individual purposes.

Mathematics

NCTM Number and Operations Compute fluently and make reasonable estimates.

Social Studies

NCSS IV I Power, Authority, and Governance Evaluate the extent to which governments achieve their stated ideals and policies at home and abroad.

Ways to Prevent Falls

 Graphic Organizer Go to this book's Online Learning Center at **glencoe.com** to print out this graphic organizer.

NCTE *National Council of Teachers of English*
NCTM *National Council of Teachers of Mathematics*
NSES *National Science Education Standards*
NCSS *National Council for the Social Studies*

Prevent Home Accidents

An important part of home care involves keeping the home safe. Every year, millions of Americans are injured and thousands die in their home, the very place where most people feel safest. The most common types of home accidents are falls, cuts, electrical shocks, poisonings, and burns. Most accidents that happen in the home can be prevented. It is every individual's responsibility to understand potential dangers and take steps to prevent accidents.

As You Read

Connect Have you ever been in an accident in your home? If so, how did it happen?

Prevent Falls

Falls are the **leading**, or main, cause of injuries and deaths in the home. Although children and older people fall most often, anyone can fall. Falls are most likely to occur on cluttered or slippery surfaces. Most falls occur in bathrooms, in kitchens, and on stairs. Follow these tips to minimize the risk of falling:

- Use a stepladder, not a chair, to reach high places.
- Keep toys and clutter off the floor in heavy traffic areas.
- Install safety gates at the top and bottom of stairs when toddlers are present.
- Keep rooms and hallways well lighted, especially near stairs.
- Anchor throw rugs with carpet tape or nonskid mats.
- Arrange furniture to be out of the path of traffic.
- Wipe up spills immediately. Warn others when you have just washed a floor.
- Use a tub mat or adhesive-backed strips on the bottom of the bathtub to prevent slips. Install grab rails for older family members.

Vocabulary

You can find definitions in the glossary at the back of this book.

Prevent Cuts

Cuts from tools and equipment occur most often in the kitchen, workrooms, and outdoor areas. Always pay close attention to what you are doing when you use knives and other tools. Use the tools only as intended. Here are some additional ways to prevent cuts:

- Store knives with their handles toward the front of the drawer or use a wooden knife block.
- Keep knives and scissors away from young children.
- Wear gloves and goggles when you operate power tools. Store power tools and saws in a safe place, and cover the blades.
- Wear closed-toe shoes when using a lawn mower or trimmer.
- Unplug any tool or appliance before you try to adjust or fix it.

Financial *Literacy*

Appliance Costs

You spend $15 a month on electricity to run your dishwasher, and you want to buy a new dishwasher. Dishwasher A costs $425.72 and will cut your monthly electric bill in half. Dishwasher B costs $173.84 and will not change your monthly electric bill. Round the price of each dishwasher up or down to the nearest dollar. Then calculate the cost of each one after a year.

Math Concept **Rounding Decimals** Look at the digit to the right of the place value you want to round up to. If that number is greater than or equal to five, add a one to the place value, and drop all digits to the right. If that number is less than five, drop all digits to the right, but do not add a one to the place value.

Starting Hint The price of dishwasher A can be rounded up to $426 because the digit to the right of the five is a seven. Remember to add the monthly electricity cost of each dishwasher.

 For more math practice, go to the Math Appendix at the back of the book.

NCTM Number and Operations Compute fluently and make reasonable estimates.

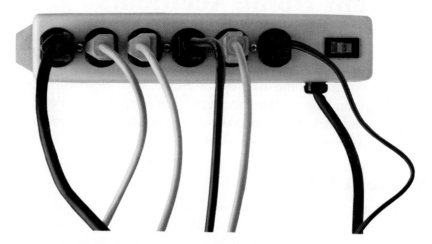

Prevent Electrical Shocks

Most electrical shocks occur because of problems with plugs, outlets, wiring, and extension cords or because of appliance misuse. Precautions to prevent electrical shocks include:

- **Plugs and Outlets** Inspect cords for loose plugs or exposed wiring. When there are children around, use outlet covers. Install a **ground fault circuit interrupter (GFCI)**, a device used near water that automatically turns off electricity to guard against electrical shock, in kitchens and bathrooms.
- **Extension Cords** To prevent circuit overload, do not plug too many appliances into the same outlet. Instead, use power strips, extension cords, or two or more outlets. Keep all electrical cords out of areas where people might trip on them, but do not place them under rugs or carpets as this could cause a fire.
- **Appliances** Never use electrical appliances when you have wet hands, are standing on a wet surface, or are near a full bathtub or sink. Make sure appliance cords are well insulated and not frayed. Unplug small appliances when they are not in use.

Prevent Poisonings

Most accidental poisonings happen in the bathroom, kitchen, and bedroom. Young children are most at risk because they are naturally curious and do not always recognize danger. Medicines are particularly dangerous. Choose childproof containers, and keep all medicines out of reach.

Be aware of other poisons in your home, including cleaning products, gasoline, kerosene, fertilizer, paint, and insect and weed killers. Use locks or childproof latches to secure all poisons. Be sure to keep all poisonous products in their original containers.

Gases can also be poisonous. Carbon monoxide is a poisonous gas produced by defective gas appliances such as a furnace or fireplace. All gas heating devices should be checked regularly, and you should install a **carbon monoxide detector**, a device that sounds an alarm when a dangerous level of carbon monoxide is reached.

Be Smart Be Safe

Safety Starts at Home Discouraging crime starts at home. Keep entrances well lit at night, lock doors and windows, never hide a key in an easy-to-find place, do not allow shrubs to grow tall around entryways, and keep expensive items such as jewelry in a safe place.

Write About It Think about other ways you might keep your home safe. Research home safety information, and make a list detailing some ideas.

Prevent Fires and Burns

Many of the guidelines for preventing electrical shocks will also help prevent fires and burns. In addition, you can reduce the risk of fires by being especially careful when using matches and candles. Make sure that no one in your home smokes in bed. Before throwing away burned matches, be sure they are properly extinguished. Do not place candles near anything that could catch fire or in a place where they could be knocked over. Never leave lighted candles in an empty room. If you have candles in a bedroom, make sure you put them out before you go to sleep.

If you use a portable space heater, place it well away from furniture, drapes, and anything else that could catch fire. Always follow the manufacturer's directions. Never leave the heater unattended.

Most fires and burns occur in the kitchen. Fire and burn prevention in the kitchen is discussed in Chapter 29. Turn pot handles toward the center of the range, and be aware that children do not necessarily know what is hot and could burn them. If you smell gas in your home, leave immediately, and call the gas company from a neighbor's home.

✓ **Reading Check** **Identify** What things cause most of the electrical shocks that occur in the home?

Preparing for Emergencies

You need to know what kinds of emergencies might happen in your home and prepare for them. This includes weather-related emergencies like hurricanes, tornadoes, floods, or snowstorms that can occur in your **region**, or area. General measures you can take to prepare for emergencies are:

- Keep fire extinguishers in the kitchen and garage, and learn how to operate them.
- Install smoke detectors on every level.
- Develop a fire escape plan with family members, and practice using it.
- Assemble a disaster preparedness kit with a flashlight, battery-operated radio, extra batteries, candles, first aid kit, bottled water, and canned food.
- Practice any recommended procedures for the disasters that might happen in your region.
- Find and label shut-off valves for water, electricity, and gas. Learn how to operate them.
- Keep telephone numbers for the police, fire department, ambulance, closest hospital, and poison control next to each phone in your home.

✓ **Reading Check** **Describe** What types of items should be in a disaster preparedness kit?

Succeed in SCHOOL and LIFE

Talk It Through

Being stressed can be a distraction. If you are worried about something, such as safety, you might have trouble focusing on your schoolwork. If something is really bothering you, find someone to talk to, such as a friend, parent, teacher, or counselor.

In Case of Emergency

To stay safe in your living space, be prepared for emergencies. One way to do this is to keep fire extinguishers handy. *How else might you stay safe in your living space?*

Community Safety

You can contribute to the safety of your community. Start by getting to know your neighbors. If you know who belongs in your neighborhood, it is easier to spot suspicious activity. Pay attention to what is happening around you. If you see unfamiliar parked vehicles, strangers loitering, or cars driving by slowly, stay extra alert. If you see suspicious activity, call the police.

You might also want to start or join a **Neighborhood Watch program**, an organized community group that watches for suspicious activity and reports problems to the police. These programs have been effective in promoting safety and preventing crime. Some Neighborhood Watch groups also focus on preparing for emergencies and being on the lookout for terrorism.

Protect Yourself from Crime

You cannot assume that you are safe from crime. What you can do, though, is take precautions that will help protect you. Wherever you are, stay aware of your surroundings. Do not put yourself in harm's way unnecessarily.

- **At Home** You should feel safe at your home. Always keep doors and windows locked. If you ever experience violence within the home, seek help from a counselor or other trusted adult.
- **Online** Never give out personal information to strangers you meet online. If someone you know only through the Internet wants to meet you in person, tell an adult in your family.
- **At School** Safety at school is essential for learning. If you know of crimes or situations that may cause violence, it is your responsibility to let administrators know. Think about starting or joining a committee to improve harmony at school.
- **In the Community** Avoid any places known for high crime rates. On public transportation, be alert for dangerous situations. On the street, walk with confidence, and scan the area as you walk. If you must walk at night, walk with someone else and choose a well-traveled and well-lighted route. If you get lost in an unfamiliar area, ask a police officer for help or stop at a restaurant or store. Keep valuables out of sight. If someone demands your purse or wallet, you should give it to the person instead of refusing or trying to fight.

Meet Your Neighbors

Getting to know your neighbors is a good idea because it contributes to community safety. *What are some other benefits of getting to know your neighbors?*

✓ **Reading Check** **Explain** Why is it smart to get to know your neighbors?

Safety on the Road

The largest proportion of teen deaths and injuries result from motor vehicle crashes. Following basic safety precautions can help prevent accidents and injuries on the road.

- **Wear a Safety Belt** Teens are least likely to wear safety belts, yet they also take the greatest risks when driving or riding in a car. Always wear a safety belt, and insist that others do, too.
- **Follow Traffic Laws** Speeding, running red lights, and making illegal turns are all against the law. Whether you drive, walk, or bike, take traffic laws seriously. They protect you and others.
- **Never Mix Alcohol and Vehicles** Alcohol is involved in more than one-third of deaths involving teen drivers. Do not ever drive after drinking alcohol or let someone who has been drinking alcohol drive you. Take away their keys, if necessary.
- **Stay Focused** When driving, concentrate on driving and on traffic and road conditions. Eating, changing music, talking to friends, and using a cell phone are dangerous distractions.
- **Drive Defensively** When you practice defensive driving, you take steps to minimize the chances of an accident. For example, keep a safe distance from the vehicle ahead of you. If it stops suddenly, you will have enough time to stop, too. Anticipate dangerous situations, and be ready to react.

Health & Wellness TIPS

Home Health and Safety

When looking for a place to live, consider these health and safety issues:

- ▶ Standing water or water damage can result in mold or structural problems.
- ▶ Cracks in a home's structure due to age or earthquakes could lead to parts of the home falling.

 Podcasts Access the Online Learning Center to download *Managing Life Skills* podcasts.

Section 36.2

After You Read

Review Key Concepts

1. **Assess** how to keep poisons out of the hands of children.
2. **List** what telephone numbers should be kept by home phones.
3. **Describe** the purpose of a Neighborhood Watch group.
4. **Define** defensive driving.

 Check Your Answers Check your answers at this book's Online Learning Center at **glencoe.com**.

Practice Academic Skills

 English Language Arts

5. Use print and online resources to research how to make a fire safety escape plan for your home. Plan at least two escape routes, and consider a buddy system for small children, older people, and anyone with a disability. Then write an outline of the escape plan, including where all family members would meet outside.

> **NCTE 12** Use language to accomplish individual purposes.

 Social Studies

6. With your teacher's permission, use the Internet to research the Environmental Protection Agency's "Read the Label First" program. Take notes on the different parts of a pesticide label and what information they provide. Write a summary of the label information, and write two paragraphs on whether you think that the information listed on the label is enough to keep people safe from accidental poisoning.

> **NCSS VI I** Evaluate the extent to which governments achieve their stated ideals and policies at home and abroad.

Pathway to College   Finding Housing

How Do I Find Housing?

There are many college housing options, and there is a lot of information to wade through. You might live at home, in a dorm, or off campus. If you live in a dorm, you will probably have a roommate and possibly less privacy than you are used to. If you live off campus, you will need to find a place and sign a lease for probably the first time in your life.

What do I need to think about when deciding between living on or off campus?

If you can, it is usually a good idea to live in the dorms for at least your first year of college. Many colleges require it. Even if your school allows off-campus housing your first year, living in the dorms can be really helpful. Dorms are usually centrally located, and they can help you jump-start your social life and ease the transition to life on your own.

If I decide to live off campus, how do I find housing?

Finding housing that matches your needs will require patience and persistence. The good news is that you have plenty of resources to help you with your search, including the Internet, neighborhood listings, your school's housing office, and real estate agents. Be prepared for plenty of competition for off-campus housing. Do research, decide what you want, and start your search as early as possible.

What do I need to know about signing a lease?

A lease is a binding, legal contract between you and your landlord, outlining the rights and responsibilities of both parties. It is really important that you, and your parents if possible, read it carefully and understand and agree to everything before signing. Your college's off-campus housing office may also be able to review your lease and give you advice.

College Readiness Choose a city or town you think you might attend college in or near. If you already know where you are going or have a specific college in mind, use that city. With your teacher's permission, go online and research housing options, both on-campus at the school and off-campus in the city or town where the school is located. Pick the three options that you think are the best, and explain your decision.

Path to Success

CCR ★ College & Career Readiness

Give It Some Thought Housing is a very important part of the college experience. Take the decision seriously.

Be Realistic Set your housing sights on housing you can realistically find and afford.

Read It Never sign anything without reading and understanding it.

Consider a Roommate Roommates can be fun and help you save money. Just be sure you are compatible.

Research and Read There is a lot of information and literature about college housing options. The more you know, the better prepared you will be.

Set Ground Rules If you live with roommates, have a discussion about bills, cleaning, and privacy before they become issues.

 Go to this book's Online Learning Center at **glencoe.com** to learn more about college and career readiness.

CHAPTER SUMMARY

Section 36.1
Caring for Your Home

Home care means keeping the home clean, doing routine maintenance, and preventing accidents. Establish a routine, and perform daily and weekly cleaning tasks. Basic cleaning items include a vacuum, broom, cleaning cloths, sponge, bucket, and basic cleaning products. Maintain outdoor areas regularly. Perform seasonal and annual maintenance tasks to prevent larger problems. Other tasks can be performed on an as-needed basis.

Section 36.2
Staying Safe

Common household accidents include falls, cuts, electrical shocks, poisonings, and burns. Most home accidents can be prevented. Prepare for the types of emergencies that can happen in a home. Contribute to the safety of your community by getting to know your neighbors and participating in Neighborhood Watch programs. Protect yourself and others from violence and crime. Practice safe driving skills on the road, and never drink alcohol and drive.

Vocabulary Review

1. Write a sentence using two or more of these vocabulary words. The sentence should clearly show how the words are related.

Content Vocabulary
◇ home care (p. 737)
◇ preventive maintenance (p. 740)
◇ ground fault circuit interrupter (GFCI) (p. 744)
◇ carbon monoxide detector (p. 744)
◇ Neighborhood Watch program (p. 746)

Academic Vocabulary
■ routine (p. 738)
■ slew (p. 740)
■ leading (p. 743)
■ region (p. 745)

Review Key Concepts

2. **List** some of the benefits of home care.
3. **Describe** how establishing a routine can help with cleaning.
4. **Name** seasonal and annual preventive maintenance tasks.
5. **Describe** where falls, cuts, and poisonings are most likely to happen.
6. **List** general measures you can take to prepare for emergencies.
7. **Identify** ways to help keep your community safe.
8. **Discuss** ways to stay safe on the road.

Critical Thinking

9. **Apply** Your friend Tray has a dog that sheds. He wants to set up a schedule for cleaning his carpets. What advice would you give him?
10. **Predict** Tara needs to put away summer patio items in her garage. She must use a ladder to reach the storage space. Should she do this task alone? Why or why not?
11. **Assess** What types of weather-related emergencies are most likely to happen in your area? What can you do to prepare for them?

ACTIVE LEARNING

Family & Community Connections

12. **Develop a Lesson Plan** Follow your teacher's instructions to form groups. As a group, plan and prepare a presentation for grade school-age children about ways to avoid injuries at home. Use information from this chapter as the basis for your presentation. A key component should be teaching children to not leave skateboards, scooters, and other belongings where they could be a hazard to others. You may also focus on other safety tips, such as staying away from household cleaners and preventing burns. Give your presentation to your class. If possible, give your presentation to a grade school class.

13. **Create Cleanliness Slogans** Use the information found in this chapter to create at least three advertising slogans that might encourage people to keep their homes clean and tidy. Once you have created your list of slogans, make a survey to ask people at school or in your neighborhood which slogan they prefer and think would be most convincing. Ask survey participants why they chose a particular slogan. Survey at least 10 people for their opinions. Once you have completed the survey, count the results to figure out which slogan people liked most and thought would be most effective. Create a poster using the winning slogan. Share your slogan and poster with the class, and give a short presentation on why this slogan was the most preferred.

★ 21st Century Skills

Technology Skills

14. **Cleaning Tips** Use a spreadsheet program to create a chart with the headings: Tips, Area, and Schedule. List home maintenance tips in the Tips column. List which part of the home would benefit in the Area column. List how often the task would be done in the Schedule column.

Information Skills

15. **Read Product Labels** Check the warning labels on cleaning products, household chemicals, large and small appliances, and power tools used in or around your home. Take notes on information you did not know before reading the label, and write a one-page summary on the information found on labels and why reading it is important.

FCCLA Connections

Self-Management Skills

16. **Develop Good Habits** As part of its mission, FCCLA encourages students to manage opportunities for personal development and preparation for adult life. Over the next few days, notice a cleaning habit of yours that needs improvement. Write down the habit on a piece of paper. Then make a list of ways to change your habit.

Academic Skills

 English Language Arts

17. Examine a Crime Story Choose a short story or novel that depicts a crime. In your opinion, could the crime have been prevented? What steps could the story or novel character have taken to avoid the crime? Write your opinion in a two-paragraph summary.

> **NCTE 2** Read literature to build an understanding of the human experience.

 Science

18. Research Health Effects Mold in a home can cause many health problems. Mold infestation can result from water damage and wet climates.

Procedure Research the health effects of mold exposure and how it can be prevented. Include details on how mold affects different body systems.

Analysis Detail your findings in a report. Cite your sources. Include images of mold, if possible.

> **NSES F** Develop an understanding of personal and community health.

 Mathematics

19. Find an Average You are planning spring cleaning with a friend. You want to clean for two and one-half hours, but your friend wants to clean for only 45 minutes. You suggest that you both compromise and split the difference. What amount of time should you suggest as a compromise?

Math Concept **Averages** To find the average of a group of numbers, add the numbers together, and divide the total by the quantity of numbers.

Starting Hint Convert the 2½ hours you want to spend cleaning into minutes. There are 60 minutes in an hour, so 150 minutes would equal 2.5 hours (60×2.5). Add 150 minutes to the 45 minutes your friend wants to spend cleaning. Then divide by the number of items you added (2).

 For more math practice, go to the Math Appendix at the back of the book.

> **NCTM Algebra** Use mathematical models to represent and understand quantitative relationships.

 Standardized Test Practice   **CCR College & Career Readiness**

MATH WORD PROBLEMS
Read the problem. Then calculate the correct answer.

> **Test-Taking Tip** In a math word problem, first identify the information you need to solve the problem. Then convert this information into a mathematical equation necessary to solve the problem. After solving the equation, translate the numbers back into words. Present your answer in the wording of the question.

20. You have been asked to purchase cleaning supplies for your home. You must buy window cleaner for $5.95, a mop for $10.50, a bucket for $3.95, paper towels for $5, and floor cleaner for $4.75. You have a $20 bill. Will you have enough money to purchase all the supplies? If so, how much change will you get? If not, how much more do you need?

Chapter 37

Protect the Environment

Chapter Objectives

Section 37.1 Conserve Resources

- **Identify** the two categories of natural resources, and give examples of each.
- **Describe** the different ways in which you can conserve energy.
- **List** tips for conserving water.

Section 37.2 Clean Up the Earth

- **Explain** why and how pollution has become a problem on our planet.
- **Summarize** a plan for managing waste.

▶Explore the Photo

Every person needs to do what is necessary to protect our global environment. *What are the possible consequences of neglecting our responsibility to the environment?*

Writing Activity

Letter to the Editor

Everyone Can Help Our society is designed to give people the freedom to express their opinions. When you respectfully communicate what you think, you invite others to join in a dialogue. Imagine you are writing a letter to the editor of your local newspaper about how important it is for everyone to participate in protecting the environment.

Writing Tips To write a letter to the editor:
- Use letter format with a date, salutation, and closing.
- Write a topic sentence that clearly states your opinion
- Support your views with valid reasons and facts.
- Conclude your letter by restating your opinion.

Section 37.1

Conserve Resources

The future of the earth's resources is in your hands.

Reading Guide

Before You Read

Stay Engaged One way to stay engaged when reading is to turn each of the headings into a question, and then read the section to find the answers to the questions.

Read to Learn
Key Concepts
- **Identify** the two categories of natural resources, and give examples of each.
- **Describe** the different ways in which you can conserve energy.
- **List** tips for conserving water.

Main Idea

Our natural resources are vital to our survival and way of life. Conserving energy and water is an important part of protecting our environment.

Content Vocabulary
◇ global environment
◇ renewable resources
◇ nonrenewable resources
◇ fossil fuels
◇ conservation
◇ biodegradable

Academic Vocabulary

You will find these words in your reading and on your tests. Use the glossary to look up their definitions if necessary.
■ harness
■ accumulate

Academic Standards

English Language Arts

NCTE 3 Apply strategies to interpret texts.

Science

NSES F Develop an understanding of natural resources; environmental quality; science and technology in local, national, and global challenges.

Social Studies

NCSS III F People, Places, and Environments Use knowledge of physical system changes such as seasons, climate and weather, and the water cycle to explain geographic phenomena.

NCTE *National Council of Teachers of English*
NCTM *National Council of Teachers of Mathematics*
NSES *National Science Education Standards*
NCSS *National Council for the Social Studies*

Graphic Organizer

As you read, look for the three categories of a household's biggest energy users and three examples of each category. Use a cluster graphic like the one shown to help you organize your information.

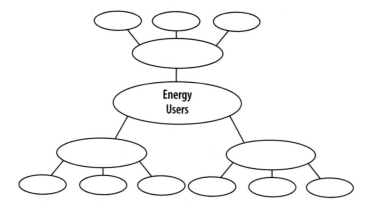

Energy Users

 Graphic Organizer Go to this book's Online Learning Center at **glencoe.com** to print out this graphic organizer.

Earth's Natural Resources

Where do you live? You live in your house, but you also live in a city or town, in a state, in a country, on a continent, and on planet earth. The earth is our home, and just as we protect and take care of our house, we also need to protect and take care of the earth and our environment. All local environments are parts of one greater environmental system. The **global environment** makes up the life support systems of the whole planet. This is why an event in any one place can affect much broader areas. Yet for many years, people have been misusing the very elements that keep them alive.

The resources found in nature include air, water, soil, plants, and minerals. Some, such as clean air and drinking water, are necessary for survival. Others, such as gas, oil, and coal, have become important for maintaining our way of life. Without natural resources, our options would be severely limited. For these reasons and more, natural resources, like any other resources, need to be used wisely.

Types of Resources

The world's natural resources can be divided into two broad categories: renewable and nonrenewable. **Renewable resources**, such as plants, trees, and soil, replace themselves naturally over time. **Nonrenewable resources** cannot be replaced once they are used. Fossil fuels fall into this category. **Fossil fuels** are fuels that come from living matter from a previous geologic time. They include coal, oil, and natural gas. If people continue to rely on fossil fuels for heating, energy production, and transportation, supplies could run dangerously low.

Alternative Energy

Alternative sources of energy, such as wind and solar, are important solutions to the challenge of limited nonrenewable resources. *In what areas can these energy sources replace traditional sources?*

As You Read

Connect What actions have you already taken to protect the environment?

Vocabulary

You can find definitions in the glossary at the back of this book.

Succeed in SCHOOL and LIFE

Be a Conscientious Consumer

One of the most powerful ways you can demonstrate your commitment to protecting the environment is with your purchasing decisions. If you feel strongly about recycling, make sure you buy products from companies that use recyclable packaging. If you are concerned about conserving natural resources, research companies that share your concern, and purchase products from them.

There are limited supplies of nonrenewable resources, so active conservation is necessary. **Conservation** is the careful management and protection of natural resources. The challenge in managing natural resources is to meet present-day needs without sacrificing the well-being of citizens in the future. Most conservation efforts focus on using fewer nonrenewable resources. One strategy is to use renewable resources instead. Governments and industries continue to investigate alternative forms of energy that **harness**, or capture, the power of wind, waves, and the sun.

It is easy to assume that governments will take care of environmental problems, but governments cannot do it alone. People must be willing to help steer their governments and cooperate with government rulings trying to protect the environment. There are many ways in which individuals like you can make a difference.

✓ **Reading Check** **Give Examples** What are some commonly used fossil fuels?

HOW TO . . . . Conserve Energy

Every day brings an opportunity to develop your energy conserving habits. Your efforts to conserve, along with the efforts of millions of other people, will lead to real results. Remember, it only takes a few simple changes to make a world of difference. Here are a few suggestions:

Lower the Heat During cold weather, set the thermostat no higher than 68°F (20°C) while people are home. Lower the thermostat even more at night and when no one will be home for four hours or more.

Close Off the Fireplace If you have a fireplace, close the damper when it is not in use. This will prevent warm air from escaping up the chimney.

Close Doors Close off rooms that are not being used by shutting the door and closing any vents and registers. Keep closet doors closed throughout the home.

Get the Most Out of the Water Heater Keep your water heater set at "normal" or 120°F (49°C). Wrap insulation around the water heater and the pipes that lead to it. The insulation will save additional energy by holding in the heat.

Go Easy on the A/C In warm weather, try to use fans instead of an air conditioner. When you run central air conditioning, set the thermostat to no more than 15 degrees below the outside temperature. Never set it lower than 78°F (26°C).

Use Window Coverings On cold days, open blinds or draperies on the sunny side of the home, and close them when the sun sets. On hot days, keep the sunshine out and your home cooler by closing drapes and shades.

Conserving Energy

When you take steps to conserve energy, you help reduce the demand for fossil fuels so that the supply of these nonrenewable resources will last longer.

How much energy does your family use? The answer depends on some unchangeable factors such as the size of your family, the age and condition of your home, and the climate where you live.

Heating and cooling systems, water heaters, refrigeration, and laundry appliances consume most of the energy used in the typical home. Lighting, cooking, computers, appliances, and entertainment account for the rest. The energy used for transportation depends on where you live and your family's general lifestyle. If your family is like most, you can save energy by following some basic conservation measures.

Science For Success

Alternative Energy

Natural resources can provide alternative sources of energy. Alternative energy sources can be used instead of fossil fuels, coal, wood, and uranium. Alternative energy sources should be renewable, nonpolluting, easy to get, and affordable.

Procedure Collect data about alternative power sources. Create a chart that includes the alternative sources of energy and how they are used.

Analysis Which alternative energy sources are used most? Which do you think could be used more?

> **NSES F** Develop an understanding of natural resources; environmental quality; science and technology in local, national, and global challenges.

Heating and Cooling

Heating systems, air conditioners, and water heaters use a lot of energy, so they are effective targets for your conservation efforts. Families can conserve energy by making the following basic home improvements:

- Seal joints in your heating system to stop leaks.
- Install weather stripping around doors and windows.
- Add insulation to the attic.

Appliances and Lighting

When you get home today, check to see how many appliances are running needlessly. Is a television playing to an empty room? Is a fan cooling a room that nobody is using? You can save energy by switching off electrical appliances when you are not using them. Here are some additional opportunities for saving energy on appliances:

- **Refrigerator** Do not leave the refrigerator door open any longer than necessary. Take out or put away your items, and promptly close the door.
- **Dishwasher** Run the dishwasher only when you have a full load. Use the energy-saver cycle.
- **Oven** Avoid using the oven in hot weather. Use a microwave oven or toaster oven for heating small quantities of food. Avoid opening the oven while food is cooking.
- **Washer and Dryer** Accumulate, or collect, laundry until you have a full load. Run the dryer only as long as necessary. Be sure to clean the lint filter after each load.

Be Smart Be Safe

Mass Transit Safety Using mass transit helps protect the environment. However, when you take the bus or train, make sure you are protecting yourself as well. It is important to be aware of what is around you at all times.

Write About It Write a list of safety tips for teens who take mass transit. Include advice for staying safe while waiting and while onboard the vehicle.

You can also take a major step toward saving energy by choosing energy-efficient appliances. When shopping for appliances, take time to compare the EnergyGuide labels, which estimate the cost of running the appliance for one year. Also look for Energy Star labels on major appliances.

Lighting provides another opportunity to conserve. Get into the habit of turning off lights when they are not needed. Do not keep several lights on in a room if you need just one near you. You might also replace standard bulbs with compact fluorescent bulbs that use less energy and last longer.

Transportation

Driving alone to school or work is the least energy-efficient form of transportation. Mass transit, carpools, and bicycles are three means of transportation that help people conserve energy and reduce air pollution.

When you must use a car, choose a vehicle that is fuel efficient, meaning it has high gas mileage. The more miles to the gallon a vehicle gets, the less fuel it will need to use. The size of a vehicle and its engine determine the gas mileage that you can expect. Trucks, sport utility vehicles, and large cars generally require the most fuel. Hybrid electric vehicles, or HEVs, are able to achieve superior fuel economy.

✓ **Reading Check** **Illustrate** What are some ways to save energy on lighting?

Life On Your Own

Purchase Appliances

It is likely that at some point in your life, you will need to purchase a major appliance such as a refrigerator or a washing machine. When that time comes, you will need to know what to look for in an appliance, taking into consideration your own needs and the environmental impact of the item you purchase. Whether you make the right choice will depend on how much you know before you enter the appliance store.

How It Works To make a wise appliance purchase, it pays to do some "homework." Research various brands and models of that appliance, taking into account factors such as size, features, warranty, and energy savings. Look for appliances that have met the Energy Star energy-saving standards. When you go to the store, look at The EnergyGuide label on the appliance for precise information on how energy efficient the appliance is.

Try It Out You have just moved into your own place. It came with a dryer but no washing machine, so you are going to have to buy one. You know that you need a machine that can handle a medium load of heavily soiled laundry every week, but you also need to watch your water and energy bills. You have a limited about of space and a tight budget.

Your Turn What is the first thing you would do in this situation? What process would you undertake in looking for the right machine? How long do you think it would take you to find it?

Conserve Water

Whether or not you live in an area affected by water shortages, you should always try to conserve water. Conserving water saves energy and ensures that there is an adequate supply for everyone. Follow these suggestions to conserve water:

- Take a quick shower instead of a bath. On average, a bath uses 20 gallons of water, while a short shower uses 8 to 12 gallons.
- Install low-flow showerheads and faucet aerators. This will allow you to use only about half as much water, but the water will feel as though it is running full force.
- Do not let water run continuously while you brush your teeth, shave, or shower. Instead, run water only while you need it.
- While washing dishes, fill a dishpan or sink for washing and another for rinsing. Washing and rinsing dishes under continuously running water wastes about 30 gallons of water per meal.
- Fix dripping faucets and other water leaks promptly.
- Do not overwater your lawn or garden. If you water with sprinklers, use them during early morning hours. Choose plants that thrive in your region without frequent watering.
- Use biodegradable detergents. A **biodegradable** product is formulated to break down easily in the environment.
- Do not dump hazardous wastes into drains or sewers.

Go Green

Stay informed by following environmental issues at the community, state, national, and international levels. Consider donating time or money to worthwhile environmental organizations.

 Podcasts Access the Online Learning Center to download *Managing Life Skills* podcasts.

Section 37.1 — After You Read

Review Key Concepts

1. **Explain** how an environmental event in one town affects people in towns far away.
2. **Identify** the unchangeable factors that influence how much energy your family uses.
3. **Calculate** how much water is saved by taking a short shower instead of a bath.

 Check Your Answers Check your answers at this book's Online Learning Center at **glencoe.com**.

Practice Academic Skills

 English Language Arts

4. Find a poem or short essay that expresses concern for the natural environment. Create an art project that represents the written piece. It may be a drawing, poster, collage, sculpture, or any other visual interpretation. Give a presentation displaying your project while you read the poem or essay aloud.

NCTE 3 Apply strategies to interpret texts.

 Social Studies

5. Visit the home page of the Environmental Protection Agency's Web site. Enter your zip code to access environmental information about your area. Write a summary describing what you learn.

NCSS III F Use knowledge of physical system changes such as seasons, climate, and weather, and the water cycle to explain geographic phenomena.

Clean Up the Earth

What is more important than the air that you breathe?

Reading Guide

Before You Read

Vocabulary To gain a better understanding of vocabulary, divide a piece of paper into three columns. Label the columns, Vocabulary, What is it?, and What else is it like? Write down each word, and answer the questions as you read.

Read to Learn

Key Concepts

- **Explain** why and how pollution has become a problem on our planet.
- **Summarize** a plan for managing waste.

Main Idea

Protecting our environment involves taking steps to control air, water, and land pollution. You can use a "reduce, reuse, and recycle" strategy to minimize waste.

Content Vocabulary

◇ pollution
◇ pollutant
◇ global warming
◇ ozone layer
◇ acid rain
◇ landfill
◇ precycling
◇ recycled-content products

Academic Vocabulary

You will find these words in your reading and on your tests. Use the glossary to look up their definitions if necessary.

■ generate
■ transform

Academic Standards

English Language Arts

NCTE 4 Use written language to communicate effectively.

Mathematics

NCTM Number and Operations Compute fluently and make reasonable estimates.

Social Studies

NCSS VI B Power, Authority, and Governance Explain the purpose of government and analyze how its powers are acquired, used, and justified.

Graphic Organizer

As you read, look for the ways in which you can reuse everyday items. Use a before-and-after graphic like the one shown to help you organize your information.

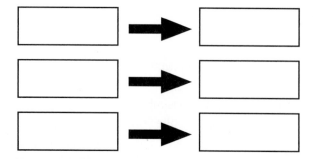

 Graphic Organizer Go to this book's Online Learning Center at **glencoe.com** to print out this graphic organizer.

NCTE *National Council of Teachers of English*
NCTM *National Council of Teachers of Mathematics*
NSES *National Science Education Standards*
NCSS *National Council for the Social Studies*

How Pollution Occurs

A major component to protecting our environment is taking steps to control pollution. **Pollution** is the presence of harmful substances in the environment. One of these harmful substances is referred to as a **pollutant**. Some pollution occurs naturally, like when a volcano erupts. Most pollution, however, is caused by people. Industrial nations are responsible for most of the world's pollution. Industry, automobiles, intensive agriculture, and other human activities all release pollutants into the environment. Each type of pollution, whether it occurs in the air, water, or land, has many harmful effects.

Air pollution occurs when harmful gases and chemicals are released into the air. Breathing polluted air has been linked to medical conditions ranging from asthma and bronchitis to cancer and damage to the nervous system. Like water pollution, air pollution can affect areas far from the source of the pollution.

Air pollution is linked to wider environmental concerns such as global warming, the depletion of the ozone layer, and acid rain. **Global warming** is the gradual increase in the earth's surface temperature caused by depletion of the earth's ozone layer. Global warming has a far-reaching effect on all forms of life on our planet. The **ozone layer** is a layer in the earth's upper atmosphere that is meant to block and protect the earth from most of the sun's harmful ultraviolet rays. **Acid rain** is the environmentally damaging and physically harmful rain that results from the combination of fossil fuel emission and water in the atmosphere.

⚠ The Pollution Problem

Pollution of our air, water, and land ultimately affects everyone. *Why might some people not want to admit that pollution is a problem?*

As You Read

Connect Think of a recent example of pollution that you saw or read about. How did it make you feel?

◇ Vocabulary

You can find definitions in the glossary at the back of this book.

Succeed in SCHOOL and LIFE

Become a Recycling Expert

Schools are ideal places for recycling. From notebook paper to juice bottles, students use a lot of materials in the course of a day. Talk to an administrator about your school's current recycling program, if you have one. Find out how you can become a resource for students, providing recycling information and opportunities to step up their efforts.

Math For Success

Water pollution comes from chemicals and other waste products that make their way into oceans, rivers, lakes, streams, and groundwater. Water is categorized as a renewable resource, yet the supply is limited. Only about 1 percent of the planet's water is fresh water. Polluted water can kill fish and other forms of marine life and can cause serious health problems for humans. Once polluted, water is difficult and costly to clean.

Land pollution results from the disposal of household and industrial waste. Humans produce millions of tons of garbage each year. Most solid waste goes into a **landfill**, a huge pit where waste is dumped and buried. The landfills in many areas are filling up, and there is a shortage of available land for additional landfills. No one wants a landfill near their house or in their neighborhood, but all the garbage has to go somewhere.

The United States already works with many other countries to limit waste and control pollution. Within the United States, numerous programs have been established at the federal, state, and local levels to protect the environment. The Clean Water Act and the Clean Air Act, for example, regulate the amount of pollution-causing substances that can be discharged into the water and air. Other acts ban the use of certain harmful chemicals and set controls on the exhaust emissions from vehicles.

However, it is up to individuals like you to work within your home and community to cut down on the waste that contributes to our global pollution problem. Try to keep this in mind every day, as you decide whether it is worth the effort to recycle an aluminum can or how many paper towels to use to clean up a spill.

✓ Reading Check **Recall** What portion of our planet's water supply is considered fresh water?

Reduce, Reuse, Recycle

You are probably familiar with the slogan, "Reduce, Reuse, and Recycle." But how well are you putting that slogan into practice? American families continue to **generate**, or produce, enormous amounts of waste that must be sent to landfills. As you read the suggestions that follow, identify the changes that could be made in your home to reduce the amount of waste that your family generates.

Reduce

As a consumer, you can reduce waste by making environmentally responsible choices. This practice is called **precycling**. In the grocery store, for example, avoid items with excess packaging, and instead look for products with minimal packaging. Your choices will send a message to manufacturers and influence their packaging designs in the future. Here are some additional suggestions for reducing waste:

- When going grocery shopping, bring your own cloth or plastic bags to the store in which to take your groceries home. Use these bags over and over again.
- Buy the items that you use frequently in large quantities to cut down on packaging.
- Buy foods such as dried fruits and grains from bulk containers whenever possible.
- Cut back on single-use disposable products, such as plastic and paper cups and plates.
- Reuse lunch bags and water bottles.
- Use reusable containers and cloth napkins that you can use, wash, and use again.
- Rent or borrow items that you use only occasionally, and offer to loan items you have to others.

Two Views One World

Is Conservation Good for the Economy?

While everyone supports the health of the planet, many feel that some measures may hurt businesses and have a negative impact on our economy.

Erica: I think that the only way we're going to clean up our planet is if companies cut back on manufacturing so many goods. We really don't need all of the products that are made, and the factories pump out tons of pollutants that are ruining our environment. We'd be better off planting more trees and crops and making fewer unnecessary items that are just for our amusement.

Antonio: It's not going to do us any good to have fewer factories if it's going to put a lot of people out of work. I agree that people need clean air and water, but they also need jobs. If we cut back on manufacturing, we'll end up with more unemployment. Then people will have less money, and our economy will go down the drain. It won't matter how clean our air is if no one has a job and our economy is in horrible shape.

Seeing Both Sides
Is there a way you can imagine a cleaner environment that would not create economic problems? Is it possible to keep the jobs while reducing the pollutants in the air and water?

Responsible Choices

Your manager has asked you to order and serve lunch for 12 people at a workplace meeting. The restaurant offers you two choices: twelve boxed lunches in individual containers, which can be easily served but would create a lot of non-biodegradable trash, or one extra-large serving of salad and an extra-large lasagna casserole, which would need to be dished into individual plates.

You Decide

What are the pros and cons of each option? How might you minimize the downside of each? What would you eventually choose and why?

Reuse

The night before trash is picked up in Ernest's neighborhood, the residents set useful items by the curbside. Ernest has seen a computer monitor, old patio chairs, a barbecue grill, and even a guitar and drum kit. By morning, the unwanted items are usually gone. Whether the recipients needed the items for their own use or hoped to sell them, the end result benefits the environment. The item is reused and stays out of the landfill.

Every time you reuse items, you cut down on the need to discard and replace them. For example, instead of buying special boxes in which to store photographs and keepsakes, Malika creates her own made of shoe boxes covered with fabric remnants. Perhaps you could save used printer paper, and use the back of it for jotting down notes or shopping lists. What are some other ideas for reusing everyday items in your home?

Another way to reuse is to share. For example, do not dispose of leftover paint or varnish. Instead, pass it on to a friend who can use it. Give household items and clothing to someone you know or to charitable groups that will distribute them to people who can use them. Find out whether your library accepts used books. Nursing homes, primary schools, and organizations such as Scout troops and 4-H clubs may appreciate your old greeting cards for use in craft projects.

Buying used goods at vintage stores and garage sales is another way to reuse products that already exist. You should also consider switching from disposable products to reusable products. Keep this in mind next time you are buying cups, plates, food and beverage containers, pens, razors, diapers, towels, or shopping bags.

Recycle

Recycling is a way to **transform**, or change, an item in some way so that the materials in it can be used again. Aluminum cans, for example, can be melted down and made into sheets of aluminum that can be used to make more cans. Many communities have programs for recycling aluminum, paper, plastics, and glass.

Recycling has three main advantages: it conserves energy, it conserves natural resources, and it helps reduce waste. Thanks to individual and community efforts, millions of tons of items that might have ended up in landfills have been made into something useful instead.

◀ **Reduce, Reuse, Recycle**

Everyone in the family can get in the habit of recycling.
How does the recycling program in your community work?

If your community has a recycling program, be sure you and your family make full use of it. Look for other opportunities to recycle too. You might find businesses or organizations in your community that collect items such as used plastic bags, batteries, or printer cartridges for recycling.

Remember that for recycling to be successful, there must be a strong market for the products made with recovered materials. **Recycled-content products** are items made partially or totally from materials that might have ended up in a landfill. The products range from plastic lumber and deck furniture to egg cartons and paper towels. Products made from recovered materials and products that can be recycled are both marked by symbols. Choose these products whenever possible.

While many things are able to be recycled, it is also important to know what cannot be recycled. Read up on the recycling rules for your area to make sure you do not try to recycle anything that cannot be processed as this just slows down the recycling process.

Recycling offers an opportunity to demonstrate your commitment with everyday actions. This sends a powerful message. The example you set will have a positive effect on classmates, friends, and family members. When you see others taking responsibility for the environment, show that you support them. Remember that everything you do counts and that you can make a difference.

Get Involved!

Start Your Own Organization

If you want to volunteer at a specific type of environmental organization, but it does not exist in your community, why not start your own? If you think it is a good idea, chances are other people in your community will too. It is a great way to give back to your community while also taking on a leadership role.

 Podcasts Access the Online Learning Center to download *Managing Life Skills* podcasts.

Section 37.2   After You Read

Review Key Concepts

1. **Identify** the kinds of health problems that are associated with air pollution.
2. **List** the ways in which you can reduce waste.

Practice Academic Skills

 English Language Arts

3. Write a descriptive essay about a natural environment that you have visited and enjoyed. Use details inspired by all five of the senses to create a strong sense of place for the reader. Make sure to title your essay.

 Social Studies

4. The 1990 Clean Air Act was enacted by the Environmental Protection Agency to protect human health and the environment. Research this important environmental law. Then create a list of at least three major goals of the law. Be prepared to discuss the role of government agencies in regulating activities that affect the environment.

Check Your Answers Check your answers at this book's Online Learning Center at **glencoe.com**.

NCTE 4 Use written language to communicate effectively.

NCSS VI B Explain the purpose of government and analyze how its powers are acquired, used, and justified.

Pathway to Your Career

Environmental Engineer

What Does an Environmental Engineer Do?

Environmental engineers work to find solutions to environmental problems, such as water and air pollution, using chemistry, biology, and other sciences. They work on recycling, pollution control, waste disposal, and public health issues. They also conduct research to predict the environmental impact of proposed projects, and they attempt to minimize the effects of global warming, acid rain, automobile emissions, and ozone depletion.

Career Readiness Skills Environmental engineers should be creative, inquisitive, and detail oriented. They need to have a strong interest in and head for science and mathematics and excellent analytical skills. They should also have good teamwork skills.

Education and Training A bachelor's degree in engineering is required for many entry-level jobs. Engineers trained in one branch often end up working in related branches, allowing engineers to shift to fields with better employment prospects or that they are more interested in. A graduate degree is essential for many faculty positions and research programs.

Job Outlook Environmental engineer job prospects should grow 25 percent during the next decade, much faster than the average. This growth will be due to more environmental regulations, increasing public health concerns, and a general increase in awareness of and concern for our environment.

Critical Thinking Think of one of the environmental problems that we are currently dealing with. Relate this problem to your own life. How does it affect you? Is there anything you can do personally to help with the problem?

Career Cluster

CCR College & Career Readiness

Manufacturing Environmental engineers work in the Health, Safety & Environmental Assurance pathway of this career cluster. Other jobs in this cluster include:

- Painter
- Tool Maker
- Welder
- Safety Coordinator
- Electrician
- Inspector
- Lab Technician
- Sheet Metal Worker
- Industrial Engineer
- Shipping and Receiving Clerk
- Plumber
- Safety Engineer

Explore Further The Manufacturing career cluster contains six pathways: Production; Manufacturing Production Process Development; Maintenance, Installation & Repair; Quality Assurance; Logistics & Inventory Control; and Health, Safety & Environmental Assurance. Choose one of these pathways to explore further.

 Career Clusters To learn more about career clusters, go to this book's Online Learning Center at **glencoe.com**.

CHAPTER SUMMARY

Section 37.1
Conserve Resources

Everyone must work to solve global environmental problems. Renewable resources can replace themselves over time, and nonrenewable resources cannot. Active conservation is needed to protect natural resources. Energy conservation reduces fuel consumption and cuts back on air pollution. You can conserve energy and water by paying attention to your usage patterns and changing wasteful habits.

Section 37.2
Clean Up the Earth

Pollution of the air, water, and land results mainly from human activities. Air pollution is linked to global warming, the depletion of the ozone layer, and acid rain. Our supply of fresh water is limited, and so it is important to conserve water. Land pollution results from the disposal of household and industrial waste. You can cut back on waste by reducing, reusing, and recycling.

Vocabulary Review

1. Find a visual example in the textbook or bring one in from home of each of these vocabulary words: global environment; renewable resources; nonrenewable resources; pollutant.

Content Vocabulary
◇ global environment (p. 755)
◇ renewable resources (p. 755)
◇ nonrenewable resources (p. 755)
◇ fossil fuels (p. 755)
◇ conservation (p. 756)
◇ biodegradable (p. 759)
◇ pollution (p. 761)

◇ pollutant (p. 761)
◇ global warming (p. 761)
◇ ozone layer (p. 761)
◇ acid rain (p. 761)
◇ landfill (p. 762)
◇ precycling (p. 763)
◇ recycled-content products (p. 765)

Academic Vocabulary
■ harness (p. 756)
■ accumulate (p. 757)
■ generate (p. 762)
■ transform (p. 764)

Review Key Concepts

2. **Identify** the two categories of natural resources, and give examples of each.
3. **Describe** the different ways in which you can conserve energy.
4. **List** tips for conserving fresh water.
5. **Explain** why and how pollution has become a problem on our planet.
6. **Summarize** a plan for managing waste.

Critical Thinking

7. **Generalize** Which conservation measure do you think could bring about the greatest benefit to the environment if everyone practiced it? Why?
8. **Hypothesize** What can happen if some nations agree to follow strict environmental guidelines while others do not?
9. **Conclude** Why do some people end up living near landfills, even though they may pose health risks?
10. **Draw Conclusions** Do you think that using 100 percent of our conservation and waste management options would cost or save money?
11. **Analyze** Can one person make a difference in a global problem?

ACTIVE LEARNING

Family & Community Connections

12. School-Wide Conservation Sometimes in large facilities like schools, natural resources are wasted because everyone is too busy doing their jobs to spot opportunities to conserve. Follow your teacher's instructions to form into small groups. As a group, identify ways in which your school might be wasting energy. Take into account the suggestions mentioned in this chapter. Make a list of specific actions that teachers, students, school administrators, and other workers could take to conserve. Write your recommendations in a proposal, and submit it to the appropriate school administrators.

13. Household Waste Families can produce a lot of unnecessary waste in a brief amount of time. In most cases, the larger the household, the greater the waste management problem. Fortunately, this can often be remedied with an agreed-upon family policy. Call a family meeting to discuss specific ways to reduce the amount of waste your family throws out weekly. Pinpoint the areas where the greater waste occurs. Is it in beverage packaging? Food wrappers and boxes? Junk mail? Newspapers? Paper goods? Encourage everyone to contribute ideas. Choose the three best suggestions by taking a vote. Follow those suggestions for one week, and then evaluate how effective they were. Report on your results in class. Discuss how the program may be improved.

★ 21ˢᵗ Century Skills

Creativity Skills

14. Recycling Containers Use recyclable material to create at-home recycling containers for paper, glass, plastic, and aluminum. Decorate the containers with eye-catching words and pictures. Take digital pictures of the bins to share online with other environmentally aware teens.

Technology Skills

15. CFL Savings Compact fluorescent light bulbs, or CFLs, can use as much as 75 percent less energy and last about 10 times longer than typical incandescent light bulbs. How do they do this? Research the technology behind CFLs. Explain it in a short written report.

FCCLA Connections

Responsibility Skills

16. Organizational Involvement As part of its mission, FCCLA encourages students to help achieve global cooperation and harmony. Find out how you can become involved in environmental protection efforts in your community. Investigate existing programs run by the state and local government, public utilities, industry, and environmental organizations. Share your findings.

Academic Skills

 English Language Arts

17. Earth's Point of View If the earth could talk to us, what would it say? Suppose you were the earth itself. Imagine what it would feel like to be the air, water, and land in their current condition. Speaking as the earth, write a letter to your inhabitants about the environment, asking for action on your behalf.

> **NCTE 5** Use different writing process elements to communicate effectively.

 Science

18. Water Pollution When we use a chemical in our home, there is a chance it will end up in our water supply. Once an acidic chemical has been dissolved into fresh water, how hard is it to remove?

Procedure Test 50 mL of water with litmus paper for acid levels. Then add 50 mL of vinegar, and retest the water. Pour the water and vinegar solution through filter paper, and test it again.

Analysis Analyze the three pieces of litmus paper and the filter. Did the filter remove the acid from the water?

> **NSES B** Develop an understanding of the properties of matter.

 Mathematics

19. Cutting Energy Costs Using energy efficient appliances, monitoring heating and cooling, and using energy-saving light bulbs can greatly reduce your energy costs. You are trying to use less energy. Imagine that presently, your appliances cost you $850 per year to operate. However, you have discovered that if you buy energy efficient appliances, you can save 15 percent a year. How much will you save if you use the appliances for ten years?

Math Concept **Percent Calculation** A percent is a ratio that compares a number to 100. To find the percentage of a number, take the percent and convert it to a decimal by moving the decimal point two places to the right.

Starting Hint Take the $850 and multiply by 0.15 to find the yearly savings. Then multiply this answer by 10 years to get the total savings.

 For more math practice, go to the Math Appendix at the back of the book.

> **NCTM Number and Operations** Understand numbers, ways of representing numbers, relationships among numbers, and number systems.

 ## Standardized Test Practice

 CCR College & Career Readiness

TRUE/FALSE
Based on what you read in this chapter, decide whether this statement is true or false.

> **Test-Taking Tip** Make sure you understand the full statement. All parts of a statement must be correct for the statement to be true.

20. The more miles to the gallon a vehicle gets, the more fuel it will use.

  a. True

  b. False

Prepare for an Interview

In this project, you will work with a partner to find a job lead that appeals to both of you. You will interview a hiring manager to find out more about effective job interviews and then prepare for a mock job interview. Finally, you and your partner will interview each other.

My Journal

If you completed the journal entry from page 694, refer to it to see if your thoughts have changed after reading the unit.

Project Assignment

In this project you will:

- Choose a partner, and find an appropriate job lead.
- Research information about the hiring company.
- Write three questions about the company and job duties.
- Participate in mock interviews with your partner.
- Take notes about the experience.
- Give a presentation to the class with your partner about the experience.

THE SKILLS BEHIND THE PROJECT

Key personal and relationship skills you will use in this project include:

- Gathering and consolidating information
- Working together with a partner
- Communicating respectfully

Academic Skills

English Language Arts

NCTE 7 Conduct research and gather, evaluate, and synthesize data to communicate discoveries.

NCTE 12 Use language to accomplish individual purposes.

STEP 1 Find an Appropriate Job Lead

Follow your teacher's instructions to form pairs. With your partner, search for a job lead. You may find the lead online, in a newspaper, or in a magazine. Use these guidelines to help you find a job lead:

- Choose a lead that lists the name of the hiring company.
- Choose a job that appeals to both you and your partner.
- Choose a lead that lists specific information about the duties required for the job.

STEP 2 Research the Hiring Company

Use print and online resources to research information about the hiring company you and your partner have chosen. Take notes on the information, and write a summary of your findings. Develop three questions to find out more about the company and the job lead. Write down your questions using word processing software.

Research Skills

- Perform research using a variety of resource materials.
- Synthesize and organize information.
- Take notes on your research, and write a summary of your findings.

STEP 3   Connect with Your Community

Take turns with your partner in a mock interview. One of you should play the role of the hiring manager, while the other plays the role of the job candidate. Then, switch roles so you can each experience both sides of the interview. Prepare a cover letter for your interview, and use your job portfolio. Ask the questions you have developed, and take notes on your experiences in both roles.

Interview Skills

- Use standard English to communicate.
- Listen respectfully.
- Record responses, and take notes during the interview.

STEP 4   Build Your Portfolio Project

Use the Portfolio Project Checklist to create a presentation with your partner on what you learned about both roles during the interview.

Interpersonal Skills

- Work cooperatively with your partner.
- Be sensitive to the needs of your audience.
- Be aware of nonverbal communication.

STEP 5   Evaluate Your Project

Your portfolio project will be evaluated based on:

Academic Skills

- Extent of your research
- Preparation for your interview
- Interviewing skills
- Clarity of your presentation
- Speaking and listening skills

Evaluation Rubric Go to this book's Online Learning Center at **glencoe.com** for a rubric you can use to evaluate your final project.

PORTFOLIO PROJECT CHECKLIST

Plan

✔ Write a cover letter, and prepare your job portfolio for use during your mock interview.

✔ Be respectful during your interview as a candidate, and highlight your experience and skills that match the job duties. Take notes about the experience.

✔ Be courteous during your interview as a hiring manager, and create answers to the candidate's questions to the best of your ability. Take notes about the experience.

Present

✔ Compile your notes, and create a presentation with your partner to share your experiences with the class.

✔ Invite the students to ask questions. Answer the questions. Demonstrate in your answers that you respect their perspectives.

✔ Turn in your research summary, interview notes, and cover letter to your teacher.

Portfolio Highlights

Preparing Answers

Different employers will ask different questions during a job interview. You should prepare answers to all types of questions so you will be ready, even if you are nervous.

Consider Everyday Job Situations

More and more employers are asking job candidates to describe the actions they would take in certain situations on the job. Before you go for an interview, think about what situations you might face on the job and how you might handle them.

Benefit to the Company

Use your experience and skills to think of ways you might benefit the company. Then prepare for an interview by using statements that highlight this. For example, rather than saying, "I have excellent writing skills," you might say, "I can use my writing skills to better communicate with vendors."

Turn Weaknesses into Strengths

A common interview question is, "What is your greatest weakness?" This can be hard to answer positively, but it is an opportunity to showcase your problem-solving skills. Explain a weakness along with how you compensate for it or overcome it.

Number and Operations

▶ Understand numbers, ways of representing numbers, relationships among numbers, and number systems

Fraction, Decimal, and Percent

A percent is a ratio of a number to 100. To write a percent as a fraction, drop the percent sign, and use the number as the numerator in a fraction with a denominator of 100. Simplify, if possible. For example, $76\% = \frac{76}{100}$, or $\frac{19}{25}$. To write a fraction as a percent, convert it to an equivalent fraction with a denominator of 100. For example, $\frac{3}{4} = \frac{75}{100}$, or 75%. A fraction can be expressed as a percent by first converting the fraction to a decimal (divide the numerator by the denominator) and then converting the decimal to a percent by moving the decimal point two places to the right.

Comparing Numbers on a Number Line

In order to compare and understand the relationship between real numbers in various forms, it is helpful to use a number line. The zero point on a number line is called the origin. The points to the left of the origin are negative, and those to the right are positive. The number line below shows how numbers in fraction, decimal, percent, and integer form can be compared.

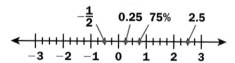

Percents Greater Than 100 and Less Than 1

Percents greater than 100% represent values greater than 1. For example, if the weight of an object is 250% of another, it is 2.5, or $2\frac{1}{2}$, times the weight.

Percents less than 1 represent values less than $\frac{1}{100}$. In other words, 0.1% is one tenth of one percent, which can also be represented in decimal form as 0.001, or in fraction form as $\frac{1}{1,000}$. Similarly, 0.01% is one hundredth of one percent or 0.0001 or $\frac{1}{10,000}$.

Ratio, Rate, and Proportion

A ratio is a comparison of two numbers using division. If a basketball player makes 8 out of 10 free throws, the ratio is written as 8 to 10, 8:10, or $\frac{8}{10}$. Ratios are usually written in simplest form. In simplest form, the ratio 8 out of 10 is 4 to 5, 4:5, or $\frac{4}{5}$. A rate is a ratio of two measurements having different kinds of units—cups per gallon, or miles per hour, for example. When a rate is simplified so that it has a denominator of 1, it is called a unit rate. An example of a unit rate is 9 miles per hour. A proportion is an equation stating that two ratios are equal. $\frac{3}{18} = \frac{13}{78}$ is an example of a proportion. The cross products of a proportion are also equal. $\frac{3}{18} = \frac{13}{78}$ and $3 \times 78 = 18 \times 13$.

Representing Large and Small Numbers

In order to represent large and small numbers, it is important to understand the number system. Our number system is based on 10, and the value of each place is 10 times the value of the place to its right. The value of a digit is the product of a digit and its place value. For instance, in the number 6,400, the 6 has a value of six thousands and the 4 has a value of four hundreds. A place value chart can help you read numbers. In the chart, each group of three digits is called a period. Commas separate the periods: the ones period, the thousands period, the millions period, and so on. Values to the right of the ones period are decimals. By understanding place value you can write very large numbers like 5 billion and more, and very small numbers that are less than 1, like one-tenth.

Scientific Notation

When dealing with very large numbers like 1,500,000, or very small numbers like 0.000015, it is helpful to keep track of their value by writing the numbers in scientific notation. Powers of 10 with positive exponents are used with a decimal between 1 and 10 to express large numbers. The exponent represents the number of places the decimal point is moved to the right. So, 528,000 is written in scientific notation as 5.28×10^5. Powers of 10 with negative exponents are used with a decimal between 1 and 10 to express small numbers. The exponent represents the number of places the decimal point is moved to the left. The number 0.00047 is expressed as 4.7×10^{-4}.

Factor, Multiple, and Prime Factorization

Two or more numbers that are multiplied to form a product are called factors. Divisibility rules can be used to determine whether 2, 3, 4, 5, 6, 8, 9, or 10 are factors of a given number.

Multiples are the products of a given number and various integers.

For example, 8 is a multiple of 4 because $4 \times 2 = 8$. A prime number is a whole number that has exactly two factors: 1 and itself. A composite number is a whole number that has more than two factors. Zero and 1 are neither prime nor composite. A composite number can be expressed as the product of its prime factors. The prime factorization of 40 is $2 \times 2 \times 2 \times 5$, or $2^3 \times 5$. The numbers 2 and 5 are prime numbers.

Integers

A negative number is a number less than zero. Negative numbers like -8, positive numbers like $+6$, and zero are members of the set of integers. Integers can be represented as points on a number line. A set of integers can be written $\{\dots, -3, -2, -1, 0, 1, 2, 3, \dots\}$ where $\dots$ means continues indefinitely.

Real, Rational, and Irrational Numbers

The real number system is made up of the sets of rational and irrational numbers. Rational numbers are numbers that can be written in the form $\frac{a}{b}$ where a and b are integers and $b \neq 0$. Examples are 0.45, $\frac{1}{2}$, and $\sqrt{36}$. Irrational numbers are non-repeating, non-terminating decimals. Examples are $\sqrt{71}$, π, and $0.020020002\dots$.

Complex and Imaginary Numbers

A complex number is a mathematical expression with a real number element and an imaginary number element. Imaginary numbers are multiples of i, the imaginary square root of -1. Complex numbers are represented by $a + bi$, where a and b are real numbers and i represents the imaginary element. When a quadratic equation does not have a real number solution, the solution can be represented by a complex number. Like real numbers, complex numbers can be added, subtracted, multiplied, and divided.

Vectors and Matrices

A matrix is a set of numbers or elements arranged in rows and columns to form a rectangle. The number of rows is represented by m and the number of columns is represented by n. To describe the number of rows and columns in a matrix, list the number of rows first using the format $m \times n$. Matrix A is a 3×3 matrix because it has 3 rows and 3 columns. To name

an element of a matrix, the letter i is used to denote the row and j is used to denote the column, and the element is labeled in the form $a_{i,j}$. In matrix A below, $a_{3,2}$ is 4.

$$\text{Matrix A} = \begin{pmatrix} 1 & 3 & 5 \\ 0 & 6 & 8 \\ 3 & 4 & 5 \end{pmatrix}$$

A vector is a matrix with only one column or row of elements. A transposed column vector, or a column vector turned on its side, is a row vector. In the example below, row vector b' is the transpose of column vector b.

$$b = \begin{pmatrix} 1 \\ 2 \\ 3 \\ 4 \end{pmatrix}$$

$$b = \begin{pmatrix} 1 & 2 & 3 & 4 \end{pmatrix}$$

▶ Understand meanings of operations and how they relate to one another

Properties of Addition and Multiplication

Properties are statements that are true for any numbers. For example, $3 + 8$ is the same as $8 + 3$ because each expression equals 11. This illustrates the Commutative Property of Addition. Likewise, $3 \times 8 = 8 \times 3$ illustrates the Commutative Property of Multiplication.

When evaluating expressions, it is often helpful to group or associate the numbers. The Associative Property says that the way in which numbers are grouped when added or multiplied does not change the sum or product. The following properties are also true:

- **Additive Identity Property:** When 0 is added to any number, the sum is the number.

- **Multiplicative Identity Property:** When any number is multiplied by 1, the product is the number.

- **Multiplicative Property of Zero:** When any number is multiplied by 0, the product is 0.

Rational Numbers

A number that can be written as a fraction is called a rational number. Terminating and repeating decimals are rational numbers because both can be written as fractions. Decimals that are neither terminating nor repeating are called irrational numbers because they cannot be written as fractions.

Terminating decimals can be converted to fractions by placing the number (without the decimal point) in the numerator. Count the number of places to the right of the decimal point, and in the denominator, place a 1 followed by a number of zeros equal to the number of places that you counted. The fraction can then be reduced to its simplest form.

Writing a Fraction as a Decimal

Any fraction $\frac{a}{b}$, where $b \neq 0$, can be written as a decimal by dividing the numerator by the denominator. So, $\frac{a}{b} = a \div b$. If the division ends, or terminates, when the remainder is zero, the decimal is a terminating decimal. Not all fractions can be written as terminating decimals. Some have a repeating decimal. A bar indicates that the decimal repeats forever. For example, the fraction $\frac{4}{9}$ can be converted to a repeating decimal, 0.4

Adding and Subtracting Like Fractions

Fractions with the same denominator are called like fractions. To add like fractions, add the numerators and write the sum over the denominator. To add mixed numbers with like fractions, add the whole numbers and fractions separately, adding the numerators of the fractions, then simplifying if necessary. The rule for subtracting fractions with like denominators is similar to the rule for adding. The numerators can be subtracted and the difference written over the denominator. Mixed numbers are written as improper fractions before subtracting. These same rules apply to adding or subtracting like algebraic fractions. An algebraic fraction is a fraction that contains one or more variables in the numerator or denominator.

Adding and Subtracting Unlike Fractions

Fractions with different denominators are called unlike fractions. The least common multiple of the denominators is used to rename the fractions with a common denominator. After a common denominator is found, the numerators can then be added or subtracted. To add mixed numbers with unlike fractions, rename the mixed numbers as improper fractions. Then find a common denominator, add the numerators, and simplify the answer.

Multiplying Rational Numbers

To multiply fractions, multiply the numerators and multiply the denominators. If the numerators and denominators have common factors, they can be simplified before multiplication.

If the fractions have different signs, then the product will be negative. Mixed numbers can be multiplied in the same manner, after first renaming them as improper fractions. Algebraic fractions may be multiplied using the same method described above.

Dividing Rational Numbers

To divide a number by a rational number (a fraction, for example), multiply the first number by the multiplicative inverse of the second. Two numbers whose product is 1 are called multiplicative inverses, or reciprocals. $\frac{7}{4} \times \frac{4}{7} = 1$. When dividing by a mixed number, first rename it as an improper fraction, and then multiply by its multiplicative inverse. This process of multiplying by a number's reciprocal can also be used when dividing algebraic fractions.

Adding and Subtracting Integers

To add integers with the same sign, add their absolute values. The sum takes the same sign as the addends. An addend is a number that is added to another number (the augend). The equation $-5 + (-2) = -7$ is an example of adding two integers with the same sign. To add integers with different signs, subtract their absolute values. The sum takes the same sign as the addend with the greater absolute value. The rules for adding integers are extended to the subtraction of integers. To subtract an integer, add its additive inverse. For example, to find the difference $2 - 5$, add the additive inverse of 5 to 2: $2 + (-5) = -3$. The rule for subtracting integers can be used to solve real-world problems and to evaluate algebraic expressions.

Additive Inverse Property

Two numbers with the same absolute value but different signs are called opposites. For example, -4 and 4 are opposites. An integer and its opposite are also called additive inverses. The Additive Inverse Property says that the sum of any number and its additive inverse is zero. The Commutative, Associative, and Identity Properties also apply to integers. These properties help when adding more than two integers.

Absolute Value

In mathematics, when two integers on a number line are on opposite sides of zero, and they are the same distance from zero, they have the same absolute value. The symbol for absolute value is two vertical bars on either side of the number. For example, $|-5| = 5$.

Multiplying Integers

Since multiplication is repeated addition, $3(-7)$ means that -7 is used as an addend 3 times. By the Commutative Property of Multiplication, $3(-7) = -7(3)$. The product of two integers with different signs is always negative. The product of two integers with the same sign is always positive.

Dividing Integers

The quotient of two integers can be found by dividing the numbers using their absolute values. The quotient of two integers with the same sign is positive, and the quotient of two integers with a different sign is negative. $-12 \div (-4) = 3$ and $12 \div (-4) = -3$. The division of integers is used in statistics to find the average, or mean, of a set of data. When finding the mean of a set of numbers, find the sum of the numbers, and then divide by the number in the set.

Adding and Multiplying Vectors and Matrices

In order to add two matrices together, they must have the same number of rows and columns. In matrix addition, the corresponding elements are added to each other. In other words $(a + b)_{ij} = a_{ij} + b_{ij}$. For example,

$$\begin{pmatrix} 1 & 2 \\ 2 & 1 \end{pmatrix} + \begin{pmatrix} 3 & 6 \\ 0 & 1 \end{pmatrix} = \begin{pmatrix} 1+3 & 2+6 \\ 2+0 & 1+1 \end{pmatrix} = \begin{pmatrix} 4 & 8 \\ 2 & 2 \end{pmatrix}$$

Matrix multiplication requires that the number of elements in each row in the first matrix is equal to the number of elements in each column in the second. The elements of the first row of the first matrix are multiplied by the corresponding elements of the first column of the second matrix and then added together to get the first element of the product matrix. To get the second element, the elements in the first row of the first matrix are multiplied by the corresponding elements in the second column of the second matrix then added, and so on, until every row of the first matrix is multiplied by every column of the second. See the example below.

$$\begin{pmatrix} 1 & 2 \\ 3 & 4 \end{pmatrix} \times \begin{pmatrix} 3 & 6 \\ 0 & 1 \end{pmatrix} = \begin{pmatrix} (1\times3)+(2\times0) & (1\times6)+(2\times1) \\ (3\times3)+(4\times0) & (3\times6)+(4\times1) \end{pmatrix} = \begin{pmatrix} 3 & 8 \\ 9 & 22 \end{pmatrix}$$

Vector addition and multiplication are performed in the same way, but there is only one column and one row.

Permutations and Combinations

Permutations and combinations are used to determine the number of possible outcomes in different situations. An arrangement, listing, or pattern in which order is important is called a permutation. The symbol $P(6, 3)$ represents the number of permutations of 6 things taken 3 at a time. For $P(6, 3)$, there are $6 \times 5 \times 4$ or 120 possible outcomes. An arrangement or listing where order is not important is called a combination. The symbol $C(10, 5)$ represents the number of combinations of 10 things taken 5 at a time. For $C(10, 5)$, there are $(10 \times 9 \times 8 \times 7 \times 6) \div (5 \times 4 \times 3 \times 2 \times 1)$ or 252 possible outcomes.

Powers and Exponents

An expression such as $3 \times 3 \times 3 \times 3$ can be written as a power. A power has two parts, a base and an exponent. $3 \times 3 \times 3 \times 3 = 3^4$. The base is the number that is multiplied (3). The exponent tells how many times the base is used as a factor (4 times). Numbers and variables can be written using exponents. For example, $8 \times 8 \times 8 \times m \times m \times m \times m \times m$ can be expressed $8^3 m^5$. Exponents also can be used with place value to express numbers in expanded form. Using this method, 1,462 can be written as $(1 \times 10^3) + (4 \times 10^2) + (6 \times 10^1) + (2 \times 10^0)$.

Squares and Square Roots

The square root of a number is one of two equal factors of a number. Every positive number has both a positive and a negative square root. For example, since $8 \times 8 = 64$, 8 is a square root of 64. Since $(-8) \times (-8) = 64$, -8 is also a square root of 64. The notation $\sqrt{}$ indicates the positive square root, $-\sqrt{}$ indicates the negative square root, and $\pm\sqrt{}$ indicates both square roots. For example, $\sqrt{81} = 9$, $-\sqrt{49} = -7$, and $\pm\sqrt{4} = \pm2$. The square root of a negative number is an imaginary number because any two factors of a negative number must have different signs, and are therefore not equivalent.

Logarithm

A logarithm is the inverse of exponentiation. The logarithm of a number x in base b is equal to the number n. Therefore, $b^n = x$ and $\log_b x = n$. For example, $\log_4(64) = 3$ because $4^3 = 64$. The most commonly used bases for logarithms are 10, the common logarithm; 2, the binary logarithm; and the constant e, the natural logarithm (also called $ln(x)$ instead of $\log_e(x)$). Below is a list of some of the rules of logarithms that are important to understand if you are going to use them.

$$\log_b(xy) = \log_b(x) + \log_b(y)$$
$$\log_b \frac{x}{y} = \log_b(x) - \log_b(y)$$
$$\log_b \frac{1}{x} = -\log_b(x)$$
$$\log_b(x)y = y\log_b(x)$$

▶ *Compute fluently and make reasonable estimates*

Estimation by Rounding

When rounding numbers, look at the digit to the right of the place to which you are rounding. If the digit is 5 or greater, round up. If it is less than 5, round down. For example, to round 65,137 to the nearest hundred, look at the number in the tens place. Since 3 is less than 5, round down to 65,100. To round the same number to the nearest ten thousandth, look at the number in the thousandths place. Since it is 5, round up to 70,000.

Finding Equivalent Ratios

Equivalent ratios have the same meaning. Just like finding equivalent fractions, to find an equivalent ratio, multiply or divide both sides by the same number. For example, you can multiply 7 by both sides of the ratio 6:8 to get 42:56. Instead, you can also divide both sides of the same ratio by 2 to get 3:4. Find the simplest form of a ratio by dividing to find equivalent ratios until you can't go any further without going into decimals. So, 160:240 in simplest form is 2:3. To write a ratio in the form *1:n*, divide both sides by the left-hand number. In other words, to change 8:20 to *1:n*, divide both sides by 8 to get 1:2.5.

Front-End Estimation

Front-end estimation can be used to quickly estimate sums and differences before adding or subtracting. To use this technique, add or subtract just the digits of the two highest place values, and replace the other place values with zero. This will give you an estimation of the solution of a problem. For example, 93,471 – 22,825 can be changed to 93,000 – 22,000 or 71,000. This estimate can be compared to your final answer to judge its correctness.

Judging Reasonableness

When solving an equation, it is important to check your work by considering how reasonable your answer is. For example, consider the equation $9\frac{3}{4} \times 4\frac{1}{3}$. Since $9\frac{3}{4}$ is between 9 and 10 and $4\frac{1}{3}$ is between 4 and 5, only values that are between 9×4 or 36 and 10×5 or 50 will be reasonable. You can also use front-end estimation, or you can round and estimate a reasonable answer. In the equation 73×25, you can round and solve to estimate a reasonable answer to be near 70×30 or 2,100.

Algebra

▶ *Understand patterns, relations, and functions*

Relation

A relation is a generalization comparing sets of ordered pairs for an equation or inequality such as $x = y + 1$ or $x > y$. The first element in each pair, the x values, forms the domain. The second element in each pair, the y values, forms the range.

Function

A function is a special relation in which each member of the domain is paired with exactly one member in the range. Functions may be represented using ordered pairs, tables, or graphs. One way to determine whether a relation is a function is to use the vertical line test. Using an object to represent a vertical line, move the object from left to right across the graph. If, for each value of x in the domain, the object passes through no more than one point on the graph, then the graph represents a function.

Linear and Nonlinear Functions

Linear functions have graphs that are straight lines. These graphs represent constant rates of change. In other words, the slope between any two pairs of points on the graph is the same. Nonlinear functions do not have constant rates of change. The slope changes along these graphs. Therefore, the graphs of nonlinear functions are *not* straight lines. Graphs of curves represent nonlinear functions. The equation for a linear function can be written in the form $y = mx + b$, where m represents the constant rate of change, or the slope. Therefore, you can determine whether a function is linear by looking at the equation. For example, the equation $y = \frac{3}{x}$ is nonlinear because x is in the denominator and the equation cannot be written in the form $y = mx + b$. A nonlinear function does not increase or decrease at a constant rate. You can check this by using a table and finding the increase or decrease in y for each regular increase in x. For example, if for each increase in x by 2, y does not increase or decrease the same amount each time, the function is nonlinear.

Linear Equations in Two Variables

In a linear equation with two variables, such as $y = x - 3$, the variables appear in separate terms and neither variable contains an exponent other than 1. The graphs of all linear equations are straight lines. All points on a line are solutions of the equation that is graphed.

Quadratic and Cubic Functions

A quadratic function is a polynomial equation of the second degree, generally expressed as $ax^2 + bx + c = 0$, where a, b, and c are real numbers and a is not equal to zero. Similarly, a cubic function is a polynomial equation of the third degree, usually expressed as $ax^3 + bx^2 + cx + d = 0$. Quadratic functions can be graphed using an equation or a table of values. For example, to graph $y = 3x^2 + 1$, substitute the values -1, -0.5, 0, 0.5, and 1 for x to yield the point coordinates $(-1, 4)$, $(-0.5, 1.75)$, $(0, 1)$, $(0.5, 1.75)$, and $(1, 4)$. Plot these points on a coordinate grid and connect the points in the form of a parabola. Cubic functions also can be graphed by making a table of values. The points of a cubic function from a curve. There is one point at which the curve changes from opening upward to opening downward, or vice versa, called the point of inflection.

Slope

Slope is the ratio of the rise, or vertical change, to the run, or horizontal change of a line: slope = rise/run. Slope (m) is the same for any two points on a straight line and can be found by using the coordinates of any two points on the line:

$$m = \frac{y_2 - y_1}{x_2 - x_1}, \text{ where } x_2 \neq x_1$$

Asymptotes

An asymptote is a straight line that a curve approaches but never actually meets or crosses. Theoretically, the asymptote meets the curve at infinity. For example, in the function $f(x) = \frac{1}{x}$, two asymptotes are being approached: the line $y = 0$ and $x = 0$. See the graph of the function below.

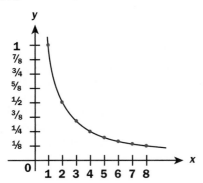

Represent and analyze mathematical situations and structures using algebraic symbols

Variables and Expressions

Algebra is a language of symbols. A variable is a placeholder for a changing value. Any letter, such as x, can be used as a variable. Expressions such as $x + 2$ and $4x$ are algebraic expressions because they represent sums and/or products of variables and numbers. Usually, mathematicians avoid the use of i and e for variables because they have other mathematical meanings ($i = \sqrt{-1}$ and e is used with natural logarithms). To evaluate an algebraic expression, replace the variable or variables with known values, and then solve using order of operations. Translate verbal phrases into algebraic expressions by first defining a variable: Choose a variable and a quantity for the variable to represent. In this way, algebraic expressions can be used to represent real-world situations.

Constant and Coefficient

A constant is a fixed value unlike a variable, which can change. Constants are usually represented by numbers, but they can also be represented by symbols. For example, π is a symbolic representation of the value $3.1415\ldots$. A coefficient is a constant by which a variable or other object is multiplied. For example, in the expression $7x^2 + 5x + 9$, the coefficient of x^2 is 7 and the coefficient of x is 5. The number 9 is a constant and not a coefficient.

Monomial and Polynomial

A monomial is a number, a variable, or a product of numbers and/or variables such as 3×4. An algebraic expression that contains one or more monomials is called a polynomial. In a polynomial, there are no terms with variables in the denominator and no terms with variables under a radical sign. Polynomials can be classified by the number of terms contained in the expression. Therefore, a polynomial with two terms is called a binomial ($z^2 - 1$), and a polynomial with three terms is called a trinomial ($2y^3 + 4y^2 - y$). Polynomials also can be classified by their degrees. The degree of a monomial is the sum of the exponents of its variables. The degree of a nonzero constant such as 6 or 10 is 0. The constant 0 has no degree. For example, the monomial $4b^5c^2$ had a degree of 7. The degree of a polynomial is the same as that of the term with the greatest degree. For example, the polynomial $3x^4 - 2y^3 + 4y^2 - y$ has a degree of 4.

Equation

An equation is a mathematical sentence that states that two expressions are equal. The two expressions in an equation are always separated by an equal sign. When solving for a variable in an equation, you must perform the same operations on both sides of the equation in order for the mathematical sentence to remain true.

Solving Equations with Variables

To solve equations with variables on both sides, use the Addition or Subtraction Property of Equality to write an equivalent equation with the variables on the same side. For example, to solve $5x - 8 = 3x$, subtract $3x$ from each side to get $2x - 8 = 0$. Then add 8 to each side to get $2x = 8$. Finally, divide each side by 2 to find that $x = 4$.

Solving Equations with Grouping Symbols

Equations often contain grouping symbols such as parentheses or brackets. The first step in solving these equations is to use the Distributive Property to remove the grouping symbols. For example $5(x + 2) = 25$ can be changed to $5x + 10 = 25$, and then solved to find that $x = 3$.

Some equations have no solution. That is, there is no value of the variable that results in a true sentence. For such an equation, the solution set is called the null or empty set, and is represented by the symbol $\varnothing$ or {}. Other equations may have every number as the solution. An equation that is true for every value of the variable is called the identity.

Inequality

A mathematical sentence that contains the symbols < (less than), > (greater than), ≤ (less than or equal to), or ≥ (greater than or equal to) is called an inequality. For example, the statement that it is legal to drive 55 miles per hour or slower on a stretch of the highway can be shown by the sentence $s \leq 55$. Inequalities with variables are called open sentences. When a variable is replaced with a number, the inequality may be true or false.

Solving Inequalities

Solving an inequality means finding values for the variable that make the inequality true. Just as with equations, when you add or subtract

the same number from each side of an inequality, the inequality remains true. For example, if you add 5 to each side of the inequality $3x < 6$, the resulting inequality $3x + 5 < 11$ is also true. Adding or subtracting the same number from each side of an inequality does not affect the inequality sign. When multiplying or dividing each side of an inequality by the same positive number, the inequality remains true. In such cases, the inequality symbol does not change. When multiplying or dividing each side of an inequality by a negative number, the inequality symbol must be reversed. For example, when dividing each side of the inequality $-4x \geq -8$ by -2, the inequality sign must be changed to ≤ for the resulting inequality, $2x \leq 4$, to be true. Since the solutions to an inequality include all rational numbers satisfying it, inequalities have an infinite number of solutions.

Representing Inequalities on a Number Line

The solutions of inequalities can be graphed on a number line. For example, if the solution of an inequality is $x < 5$, start an arrow at 5 on the number line, and continue the arrow to the left to show all values less than 5 as the solution. Put an open circle at 5 to show that the point 5 is *not* included in the graph. Use a closed circle when graphing solutions that are greater than or equal to, or less than or equal to, a number.

Order of Operations

Solving a problem may involve using more than one operation. The answer can depend on the order in which you do the operations. To make sure that there is just one answer to a series of computations, mathematicians have agreed upon an order in which to do the operations. First simplify within the parentheses, often called graphing symbols, and then evaluate any exponents. Then multiply and divide from left to right, and finally add and subtract from left to right.

Parametric Equations

Given an equation with more than one unknown, a statistician can draw conclusions about those unknown quantities through the use of parameters, independent variables that the statistician already knows something about. For example, you can find the velocity of an object if you make some assumptions about distance and time parameters.

Recursive Equations

In recursive equations, every value is determined by the previous value. You must first plug an initial value into the equation to get the first value, and then you can use the first value to determine the next one, and so on. For example, in order to determine what the population of pigeons will be in New York City in three years, you can use an equation with the birth, death, immigration, and emigration rates of the birds. Input the current population size into the equation to determine next year's population size, then repeat until you have calculated the value for which you are looking.

▶ Use mathematical models to represent and understand quantitative relationships

Solving Systems of Equations

Two or more equations together are called a system of equations. A system of equations can have one solution, no solution, or infinitely many solutions. One method for solving a system of equations is to graph the equations on the same coordinate plane. The coordinates of the point where the graphs intersect is the solution. In other words, the solution of a system is the ordered pair that is a solution of all equations. A more accurate way to solve a system of two equations is by using a method called substitution. Write both equations in terms of y. Replace y in the first equation with the right side of the second equation. Check the solution by graphing. You can solve a system of three equations using matrix algebra.

Graphing Inequalities

To graph an inequality, first graph the related equation, which is the boundary. All points in the shaded region are solutions of the inequality. If an inequality contains the symbol $\leq$ or $\geq$, then use a solid line to indicate that the boundary is included in the graph. If an inequality contains the symbol $<$ or $>$, then use a dashed line to indicate that the boundary is not included in the graph.

▶ Analyze change in various contexts

Rate of Change

A change in one quantity with respect to another quantity is called the rate of change. Rates of change can be described using slope:

$$\text{slope} = \frac{change\ in\ y}{change\ in\ x}$$

You can find rates of change from an equation, a table, or a graph. A special type of linear equation that describes rate of change is called a direct variation. The graph of a direct variation always passes through the origin and represents a proportional situation. In the equation $y = kx$, k is called the constant of variation. It is the slope, or rate of change. As x increases in value, y increases or decreases at a constant rate k, or y varies directly with x. Another way to say this is that y is directly proportional to x. The direct variation $y = kx$ also can be written as $k = \frac{y}{x}$. In this form, you can see that the ratio of y to x is the same for any corresponding values of y and x.

Slope-Intercept Form

Equations written as $y = mx + b$, where m is the slope and b is the y-intercept, are linear equations in slope-intercept form. For example, the graph of $y = 5x - 6$ is a line that has a slope of 5 and crosses the y-axis at $(0, -6)$. Sometimes you must first write an equation in slope-intercept form before finding the slope and y-intercept. For example, the equation $2x + 3y = 15$ can be expressed in slope-intercept form by subtracting $2x$ from each side and then dividing by 3: $y = -\frac{2}{3}x + 5$, revealing a slope of $-\frac{2}{3}$ and a y-intercept of 5. You can use the slope-intercept form of an equation to graph a line easily. Graph the y-intercept and use the slope to find another point on the line, then connect the two points with a line. Analyze characteristics and properties of two- and three-dimensional geometric shapes and develop mathematical arguments about geometric relationships

Geometry

▶ Analyze characteristics and properties of two- and three-dimensional geometric shapes and develop mathematical arguments about geometric relationships

Angles

Two rays that have the same endpoint form an angle. The common endpoint is called the vertex, and the two rays that make up the angle are called the sides of the angle. The most common unit of measure for angles is the degree. Protractors can be used to measure angles or to draw an angle of a given measure. Angles can be classified by their degree measure. Acute angles have measures less than 90° but greater than 0°. Obtuse angles have measures greater than 90° but less than 180°. Right angles have measures of 90°.

Triangles

A triangle is a figure formed by three line segments that intersect only at their endpoints. The sum of the measures of the angles of a triangle is 180°. Triangles can be classified by their angles. An acute triangle contains all acute angles. An obtuse triangle has one obtuse angle. A right triangle has one right angle. Triangles can also be classified by their sides. A scalene triangle has no congruent sides. An isosceles triangle has at least two congruent sides. In an equilateral triangle all sides are congruent.

Quadrilaterals

A quadrilateral is a closed figure with four sides and four vertices. The segments of a quadrilateral intersect only at their endpoints. Quadrilaterals can be separated into two triangles. Since the sum of the interior angles of all triangles totals 180°, the measures of the interior angles of a quadrilateral equal 360°. Quadrilaterals are classified according to their characteristics, and include trapezoids, parallelograms, rectangles, squares, and rhombuses.

Two-Dimensional Figures

A two-dimensional figure exists within a plane and has only the dimensions of length and width. Examples of two-dimensional figures include circles and polygons. Polygons are figures that have three or more angles, including triangles, quadrilaterals, pentagons, hexagons, and many more. The sum of the angles of any polygon totals at least 180° (triangle), and each additional side adds 180° to the measure of the first three angles. The sum of the angles of a quadrilateral, for example, is 360°. The sum of the angles of a pentagon is 540°.

Three-Dimensional Figures

A plane is a two-dimensional flat surface that extends in all directions. Intersecting planes can form the edges and vertices of three-dimensional figures or solids. A polyhedron is a solid with flat surfaces that are polygons. Polyhedrons are composed of faces, edges, and vertices and are differentiated by their shape and by their number of bases. Skew lines are lines that lie in different planes. They are neither intersecting nor parallel.

Congruence

Figures that have the same size and shape are congruent. The parts of congruent triangles that match are called corresponding parts. Congruence statements are used to identify corresponding parts of congruent triangles. When writing a congruence statement, the letters must be written so that corresponding vertices appear in the same order. Corresponding parts can be used to find the measures of angles and sides in a figure that is congruent to a figure with known measures.

Similarity

If two figures have the same shape but not the same size they are called similar figures. For example, the triangles below are similar, so angles A, B, and C have the same measurements as angles D, E, and F, respectively. However, segments AB, BC, and CA do not have the same measurements as segments DE, EF, and FD, but the measures of the sides are proportional.

For example, $\dfrac{\overline{AB}}{\overline{DE}} = \dfrac{\overline{BC}}{\overline{EF}} = \dfrac{\overline{CA}}{\overline{FD}}$.

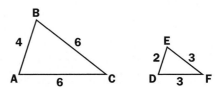

Solid figures are considered to be similar if they have the same shape and their corresponding linear measures are proportional. As with two-dimensional figures, they can be tested for similarity by comparing corresponding measures. If the compared ratios are proportional, then the figures are similar solids. Missing measures of similar solids can also be determined by using proportions.

The Pythagorean Theorem

The sides that are adjacent to a right angle are called legs. The side opposite the right angle is the hypotenuse.

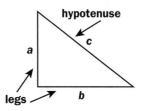

The Pythagorean Theorem describes the relationship between the lengths of the legs a and b and the hypotenuse c. It states that if a triangle is a right triangle, then the square of the length of the hypotenuse is equal to the sum of the squares of the lengths of the legs. In symbols, $c^2 = a^2 + b^2$.

Sine, Cosine, and Tangent Ratios

Trigonometry is the study of the properties of triangles. A trigonometric ratio is a ratio of the lengths of two sides of a right triangle. The most common trigonometric ratios are the sine, cosine, and tangent ratios. These ratios are abbreviated as *sin*, *cos*, and *tan*, respectively.

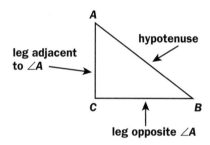

If $\angle A$ is an acute angle of a right triangle, then

$$sin\ \angle A = \frac{\text{measure of leg opposite } \angle A}{\text{measure of hypotenuse}},$$

$$cos\ \angle A = \frac{\text{measure of leg adjacent to } \angle A}{\text{measure of hypotenuse}}, \text{ and}$$

$$tan\ \angle A = \frac{\text{measure of leg opposite } \angle A}{\text{measure of leg adjacent to } \angle A}.$$

▶ Specify locations and describe spatial relationships using coordinate geometry and other representational systems

Polygons

A polygon is a simple, closed figure formed by three or more line segments. The line segments meet only at their endpoints. The points of intersection are called vertices, and the line segments are called sides. Polygons are classified by the number if sides they have. The diagonals of a polygon divide the polygon into triangles. The number of triangles formed is two less than the number of sides. To find the sum of the mea-sures of the interior angles of any polygon, multiply the number of triangles within the polygon by 180. That is, if n equals the number of sides, then $(n - 2)$ 180 gives the sum of the measures of the polygon's interior angles.

Cartesian Coordinates

In the Cartesian coordinate system, the y-axis extends above and below the origin and the x-axis extends to the right and left of the origin, which is the point at which the x- and y-axes intersect. Numbers below and to the left of the origin are negative. A point graphed on the coordinate grid is said to have an x-coordinate and a y-coordinate. For example, the point $(1, -2)$ has as its x-coordinate the number 1, and has as its y-coordinate the number -2. This point is graphed by locating the position on the grid that is 1 unit to the right of the origin and 2 units below the origin.

The x-axis and the y-axis separate the coordinate plane into four regions, called quadrants. The axes and points located on the axes themselves are not located in any of the quadrants. The quadrants are labeled I to IV, starting in the upper right and proceeding counterclockwise. In quadrant I, both coordinates are positive. In quadrant II, the x-coordinate is negative and the y-coordinate is positive. In quadrant III, both coordinates are negative. In quadrant IV, the x-coordinate is positive and the y-coordinate is negative. A coordinate graph can be used to show algebraic relationships among numbers.

▶ Apply transformations and use symmetry to analyze mathematical situations

Similar Triangles and Indirect Measurement

Triangles that have the same shape but not necessarily the same dimensions are called similar triangles. Similar triangles have corresponding angles and corresponding sides. Arcs are used to show congruent angles. If two triangles are similar, then the corresponding angles have the same measure, and the corresponding sides are proportional. Therefore, to determine the measures of the sides of similar triangles when some measures are known, proportions can be used.

Transformations

A transformation is a movement of a geometric figure. There are several types of transformations. In a translation, also called a slide, a figure is slid from one position to another without turning it. Every point of the original figure is moved the same distance and in the same direction. In a reflection, also called a flip, a figure is flipped over a line to form a mirror image. Every point of the original figure has a corresponding point on the other side of the line of symmetry. In a rotation, also called a turn, a figure is turned around a fixed point. A figure can be rotated 0°–360° clockwise or counterclockwise. A dilation transforms each line to a parallel line whose length is a fixed multiple of the length of the original line to create a similar figure that will be either larger or smaller.

▶ Use visualizations, spatial reasoning, and geometric modeling to solve problems

Two-Dimensional Representations of Three-Dimensional Objects

Three-dimensional objects can be represented in a two-dimensional drawing in order to more easily determine properties such as surface area and volume. When you look at the triangular prism, you can see the orientation of its three dimensions, length, width, and height. Using the drawing and the formulas for surface area and volume, you can easily calculate these properties.

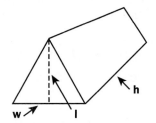

Another way to represent a three-dimensional object in a two-dimensional plane is by using a net, which is the unfolded representation. Imagine cutting the vertices of a box until it is flat then drawing an outline of it. That's a net. Most objects have more than one net, but any one can be measured to determine surface area. Below is a cube and one of its nets.

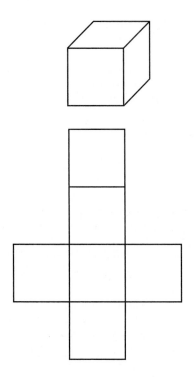

Measurement

▶ Understand measurable attributes of objects and the units, systems, and processes of measurement

Customary System

The customary system is the system of weights and measures used in the United States. The main units of weight are ounces, pounds (1 equal to 16 ounces), and tons (1 equal to 2,000 pounds). Length is typically measured in inches, feet (1 equal to 12 inches), yards (1 equal to 3 feet), and miles (1 equal to 5,280 feet), while area is measured in square feet and acres (1 equal to 43,560 square feet). Liquid is measured in cups, pints (1 equal to 2 cups), quarts (1 equal to 2 pints), and gallons (1 equal to 4 quarts). Finally, temperature is measured in degrees Fahrenheit.

Metric System

The metric system is a decimal system of weights and measurements in which the prefixes of the words for the units of measure indicate the relationships between the different measurements. In this system, the main units of weight, or mass, are grams and kilograms. Length is measured in millimeters, centimeters, meters, and kilometers, and the units of area are square millimeters, centimeters, meters, and kilometers. Liquid is typically measured in milliliters and liters, while temperature is in degrees Celsius.

Selecting Units of Measure

When measuring something, it is important to select the appropriate type and size of unit. For example, in the United States it would be appropriate when describing someone's height to use feet and inches. These units of height or length are good to use because they are in the customary system, and they are of appropriate size. In the customary system, use inches, feet, and miles for lengths and perimeters; square inches, feet, and miles for area and surface area; and cups, pints, quarts, gallons or cubic inches and feet (and less commonly miles) for volume. In the metric system use millimeters, centimeters, meters, and kilometers for lengths and perimeters; square units millimeters, centimeters, meters, and kilometers for area and surface area; and milliliters and liters for volume. Finally, always use degrees to measure angles.

▶ Apply appropriate techniques, tools, and formulas to determine measurements

Precision and Significant Digits

The precision of measurement is the exactness to which a measurement is made. Precision depends on the smallest unit of measure being used, or the precision unit. One way to record a measure is to estimate to the nearest precision unit. A more precise method is to include all of the digits that are actually measured, plus one estimated digit. The digits recorded, called significant digits, indicate the precision of the measurement. There are special rules for determining significant digits. If a number contains a decimal point, the number of significant digits is found by counting from left to right, starting with the first nonzero digit. If the number does not contain a decimal point, the number of significant digits is found by counting the digits from left to right, starting with the first digit and ending with the last nonzero digit.

Surface Area

The amount of material needed to cover the surface of a figure is called the surface area. It can be calculated by finding the area of each face and adding them together. To find the surface area of a rectangular prism, for example, the formula $S = 2lw + 2lh + 2wh$ applies. A cylinder, on the other hand, may be unrolled to reveal two circles and a rectangle. Its surface area can be determined by finding the area of the two circles, $2\pi r^2$, and adding it to the area of the rectangle, $2\pi rh$ (the length of the rectangle is the circumference of one of the circles), or $S = 2\pi r^2 + 2\pi rh$. The surface area of a pyramid is measured in a slightly different way because the sides of a pyramid are triangles that intersect at the vertex. These sides are called lateral faces and the height of each is called the slant height. The sum of their areas is the lateral area of a pyramid. The surface area of a square pyramid is the lateral area $\frac{1}{2}bh$ (area of a lateral face) times 4 (number of lateral faces), plus the area of the base. The surface area of a cone is the area of its circular base (πr^2) plus its lateral area (πrl, where l is the slant height).

Volume

Volume is the measure of space occupied by a solid region. To find the volume of a prism, the area of the base is multiplied by the measure of the height, $V = Bh$. A solid containing several prisms can be broken down into its component prisms. Then the volume of each component can be found and the volumes added. The volume of a cylinder can be determined by finding the area of its circular base, πr^2, and then multiplying by the height of the cylinder. A pyramid has one-third the volume of a prism with the same base and height. To find the volume of a pyramid, multiply the area of the base by the pyramid's height, and then divide by 3. Simply stated, the formula for the volume of a pyramid is $V = \frac{1}{3}bh$. A cone is a three-dimensional figure with one circular base and a curved surface connecting the base and the vertex. The volume of a cone is one-third the volume of a cylinder with the same base area and height. Like a pyramid, the formula for the volume of a cone is $V = \frac{1}{3}bh$. More specifically, the formula is $V = \frac{1}{3}\pi r^2h$.

Upper and Lower Bounds

Upper and lower bounds have to do with the accuracy of a measurement. When a measurement is given, the degree of accuracy is also stated to tell you what the upper and lower bounds of the measurement are. The upper bound is the largest possible value that a measurement could have had before being rounded down, and the lower bound is the lowest possible value it could have had before being rounded up.

Data Analysis and Probablity

▶ *Formulate questions that can be addressed with data and collect, organize, and display relevant data to answer them*

Histograms

A histogram displays numerical data that have been organized into equal intervals using bars that have the same width and no space between them. While a histogram does not give exact data points, its shape shows the distribution of the data. Histograms also can be used to compare data.

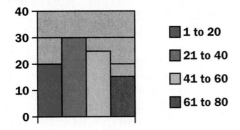

- ■ 1 to 20
- ■ 21 to 40
- ■ 41 to 60
- ■ 61 to 80

Box-and-Whisker Plot

A box-and-whisker plot displays the measures of central tendency and variation. A box is drawn around the quartile values, and whiskers extend from each quartile to the extreme data points. To make a box plot for a set of data, draw a number line that covers the range of data. Find the median, the extremes, and the upper and lower quartiles. Mark these points on the number line with bullets, then draw a box and the whiskers. The length of a whisker or box shows whether the values of the data in that part are concentrated or spread out.

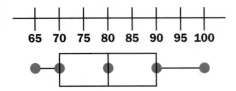

Scatter Plots

A scatter plot is a graph that shows the relationship between two sets of data. In a scatter plot, two sets of data are graphed as ordered pairs on a coordinate system. Two sets of data can have a positive correlation (as x increases, y increases), a negative correlation (as x increases, y decreases), or no correlation (no obvious pattern is shown). Scatter plots can be used to spot trends, draw conclusions, and make predictions about data.

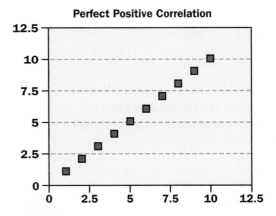

Randomization

The idea of randomization is a very important principle of statistics and the design of experiments. Data must be selected randomly to prevent bias from influencing the results. For example, you want to know the average income of people in your town but you can only use a sample of 100 individuals to make determinations about everyone. If you select 100 individuals who are all doctors, you will have a biased sample. However, if you chose a random sample of 100 people out of the phone book, you are much more likely to accurately represent average income in the town.

Statistics and Parameters

Statistics is a science that involves collecting, analyzing, and presenting data. The data can be collected in various ways—for example through a census or by making physical measurements. The data can then be analyzed by creating summary statistics, which have to do with the distribution of the data sample, including the mean, range, and standard error. They can also be illustrated in tables and graphs, like box-plots, scatter plots, and histograms. The presentation of the data typically involves describing the strength or validity of the data and what they show. For example, an analysis of ancestry of people in a city might tell you something about immigration patterns, unless the data set is very small or biased in some way, in which case it is not likely to be very accurate or useful.

Categorical and Measurement Data

When analyzing data, it is important to understand if the data is qualitative or quantitative. Categorical data is qualitative and measurement, or numerical, data is quantitative. Categorical data describes a quality of something and can be placed into different categories. For example, if you are analyzing the number of students in different grades in a school, each grade is a category. On the other hand, measurement data is continuous, like height, weight, or any other measurable variable. Measurement data can be converted into categorical data if you decide to group the data. Using height as an example, you can group the continuous data set into categories like under 5 feet, 5 feet to 5 feet 5 inches, over 5 feet five inches to 6 feet, and so on.

Univariate and Bivariate Data

In data analysis, a researcher can analyze one variable at a time or look at how multiple variables behave together. Univariate data involves only one variable, for example height in humans. You can measure the height in a population of people then plot the results in a histogram to look at how height is distributed in humans. To summarize univariate data, you can use statistics like the mean, mode, median, range, and standard deviation, which is a measure of variation. When looking at more than one variable at once, you use multivariate data. Bivariate data involves two variables. For example, you can look at height and age in humans together by gathering information on both variables from individuals in a population. You can then plot both variables in a scatter plot, look at how the variables behave in relation to each other, and create an equation that represents the relationship, also called a regression. These equations could help answer questions such as, for example, does height increase with age in humans?

▶ Select and use appropriate statistical methods to analyze data

Measures of Central Tendency

When you have a list of numerical data, it is often helpful to use one or more numbers to represent the whole set. These numbers are called measures of central tendency. Three measures of central tendency are mean, median, and mode. The mean is the sum of the data divided by the number of items in the data set. The median is the middle number of the ordered data (or the mean of the two middle numbers).

The mode is the number or numbers that occur most often. These measures of central tendency allow data to be analyzed and better understood.

Measures of Spread

In statistics, measures of spread or variation are used to describe how data are distributed. The range of a set of data is the difference between the greatest and the least values of the data set. The quartiles are the values that divide the data into four equal parts. The median of data separates the set in half. Similarly, the median of the lower half of a set of data is the lower quartile. The median of the upper half of a set of data is the upper quartile. The interquartile range is the difference between the upper quartile and the lower quartile.

Line of Best Fit

When real-life data are collected, the points graphed usually do not form a straight line, but they may approximate a linear relationship. A line of best fit is a line that lies very close to most of the data points. It can be used to predict data. You also can use the equation of the best-fit line to make predictions.

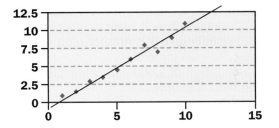

Stem and Leaf Plots

In a stem and leaf plot, numerical data are listed in ascending or descending order. The greatest place value of the data is used for the stems. The next greatest place value forms the leaves. For example, if the least number in a set of data is 8 and the greatest number is 95, draw a vertical line and write the stems from 0 to 9 to the left of the line. Write the leaves from to the right of the line, with the corresponding stem. Next, rearrange the leaves so they are ordered from least to greatest. Then include a key or explanation, such as 1|3 = 13. Notice that the stem-and-leaf plot below is like a histogram turned on its side.

```
0|8
1|3 6
2|5 6 9
3|0 2 7 8
4|0 1 4 7 9
5|1 4 5 8
6|1 3 7
7|5 8
8|2 6
9|5
```

Key: **1|3 = 13**

▶ Develop and evaluate inferences and predictions that are based on data

Sampling Distribution

The sampling distribution of a population is the distribution that would result if you could take an infinite number of samples from the population, average each, and then average the averages. The more normal the distribution of the population, that is, how closely the distribution follows a bell curve, the more likely the sampling distribution will also follow a normal distribution. Furthermore, the larger the sample, the more likely it will accurately represent the entire population. For instance, you are more likely to gain more representative results from a population of 1,000 with a sample of 100 than with a sample of 2.

Validity

In statistics, validity refers to acquiring results that accurately reflect that which is being measured. In other words, it is important when performing statistical analyses, to ensure that the data are valid in that the sample being analyzed represents the population to the best extent possible. Randomization of data and using appropriate sample sizes are two important aspects of making valid inferences about a population.

▶ Understand and apply basic concepts of probability

Complementary, Mutually Exclusive Events

To understand probability theory, it is important to know if two events are mutually exclusive, or complementary: the occurrence of one event automatically implies the non-occurrence of the other. That is, two complementary events cannot both occur. If you roll a pair of dice, the event of rolling 6 and rolling doubles have an outcome in common (3, 3), so they are not mutually exclusive. If you roll (3, 3), you also roll doubles. However, the events of rolling a 9 and rolling doubles are mutually exclusive because they have no outcomes in common. If you roll a 9, you will not also roll doubles.

Independent and Dependent Events

Determining the probability of a series of events requires that you know whether the events are independent or dependent. An independent event has no influence on the occurrence of subsequent events, whereas, a dependent event does influence subsequent events. The chances that a woman's first child will be a girl are $\frac{1}{2}$, and the chances that her second child will be a girl are also $\frac{1}{2}$ because the two events are independent of each other. However, if there are 7 red marbles in a bag of 15 marbles, the chances that the first marble you pick will be red are $\frac{7}{15}$ and if you indeed pick a red marble and remove it, you have reduced the chances of picking another red marble to $\frac{6}{14}$.

Sample Space

The sample space is the group of all possible outcomes for an event. For example, if you are tossing a single six-sided die, the sample space is {1, 2, 3, 4, 5, 6}. Similarly, you can determine the sample space for the possible outcomes of two events. If you are going to toss a coin twice, the sample space is {(heads, heads), (heads, tails), (tails, heads), (tails, tails)}.

Computing the Probability of a Compound Event

If two events are independent, the outcome of one event does not influence the outcome of the second. For example, if a bag contains 2 blue and 3 red marbles, then the probability of selecting a blue marble, replacing it, and then selecting a red marble is $P(A) \times P(B) = \frac{2}{5} \times \frac{3}{5}$ or $\frac{6}{25}$.

If two events are dependent, the outcome of one event affects the outcome of the second. For example, if a bag contains 2 blue and 3 red marbles, then the probability of selecting a blue and then a red marble without replacing the first marble is $P(A) \times P(B$ following $A) = \frac{2}{5} \times \frac{3}{4}$ or $\frac{3}{10}$. Two events that cannot happen at the same time are mutually exclusive. For example, when you roll two number cubes, you cannot roll a sum that is both 5 and even. So, $P(A$ or $B) = \frac{4}{36} + \frac{18}{36}$ or $\frac{11}{18}$.

Career Appendix

MAKING CAREER CHOICES

A career differs from a job in that it is a series of progressively more responsible jobs in one field or a related field. You will need to learn some special skills to choose a career and to help you in your job search. Choosing a career and identifying career opportunities require careful thought and preparation.

STEPS TO MAKING A CAREER DECISION

The *Career Plan Project Workbook* is available at this book's Online Learning Center at **glencoe. com**. It provides information and worksheets that can help you develop the essential elements of a career plan. You can use this workbook to explore the three core areas of career decision making: self-assessment, career exploration, and goal setting. Then you can follow step-by-step directions to create your own career plan. These are the five basic steps to making a career decision:

1. Create a self-profile with these headings: lifestyle goals, values, interests, aptitudes, skills and abilities, personality traits, learning styles. Fill in information about yourself.

2. Identify possible career choices based on your self-assessment.

3. Gather information on each choice, including future trends.

4. Evaluate your choices based on your self-assessment.

5. Make your decision.

After you make your decision, create a career plan that explains how you will reach your goal. Include short-term, medium-term, and long-term goals. In making your choices, explore the future opportunities in this field or fields over the next several years. What impact will new technology and automation have on job opportunities in a rapidly evolving workplace environment? Remember, if you plan, you make your own career opportunities.

COLLEGE AND CAREER PORTFOLIO

A college and career portfolio is a collection of information about a person, including documents, projects, and work samples that show a person's skills, talents, and qualifications. It includes information needed for a job search or to apply for college. Turn to the end of this Career Skills Handbook for more information and instructions for creating your own college and career portfolio.

CAREER RESEARCH RESOURCES

In order to gather information on various career opportunities, there are a variety of sources to research:

- **Libraries.** Your school or public library offers books, magazines, pamphlets, videos, and other print, online, and multimedia reference materials on careers. The U.S. Department of Labor publishes the *Dictionary of Occupational Titles (DOT),* which describes about 20,000 jobs and their relationships with data, people, and things; the *Occupational Outlook Handbook (OOH),* with information on more than 200 occupations; and the *Guide for Occupational Exploration (GOE),* a reference that organizes the world of work into interest areas that are subdivided into work groups and subgroups.

- **The Internet.** The Internet is a primary source of research on any topic. It is especially helpful in researching careers.

- **Career Consultations.** Career consultation, an informational interview with a professional who works in a career that interests you, provides an opportunity to learn about the realities of a career.

- **On-the-Job Experience.** On-the-job experience can be valuable in learning firsthand about a job or career. You can find out if your school has a work-experience program, or look into a company or organization's internship opportunities. Interning gives you direct work experience and often allows you to make valuable contacts.

THE JOB SEARCH

To aid you in your actual job search, there are various sources to explore. You should contact and research all the sources that might produce a job lead, or information about a job. Keep a contact list as you proceed with your search. Some job search resources include:

- **Networking with family, friends, and acquaintances.** This means contacting people you know personally, including school counselors, former employers, and professional people.

- **Cooperative education and work-experience programs.** Many schools have programs in which students work part-time on a job related to one of their classes. Many also offer work-experience programs that are not limited to just one career area, such as marketing.

- **Newspaper ads.** Reading the Help Wanted advertisements in your local papers will provide a source of job leads, as well as teach you about the local job market.

- **Employment agencies.** Most cities have two types of employment agencies, public and private. These employment agencies match workers with jobs. Some private agencies may charge a fee, so be sure to know who is expected to pay the fee and what the fee is.

- **Company personnel offices.** Large and medium-sized companies have personnel offices to handle employment matters, including the hiring of new workers. You can check on job openings by contacting the office by telephone or by scheduling a personal visit.

- **Searching the Internet.** Cyberspace offers multiple opportunities for your job search. Many Web sites provide lists of companies offering employment. There are thousands of career-related Web sites, so find those that have jobs that interest you. Companies that interest you may have a Web site, which may provide information on their benefits and opportunities for employment.

APPLYING FOR A JOB

When you have contacted the sources of job leads and found some jobs that interest you, the next step is to apply for them. You will need to complete application forms, write letters of application, and prepare your own résumé. Before you apply for a job, you will need to have a work permit if you are under the age of 18 in most states. Some state and federal labor laws designate certain jobs as too dangerous for young workers. Laws also limit the number of hours of work allowed during a day, a week, or the school year. You will also need to have proper documentation, such as a green card if you are not a U.S. citizen.

JOB APPLICATION

You can obtain the job application form directly at the place of business, by requesting it in writing, or over the Internet. It is best if you can fill the form out at home, but some businesses require that you fill it out at the place of work.

Fill out the job application forms neatly and accurately, using standard English, the formal style of speaking and writing you learned in school. You must be truthful and pay attention to detail in filling out the form.

PERSONAL FACT SHEET

To be sure that the answers you write on a job or college application form are accurate, make a personal fact sheet before filling out the application:

- Your name, home address, and phone number
- Your Social Security number
- The job you are applying for
- The date you can begin work
- The days and hours you can work
- The pay you want
- Whether or not you have been convicted of a crime
- Your education
- Your previous work experience
- Your birth date

- Your driver's license number if you have one
- Your interests and hobbies, and awards you have won
- Your previous work experience, including dates
- Schools you have attended
- Places you have lived
- Accommodations you may need from the employer
- A list of references—people who will tell an employer that you will do a good job, such as relatives, students, former employers.

LETTERS OF RECOMMENDATION

Letters of recommendation are helpful. You can request teachers, counselors, relatives, and other acquaintances who know you well to write these letters. They should be short, to the point, and give a brief overview of your important accomplishments or projects. The letter should describe your character and work ethic.

LETTER OF APPLICATION

Some employees prefer a letter of application, rather than an application form. This letter is like writing a sales pitch about yourself. You need to tell why you are the best person for the job, what special qualifications you have, and include all the information usually found on an application form. Write the letter in standard English, making certain that it is neat, accurate, and correct.

RÉSUMÉ

The purpose of a résumé is to make an employer want to interview you. A résumé tells prospective employers what you are like and what you can do for them. A good résumé summarizes you at your best in a one- or two-page outline. It should include the following information:

1. **Identification.** Include your name, address, telephone number, and e-mail address.

2. **Objective.** Indicate the type of job you are looking for.

3. **Experience.** List experience related to the specific job for which you are applying. List other work if you have not worked in a related field.

4. **Education.** Include schools attended from high school on, the dates of attendance, and diplomas, degrees, licenses, or certifications earned. A professional certification is a designation earned by a person to assure qualification to perform a job or task. You may also include courses you are taking or have taken that are related to the job you are applying for.

5. **References.** Include up to three references or indicate that they are available. Always ask people ahead of time if they are willing to be listed as references for you.

A résumé that you put online or send by e-mail is called an electronic résumé. Some Web sites allow you to post them on their sites without charge. Employers access these sites to find new employees. Your electronic résumé should follow the guidelines for a print résumé. It needs to be accurate. Stress your skills and sell yourself to prospective employers.

COVER LETTER

If you are going to get the job you want, you need to write a great cover letter to accompany your résumé. Think of a cover letter as an introduction: a piece of paper that conveys a smile, a confident hello, and a nice, firm handshake. The cover letter is the first thing a potential employer sees, and it can make a powerful impression. The following are some tips for creating a cover letter that is professional and gets the attention you want:

- **Keep it short.** Your cover letter should be one page, no more.
- **Make it look professional.** Key your letter on a computer and print it on a laser printer. Use white or buff-colored paper. Key your name, address, phone number, and e-mail address at the top of the page.
- **Explain why you are writing.** Start your letter with one sentence describing where you heard of the opening. "Joan Wright suggested I contact you regarding a position in your marketing department," or "I am writing to apply for the position you advertised in the Sun City Journal."

- **Introduce yourself.** Give a short description of your professional abilities and background. Refer to your attached résumé: "As you will see in the attached résumé, I am an experienced editor with a background in newspapers, magazines, and textbooks." Then highlight one or two specific accomplishments.

- **Sell yourself.** Your cover letter should leave the reader thinking, "This person is exactly who we are looking for." Focus on what you can do for the company. Relate your skills to the skills and responsibilities mentioned in the job listing. If the ad mentions solving problems, relate a problem you solved at school or work. If the ad mentions specific skills or knowledge required, mention your mastery of these in your letter. (Also be sure these skills are included on your résumé.)

- **Provide all requested information.** If the Help Wanted ad asked for "salary requirements" or "salary history," include this information in your cover letter. However, you do not have to give specific numbers. It is okay to say, "My wage is in the range of $10 to $15 per hour." If the employer does not ask for salary information, do not offer any.

- **Ask for an interview.** You have sold yourself, now wrap it up. Be confident, but not pushy. "If I would be an asset to your company, please call me at [insert your phone number]. I am available for an interview at your convenience." Finally, thank the person. "Thank you for your consideration. I look forward to hearing from you soon." Always close with a "Sincerely," followed by your full name and signature.

- **Check for errors.** Read and re-read your letter to make sure each sentence is correctly worded and there are no errors in spelling, punctuation, or grammar. Do not rely on your computer's spell checker or grammar checker. A spell check will not detect if you keyed "tot he" instead of "to the." It is a good idea to have someone else read your letter, too. He or she might notice an error you overlooked.

 **INTERVIEW**

Understanding how to prepare for and follow up on interviews is critical to your career success. At different times in your life, you may interview with a teacher or professor, a prospective employer, a supervisor, or a promotion or tenure committee. Just as having an excellent résumé is vital for opening the door, interview skills are critical for putting your best foot forward and seizing the opportunity to articulate why you are the best person for the job.

RESEARCH THE COMPANY

Your ability to convince an employer that you understand and are interested in the field you are interviewing to enter is important. Show that you have knowledge about the company and the industry. What products or services does the company offer? How is it doing? What is the competition? Use your research to demonstrate your understanding of the company.

PREPARE QUESTIONS FOR THE INTERVIEWER

Prepare interview questions to ask the interviewer. Some examples include:

- "What would my responsibilities be?"
- "Could you describe my work environment?"
- "What are the chances to move up in the company?"
- "Do you offer training?"
- "What can you tell me about the people who work here?"

DRESS APPROPRIATELY

Nonverbal communication is 90 percent of communication, so dressing appropriately is of the utmost importance. Wear clothing that is appropriate for the job for which you are applying. In most situations, you will be safe if you wear clean, pressed, conservative business clothes in neutral colors. Pay special attention to grooming. Keep makeup light and wear very little jewelry. Make certain your nails and hair are clean, trimmed, and neat. Do not carry a large purse, backpack, books, or coat. Simply carry a pad of paper, a pen, and extra copies of your résumé and letters of reference.

EXHIBIT GOOD BEHAVIOR

Conduct yourself properly during an interview. Go alone; be courteous and polite to everyone you meet. Relax and focus on your purpose: to make the best possible impression.

- Be on time.
- Be poised and relaxed.
- Avoid nervous habits.
- Avoid littering your speech with verbal clutter such as "you know," "um," and "like."
- Look your interviewer in the eye and speak with confidence.
- Use nonverbal techniques to reinforce your confidence, such as a firm handshake and poised demeanor.
- Convey maturity by exhibiting the ability to tolerate differences of opinion.
- Never call anyone by a first name unless you are asked to do so.
- Know the name, title, and the pronunciation of the interviewer's name.
- Do not sit down until the interviewer does.
- Do not talk too much about your personal life.
- Never bad-mouth your former employers.

BE PREPARED FOR COMMON INTERVIEW QUESTIONS

You can never be sure exactly what will happen at an interview, but you can be prepared for common interview questions. There are some interview questions that are illegal. Interviewers should not ask you about your age, gender, color, race, or religion. Employers should not ask whether you are a parent, married or pregnant, or question your health or disabilities.

Take time to think about your answers now. You might even write them down to clarify your thinking. The key to all interview questions is to be honest, and to be positive. Focus your answers on skills and abilities that apply to the job you are seeking. Practice answering the following questions with a friend:

- "Tell me about yourself."
- "Why do you want to work at this company?"

- "What did you like/dislike about your last job?"
- "What is your biggest accomplishment?"
- "What is your greatest strength?"
- "What is your greatest weakness?"
- "Do you prefer to work with others or on your own?"
- "What are your career goals?" or "Where do you see yourself in five years?"
- "Tell me about a time that you had a lot of work to do in a short time. How did you manage the situation?"
- "Have you ever had to work closely with a person you didn't get along with? How did you handle the situation?"

AFTER THE INTERVIEW

Be sure to thank the interviewer after the interview for his or her time and effort. Do not forget to follow up after the interview. Ask, "What is the next step?" If you are told to call in a few days, wait two or three days before calling back.

If the interview went well, the employer may call you to offer you the job. Find out the terms of the job offer, including job title and pay. Decide whether you want the job. If you decide not to accept the job, write a letter of rejection. Be courteous and thank the person for the opportunity and the offer. You may wish to give a brief general reason for not accepting the job. Leave the door open for possible employment in the future.

FOLLOW UP WITH A LETTER

Write a thank-you letter as soon as the interview is over. This shows your good manners, interest, and enthusiasm for the job. It also shows that you are organized. Make the letter neat and courteous. Thank the interviewer. Sell yourself again.

ACCEPTING A NEW JOB

If you decide to take the job, write a letter of acceptance. The letter should include some words of appreciation for the opportunity, written acceptance of the job offer, the terms of employment (salary, hours, benefits), and the starting date. Make sure the letter is neat and correct.

⬤ STARTING A NEW JOB

Your first day of work will be busy. Determine what the dress code is and dress appropriately. Learn to do each task assigned properly. Ask for help when you need it. Learn the rules and regulations of the workplace.

You will do some paperwork on your first day. Bring your personal fact sheet with you. You will need to fill out some forms. Form W-4 tells your employer how much money to withhold for taxes. You may also need to fill out Form I-9. This shows that you are allowed to work in the United States. You will need your Social Security number and proof that you are allowed to work in the United States. You can bring your U.S. passport, your Certificate of Naturalization, or your Certificate of U.S. Citizenship. If you are not a permanent resident of the United States, bring your green card. If you are a resident of the United States, you will need to bring your work permit on your first day. If you are under the age of 16 in some states, you need a different kind of work permit.

You might be requested to take a drug test as a requirement for employment in some states. This could be for the safety of you and your coworkers, especially when working with machinery or other equipment.

EMPLOYABILITY SKILLS

You will need employability skills to succeed in a rapidly evolving workplace environment. These skills include personal and interpersonal skills, such as functioning effectively as part of a team and demonstrating leadership skills, no matter what position you are in. There are also certain qualities and behaviors that are needed to be a good employee.

- Attend work regularly.
- Be prompt.
- Make the most productive use of your time.
- Be cooperative, responsible, and honest.
- Obey company rules.
- Have a positive attitude.
- Show enthusiasm and pride.
- Tolerate differences.
- Be open-minded.

- Show respect.
- Be flexible.
- Take initiative.
- Be willing to learn new skills.
- Listen attentively.
- Use an appropriate voice.
- Demonstrate planning and time-management skills.
- Keep your workplace clean and safe.
- Understand the legal and ethical responsibilities related to your job.
- Understand the relationship between health and achievement.
- Understand and avoid the implications of substance abuse.

LEAVING A JOB

If you are considering leaving your job or are being laid off, you are facing one of the most difficult aspects in your career. The first step in resigning is to prepare a short resignation letter to offer your supervisor at the conclusion of the meeting you set up with him or her. Keep the letter short and to the point. Express your appreciation for the opportunity you had with the company. Do not try to list all that was wrong with the job.

You want to leave on good terms. Do not forget to ask for a reference. Do not talk about your employer or any of your coworkers. Do not talk negatively about your employer when you apply for a new job.

If you are being laid off or face downsizing, it can make you feel angry or depressed. Try to view it as a career-change opportunity. If possible, negotiate a good severance package. Find out about any benefits you may be entitled to. Perhaps the company will offer services for finding new employment.

⬤ TAKE ACTION!

It is time for action. Remember the networking and contact lists you created when you searched for this job. Reach out for support from friends, family, and other acquaintances. Consider joining a job-search club. Assess your skills. Upgrade them if necessary. Examine your attitude and your career choices. Decide the direction you wish to take and move on!

BUILD YOUR COLLEGE AND CAREER PORTFOLIO

A college and career portfolio is a collection of information about a person, including documents, projects, and work samples that showcase a person's academic and professional skills, talents, accomplishments, and qualifications. It includes the information needed for a job search or for applying for college. Your portfolio can be a paper portfolio in a folder, a digital portfolio with electronic files, or a combination of both. You can use your college and career portfolio throughout your life to keep track of your academic and career goals and accomplishments.

- **Personal Fact Sheet** When you apply for a job, you will probably fill out an application that asks for information that may not be on your résumé. For that reason you should include a personal fact sheet in your college and career portfolio. Include all of the items listed on pages 788–789.

- **Evaluate Yourself** The information you know about yourself can help you choose a career that is right for you. Update your self evaluation periodically to make sure you are on the right path.

- **Conduct Career Research** Create a section for your portfolio called Career Research. Include information about career clusters and careers that interest you and sources of information you find helpful. Also include notes from career interviews and career evaluations. Update the Career Research section of your portfolio as you continue to explore your career options.

- **Prepare a Career Plan** After you have made a career decision, you can make a career plan. Create a section for your portfolio called career plan. Your first step in making your career plan is setting a career goal. Then you can set the short-term goals, medium-term goals, and long-term goals that will lead you to your career goal. Include goals related to education or training and other experiential learning. Review, update, or create new career plans as you continue to explore your career options.

- **Résumé and Cover Letter** Your college and career portfolio should include your résumé and a sample cover letter that you can use when following up job leads. When you find a job that interests you, note the qualifications required. Then customize your cover letter and résumé so that they are tailored to the job. Relate the skills you have to the skills required for the job.

- **Develop References** You should supply references when you apply for a job. You may also need them when applying for college. Include a list of your references in your college and career portfolio. Include each person's name, title and company, address, phone number, and e-mail address. If your references will provide written letters of reference, include copies in your portfolio. People to ask include former managers, teachers, counselors, or other trusted adults in the community who can comment on your reliability and attitude.

- **Showcase Your Technology Skills** The best way to show an employer what you know about technology is by demonstrating your technology skills! As you research the career that interests you, take note of the hardware, software, and other technology tools that are current in the field. Then, learn to use the technologies and include examples that show your mastery of these tools in your college and career portfolio. Include a list of hardware and software that you know how to use.

- **Awards, Honors, and Certifications** If you have received awards or honors, include any relevant information about them in your college and career portfolio. Also, if you have any licenses or certifications related to your continuing education or job search, also include these in your portfolio.

CAREER APPENDIX

REVIEW KEY CONCEPTS

1. What are the five steps to making a career decision?

2. What three types of goals should a career plan include?

3. Why is a personal fact sheet useful?

4. What are employability skills?

5. What is the role of professional certifications in a career search?

6. What is the role of a career and college portfolio?

7. What are the functions of résumés and portfolios?

8. Why is it important to demonstrate leadership skills?

9. What are five positive work qualities?

10. What are three questions you should be prepared to answer in a job interview?

CRITICAL THINKING

11. Compare and contrast the role of a résumé and a cover letter.

12. Analyze why your career choice might change as you get older.

13. Predict the consequences of choosing a career that conflicts with your personal values.

14. Evaluate how tracking employment trends and technology trends can help you manage your own career.

15. Explain why you think it is important to think critically, demonstrate strong communication skills, and function effectively as part of a team in order to be successful in the workplace.

16. Analyze the importance of time management and project management skills in your chosen career field. Explain your answer.

CHALLENGE YOURSELF!

17. Imagine that you have been asked to work on a project team either at school or where you work.

   - Think about the leadership and teamwork skills that you would need to be a successful member of the project team.

   - Demonstrate your knowledge of leadership and teamwork skills by creating a checklist that outlines what these skills are.

   - Work with a partner to identify how you would demonstrate these skills and behaviors in a work or school environment. Relate the skills to the "Employability Skills" section elsewhere in this handbook. For example, offering to perform a task that another team member cannot complete may demonstrate initiative and support for a fellow team member.

18. Research careers of personal interest to you. Look at career Web sites to find job opportunities and accompanying duties.

   - Find out what type of education, certification, job training, and experience are required to meet your career goals.

   - Create a five-year plan that breaks down your goals.

   - What do you need to do now in order to meet your goals? What will you need to do next year? How will you assess your progress?

Go Online e-RESOURCES
glencoe.com

Go to the **Online Learning Center** to find career resources, including information about résumés, portfolios, and interview and workplace tips. Use the *Career Plan Project Workbook* to help you create a career plan.

Glossary

How to Use This Glossary

- Content vocabulary terms in this glossary are words that relate to this book's content. They are **boldfaced** and **highlighted yellow** in your text.

- Words in this glossary that have an asterisk (*) are academic vocabulary terms. They help you understand your school subjects and are used on tests. They are **boldfaced blue** in your text.

- Some of the vocabulary words in this book include pronunciation symbols to help you sound out the words. Use the pronunciation key to help you pronounce the words.

Pronunciation Key

a . . . . **a**t	**ô** . . . . f**o**rk, **a**ll	**ⁿ** . . . . indicates preceding sound is pronounced with an open nasal passage
ā . . . . **a**pe	**oo** . . . w**oo**d, p**u**t	**th** . . . **th**in
ä . . . . f**a**ther	**ō͞o** . . . f**oo**l	**th** . . . **th**is
e . . . . **e**nd	**oi** . . . **oi**l	**zh** . . . trea**s**ure
ē . . . . m**e**	**ou** . . . **ou**t	**ə** . . . . **a**go, tak**e**n, penc**i**l, lem**o**n, circ**u**s
i . . . . **i**t	**u** . . . . **u**p	**'** . . . . indicates primary stress (symbol in front of and *above* letter)
ī . . . . **i**ce	**ū** . . . . **u**se	**,** . . . . indicates secondary stress (symbol in front of and *below* letter)
o . . . . h**o**t	**ü** . . . . r**u**le	
ō . . . . h**o**pe	**u̇** . . . . p**u**ll	
o̍ . . . . s**a**w	**ŋ** . . . . si**ng**	

#

401(k) A specific type of retirement plan offered by many companies. (p. 271)

A

abstinence ('ab-stə-nen(t)s) A deliberate decision to avoid high-risk behaviors, including sexual activity and the use of tobacco, alcohol, and other drugs. (p. 11)

abuse When a person threatens the physical or mental health of another. (p. 386)

*accommodate Help. (p. 554)

accountability The willingness to accept the consequences of your actions and words. (p. 46)

*accountable Responsible. (p. 14)

*accumulate Collect or gather. (p. 757)

acid rain The environmentally damaging and physically harmful rain that results from the combination of fossil fuel emissions and water in the atmosphere. (p. 761)

active listening Concentrating on what is said so you understand and remember it. (p. 73)

active play Physical activities that use large motor skills. (p. 486)

adapt Change to fit. (p. 131)

*adequate Enough or sufficient. (p. 528)

adoption A legal process by which people acquire the rights and responsibilities of parenthood for children who are not biologically their own. (p. 508)

adrenaline (ə-'dre-nə-lən) A stress hormone that increases the heartbeat and breathing rate. (p. 530)

*advance Ahead of time. (p. 619)

aerobic activities (,er-'ō-bik) Continuous, rhythmic activities that help improve heart, lung, and muscle function. (p. 521)

age appropriate Suitable for the age and developmental needs of a child. (p. 477)

*aggressive Forceful and pushy. (p. 72, 108)

alcoholism A physical and mental dependence on alcohol. (p. 386) *alert Warn or make aware. (p. 398)

allergen A protein substance in food that triggers an allergic reaction. (p. 573)

*alter Change. (p. 679)

*alternate Back-up or alternative. (p. 448)

*alternative Another option. (p. 90)

annual percentage rate (APR) The annual rate of interest that a company charges you for using credit. (p. 277)

annulment Invalidation of a marriage. (p. 423)

*anonymous Unidentified. (p. 631)

anorexia nervosa (ˌa-nə-ˈrek-sē-ə (ˌ)nər-ˈvō-sə) An extreme urge to lose weight by starving oneself. (p. 524)

*apparent Clear or obvious. (p. 8)

application form A form used to list personal information, such as your address, phone number, and Social Security number. (p. 320)

apprenticeship A training program that combines classroom instruction with on-the-job learning. (p. 296)

aptitude (ˈap-tə-ˌtüd) A natural talent or potential for learning a skill. (p. 299)

*aspect Part. (p. 172)

assertive Expressing your ideas and opinions firmly and with confidence. (p. 72)

*asset Advantage or resource. (p. 618)

*assume Take on or undertake. (p. 530)

attention span The length of time a person can concentrate on a task without getting distracted. (p. 487)

B

*bare Minimum or without extra. (p. 585)

*barrier An obstacle. (p. 69)

*baste Hold pieces of fabric together temporarily. (p. 675)

binge eating Compulsive overeating, often without being hungry. (p. 524)

biodegradable Formulated to break down easily in the environment. (p. 759)

blend Yarn made from two or more different fibers. (p. 659)

bobbin A small metal or plastic spool positioned beneath the needle on a sewing machine. (p. 673)

body image An individual's personal view of their own size and shape. (p. 522)

body language A person's posture, facial expressions, gestures, and way of moving. (p. 70)

Body Mass Index (BMI) A person's appropriate weight range determined by weight, height, and age. (p. 523)

bonding The act of forming emotional ties between parents and child. (p. 461)

book value The estimated value of a car of a specific make, model, and year. (p. 725)

*boundaries Limits. (p. 414)

budget A plan for spending and saving money. (p. 192)

buffet service ((ˌ)bə-ˈfā) A food service style in which bowls and platters of food are arranged on a serving table, with dinner plates at one end, and people serve themselves as they walk along the table. (p. 616)

bulimia (bü'lē-mē-ə) Bouts of extreme and often secret overeating followed by attempts to get rid of the food eaten by using laxatives or vomiting. (p. 524)

bully An aggressive person who intimidates, abuses, or mistreats people. (p. 129)

C

campaign ((ˌ)kam-ˈpān) A series of actions designed to bring about a specific result. (p. 245)

*capacity Maximum amount possible or potential. (p. 45)

carbohydrate (ˈkär-(ˌ)bō-ˈhī-ˌdrāt) A nutrient that provides your body with energy. (p. 541)

carbon monoxide detector A device that sounds an alarm when a dangerous level of carbon monoxide is reached. (p. 744)

cardiopulmonary resuscitation (CPR) A first aid procedure that combines rescue breathing with chest compressions. (p. 480)

career A series of related jobs or occupations in a particular field. (p. 291)

career cluster A large grouping of occupations that have certain characteristics in common. (p. 300)

career ladder A visualization of your chosen career path. (p. 303)

career path All of the career moves and job experience that a person gains as he or she works toward a career goal. (p. 291)

caregiver Anyone who takes care of a child. (p. 475)

carpool An arrangement in which a group of people commute together by car. (p. 720)

*casual Informal. (p. 355)

chain letter A letter or an e-mail message that encourages people to send copies of the letter to additional people, often along with money. (p. 235)

*chair An office or position of authority. (p. 46)

character The development and application of commonly held principles that promote personal growth, establish good citizenship, and support society. (p.27)

childproof Take steps to protect a child from possible dangers. (p. 477)

cholesterol (kə-ˈles-tə-ˌrōl) A white, wax-like substance that plays a part in transporting and digesting fat. (p. 542)

chronological résumé A résumé in which the information is organized by work experience in reverse time order. (p. 311)

citizen A member of a community. (p. 45)

citizenship The way that you handle your responsibilities as a citizen. (p. 45)

clarification To make something clearer with further explanation. (p. 79)

classic A clothing style that stays popular for a long time. (p. 653)

clique ('klik) A small, exclusive group that restricts who can join. (p. 403)

closed adoption An adoption in which the birth parents do not know the names of the adoptive parents. (p. 508)

closing cost All the various fees due at the time of the purchase of a house or other property. (p. 704)

clothing inventory An organized list of the garments you own. (p. 641)

collaboration (kə-ˌla-bə-'rā-shən) The cooperative efforts of everyone in a group. (p. 50)

*collectively As a group or together. (p. 225)

colorfast Clothing with colors that will remain the same over time. (p. 660)

commitment Acceptance of an obligation and responsibility. (p. 93, 421)

communication The process of sending and receiving messages between people. (p. 69)

commute Travel regularly from one place to another, especially between home and work. (p. 720)

comparison shopping Comparing prices of different forms, container sizes, brands, and stores to get the best value for your dollar. (p. 568)

*compatible Well-matched. (p. 413)

*compelling Strong or demanding attention. (p. 106)

compensation package Pay and any additional benefits that an employer offers. (p. 322)

competence ('käm-pə-tən(t)s) Having the skills and qualities needed to perform a task or participate fully in an activity. (p. 14)

*composition The ratio of fat to lean tissue in your body. (p. 523)

compound interest Interest that is calculated on the deposits you make and on the interest you have already earned. (p. 269)

*comprise Consist or be made up of. (p. 658)

compromise A settlement of differences in which each side makes concessions. (p. 90)

*concentrated Intense or condensed. (p. 542)

*condition State of readiness for use. (p. 725)

*conduct Behavior. (p. 33)

*confidential Private. (p. 378)

conflict A clash among people who have opposing ideas or interests. (p. 125)

*congestion Clog or traffic jam. (p. 719)

conscience ('kän(t)-shən(t)s) The inner voice that tells you what is morally right and wrong. (p. 31)

consensus (kən-'sen(t)-səs) An agreement by the entire group in which everyone's ideas are taken into account. (p. 90)

consequence Something that follows as a result of an action or choice. (p. 27)

conservation The careful management and protection of natural resources. (p. 756)

*consider Think about carefully. (p. 156)

*consideration Matter taken into account. (p. 653)

*consistency Reliability and stability. (p. 483)

constructive criticism Helpful feedback that includes suggestions for ways you can learn and improve. (p. 333, 435)

consumer Someone who buys and uses products or services. (p. 225)

consumer advocate A person or organization who works on behalf of consumers. (p. 230)

*contact Touch or connection. (p. 590)

context All of the conditions surrounding a problem or situation. (p. 173)

contingency plan (kən-'tin-jən(t)-sē 'plan) A different course of action that could help you overcome potential obstacles. (p. 156)

*contribute Play a significant part in bringing about a result. (p. 433)

convenience food Food that has been partially or fully prepared or processed to make it easier and faster to use. (p. 604)

*convey Express or deliver a message. (p. 77)

cooperation Associating with others for mutual benefit. (p. 88)

*conviction Confidence and certainty. (p. 115)

cooperative play A type of play in which children play and interact with one another. (p. 463)

*coordinate Organize to work together. (p. 204)

copyright Legal rights of the people and companies that produce original works. (p. 213)

cost per wearing An estimate of how much it actually costs you each time you wear an item of clothing. (p. 653)

cover letter A letter telling an employer that you are applying for a position with the company. (p. 318)

*credit Praise and recognition. (p. 521)

credit Money, goods, or services obtained now based on the promise to pay for them in the future. (p. 274)

credit rating An evaluation of a consumer's credit history. (p. 276)

credit report A record of a particular consumer's transactions and payment patterns. (p. 276)

creditor Banks, finance companies, and stores that extend credit to consumers with the understanding that the loan will be paid back over a specified period of time. (p. 274)

crisis An event or situation that overwhelms the usual coping methods and causes severe stress. (p. 385)

*criteria (krī-'tir-ē-ə) Standards. (p. 315)

*critical Extremely important. (p. 396)

GLOSSARY

critical thinking Applying reasoning strategies to make sound judgments. (p. 210)

cross-contamination The spreading of harmful bacteria from one food to another food. (p. 590)

crush A temporary romantic attraction, common among teens and young people. (p. 417)

*****cue** Sign, signal, or hint. (p. 363)

*****cultivate** Encourage. (p. 57)

custody The legally assigned responsibility for the care of children and the decisions that affect them. (p. 385)

*****customary** Traditional or usual. (p. 638)

customary measurement system The system of measurement used in the United States. (p. 606)

D

Daily Values The recommended amounts of nutrients in an eating plan. (p. 573)

danger zone Temperatures between 40°F (4°C) and 140°F (60°C) that allow bacteria to grow to dangerous levels most rapidly. (p. 590)

dart A triangular fold used to give shape to a garment. (p. 683)

deadline A time or date by which a task must be completed. (p. 186)

debit card A card that deducts the cost of a purchase from the user's bank account at the time of purchase. (p. 268)

decision-making process A six-step procedure for making thoughtful choices. (p. 167)

deduction (di-'dək-shən) Anything that is subtracted from gross pay. (p. 265)

*****deficiency** Shortage or not enough. (p. 505)

*****define** Outline. (p. 155)

*****degree** Amount. (p. 381)

*****delay** Put off. (p. 425)

delegate Assign tasks to other team members. (p. 94)

dependent Relying too much on someone else for one's own happiness. (p. 364)

*****determine** Decide. (p. 212)

developmental tasks Skills and abilities that are mastered as part of the maturing process. (p. 461)

diabetes (ˌdī-ə-'bē-tēz) A condition caused by inadequate production or use of the hormone insulin. (p. 559)

*****dictate** Determine. (p. 632)

Dietary Guidelines for Americans Guidelines for healthful eating habits developed jointly by the U.S. Department of Agriculture (USDA) and the Department of Health and Human Services. (p. 548)

dietary supplement An extra vitamin, mineral, or other nutrient in the form of pills, capsules, or powders. (p. 546)

dilemma A problem involving a difficult choice with serious consequences. (p. 165)

direct mail advertising The practice of delivering ads to consumers' homes by mail. (p. 247)

*****discipline** Self-control. (p. 192)

discretion The good judgment and sensitivity needed to avoid embarrassing others and to keep sensitive information private. (p. 34)

discrimination The unfair treatment of a person or group, usually because of prejudice about race, ethnicity, age, religion, or gender. (p. 360)

*****distant** Detached. (p. 401)

*****distributor** A store or person who markets a commodity. (p. 651)

*****diversify** Spread or increase variety. (p. 271)

diversity A variety of something, such as ethnicity, culture, age, gender, or opinions. (p. 399)

*****dovetail** ('dəv-ˌtāl) Overlap tasks to save time. (p. 188, 605)

down payment A portion of the purchase price of a property that a buyer pays up front in cash. (p. 704)

downsizing Eliminating jobs to reduce costs. (p. 295)

dress code A set of rules describing required or appropriate clothing. (p. 639)

dry-heat cooking A method used to cook food uncovered without adding liquid or fat. (p. 610)

E

*****economic** Cost-related. (p. 567)

*****effective** Successful or efficient. (p. 87)

embryo ('em-brē-ˌō) The developing baby during the first eight weeks of pregnancy. (p. 461)

emotional maturity Being responsible enough to consistently put someone else's needs before your own needs. (p. 500)

empathy The ability to identify with and understand someone else's feelings. (p. 395)

emphasis ('em(p)-fə-səs) The technique of drawing attention to a specific area. (p. 633, 709)

*****enable** Help or make possible. (p. 204, 573)

endorse Approve or support a product. (p. 248)

endurance The ability to use energy over a period of time without getting tired. (p. 521)

Energy Star label A blue and green label that shows that a product meets government standards for energy efficiency. (p. 710)

EnergyGuide label A black and yellow label that shows the estimated annual energy consumption of a specific product. (p. 710)

*****engage** Participate. (p. 404)

engagement period The time a couple uses to test their relationship, make sure that marriage is the right decision, and plan for their wedding and married life. (p. 421)

*enlist Agree to serve. (p. 296)

*entail Require you to do or make necessary. (p. 332)

enthusiasm Strong feeling of excitement. (p. 332)

entrepreneur (ˌän-trə-p(r)ə-ˈnər) Someone who sets up and operates a business. (p. 294)

environment The people, places, and things that surround and influence a person, including family, home, school, and community. (p. 459)

equivalent measurement The same amount expressed using a different unit of measure. (p. 607)

*essential Necessary. (p. 147)

*estimate Use knowledge to guess. (p. 569)

ethical leadership Leadership that is based on ethical principles. (p. 95)

ethics The principles and values that guide the way you live. (p. 36)

etiquette Behavior based on showing consideration and respect for other people. (p. 434)

*evaluate Assess and examine. (p. 9)

expectation A want or need that each person hopes will be met in a relationship. (p. 356)

expenses The items on which you spend money. (p. 193)

expiration date The last day a product should be eaten. (p. 574)

external pressures Pressures that come from outside sources. (p. 106)

eye contact Direct visual contact with another person's eyes. (p. 70)

F

fabric finish Any special treatment that improves the appearance, feel, or performance of a fabric. (p. 660)

*facilitate Make easier or bring about. (p. 337)

facing A shaped piece of fabric used to finish the raw edge of a garment. (p. 683)

fad A style that remains popular for only a short time. (p. 653)

family life cycle The process of growth and change in a family over the years. (p. 375)

family style A serving style in which food is brought to the table in serving dishes, which are passed from person to person. (p. 615)

fashion Design characteristics that are popular at a particular point in time. (p. 631)

*favorable Positive. (p. 321)

feedback Occurs when a listener lets a speaker know that he or she is trying to understand the message being delivered. (p. 74)

fetus (ˈfē-təs) The developing baby from the ninth week until birth. (p. 461)

fiber A material in food that helps move food through the digestive system and may reduce the risk of heart disease and cancer. (p. 541)

fiber A very fine, hair-like strand. (p. 658)

fiber content The percentage of each type of fiber by weight in cloth. (p. 655)

finance charge Interest or an additional fee, such as a charge for a late payment. (p. 275)

fine motor skills Skills involving the smaller muscles of the body such as those in fingers. (p. 456)

first aid Emergency care or treatment given right away to an ill or injured person. (p. 478)

fitness When your body works at its peak, you look your best, and you are healthy, strong, and well. (p. 521)

fixed goal A goal that can be met only at a certain time. (p. 148)

flatware The knives, forks, and spoons for eating. (p. 617)

*flavor Interest and variety. (p. 355)

flexible goal A goal with no time limit. (p. 149)

flexibility Willing to adapt to new or changing requirements. (p. 331)

flexibility The ability of your joints to make the full range of movements available to them. (p. 521)

flextime A system that allows workers to choose when they will begin and end their working day. (p. 342)

floor plan A diagram that shows the main structural elements of a home or room. (p. 706)

*flourish Be successful. (p. 210)

food allergy When the body's immune system reacts to a particular food substance. (p. 558)

food intolerance Trouble digesting a food or food component. (p. 558)

foodborne illness A sickness caused by eating food that contains a contaminant, or harmful substance. (p. 590)

fortify Add a nutrient to a food that is not naturally present in that food. (p. 549)

fossil fuels Fuels gained from living matter from a previous geologic time. (p. 755)

*foster Encourage a relationship. (p. 79)

*foundation Base or support. (p. 166)

fraud Deceitful conduct for personal gain. (p. 234)

free play A type of play during which children choose any safe activity they want. (p. 486)

freezer burn A condition caused by moisture loss due to improper or inadequate packaging of food before freezing. (p. 594)

*function Operate properly. (p. 364)

G

*gauge Measure the distance or size or something. (p. 685)

*generate Produce or make. (p. 762)

generic brand A brand that usually has a plain label and no brand name. (p. 568)

global economy The way national economies around the world are linked by trade. (p. 295)

global environment The life support systems of the whole planet. (p. 755)

global warming The gradual increase in the earth's surface temperature caused by depletion of the earth's ozone layer. (p. 762)

goal Something you consciously aim to achieve and are willing to plan and work for. (p. 148)

*goods Products. (p. 237)

grain The directions in which the lengthwise and crosswise yarns run in a fabric. (p. 678)

grief The sorrow caused by the death of a loved one and the emotional adjustment to that loss. (p. 386)

gross motor skills Skills that use the large muscles of the body, such as those of the legs and shoulders. (p. 456)

gross pay The total amount you earn. (p. 265)

ground fault circuit interrupter (GFCI) A device used near plumbing or water that automatically turns off electricity to guard against electrical shock. (p. 744)

groupthink A faulty decision-making process caused by a strong desire for group agreement. (p. 91)

guidance Using firmness and understanding to help children learn how to behave. (p. 483)

hand-eye coordination The ability to move the hands and fingers precisely in relation to what is seen. (p. 461)

hang tag A tag on an item of clothing that lists the brand name, size, any warranty, and a bar code. (p. 655)

harassment A persistent, hostile behavior directed at a specific person. (p. 404)

*harness Capture and use. (p. 756)

heredity The set of characteristics that you inherit from your parents and ancestors. (p. 459)

*hinder Get in the way of. (p. 72)

home care Routine maintenance tasks done to keep the home clean and prevent home accidents. (p. 737)

hue (ˈhyü) A specific color that can be identified by name, such as green or red. (p. 635)

I

"I" message A statement that allows you to say how you feel and what you think, rather than criticizing someone else. (p. 71)

identity theft The illegal use of an individual's personal information. (p. 232)

illusion An image that fools the eye. (p. 632)

immunization A shot of a small amount of a dead or weakened disease-carrying germ given so that the body may build resistance to the disease. (p. 476)

*impact The effect that something has. (p. 166)

*impartial Unbiased or neutral. (p. 248)

implement Put a plan into action. (p. 157)

*improvise Make the best of what you have or to use what is on hand. (p. 710)

impulse buying Making unplanned purchases with little or no thought. (p. 252)

*inadequate Failing to meet an expectation or not enough. (p. 364, 545)

income The money you make. (p. 193)

infatuation An intense, short-lived, and sometimes irrational passion. (p. 418)

*inflate Raise the price of something. (p. 726)

infomercial A television or radio advertisement that lasts 30 minutes or more and is designed to seem like regular programming. (p. 246)

*initiate (i-ˈni-shē-ˌāt) Cause something to happen or begin. (p. 16)

initiative (i-ˈni-shə-tiv) The desire and willingness to do what needs to be done without being asked. (p. 331, 435)

insurance Financial protection in the case of loss or harm. (p. 269)

*insure Cover through an insurance policy. (p. 699)

intensity The brightness or dullness of a color. (p. 636)

interest A fee the bank pays you for the opportunity to use your money. (p. 267)

*interfere Negatively affect or get in the way of. (p. 187)

intergenerational Including family members from multiple generations. (p. 375)

interject Insert a comment or gesture into a discussion. (p. 74)

internal pressures Pressures that come from within you. (p. 106)

internship Short-term work for little or no pay in exchange for an opportunity to work and learn. (p. 296)

*interrelated Affected by the others or linked. (p. 458)

*intervene Get involved or step in. (p. 386)

introspective (ˌin-trə-ˈspek-tiv) Examining your own feelings, thoughts, and motives. (p. 7)

invest Using money to participate in a business enterprise that offers the possibility of profit. (p. 271)

invoice price Roughly the price the dealer paid the manufacturer for a vehicle. (p. 726)

irregular Slight imperfections in clothing that are generally not noticeable and do not affect use or wear. (p. 253, 651)

isolated Separated and cut off. (p. 363)

jealousy The feeling that the person you care about is more interested in something or someone else than in you. (p. 418)

job lead Information about a specific job opening. (p. 314)

job shadowing Spending time in the workplace with someone as he or she goes through a normal workday. (p. 301)

job sharing Two part-time workers sharing one full-time job. (p. 342)

K

*****key** Very important. (p. 466)

L

lactose intolerance An inability to digest lactose, the form of sugar that is found in milk. (p. 558)

landfill An area where waste is dumped and buried. (p. 762)

landlord The owner of a rental property. (p. 702)

leadership The ability to direct and motivate a team or group to achieve its goals. (p. 49)

leadership style A leader's pattern of behavior when directing a team. (p. 96)

*****leading** Main or foremost. (p. 743)

lease A legal document that specifies the rights and responsibilities of the landlord and tenant in a housing agreement. (p. 703)

lease A monthly fee in exchange for exclusive use of a vehicle for a specific length of time. (p. 722)

life-span development The growth and change that occurs during a person's life. (p. 455)

lifestyle The way you live. (p. 292)

long-term goal Something you plan to complete in the future, possibly spanning years. (p. 148)

low birth weight Weighing fewer than 5 pounds, 8 ounces at birth. (p. 505)

M

major appliance A large tool or piece of equipment. (p. 585)

majority rule A democratic process in which decisions are made by voting. (p. 90)

make A car's brand name. (p. 725)

management process A system to manage the steps needed to accomplish something. (p. 155)

manipulate (mə-'ni-pyə-,lāt) Control or influence somebody or something in a deceptive way. (p. 249)

manufactured fiber A strand formed either completely or in part by chemicals. (p. 658)

markdown Item with a reduced price or the amount a price is reduced. (p. 652)

*****market** Potentially interested in buying. (p. 722)

mass transit A transportation system designed to carry large numbers of people. (p. 719)

media Channels of mass communication, such as newspapers, magazines, radio, television, movies, and Web sites. (p. 106)

mediation Settling a conflict with the help of a neutral third party. (p. 134)

medium-term goal A goal that will take six months to a few years to achieve. (p. 148)

mentor A person who acts as a teacher and guide. (p. 27)

metric system A system of measurement based on multiples of ten. (p. 606)

mildew A fungus that shows up as small black dots. (p. 664)

mineral A nutrient that regulates body processes and forms parts of tissues. (p. 543)

mixed message When your words and body language do not communicate the same thing. (p. 71)

*****mobile** Movable. (p. 376)

*****model** Demonstrate or show. (p. 27)

model Type or design of a car. (p. 725)

moist-heat cooking A cooking method that uses hot liquid, steam, or both. (p. 609)

monogamy Faithful to one person. (p. 423)

morality A sense of right and wrong that guides decisions and actions. (p. 8)

mortgage A long-term home loan. (p. 699)

*****motivation** Driving force or incentive. (p. 185)

MyPyramid A system developed by the U.S. Department of Agriculture (USDA) to help individuals make wise decisions about food and physical activity. (p. 549)

N

national brand A brand sold and marketed by major food companies. (p. 568)

natural fiber A strand that comes from plants or animals. (p. 658)

neglect The failure to give the proper or required care and attention to somebody, including children, older adults, and those who cannot care for themselves. (p. 386)

negotiation Communication about a problem with the goal of finding a solution. (p. 133)

Neighborhood Watch Program An organized community group that watches for suspicious activity and reports it to the police. (p. 746)

net pay The amount of pay you receive after deductions. (p. 265)

networking Using personal contacts to find a job. (p. 314)

*****neutral** Impartial and unbiased. (p. 439)

nonrenewable resources Resources that cannot be replaced once they are used. (p. 755)

nonverbal communication Communication without words through the use of facial expressions and gestures. (p. 69)

notions The smaller supplies necessary to complete a sewing project. (p. 676)

nurture Provide the care and attention needed to promote development. (p. 373)

nutrient A chemical found in food that helps the body work properly. (p. 541)

O

*objective Detached or fair. (p. 437)

obsolete Out of date and no longer useful. (p. 208)

open adoption An adoption in which the birth parents and adoptive parents know something about each other. (p. 509)

osteoporosis (ˌäs-tē-ō-pə-ˈrō-səs) A condition in which bones are weakened because they lose the calcium that keeps them strong. (p. 543)

outreach program A program that offers assistance or services to the community, usually as an act of charity or goodwill. (p. 52)

outsourcing Contracting out certain tasks to other companies. (p. 295)

over scheduling Trying to accomplish too many things in a limited amount of time. (p. 188)

ozone layer A layer in the earth's upper atmosphere that is meant to block out and protect the earth from most of the sun's harmful ultraviolet rays. (p. 761)

P

parallel play When children play near, but not actually with, other children. (p. 462)

parenting The process of caring for children and helping them grow and develop. (p. 475)

parenting readiness The level of someone's emotional, financial, and personal preparation to be a child's parent. (p. 499)

parliamentary procedure Rules for conducting meetings in an orderly way. (p. 90)

passive A communication style characterized by keeping opinions to oneself and being vulnerable to the influence of others. (p. 72)

pasteurized Heat-treated to kill bacteria that could cause disease or spoilage. (p. 576)

paternity The legal identification of a man as the biological father of a child. (p. 506)

pattern guide sheet A sheet in a sewing pattern that gives specific instructions for cutting and sewing the project. (p. 678)

peer education A program that is based on the principle of teens teaching teens. (p. 132)

peer mediation A process in which specially trained students help other students resolve conflicts peacefully. (p. 135)

peer pressure Influence of others in your age group. (p. 33)

perishable Easily spoiled. (p. 574)

perseverance (ˌper-sə-ˈvir-ən(t)s) Working patiently to overcome challenges and sticking to an action or belief, even when it is difficult. (p. 18)

personal boundaries Limits you set for yourself based on your priorities. (p. 339)

personal growth Learning and practicing new skills as you progress toward reaching your full potential. (p. 12)

personal standard A rule or principle you set for yourself. (p. 33)

personality The combination of characteristics that makes you different from other people. (p. 7)

*perspective A position or viewpoint. (p. 339)

persuade (ˈpər-ˈswād) Urge others in a direction. (p. 89)

place setting The arrangement of tableware for one person. (p. 617)

plagiarism When someone takes part of another person's original work and uses it as if it were his or her own work. (p. 213)

plate service When food is placed on each person's plate in the kitchen, and the plates are brought to the table. (p. 615)

pollutants Harmful substances. (p. 761)

pollution The presence of harmful substances in the environment. (p. 761)

Ponzi scheme A type of pyramid scheme that promises investors high profits from fake sources. (p. 235)

portfolio A collection of work samples that demonstrates your skills. (p. 313)

potential The capacity to develop, succeed, or become something more than you are right now. (p. 11)

power struggle When multiple individuals or groups feel a need to be in control. (p. 125)

*practical Useful. (p. 700)

practical problem A complex situation with many elements that involves making several choices that are related to one another. (p. 171)

practical reasoning The process of examining and asking questions about a practical problem. (p. 173)

precycling Reducing waste with environmentally responsible consumer choices. (p. 763)

prejudice (ˈpre-jə-dəs) An unfair judgment made without knowing all the facts. (p. 125)

premature Born before 37 weeks of development. (p. 505)

prenatal Before birth. (p. 461)

preventive maintenance Taking action to prevent problems or to keep minor problems from becoming major ones. (p. 740)

*pride Pleased and satisfied. (p. 497)

primary care physician A doctor who provides general care and performs checkups. (p. 532)

*primary Main or first. (p. 475)

*principal The original loan amount borrowed. (p. 274)

prioritize Decide what is most important. (p. 147)

private-label Made by an unnamed manufacturer, especially for the distributor. (p. 651)

proactive The initiative to think and plan ahead for situations. (p. 33)

procrastination (prō-ˌkras-tə-ˈnā-shən) Putting off doing something until later. (p. 11)

***progress** Move forward or advance. (p 126)

***prohibit** Ban or disallow. (p. 423, 639)

***project** Display outwardly. (p. 131)

***promote** Encourage or advance. (p. 245, 475)

***prone** Sensitive or likely to. (p. 463)

proportion The relationship in size of one part of a design to another part and to the whole. (p. 634, 708)

***prospective** Likely or expected. (p. 500)

***prospects** Possibilities. (p. 302)

protein A nutrient your body uses to build and repair body tissues. (p. 541)

puberty Hormonally triggered changes that result in a physically mature body that is able to reproduce. (p. 464)

pyramid scheme A get rich quick plan based on recruiting other participants. (p. 235)

Q

***quality** Characteristic or attribute. (p. 95)

quiet play Activities that engage the mind and use small motor skills. (p. 486)

R

***range** A cooking stove. (p. 585)

***rate** Speed. (p. 458)

REASON process Process to help you think through and solve problems. (p. 174)

rebate A refund of part of the purchase price of a product. (p. 256)

recipe A list of ingredients and instructions for making a food or beverage. (p. 603)

reciprocity (ˌre-sə-'prä-s(ə-)tē) A mutual exchange in which each person gives as well as receives. (p. 395)

reconcile ('re-kən-ˌsī(-ə)l) Compare accounts for accuracy. (p. 269)

***recover** To get back or regain. (p. 234)

recycled-content products Items made partially or totally from materials that might have ended up in a landfill. (p. 765)

redress The right to seek legal remedy when laws are violated. (p. 226)

reference A person your potential employer can contact to learn more about you. (p. 311)

***reflect** Reveal or show. (p. 28)

reflex An instinctive, automatic response in infants, such as grasping and sucking. (p. 461)

***refurbish** Repair or renovate. (p. 687)

refusal skills Communication strategies that help you say no when you are urged to take part in behaviors that are unsafe, unhealthful, or go against your values. (p. 115)

***region** Area or district. (p. 745)

***regulates** Controls. (p. 573)

rejection Feeling dismissed by others. (p. 398)

relationship The connection you have with other people. (p. 355)

***reliable** Trustworthy and dependable. (p. 175)

renewable resources Resources, such as plants, trees, and soil, that replace themselves naturally over time. (p. 755)

***representative** Someone who acts on behalf of someone else. (p. 332)

resentment Ongoing anger caused by a sense of having been badly treated. (p. 441)

resiliency The ability to overcome disappointment and stress. (p. 18, 483)

resource Something or someone that can help you achieve a goal. (p. 150)

resourceful Using creative problem solving to manage available resources. (p. 153)

responsibility A required task. (p. 185)

***restrict** Limit. (p. 56)

résumé ('re-zə-ˌmā) A written summary of a job seeker's work experience, education, skills, and interests. (p. 311)

return policy The rules for returning or exchanging purchased merchandise. (p. 236)

rivalry A situation in which people compete to gain an advantage. (p. 441)

role conflict When one role has a significant negative impact on another role. (p. 337)

role model A person who sets an example for others. (p. 93)

rotation Storage system that ensures that older supplies are used before newer ones. (p. 593)

***routine** A regular procedure. (p. 738)

S

saturated fats Fats that are usually in solid form at room temperature and are found mostly in animal products such as meat, milk, cheese, and butter. (p. 542)

scale drawing A drawing in which a given number of inches represents a given number of feet. (p. 706)

***scratch** The use of basic ingredients in cooking instead of a prepared mix. (p. 556)

***second** A clothing item with a noticeable flaw, such as a small hole. (p. 253, 651)

security deposit A fee paid before renting a property to cover any damage you might cause. (p. 699)

***seldom** Not often, or rare. (p. 711)

self-concept The way you see yourself and the way you believe others see you. (p. 8)

self-esteem The value or importance you place on yourself. (p. 9)

sell-by date The last day a product may be sold. (p. 574)

selvage The finished edge of fabric. (p. 678)

sense of self Your idea of who you are. (p. 112)

***sequence** Order. (p. 605)

serger A machine that sews, trims, and finishes a fabric edge in one step. (p. 675)

service Work performed for a fee. (p. 257)

service learning Taking classroom learning and using it to meet a community need. (p. 55)

sewn-in label A label with information such as manufacturer name, country of manufacture, fiber content, and care instructions. (p. 655)

sew-through button A button with two or four visible holes. (p. 686)

sexual harassment Objectionable behavior of a sexual nature. (p. 404)

sexually transmitted infections (STIs) Diseases spread through sexual contact. (p. 415)

shade A darker color value. (p. 636)

shank button A button with a built-in loop on the back. (p. 686)

*__shares__ Individual units of ownership. (p. 272)

shoplifting The theft of merchandise from a store. (p. 237)

short-term goal A goal you want to complete soon. (p. 148)

*__signal__ Indicate or show. (p. 397)

*__significant__ Important. (p. 322)

silhouette (ˌsi-lə-ˈwet) The shape or form created when lines are combined. (p. 633)

skills-based résumé A résumé focusing on workplace skills and giving examples of how you have used the skills. (p. 311)

*__slew__ A large number or many. (p. 740)

small claims court A court in which claims under a certain dollar amount are settled by a judge. (p. 230)

socialization Learning how to interact with other people. (p. 374)

specialist A doctor trained to treat specific diseases or medical conditions. (p. 532)

*__spontaneous__ (spän-ˈtā-nē-əs) Impulsive or acting without restraint. (p. 191)

standing time A period of time when food continues to cook after microwaving. (p. 613)

staples Basic food items, such as rice or flour. (p. 570)

status symbol A sign of social position or rank. (p. 632)

staystitching A row of regular machine stitches through a single layer of fabric. (p. 683)

stereotype An expectation that all people in a particular group will have the same qualities or act in the same way. (p. 362)

sticker price The dealer's initial asking price as shown on the sticker attached to the vehicle. (p. 726)

stimulating environment An environment in which one has a wide variety of things to see, taste, smell, hear, and touch. (p. 483)

store brand A supermarket's product. (p. 568)

stress A body's response when one feels overwhelmed. (p. 530)

style A distinctive form of a clothing item. (p. 631)

substance abuse The use of illegal drugs or the misuse of legal drugs or substances. (p. 386, 525)

*__substantial__ Large. (p. 255)

*__suit__ Match or fit your needs. (p. 299)

*__suitable__ Right for the circumstances. (p. 314)

supervisor The person responsible for making sure people do the work necessary to complete projects and achieve goals. (p. 436)

support system All the people and organizations a person can turn to for help. (p. 379)

*__support__ Pay the costs of. (p. 506)

T

target market A group of consumers to whom a company is trying to appeal with its products. (p. 631)

task management Keeping track of the tasks you need and want to accomplish and making sure you get them all done in a timely way. (p. 185)

teamwork Working with others to achieve a common goal. (p. 87)

technology The application of science to help people meet their needs and wants. (p. 203)

telecommute (ˈte-li-kə-ˌmyüt) Work from home using technology to link to one's job. (p. 342)

telemarketing The act of marketing goods and services by telephone. (p. 234)

temperament An inborn style of reacting to the world and relating to others. (p. 457)

tenant Person who rents a property. (p. 702)

*__terms__ Conditions. (p. 277)

testimonial A positive statement about or endorsement of a product based on personal experience. (p. 248)

text message A short typed message sent between cellular telephones. (p. 76)

third party A person who is not directly involved in or affected by a situation. (p. 439)

tint A lighter color value. (p. 636)

title A legal document showing ownership. (p. 722)

tolerance Respecting other people's beliefs and customs. (p. 359)

tone The way a message would sound if it were read aloud. (p. 71)

traffic pattern The route people use to move through a room or from one part of a home to another. (p. 706)

trans fats A type of fat formed when food manufacturers turn liquid oils into solid fats in a process known as hydrogenation. (p. 542)

*__transfer__ Move or convey. (p. 595)

transferable skill A general skill that can be used in many different situations. (p. 296)

*__transform__ Change or alter. (p. 764)

*__trivial__ Minor or unimportant. (p. 125)

*__true__ Unchanged or consistent. (p. 661)

U

*__unique__ (yù-ˈnēk) Different or distinguished from the rest. (p. 150)

unit price The price per ounce, pound, or other unit of measure. (p. 569)

unsaturated fats Fats that are usually in liquid form at room temperature and are found mainly in oils from vegetables, nuts, and seeds. (p. 542)

use-by date The last day a product is considered fresh. (p. 574)

V

vaccine The disease-causing germ that is injected in the body so that the body can create antibodies. (p. 476)

*****vacuum** A state of isolation from outside influences. (p. 225)

*****value** Attach importance. (p. 34)

value An accepted principle or standard held by a person or a group. (p. 8)

value The lightness or darkness of a hue. (p. 636)

vegetarian A person who does not eat meat, poultry, and fish. (p. 558)

verbal communication Sending messages with words. (p. 69)

vintage clothes Clothing items and accessories from a previous era, generally representing decades from the 1930s to the not-so-distant past. (p. 652)

violence Physical force used to injure or abuse someone. (p. 127)

*****vision** The ability to imagine. (p. 93)

vitamin A nutrient that helps your body function properly and process other nutrients. (p. 542)

volume The amount of space taken up by something. (p. 606)

volunteer Someone who offers services free of charge to help others. (p. 53)

vulnerable Especially open to physical or emotional harm or easily persuaded by pressure. (p. 364)

W

wardrobe Personal collection of clothes. (p. 641)

warranty A guarantee that provides protection against faulty products. (p. 255)

*****waver** Change opinion. (p. 114)

wellness An approach to life that emphasizes taking positive steps toward overall good health and well-being. (p. 521)

win-win solution A solution that benefits everyone involved and has no real drawbacks for anyone. (p. 133)

work center An area devoted to a certain type of task. (p. 586)

work ethic The self-imposed obligation to work hard and complete tasks efficiently and well. (p. 331)

work triangle In a kitchen, the imaginary lines connecting the three work centers, which are storage, cooking, and cleanup. (p. 586)

workplace culture An atmosphere based on the attitudes, behavior, habits, and expectations of the company's owners and employees. (p. 332)

Y

yarn The thread-thin product of fibers that have been twisted together. (p. 659)

yield The number of servings a recipe makes. (p. 603)

Index

INDEX